THE DIVINE COMEDY

ALMA CLASSICS
an imprint of

ALMA BOOKS LTD
Thornton House
Thornton Road
Wimbledon Village
London SW19 4NG
United Kingdom
www.almaclassics.com

This translation of the complete *Divine Comedy* first published by Alma Classics in 2012
A paperback edition first published in 2013. Reprinted 2017
This new edition first published by Alma Classics in 2021
The translation of *Inferno* first published by Hesperus Press in 2005; published in a revised edition by Alma Classics in 2010
The translation of *Purgatory* first published by Alma Classics in 2011
Translation, notes and extra material © J.G. Nichols, 2012

Cover: nathanburtondesign.com

Printed in Great Britain by CPI Group (UK) Ltd, Croydon, CR0 4YY

MIX
Paper | Supporting
responsible forestry
FSC® C171272

ISBN: 978-1-84749-876-2

THE DIVINE COMEDY

DANTE ALIGHIERI

A new translation by
J.G. Nichols

With twenty-four
illustrations by
Gustave Doré

ALMA CLASSICS

CONTENTS

THE DIVINE COMEDY

INFERNO

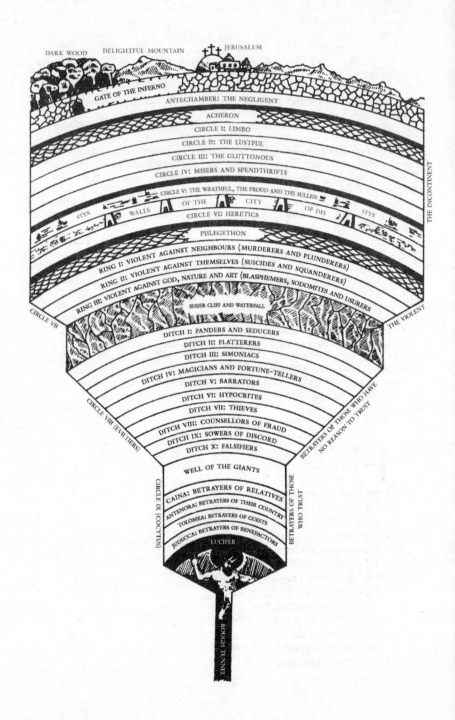

CANTO I

This canto, the prologue to Dante's journey through the Inferno, acts also as an introduction to *The Divine Comedy* as a whole.

At the age of thirty-five Dante realizes he is lost in a dark, terrifying wood. He takes heart when he sees in front of him a hilltop shining in sunlight. But, as he starts to climb the hill, he is frightened by a leopard which obstructs him in a threatening manner, and then by an angry lion, and finally by a she-wolf – the most alarming animal of the three. So Dante is driven back into the darkness which – as we soon come to realize about everything in this poem – is both real and allegorical. (There are, throughout this poem, many kinds of allegory. For instance, the leopard, the lion and the she-wolf – emblems rather than symbols, and therefore in need of interpretation – are of a different order from the dark wood, whose import is obvious.)

A human figure approaches, and Dante, uncertain whether it is a living being or a ghost, implores its help. The figure explains that he is the shade of Virgil. This is the poet whom Dante, as he is quick to declare, admires more than any other. Virgil encourages Dante, and explains that he must travel by a different road if he is to find a way out of his difficulties.

After making an obscure prophecy about the coming of a hound which will kill the she-wolf and also be the saviour of Italy, Virgil says that he will guide Dante through the realms of the Inferno, inhabited by the souls of the damned, who are beyond all hope; and also through Purgatory, where the souls of those now doing penance for their sins are residing, glad to suffer because they have the certain hope of going ultimately to Paradise. Virgil, because he was a pagan who lived and died before Christ and so could not believe in Him, cannot accompany Dante into Paradise. But he says there is another guide who will take Dante there. Dante accepts Virgil's guidance, and they set off.

Halfway along our journey to life's end
   I found myself astray in a dark wood,
   Since the right way was nowhere to be found.
How hard a thing it is to express the horror
   Of that wild wood, so difficult, so dense!
   Even to think of it renews my terror.
It is so bitter death is scarcely more.
   But to convey what goodness I discovered,
   I shall tell everything that I saw there.
How I got into it I cannot say: 10
   I'd fallen into such a heavy sleep
   The very instant that I went astray.
But when I came beneath a steep hillside –
   Which rose at the far end of that long valley
   That struck my stricken heart with so much dread –
I lifted up my eyes, and saw the height

Covered already in that planet's rays[1]
Which always guides all men and guides them right.
And then the fear I felt was somewhat less,
   Though it had filled my heart to overflowing   20
   The whole night I had spent in such distress.
And as somebody, trying to get his breath,
   Emerging from the sea, now safe on shore,
   Turns round to look at where he cheated death,
Just so inside my mind, which was still fleeing,
   I turned to look again upon that pass
   Which never left alive one human being.
When I'd rested my body for a time,
   I made my way across deserted foothills,
   Keeping my low foot always the more firm.[2]   30
And then, just where the hill began to rise,
   I saw a leopard, light upon its paws,
   Covered all over in a spotted hide![3]
It would not move, but stood in front of me,
   And so obstructed me upon my journey
   I kept on turning round to turn and flee.
By then it was the first hour of the morning,
   With the sun rising in the constellation
   That came with him when stars we still see burning
Were set in motion by divine love first.[4]   40
   And so I had good cause to feel encouraged –
   About the lithe and gaily coloured beast –
By that glad time of day and time of year.
   But not so much encouraged that a lion
   Failed to inspire alarm as it drew near.
It did seem that the beast was drawing near,
   With head held high, and so irate with hunger
   The air itself seemed shivering in fear.[5]
And then a she-wolf! Though she was so lean,
   She looked about to burst, being crammed with cravings, 50
   She who'd made many draw their breath in pain.[6]
The pain she caused me was so terrible,
   And such the terror coming from her sight,
   I lost all hope of climbing up the hill.

---

1   According to the Ptolemaic system, accepted in Dante's time, the sun was one of several
    planets revolving round the earth. The dark wood and the comforting sunlight mark the
    beginning of that symbolism of light and darkness which runs through the whole *Comedy*.
2   He was climbing.
3   This leopard is an embodiment of the sin of lust, or sensuality in general, commonly
    associated with youth.
4   It was a common medieval belief that, when the world was created, the season was
    early spring, with the sun in the constellation of Aries.
5   The lion embodies the sins of wrath and pride, commonly associated with middle age.
6   The she-wolf embodies the sin of avarice, commonly associated with old age.

And like that miser, happy while he's gaining,
   Who when luck changes and he starts to lose,
   Gives himself up to misery and moaning –
That's how I was, faced by that restless brute,
   Which always coming nearer, step by step
   Drove me back down to where the sun is mute.[1]   60
Then suddenly, as I went slipping down,
   Someone appeared before my very eyes,
   Seemingly through long silence hoarse and wan.[2]
When I caught sight of him in that wide waste,
   "Take pity on me," I shouted out to him,
   "Whatever you are, a real man or a ghost!"
He answered: "Not a man, though I was once.
   Both of my parents came from Lombardy,
   And both of them were native Mantuans.
I came to birth *sub Julio*, rather late,[3]   70
   And lived in Rome under the good Augustus[4]
   When false, deceptive gods still held their state.
I was a poet, and I sang the good
   Son of Anchises who came out of Troy
   When Ilium was burned in all its pride.[5]
But you, why d'you go back to misery?
   Why don't you climb up the delightful mountain,
   The origin and cause of perfect joy?"
"Then are you Virgil, you, that spring, that stream
   Of eloquence, that ever-widening river?"   80
   I answered, red with reverence and shame.
"Oh every poet's glory and guiding light!
   May I be aided by the love and zeal
   That made me turn your pages day and night.
You are my only master and my author,
   You only are the one from whom I took
   That style which has bestowed on me such honour.
You see the beast that made me turn in flight.
   Save me from her, O famous fount of wisdom!
   She makes the blood run from my veins in fright."   90
"Now you must travel by a different road,"
   He answered when he saw that I was weeping,
   "If you wish to escape from this wild wood.

---

1   As an example of synaesthesia this may at first seem more striking than apt, but during
    the course of the *Comedy* light, or the lack of it, "speaks" volumes.
2   This is the shade of someone who has been dead a long time.
3   When Caesar was dominant in Rome, but too late to be acquainted with him.
4   The Emperor Augustus.
5   This is Virgil, and the poem he refers to is his *Aeneid*, whose hero, Aeneas, a refugee
    from Troy (or Ilium), is the son of Anchises. The theme of the *Aeneid*, the events leading
    up to the foundation of Rome, was particularly dear to Catholic Europe because Rome
    eventually became the seat of the Papacy.

This beast, the reason that you cry out loud,
    Will not let people pass along this way,
    But hinders them, and even has their blood.
She is by nature such an evildoer
    Her avid appetite is never slaked,
    And after food she's hungrier than before.
And many are the beasts she's mating with,[1]   100
    And there'll be many more, until the hound[2]
    Arrives, to bring her to a painful death.
This hound will not be fed with land or pelf,
    But rather feed on wisdom, love, and valour.
    He will originate in folds of felt.[3]
He'll be the saviour of low-lying lands
    Of Italy for which Camilla died,
    Turnus, Nisus, Euryalus, of their wounds.[4]
This hound will hunt that creature high and low
    Until he thrusts her back in the Inferno,   110
    Whence envy freed her first and let her go.
I therefore think and judge it would be best
    For you to follow me. And I shall lead
    You to a region that will always last,
Where you will hear shrieks of despair and grief,
    And see the ancient spirits in their pain,
    As each of them begs for their second death.
And you'll see spirits happy in the fire,
    Because they live in hope that they will come,
    Sooner or later, where the blessèd are.   120
And if you wish to join that company,
    One worthier than I will take you up.[5]
    I'll leave you with her when I go away.
That Emperor who has His kingdom there[6]
    Lets no one come through me into his city,
    Because I was a rebel to his law.[7]
He governs all creation, ruling where
    He has His capital and His high throne.
    Happy are those he chooses to have there!"
I answered: "What I beg of you is this –   130

---

1   Many people will indulge in the sin of avarice.
2   Variously interpreted as a political or religious saviour (there are many candidates) or
    – most satisfactorily – as a prophecy left deliberately vague.
3   Again obscure, but as translated here it suggests a humble origin.
4   All characters in the *Aeneid*.
5   Beatrice, the woman loved by Dante in his youth and a lasting means of grace leading
    him to God. Dante's own account of his love, *Vita Nuova* (*New Life*), a work in prose
    with lyrics interspersed, is by far the best introduction to the *Comedy*.
6   God. In the Inferno God tends to be alluded to rather than named, while Christ is never
    named.
7   Virgil was a pagan.

By that God whom you never knew – so that
I may escape this evil and much worse,
Take me to both those places as you said,
   To see the gate kept by St Peter[1] and
   Those souls you say are desperately sad."[2]
Then he set off. I followed on behind.

---

1   Either the gate of Purgatory, guarded by an angel obedient to St Peter, or the gate of
     Paradise.
2   Those in the Inferno.

CANTO II

The sun is now setting. This is a time when most creatures settle down to rest. Dante, however, is preparing himself for the coming day-long journey and its hardships.

   He invokes the Muses to help him give a true account of his journey. Then he tells Virgil how he doubts his own ability to complete the task, and expresses his perplexity as to why he has been chosen for such an unusual enterprise. He can understand why Aeneas was chosen, the man of destiny who was to found the race that founded Rome, the ruling city of a great empire and the seat of the Holy See. But Dante cannot think that any such destiny is prepared for him. He can understand too why St Paul was taken temporarily into Heaven while still alive. But no one could believe that Dante is worthy of such a favour.

   To these doubts Virgil replies by saying that Dante is simply afraid. To combat Dante's fear he will explain how he came to help him. Beatrice came to him in Limbo and asked for his help to save Dante from damnation. She promised in return to praise Virgil frequently in the presence of God. In answer to Virgil's question, Beatrice explains how she was not afraid to venture down from Heaven: the souls in bliss are not tormented by earthly things. Beatrice describes how Mary, the Mother of Christ, had asked St Lucy to help Dante, and St Lucy then asked her.

   With three such ladies caring for him (an outstanding example of the communion of the saints, in contrast to the lack of a sense of community we find in the Inferno) Dante must have nothing to fear. Duly encouraged, Dante sets off with Virgil.

T he light was failing, and the growing gloom
    Relieving every creature on the earth
    Of all its toil and trouble. I alone
Was getting ready to endure the stress
    Both of the road and the resultant anguish,
    Which never-erring memory will rehearse.
O Muses, O my genius, lend me aid!
    O memory, who wrote down what I saw,
    Here your capacity will be well tried!
I started: "Poet, you who are my guide,   10
    Consider if I have the strength and skill,
    Before you set me on this rugged road.
The father of Silvius,[1] as you tell it, while
    He was corruptible, travelled beyond
    This world of ours, being still corporeal.
And, if the enemy of all that's bad
    Did favour him, because of who he was
    And what he was, and what at last he did,
That must, to men of sense, seem not unfair,
    Since he was chosen in the highest heaven   20

---

1   Aeneas, the hero of the *Aeneid*. In the sixth book of that poem Aeneas journeys through
    the underworld and is rewarded with a prophecy of the future glory of Rome.

As father of great Rome and Rome's Empire.
The City of Rome, to tell the truth of it,
    Was destined to become that sacred place
    Where his successor[1] sits in Peter's seat.
On this strange journey you ascribe to him,
    He heard of things that were to bring about
    His triumph and the papal power in Rome.
That is a road the Vessel of Election[2]
    Went upon also, strengthening the faith
    Which starts us on our journey to salvation.   30
But why should I go there? By whose decree?
    Aeneas I am not, and not Paul either.
    That I am worthy no one would agree.
And so, if I agree to go that way,
    I am afraid of being overbold.
    You're wise. You understand more than I say."
Just as one is who unmeans what he meant,
    Changing that mind of his on second thoughts,
    Wholly diverted from his first intent –
That's how I stood upon that gloomy slope: 40
    By thinking through it, I'd consumed the venture
    For which I was so eager starting up.
"If I have understood your words aright,"
    Answered the shade of that high-minded man,
    "Your cowardly soul has simply taken fright.
Fear often faces men with obstacles
    To make them turn from honourable endeavours,
    As beasts fear shadows when the daylight fails.
That you may lose this fear and so come through,
    I'll tell you why I came, and what I learnt   50
    At the first instant when I pitied you.
I was among those souls who are suspended.[3]
    A lady called to me, so bright and blessed
    I asked her to make known what she commanded.
Her eyes were shining brighter than the stars.
    She spoke in her own tongue, in gentleness,
    And said in that angelic voice of hers:
'O Mantuan soul, the soul of courtesy,
    Whose glory is still current in the world,
    And shall endure till this world cease to be,   60
This friend of mine (though not a friend of fate)
    Is so encumbered on the lonely hillside

---

1   St Peter's successor, the Pope.

2   St Paul, the "chosen vessel" mentioned in Acts 9:15. Paul himself describes how "he was
    caught up into paradise" (2 Cor. 12:2–4).

3   In Limbo, described in *Inf.* IV. Limbo is the part of the Inferno reserved for those who
    had lived virtuously but were not baptized, and so are held in suspense between their
    desire for God and the impossibility of ever seeing Him.

He has been driven from his path in fright.
It could be that he has already strayed
   So far I'm here too late to give him succour,
   Judging by what in heaven I have heard.
Now go, and with your noted eloquence,
   And everything he needs for his escape,
   Come to his aid. I shall take comfort thence.
For I am Beatrice putting you to work.   70
   I come from where I'm anxious to return.
   Love urged me on to this – Love makes me speak.
When I'm once more in presence of my Lord,
   I'll sing your praises to him frequently.'
   At that point she fell silent. Then I said:
'O lady full of virtue, and through whom
   The human race surpasses everything
   Beneath the narrow circle of the moon,[1]
I am so gratified by what you order,
   If I'd obeyed already I'd be tardy.   80
   There is no need to express your wishes further.
But tell me first the reason you don't spurn
   Descending to this centre from broad spaces[2]
   Where, as you say, you're anxious to return.'
'Because you feel the urge to understand,
   I shall explain quite briefly,' she replied,
   'Why I am not too frightened to descend.
We should be frightened of those things alone
   Which have the ability to do us evil.
   Things are not frightening if they do no harm.   90
I'm formed in such a fashion, by God's grace,
   That your unhappiness does not affect me.
   Nor do the fires that rage throughout this place.
A lady in heaven[3] has such great sympathy,
   Given the encumbrances through which I send you,
   That the stern judgement up above gives way.
She called on Lucy, and she said to her:
   "One who is faithful to you now has need
   Of you, and I commend him to your care."
St Lucy,[4] foe to all malignity,   100
   Rose at those words and, coming where I sat
   With venerable Rachel, said to me:

---

1   The moon was considered to be the planet nearest to the earth. All above its orbit was
   considered everlasting, and all below mortal.

2   "This centre" is the earth, seen in the Ptolemaic system as the centre of the universe.
   The "broad spaces" refers to the Empyrean, the highest heaven, the sphere farthest from
   the earth.

3   The Virgin Mary.

4   A saint to whom Dante was particularly devoted. Her name is derived from the Latin
   "*lux*" meaning light.

HALFWAY ALONG OUR JOURNEY TO LIFE'S END
I FOUND MYSELF ASTRAY IN A DARK WOOD...

INFERNO I, 1–2

AT THAT THERE CAME TOWARDS US IN A BOAT
AN OLD OLD MAN, WHOSE HAIR WAS WHITE WITH AGE...

INFERNO III, 82–83

"Beatrice, veritable praise of God,
   Why do you not help him who loved you so
   That for your sake he stood out from the crowd?
Can you not hear his cries of misery?
   Can you not see him caught in a death struggle
   Upon that flood as fearful as the sea?"
Nobody in the world was ever so quick
   To seek advantage and to run from loss   110
   As I, the instant I had heard her speak,
Was quick to leave my seat among the blessed,
   Putting my faith in your fine honest speech,[1]
   Which honours you and those who read it best.'
As soon as she had said these words to me,
   She turned her eyes, shining with tears, aside,
   Which made me the more eager to obey.
And so I came since she requested it,
   And saved you from that savage beast that barred
   The short way up the mountain of delight.   120
What is it then? Why do you hesitate?
   Why do you relish living like a coward?
   Why cannot you be bold and keen to start?
Are not three blessèd ladies, after all,
   Concerned and speaking up for you in heaven?
   And does not what I've said promise you well?"
As tiny blossoms, when the cold night air
   Has made them droop and close, lift up their heads
   And spread their petals once it's dawn once more,
So I did also, after being exhausted.   130
   And such great ardour streamed into my heart
   That like somebody freed from fear I started:
"Oh how compassionate to bring me aid!
   And you, how courteous you were! When she
   Spoke those true words, how swiftly you obeyed!
You have instilled such longing in my heart
   To come with you, because of all you say,
   That I have now gone back to my first thought.
Now go, for we are thoroughly at one.
   You are my leader, my master, and my lord."   140
   Those were my words. And so, as he went on,
I started on that rugged, savage road.

---

1   Virgil's poetry, especially the *Aeneid*.

CANTO III

Dante sees the terrible words written over the gate of the Inferno, stressing divine justice and the everlasting nature of the punishment which it inflicts.

Dante is understandably perturbed, and Virgil has once again to remind him of the need for courage to face what lies ahead.

Inside the gate there is no light, no quiet, no rest. The damned are running continually, and to no purpose, after a banner whose significance is not specified. The souls here are of those who were neither for God nor against Him. Having shown neither the courage nor the energy to act decisively, they are now not good enough for heaven, and not evil enough for hell. So they exist in a sort of antechamber of the Inferno. As if to emphasize the contempt in which they should be held, not one of these souls is named.

Then Dante sees a crowd gathering on the bank of a river, the Acheron. A frightening, demonic boatman, Charon, comes towards them from the opposite bank to ferry them over. He curses them. He also tells Dante that, since he is still alive, he cannot go in this boat. Virgil silences Charon by mentioning the inescapable nature of the decision which has brought Dante there. He explains to Dante that normally only the damned can go that way.

As Charon's boat moves off, another crowd of damned souls is already gathering to be ferried across.

Suddenly, the earth quakes, there is thunder and lightning, and Dante falls down in a faint.

✳

"YOU GO THROUGH ME TO A CITY OF LAMENTATION.
YOU GO THROUGH ME TO EVERLASTING PAIN.
YOU GO THROUGH ME TO THE FORSAKEN NATION.
JUSTICE INSPIRED MY MAKER UP ABOVE.
I WAS ESTABLISHED BY OMNIPOTENCE,
THE HIGHEST WISDOM AND THE PRIMAL LOVE.
NOTHING BEFORE ME WAS CREATED EVER
BUT EVERLASTING THINGS.[1] AND I SHALL LAST.
ABANDON HOPE ENTIRELY, YOU WHO ENTER."
These were the very sentences I eyed,   10
    Set out in sombre black above a gate.
    Then I said: "Master, this seems very hard."
Then he to me, being quick to catch my mood:
    "Here all misgivings must be left behind,
    And all your cowardice be left for dead.
We come now to the region, as I said,
    Where you will see the people steeped in sorrow,
    Those who have lost all intellectual good."[2]
And then, when he had looked at me and smiled

---

1   The angels were created first (creatures who, not being corporeal, are not subject to mortality), and the Inferno was created to receive those angels who rebelled against God.
2   Nothing but the truth, which is God, can satisfy the intellectual longings with which human beings are born.

I4

And pressed my hand, from which I drew some comfort,   20
   He introduced me to the secret world.
From this point, sighs, laments, and piercing groans
   Were echoing throughout the starless air.
   Hearing them this first time, I wept at once.
Deformed and diverse tongues, terrible sounds,
   Words venting misery, outbursts of rage,
   Loud voices, soft ones, sounds of slapping hands
Combined into a turmoil always swirling
   Throughout that unrelieved black atmosphere,
   Like sand which rises at a whirlwind's whirling.   30
And I, my head surrounded by that horror,
   Said: "Master, what's this noise that I can hear?
   Who are these people crushed by what they suffer?"
He said: "This is the wretched way of these
   Sorry creatures: the lives they lived were such
   They earned no infamy, and earned no praise.
Now they are mingled with that wicked sort
   Of angels who were neither with the rebels,
   Nor true to God, but simply stood apart.
The heavens, lest their beauty should be flawed,   40
   Reject them, whom deep hell cannot receive
   Lest it should gain some glory on that head."
I asked: "What is it hitting them so hard
   That they must answer with such loud laments?"
   And he replied: "I'll tell you in a word.
These people have no hope of dying ever,
   And their blind life is so contemptible
   That they would barter it for any other.
The world accords them not the least renown.
   Pity and justice scorn them equally.   50
   Enough of this – you've seen them, now pass on."
I saw some kind of banner that was wheeled
   Around, and racing round at such a rate
   It seemed there was no breathing time allowed.
And after it there ran so long a line
   Of people that I never would have thought
   That death had gathered such a number in.
When I had recognized some of them there,
   I saw and recognized the shade of him
   Who made the great refusal, out of fear.[1]   60

---

1   There has been much discussion as to who this is. Some say it is Pope Celestine V (r.1294), who resigned the Papacy only five months after his election. Others suggest Pontius Pilate, who washed his hands at the trial of Christ. The second seems more appropriate, since this is the only shade in this canto who receives an individual mention, and Pilate's role in the Passion was so important. The point is that Dante leaves this character un-named (in a poem which includes so many names) to imply that, since he is one of those who lived so unworthily that they "never really existed", he does not deserve to be named.

Immediately I understood how those
　　Were members of that dire denomination
　　Displeasing both to God and to his foes.
All these wretches, who'd never really existed,
　　Went naked and were fiercely goaded on
　　By blowflies and by wasps that buzzed and twisted.
These insects went on stinging them and streaking
　　Their faces with their blood which, mixed with tears,
　　Flowed down to where obnoxious worms were licking.
And then I saw, some way beyond all these,　　　　　　　　70
　　A crowd upon the bank of a broad river.
　　That made me beg of Virgil: "Master, please
Tell me. Who are they? And what can incite
　　Them with such eagerness to cross the river,
　　As far as I can see in this dim light?"
And he replied: "All will be made quite plain
　　When we suspend our journey for a while
　　Upon the gloomy banks of Acheron."[1]
So then, with eyes cast down and full of shame,
　　Afraid that I might irk him with my speech,　　　　　　80
　　I kept from talking till we reached the stream.
At that there came towards us in a boat
　　An old old man, whose hair was white with age.[2]
　　"Woe to you, wicked souls!" he shouted out.
"Do not expect to see the sky again!
　　I'm here to take you to the further bank,
　　To everlasting darkness, ice and flame.
And you, you over there, you living soul!
　　Keep well away from these. All these are dead."
　　But when he saw I made no move at all,　　　　　　　90
He said: "By other ways, another port,
　　You will arrive on shore, and not this way.
　　You must be carried in a lighter boat."[3]
My guide said: "Charon, do not fret and fuss.
　　This is wished there where whatsoever is wished
　　Is always done. There's nothing to discuss."
The shaggy jowls went silent. Nothing more
　　Came from the pilot of the muddy river,
　　Who had around his eyes such rings of fire.
But those souls – every troubled naked wretch –　　　　100
　　Changed colour and their teeth began to chatter
　　Soon as they heard his rough-and-ready speech.
They cursed their God, their parents in one breath,

1　The classical river of the dead, which must be crossed to reach the underworld. Its name
　　is derived from a Greek word meaning "pain" or "distress".
2　The classical ferryman of the dead. His Greek name is derived from his bright, fierce
　　eyes.
3　The boat which carries the souls of the saved to the island of Purgatory.

All humankind, the time, the place, the seed
   Of their conception and their very birth.
And they huddled together in a crowd,
   Weeping loudly beside that wicked river
   Which waits for all who have no fear of God.
The demon Charon, eyes like glowing embers,
   Beckons to them and gathers them together,   110
   And with his oar he beats whoever lingers.
As in the autumn, when the leaves descend
   One after the other, till the boughs are left
   With all that clothed them lying on the ground,
In the same fashion Adam's evil seed
   Flew down towards the river one by one,
   At Charon's nod, as birds do when they're lured.
They move away across the murky river,
   And well before they reach the other bank
   Another crowd on this side starts to gather.   120
"My son," my courteous master then explained,
   "Those who have died still subject to God's anger
   All come together here from every land.
And they are keen to reach the other shore,
   Because celestial justice spurs them on
   Until their fear is turned into desire.[1]
No soul that has been good passes this way.
   So now, if Charon was annoyed with you,
   You know exactly what he meant to say."
The instant this was said, the darkened land   130
   Shuddered, so violently that once again
   I'm bathed in sweat, calling it back to mind.
Out of the tearful, sodden earth a wind
   Burst with the sound of thunder, sending up
   Sudden vermilion flashes. I was stunned,
And sank like someone overcome by sleep.

---

1   It is as though the damned, in a very human way, wish to get the suspense over with,
   even though they are going to their punishment. There is also here a hint of something
   which becomes clearer and clearer in the course of the poem: divine justice consists in
   allowing people to have what they really want, and the damned have chosen damnation.

CANTO IV

Dante is aroused by a clap of thunder, to find himself on the other side of Acheron. He and Virgil are on the edge of the abyss which is the Inferno proper. Dante's fear is increased by the sight of Virgil's pallor. However, as Virgil explains, this pallor is not the result of fear, but of compassion for those who are suffering below. And so they enter Limbo, the first circle of the Inferno.

Here nothing can be distinguished at first but the sighs of the damned, who are not here because they have sinned, but because they were not baptized. Virgil himself is one of them. They sigh because of their spiritual grief: they endure no physical pain, but a strong and hopeless desire for God.

Dante asks if anyone was ever taken from this place to bliss, and finds that Virgil understands what is in his mind. Virgil describes the Harrowing of Hell – the rescue by Christ, after His resurrection, of Old Testament patriarchs, one matriarch and others too many to mention. These people worshipped the true God, even though they were not baptized, and they were the first to go to heaven.

Dante and Virgil see ahead of them a hemisphere of light, in which Dante imagines there may be great spirits. Virgil confirms this, and says a special place is allotted to them. A lone voice cries out to announce Virgil's return. Then they are approached by the shades of Homer, Horace, Ovid and Lucan, who welcome Dante because he too is a poet.

When they reach the light, they see it is a castle with seven high walls and a moat. Inside the castle are the shades of many celebrated people. These include, apart from the four classical poets, Trojan and Roman heroes, pagan intellectuals and three Muslims.

Dante and Virgil leave the four famous poets and go down to the second circle of the Inferno, where there is no light at all.

✻

A sudden thunder broke the heavy sleep
    I'd fallen into, and I shook myself,
    As people do when roughly woken up.
From side to side I moved my rested eyes,
    Standing erect, and staring fixedly,
    In an attempt to find out where I was.
The truth is I was standing on the brow
    Over the valley and the sad abyss,
    Receptacle of never-ending woe.
It was so deep, profoundly dark, and full   10
    Of mist that, though I peered and peered again,
    I could not make out anything at all.
"Now down into a world where all is blind,"
    Said then the poet, who was deathly pale.
    "I shall go first, you follow on behind."
And I, who'd seen the pallor in his face,
    Answered, "How can I come, when you're afraid
    Who've always comforted my fearfulness?"

Then he to me, "The thought of those down there
   In misery has painted on my face   20
   That agony which you mistake for fear.
We must go now. The long way urges us."
   And so he entered, and he made me enter
   On the first circle that goes round the abyss.[1]
So far as I could tell by listening, here
   There was no lamentation but of sighs,
   That trembled through the everlasting air,
Arising from the grief, which is not pain,
   Of all the innumerable multitudes
   Of babies and of women and of men.   30
"You do not ask," my gentle master said,
   "Who these spirits are that you are looking at?
   You ought to know, before you go ahead,
They did not sin. And if they have some worth,
   That's not enough, since they were not baptized:
   Baptism is essential in your faith.[2]
They lived too early to be Christian,
   And failed to worship God as people should.[3]
   Among such spirits I myself am one.[4]
It is for such defects, not sin, we're here   40
   Among the lost, and punished but in this:
   That without hope we languish in desire."
My heart was sickened when I caught his sense,
   Because I recognized some men of worth
   Inhabiting that limbo in suspense.
"Tell me, my master and my lord, tell me,"
   I said, because I wanted to be sure,
   With faith that conquers all uncertainty:
"Has anyone ever, through the good he did,
   Or others' help, gone out from here to bliss?"   50
   And he, who knew what I had left unsaid,
Answered: "When I'd arrived but recently
   I saw the coming of a mighty lord,[5]
   Bearing the evidence of victory.[6]

---

1   The Inferno is in the shape of a hollow inverted cone. See the illustration on p. 4.

2   The Jews of the Old Testament – those who worshipped the true God and lived in hope
   of a Messiah – are exempted from this requirement. The exclusion of unbaptized virtu-
   ous pagans from heaven clearly troubled Dante.

3   That is, as was done by the Jews of the Old Testament who were faithful to their covenant
   with God.

4   The inclusion in Limbo of even Virgil, who was for centuries revered by Christians as
   a poet and a sage, stresses the limitations of human reason without God's grace.

5   Christ after His resurrection.

6   Medieval representations of the resurrected Christ often show him with a halo which
   encircles a cross.

He took from here our primal father's shade,[1]
    The shade of Abel and the shade of Noah,
    And Moses, who made laws and who obeyed,
The patriarch Abraham, David the King,
    Israel with his father and his children,
    And Rachel, won with so much labouring,[2]   60
And many others, whom he took to bliss.
    And you must know, no human spirits ever
    Were taken up to glory before this."
While he explained these things, we did not pause,
    But kept on making progress through the wood –
    I mean the wood of shades crowded like trees.
When we had still not travelled very far
    From the circle's highest point, I saw a blaze
    That overcame a gloomy hemisphere.
As yet we were some way away from it,   70
    But not so far that I could not perceive
    That there were honoured people in that light.
"O you who honour both knowledge and art,
    Who are these men who are so highly honoured
    Above the others that they're set apart?"
And he to me: "Their honourable name,
    Still echoing throughout the world above,
    Wins grace in heaven and thus advances them."
He'd scarcely finished when I heard a voice:
    "Give honour to the celebrated poet!   80
    His shade returns which had abandoned us!"
Then, when the voice had stopped and all was still,
    I saw four lofty shades approaching us.
    And they seemed neither glad nor sorrowful.[3]
My kindly master, when he saw them, said:
    "Look well at him who has a sword in hand,[4]
    And comes before the other three as lord.
Homer, the sovereign poet, is the first,
    Satirical Horace is the next to come,
    Ovid is third, and Lucan is the last.[5]   90
Since they, as well as I do, have by right
    That name[6] the single person has pronounced,
    They do me honour, and in that do right."
And as I watch, the glorious circle gathers

---

1   Adam.
2   Jacob, later called Israel, served Rachel's father for fourteen years to win her as his bride.
3   Because they were not physically tormented, but not in bliss either. Also, one traditional notion of a sage was of someone not subject to emotion.
4   Indicating his authorship of the warlike epic, The Iliad.
5   Homer's work was known to Dante only by reputation, but the three Roman poets were among his favourite writers.
6   The name of poet.

Around that master of the highest style[1]
  Who like an eagle soars above all others.
When they had talked a little while together,
  They turned to me and made a sign of welcome,
  At which my master smiled in simple pleasure.
An even higher honour came my way,   100
  For they invited me to join their circle:
  I was the sixth, with such great minds as they.[2]
So we continued till we reached the light,
  Speaking of things of which I must be silent,
  Just as to talk about them then was right.
We came at last to a noble castle's foot,
  Surrounded seven times by soaring walls,[3]
  Round which a little stream served as a moat.
We went across this stream as on dry land –
  I went through seven gateways with these sages.   110
  We reached a meadow growing green, and found
People there whose eyes were grave and slow:
  They looked as though they had authority –
  They seldom spoke, and then gently and low.
We drew apart onto some rising ground,
  Into an open area full of light,
  From which we could see everyone around.
In front of me, on the enamelled green,
  All those great spirits were revealed to me:
  I still rejoice to think what I have seen.   120
I saw Electra there, with all her seed,
  Among whom there were Hector and Aeneas,
  And Caesar, all in armour and hawk-eyed.[4]
I saw Camilla and Penthesilea,
  And King Latinus on the other side,
  Sitting beside his child, Lavinia, there.[5]
I saw that Brutus who drove Tarquin out,
  Lucrece and Julia, Marcia and Cornelia.
  And I saw Saladin, alone, apart.[6]
I had to raise my eyes somewhat to see   130
  Where the great master of the men who know[7]

---

1   The epic style.
2   Dante is welcomed by them as a fellow poet.
3   Opinions vary, but probably best interpreted as referring to the seven liberal arts – grammar, rhetoric, logic, arithmetic, music, geography and astronomy.
4   In this tercet: mother of Troy's founder; defender of Troy; refugee from Troy who founded the Latin race; Julius Caesar.
5   In this tercet: queen killed by Aeneas; Amazon killed by Achilles; King of Latium before Aeneas; Aeneas's third wife.
6   In this tercet: Junius Brutus; four virtuous women of republican Rome; Sultan of Egypt who inflicted severe defeats on crusaders, yet had a high reputation in Europe.
7   Aristotle.

Sat with his philosophic family.
They all look up to him, all do him honour:
I saw both Socrates and Plato there,
Standing closer to him than any other,
Democritus, who puts all down to chance,
Diogenes, Empedocles and Zeno,
Heraclitus and Thales, Anaxagoras.[1]
I also saw the worthy herbalist
Dioscorides; Linus and Orpheus,   140
Tully and Seneca the moralist,[2]
Euclid the geometer and Ptolemy,
Hippocrates, Galen and Avicenna,
Averroës who wrote the Commentary.[3]
I cannot now give details of them all:
My long theme urges me, and very often
What's said falls short of what there is to tell.
The company of six now disassembles.
My leader takes me on a different trail,
Out of that calm, into the air that trembles.   150
I come to where there is no light at all.

---

1   Greek philosophers of the pre-Christian era.

2   In this tercet: Greek physician of the first century AD; two mythical Greek poets; Cicero (Roman statesman and orator); Roman tragedian (d.65 AD).

3   In this tercet: Greek mathematician (c.300 BC); Greek astronomer (second century AD); Greek physician (c.400 BC); Greek physician (second century AD); Arab philosopher (d.1037); Arab philosopher from Spain whose Commentary was on Aristotle.

CANTO V

Dante has left Limbo behind: now all the shades he meets have damned themselves by their own actions. This second circle contains the lustful: worse sins are punished lower down in the Inferno. King Minos of Crete is here as judge, and he consigns the damned to an appropriate circle of the Inferno, winding his tail around himself a certain number of times to indicate how many circles down the sinner must go. Like Charon, he tries to warn Dante off, but is rebuked with the same words which Virgil used to Charon.

This circle resounds with cries of lamentation, mixed with the bellowing of opposing winds on which the spirits are carried higgledy-piggledy, as once they allowed themselves to be swept along by their passions.

Virgil names some of these spirits, all of them more or less legendary people, for whom the reader may well feel sympathy, so striking are their stories. But then Dante speaks to two people who had certainly existed and died during his lifetime – Paolo Malatesta and Francesca da Rimini. It is clear why these two spirits are associated with the others: the immediate cause of their sin was their reading of a romantic episode of the Arthurian legends. Their fate is pitiful, and it disturbs Dante so much (he has, after all, himself been much concerned with literary depictions of love) that he faints.

This, justly one of the most famous episodes in the *Comedy*, has itself become part of the literature of romantic love. But a merely romantic interpretation of it would be inadequate. Francesca is damned out of her own mouth. All the souls have to reveal their unvarnished sins to Minos; but when she is speaking to Dante, Francesca tries subtly to exculpate herself, revealing the very irresponsibility which led to the damnable sinful act. We find ourselves sympathizing with Francesca, not because the judgement on her is too hard, but because we have similar defects ourselves. The seriousness of the sin, with its dreadful consequence of three damnations, is neither glossed over by Dante nor blurred in a legendary mist.

A nd so from the first circle I descended
    Into the second, which contains less space[1]
    And much more woe, whence shouts of pain ascended.
Minos[2] is there, most horribly, and grinding
    His teeth. He judges guilt as people enter,
    And places them according to his winding.
I mean that when the spirit born for ill
    Comes in his sight, it makes a full confession;
    And then that expert on all sin can tell
What depth of Hell is most appropriate,   10
    Winding his long tail round himself to number
    How many circles down it must be put.
Always there are large crowds. Each one in turn
    Must stand in front of him to hear his judgement.

---

1   All the circles become smaller as Dante descends further into the Inferno. See *Inf.* IV, 24 and note.
2   Mythical King of Crete, generally regarded as a just ruler who became judge of the dead in Hades.

They speak, they hear, they're straight away sent down.
"O you, arriving where the wretched dwell,"
    Cried Minos when he saw me there, neglecting
    To carry out his task as usual,[1]
"Watch how you enter and in whom you trust!
    The entrance is so wide it may deceive you!"   20
    My leader answered him: "Why this outburst?
Do not obstruct his fated journey thus.
    This is wished there where whatsoever is wished
    Is always done. There's nothing to discuss."[2]
And now there is the sound of voices, loud
    With lamentation, and I have arrived
    Where outcries strike my ears from every side.
I have come somewhere where all light is mute,
    Where there is bellowing like a storm at sea,
    With wild opposing winds fighting it out.   30
This hellish storm, that does not slacken ever,
    Whirls all the spirits irresistibly
    Along with it, and beats and bowls them over.
And when they come where rocks have fallen down,[3]
    Why then what outcries, wailings, and laments!
    And how they curse the power that is divine.
I understood how all such torments are
    Destined for those whose sins are of the flesh,
    Those who subject their reason to desire.
And like a flock of starlings on the wing   40
    In the cold season, crowded all together,
    So the bad spirits in that blustering
Are carried here and there and up and down:
    They are not comforted by thoughts of rest,
    Or even diminution of their pain.
And like a flock of loud lamenting cranes
    Making themselves a long line in the air,
    I saw shades coming and emitting groans,
Borne on the onrush of that windy war.
    So that I questioned: "Master, who are these,   50
    Punished so hard in this black atmosphere?"
My master answered me: "The first of those
    Of whom you wish to be informed was empress
    Of many lands and many languages.
She was so vicious, unrestrained, and lewd
    That she made licence licit in her laws
    To take away the blame she had incurred.[4]

---

1   His allocation of the damned to their appropriate circle.
2   See *Inf.* III, 95–96.
3   The result (as we are told in *Inf.* XII) of the earthquake which occurred at the time of the Crucifixion.
4   By her incest with her son.

She was Semiramis – we read of her
    That she was Ninus' wife and his successor.
    She ruled the land now in the Sultan's power.[1]   60
That other killed herself in love's despair,
    Breaking her faith with the ashes of Sychaeus.[2]
    Then Cleopatra[3] is the next one there.
See Helen, for whose sake the times were cursed
    With crime and woe, and see the great Achilles:
    He too was overcome by love at last.[4]
See Paris,[5] and see Tristan."[6] And he showed
    A thousand shades and more to me, and named them,
    Of those whom love and lust had left for dead.
When I had heard my teacher to the end,   70
    Naming the ancient ladies and the knights,
    Such horror seized me that I almost swooned.
I started: "Poet, I would be inclined
    To talk with those two who go yoked together
    And seem to be so light upon the wind."
Then he to me: "You try it when those two
    Have come much nearer. Beg them by that love
    Which drives them on, and they will turn to you."
Once they were blown towards us by the wind,
    I spoke: "O terribly tormented souls,   80
    Come here and speak to us, if that's not banned!"
And just as doves, attracted by desire
    Into their nest, their wings outspread and still,
    Glide with a clear intention through the air,
So these two left the throng where Dido was,
    And came to us through that foul atmosphere,
    Such was the power of my affectionate cries.
"O living being, so gracious and so good
    That you come visiting, through pitch-black air,
    Us who once stained this world of ours with blood,   90
Oh, if the Lord of all were but our friend,
    We would appeal to Him to give you peace,
    Since you show sympathy with our sad end.
And anything you wish to talk about,
    Whatever it is, we'll talk of it with you,

---

1   Egypt.

2   In the *Aeneid*, Dido Queen of Carthage had vowed to remain faithful to the memory of her dead husband. She violated this oath by her love for Aeneas, and killed herself when Aeneas forsook her.

3   Queen of Egypt, lover of Julius Caesar and later Mark Antony, who killed herself to avoid being captured by Octavius after the Battle of Actium.

4   Because of his love for Polyxena, daughter of Priam, King of Troy, he let himself be ambushed and killed.

5   The son of Priam, he stole Helen from Menelaus, causing the Trojan wars.

6   The adulterous lover of Isolde, who was killed by her husband.

In these few moments while the storm is mute.
I must explain my native city lies
   Upon that seacoast where the Po descends
   To the calm sea with all its tributaries.[1]
Love, kindling quickly in the noble heart,   100
   Seized him: he was enamoured of this body
   Killed in a way from which I suffer yet.[2]
Love, who insists all loved ones must requite
   Their lovers, seized me so with love's enjoyment
   That, as you see, love does not leave me yet.
Love chose a single death for both of us.
   Caïna[3] waits for him who took our lives."
   Such were the words of hers which came across.
I, when I'd heard these stricken souls, inclined
   My head, and for a long time held it down.   110
   At length the poet asked: "What's in your mind?"
Then I replied to him and said: "Alas!
   How many pleasant thoughts, and how much ardour
   Have brought this wretched pair to such a pass!"
And then once more I turned to them to speak
   And said: "Francesca, seeing how you suffer
   Makes me weep tears of sympathy and grief.
But tell me: in the time of gentle sighs,
   By what and in what way did Love permit you
   To recognize your dubious desires?"   120
She said: "There is no greater wretchedness
   Than calling back to mind a happy time
   In misery – your teacher[4] too knows this.
But, if you want to understand the root
   Cause of our love – it seems you really want to –
   I'll tell you, though I weep describing it.
We were reading one day for delectation
   Of Lancelot and how love held him close.[5]
   We were alone and quite without suspicion.
At several points that reading drew our eyes   130
   Together, drained the colour from our cheeks.
   But one point only took us by surprise.
When we read how the smile of the belovèd
   Was kissed by such a celebrated lover,[6]

---

1   The speaker is Francesca da Rimini. Born in Ravenna, she was married to Gianciotto
     Malatesta, but fell in love with his brother Paolo. Her husband came upon the guilty
     pair and killed them.
2   Not only was her death violent, but it allowed her no time to repent.
3   A zone of the lowest circle of the Inferno (XXXII), reserved for those who betray their
     relatives. It is named after Cain, who murdered his brother Abel (Gen. 4:8).
4   Virgil.
5   The adulterous love of Lancelot for Guinevere, the wife of his lord King Arthur.
6   Guinevere was kissed by Lancelot.

This one,[1] from whom I never will be severed,
Kissed me upon the mouth, trembling all over.
    That book's a pander, and the man who wrote it:
    And on that day we read in it no further."
While the one spirit said all this to me,
    The other wept, and my disquietude   140
    Brought on a fainting fit. I seemed to die,
And fell down as a body does when dead.

---

1   Paolo.

CANTO VI

Dante is now in the third circle of the Inferno, that of the gluttonous. Their shades are prostrated in fetid mud where hail, dirty rain and snow fall upon them with unvarying intensity. They are deafened by the continual howling of Cerberus, the three-headed monster, who also tears them apart and flays them with his claw-like hands. There is little that seems human in this circle: only one shade speaks, and he lacks individuality. The damned here are what their gross appetites have made them – subhuman, almost sub-bestial.

The one shade who is interested enough in the visitors to speak to them is Ciacco: he recognizes Dante as a fellow Florentine. In response to Dante's questions, he discusses the troubles in their native city and hints at Dante's coming exile. It is noteworthy that he attributes all the discord in Florence to the moral faults of the citizens, and does not discuss policies at all. We have here the start of one of the great themes of the *Comedy* – the history of Florence.

As the companions continue to walk through this circle, they discuss the life to come, and Virgil explains what the state of the damned will be after the Last Judgement.

They then descend to the fourth circle, which is dominated by Pluto, god of wealth.

On coming to my senses, lost when faced
  With all the wretchedness of those in-laws
  Whose sad plight left me totally confused,
I see new torments, new tormented shades
  Rising around me as I move around,
  Wherever I turn myself, wherever I gaze.
I've come to the third circle,[1] that of heavy
  Rain which goes on for ever, coldly cursed,
  Whose nature and whose volume never vary.
Huge hail, with water of a filthy texture   10
  And snow, comes pouring down through murky air –
  The earth is stinking that receives this mixture.
And Cerberus,[2] a strange and cruel beast,
  Is growling like a dog through all three gullets
  Over the people who lie here immersed.
He has red eyes, a black and greasy beard,
  A swollen belly, and great claws for hands,
  By which the shades are rent apart and flayed.
The spirits howl like hounds under the rain:
  They have to shelter one flank with the other,   20
  And so the sinners turn and turn again.
When Cerberus perceived us, the great worm,
  He opened all his mouths and bared his fangs.
  There was no part of him that did not squirm.

---

1 That of the gluttonous.
2 The classical poets represent Cerberus, the guardian of their underworld, as a three-headed dog. So does Dante, but he adds grotesque details of his own.

And then my leader spreads his hands out, tears
   Up earth until his fists are overflowing
   And thrusts it in those gaping apertures.[1]
Then like a dog that, barking for a bone,
   Calms down immediately it gnaws its food,
   Solely intent on gobbling it all down,   30
Just so did the three filthy faces there
   Of Cerberus, the demon dog who stuns
   The spirits till they wish they could not hear.
We walked across those shades the constant flood
   Goes beating down upon, placing our feet
   On nothingness which seems like flesh and blood.
They went on lying prostrate, all of them
   Except for one who sat up suddenly
   The instant that he saw us passing him.
"O you," he called, "who are now being led   40
   Through this Inferno, please call me to mind,
   For you were born a while before I died."
And I to him: "The torment that you suffer
   Appears to drive you from my memory,
   So that it seems we never knew each other.
But tell me who you are, you who are placed
   In such a spot, with such a penalty
   That if there's worse, none rouses more disgust."
And he replied: "While I lived in the sun,
   That city,[2] overflowing with its envy,   50
   Which is your city still, was also mine.
Ciacco[3] was what you citizens called me.
   You see me here, a broken man in rain,
   And ruined by the sin of gluttony.
And, sad soul that I am, I'm not alone,
   Since all these suffer the same penalty
   For the same sin." He did not carry on,
And so I said: "Ciacco, your wretched state
   So weighs upon me that it makes me weep.
   But tell me, if you can, the future fate   60
Of the divided city's citizens.[4]
   Is there one man who's just? Tell me the reason
   Why it's a prey to so much dissidence."
And then he answered: "After much dispute
   There will be bloodshed, and the rural party[5]

---

1   A parody of the feeding of Cerberus in the *Aeneid* with a sop of honey and drugged
    meal to soothe him, so that he may allow Aeneas to enter the underworld.
2   Florence.
3   Possibly a nickname meaning "swine".
4   Divided politically into Guelfs and Ghibellines, and subdivided, as we learn in the next
    few lines, into White Guelfs (of whom Dante is one) and Black Guelfs.
5   White Guelfs.

Will use brute force to drive the other out.
Then this party will lose its dominance
    Inside three years, and the other party[1] triumph
    With help from him who's sitting on the fence.[2]
This party then will hold the other down,   70
    And hold its own head high, with gross inflictions[3]
    For many years, however they complain.
There are two just men,[4] but they're never heard.
    For three sparks only have set hearts on fire:
    Envy I mean, and avarice, and pride."
And so he ended on a cheerless note.
    But I said: "I would like more information.
    Therefore I beg you, tell me more than that.
Farinata, Tegghiaio – men of honour –
    Jacopo Rusticucci, Arrigo, Mosca,   80
    And all who set their hearts on right behaviour –
Say where they are that we may come together.
    I have a longing to be told if Heaven
    Comforts them, or the Inferno makes them bitter."
"Among the blackest souls is where they are,
    For different sins have sent them to the depths.[5]
    You'll see them there, if you go down so far.
But when you're back in the sweet world again,
    I beg you to remember me to people.
    I'll say no more to you. You'll ask in vain."   90
With that he turned aside his steady glance,
    Squinnied at me a while, then bent his head,
    And fell down with the other blinded ones.[6]
"He will not rise," my leader said to me,
    "Until the blast of the angelic trumpet
    Heralds the inimical authority,[7]
When all will reassume their flesh and figure[8]
    (Once they have found the place where they are buried)
    And hear the sentence that resounds for ever."
And so we passed across the squalid slime,   100
    A mix of shades and mud – and we walked slowly,
    Touching a little on the life to come.
And so I asked him: "Master, these torments,

---

1   Black Guelfs.
2   Probably Pope Boniface VIII, a *bête noire* of Dante's. See also *Inf.* XIX, 52–57.
3   Including Dante's banishment from his native city.
4   We are left to guess who they may be. Possibly all that is intended is an indefinite small
    number.
5   Of these five prominent Florentines, Farinata is mentioned again in *Inf.* x, Tegghiaio
    and Rusticucci in *Inf.* xvi, and Mosca in *Inf.* xxvIII. No more is heard of Arrigo.
6   Face down in mud, of course, but spiritually blind also.
7   Christ.
8   A reference to the dogma of the resurrection of the body.

Will they grow greater from the Judgement Day,
   Or lessen, or be simply as intense?"
Then he to me: "Your learning makes it plain:
   The nearer something comes to its perfection,
   The greater is its pleasure and its pain.
And these accursèd people here, although
   They'll never ever reach their true perfection,   110
   Expect to be much nearer then than now."[1]
We went on walking that circumference,
   Talking of more things than I care to say,
   And came at last to where the road descends.[2]
Here we found Pluto,[3] the great enemy.

---

1   They cannot, since they are damned, ever be perfect. But they will be nearer to perfection when their souls are reunited with their bodies at the Last Judgement.
2   From the third to the fourth circle.
3   The classical god of wealth. He is "the great enemy" because "the love of money is the root of all evil" (2 Timothy 6:10).

CANTO VII

At the entrance to the fourth circle is Pluto, the mythical god of the underworld, personi-
fying wealth, the love of which is "the root of all evil". He is angry at Dante's arrival, but
Virgil immediately takes the wind out of his sails, and the travellers are able to descend into
the fourth circle.

Here are the souls of misers and spendthrifts, guilty of sins which at first sight seem op-
posite, and yet are very similar because they both involve a lack of judgement in the use of
riches. They are in two groups, rolling great weights towards each other with their chests,
upbraiding each other as they do so. When the two groups have clashed together, they turn
back to where they started from, describe a semicircle, and then once more roll their weights
towards each other, to clash again in the middle. It is a striking image of futile effort. Dante
wishes to see if he can identify any of them, but they are so disfigured by their sins that they
are unrecognizable.

In answer to Dante's question, Virgil explains the function of Fortune, seen here as an
angel appointed by God to move this world's wealth about. Virgil stresses that the reasons
for her actions are quite beyond human comprehension.

Following a watercourse which runs from the fourth circle, Dante and Virgil arrive at a
marsh, the Styx. The wrathful are here, naked and covered in mud, and attacking each other
savagely with their teeth and every other part of their bodies.

Submerged in the marsh – their presence revealed by bubbles which rise to the surface –
are the souls of the sullen, whose anger is turned inward on themselves. They cannot speak
properly, because of the mud in their throats, but Virgil explains to Dante what they are
trying to say: they wilfully lived in gloom.

As Dante and Virgil continue to walk round the circle, they come across a tower.

✳

"Papé Satàn, papé Satàn, aleppe!"[1]
   That is what Pluto rasped in raucous tones.
   But that all-knowing sage, keeping me happy,
Said: "Never let the sound of him perplex
   Or frighten you. Whatever power he has,
   He cannot stop us climbing down these rocks."
He turned back to that bloated face and said:
   "Silence, cursed wolf! If you must be consumed
   With anger, let it gobble you inside.
This is no pointless journey into dark.   10
   It is decided there on high, where Michael
   Left arrogant rebellion thunderstruck."[2]
As sails, once proudly swollen in the wind,

---

1   Like others with posts of responsibility in the Inferno, Pluto is annoyed at Dante's ar-
rival. He seems to be addressing his chief, Satan.

2   "And there was war in heaven: Michael and his angels fought against the dragon; and
the dragon fought and his angels, and prevailed not... And the great dragon was cast
out, that old serpent, called the Devil, and Satan, which deceiveth the whole world: he
was cast out into the earth, and his angels were cast out with him." (Revelation 12:7–9)

Slump in a tangle with the snapping mast,
So that outrageous beast dropped to the ground.
We went to the fourth level, and ahead
  Along the edge of the abyss where all
  The evils of the world are pocketed.
Justice of God! Who's ever seen amassed
  So many uncouth torments as I saw?   20
  Why does this guilt of ours so lay us waste?
As near Charybdis,[1] where the waters, once
  They batter the opposing waters, shatter,
  The people here are led a merry dance.
Here I saw shades more numerous than ever,
  Rolling great weights by pushing with their chests,
  Howling out loud, from one side to the other.
They struck against each other, and then they
  All turned around and rolled the weights back shouting:
  "Why do you hoard?" and "Why d'you throw away?"[2]   30
Describing a half-circle in the gloom,
  They went from each side to the opposite,
  Once more repeating their opprobrium.
Then each lot turned, when they had reached the spot
  Half round the circle, for another joust.
  And I, who felt so very sick at heart,
Said: "Master, I would like all this explained.
  Who are these people here? Were they all clerics,
  These here, the tonsured ones on our left hand?"
And he to me: "All of them used to squint –   40
  Squint mentally I mean – while they were living:
  There was no golden mean in how they spent.
Their own loud voices bark this clearly out
  Whenever they reach those two points on the circle
  Where their opposing faults show them apart.
Those on the left were clerics (those with less
  Hair on the top), and popes and cardinals,
  Among whom there is endless avarice."
And then I said: "Master, among all these,
  Who fouled themselves with either of the sins,   50
  There should be some whom I can recognize."
And he replied: "You think such thoughts in vain.
  The undiscerning life that made them filthy
  Now makes their features harder to discern.
To all eternity these weights are rolled.
  This lot will one day leave their sepulchres

---

1   The whirlpool in the Straits of Messina.
2   Misers and spendthrifts are punished together and in the same way, because both have
    failed to observe moderation in their use of wealth.

With fists clenched tight,[1] and those with heads quite bald.[2]
Ill-giving and ill-keeping took away
  The bright world from them, leaving them these clashes
  I will not scrat around to beautify.   60
And now, my son, you see the brief illusion
  Of this world's wealth, which is in Fortune's hands,
  And brings the human race to such confusion.
For all the gold that is beneath the moon,
  Or ever was, could never pacify,
  Among these weary spirits, even one."[3]
"Master," I asked him then, "tell me, who is
  This so-called Fortune you have touched upon,
  Who has all this world's riches in her claws?"
And he replied: "How much sheer ignorance   70
  Are foolish human beings the victims of!
  Now, as I feed it you, digest my sense.
He whose wisdom is utterly transcendent
  Made the heavens, and gave them guides[4] so that
  Each part to every other was resplendent,
With all the light apportioned equally.
  And he ordained a guide and minister
  For worldly wealth and fame in the same way,
To move these empty goods, when time was right,
  From race to race, and over families,   80
  Beyond the influence of human wit.
So, while one people rules, another's weak,
  Exactly as that minister decides,
  Whose judgement's hidden in long grass, a snake.
Your wisdom cannot come to grips with hers.
  For she foresees and judges, and maintains
  Her kingdom as the other gods[5] do theirs.
Her permutations never know a truce.
  Necessity compels her to be swift,
  So often do men have to change their place.   90
So this is she who is reviled and cursed,
  Even by those who ought to give her praise,
  And blamed without being guilty, and traduced.
But she is blessèd, and she does not hear:
  With the other primal creatures[6] she is happy –

---

1 The misers, on the Day of Judgement.
2 The spendthrifts. The idea is that they are so wasteful that they have thrown away even
   the hair from their heads.
3 No amount of wealth could pacify them in Hell, any more than it could in life.
4 The angelic intelligences who rule the heavenly spheres.
5 Virgil is using the term a pagan would use to refer to the angelic intelligences.
6 The angels, the first beings to be created.

Rejoicing in her bliss, she turns her sphere.[1]
Now let's descend to greater misery,
    For every star is setting that was rising
    When I set out, and we must not delay."
We crossed onto the further bank, from which   100
    There is a spring that gurgles and pours out
    Into a sort of effluential ditch.
The water was obscure rather than black.
    And we, together with those murky waves,
    Went down along a rough, uneven track.
This melancholy stream descends, and makes –
    Beyond the foot of that accursèd slope –
    Its way into a swamp known as the Styx.[2]
And I, who'd come to a halt to stand and gaze,
    Saw muddied people wallowing in the mire,   110
    All of them naked, all with looks of rage.
And these, not only did they beat and beat
    Each other with their fists, heads, breasts and feet,
    But tore each other piecemeal with their teeth.[3]
My kindly teacher said: "My son, you see
    The souls of those whom anger overmastered.
    And what is more – I hope you'll credit me –
Beneath the surface many people sigh,
    With lots of little bubbles rising up,
    As you can see, wherever you cast your eye.   120
They say, stuck in the mud: 'Our minds stayed dark
    In the sweet air enlightened by the sun.
    Inside us was a sort of sluggish smoke.
Now we are sullen in the gloomy mud.'[4]
    This is the hymn they're gurgling in their gullets,
    Because they can't sing words out as they should."[5]
So, in a wide arc round the mire, we came –
    Between the dry bank and the filthy moist,
    Our eyes upon the gulpers-down of slime –
Right to the foot of a lofty tower at last.   130

---

1   As other angelic intelligences guide the heavenly spheres, so Fortune regulates those
    things (worldly wealth and status) which are within her sphere of influence. There is
    also a hint of the traditional notion of Fortune's wheel.
2   One of the rivers of the classical underworld.
3   The wrathful act in the Inferno as they did on earth, but in the Inferno there is no
    disguising the essential nature of their actions.
4   They, like the other souls in this circle, are wrathful, but their wrath turns inward on
    themselves.
5   Because of the mud in their throats.

CANTO VIII

Here, in the fifth circle (that of the wrathful, the proud and the sullen), Dante goes back in his account to the time before he and Virgil reached the tower. They could see two fires burning at the top of the tower, and another fire in the distance apparently answering them.

A boat arrives, guided by the angry demon Phlegyas. When Dante steps into the boat, it sinks lower in the water because of his body's weight.

A figure rears up out of the water, demanding to know who they are. Dante brusquely retorts with the same question and then reveals he knew him all along. Virgil praises Dante for his harshness towards the shade, who to Dante's delight is attacked by his fellow sufferers in the swamp. He is Filippo Argenti, a proud and foul-tempered Florentine.

Dante is here showing himself full of a righteous indignation at evil, which is sharply distinguished from unwarranted and excessive anger. Virgil certainly approves of his attitude.

The sound of lamentation is heard, and then we are back to the moment when Dante and Virgil arrived beneath the high tower. This is the city of Dis, named after a classical god of the underworld. Virgil explains that the towers of the city look red because of the fires always burning inside them.

On the city walls are more than a thousand devils. They say that Virgil may proceed, but Dante must go back. Virgil attempts to encourage Dante, and goes forward to speak with the devils alone. Their conversation does not last long. The devils run back into the city and shut its gates in Virgil's face. Virgil walks slowly back to where Dante is waiting in trepidation. Virgil, although he is clearly not so confident as he was, again tries to encourage Dante by describing how the gates of the Inferno were broken at Christ's Harrowing of Hell, and by saying that help is on its way.

To go back quite a way – when we'd not yet
    Come to the high tower's foot, as I have mentioned,
    Our eyes were drawn up to the top of it
By two small flames which somebody placed there,
    And yet another answering their signal,
    So far away it seemed much tinier.[1]
And I turned to the ocean of good sense:
    "What does this mean? What does that other fire
    Reply? And who are they who send the signs?"
And he replied: "Over these muddy waves   10
    You can already see what to expect,
    Unless the marsh mist hides it from your eyes."
No arrow from a bowstring ever shot
    Away so rapidly through yielding air
    As I could see a very little boat
Coming towards us through the waves meanwhile,
    Under the guidance of a single boatman.

---

1   In Dante's day such signals suggested military activity.

"I've got you now," he shrieked, "you wicked soul!"[1]
"O Phlegyas,[2] O Phlegyas, you waste
   Your breath," my master said, "on this occasion: 20
   You've only got us till the marsh is crossed."
Like one who has uncovered some foul plot
   He's been the victim of, which makes him angry,
   Just so was Phlegyas, choking in defeat.
My leader stepped into the little boat,
   And made me follow after. Only then
   Did it sink lower, underneath my weight.[3]
And once we two were in the boat together,
   The ancient prow went cutting through the waves,
   Plunging more deeply than it had done ever.   30
While we were moving through the stagnant slime,
   There rose before me someone caked in mud
   Who asked: "Who are you, here before your time?"[4]
"I'm here," I said, "but I shall not remain.
   And who are you, who've made yourself so filthy?"
   His answer was: "You see me weep for sin."
Then I to him: "With weeping and regret,
   Accursèd spirit, you're here and must remain.
   For I know who you are, despite the dirt."
He stretched up both his hands to grip the boat –   40
   At this, my wary master pushed him off,
   And said: "Back to the other dogs! Off! Out!"
My lord then threw his arms around my neck,
   Kissed me and said: "Indignant soul, how blessed
   The womb that bore, the paps that gave you suck![5]
That man was, in the world, presumptuous;
   No kindly acts adorn his memory:
   Therefore down here his shade is furious.
How many now up there are full of pride,
   Who will one day be here like pigs in mud,   50
   Leaving behind but scorn for what they did!"
I answered: "Master, I would really like
   To see this fellow drenched in this pigswill
   Before we end our voyage on the lake."
And he: "Before the shore comes into sight
   That aspiration will be satisfied:
   To grant you such a wish is only right."

---

1   The boatman presumes that Dante is a damned soul.
2   A character from Greek myth who, to avenge his daughter's death at the hands of Apollo,
     set fire to Apollo's temple at Delphi. He is therefore included here as an embodiment
     of impious and uncontrolled rage.
3   Virgil, who went into the boat before Dante, is a weightless shade.
4   This shade is more perceptive than Phlegyas, since he realizes Dante is still alive.
5   An echo of Luke 11:27: "Blessed is the womb that bare thee, and the paps which thou
     hast sucked." In the Gospel these words are addressed to Christ.

I saw that spirit grabbed, soon after that,
   As I had wanted, by more muddy people,
   And I'm still giving thanks to God for it.   60
"Filippo Argenti! Grab him!"[1] they all cried,
   At which the shade of the waspish Florentine
   Tore at himself, being eaten up inside.
We left him then, with no more to be said,
   But sudden lamentation strikes my ears,
   And I, my eyes wide open, peer ahead.
My kindly master told me: "Now, my son,
   We're getting near that city known as Dis,[2]
   With its grave citizens and garrison."
"Master," I said, "already I discern   70
   Its mosques[3] down in the valley quite distinctly,
   Bright-red, as though they'd recently been drawn
From fire." He answered: "Fire eternally
   Glowing, red-hot within them, turns them red
   Down in these nether regions, as you see."
At last we came to where deep trenches made
   A ring of moats round this despondent city:
   Its walls were built of iron, it appeared.
Not without ranging first in a wide turn,
   We came to somewhere where the blatant boatman   80
   Shouted: "Get out! This is where you go in."
I saw a thousand or more, all ranged above,[4]
   Poured down like rain from heaven,[5] angrily
   Wanting to know: "Who is this, still alive,
Who's coming through the kingdom of the dead?"
   My master made a sign to show his wish
   To speak with them, a little to one side.
Then they clamped down somewhat on their disdain
   And said: "Come by yourself, and let him go.
   He's over-bold, to enter this domain.   90
Let him retrace his steps on his mad road –
   That's if he can! For you are staying here,
   You who have been, through this dark realm, his guide."
Imagine, Reader, if you can, my fear,
   Hearing them saying those accursèd words.
   I thought I'd never find my way back here.
"O my dear leader, who have frequently

---

1   A Florentine, contemporary with Dante, easily aroused to anger. He was said to have
been so proud that he had his horse shod with silver, and his surname (from *argento*,
silver) seems to allude to this.

2   On several occasions in the Inferno Dante uses this name for Satan.

3   These are the city's towers, which rise above its walls. Dante and his contemporaries
considered Islam a Christian heresy.

4   On the walls of the city.

5   The rebel angels, who were cast out of heaven, became devils.

Given me confidence, and snatched me safe
Out of the dangers that stood in my way,
Don't leave me in this plight," I tried to say,   100
"And, if we are forbidden to go further,
Then let's go back together, straight away!"
He who had guided me so far replied:
"You need not fear. None can prevent our passage:
Consider him by whom it's guaranteed![1]
Wait for me here, and let your heart be filled
And nourished with good hope and comfort. I
Shall not forsake you in this nether world."
He leaves me there, while he goes on ahead,
My kindly guide leaves me in dreadful doubt,   110
With yes and no contending in my head.
I could not make out what it was he said,
But he had not been with them very long
Before they all went running back inside.
They slammed the city gates, our enemies,
Full in my master's face. He, left outside,
Turned back and walked towards me by degrees.
His eyes cast down, no sign left on his face
Of former confidence, he sighed and said:
"And these have barred me from this mournful place!"   120
Then turned to me: "Because I seem dismayed,
Don't be cast down, for I shall win this battle,
Whatever defence is organized inside.
This insolence of theirs is nothing new.
They showed it at a less secluded gate,[2]
Which stays unbarred since it was broken through.[3]
You saw that gate and saw its deadly word.[4]
Already inside it, coming down the abyss,
Through circle after circle with no guide,
Is one who'll open up the way for us."[5]   130

---

1   God.
2   The entrance to the Inferno. See the beginning of *Inf.* III.
3   By Christ, at the Harrowing of Hell. See *Inf.* IV, 46–63 and notes.
4   The inscription on the gate at the entrance to the Inferno.
5   There has been repeated emphasis on the difficulty of the way by which Dante and Virgil
    have travelled. The ease with which this new arrival moves is therefore all the more
    mysterious and significant. His identity and purpose are not made clear until halfway
    through the next canto.

CANTO IX

Dante and Virgil are left in suspense outside the City of Dis and, despite Virgil's suggestion in the previous canto that help is on the way, their consternation increases. Virgil, the embodiment of human reason unaided by divine grace, remains baffled in the face of unmotivated malevolence, and his bewilderment is communicated to Dante.

In reply to Dante's fearful question, Virgil says that he has been right down to the lowest depth of the Inferno once before, and he therefore knows the way. However, any comfort this might have brought to Dante is cancelled by the appearance on the city walls of the three Furies, grotesque and terrifying personifications of the spirit of vengeance.

Even more frightening is the appearance of the Gorgon Medusa, who has the power to petrify people. Virgil warns Dante to turn his back on her, and adds his own hands to Dante's to cover Dante's eyes. The terror caused by all this is converted to awe when, heralded by a great wind, a figure is seen moving without effort across the marsh. The shades of the damned in the marsh scuttle away at this angel's approach. The angel then opens the gates of the City of Dis by the mere touch of a little wand, rebukes the devils and goes away. Divine grace has achieved effortlessly what no human endeavours could.

Dante and Virgil are now able to enter the city unopposed. Inside it they see a large stretch of countryside (the sixth circle) covered with monumental tombs. The lids of the tombs are propped open, and wailing is heard from within them. The tombs are heated by flames scattered among them. Inside the tombs are heretics, punished by greater or less heat according to the gravity of the heresy of which they were guilty.

T hat I through cowardice had lost my colour,
 Seeing my leader turning slowly back,
 Made him dissemble his unwonted pallor.
He paused like an attentive listener,
 Because he could not see into the distance
 Through the dense fog and the benighted air.
"'There is no question: we must win this fight,"
 He said. "If not... But think who's interceded...
 I can't but fear it's being left too late!"
I saw quite clearly how he tried to hide   10
 What he'd begun to say with further words
 Of different meaning from the first he said.
That hardly stopped his words from rousing fear,
 Because I gave the sentence he'd cut short
 A meaning worse perhaps than it could bear.
"Does anybody ever come so deep
 Into this hollow from the highest circle,
 Whose only torment is his lack of hope?"[1]
That was my question, and he said, "Although
 It seldom happens any one of us   20

---

1 Dante's question reveals his uncertainty as to Virgil's knowledge of the way.

40

Goes on the road on which I'm going now,
The truth is that I have been here before,
    Under the spell of pitiless Erichtho,[1]
    Who called shades back to where their bodies were.
My flesh had not been parted from my soul
    For long when she sent me inside this city
    To draw a spirit from the depth of Hell.[2]
I mean the lowest, darkest place of all,
    Furthest from the all-motivating sphere.[3]
    Be reassured: I know the way there well.   30
This swamp which breathes out such a stinking mist
    Goes all the way around the cheerless city
    Which now we cannot enter unopposed."
Though he said more, I don't remember it,
    Because my eyes directed my attention
    Towards the high tower where it glowed red-hot,
Where, on a sudden, there before my eyes
    Stood three infernal Furies stained with blood.
    They looked like women and had women's ways,
With bright green hydras twisted round the waist,   40
    With thin serpents and two-horned snakes for hair,
    Bound round their savage heads and interlaced.
And he, so cognizant of old of these
    Slaves of the queen of eternal lamentation,
    Said to me: "Look! The fierce Erinyes![4]
That is Megaera on the left; the one
    Who's weeping on our right hand is Alecto;
    Tisiphone's between." Then he was done.
They tore their breasts with fingernails – they clawed
    And slapped themselves – their shrieking was so loud   50
    I clutched the poet: I was terrified.
"When Medusa[5] is here, he'll turn to stone,"
    They all three said, as they looked down at us.
    "When Theseus challenged, we were too humane."[6]
"Now turn right round, and keep your eyes shut tight,
    For if the Gorgon comes and you see her,
    There'll be no way back to the world of light."

---

1   A mythical Thessalian witch.
2   Judecca, where Judas Iscariot is.
3   The Primum Mobile, so called because it is the first of the heavenly spheres to be set
    in motion (by God). It surrounds all the other moving spheres and itself sets them in
    motion.
4   Classical embodiments of the spirit of vengeance, and often, to those who saw them,
    of remorse.
5   One of the three Gorgons, monsters who petrified whoever looked at them. Possibly
    she is here a symbol of despair, the worst sin of all.
6   When Theseus entered the underworld, in an attempt to abduct Proserpine, he was
    captured, but not killed. He had to be rescued by Hercules.

My master said this, and he made me turn,
   And not content that I should use my hands,
   He covered up my eyes with both his own.   60
O you, whose minds are sound and full of sense,
   Notice the deeper meaning hidden here,
   Veiled by these lines that speak of strange events.
And now a noise across the muddy water
   Rang out, re-bellowed – and so terribly
   It caused the river banks to shake and shudder.
Exactly like the sound made by a wind
   Enticed and driven wild by adverse warmth;
   It strikes a forest – nothing can withstand
It – breaking boughs, and bearing them away,   70
   It proudly sweeps along a cloud of dust
   And makes wild beasts and shepherds turn and flee.
He took his hands away: "Now look your fill
   Across that prehistoric foam or scum,
   There where the mist is thickest and most foul."
Like frogs, scared by their enemy the snake,
   Retreating rapidly across the water,
   To pile up on the land in one great stack,
So I saw hordes of the ruined people flee
   In front of one who passed over the marsh   80
   And crossed the Styx, keeping his feet quite dry.
He brushed the viscid atmosphere from time
   To time out of his face with his left hand,
   And that was all that seemed to trouble him.
I had no doubt at all that he was one
   Sent down from heaven, and turned towards my master,
   Who signed me to be silent and bow down.
How magisterial he seemed to me!
   He reached the gate, and with a little wand
   He opened it, and none stood in his way.   90
"O you, outcasts of heaven, wretched race,"
   He said, when he was standing on the threshold,
   "What is it in you breeds such arrogance?
Why do you kick against the pricks again?
   That will is not diverted from its end,
   And more than once it has increased your pain.[1]
Why bang your heads against the wall of fate?
   That Cerberus of yours, if you remember,
   Still has the flesh scraped off his chin and throat."[2]
Then he turned back upon the filthy road   100

---

1   An allusion to the descent into the underworld of Theseus and Hercules and, more
    importantly, Christ's Harrowing of Hell.
2   When Cerberus opposed him, Hercules tied him with a chain and dragged him away.
    It was this chain's attrition which removed the flesh from his chin and throat.

And said no word to us, but had the look
Of someone whom some other care devoured[1]
Than that of those who stood before him there.
And so we turned our steps towards the city:
After his holy speech we were secure.
We went inside, and there was no dispute.
And I, who had a longing to discover
What kind of things were locked in such a fort,
Cast my eyes round it, once I was within,
And saw, on every side, a rural region   110
Of lamentation and of cruel pain.
And as at Arles, there where the Rhône stagnates,
Or as at Pola, near to where Quarnero
Washes that Italy it demarcates,
Sepulchres make the ground irregular,
So they did here on every hand, except
The circumstances were much crueller.
For here and there among the tombs a scatter
Of fire and flame made every tomb so hot
No smith would need his iron to be hotter.   120
All of the lids were open and upended,
And from them came such direful lamentation
As only from the grievously tormented.
I asked him: "Master, tell me, who are these
Who, laid to rest in monumental tombs,
Make themselves heard with lamentable sighs?"
He said: "Heresiarchs, and their followers
Of every sect, are here. And many more
Than you might think are in these sepulchres.
Of all the sects, like is entombed with like,   130
With heat that varies through the monuments."[2]
We went on then and, turning to the right,
Passed between torments and high battlements.

---

1 Perhaps his wish to return to Heaven or the thought of his next task.
2 The heat is greater or less according to the gravity of the particular heresy. In Dante's
   day a common punishment for heresy was to be burnt alive.

CANTO X

Virgil and Dante are now in the area reserved for those heretics who insisted that the soul died with the body.

One of the shades, realizing from his speech that Dante is a fellow citizen of Florence, wishes to talk with him. This is Farinata degli Uberti, one-time leader of the Ghibelline faction: Dante's family were Guelfs. The feud is continued in Hell, as Farinata boasts of twice routing the Guelfs, and Dante retorts that his party recovered, whereas Farinata's did not.

They are interrupted by the shade of Cavalcante de' Cavalcanti, who cannot understand – if Dante can visit the Inferno by the power of his intellect – why his son Guido, Dante's friend, is not with him. Cavalcante fears that his son is dead and, when Dante hesitates to reply to his questions, Cavalcante falls back into his tomb, and is not seen or heard again.

Farinata alludes to Dante's future exile from Florence. He asks why the Florentines are so set against his family, and Dante recalls the rout of the Guelf forces at Montaperti. Farinata insists that it was he alone who prevented the destruction of Florence after that battle.

Farinata explains that the damned can see the future, but not the present: at the end of time they will know nothing.

Dante asks Farinata to explain to Cavalcante that his son is still alive; but there is no indication that Farinata even tries to do this.

With Virgil impatient to continue their journey, Dante pauses only long enough to learn from Farinata that his tomb contains also the shades of the Emperor Frederick II and "the Cardinal".

Virgil, told by Dante of his worries over his own future, advises him to wait until he meets Beatrice, when the course and purpose of his life will be revealed.

Virgil and Dante now move away from the walls of Dis towards the centre of the sixth circle. Their path leads to a valley which will take them down to the seventh circle. The stench from this valley is already rising to meet them.

W e passed along a narrow, hidden track
　　Between the tortured people and the wall,
　　My master first, and I behind his back.
"O you, most virtuous man, bringing me through
　　These sacrilegious gyres, as you think best,
　　Please speak, and tell me what I long to know.
Are any visible, of all those laid
　　Within these sepulchres? I see the lids
　　Are lifted, and there's nobody on guard."
He said: "The sepulchres will all be sealed　　　　　　　　　10
　　When these[1] return here from Jehoshaphat
　　Bringing their bodies from the upper world.[2]
This region is the burial ground of those –

1　The shades of the dead.
2　On the Day of Judgement all the souls of the dead will be reunited with their bodies. See Joel 3:2: "I will also gather all nations, and bring them down into the valley of Jehoshaphat…"

Epicurus[1] and all his followers –
Who say the soul dies when the body does.
And now the question you have asked of me
    Will quickly find its answer in this circle,
    As will the longing which you hide away."[2]
I answered: "My kind guide, this reticence
    Comes simply from a wish to guard my tongue,   20
    As you've admonished me – and more than once."
"O Tuscan walking through this land of fire,
    While still alive, and with such courteous speech,
    May it please you to pause and linger here.
To me your way of speaking makes it clear
    That you're a native of that noble city
    Where I perhaps was too unpopular."
This sound came all of a sudden from inside
    One of the sepulchres, and in my fear
    I crept a little closer to my guide.   30
He said to me: "Turn round! Why be distressed?
    Look there: it's Farinata who has risen;
    You will see all of him above the waist."[3]
I had already caught his eye, meanwhile
    He held his chest and held his head up high,
    As though he had a huge contempt for Hell.
And my leader, whose hands were prompt and quick,
    Pushed me to Farinata through the tombs
    And said: "Think carefully before you speak."
When I was at his sepulchre then he   40
    Looked at me for a while. Then, with some pride,
    He wished to know: "What is your ancestry?"
I, who was all too keen to answer that,
    Hid nothing from him, but made all quite clear.
    Which when he heard, he raised his brows somewhat
And said: "They were so savagely adverse
    To me and to my forebears and my party,
    I had to scatter them – and do it twice!"[4]
"Yes, they were scattered, but they all returned
    From all around," I said, "and did that twice –   50
    A skill your party never really learned!"[5]
And then nearby another shade arose[6]
    Till it was visible down to the chin:

---

1   A Greek philosopher (341–270 BC). His philosophy was essentially materialist.
2   Dante's wish to see Farinata.
3   Farinata degli Uberti (who died about a year before Dante's birth) was a leader of the
    Ghibelline faction in Florence.
4   The Guelfs were driven from Florence in 1248 and 1260.
5   The Ghibellines were ultimately defeated.
6   That of Cavalcante de' Cavalcanti, a Florentine Guelf, father of Dante's great friend,
    the poet Guido Cavalcanti. Both father and son had the reputation of being heretics.

I think he must have got up on his knees.
He looked all round, as if he really wanted
  To find somebody in my company;
  And when he was completely disappointed,
He said in tears: "If you can tread this blind
  Prison by virtue of your intellect,
  Where is my son? Why is he not at hand?"   60
I answered him: "My strength is not my own:
  He who is waiting there, perhaps will guide me
  To one[1] for whom your Guido felt disdain."
What he said, and the way he was tormented,
  Immediately informed me who this was;
  And that was why my answer was so pointed.
He started up, and cried: "What? Did you say
  He '*felt* disdain'? Is he not still alive?
  Does he no longer see the light of day?"[2]
When he perceived there was a pause before   70
  I found the words in answer to his question,
  He fell back, and he failed to reappear.
But that other great soul, at whose demand
  I'd stopped to speak, did not change his expression,
  Or turn his face, or any way unbend,
Adding to what he had already said:
  "If they have failed to learn that skill correctly,
  That is a greater torment than this bed.
And yet, before the fiftieth time the queen
  Who rules down here has found her face rekindled,[3]   80
  You'll know how hard a skill that is to learn.[4]
And – may you get back to the world – tell me:
  Why are that city's citizens so savage
  In all their laws against my family?"[5]
I answered him: "The slaughter at the rout
  Which left the River Arbia running red[6]
  Is what brought all such orisons about."
He sighed and shook his head: "You know I was
  Hardly alone in that. Nor certainly
  Would I have joined the others without cause.   90

---

1 Probably Beatrice, as a representative of the Christian faith, but this could equally refer
   to God.
2 As Dante explains later, Guido Cavalcanti was alive at the date given to Dante's vision
   (the spring of 1300). He died in August of that year.
3 Proserpine, the wife of Pluto, is identified with the moon. Farinata is saying his prophecy
   will come true before there have been fifty more full moons (i.e. months).
4 A hint of Dante's exile from Florence, which is often referred to later in the *Comedy*.
5 The Uberti were excluded from all amnesties.
6 The Battle of Montaperti (1260), at which the Guelfs were utterly defeated by the
   Ghibellines.

Yet there at Empoli[1] I was the one –
    When all agreed on Florence's destruction –
    Who set his face against it, I alone."
"So may your seed eventually have rest,"
    I begged him, "please undo a tangled knot,
    This doubt which keeps my mind in such a twist.
You see beforehand, if I hear aright,
    Those things which time brings with it in its course,
    But with things present it is not like that."
"We see, as people do who have long sight,   100
    Things," he replied, "that are remote from us:
    The supreme lord still gives us that much light.
When things are near, or here, our minds are quite
    Empty; and, if there's none to bring us word,
    Then we know nothing of your human state.
Therefore we shall be utterly without
    Knowledge or understanding from the moment
    The gate into the future has been shut."[2]
I then said, feeling guilty for not giving
    This answer earlier, "Tell the stricken shade[3]   110
    That son of his[4] is still among the living.
And if I was, before, slow to reply,
    Tell him that I was busy thinking over
    That problem which you have resolved for me."
My master was now wanting me to come;
    And therefore I was quick to beg that spirit
    To name, and quickly, those entombed with him.
He said: "I'm lying here with thousands more.
    In my tomb is the second Frederick,[5] and
    The Cardinal:[6] other names I forbear."   120
With that he hid himself – I turned to walk
    Back to the ancient poet, thinking over
    Words that had seemed to prophesy ill luck.[7]
He started off and, as he walked, he said:
    "I want to know why you are so confused."
    And I made quite sure that he understood.
"Remember everything that you have heard
    To your distress," that wise man recommended.

---

1   A town some twenty miles from Florence where, after their victory at Montaperti, the
    Tuscan Ghibellines met to decide the fate of Florence.
2   At the Day of Judgement, when time will give way to eternity.
3   Cavalcante de' Cavalcanti.
4   Guido Cavalcanti.
5   The Holy Roman Emperor Frederick II (r.1220–50), who was reputed to be a heretic.
    He engaged in a long political struggle with the Papacy.
6   Cardinal Ottaviano degli Ubaldini (d.1273), generally credited with the remark: "I can
    say that, if there is a soul, I have lost mine for the Ghibellines."
7   See ll. 79–81 above.

"Now mark my words!" He raised his finger, said:
"When you are standing in the radiance   130
 Of her[1] whose lovely eyes see everything,
 You'll know from her the course of your life hence."
With that he turned his feet to the left hand,
 Towards the circle's centre, from the wall,
 Along a path with a valley at the end.
Even up there, that valley's stench was foul.

---

1 Beatrice.

CANTO XI

Virgil and Dante look down into the abyss, where they see more shades heaped up. The stench rising from this abyss makes them draw back behind the tomb of Pope Anastasius II, who reputedly had heretical tendencies.

Virgil suggests that they pause awhile, to accustom themselves to the stench, before they descend. So that their time may not be wasted, he will spend it describing what sort of sinners they will find below and, indeed, outlining the plan of the Inferno as a whole.

There are three main divisions of the Inferno: that of incontinence (above and outside the City of Dis, and already visited by Dante), that of violence and that of fraud. One important distinction here is that those who sin through incontinence are less culpable than those whose sin necessarily involves a clear decision. Throughout the Inferno, the worse the sin the lower the sinner is placed, and so violence and fraud are inside the City of Dis.

The violent are in the first circle immediately below Dante and Virgil, which is the seventh of the circles in the Inferno as a whole. Those guilty of defrauding people who have no particular reason to trust them are in the second circle below, the eighth from the beginning. Finally, those who defraud, or betray, people who have good reason to trust them, are in the last circle below, the lowest place of all. There are many subdivisions also.

In this almost entirely didactic canto Dante relies very much, for his classification of the sins, on pagan authorities, particularly Aristotle. This has the effect of implying that the world is, and always has been, essentially a moral system, the basic understanding of whose nature does not depend on Christian faith.

Finally, Virgil mentions the present position of the stars, which indicates that it is nearly dawn in the world above, where those stars may be seen. It is therefore time for them to move on and down.

> W e – from the very edge of a high steep,
>   Made by a circle of huge broken rocks –
>   Looked down at shades more cruelly heaped up.
> And here, because of the extremely bad
>   Odour arising from the deep abyss,
>   We drew together, back behind the lid
> Of a great tomb, where I saw words which say:
>   "Here lies Pope Anastasius, whom Photinus
>   Persuaded from the straight and narrow way."[1]
> "Before going down we must delay somewhat,   10
>   So that our nostrils may grow more accustomed
>   To the foul breath, which then we can forget."
> So said my master. And I said: "Then find
>   Some compensation, lest our time be wasted."
>   And he: "Something's already in my mind.
> My son, within this band of broken stone,"

---

1   Pope Anastasius, who reigned 496–98, was said to have been led by Photinus, a deacon from Thessalonica, into denying the divine origin of Christ.

So he began, "there are three smaller circles,[1]
Like those you've left, and always going down.
They are all full of spirits that are cursed;
   And for your understanding when you see them,   20
   Hear for what cause and whereabouts they're placed.
Of every sin that earns the hate of God
   The end's injustice, and all such injustice
   Harms somebody, either by force or fraud.
But, since fraud is peculiar to man,
   It grieves God more; and so the fraudulent
   Are lower down, subject to greater pain.
And the first circle under us belongs
   To the violent; but since force is threefold,
   The circle's made of three concentric rings.   30
On God, oneself, one's neighbour one may use
   Force – on them or on what they own, I mean –
   As I intend more fully to disclose.
A violent death or grievous wounds may be
   Inflicted on a neighbour; on his goods
   Ruin, arson, extortion and robbery.
Killers, and all who use force sinfully,
   Looters and pillagers, are all tormented
   In the first ring, but punished differently.
A man may raise his hand in violence   40
   Against himself or his own goods. Therefore
   In the next ring, in pointless penitence,
Lie those who up in your world did away
   With themselves, or dissipated wealth in gambling
   Till lamentation took the place of joy.
One may use force, and use it against God,
   Denying him in secret, or blaspheming,
   Or scorning nature and her plenitude;
And so the smallest of the rings has set
   Its seal on Sodom, Cahors[2] and everyone   50
   Who blasphemes, scorning God within his heart.
Now fraud, by which the conscience *must* be pierced,[3]
   May be practised on one who trusts the trickster,
   Or else on one who has no call to trust.
Clearly this latter merely cuts across

---

1   The Inferno consists of nine circles, one below the other, which – since the Inferno is
   shaped like an inverted cone – become smaller the lower one goes. See illustration on
   p. 4.
2   Sodom, one of the "cities of the plain" (Gen. 19:29) destroyed by God. It gave its name
   to sodomy. Cahors, a city in southern France, proverbial for usury.
3   Those who practise fraud are bound by the nature of their actions to be conscious of
   what they do, since it requires the concurrence of their reason. Their sin is therefore
   the more grievous.

MY KINDLY TEACHER SAID: "MY SON, YOU SEE
THE SOULS OF THOSE WHOM ANGER OVERMASTERED"...

INFERNO VII, 115–16

"LOOK THERE: IT'S FARINATA WHO HAS RISEN;
YOU WILL SEE ALL OF HIM ABOVE THE WAIST"...

INFERNO X, 32–33

The bonds by which we're bound by nature.[1] So
    Down in the second circle under us[2]
Hypocrites, flatterers and sorcery
    Must nestle, forgers, thieves, simoniacs,
    Pimps, barrators and suchlike blackguardry.   60
But, by the other kind of fraud,[3] not just
    Love formed by nature is forgotten, but
    That added love which makes for special trust.
So in the smallest circle,[4] at the centre
    Of all the universe, the seat of Dis,
    All who are traitors are consumed for ever."
And I: "Master, your reasoning is precise,
    And it distinguishes most carefully
    Among the people held in this abyss.
But tell me now: those in the slimy marsh,   70
    Or blown on the wind, or beaten by the rain,
    Or those whose altercations are so harsh[5] –
Whyever in this city's[6] conflagration
    Are they not punished too, if loathed by God?
    If not, why are they plagued in such a fashion?"
Then he replied: "Why does your reasoning take,
    So unaccustomedly, this deviant course?
    Or are you off upon a different tack?[7]
Are you oblivious then of what is said
    In detail in your *Ethics*[8] of the three   80
    Dispositions which are opposed to God –
Incontinence and malice, and insane
    Brutality? And how incontinence
    Offends God less and so incurs less blame?
If you consider well what has been said,
    And if you then remember who they are
    Who suffer punishment above outside,[9]
You will see clearly why they're kept away
    From evil souls like these, and why God's anger

---

1   The love for each other, which is inborn in human beings, since man is by nature a social
    creature.
2   That is, the eighth circle in the Inferno as a whole.
3   That practised against those who have a particular reason (e.g. a close relationship) to
    trust us.
4   The ninth and last.
5   In the last tercet, Virgil refers to, respectively, the wrathful (*Inf.* VII and VIII), the lustful
    (V), the gluttonous (VI), the avaricious and prodigals (VII).
6   The City of Dis.
7   Virgil suggests that Dante is either foolishly forgetting here to distinguish between
    degrees of culpability in sinning, or else deliberately adopting the Stoic view that all
    faults are equally culpable.
8   Aristotle's *Nicomachean Ethics*, which Virgil implies is one of Dante's favourite books.
9   In the first five circles, which lie above and outside the City of Dis.

Strikes them indeed, but much less heavily."   90
"O sun, clearing the clouds from troubled sight,
   You make me so contented with your answers
   That, much as knowledge pleases, so does doubt.
Go back," I said, "a little way, to that
   Point where you said that usury was offensive
   To God's own goodness, and undo the knot."
"For one who understands, philosophy
   Points out," he said, "not only in one passage,
   How nature, in her working, makes her way
After divine intelligence and art.   100
   Then, if you've read your *Physics*[1] with some care,
   You'll find this noted, and quite near the start:
Human skill works, as closely as it may,
   Following nature, as a child his teacher;
   So your skill is God's grandchild, one might say.
So from these two – remember the beginning
   Of Genesis[2] – it follows that mankind
   Should make its way in the world and make a living.
That's not the method of the usurer,
   For he must slight both nature and her pupil,   110
   Hard human work, placing his hopes elsewhere.[3]
Follow me now, because I think it best.
   The Fish[4] flash up on the horizon, and
   The Wain[5] is lying over the north-west.
Further on is the place where we descend.[6]

---

1   Aristotle's *Physics*.

2   For example, "And the Lord God took the man, and put him into the garden of Eden to dress and keep it" (Gen. 2:15), and "In the sweat of thy face shalt thou eat bread" (Gen. 3:19).

3   The argument against usury here is essentially that the usurer does not produce anything by working, as he should, in co-operation with God and God's creation. Instead, he uses money (which is not wealth in itself but merely a means of exchange, a token of wealth) to take for himself, in Shakespeare's words, "a breed for barren metal".

4   The constellation Pisces.

5   The constellation Ursa Major, the Great Bear.

6   To the seventh circle.

CANTO XII

Dante and Virgil scramble down a mass of fallen rocks into the seventh circle, that of the violent, and into the first ring of this circle, reserved for those who were violent against their neighbour. Virgil explains that the landslip was caused by the earthquake at the time of the Crucifixion. The Minotaur, the guardian of this circle, is angry at their arrival, but Virgil provokes the monster to a blind frenzy which enables them to evade it.

Around the circle runs a river of boiling blood. This is the Phlegethon, the fiery river of the classical underworld, although Dante does not name it until *Inf.* xiv. The banks of the river are patrolled by centaurs armed with bows and arrows, who shoot any of the damned who rise too far out of it, for the violent are immersed in it to a greater or less depth according to the gravity of their sin.

The centaurs are at first suspicious of Virgil and Dante, but their leader, Chiron, obeys Virgil's orders and gives them Nessus to be their guide and to carry Dante on his back when they ford the river. Nessus explains the way the damned are punished here, and points many of them out. Then Nessus goes back across the ford.

This canto is a good example of how Dante develops imaginatively what are basically very simple, even obvious, images. The centaurs, who have both human and animal attributes, clearly symbolize the state of those human beings who have acted bestially. Then the river of boiling blood is a development of the common metaphor we use when we say something like, "It makes my blood boil" (a metaphor also used in Italian of course). The grotesque features of this circle mirror the grotesque nature of the sins involved, the "blind cupidity and senseless anger" which cause us to sin in our short lives and so merit a punishment which lasts for ever.

T he place we came to, for our journey down,
  Was strewn with rocks; and there was something else,
  And such as anybody's eyes would shun.[1]
Like that landslip, this side of Trent, which struck
  The River Adige on its left bank –
  Whether through faulty shoring or earthquake –
Where from the mountain top down to the plain
  The rocks are shattered and all heaped up so
  They give some footing to one climbing down –
Such was the way to get into that pit.   10
  And on the broken chasm's very brink,
  Spreadeagled, lay the infamy of Crete,
Who was conceived inside a cowlike cage;[2]
  And catching sight of us, he bit himself,
  Like somebody consumed with inward rage.

---

1 What this "something else" is becomes clear only in ll. 11–13.
2 The Minotaur, half man and half bull, the offspring of Pasiphaë (wife of King Minos of Crete) and a bull. Pasiphaë ordered the construction of a wooden cow, into which she placed herself to receive the bull.

My sage called out to him: "Could it be said
    That you believe this is the Duke of Athens[1]
    At whose hands, in the world above, you died?
But no! Be off! This man has not come here
    Under your sister's artful tutelage,[2]   20
    But to observe the torments you endure."
Now like a bull that breaks its bondage at
    The instant it receives the fatal blow,
    And cannot walk, but goes plunging about –
That's how I saw the Minotaur behave.
    Quickly my guide cried out: "Make for the pass –
    You'd best descend while he is in this rage."
And so we made our way: under my feet
    Rocks and stones were frequently dislodged,
    Because of all the unaccustomed weight.[3]   30
I went on, lost in thought. He said: "You will
    Be thinking of that fall of rocks watched over
    By the brute wrath I managed to control.
Now I would have you know, the first time when
    I came down here and into nether hell,[4]
    This mass of rocks had not yet fallen down.
But, if I'm not mistaken, a short while
    Before *He* came, who took away from Dis,
    And from the highest circle, glorious spoil,[5]
This deep and dirty hollow all around   40
    Shuddered so much I think the universe
    Felt love, by which it has been often turned,
As some believe, to chaos once again.
    And at that point this ancient mass of rocks,
    Both here and elsewhere like this, tumbled down.[6]
But look down there, and look intently: we'll
    Soon be beside the stream of blood, where those
    Who in their violence injure others boil."
O blind cupidity and senseless anger,
    Which goad us on throughout our little life,   50
    Then soak us in such anguish, and for ever!

---

1   Theseus.
2   Theseus was provided by Ariadne, the Minotaur's half-sister, with a sword to kill the
    monster, and a ball of thread by which to retrace his steps out of the labyrinth where
    the monster was kept.
3   One of several reminders that Dante, being still alive, is not a shade.
4   See *Inf.* IX, 22–27.
5   A reference to Christ's Harrowing of Hell after the Crucifixion, His rescue of the souls
    of patriarchs and prophets from Limbo ("the highest circle").
6   A reference to the earthquake which accompanied the Crucifixion. Virgil, a pagan, tries to
    understand this in the light of the Empedoclean idea that the supervention of harmony,
    or love, in creation results in disorder. Virgil speaks more truly than he realizes, in that
    the Crucifixion is love in action.

I saw a ditch bent in a curve and broad,
   Encircling as it went the entire level,
   Just as my guide, some time before, had said.
Between it and the scarp I saw some running:
   A file of centaurs,[1] armed with bows and arrows,
   As, in the world above, they went out hunting.
As we came down, they stopped and stood there steady,
   And three of them broke ranks and stared at us,
   Holding their bows and arrows at the ready.   60
One shouted from far off: "Tell me to what
   Punishment you are coming down the slope.
   Tell me from where you are. If not, I'll shoot."
My master said: "Our answer will be made
   To Chiron, when we get to where he is:
   You always were too quick for your own good."
Then he nudged me. "That was Nessus," he said,
   "Who died for the lovely Deianira and
   Took vengeance for himself when he was dead.[2]
That big one in the middle, with bowed head,   70
   Is the great Chiron, guardian of Achilles.
   The other's Pholus, known for his bad blood.[3]
They run in thousands by the stream, and shoot
   At any guilty soul who lifts himself
   Out of the blood beyond what is his lot."[4]
And now, as we were getting near to those
   Quick creatures, Chiron, with an arrow's nock,
   Brushed back his beard on both sides from his jaws.
And when his big mouth was disclosed for speech,
   He said to his companions: "Have you noticed   80
   The one behind moving what his feet touch?
Feet of the dead don't usually do that."
   And my good guide, already at that breast
   Where the two natures of the creature meet,
Answered: "He's certainly alive, and he
   Comes here that I may show him this dark valley.
   Not pleasure brings him, but necessity.
She[5] came from singing songs of praise who laid
   This charge upon me, novel as it was:
   He is no robber, I'm no thieving shade.   90

---

1 As creatures with both human and bestial attributes, the centaurs are well placed in the
    circle of the violent.
2 He tried to rape Deianira, and was killed by her husband, Heracles. Before he died Nessus
    told Deianira to take his shirt covered with his blood to use as a love charm. She gave it
    to Heracles, and when he put it on, it turned out to be poisonous and he was killed.
3 He provoked the famous fight, at a wedding feast, between the centaurs and Lapiths.
4 The depth to which the violent are immersed in the boiling blood varies according to
    the gravity of their sin.
5 Beatrice.

But by that power through which I am allowed
  To go on such a rugged journey, give us
  One of your band whom we may stay beside,
And following the stream let him show where
  To ford it, bearing this man on his crupper:
  He is no spirit to fly through the air."
Then Chiron turned and wheeled to the right hand,
  Commanding Nessus: "Come, and be their guide,
  And clear the way of any other band."[1]
And so, together with our faithful guide,   100
  We went beside the boiling, crimson river;
  I heard the high-pitched shrieks of those being boiled.
I saw some there up to their eyebrows under;
  And the huge centaur told us: "They are tyrants
  Who liked to soak their hands in blood and plunder.
They pay for pitiless brutality –
  Alexander,[2] and fierce Dionysius,[3]
  Who gave such years of grief to Sicily.
That brow on which the hair is very black
  Is Ezzelino;[4] and the other, fair,   110
  Obizzo da Este,[5] who indeed was struck
Down by the hand of his unnatural son."[6]
  I then turned to the poet, and he said:
  "Listen to him now, and me later on."
A little further and the centaur stood
  Beside a group that even to their necks
  Appeared to rise above the boiling blood.
He pointed to one separated shade,
  Saying: "That man, within God's bosom, pierced
  The heart that by the Thames still drips with blood."[7]   120
Then I saw people keeping their heads raised,
  And even their whole chests, above the river;
  And quite a few of these I recognized.
So bit by bit I saw the boiling blood
  Go shallower, until it scalded feet
  And nothing else; and here we crossed the ford.
"Just as on this side, as you must have seen,
  The stream goes shallower and shallower,"

---

1   These centaurs are reminiscent of the roving bands of mercenaries and brigands who
     troubled Italy in Dante's day.
2   Presumably, since the name lacks any qualification, Alexander the Great.
3   Dionysius the Elder, who died in 367 BC, after a tyrannous reign of thirty-eight years.
4   Ezzelino III da Romano (1194–1259).
5   Obizzo da Este (c.1247–93).
6   The centaur confirms the rumour that Obizzo was killed by his son.
7   Guy de Montfort, son of the famous Simon de Montfort, in 1271 murdered his first
     cousin in a church. The heart of his victim was kept in a reliquary in London: it is said
     to be still bleeding because the death went unavenged.

The centaur said, "so now I must explain
That on the other side its bed sinks down   130
   Deeper and deeper, till we come once more
   To there where tyranny is made to groan.
And so God's justice on the far side stings
   That Attila[1] who was a scourge on earth,
   Pyrrhus[2] and Sextus;[3] and forever wrings
Tears out from those being boiled – Rinier de' Pazzi
   And Rinier da Corneto,[4] two who made
   Our roads the scene of action in their wars."
Then he turned round, and back across the ford.

1   King of the Huns (r. 434–53), known as "the scourge of God".
2   Probably the son of Achilles, whose cruelty after the fall of Troy is described by Virgil
   in his *Aeneid*.
3   Probably the son of Pompey the Great, a pirate who was put to death in 35 BC.
4   Rinieri de' Pazzi, a notorious highway robber, died before 1280; Rinieri da Corneto, a
   contemporary of Dante, was a bandit chief who operated on the roads leading into
   Rome.

CANTO XIII

Virgil and Dante make their way through a tangled wood of gnarled and twisted bushes – the wood of the suicides and profligates. This wood is inhabited by the Harpies – eerie birds with the faces of women. Virgil explains that they are now in the second ring of the seventh circle, reserved for those who used violence against themselves – either their own bodies or their own goods.

Around them is the sound of groaning, but nobody seems to be there to make the sound. Acting on Virgil's suggestion, Dante plucks a twig from a thorn bush and hears the bush complaining of that ill treatment. The bush, speaking through the wound left by its mutilation, says that it is the shade of the poet Pier della Vigna, who died by his own hand after his political disgrace. He insists he was innocent of the charges made against him, but admits he sinned in killing himself. He explains that, when a soul deliberately separates itself from its body, it is condemned to the seventh circle of the Inferno, where it falls into this wood like a seed, and sprouts and becomes a bush. It is tormented by the Harpies, who eat its leaves, thereby leaving wounds through which the bush groans. On the Day of Judgement these souls will regain their bodies, but they will not put them on again. Instead, the bodies will hang on the bushes which are their souls. It would not be right for body and soul to be reunited when the human being they formed has deliberately willed their separation.

Suddenly there is the noise of hunting, and two naked and lacerated shades run through the wood, chased by hounds which catch them and tear them. These shades are the spendthrifts, who are now laid waste as their goods were once.

One of these shades explains that he was a Florentine, and he attributes the troubles of that city to its change of patron from Mars to John the Baptist. He says he hanged himself in his own home.

N essus has not yet reached the other side,
    And we've already started on our way
    Through what's apparently a trackless wood.[1]
No fresh green leaves, but only sable ones;
    No smooth, straight boughs, but only gnarled and twisted;
    And no fruit either, only poison thorns:
Wild creatures loathing cultivated earth,
    Living near Cecina and Corneto, never
    Come across such unyielding, tangled growth.
And here the filthy Harpies make their home,   10
    Who drove the Trojans from the Strophades
    With dark announcements of their future doom.[2]
They have broad wings; their faces are of women;

---

1   The wood of the suicides. Dante and Virgil are in the second ring of the seventh circle, where those who were violent against themselves are punished.

2   In his *Aeneid* (III, 209*ff*), Virgil describes how Aeneas and his companions, when they came to the islands of the Strophades, were unable to eat because the Harpies swooped down, snatched food from the table and fouled everything with their droppings. One of the Harpies, Celaeno, also prophesied further trouble for the Trojans.

Their feet have talons, their big bellies feathers;
  Their wailing in the trees seems less than human.
My master said: "Before you penetrate
  The wood much further, know that you're within
  The second ring,¹ and will remain in it
Until you come upon the sand of dread.²
  So study all you see: you will see things   20
  For which I know you'd never take my word."
I could hear groaning coming from all round,
  Which stopped me in my tracks and in confusion,
  Because I saw nobody make the sound.
I think that he was thinking that I thought
  That all those voices in among the trunks
  Issued from people hidden from our sight.
Therefore my master told me: "Tear a bit,
  A little twig, from any of these branches:
  You'll find your thoughts will also be cut short."   30
I stretched my hand a short way out before me,
  And snapped a tiny branch from off a thorn;
  And then the trunk screamed out: "Why do you tear me?"
And when a stream of blood had blackened it,
  It started off again: "Why do you rend me?"
  Have you no drop of pity in your heart?
Once we were men, and now we're stumps and stocks:
  Your hand might well have shown us greater mercy,
  If we'd turned out to be the souls of snakes."
As from a firebrand, at one end on fire –   40
  While from the other, since it is still green,
  It drips and hisses with the escaping air –
So, from the stump that I had injured, blood
  Came out mixed up with words. I let the twig
  Drop, and I stood like somebody afraid.
"If he'd been able to believe at first,
  O damaged soul," my sage replied to him,
  "What he'd seen only as he found it versed,³
He never would have laid his hand on you;
  But such a thing, so incredible, required   50
  Persuasion to this deed which hurts me too.
Say who you were. He will, in recompense,
  Restore you to your worldly reputation,
  Once he, who is allowed up there, returns."
The trunk replied: "Your words to me are such
  I can't keep silent; but I beg indulgence
  If for a while I'm tempted into speech.

---

1   Of the seventh circle.
2   In the third ring of the seventh circle, which Virgil and Dante reach in the next canto.
3   In the *Aeneid* (III, 19–68) there is a comparable episode, which Dante used as his source.

I am the man who used to hold both keys
    Of Emperor Frederick's heart,[1] and used to turn them,
    Locking, unlocking, with such practised ease   60
That I kept almost all men from his thought,
    And was so conscientious in that office
    I lost both sleep and health because of it.
That whore[2] who never turned her harlot's eyes
    Away from Caesar's household[3] – always fatal
    Throughout the world, in courts a special vice –
Inflamed men's minds against me and my state,
    And all those so inflamed inflamed Augustus,[4]
    And joyful honour turned to foul despite.
For all of this my mind had such disgust   70
    It hoped by death to flee distaste, and made me
    Unjust against myself, though I was just.
Now, by the roots of this abnormal timber,
    I swear to you I never broke my faith
    To my great lord, so worthy of all honour.
If one of you gets back into the world,
    Let him revive my glorious memory,
    Still prostrate from the darts that envy hurled."
My poet waited and, "Since he's not speaking,"
    He said to me, "then do not waste your time,   80
    But question him according to your liking."
To this I answered: "Please go on with it,
    And ask him what you think I need to know;
    I cannot, there's such anguish in my heart!"
So he began once more: "All will be done,
    And willingly, that you have begged of us,
    Imprisoned spirit, if you speak again,
And tell us how the soul comes to be tied
    In knots like these; and tell us, if you can,
    If there was ever anybody freed."   90
And then the hapless trunk hissed very hard
    Until its wheezing breath became a voice:
    "To that you'll have your answer in a word.
The cruel soul – when it has torn itself
    Out of its body, which it leaves behind,
    And Minos sends it to the seventh gulf[5] –
Falls in the wood, in no particular part;
    Merely where random fortune slings or flings it,

---

1   This is the poet Pier della Vigna (c.1190–1249) who, after being chief adviser to the
    Emperor Frederick II, was disgraced and imprisoned. His death in prison was attributed
    to suicide.
2   Envy.
3   A flattering way of referring to Frederick II's court.
4   It is a compliment to Frederick II to equate him with Augustus, the first Roman Emperor.
5   The seventh circle, reserved for the violent.

It sprouts and springs up like a grain of spelt.
It rises as a tender woodland plant: 100
    The Harpies, who are feeding on its foliage,
    Cause pain, and for the pain provide a vent.[1]
We'll come for our remains, like everyone,
    But not that we may put them on once more:
    What men renounce they cannot have again.[2]
No, we shall drag them here: throughout the sad
    Wood all our bodies will be left to hang,
    Each on the thorn bush of its harmful shade."
We were all eyes and ears, waiting upon
    The trunk, believing he had more to say,   110
    When straight we were distracted by a din,[3]
Like somebody made all at once aware,
    From where he stands, of wild boar being hunted,
    Who hears the hounds, and hears the bushes stir.
And suddenly, upon our left, there went
    Two beings, scratched and naked, through the wood,
    So fast they broke through all entanglement.
The one in front cried out: "O death, come quick!"
    The other one, who seemed to lag behind,
    Shouted out: "Lano, you were not so slick   120
When jousting near the Toppo!"[4] and at that,
    Perhaps because his breath was coming short,
    Melted into a bush and made one knot.
Behind them, and throughout the wood, there rushed
    A horde of sable bitches, hungry, rapid,
    Like greyhounds that are suddenly unleashed.
They, where he crouched, got their teeth into him,
    And mangled all his body inch by inch,
    Then carried off each lacerated limb.
And now my guide has grasped my hand, and taken   130
    Me to the blackthorn bush that is lamenting
    Uselessly through the bleeding where it's broken.
    "O Jacopo da Sant'Andrea,"[5] said

---

1   The bushes are able to speak through the wounds left in them by their mutilation.

2   On the Day of Judgement these souls, like all the others, will assemble in the valley of
Jehoshaphat with their bodies (see *Inf.* x, 10–12). They alone, however, will not be allowed
to put their bodies on once more, since they chose to separate their souls from their bodies.

3   We now see those who did violence to themselves, not by suicide, but by squandering
their wealth. Dante also gives examples of conspicuous consumption and deliberate
waste in *Inf.* xxix, 121–32.

4   Lano was a Sienese spendthrift killed in battle near the River Toppo in 1288. The reference
to the battle as "jousting" is ironical. Lano is thought to have belonged to the "*brigata
spendereccia*" ("brotherhood of big spenders"), whose aim in life was to waste as much
as possible.

5   Died 1239. Notorious for wasting his inheritance. For example, he is said to have sailed
on the River Brenta, dropping coins into the water.

The thorn bush, "Did I make a helpful shelter?
Am I to blame because your life was bad?"
My master came, stood over it and said:
    "Who were you once, who through so many wounds
    Breathe out such grievous language with your blood?"[1]
And he to us: "O souls who've made your way
    To look upon this horrifying havoc,   140
    And see my leaves have all been torn away,
Gather them at the wretched bush's foot.
    I'm from the city which for John the Baptist
    Changed its first patron[2] – who, because of that,
Now uses all his skill to make her mourn;
    And if, close by the bridge across the Arno,
    Some semblance of that god did not remain,[3]
Those citizens who laboured to refound
    The town on ash Attila left for them[4]
    Would certainly have laboured to no end.   150
I made myself a scaffold in my home."

---

1   This soul says many things, but not his name. We are left to speculate why this should
    be so. Perhaps Dante includes him as a representative of all those suicides not famous
    enough to be remembered.
2   It is said that the first patron of Florence was Mars, who resented the change of patron.
    His "skill" was of course in warfare, and the Florentines were notoriously quarrelsome.
3   In Dante's time part of a statue of Mars still survived near the Ponte Vecchio.
4   Attila the Hun, according to legend, sacked Florence. See *Inf.* XII, 134.

CANTO XIV

Dante gathers up the leaves which have fallen from the bush which was his fellow citizen and places them at the foot of the bush. Then the two travellers move from the second ring of the seventh circle into the third ring.

This is a bare sandy plain onto which flakes of fire are falling continually. Some damned souls (those who have been violent against God) are lying there supine, some (the usurers, violent against art or industry) are crouching, and some (the sodomites, who have done violence to nature) are continually in motion.

The pilgrims see the shade of Capaneus, one of the seven kings against Thebes, who is still unrepentantly cursing God. Virgil explains to him, and to Dante, that his anger is its own punishment. (The god whom Capaneus blasphemes is, of course, Jove. It is characteristic of Dante's all-embracing vision that this does not stop him using Capaneus as a symbol of the person who sins by refusing to accept the nature of things.)

A red stream issues from the wood of the suicides and runs across the burning sand. This is Phlegethon, which the travellers have seen before. Virgil explains how all the rivers of the Inferno originate in a fissure in a giant statue of an old man in Crete, composed of various metals, except for one of his feet, which is of baked clay. The interpretation of this image – even if we realize its biblical origin and know the interpretation offered there – is difficult. It may be contrasted with the boiling blood of Phlegethon, whose interpretation is obvious.

The stream protects the air above and the margins alongside it from the rain of fire. Virgil now tells Dante to move away from the wood and onto the edge of the stream, where they may walk safely.

*

O nly affection for my native place
    Urged me to gather up the scattered leaves
    For him who had already lost his voice.
From there we came at last to the division
    Between the second and third rings, there where
    Justice is seen in fearful operation.
To bring to light a scene unseen as yet,
    I say that we had come upon a plain
    Which gives no green thing leave to grow on it.
The wood of sorrow[1] garlands it about,   10
    Like the grim stream[2] around the wood itself:
    We paused upon the very edge of it.
The ground was dry, compacted sand, like that
    Which on his journey through the Libyan desert
    Cato of Utica[3] trod underfoot.
Vengeance of God, how greatly you should be

---

1   The wood of the suicides (*Inf.* XIII).
2   Phlegethon, the river of boiling water.
3   A Roman renowned for his integrity, Cato (95–46 BC) appears later in the *Comedy* as the guardian of the entrance to Purgatory.

Dreaded by all who merely read about
What was here made so manifest to me!
Here I saw many herds of naked souls,
   All weeping, and all weeping wretchedly,   20
   All subject, so it seemed, to different rules;
For some were lying supine on the ground,[1]
   Some sitting all bent up within themselves[2]
   And some of them were moving round and round.[3]
Those who were moving were most numerous;
   Those least who took their torment lying down,
   And yet these were the ones whose tongues were loose.
Over that stretch of sand, a gentle fall
   Of fire in broadest flakes was drifting down,
   Like snow in mountains with no wind at all.   30
As Alexander[4] in hot India once
   Saw unextinguished flames of fire descending
   Onto the earth and his battalions,
And therefore told his men to trample on
   The ground, so that the flaming flakes of fire
   Would be extinguished swiftly one by one –
Just so the everlasting heat came down;
   And so the sand was set on fire, like tinder
   Under the flint, to give them double pain.
No let-up in the twisting and the turning   40
   Of the poor hands, on this side and on that,
   Trying to beat away the freshest burning.
I said: "O master, able to defeat
   All enemies except those stubborn devils
   Who came against us at the city gate,[5]
Who is that giant who seems not to care
   About the burning, but lies scornful, scowling,
   As though not tortured by the rain of fire?"
And he who lay there, knowing what I said
   Referred to him, forestalled my guide and shouted: 50
   "What I was when alive, such am I dead!
Though Jove tire out that smith[6] from whom he took
   In his great rage the piercing flash of lightning
   Whence I, on my last day, was thunderstruck;
Or if he tire the others[7] taking turns
   In Mongibello[8] at the filthy forge,

---

1   The violent against God, the blasphemers.
2   The usurers.
3   The sodomites.
4   Alexander the Great.
5   The entrance to Dis (*Inf.* VIII, 82*ff*).
6   Vulcan, the blacksmith of the classical gods.
7   The Cyclopes, who worked for Vulcan in his forge.
8   Beneath Mount Etna.

Crying out, 'Help me, Vulcan, just this once!',
Just as he did upon the field of Phlegra,[1]
  And hurled his bolts at me with all his strength –
  His vengeance would not give him any pleasure."   60
And then my leader, with such vehemence
  As I had never heard before, spoke out:
  "You are, Capaneus, since your arrogance
Is unextinguished, punished all the more:
  No torment but this ranting and this raving
  Could be commensurate with your own ire."
And then, turning to me, my master said,
  More gently now: "This man was of the seven
  Besieging Thebes.[2] He held, and still holds, God
In high disdain, and not of much account;   70
  But, as I told him, such scorn only makes,
  For breasts like his, a fitting ornament.
Now come behind me. Take care not to tread,
  At this stage even, on the burning sand;
  But always keep your feet close to the wood."
We came in silence where there gushes out
  A very tiny streamlet from the wood,
  A stream whose redness makes me shudder yet.
As from the spring of Bulicame runs
  A watercourse used only by the carders,[3]   80
  So did this stream run down across the sands.
The stream's bed and its sloping banks were made
  Of stone, as were the margins running by them;
  And so I saw that as the place to tread.
"Of all the other things that I have shown
  Since first we came together through that gate
  Whose threshold's crossing is denied to none,[4]
Nothing has ever been exhibited
  To you as striking as this present river
  Quenching the conflagration overhead."   90
These words were spoken by my guide. At that
  I begged him to be generous with the feast[5]
  For which he had aroused my appetite.
"Mid-sea there lies an island, now a waste,"
  He answered me, "an island known as Crete,
  Under whose King the world was one time chaste.[6]

---

1 Where Jove fought with the Titans who were trying to scale Mount Olympus.
2 This siege is the subject of a tragedy by Aeschylus. According to the myth, Capaneus
    was struck dead by a thunderbolt when he was in the act of scaling the city walls.
3 Bulicame is a hot sulphurous spring near Viterbo, about 80 km north of Rome, whose
    waters were used by carders of flax and hemp.
4 The entrance to the Inferno. See the beginning of *Inf.* III.
5 A "feast" of explanation.
6 This refers to the fabled Golden Age, during the reign of Saturn.

There is a mountain there that was well covered
  With leaves and running water, known as Ida,
  Abandoned now, like something old and withered.
Rhea once chose this place, as a safe cot   100
  For her young son and, to disguise his presence
  When he was crying, used to raise a shout.[1]
A huge old man stands in the mountain's mass,
  Holding his shoulders turned towards Damietta,[2]
  Gazing at Rome as on his looking glass.
The finest gold has gone to form his head;
  His arms and breast are fashioned from pure silver;
  Then all is brass to where his legs divide;
All's iron unalloyed from that point down,
  Except his right foot, made of terracotta,   110
  On which he rests more than the other one.[3]
Through all, except the gold, there runs a crack,
  And tears are always dripping down that fissure
  To gather at his feet and pierce the rock,
Dropping down crags till they turn out to be
  The Acheron, the Styx, the Phlegethon;
  Then, through this narrow gap, till finally
They come to where there is no going down.[4]
  That is Cocytus – what that pool is like
  You'll shortly see, and so I'll not explain."   120
And I to him: "Why, if the course is such
  That this stream follows, coming from our world,
  Is it not seen until this utmost verge?"
He said: "You know this place is circular;
  And even though you've come in a great arc
  Towards the left, descending more and more,
You have not yet completed the whole round.
  So, if we come on something that is new,
  That surely is not something to astound."
I questioned him again: "Master, where is   130
  Lethe? Where Phlegethon? You ignore the first,
  And say that Phlegethon's a rain of tears."
"I'm pleased you ask these questions, certainly,"
  He answered, "but the stream of boiling blood
  Should have solved one that you've just put to me.

---

1 Rhea, to save her son Jove from Saturn (who was accustomed to eat his children), hid
   him on Mount Ida and ordered her priests to make a noise to drown the infant's cries.
2 In Egypt. The statue is therefore looking west.
3 The image of the old man of Crete – open to apparently endless allegorical interpreta-
   tion, particularly in its details – is primarily an image of the progressive deterioration of
   mankind. Its source is biblical – Nebuchadnezzar's dream in the second chapter of the
   Book of Daniel. In that chapter Daniel interprets the King's dream; but his interpretation
   is not necessarily to be taken to coincide with Dante's intention.
4 The lowest part of the Inferno, at the centre of the world.

You will see Lethe, not in this abyss,
    But where souls go to purify themselves
    When all their guilt's repented and dismissed."[1]
Then he went on: "It's time that we were turning
    Out of the wood – now follow where I lead: 140
    The margins make a road, for they're not burning:
The flames are all extinguished overhead."

---

1   The River Lethe is in the Earthly Paradise (*Purg.* XXVIII, 25–33).

CANTO XV

As Dante and Virgil move along the river's margin, they encounter a group of shades run-ning towards them on the burning sand, one of whom plucks at the hem of Dante's robe.

This is Brunetto Latini, once Dante's mentor and friend, but now damned for the sin of sodomy. The meeting is joyful, but distressing also in that their situations are now so different. It is forbidden for these shades to pause, but Brunetto walks along with Dante for a while.

Brunetto regrets that he cannot now help Dante in his work. Like Farinata in the circle of the heretics, Brunetto prophesies, in a rather vague way, future trouble for Dante. Dante says that he hopes for some explication of these prophecies when he meets Beatrice. Brunetto says his group is made up entirely of clerics, all famous men of letters, and all guilty of the one sin. (Very many, perhaps most, educated men in Dante's day were in minor orders at least, and not all of these "clerics" performed religious duties. So far as is known, Brunetto himself did not.)

As they see another group of sinners approaching, Brunetto, fearful of the punishment he will incur if he does not rejoin his group, races away.

This canto, a striking rebuttal of any notion that Dante merely "put his enemies in hell", arouses many, apparently contradictory, reactions. The love and respect on both sides is clear, but so is the gulf between the old friends; worldly fame is valued, but it is seen to be noth-ing compared to one's eternal fate; Brunetto's intellectual and artistic qualities are stressed, but so is the foulness of his sin. The final image of Brunetto racing away "like the winning, not the losing, runner", with the sad undertone of the literal reason for his speed – one of the most famous images in the *Comedy* – summarizes implicitly much that has gone before.

✳

N ow the hard margin takes us on from there:
   Steam from the river darkens overhead,
   Shielding the shores and water from the fire.
As the Flemings, from Wissant up to Bruges,
   Fearing the ocean rushing in on them,
   Have built a dyke along the water's edge;
And like the Paduans where the Brenta flows,
   In order to defend their towns and castles,
   Before warm weather melts Carinthia's snows,
In the same fashion were these margins made –   10
   Whoever was the builder who designed them –
   Except not raised so high and not so broad.[1]
We had already left the wood behind
   So far that I could not have any longer
   Seen where it was, if I had turned around;
We met up with a company of shades
   Coming along the riverside,[2] who all
   Stared hard at us as, when the daylight fades,

---

1   We gather during the course of this canto that the margins are about the height of a man.
2   These shades are moving in the opposite direction to Dante and Virgil.

Men stare if there is no moon in the sky;
   They knit their brows and squinnied up at us   20
   Like an old tailor at a needle's eye.
Then, as the group of shades stared up like this,
   One recognized me, and caught hold of me
   By my gown's hem and cried: "What a surprise!"
And I, as he was stretching out his hand
   Towards me, fixed my eyes on his baked features,
   Till the scorched face could not prevent my mind
Recalling him, and all became quite clear;
   And as I bent my face towards his face,
   I said: "O Ser Brunetto, are you here?"[1]   30
And he replied: "Don't be displeased, my son,
   If Brunetto Latini for a while
   Turns back to you and lets the rest pass on."
I said: "With all my heart, I beg of you!
   And should you wish that I should pause, I will,
   If he with whom I've come allows me to."
"O son," he said, "whoever of this flock
   Pauses at all, must lie one hundred years
   Without defence as flakes of fire attack.
Therefore walk on; I'll keep close by your gown   40
   Down here; and then I must rejoin my troop
   Who go on mourning their eternal pain."
I did not dare descend from off my road
   To where he walked; and yet, like somebody
   Who's full of reverence, I bowed my head.
Then he began: "What chance or destiny
   Brings you down here before your final hour?
   And who is this who's showing you the way?"
"There, up above, in the world of living men,"
   I said, "I strayed off in a gloomy valley,   50
   Before the midpoint of my life had come.
At dawn but yesterday I turned my back
   Upon it – then returned – this man appeared
   To put me once again on the right track."
And he replied: "If you follow your star,
   You cannot fail to reach a glorious haven,
   If my opinion while I lived was fair.
Had it not happened that I died too soon,
   Seeing that heaven was benign towards you,
   I would have helped in all that you took on.   60
But those ungrateful and malicious folk –

---

1   Brunetto Latini (*c.*1220–94) was a Florentine Guelf and, as the title *"Ser"* suggests, a
notary. His most famous literary works were *Li livres dou tresor* (*The Treasury*, an ency-
clopedia written in French), and *Il tesoretto* (*The Little Treasury*, an unfinished narrative
poem written in Italian). He was almost certainly not an official teacher of Dante, but
rather a well-loved mentor; he was, of course, much older than Dante.

Descending in the past from Fiesole,
  Still with some trace of mountain and of rock –
Will be, for your good works, your enemy:
  And with good reason: among bitter rowans
  Sweet fig trees were not meant to fructify.[1]
They are of old reputed to be blind –
  And they are greedy, envious, and presumptuous.
  Avoid the faults to which they are inclined!
Such honour is reserved for you by fate,   70
  That both sides[2] will be eager to devour you;
  But grass will be kept distant from the goat.[3]
Let beasts of Fiesole forage among
  Themselves, and leave untouched the family tree –
  If any still arises from their dung –
In which there lives once more the sacred seed
  Of those first Romans who remained there when
  It turned into a nest of such bad blood."
"If all my prayers were answered utterly,"
  I said in my reply, "you would not yet   80
  Have been excluded from humanity;
For still I have in mind, to my great pain,
  The dear, the kindly, the paternal image
  Of you who, in the world, time and again
Taught me how man becomes eternal:[4] while
  There's breath in me, my gratitude for that
  Is something that my language must reveal.
What you say of my future I shall store
  Beside another text,[5] to be expounded
  By one[6] who will know how, if I reach her.   90
This much I'd have you understand quite clearly –
  Provided that my conscience does not chide –
  Whatever Fortune brings me, I am ready.
Such prophecies to me are nothing new:
  And so I say, let Fortune turn her wheel
  As she thinks best, the peasant wield his hoe."[7]

---

1 According to old tradition the Romans conquered Fiesole and founded Florence on
   the plain below it, and the new city was inhabited first by a few Roman settlers and by
   refugees from Fiesole who brought their uncivilized ways with them. The vices of the
   Florentines, so often mentioned by Dante, are attributed by Brunetto to their Fiesolan
   ancestry.
2 Black and White Guelfs.
3 This sounds like a proverb. Dante, a White Guelf, incurred the enmity of both factions
   of the Florentine Guelfs.
4 Lives on after death because of his renown. Dante was not indifferent to worldly fame,
   and Brunetto is still very anxious for it even in the Inferno (see ll. 119–20 below).
5 Farinata's prophecy in *Inf.* x, 79–81.
6 Beatrice.
7 Fortune's wheel is a traditional image of the uncertainty of worldly affairs.

My master turned his head towards the right
  At this, and then right round to look at me,
  And said: "He listens well who takes good note."
Nevertheless I wished to talk some more   100
  With Ser Brunetto, so I asked about
  Those in his flock most famed and with most power.
And he replied: "It's well to know of some;
  As for the others, we had best be silent:
  There is not time enough to talk of them.
In short, know they were clerics, one and all,
  Great men of letters, and men of renown,
  Whom in the world above one sin[1] made foul.
You see there Priscian[2] running with that grim
  Crowd, and Francesco d'Accorso;[3] and also,   110
  If you had any wish to see such scum,
The bishop whom God's servant[4] ordered on,
  Who left the Arno for the Bacchiglione,
  Where he gave up that body strained by sin.[5]
I would say more – but not another word
  Am I allowed, another inch: I see
  A fresh cloud[6] rising from the sand of dread.
People are here with whom I must not be.
  I recommend to you my *Treasury*,[7]
  In which I'm still alive: that's all I'll say."   120
Then he turned round, and looked like one of those
  Who race, to win the green cloth at Verona,
  Across the fields; and looked, among all these,
Most like the winning, not the losing, runner.[8]

---

1 The "one sin" is sodomy. This seems clear from what Virgil has said in *Inf.* xi, 49–51.
  However, there is no other known independent evidence that Brunetto was guilty of
  this sin, and Dante strangely does not name it in this present canto. Other suggestions
  have therefore been made, but unpersuasively.
2 Probably the famous Latin grammarian (fl. *c.*500).
3 Francesco d'Accorso (1225–93) was a celebrated lawyer from Bologna; he lectured for
  some time at Oxford.
4 The Pope. The description *servus servorum Dei* (servant of the servants of God) is still
  used.
5 Andrea de' Mozzi, Bishop of Florence on the River Arno, was moved to Vicenza, on the
  River Bacchiglione, on account of his scandalous way of life. He died in 1296.
6 This probably refers to the cloud of sand raised by the shades running towards them.
7 See note to l. 30 above. The book mentioned here is probably Brunetto's large encyclo-
  pedia rather than his short narrative poem.
8 In this race the winner received a piece of green cloth, and the last runner a booby prize
  which exposed him to derision. The episode finishes on an apparently triumphant note:
  we may momentarily forget why he is racing back.

CANTO XVI

Dante hears falling water in the distance. Then three figures detach themselves from one of the bands of sinners: they have gathered from Dante's clothes that he is a Florentine, and they ask him to stop and talk.

Virgil warns Dante to show respect to these shades; but as they approach, they form themselves into a ridiculous circle and wheel round while still keeping their faces towards Dante. One of them, Jacopo Rusticucci, introduces the other two and then himself: they are all to be respected for the good qualities they showed in their lives. Only the thought of being tormented like them prevents Dante from rushing down to embrace the three, so great is his love and respect.

Jacopo Rusticucci is anxious for news of Florence, since a fellow citizen, a new arrival in their circle of the Inferno, has come with disturbing reports. Dante replies by saying that newcomers into Florence and a sudden access of profits have brought about the city's moral decadence. Rusticucci asks Dante to keep the memory of him and his companions alive, if he should ever return to Florence. Then the shades rush away to rejoin their band of sinners.

The sound of falling water is now deafeningly near. Dante is wearing a cord around his waist, and he obeys Virgil's command by undoing it and handing it over. Virgil throws it down into the gulf beneath them, and they wait to see what will happen.

Dante explains to the reader that what is about to appear would tax anyone's credulity. A shape comes up from the depths of the Inferno, an eerie sight; but we have to wait until the next canto for a description.

Brunetto Latini in the previous canto was a representative of the clerisy, and now in this canto we see lay Florentines, like him justly famed and like him damned. In both cantos we see that there is a higher judgement than man's, but also that man's judgement is not to be despised.

✳

I was in earshot of re-echoing waves
   Cascading to the circle lying under,[1]
   Like the faint thunder of unnumbered hives,
When suddenly we saw three shades that came
   Towards us, running from a crowd that passed
   Beneath the bitter torment of hot rain.
They raced to us, and shouted out as one:
   "Stop, you who by your clothing seem to be
   Someone who comes from our degenerate town!"[2]
What gaping wounds their bodies showed, alas,   10
   Old or just opened by the excessive heat!
   It grieves me merely to remember this.
My teacher listened carefully to their cries;
   Then turned to face me, and he said: "Now wait.
   One must show courtesy to such as these.

---

1   The eighth circle of the Inferno.
2   Florence.

Were it not for this fire that shoots down, through
　　The nature of the place, I'd think it fitter
　　For you to run to them than they to you."
As soon as we stood still, their usual noises[1]
　　Began again; when they arrived, the three　　　　　　20
　　Made up a wheel, a sort of ring o' roses.
As wrestlers who are oiled and naked do,
　　Looking for where to grasp and take advantage,
　　Before it comes to kick and punch and blow,
So these wheeled round; and each one always bent
　　His face towards me, and he turned his neck
　　Contrariwise to how his footsteps went.
And "If our plight upon this shifting sand
　　Makes us and what we ask provoke disdain,"
　　One said, "and these our faces skinned and browned,　　30
Then may our fame on earth incline you yet
　　To tell us who you are, who go so safely
　　Through the Inferno, and on living feet.
He, in whose footsteps now you see me walk,
　　Although his skin is peeled and he goes naked,
　　Was greater in degree than you'd have thought:
He was a grandson of the good Gualdrada;[2]
　　His name was Guido Guerra;[3] all his life
　　He was, with sword and thought, a worthy leader.
The other one who's with me, pounding sand,　　　　　　40
　　Is Tegghiaio Aldobrandi,[4] whose opinion
　　Ought to have been more often kept in mind.[5]
And I, who with them hang upon a cross,
　　Was Jacopo Rusticucci; it was my
　　Shrewish wife who brought me down to this."
Now, were it not for fire and flames, I would
　　Have thrown myself down there to be among them,
　　Which I believe my guide might have allowed;
But since that would have been to bake and burn,
　　Sheer terror overcame my fine intention　　　　　　50
　　Of running to embrace them there and then.
"No, not disdain, but simple grief to see
　　The state you're in," I said, "entered my heart –
　　Grief that will take some time to fade away –
The instant that the words of my lord here
　　Gave me good reason to believe that people

1　Weeping and lamentation.
2　Known for her domestic virtues.
3　A leader of the Florentine Guelfs, he fought at Montaperti (1260), was exiled after that
　　battle, fought at Benevento (1265) and returned to Florence.
4　A Florentine Guelf, who died before 1266. Dante has already enquired about him and
　　the present speaker (Jacopo Rusticucci) in *Inf.* VI, 79–84.
5　He advised the Florentines not to fight at Montaperti, where they were defeated.

Of such renown as yours were coming near.
Your fellow citizen, I've never failed
  To dwell with great affection on your honoured
  Names and great deeds as I have heard them told.   60
I leave the bitter for the sweetest taste,[1]
  Just as my truthful guide has promised me;
  But I must drop down to the centre[2] first."
"Now may your soul direct your body on
  For many years," he spoke to me once more,
  "And may your fame shine out when you are gone!
Tell us if courtesy and valour still
  Live in our city as they used to do,
  Or if they've gone outside the city wall:
Guglielmo Borsiere[3] only recently   70
  Has felt our pains,[4] and goes there in our band,
  Disturbing us with what he has to say."
"Newcomers and quick profits generate
  Such arrogance and such excess, O Florence,
  That you already have to weep for it."
So I cried out, with my face elevated;[5]
  At this reply, they stared at one another,
  As men do when they hear the truth being stated.
"If you can offer such a free and full
  Answer on all occasions," they replied,   80
  "Then happy you who speak out as you will!
And so, if you can but escape from here,
  And go from this dark land to see the stars,
  When you can say with pleasure, 'I was there',
Please speak of us, that our renown may last."
  They broke the wheel up then, and as they fled,
  Those legs of theirs seemed wings, they moved so fast.
No one could possibly have said "Amen"
  In less time than they took to disappear:
  My master thought it time that we went on.   90
I follow him; and we have not gone far
  Before the sound of water[6] comes so close
  That any conversation's hard to hear.

---

1 Dante is going to leave sin behind in the Inferno, and travel to Paradise.
2 The centre of the earth (pictured by Dante as a globe), and the uttermost depth of the Inferno.
3 Another Florentine with a good reputation.
4 He has died recently. He must therefore have died before the date (the spring of 1300) which Dante assigns to his journey.
5 To emphasize the importance of the generalized statement he is making. When speaking to shades in this circle, Dante normally looks *down*, since they are below him.
6 The waterfall mentioned as at some distance from them at the beginning of this canto.

Like that first river[1] which flows on its own[2]
  Down the left side of the high Apennines
  From the Monviso to the east (and known
Up above as the Acquacheta first,
  Before it drops into its lower bed,
  Where at Forlì that former name is lost),
Making thunderous echoes near to San   100
  Benedetto in Alpe, where with one
  Fall, not a thousand, it goes hurtling down –
So from a rocky precipice we found
  That blackened water falling and resounding:
  We would have been, if we had stayed there, stunned.
Around my waist I had a knotted cord,
  With which one time it had been my intention
  To catch the leopard with the speckled hide.[3]
As soon as I had got the cord undone,
  Just as my leader had commanded me,   110
  I gave it to him, in a hank or skein.
At that he turned away to his right hand,
  And at a certain distance[4] from the brink
  He flung it, down into the vast profound.
"Something that's very strange must make reply,"
  I told myself, "to this unwonted signal
  Which my master is following with his eye."
How cautious we should be who chance to find
  Ourselves with others who don't stop at actions,
  But have the wit to see inside the mind![5]   120
"Something," he said to me, "will soon emerge –
  Something I'm waiting for and you but dream of:
  Something will come in sight out of this gorge."
Faced with that truth which seems to be a lie,
  A man should keep his mouth shut, if he can,
  Or he'll be brought to shame quite guiltlessly;
But here I can't be silent. By the verse
  Of this my comedy,[6] I, Reader, swear –
  May it find favour over many years! –
That through that murky atmosphere I saw   130
  A shape swim up towards us – and a shape
  To strike the most self-confident with awe!

---

1 The Montone.

2 That is, it flows into the sea without joining another river.

3 The cord presumably represents some means Dante had used to combat the sins of
   incontinence (see *Inf.* 1); but its allegorical significance here is uncertain.

4 To avoid its catching on the edge of the chasm.

5 As we see from the next tercet, and have seen previously, Virgil is often able to read
   Dante's thoughts.

6 Dante uses the word "comedy" to denote poetry written in a humble style in the ver-
   nacular, which ends happily.

It moved most like a mariner, when he –
    Being down to free an anchor that was caught
    Upon a rock or something in the sea –
Shoots to the surface and draws in his feet.

CANTO XVII

What turns out to be a strange composite beast comes to rest on the edge of the pit, after flying up from the depths of the Inferno. It is described in ways that make clear its nature as the embodiment of fraud. Virgil goes to speak with it, and he arranges for it to carry Dante and himself down into the eighth circle.

Meanwhile Dante walks among the usurers who are crouching in this third ring of the seventh circle. Each of them has hanging from his neck a purse which bears his family's coat of arms, and they are, as one might expect with usurers, feasting their eyes on their purses. When they were alive, they were all of high social rank, but they were guilty of what Dante clearly regards as a particularly low sin. One of them, a Paduan, takes pleasure in mentioning that all but himself in that place are Florentines, and says a few more unpleasant words to Dante. Dante's disgust at these sinners is such that he does not deign to reply.

Dante returns to where Virgil is already on the back of the monster, whose name we discover is Geryon. On Virgil's advice Dante, who is terrified, mounts in front of Virgil, who is then able to defend him from Geryon's harmful tail.

Their flight down is described. Geryon, on Virgil's orders, circles as he descends, which makes the descent more gradual and somewhat easier for Dante. Dante is so frightened that he has difficulty at first in gathering what is happening. Gradually, however, he becomes aware of the fires and lamentation below them. Geryon lands at the foot of some jagged rock and, once his passengers have disembarked, flies away like an arrow from a bow.

"See there the monster with the stinging tail,
    That scales the heights, and shatters all defence!
    See there the beast that makes the whole world foul!"
That was an exclamation from my guide,
    Who beckoned to the beast to come ashore
    Close by the end of our hard stony road.
And that unclean embodiment of fraud
    Did draw up on the land his head and chest,
    But did not bring his tail up on the side.[1]
His countenance was of an honest man,   10
    Someone to all appearance well-disposed,
    And then the rest of him was serpentine;
He had two paws, with hair to the armpits –
    And back and breast and both his sides were painted
    With circles and with complicated knots:
Less colourful, less complex in design,
    Are fabrics from the Tartars and the Turks;

---

1   A notable example – one of many in the descriptions of Geryon – of how details are apt and realistic in the narrative and also allegorical: it is an essential characteristic of fraud to conceal its intended harm.

Nor did Arachne weave such on her loom.[1]
As we sometimes see vessels left to lie
   Half drawn up on the shore and half in water,   20
   And as up there in gluttonous Germany[2]
The beaver sits to hunt, half on the land,[3]
   So did that worst of beasts stay on the margin
   Made out of stone enclosing the hot sand.
The whole tail in the void was quivering
   And writhing upwards its envenomed pincers
   Which, like the scorpion's tail, contain a sting.
My leader said: "It's necessary here
   To deviate somewhat to arrive at that
   Malevolent creature lying over there."   30
So we went down a little to the right,
   And walked ten paces on the very edge,
   Avoiding carefully the sand and heat.
And when we came to where the monster lay,
   I saw, a little further on the sand,
   People crouching near where it falls away.
My master said: "In order to obtain
   A perfect understanding of this ring,[4]
   Go over there and see the state they're in.
Be sure to place a limit on your talk.   40
   Till you return I'll have some words with this
   Creature: he'll bear us both on his broad back."
So further on, along the brink of that
   Unhappy seventh circle, all alone,
   I went to where the unhappy people sat.
Their pain gushed from their eyes; and with their hands
   They kept on trying to defend themselves
   Now from the flames, now from the burning sands:
Exactly as a dog in summer does,
   Now with its muzzle, now its paws, when bitten   50
   By irksome fleas or gnats, or by gadflies.
After I'd fixed my eyes on some of them
   On whom the painful fire is always falling,
   I recognized not one; but saw that from
The neck of each of them a purse was hanging,
   Each with its special colour and device,
   On which they seemed to feast their eyes with longing.[5]
And as I walked around and kept my eye on

---

1   Arachne was an expert mythical weaver, who challenged Athena to a contest, was
    defeated and was turned into a spider.
2   Northern Europeans were proverbially gluttonous.
3   The beaver was said, when hunting, to attract fish by waving its tail in the water.
4   The third ring of the seventh circle.
5   Their heraldic devices reveal the high social rank of the usurers, while their attitude and
    the purses about their necks emphasize their depravity.

Them all, I found a yellow purse with azure
  That had the face and bearing of a lion.[1]   60
Then, looking further as I saw things better,
  I saw another purse, as red as blood,
  That had on it a goose whiter than butter.[2]
And one, who had on his white reticule
  A pregnant sow depicted in bright blue,[3]
  Demanded: "What's your purpose in this hole?
Just go away. And since you're not yet dead,
  I'll let you know my neighbour Vitaliano[4]
  Will come and sit down here at my left side.
Among these Florentines I'm Paduan: 70
  I hear their voices ringing in my ears,
  Shouting: 'We're waiting for that honoured man,
The knight who wears the purse that shows three goats!' "[5]
  At this he writhed his muzzle and stuck out
  His tongue, as oxen do to lick their snouts.
And I, who feared that any more delay
  Might anger him who'd warned me to be quick,
  Turned from those weary souls and went away.
And then I found my leader was already
  Mounted on that repulsive animal.   80
  He told me: "Now you must be bold and steady.
From now on we'll go down by ways like this:
  Climb up in front; I must be in the middle,
  So that the tail won't be injurious."
As one who feels the approach of quartan fever,
  With nails already blue, while the mere sight
  Of cooling shade makes him tremble all over –
Such was my feeling when those words were said;
  And then I had that sense of shame which makes
  A servant brave in front of his good lord.   90
I settled on those monstrous shoulders, but
  When I began to speak, my voice would not
  Issue as planned to ask him: "Hold me tight!"
But he, who'd aided me more than one time
  In other peril, soon as I had mounted
  Wrapped me in both his arms and held me firm;
And said: "Now Geryon, take off: and make
  Wide circles in descent and travel slowly:
  Think of the novel burden on your back."
Just as a boat backs slowly from its place   100

---

1 The arms of the Florentine Gianfigliazzi family, noted usurers.
2 The arms of the Obriachi family, also Florentines and noted usurers.
3 The arms of the Scrovegni family of Padua, to which several usurers belonged.
4 Obviously another Paduan, but not certainly identified.
5 Gianni Buiamonte dei Becchi, a Florentine who died in 1310, ten years after the date
   which Dante gave to his journey.

Little by little, so the creature moved;
        And when he knew he had sufficient space,
He turned his tail to where his breast had been
        And stretched it out, and moved it like an eel,
        And gathered with his paws the soft air in.
I do believe not such tremendous fear
        Struck Phaethon when the reins slipped from his grasp
        And set the sky, as still appears, on fire;[1]
Or Icarus when the feathers fell away
        From both his sides, because the wax was melting,   110
        His father crying out: "Don't go that way!"[2] –
As struck me when I looked around and saw
        Only the monster all about me and
        No scenery except the ambient air.
Our beast goes swimming slowly, and describing
        Wide circles in descent: I'm only conscious
        Of wind brushing my face and wind arising.[3]
Already I could hear upon our right
        The torrent[4] roaring horribly below,
        And craned my neck as I looked out for it.   120
Then, being terrified that I might drop,
        Seeing such fires and hearing such laments,
        I shuddered and held on, and huddled up.
I saw what I had not seen previously –
        Our spiralling descent – now that such evils
        At every side were looming up at me.
And as a falcon – one that's lingered on
        The wing too long and sees no lure[5] or prey,
        And makes the falconer wail: "You're coming down!" –
Descends exhausted whence it went with speed,   130
        Describes a hundred circles and alights
        Far from its master, sullen and annoyed –
So, at the very foot of jagged rock,
        Geryon set us down, far down below,
        And once our weight was lifted from his back,
He shot off like an arrow from a bow.

---

1   The mythical Phaethon obtained from his father, Helios the Sun, permission to guide
the chariot of the sun across the sky. Phaethon proved unequal to this task and lost
control of the horses, and they went off course. One result of the conflagration which
followed was the Milky Way, which "still appears" in the sky. See *Purg.* XXIX, 120.

2   The mythical Icarus was provided by his father with wings made from feathers held
together by wax. He was warned not to fly too near the sun – but he did: the wax melted,
the wings fell apart and he plummeted to his death.

3   The wind brushing Dante's face is caused by Geryon's circling flight, and the wind
coming from below is caused by the fact that the beast is descending.

4   Phlegethon.

5   A device to bring a falcon back to its master.

CANTO XVIII

The canto opens with a description of the eighth circle of the Inferno, which consists of ten tiered circular ditches arranged concentrically. The ditches are all cut across by lines of bridges which radiate from the deep well or chasm at the centre of this circle. Different sins are punished in each of the ditches, but all of these sins involve cheating, deceiving, or in some way practising fraud upon people who have no particular reason to trust those who deceive them, except that there is a duty incumbent on everyone to deal honestly.

The first ditch contains pimps and seducers, who move in opposite directions, and are all being scourged by horned demons. Dante speaks with one of the pimps, with whom he was already acquainted and who tries hard to avoid his eyes. This is the Bolognese Venedico Caccianemico, who sold his own sister for gain. He is frank about his fault, and gives the impression that this sin is one of which very many Bolognese are guilty, since they are proverbially avaricious.

Now Dante and Virgil climb up one of the bridges which run off at the side of their track. They stand upon its arch to look at the seducers, and they note particularly the mythical Jason, a man of regal bearing and prowess, but a habitual seducer of women. They do not speak with him.

Dante and Virgil cross the bridge and look down into the second ditch, that of the gross flatterers. These sinners are immersed in human excrement (a symbol of the filth in which they trafficked), and so smeared with it that not much can be seen of them. This perversion of the human ability to communicate is seen as not only a serious sin, but a particularly disgusting one.

✳

There is in hell a place called Eviltiers,
   Which is throughout of iron-coloured stone,
   As the high wall that goes all round it is.
In the dead centre of this wicked space
   There yawns a broad profound abyss or well,
   Whose structure I'll describe in its due place.
The area, between the high surround
   Of hard stone and the well, is circular,
   And cut into ten pits that go all round.
And like the sort of pattern that is made   10
   By the concentric moats around a castle,
   To ensure that it is strongly fortified,
So these ten ditches make the same design;
   And as a castle from its inner gates
   To its perimeter has bridges thrown,
So from the rock wall's foot ridges run down
   Over ditches and banks: the central well
   Cuts them all short and gathers them all in.
This was the very place in which we found
   Ourselves, when Geryon set us down. The poet   20

Kept to the left, and I went on behind.
Then I saw novel misery on the right,
   Novel torments and novel torturers:
   The first of all the ditches was replete.
The sinners were all naked – on our side
   They came towards us, but the ones beyond
   Along with us, both moving with great speed:
Just as the Romans for the Jubilee,[1]
   For all the numbers on the Bridge,[2] were able
   To keep the traffic moving steadily,   30
Since on one side[3] they kept their eyes all bent
   Upon the Castle,[4] going to St Peter's;
   And, on the other, moved towards the Mount.[5]
On both sides, all along the gloomy rock,
   I saw horned demons with enormous whips
   Lashing the sinners cruelly on the back.
Oh, how the demons made those sinners kick
   Their heels up! Certainly not one was anxious
   To have a third or even second stroke.
While I went on, I was by chance aware   40
   Of one who caught my eye, and I exclaimed:
   "There's somebody I'm sure I've seen before."
And so I stopped, and tried to make him out;
   My courteous guide stopped also, and he gave
   Me his permission to go back a bit.
That scourged soul thought by lowering his gaze
   To hide himself; but it was all in vain –
   I said: "O you, who go with downcast eyes,
If your known features are not false or fickle,
   Venedico you'll be – Caccianemico![6]   50
   But what's put you in such a pretty pickle?"
Then he replied: "I do not want to say,
   But I'm compelled by your clear speech, which brings
   All the old world I lived in back to me.
I was the one who pandered, after all,
   Between Ghisolabella and the Marquis,
   However men may tell the filthy tale.
I'm not the only Bolognese this ditch
   Contains. Indeed, it's crammed so full of them

---

1   The first Jubilee of the Roman Catholic Church was instituted by Pope Boniface VIII
    in 1300. It brought many pilgrims into Rome.
2   The Sant'Angelo bridge over the Tiber, leading to St Peter's.
3   One side of the road over the bridge.
4   The Castel Sant'Angelo.
5   Monte Giordano, a small hill on the side of the Tiber opposite to the Castel Sant'Angelo.
6   A leading Guelf from Bologna who sold his own sister, Ghisolabella, to the Marquis of
    Este.

Fewer are using *sipa*[1] in their speech   60
Between the Savena and Reno Rivers;[2]
  And if you think this needs to be confirmed,
  Remember we're well known as avaricious."
And, as he spoke, a demon with a lash
  Laid on him and cried out: "Clear off, you pander!
  There are no women here for you to cash."
Then I went back and caught up with my guide;
  Not many paces and we came upon
  A ridge of rock that ran out at the side.[3]
We easily climbed up this jagged ground,   70
  And turning to the right along its arch,
  We left that everlasting moving-round.[4]
When we came where that ridge has under it
  A hollow passage for those being lashed,
  My leader said: "Now stop, and let the sight
Of still more ill-born beings catch your eye,
  None of whose faces you have seen as yet,
  Since we have all been walking the same way."
From the old bridge we looked down at the group
  Coming towards us on the other side,   80
  And like the others driven by the whip.
And my kind guide, without my asking him,
  Said: "See that mighty one who is approaching,
  And does not seem to weep, for all his pain.
How regal is his bearing still! For this
  Is Jason,[5] who by grit and guile deprived
  The men of Colchis of the Golden Fleece.
He landed at the Isle of Lemnos, when
  The bold, unpitying women who lived there
  Had given up to death all of the men.   90
There, with love signs and flattering phrases, he
  Deceived Hypsipyle, the girl who had
  Deceived the other women previously.[6]
Then he abandoned her, pregnant, alone:
  Such guilt condemns him to such punishment:

---

1   The dialect word for *si* ("yes") in Bologna.
2   That is, the area under Bolognese control. There are more dead Bolognese in this part
     of the Inferno than there are Bolognese still alive.
3   This is one of the bridges already mentioned in ll. 14–18 of this canto.
4   The constant movement of the panders and seducers punished in this first ditch of the
     eighth circle. The panders move facing Dante and Virgil, while the seducers are moving
     in the opposite direction: both groups of sinners keep to their own right hand.
5   The mythical leader of the Argonauts. They sailed to Colchis in quest of the golden
     ram's fleece which was guarded by a dragon. Jason is, despite his prowess, damned as a
     serial seducer of women.
6   She had merely pretended to kill her father, and so deceived the other women of Lemnos.

Medea is avenged at the same time.[1]
With him go all deceivers of that sort:
    That's all you need to know about this valley,
    And about everyone whom its fangs bite."
We were already where the narrow ridge   100
    Crosses the second bank,[2] and where that makes
    A shoulder which supports another bridge.
From here we're conscious of a muffled whine,
    Where people[3] snort and snuffle through their muzzles,
    And slap themselves, inside the next tier down.
Foul vapours smeared the sides as they arose
    Out of the ditch, encrusting it with mould
    Repugnant to the eyes and to the nose.
This ditch's bottom is so deep and dark
    It is not visible unless one climbs   110
    The hump to where the bridge is at its peak.
Once at that point I could look down and see
    The people weltering there in excrement,
    Channelled from earth's latrines apparently.
Soon, as I cast my eyes around it all,
    I saw one with his head so smeared with shit
    That, clerical or lay, I could not tell.
He snarled at me: "Why's your insatiable
    Stare fixed on me, when all of us are filthy?"
I answered him: "Because, as I recall,   120
I used to know you, when your hair was dry,
    Alessio Interminelli, the Lucchese![4]
    That's why I look at you especially."
Then, thumping his own forehead, he replied:
    "I'm drenched down here for all those flatteries
    Of which one time my tongue was never tired."
Then, after that, my guide said: "Try to thrust
    Your head a little further to the front,
    Until you find you're face to face at last
With that dishevelled, filthy prostitute   130
    Who's scratching at herself with shitty nails,
    And sometimes crouches, sometimes stands upright.
That is Thaïs,[5] the harlot who replied
    (Her paramour had asked her: 'Do I please
    You very much?'): 'I'm vastly overjoyed!'
    Now let that be enough of sights like these."

---

1   The daughter of the King of Colchis, who helped Jason to obtain the Golden Fleece and
    whom he promised to marry. He later abandoned her.
2   Which divides the first from the second ditch of this eighth circle.
3   Those sinners who gained their ends by gross flattery.
4   All that is known of him, apart from Dante's account, is that he was a White Guelf still
    alive in 1295.
5   A character in a play by the Roman playwright Terence.

CANTO XIX

The pilgrims can now see the third ditch, where simoniacs – those who traffic in sacred things – are punished by being placed upside down in holes in the rock. Above these holes their legs are visible, and wriggle and jerk to express their torment, while fire licks about their feet.

Dante is interested in one of these pairs of legs, which seems to belong to someone who is suffering even more than the others. So Virgil carries Dante down into the ditch, where he is able to talk with this sinner. He is Pope Nicholas III (reigned 1277–80), and he explains that other simoniac popes lie piled up under him, just as he will be pushed further down at the arrival of the next sinner, who we gather will be Pope Boniface VIII (reigned 1294–1303), himself to be pushed down in his turn by Pope Clement V (reigned 1305–14).

Dante expresses to Nicholas III his great detestation of the sin of simony, and reminds him how Christ did not ask for money from St Peter before giving him the keys of the kingdom of heaven, and the Apostles did not ask for money from Matthias before they elected him to take the place of the traitor Judas Iscariot. Dante also seizes the opportunity to deprecate the Donation of Constantine, which was thought to confer temporal power upon the popes. While Dante is speaking, the feet of Nicholas III keep on kicking, though whether to express anger or pangs of conscience Dante does not know. Dante notices that he has clearly pleased Virgil by what he has said.

Virgil picks Dante up once again and carries him onto the ridge, from where they can see into the fourth ditch, and here Virgil sets him down.

O Simon Magus![1] And all you, his brood!
    You take the things of God, which ought to be
    Wedded to good and, such is your great greed,
Prostitute them for gold – because of which
    The trumpet must be sounded for you now:
    You're in your rightful place in this third ditch!
We had already climbed upon the scarp
    To reach the tomb beyond, just at that point
    Which overhangs the centre of the dip.
O Highest Wisdom, see your skill displayed   10
    In heaven, on earth, and in this wicked world!
    How justly do you punish and reward!
I saw, along the bottom and the sides,
    The iron-coloured stone pitted with holes,
    All of them round, and all of them one size,
No narrower and no wider, to my mind,
    Than those in my beloved San Giovanni,

---

1   The word "simony" derives from his name (Acts 8:9–20).

In which the priests, when they're baptizing, stand;[1]
And one of which, not many years ago,
    I broke, to stop somebody suffocating: 20
    To this I set my seal, for all to know.[2]
Out of the mouth of each and every one
    A sinner's feet projected, and his legs
    Up to the thighs: the rest remained within.
The soles of all these feet were set on fire,
    Which made their joints so tremble, jerk and twitch
    They would have broken bonds of rope or wire.
As flames on well-greased objects only go
    Flickering along them superficially,
    So the flames flickered here, from heel to toe.   30
"Who is that shade, O master, who is kicking,
    And clearly suffering, more than all his fellows,"
    I asked, "and whom a redder flame is licking?"
He said: "If you will let me bear you down
    Along that shorter bank lying below,
    He'll tell you of himself and of his sin."
I answered him: "Your wish is my command:
    You are my lord, you know your will is mine,
    And what I do not say you understand."
We came upon the fourth bulwark; at that   40
    We turned and, keeping to the left, descended
    Into the narrow, perforated pit.
My kindly master did not set me down
    Until we came upon our goal, the hole
    Of him who used his feet to make his moan.
"O you inserted here, heels over head,
    Sad soul stuck like a pole into the ground,"
    I said, "if you are able, spare a word."
There I was bending, like the confessor
    Above the assassin who, once he is planted,
    Calls the priest back, to keep death from the door.[3]   50
He cried: "So you're already standing there,
    Already standing there, eh, Boniface?[4]

---

1   The church of San Giovanni in Florence, a few yards from the Duomo, is now better
known as the Baptistery. Nothing remains of the arrangements for baptism, but a fair
idea of them can be gained from the baptistery in Pisa, where there is a very large font
with several vertical tubes inside it for the priests to stand and remain dry.

2   No more is known of this than can be deduced from Dante's text. There seems to have
been some dispute over the rightness of Dante's action, and the language in l. 21 is legal,
as though Dante is here making an official statement of the truth.

3   Hired assassins were placed upside down in a hole which was then filled with earth once
the criminal had made his confession.

4   The sinner's mistake in thinking that Pope Boniface VIII has already come to join him
is a neat way of indicating the ultimate destination of one who was still alive in 1300.

The writing[1] must have lied by a year or more.
Are you already well and truly glutted
  With wealth you did not scruple to obtain
  Deceiving Her[2] whom you then prostituted?"
At that I stood like someone who stands dumb,
  Not understanding the reply that's made:
  Thinking he's mocked, he finds no words will come.   60
Then Virgil said: "Answer immediately:
  'I'm not the one, the one you think I am.'"
So I replied as was commanded me.
At that the spirit writhed his feet; then he,
  Sighing and with a voice full of despair,
  Replied: "What is it then you want from me?
If you've taken the trouble to climb down
  Simply to find out who I am, then listen:
  I had the mighty mantle for my own;[3]
A true son of the Bear,[4] in my great greed   70
  To advance the cubs, I pocketed great wealth
  Up in the world, as here I'm pocketed.
Already underneath my head are thrown
  All those who went before me simonizing:
  They're piled up in a heap beneath the stone.
And I like all of them will fall down too
  When he arrives, the one I thought you were[5]
  When I precipitately questioned you.
And now I have already longer stayed
  Cooking my feet and stuck here upside down   80
  Than he'll stay planted with his feet bright-red:
Since some years after him will come another,
  A worse, a lawless shepherd from the west,[6]
  One fit to cover both of us together.
He'll be a Jason, like the one we read
  About in Maccabees, whose King was kind:
  The King of France will follow that King's lead."[7]
I was perhaps at this point overbold,

---

1   In the "book of the future", which the damned are able to read.

2   Holy Mother Church.

3   He was Pope.

4   Pope Nicholas III was a member of the powerful Orsini family. Since "*orso*" means "bear", they were known as "sons of the Bear". Nicholas is a "true" son, because bears were proverbially greedy creatures.

5   Pope Boniface VIII.

6   Pope Clement V. He was born in Gascony, and after he became pope he established the Papacy at Avignon, in the notorious "Babylonian Captivity" (1309–77), and never came east to Rome.

7   In 2 Maccabees 4:7–26 we are told how Jason became high priest by bribing King Antiochus. Similarly, Clement V was said to have bought the Papacy by bribing King Philip the Fair of France.

But all I said to him was in this strain:
"Now tell me, how much treasure did Our Lord   90
Demand that Peter pay Him before He
  Delivered up the keys[1] into his care?
  Surely all that He said was: 'Follow me.'[2]
Neither did the Apostles take a toll
  From St Matthias when he was elected
  To take the place of the accursèd soul.[3]
Stay there then, for that punishment's your due;
  And take good care of the ill-gotten gain
  Which made you bold against Charles of Anjou.[4]
And did not those exalted keys restrain   100
  Me still – St Peter's keys I still revere,
  Your charge while you were living in the sun –
The language that I used would be more sharp;
  Because your avarice afflicts the world,
  Stamps on the good and lifts the wicked up.
You are the pastors Revelation[5] brings
  To mind, when she who sits upon the waters
  Is seen by John[6] to fornicate with kings;
She who had seven heads[7] when she was born,
  And from ten horns[8] drew strength and sustenance   110
  So long as virtue gladdened her bridegroom.
Between you and idolaters, what odds?
  You deify your silver and your gold:
  They worship one, and you a hundred gods.
O Constantine, what evil did you mother!
  No, not by your conversion, but the dowry
  Which you donated to the first rich father!"[9]
Now while I was still harping on that note,
  Whether he felt the sting of wrath or conscience,
  He went on kicking hard with both his feet.   120
I do believe I really pleased my guide,

---

1   "The keys of the kingdom of heaven" (Matt. 16:19).

2   See Matt. 4:19.

3   Judas Iscariot. See Acts 1:13–26.

4   Nicholas III was said to have been bribed to support the conspiracy (against the rule of Charles I of Anjou) which led to the massacre of 1282, known as the Sicilian Vespers.

5   Rev. 17. Dante's interpretation of this is that the woman is the Church and her bridegroom the Pope.

6   St John the Evangelist.

7   The Seven Sacraments.

8   The Ten Commandments.

9   Pope Sylvester I (r.314–35). The Roman Emperor Constantine the Great was converted to Christianity in 312. Legend had it that, when Constantine removed the capital of the Empire from Rome to Byzantium, he gave the whole temporal power of the West to the Church. This so-called "Donation of Constantine" was exposed as a forgery by the Italian humanist Lorenzo Valla (c.1405–57). Dante regards it as genuine, but deplores it.

Because he listened so contentedly
   To every one of those true words I said.
And then he took me in his arms again
   And, when he had me up against his breast,
   He went back by the way we had come down.
Nor did he tire, or let me slip his clutch,
   Until we reached the summit of the arch
   Which leads down from the fourth to the fifth ditch.
And here he gently set his burden down,   130
   Gently because the steep ridge would have been
   A rough road for a goat to travel on.
From there another valley could be seen.[1]

---

1   The fourth ditch.

CANTO XX

In this fourth ditch of the eighth circle we find magicians of various kinds, and especially fortune-tellers. They walk slowly and sadly in what is almost a parody of a religious procession. Since they tried to look too far ahead into the future, and tried to go beyond the limits assigned to human knowledge, they are punished by having their heads twisted right round so that, in order to see where they are going, they have to walk backwards. Their appearance is at once pathetic and ludicrous. Virgil warns Dante against having any sympathy for these sinners, explaining how that would be to question divine justice.

It is noteworthy that not one of these shades says anything: their silence now contrasts with their confident assertions while they lived. Virgil, on the other hand, has much to say, and he gives Dante all the information he needs. The inhabitants of this ditch range from legendary figures like Tiresias to historical and near-contemporary ones like Michael Scot, and notably include women, and even unnamed people in humble circumstances who practised magic.

The condemnation of magic here is forthright, but that does not preclude some subtleties in the attitude towards it. Some of the shades are blamed for practising magic (apparently with success), while others are blamed for *pretending* to be able to practise it: the reader is left in some doubt as to the efficacy of magic, although in no doubt at all as to its sinfulness. Moreover, Dante's disgust at this sin does not stop him including – especially in Virgil's descriptions of scenery in Italy – a suggestion of the fascination which magic has for all of us.

With a reminder that, in the world above them, the moon is setting and day breaking, Virgil encourages Dante to go forward on the next stage of his journey.

I must fill out my verse with further pain,
   The subject matter of this twentieth canto
   Of my first book, which is of those cast down.
I was now in a place from which I could
   Look down into the depths that opened up,
   Filled with anguished weeping like a flood;
And I saw silent weeping people pace
   Slowly along the circle of the valley
   As we at holy festivals process.
Then, as my eyes moved from their faces down,   10
   I saw (amazing thing!) each one of them
   Contorted in between the chest and chin;
I saw their faces had been turned right round,
   And of necessity they travelled backwards,
   Since looking to the front was not allowed.[1]
Perhaps in palsy's worst paralysis
   There have been people twisted in this way;
   But I don't think so: I have not seen this.
And now – God grant you profit from your reading! –

---

1   Those who wished to see into the future cannot now even look straight ahead. There is a sharp contrast between their high intellectual pretensions and their ridiculous deformity.

You may well, Reader, readily imagine   20
   If I was able to refrain from weeping
The instant that, so close at hand, I'd seen
   Our image so distorted, and the eyes
   Bathing the buttocks and the cleft between.
Of course I wept, leaning upon a scar
   Of the rugged ridge, until my guide demanded:
   "Are you as foolish as the others are?
Here pity lives when it is wholly dead:
   What is more wicked than to deprecate
   God's final judgement once it is declared?   30
Raise, raise your head, until you see the one
   For whom earth opened[1] in the Thebans' eyes;
   To whom they shouted: 'Where are you going down
To, Amphiaraus? Why leave the fight?'[2]
   And he just went on falling till he came
   To Minos by whom all of us are caught.[3]
Notice his shoulders where his chest should be:
   Because he wished to see too far ahead,
   He looks behind and he walks backwardly.
Tiresias next; he changed his looks when he   40
   Turned from the man he was into a woman,
   Which altered all his members utterly;
And after that he had to strike again
   The copulating serpents with his wand
   Before his manliness came back to him.[4]
Aruns[5] backs onto that one's paunch; he found –
   In hills of Luni where the Carrarese,
   Who live beneath them, cultivate the land –
A lonely cave within white marble stone,
   And made his home there, where the sea and stars   50
   Were always, without hindrance, to be seen.
And she who uses her loose locks to hide
   Her breasts, which are not visible to you,
   She who has hairy skin on the other side,
Was Manto,[6] who went searching far and wide;
   She settled down at last where I was born;[7]

---

1   Literally.
2   Amphiaraus was one of the seven kings who besieged Thebes (see *Inf.* xiv, 68–69, and note). He accurately foresaw his own death in that campaign.
3   See *Inf.* v, 4–12.
4   The legend is that, after separating two copulating serpents, Tiresias was turned into a woman. Seven years later he struck the same two serpents again and was changed back into a man.
5   A Tuscan soothsayer, who foretold the war between Pompey and Caesar and the latter's triumph.
6   Daughter of Tiresias.
7   Mantua.

And on this topic something must be said.[1]
When her father shook off this mortal coil,
    And Bacchus' sacred city[2] was enslaved,
    She wandered through the world for a long while.   60
There lies a lake in lovely Italy,
    North of the Tyrol, which is called Benaco,[3]
    Under the mountains bounding Germany.
A thousand streams, I think, or even more
    Bathe Garda, Val Camonica and Pennino,
    And all flow from the lake that is up there.
In that lake's centre is a place[4] where three
    Bishops – of Trent, of Brescia, of Verona –
    Might bless us, if they ever went that way.
A beautiful strong fortress to confront   70
    The Brescians and the Bergamese – Peschiera –
    Stands where the shore is at its lowest point.
There all the water that cannot be held
    Within Benaco's bosom overflows:
    This river runs through many a green field.
The moment that this water starts to flow,
    Men know it as the Mincio, not Benaco,
    Till at Governolo it joins the Po.
It comes to flat land after a short way,
    On which it spreads itself into a marsh –   80
    And sometimes in the summer it runs dry.
When she went by that way the uncouth maid
    Discovered land, in the middle of the marsh,
    Untilled and wholly uninhabited.
There, to avoid all human intercourse,
    She and her slaves stayed, to pursue her arts[5] –
    Lived there, then left her body spiritless.[6]
The people who were scattered round about
    Gathered there then, since it was fensible
    By reason of the marsh surrounding it.   90
They built the city over her dead bones,
    And called it Mantua, because she chose it,
    And sought no augury but her remains.
Once the inhabitants were more numerous,

---

1   The account of the founding of Mantua which follows is at odds with what Virgil says
in his *Aeneid* x, 198–200. The apparent digression here enables Dante to scout the notion
of deciding on the foundation of a city, or the naming of it, by casting lots or looking
for auguries.

2   Thebes.

3   The modern Lake Garda.

4   Probably the island now known as Lechi, on which there was a church subject to the
authority of three bishops.

5   Magic arts.

6   That is, when she died and soul and body were separated.

I STRETCHED MY HAND A SHORT WAY OUT BEFORE ME
AND SNAPPED A TINY BRANCH FROM OFF A THORN...

INFERNO XIII, 31–32

HE TURNED HIS TALONS ONTO HIS COMPANION,
AND GOT TO GRIPS WITH HIM ABOVE THE DITCH...

INFERNO XXII, 137–39

Before the foolishness of Casalodi
    Was caught by Pinamonte's sly device.[1]
So I suggest that, if you ever see
    A different record of my city's birth,
    You let no fable drive the truth away."
"Master," I answered, "all you've said upon   100
    This matter's so persuasive any version
    Were dust and ashes in comparison.
But say, among these people moving on,
    If you see anybody worth our notice,
    Since all my thoughts turn back to that alone."
Then he replied: "That man who lets his beard
    Spread from his cheeks and down his swarthy shoulders
    Was, at a time when Greece was so devoid
Of males that there were scarcely sons in cradles,[2]
    The augur who, in company with Calchas,[3]   110
    At Aulis fixed the time to cut the cables –
Eurypylus.[4] In my high tragedy[5]
    You'll find him mentioned in a certain passage.
    You'll know the place: you've read it thoroughly.
And that one over there was Michael Scot,[6]
    That one whose hips are slim; he really, truly
    Knew every magic trick and every sleight.
See Guido Bonatti;[7] and Asdente[8] that
    Is wishing he had stuck to thread and leather,
    But whose repentance has arrived too late.   120
See the sad women who gave up the needle,
    Shuttle and spindle to become diviners;
    They worked with herbs,[9] or sometimes a wax model.[10]
But let us go now; for already Cain's
    Touching the boundary of both hemispheres

1   Alberto da Casalodi, a Guelf Count of Mantua, was persuaded by a Ghibelline lord, Pinamonte de' Buonaccorsi, to expel many of the city's nobles. Once they were gone, Pinamonte was able, in 1272, to seize the city for himself.
2   Most of the men were embarking for Troy.
3   A famous augur, who advised a human sacrifice to gain a favourable wind for the Grecian fleet.
4   An augur sent by the Greeks to consult the oracle of Apollo at Delphi about their departure for Troy. It was one function of soothsayers to decide on the best time to begin any great undertaking.
5   Virgil calls his *Aeneid* a "tragedy" because it is written in high, epic style.
6   A Scottish doctor and philosopher at the court of Frederick II of Sicily.
7   Another astrologer at the court of Frederick II.
8   A shoemaker of Parma in the second half of the 13th century, also known for predicting the future.
9   For magic potions.
10   Effigies, into which pins could be stuck or which could be melted down, used to cast spells on people.

Below Seville, and watering his thorns;[1]
Last night the moon was full – you really should
   Remember this: the moon, you must recall,
   Was not unhelpful in the first dark wood."
Those were his words, and we walked on meanwhile.   130

---

1   Cain with a thorn bush corresponds to our Man in the Moon. The moon is now setting:
    it is about 6 a.m.

CANTO XXI

Dante and Virgil look down into the fifth ditch of the eighth circle, which is amazingly dark. It is filled with boiling pitch – a reminder to Dante of the Venetian arsenals with men working through the winter to repair their ships. At first only the surface of the pitch is visible. Later Dante learns that barrators – those traffickers in public offices and other abusers of positions of public trust for profit – are boiling in this pitch, and that there are devils at hand to push them under.

Dante is terrified to see a black demon running towards them. He is carrying over his shoulder a human body, a new arrival among the barrators. Throwing this person onto the ground for the other devils to deal with, he announces that he is rushing back to Lucca, where there are so many more barrators requiring his attention.

Virgil suggests that the frightened Dante should hide behind a rock, and goes to parley with the devils. Virgil is confident that he can deal with the situation but, even when it seems that he has come to an agreement with the devils, Dante is still afraid.

Muckrake, who is acting as a representative of the devils, restrains his followers from attacking Dante, as they are eager to do, and sends ten of them to guide Virgil and Dante on their journey. He says, truly, that the next bridge that they are looking for has been destroyed, and also, untruly, that there is another bridge further on, to which his devils will lead them.

Dante is still terrified by the devils, but Virgil, who lacks his usual caution, feels quite safe. The devils salute their leader in an unusual manner, and he sounds an unusual bugle as signal for them to depart.

The most striking feature of this canto is its harsh comedy. The demons here are reminiscent of those shown in so many medieval depictions of the Last Judgement, both terrifying and ridiculous.

And so we travelled on from bridge to bridge,
    Speaking of things with which my comedy
    Is not concerned, and when we'd climbed the ridge,
We saw the next crack open in the rock[1]
    Of Eviltiers, with all its futile weeping –
    It seemed to me exceptionally black.
As, when Venetian arsenals are working
    In winter, sticky pitch is on the boil
    For caulking any vessels that are leaking,
Since nobody can sail; and some repair   10
    Their ships and make them good as new; some others
    Strengthen a frame before it's gone too far;
Some hammer nails in prow and stern; meanwhile
    Some fashion oars, and some fresh sheets and shrouds;
    Some patch the jib and others the mainsail –
So here, though not by fire, but by God's art,

---

1   This is the fifth ditch of the eighth circle (Eviltiers), occupied by those who have trafficked
    in public offices or been in other ways guilty of the misuse of public positions.

A stretch of sticky pitch was boiling over,
  And clinging to the sides all round the pit.[1]
I saw the mass, but could not see inside it,
  Only the bubbles coming to the surface,   20
  As it all swelled, then once again subsided.
While I was staring down at this, my guide
  Said to me suddenly: "Look out! Look out!"
  And then he grabbed me up against his side.
I turned around, like somebody who is
  Eager to see what he is fleeing from,
  Whom sudden fear has weakened at the knees,
And yet does not slow down, but still looks back;
  At which I saw behind us a black devil
  Racing our way along the rocky crag.   30
And what a devil! What a savage sight!
  He looked like sheer ferocity in action,
  With wings spread wide, and light upon his feet!
Upon one shoulder, that was hunched up high,
  He had a sinner's haunches, while in front
  It was his ankle bones he held him by.
He called out from our bridge: "Look here, Clawboys!
  I've brought along an elder of St Zita![2]
  Just pop him in;[3] I'm rushing back because
The city where I got him's got so many –   40
  Barrators all, except for old Bonturo;[4]
  'Nay' there turns into 'Yea' for ready money."[5]
He flung him down upon the stony cliff,
  And turned to go: no watchdog off the leash
  Was ever in such haste to catch a thief.
The sinner plunged, then came up black as pitch;
  At which, "The Holy Face here's out of place!"[6]
  Hollered the demons hidden by the bridge.
"It's not like swimming in the Serchio[7] here!
  So, unless you have a mind to taste our hooks,   50
  Don't stick your head above the boiling tar."
They got their teeth into him hungrily,
  A hundred hooks, and said: "Stay under cover;

---

1   The simile's most obvious point of comparison is simply the boiling pitch, but the de-
     scription of the Venetian shipyards is developed far beyond this. The apparent digression
     is justified, because it sets the tone for the busy and tumultuous canto it introduces.
2   A leading citizen of Lucca. Zita was born near that city, where she died in 1272. She was
     popularly acclaimed a saint.
3   Into the boiling pitch.
4   This is said ironically, to indicate that Bonturo Dati is worse than any.
5   The reference is to the selling of votes.
6   The Holy Face is a famous crucifix of black wood still venerated in the Cathedral of San
     Martino in Lucca.
7   A river near Lucca.

Steal still, if you can steal round stealthily."
Just so do cooks, when meat is in the pot,
   Order their scullions to press it under
   With their long forks, because it must not float.
"So that your presence may remain concealed,"
   My kindly master said, "you must crouch down
   Behind a rock, to serve you as a shield.   60
And then whatever outrage I endure,
   Don't be afraid: I have it all in hand;
   I've been in such a squabble once before."[1]
With that he walked on to the bridge's end
   But, when he came upon the sixth embankment,
   Found it more effort to look unconcerned.
With all that fury and that storm of storms
   With which the dogs rush out on some poor beggar
   Who's halted at the door to beg for alms,
Out from beneath the bridge the devils flew   70
   And turned their hooks against him; but he shouted:
   "I'll have no trouble now from any of you!
Before you start to use your hooks on me,
   Let one of you step forward. Hear me out:
   Then see if it is wise to grapple me."
At this they hollered: "Muckrake ought to go!"
   And so one moved – with all the others waiting –
   Towards him, asking: "What good will this do?"
"Do you imagine, Muckrake, I have got
   As far as this already," asked my master,   . 80
   "Unharmed by you, who failed to keep me out,
Without the favour and the will of God?
   Let us pass on: it is decreed in heaven
   That I must show another this rough road."
Muckrake was now completely at a loss,
   And felt his own hook slipping through his fingers,
   And said to the others: "Leave him after this."
Then Virgil said to me: "You, crouching there
   Behind those rocky boulders on the bridge,
   You may come back: there's nothing now to fear."   90
So I came out and ran towards my guide;
   And all the devils started edging forward,
   Which made me wonder if they'd keep their word:
So I remember Pisan infantry
   Under safe conduct coming from Caprona
   In fear, surrounded by the enemy.[2]

---

1   Virgil is referring to his previous descent into the Inferno, mentioned in *Inf.* ix, 22–30
   above.
2   Dante took part in the campaign of the Tuscan Guelfs in 1289, which resulted in the
   capture of the Pisan fortress of Caprona.

I kept on drawing closer to my guide,
   And did not move my eyes away from them,
   Whose attitude seemed anything but kind.
They lowered their hooks, and "Shall I touch him up,"   100
   One asked the other devils, "on the back?"
   And all the others answered, "Make him hop!"
But Muckrake, who was having a discussion
   With my good guide, turned round at that abruptly,
   And said to him: "Boll Weevil, don't be rushing!"
"You cannot go much further on this ridge,"
   He said to us, "because down there it's broken:
   Nothing but rubble's left of the sixth bridge.
So if you really want to go ahead,
   Then make your way along this same embankment: 110
   Another bridge nearby can be your road.[1]
Yesterday, five hours later than this hour,
   One thousand and two hundred and sixty-six
   Years had passed since the bridge was broken here.[2]
I'm sending some men out there to discover
   If anybody's trying to get some air:
   You go with them; they won't be any bother."
"One pace forward, Flibbertigibbet and
   Pollutus," then he ordered, "and Hellhound;
   Take nine men, Bandersnatch, and take command.   120
Step forward, Scumbag, and Snapdragon there,
   And toothy Hogwash, and beside him Scrotter,
   And Dandiprat, and raving-mad Hacksore.
Scout everywhere around the boiling pitch.
   And keep this couple safe until that spur
   That goes across the ditches like a bridge."
"Master," I said, "alas, what's this I see?
   Can't we go on alone, without an escort?
   We don't need any, if you know the way.
And you, who up to now have been so shrewd,   130
   Haven't you noticed how they grind their teeth,
   All of them looking daggers, all black-browed?"
"I would not have you fearful," he replied.
   "Let them go grinding to their hearts' content:
   They're thinking of those wretches who are stewed."
They wheeled along the ridge to the left hand;
   But first they stuck their tongues out as a signal
   Directed to the leader of their band,
And he had made his arse blow like a bugle.

---

1   It is true that the sixth bridge has been destroyed, but not that there is another bridge
    nearby.
2   As a result of the earthquake at the time of the Crucifixion.

CANTO XXII

This canto opens with a vivid description of medieval warfare, such as Dante had himself witnessed, followed by his comment that he had never before heard on the field of battle such a signal as issued from Bandersnatch at the end of the previous canto. By recalling this signal he sets a humorous tone for the events which follow.

Dante and Virgil continue their journey, escorted by the ten demons. As Dante says, who else would one expect to be escorted by in the Inferno? The barrators are leaping into the air like dolphins – not, as dolphins do, to warn sailors of a coming storm, but in order to get some brief respite from their torment. Any sinner who appears above the surface of the boiling pitch is likely to be caught by the devils' grapnels. Soon one is caught: he is brought out of the pitch on the end of a hook, like an otter.

This sinner, whom Dante does not name but who appears to be a certain Ciampolo, explains who he is and why he is being punished, and mentions two of his companions. There is a fierce argument, and some even fiercer physical maltreatment, while the demons consider what to do with him. However, they, who delight in deceiving and tormenting, are themselves deceived and tormented by Ciampolo, who offers to call other sinners up out of the ditch by whistling and so give the devils more people to torment. It is a trick, of course, and Ciampolo manages to get away. The devils turn on each other to vent their anger and frustration. Two of them, Pollutus and Flibbertigibbet, are so intent on fighting that they tumble into the boiling pitch. This stops the fight, but they still cannot get out onto the embankment, because their wings are sticky with pitch. While the other devils are preoccupied, apparently with trying to help their two boiling companions, Dante and Virgil go on their way.

*

I had seen cavalry strike camp, move out,
　　Lead an assault, or muster on parade;
　　I'd even seen them beating a retreat;
Over your territory I'd seen the scouts,
　　O Aretines, and raiding parties ranging;[1]
　　Seen clash of tournament, seen rush of joust;
With trumpeting sometimes, and sometimes bells,[2]
　　With thud of drums, and signals from the castles,
　　Some of them ours, and some from somewhere else;
But never yet had I seen foot or horse　　　　　　　　　10
　　Move in response to such a bagpipe blast[3] –
　　Nor ship steering by landmarks or by stars.
So led by the ten demons we went on:
　　What dreadful company! But, as they say,
　　"With saints in church, with gluttons at the inn."

1　Dante was present at the Battle of Campaldino (1289), at which the Ghibellines of Arezzo were defeated by the Florentine Guelfs.
2　Each of the Italian states had at this time a *carroccio*, or war wagon, drawn by oxen, and furnished with a bell: it was a rallying point in battle.
3　This is the signal mentioned in *Inf.* XXI, 139.

All my attention was upon the pitch:
   I wanted to make out each single detail
   And all the people burning in the ditch.
Just as a dolphin, with its arching back,
   Signals to sailors that they must take care   20
   To save their vessel from impending wreck,[1]
Just so at times, to mitigate his pain,
   One of the sinners would disclose his back,
   Then quick as lightning hide it once again.
And as, just at a ditch's edge, frogs squat,
   And only poke their muzzles out of water,
   Keeping their feet and bodies out of sight,
So here on every hand the sinners crouch;
   But at the instant Bandersnatch approaches,
   They just as quickly hide in boiling pitch.   30
I saw – the memory still makes me writhe –
   One sinner slow to move, as it can happen
   One frog delays, another's quick to dive;
The nearest devil, who happened to be Scrotter,
   Got his hook into his pitch-blackened locks
   And drew him out: he looked just like an otter.
(I knew their names already: I'd been rather
   Careful to listen when I heard them chosen,
   And then I'd noted what they called each other.)
"Now Hacksore, it is up to you to sever   40
   The skin from off his back: don't waste your talons!"
   The accursèd demons shouted all together.
And I said: "Master, if you're able, please
   Find out the name of that unfortunate
   Who's just been captured by his enemies."
My leader asked him, having drawn quite near,
   About his birthplace, and the wretch replied:
   "My homeland was the kingdom of Navarre.[2]
My mother placed me in service to a lord,
   Since she had borne me to a waster who   50
   Destroyed himself and everything he had.
I found myself in good King Thibaut's[3] court;
   And there I gave myself to barratry,
   For which I pay the reckoning in this heat."
Then Hogwash, from whose mouth, each side, stuck out
   A wild boar's tusk, allowed him to discover

---

1   It was an old tradition that dolphins warned sailors of coming storms. The comparison
here of dolphins to sinners is visually exact, but in other respects deliberately at odds:
the dolphins help the sailors, while the sinners are thinking only of helping themselves
– one of Dante's many subtle ways of stressing the hellishness of hell.

2   Nothing is known of him apart from what Dante says, except that the ancient com-
mentators give his name as Ciampolo.

3   King Thibaut II of Navarre (r. 1253–70).

How just the one of them could lacerate.
Now the fiends want to play at cat and mouse.
  But Bandersnatch embraces him and cries:
  "I'll see to him! You keep away from us!"   60
Then, turning to my guide, he said: "Ask on,
  If there is something more you want to know;
  Quickly, before somebody does him in."
At that my guide said: "Tell me: do you know
  Of any sinners here who are Italian
  Under the pitch?" The shade replied: "Just now
I've come from one who lived not far away:[1]
  I wish I were still covered up with him!
  Then hooks and claws would strike no fear in me."
Then Scumbag said: "This has gone far enough!"   70
  And caught him on his arm so with his grapnel
  He tore the flesh and pulled a muscle off.
Snapdragon also seemed about to strike
  And tear his legs; at which their captain turned
  Right round, and gave them all an ugly look.
When they were calmer, and the sinner too
  Was silently still staring at his wound,
  My leader asked him without more ado:
"Who was that man from whom in evil hour,
  As you yourself have said, you separated?"   80
  The sinner then replied: "Oh, that was Friar
Gomita from Gallura, full of fraud,[2]
  Who had his lord's foes under his control,
  And dealt with them in ways that they thought good.
He took their money, and he freed them all,
  As he admits; and was in other matters
  No petty jobber, but the nonpareil.
Michele Zanche from Logodoro's there[3]
  With him; they always talk about Sardinia;
  On that one subject their tongues never tire.   90
But see that demon grind his teeth and grin!
  I would say more, but I'm afraid that he
  Is just about to scratch my scabby skin."
Their great commander turned to Dandiprat,
  Who rolled his eyes and seemed about to strike,
  And ordered: "Get away, you filthy bat!"
"If you would really like to see or hear,"
  The sinner, somewhat reassured, went on,

1 In Sardinia.
2 Deputy of Nino Visconti of Pisa, judge of the district of Gallura in Sardinia (a possession
   of Pisa at that time). When Fra Gomita connived at the escape of some prisoners who
   were under his control, Nino had him hanged.
3 Little is known about his life. He was killed treacherously by his son-in-law, Branca Doria
   (see *Inf.* XXXIII).

"Tuscans or Lombards, I can get them here.
But let the Clawboys stand apart somewhat,   100
    So my companions need not fear their vengeance;
    And I, still sitting on this selfsame spot,
For the one I am, will make seven appear,
    Simply by whistling, as our custom is
    To do whenever one of us gets clear."
Hearing this, Hellhound lifted up his snout
    And shook his head, and told them: "That's a trick:
    This is his way to get back in the pit!"
Then he, who had no shortage of devices,
    Admitted: "I'm a tricky chap indeed,   110
    Fixing to give my neighbours such surprises."
Pollutus can't restrain himself at this;
    He says, to spite the others: "If you dive,
    It won't be at a gallop I give chase:
I'll fly on faster wings above the pitch.
    To see if you are smarter than we are,
    We'll hide behind this ditch's lower edge."
Now, Reader, here's a most unusual sport!
    All of them turned their eyes the other way,
    He first, the one against it at the start.[1]   120
The sinner acted when he saw their blunder:
    He planted both his feet upon the ground,
    And leapt, and broke away from their commander.
At this they were all stricken with remorse,
    Pollutus most, the cause of the disaster;
    And yet he moved and shrieked: "You're in my claws!"
Which was no help, for wings were not as fast
    As terror was: the Navarrese went under;
    And up the fiend flew, with uplifted breast.
Just so the duck's reaction's not belated,   130
    Who, when the hawk's upon her, plunges under,
    While he flies up again, tired and frustrated.
Flibbertigibbet, furious at the bluff,
    Flew at Pollutus, glad to see the sinner
    Escape, since he was keen to cut up rough;
And once the barrator was out of touch,
    He turned his talons onto his companion,
    And got to grips with him above the ditch.
And then Pollutus was not far behind
    In clawing like a falcon, till both tumbled   140
    Into the middle of the boiling pond.
They were, so great the heat, soon disentangled;
    And yet their wings stayed so gummed up with pitch
    Every attempt they made to rise was bungled.

---

1   This is Hellhound. See ll. 106–8.

Then Bandersnatch, like all the rest annoyed,
  Sent four of them to line the other shore,
  All with their hooks; and these were soon deployed
On this side and on that, and standing to;
  And then they held their hooks out hopefully;
  But both the fiends by now were cooked right through.   150
And so we left them in that quandary.[1]

---

1   This incident, in which the duplicitous devils are themselves duped and made to fall out
with each other, reveals the Inferno as a place (and a state of mind or soul) where there
is nothing good and no one to trust, a place "where there is no light at all" (*Inf.* IV, 151).
The incident suggests also, in its grotesque comedy, that going against the moral order
is not only a repulsive, but a ridiculous thing to do.

CANTO XXIII

After the tumult of the previous canto, this one begins on a quiet note. Dante and Virgil have escaped from the demons of the fifth ditch, and now they walk on while Dante thinks over the violent scenes they have just witnessed. Soon, however, Dante has more troubling thoughts. What if the devils are coming after them?

Virgil understands Dante's concern, he snatches him up, and they slide down together into the sixth ditch of Eviltiers. There they see the hypocrites, who are punished by having to walk endlessly, weighed down by cloaks which gleam with gold outside, yet are lined with lead. Dante and Virgil walk in the same direction as these sinners.

Two of the hypocrites, the Bolognese Frisky Friars Catalano and Loderingo, are curious about Dante, since they realize he must be alive. He does not say who he is, but he does say he is a citizen of Florence. In reply the others say that they were chosen jointly to rule Florence, in order to patch up the political differences there, and that they only made matters worse. They were thought to be impartial, but they were not, and so they are punished for their hypocrisy.

Suddenly Dante notices a figure lying crucified across the road – Caiaphas, who urged the Jews to deliver Christ to the Romans for crucifixion, saying that it was right for one man to die for the good of the whole people. His father-in-law, Annas, who went along with this, is also crucified in the same manner.

Virgil asks Catalano if there is a way by which they may travel out of this ditch without calling on the dubious help of the black angels who guard the barrators. Catalano tells him they can climb up the broken rock, which was originally a bridge, and so find their way.

Virgil strides out, angered by the realization that Muckrake deceived him into believing that there was an unbroken bridge there, and also by Catalano's mocking parting words. Dante follows his beloved guide.

Alone, and silently, we went on further,
   One of us in the front and one behind,
   Like Friars Minor[1] when they walk together.
My thoughts all ran on that Aesopian fable
   Which gives the story of the frog and mouse[2]
   (Suggested to me by the recent quarrel);
For "no" and "nay" are not more like each other
   Than these two stories are, if you consider
   The start and close of each of them together.
And as one thought gives rise to a further thought,   10
   Thinking about that fable made me think
   Of something that increased my former fright.
The thought was this: "These fiends, because of us,

---

1   The Franciscans are known as Friars Minor, to indicate their humility.
2   A frog promised to carry a mouse over a river. It tied the mouse to itself, and then, once in the water, dived under in an attempt to drown it. A hawk swooped down and seized the mouse, and the frog went with it. It is the fight between Flibbertigibbet and Pollutus (*Inf.* xxii, 133–44) which reminds Dante of this fable.

Have been both injured and held up to scorn,
Which must, I think, have made them furious.
Once anger's joined with that ill will of theirs,
   They will come after us more cruelly
   Than hound hunts after hare with gaping jaws."
I felt my hair was standing up on end
   In terror, as I stood there looking back   20
   And saying: "Master, if you cannot find
Somewhere to hide us quickly, then I fear them,
   The Clawboys! They are coming up behind us:
   Already I imagine I can hear them."
He said to me: "Were I a silvered mirror
   I could not take your outer image in
   More swiftly than I've taken in your inner.[1]
Your thoughts just now were so entwined with mine,
   With the same attitude, the selfsame features,
   That from them all I soon worked out one plan.   30
If that slope on the right is not too steep,
   We can descend into the lower ditch,
   And so escape the hunt you think is up."
Well, he had hardly finished saying this
   When I could see them coming, wings outspread,
   And not far off, and keen on catching us.
My guide wasted no time at all in snatching
   Me – as a mother wakened by the roar
   Of burning, and observing flames approaching,
Snatches her son and runs and does not pause: 40
   She has such care of him (none for herself)
   She does not stop to put on any clothes;
And, down from the hard ridge, upon his back
   He slid and slithered, down the steep embankment
   Which closes on one side the lower dyke.
No rushing water in a strait mill race,
   With all its energy to turn the wheel,
   And moving faster coming near the blades,
Could move as fast as he did, sliding down,
   And always bearing me against his breast,   50
   And not as a companion, but a son.
His feet had hardly touched upon the bed
   Below, when fiends were on the ridge above us;
   But now we had no cause to feel afraid,
Because High Providence, that had assigned
   These filthy demons to the foul fifth ditch,
   Deprived them of all power to go beyond.

---

1   Dante's "inner" image is his thought. This is one of the many occasions when it is shown
that Virgil can read Dante's thoughts.

Down there we came on people who were painted,[1]
    Moving about the place with lagging steps,
    Weeping, with all the signs of being defeated.   60
They had on cloaks which had their cowls pulled down
    So low they hid their eyes, cut in the fashion
    Favoured at Cluny by the monks therein.[2]
They were gilded outside, and dazzling-bright,
    But inside all of lead, and all so heavy
    That Frederick's, weighed with them, would seem but light.[3]
A tiring mantle for eternity!
    We turned once more, as always, to the left,
    And went with them, engrossed in misery.
But, such the weight they wore, those weary folk   70
    Came on so slowly that we came upon
    Fresh company with every step we took.
I therefore begged my leader: "Try to find
    Someone whose name or history is known,
    And as we walk, please cast your eyes around."
And one behind us, who'd become aware
    That I was speaking Tuscan, shouted: "Stop!
    You who are rushing[4] through this gloomy air!
And maybe I can give you what you need."
    At this my guide turned round and told me: "Wait,   80
    And then continue walking, at his speed."
I stopped, and saw two show great urgency
    Of mind, by their expressions, to come up;
    But their weight slowed them, and the narrow way.
When they came up, they did not say a word
    For quite some time, but looked at me askance;
    Then turned to one another, and they said:
This man seems living – see him move his throat.
    "If they're alive, why are they privileged,
    When we wear heavy stoles, to go without?"   90
"Tuscan, admitted to the sacred college
    Of the sad hypocrites,"[5] they said to me,
    "Say who you are: do not conceal that knowledge."
This was my answer: "I was born and bred
    In the great city on the River Arno;
    I'm with the body I have always had.

---

1   It is their robes which are "painted" (with gold), as we see in ll. 61–66.

2   The ample and sumptuous habits worn by the monks in the Benedictine monastery at
    Cluny were well known.

3   The Emperor Frederick II (r.1220–50) was believed to put traitors into leaden robes
    which were then melted over a fire.

4   Dante and Virgil are not "rushing", but to the sinners, who are hindered by heavy robes,
    they seem to be.

5   The sinners naturally assume that Dante is being punished, as they are, for the sin of
    hypocrisy. The word "college" suggests a religious community.

But who are you, in such great misery
   That I can see it running down your cheeks?
   What punishment can shine so brilliantly?"
"All of these gilded mantles," answered one,   100
   "Are made of such thick lead that their great weight
   Makes us, like balances they're laid on, groan.
We're from Bologna, and both Frisky Friars[1] –
   I Catalano, and he Loderingo –
   And both appointed – though your city was
Accustomed to appoint a single man –
   To keep the peace; and what we did accomplish
   Is still around Gardingo to be seen."[2]
I started off: "O Friars, your evil state…"
   But said no more, because one crucified   110
   By three stakes on the ground had come in sight.
He writhed and twisted, catching sight of me,
   And mingled breaths with sighs inside his beard;
   Seeing this, Catalano said to me:
"That man impaled there, upon whom you look,
   Advised the Pharisees that it was better
   One man should suffer for the people's sake.[3]
He's stretched out naked right across the road,
   As you can see, and therefore he must feel
   All who walk over him as a great load.   120
His father-in-law[4] is suffering likewise
   In this same ditch, with the others of that council
   Which brought calamity upon the Jews."[5]
I stared at Virgil, who was standing, filled
   With sheer amazement, by him, crucified
   So vilely, and eternally exiled.[6]
Then he spoke to the friar, saying: "Let
   It not displease you, if you may, to tell us
   If any passage opens on the right
Through which we two may travel and get clear   130
   Without being forced to order the black angels

---

1   The religious order of the Cavalieri di Maria Vergine Gloriosa (Knights of the Glorious
    Virgin Mary), was founded in Bologna in 1261, to promote peace and protect the weak.
    Its members were familiarly known as Frati Gaudenti (Frisky Friars), because of their
    free-and-easy way of life.
2   Catalano and Loderingo were appointed jointly as *podestà* of Florence. They were not
    impartial, and their bias led to the destruction of the property of the Uberti family in
    the Gardingo area of the city.
3   The Jewish high priest, Caiaphas, who urged that Christ should be given up to the
    Romans for execution (John 11:49–50).
4   The high priest Annas (John 18:12–14).
5   The destruction of Jerusalem in AD 70 and the dispersion of the Jewish people.
6   Virgil had not seen Caiaphas on his previous descent into the Inferno, because that was
    before the Crucifixion.

To plumb the depths and get us out of here."
"Nearer than you may think," he answered then.
  "A rocky ridge starts from the outer wall[1]
  And crosses all the dykes as it runs down,
Except this one, for it is broken here;
  But it's still possible to climb the rubble
  Lining the side and heaped up on the floor."
My leader bowed his head – he felt unsure –
  Then said: "I heard a very different story   140
  From him who hooks the sinners over there."[2]
"Well, in Bologna everybody says,"
  The friar replied, "the Devil's bad, and even
  That he's a liar, the father of all lies."
At that my guide stalked off with giant strides,
  And he was obviously a touch irate;[3]
  I left the sinners with their heavy loads
And followed in the prints of those dear feet.

---

1 The outer wall of Eviltiers (*Inf.* XVIII:1–3).
2 Muckrake.
3 Virgil's uncharacteristic anger is caused by Muckrake's deception and Catalano's mockery
   in ll. 142–44.

CANTO XXIV

This canto begins with an unusually long simile, whose purpose is partly to emphasize how brief is Virgil's annoyance and, more importantly, to provide a homely scene from the world above to throw into relief the strange events which follow.

Virgil and Dante manage with difficulty to climb up the rubble until they can look down into the seventh ditch, reserved for the shades of thieves. Dante is intrigued by the sound of a voice below, whose words he cannot make out. Looking into the ditch, Dante sees that it is filled with repulsive serpents, of many different kinds. Terrified, naked people are running about among these monsters, without any hope of evading them. Their hands are bound behind them with serpents, which pierce their loins and are then tied in a knot in front.

Suddenly one sinner who is near them is transfixed by a serpent, and then immediately falls into a heap of ash. The ash gathers itself together, and the sinner regains his usual shape. In response to Virgil's question this sinner says he is a recent arrival in the Inferno, Vanni Fucci, a notorious murderer, thug and – something which Dante is surprised to hear – sacrilegious thief. The sacrilege he committed, for which another man was executed, is the reason that he is here among the thieves, and not higher up among the violent.

Out of sheer spite Vanni Fucci makes a prophecy to Dante. Its main theme is the coming defeat of the Florentine White Guelfs, of whom Dante is one. Vanni Fucci's assertion that all the Whites will suffer is a hint of Dante's coming exile from his native city.

When the sun, while the year is still but young,
    Is in Aquarius, warming his bright hair,
    And nights grow shorter, as the days grow long –
And Jack Frost copies out upon the ground
    A perfect semblance of his sister snow,
    Not long to last with that warm sun around –
See farmers, short of food and forage, rise,
    And go to look, and find the countryside
    All white, and turn around and slap their thighs,[1]
And go back in and grumble and despair,   10
    And moon about, with nothing to be done;
    But suddenly come back, in hope once more,
Seeing the world assume a different face
    In such short space of time, and seize their crooks
    And drive their flocks of sheep abroad to graze.
Just so my master filled me with despair
    When I saw how his brow was clouded over;
    But then the ointment came to soothe the sore,
For when we reached the broken bridge, my guide
    Turned round to face me with that calm demeanour   20
    I noticed first under the mountainside.[2]

---

1   In frustration.
2   "The delightful mountain" of *Inf.* 1, at the foot of which Dante first met Virgil.

He spread his arms – once he had carefully
   Studied the bridge's ruin and decided
   His course of action – and took hold of me.
And like one who, while working, reckons up
   What's needed next, and always thinks ahead,
   So he, placing me first upon the top
Of one great rock, would trouble to find out
   Another, saying: "You must grab that next;
   But first make sure that it will take your weight."   30
No way for someone in a leaden cloak![1]
   For we, though I was helped and he was weightless,[2]
   Could hardly make our way from rock to rock;
And if the bank had not been less in height
   On that rim than the upper one, I cannot
   Speak for my guide, but I'd have faced defeat.
But since the whole of Eviltiers[3] inclines
   Towards the well's mouth lying at its foot,
   Each valley's situation always means
One rim is higher than the other one.   40
   Well then, at length we did arrive up where
   We found the final lump of broken stone.
My lungs were utterly devoid of air
   When I got to that place – my strength was gone;
   I sat down straight away once we got there.
"From now on in this way," my master said,
   "You'll cast off laziness: no one gets fame,
   Taking it easy in a feather bed;
And he who lives without achieving fame
   Leaves no more trace of what he was on earth   50
   Than smoke in air or, in the water, foam.
And so, stand up! You're panting – you must get
   Your breath back: the strong mind wins every battle,
   Unless it sinks under the body's weight.
A longer ladder waits:[4] it's not enough
   That you have left the hypocrites behind.
   You've heard me. Now show whether you are tough."
So I stood up, pretending I had more
   Breath than I had been feeling that I had,
   And said: "Lead on! I'm strong. I have no fear."   60
We made our way up, and along the ridge,
   Which was rugged and narrow, hard to manage,

---

1   Dante is still thinking of the hypocrites whom he has just left behind.
2   There is a contradiction, with no attempt to resolve it, between the immateriality of
   the shades and their capacity for physical suffering – or, as here, Virgil's physical help for
   Dante.
3   See *Inf.* XVIII, 1–18.
4   The ascent from the lowest point of the Inferno, the centre of the globe, to the surface
   of the earth.

And much more steep than was the previous bridge.
I walked and talked, not wanting to seem faint;
   And then a voice came from the lower ditch,
   Which seemed unable to articulate.
I caught no word, although I stood above
   The ditch itself, at midpoint of the bridge;
   But he who spoke seemed to be on the move.
I stood there looking down, but living eyes   70
   Could not pierce to the depth through all that dark;
   So I said: "Master, try to get us please
To the other rim, and then descend the wall;
   I stand here hearing, and not understanding,
   And look down there and see nothing at all."
"I will not give," he said, "any reply
   Except to do it – for a fair request
   Ought to be met with action, silently."
We went on, till we came to where the bridge
   Runs down to join up with the eighth embankment,   80
   And then I could see clearly in the ditch.[1]
And saw that it was frighteningly filled
   With coiling serpents – great monstrosities:
   The mere remembrance makes my blood run cold.
Let Libya boast no more, although her sand
   Produces jacules and amphisbaenae,
   Chelydres, cenchres and *phareæ*.[2] And
The whole of Ethiopia and those regions
   That lie along the shores of the Red Sea
   Never produced such pestilential legions.   90
I could see terrified and naked folk
   Running among these cruel wicked swarms,
   Hopeless of hiding place or heliotrope;[3]
They had their hands tied up with snakes behind,
   Which threaded through their loins, with head and tail
   Knotted together on the other side.
Then suddenly one sinner where we stand
   Is savaged by a serpent and transfixed
   Just where the neck and shoulders are conjoined.
And never was *O* or *I* written so soon[4]   100
   As he caught fire and burnt up, utterly
   Dissolving into ash as he fell down;

---

1   This is the seventh ditch of Eviltiers, reserved for thieves.
2   These fabulous reptiles are taken from Lucan's *Pharsalia*. Jacules fly through the air like
    javelins; amphisbaenae have a head at each end; chelydres, amphibious creatures, leave
    a trail of smoke behind them; cenchres always move in a straight line; *phareæ*, as they
    move, cut a furrow in the ground with their tails.
3   The bloodstone, said to heal snakebites, and also to make its wearer invisible.
4   Each of these letters can be written with a single stroke of the pen, and therefore very
    quickly.

And as he lay there in a heap of ash,
  The powder drew itself up altogether
  To reassume his figure in a flash.
Just so the greatest sages all aver
  The phoenix perishes and is reborn
  When she approaches her five-hundredth year:
She feeds, lifelong, on neither grass nor grain,
  But only tears of frankincense and balsam;   110
  Her winding sheet is myrrh and cinnamon.[1]
Like someone who falls down, not knowing why –
  Whether a demon has him in a seizure,
  Or other blockage binds him physically –
Then stands and looks around as he comes round,
  Bewildered utterly by all the anguish
  He's undergone, and sighs as he looks round –
That's how this sinner was when he arose.
  And oh, the power of God, how stern it is,
  Dealing in vengeance such almighty blows!   120
My master asked the sinner who he was;
  He answered: "I poured down from Tuscany,
  And not long since, into these cruel jaws.
I lived a beast's life, not a human one,
  Mule that I was: Vanni Fucci the Beast;[2]
  Pistoia suited me: it was my den."
I begged my guide: "Tell him not to slip off,
  And ask about the fault that brought him here:
  I knew him as a man of blood and wrath."[3]
The sinner understood, and did not feign,   130
  But turned his face to me, and his attention,
  And coloured up, so dreadful was his shame;
Then said: "I am more grieved that you have found me
  In such a wretched state as you can see
  Than I was grieved to leave my life behind me.
I can't deny whatever you ask of me:
  I'm stowed here so low down because I stole
  The holy vessels from the sacristy,
For which the judgement fell upon another.[4]
  But to ensure you have no cause to gloat   140
  If you should leave these lands of darkness ever,
Prick up your ears, and hear my prophecy:

---

1   The thief is compared to the phoenix because of its unusual method of regeneration.
2   "Beast" may have been a nickname. He was a citizen of Pistoia, a Black Guelf who
    played a brutal part in the civil strife in that city.
3   Dante is surprised to find Vanni Fucci among the thieves, rather than higher up among
    the violent.
4   The truth about this sacrilege came to light only after Vanni Fucci's death, which oc-
    curred in early 1300. 1300 is the date of Dante's vision: he does not know the facts until
    Vanni Fucci tells him.

Pistoia first will weed out all her Blacks,
   Then Florence change her men and polity.[1]
Enveloped in a black and stormy cloud,
   Mars will bring lightning out of Val di Magra;
   And in a bitter tempest, and a loud,
Over Piceno's field will rage the fight;
   Sudden the lightning will break through the storm,
   And wound, successively, each single White.[2]   150
And I have told you this to make you squirm!"

---

1   In 1301 the White Guelfs were victorious in Pistoia over the Black Guelfs. Not long
     afterwards the Blacks were victorious in Florence over the Whites, and Dante was among
     those proscribed.
2   In this highly coloured and obscure language, suitable to prophecy, Vanni Fucci alludes
     to the victory of the Blacks of Florence and Lucca combined, under Moroello Malaspina
     (the "lightning out of Val di Magra"), at Piceno in 1302.

CANTO XXV

Having completed his malevolent prophecy to Dante, Vanni Fucci makes an obscene gesture to God. Dante is glad to see two serpents wind themselves around the sinner and prevent his saying anything more: what pleases Dante is the demonstration that God cannot be mocked.

There is a brief condemnation of Pistoia. Then Vanni Fucci flees, and a centaur arrives, with all his animal parts covered with reptiles. This is Cacus, condemned for theft with fraud, as Virgil explains.

More thieves arrive, Florentines, and we see the second and third metamorphoses in this part of the Inferno, both very complicated ones. (The first metamorphosis was that of Vanni Fucci in the previous canto.)

A monster grapples with one of the shades, and the two become a mysterious being, which moves away slowly. Another reptile attacks a sinner, at his navel to begin with, and gradually the man becomes a reptile and the reptile a man.

Dante rejoices in his own artistry, saying that his descriptions of metamorphoses are superior to those of Lucan and Ovid. In this canto Vanni Fucci has been blamed for pride, as Capaneus was previously. Theirs is rebellious pride in the face of God, a determination not to accept the nature of things. Dante's pride in his own workmanship – a theme which will recur in the *Comedy* – is a different matter entirely.

It would be a mistake to think of these descriptions as merely an excuse for Dante to display his verbal skill. Behind them is the conviction that a thief attacks the owner himself in depriving him of his property, which may be viewed as part of himself: theft is an offence against the person. Those who do not observe the distinction between *meum et tuum* have lost the sense of human personality. The transformed sinners have become their sin.

T hat said, the robber,[1] with no more ado,
    Lifted his hands, and made the fig with both,[2]
    Shouting: "Take that, God! They are both for you!"
The serpents were my friends from that time on,
    For one of them coiled round the sinner's neck
    As if to say: "Now all your talking's done";
Another took him into its constriction,
    And tied itself so tightly up in front
    He could not move his arms even a fraction.
Men of Pistoia, the decision's yours!   10
    Burn down your city! Leave not one stone standing!
    Your evil goes beyond your ancestors'.[3]
In all the circles of obscurest hell
    I saw no shade so blasphemously proud,

---

1   Vanni Fucci.
2   An insulting and obscene gesture, made by placing the thumb between the first two fingers.
3   Legend had it that Pistoia was founded by soldiers from the army of the Roman conspirator Catiline.

Not him who tumbled from the Theban wall.[1]
He fled and did not say another word;
   And then I saw a centaur full of anger
   That came and shouted: "Where's this rebel shade?"
Even Maremma[2] has not such a swarm
   Of snakes, I think, as it had on its haunches,   20
   Right up to where it takes on human form.[3]
On its shoulders, behind the nape, it bore
   A dragon with enormous wings outspread:
   All whom it breathes upon it sets on fire.
"Now this is Cacus here," my master said,
   "That in a cave beneath Mount Aventine[4]
   Times without number made a lake of blood.
He does not take the road his brothers take,
   Because he stole from out of the great herd
   That was nearby, and did it with a trick;[5]   30
For that his crooked ways were ended, when
   Hercules clubbed him, giving him perhaps
   A hundred blows, of which he felt not ten."
My master spoke, the centaur ran away,
   And three shades came beneath our vantage point,
   Whom my leader and I both failed to see,
Until they cried out: "Who are you?" – when we
   Immediately broke off our conversation
   And paid attention only to those three.
I did not know them; but it then occurred,   40
   As frequently by chance it does occur,
   One of them named another, and he said:
"Now where is Cianfa?[6] Is he coming?" Then,
   So that my guide might pay good heed, I rested
   My finger on my mouth from nose to chin.
If, Reader, you're unwilling to believe
   What I shall tell you, that is not surprising,
   Since I, who've seen it, can't believe I have.
While I still have my eyes fastened on them,
   A reptile with six feet[7] comes springing out   50
   In front of one of them, and fastens him.
It gripped his belly with its middle feet,

1   Capaneus, punished in the third ring of the seventh circle. See *Inf.* xiv, 43–72.
2   An unhealthy marshy area on the Tuscan coast.
3   Centaurs are usually represented as having a human upper body.
4   One of the seven hills of Rome.
5   Cacus is not with the other centaurs, guardians of the violent in the first ring of the
   seventh circle, but here among the thieves, because he stole cattle from Hercules and
   tried to disguise their whereabouts by dragging them backwards into his cave by their
   tails, so that the hoof prints seemed to lead out of the cave.
6   A Florentine of the Donati family.
7   This is Cianfa, who has been turned into a reptile.

With its forefeet laid hold of both his arms,
　　And then it sank its teeth in either cheek;
It stretched each hind foot out to either thigh,
　　Then put its tail between the sinner's legs,
　　Whence, passing by his loins, it rose on high.
Rooted ivy never became attached
　　So strongly to its tree as that foul monster
　　Was found adhering to the limbs it clutched.　　　　60
They stuck together, just as if they were
　　Of molten wax; their colours ran and mingled –
　　And neither looked like what it was before –
Just as, when paper burns, the advancing heat
　　Is steadily preceded by a darkness
　　That is not black, and yet no longer white.
The other two shades cried, as they looked on:
　　"Alas, Agnolo,[1] you are really altered!
　　Look at yourself! You're neither two nor one!"
By now the two heads had become one head,　　　　70
　　And we could see two intermingled aspects
　　In one face, where the two had disappeared.
Two arms were fashioned where four lengths had been –
　　The thighs, the legs, the bellies and the breasts
　　Became such members as were never seen.
Nothing of what had been was left to see:
　　The twisted image looked like both, yet neither.
　　Such as it was, it slowly moved away.
And like a lizard underneath the lash
　　Of the dog days, moving from hedge to hedge　　　　80
　　Over the roadway like a lightning flash,
A blazing little brute came on the scene,
　　Straight for the bellies of the other two,
　　As black and livid as a peppercorn;
And at that part through which at first he'd drawn
　　His nourishment,[2] it transfixed one of them;
　　Then, at full length in front of him, fell down.
The one transfixed stared, but he did not speak –
　　He merely stood his ground, and he was yawning,
　　As overcome by fever or by sleep.　　　　90
He and the brute were looking at each other –
　　From the shade's wound, and from the monster's jaws
　　Smoke snorted, and the two fumes came together.
Let Lucan hold his tongue now, with his tale
　　Of poor Sabellus and Nasidius,[3]

1　A Florentine.
2　The navel.
3　Lucan tells in his *Pharsalia* how these two soldiers were bitten by snakes, and Sabellus
　　was reduced to ashes, while Nasidius swelled up until he became a shapeless mass.

Until he hears what wonders I reveal.
Let Ovid hold his tongue: though he recount
    Such tales of Cadmus and of Arethusa,
    I do not envy him his snake and fount:[1]
He never brought two creatures face to face   100
    And changed them so that both of them were ready
    To swap themselves around, as in this case.
This is how they responded to each other:
    The reptile split its tail into a fork;
    The wounded sinner placed his feet together.
The legs, including the whole thigh, were soon
    So closely stuck together that their juncture
    Could not by any mark or sign be seen.
The cleft tail took the shape that disappeared
    Into itself; and the reptilian skin   110
    Grew soft and smooth; the sinner's skin grew hard.
I saw each arm shrink into its armpit,
    And saw the monster's little forepaws lengthen
    In just proportion as those arms went short.
The hindpaws after, twisted into one,
    Became that member[2] which a man conceals,
    While the wretch stretched two paws out from his own.[3]
They are still veiled in smoke, they both change colour,
    And hair has started sprouting out on one,
    While all the hair starts falling from the other.   120
One rises at the downfall of the other,
    But neither turns aside his baleful eyeballs,
    Under whose glare their snouts are now changed over.
The one erect pulled his snout up and out,
    And from the excess matter that he had
    Grew ears upon a head that was without:
Then all the matter not pulled up and out –
    Matter left over – gave the face a nose,
    And both the lips were duly swelled with it.
The fallen one thrusts out his snout instead   130
    And, as a snail withdraws into its shell,
    He draws his ears right back into his head;
The tongue, that was united once and quick
    To speak, divides; the forked tongue of the other
    Becomes united – and there's no more smoke.
The human soul that had become a brute[4]
    Went hissing off in flight along the valley;

---

1   In his *Metamorphoses*, Ovid describes in vivid detail Cadmus being changed into a snake
    and Arethusa into a spring.
2   The genitals.
3   His genitals.
4   Buoso, a Florentine.

The other followed on, to speak and spit.[1]
Then, turning his new shoulders, said to the one
    Who still remained:[2] "I must see Buoso scurry   140
    On all fours down this road, as I have done."
So I saw garbage in the seventh pit
    Changed and transformed: sheer novelty's the reason
    If my account has somewhat garbled it.
And though my mind was dreadfully disturbed,
    And my eyesight was dazzled and bewildered,
    Those who remained could not fly unobserved:
Puccio the Cripple[3] I could recognize –
    Of those we came on first, the only one
    Who had not changed in any way his guise;   150
The other one made you, Gaville, mourn.[4]

---

1   The Florentine Francesco de' Cavalcanti, the "blazing little brute" of l. 82, now restored
    to human shape. He is identified by Dante only at l. 151.
2   Puccio Sciancato, named in l. 148.
3   Of a Florentine Ghibelline family. Dante recognizes him easily because he is lame, as
    his nickname indicates.
4   Francesco de' Cavalcanti was killed by inhabitants of the Tuscan village of Gaville, and
    his death was avenged on them by his relatives.

CANTO XXVI

The canto opens with an ironic encomium of Florence, famous not only throughout our world but also the underworld. Then Dante forecasts, and even reveals his longing for, the punishment that other Tuscan states will inflict on his native city for its arrogance.

Dante and Virgil climb back up the rocks by which they had descended and leave the ditch of the thieves behind. They look down into the eighth ditch, where they can see many fires twinkling in the darkness. Every fire conceals a sinner, for this is where those who counselled fraud are punished.

One flame is moving towards them. It is divided into two horns at the top. Inside it, Virgil tells Dante, are the shades of Diomed and Ulysses, Greek commanders at the siege of Troy. They are being punished for several ruses, but particularly for that of the wooden horse, by means of which the Greeks managed to get inside Troy's walls. Dante is anxious to speak with these shades, but Virgil says that he himself must do the talking: the Greeks were proverbially a proud people, and Virgil is able to claim some respect from Diomed and Ulysses for including them in his *Aeneid*.

A voice issues from the higher of the flame's two horns, that belonging to Ulysses. He gives an account of a voyage he undertook after his return home from Troy, a voyage inspired by the desire for knowledge, which ends disastrously when his ship is sunk in sight of a lone mountain rising out of the sea. This mountain, we learn much later, is Mount Purgatory.

This canto (the source of Tennyson's *Ulysses*) exemplifies the conflict between men's desire for knowledge, which is in itself praiseworthy, and the futility of this desire when it is not backed up by the grace of God. Ulysses is probably the most sympathetic of the shades we meet in the Inferno: it is interesting that his main rival for this distinction, Brunetto Latini, displays a similar intellectual curiosity.

F lorence, rejoice, now that you have such fame,
    And over land and sea you spread your wings!
    The whole Inferno's ringing with your name!
Among the thieves I found five citizens
    Of yours, all nobles, causing me some shame,
    While you yourself take little honour thence.
And yet, if dreams we dream at dawn come true,[1]
    You shall before long feel the weight of what
    Prato desires for you, and others too.[2]
It would, if it had come, not be too soon;   10
    Since come it must, I wish that it had happened:
    It will but hurt me more as time goes on.
We left that place, and slowly, step by step,
    Using the rocks by which we had descended,
    My guide climbed up once more and drew me up;

---

1   A common belief in ancient and medieval times.
2   Prato was at this time subject to Florence, whose power was feared by other Tuscan cities also.

And so we made our solitary way
    Among the crags and splinters of the ridge:
    Feet without hands would have made no headway.
I grieved to see, and now I grieve again
    When I call back to mind the things I saw,   20
    And hold my genius on a tighter rein,
For fear it run where virtue does not guide,
    So that, if a kind star or something better[1]
    Has made me gifts, I do not make them void.
Just as some peasant – when he takes his rest
    Upon a little hillside in that season
    When he that lights the world[2] hides his face least,
That hour when mites go and mosquitoes come[3] –
    Sees countless fireflies crowded in the valley,
    His scene of husbandry and harvest home –   30
So the eighth ditch was scatteringly bright
    With countless fires, as I became aware
    The instant its depression came in sight.
And just as he who was avenged by bears[4]
    Saw, as it left, the chariot of Elijah,[5]
    Its horses rearing heavenwards as it rose,
And could not keep it under observation
    Except by following the blaze alone,
    Like a small burning cloud in its ascension –
So each flame makes its way along the inner   40
    Parts of the ditch, and none reveals the theft,
    Though each of them contains a stolen sinner.
I stood tiptoe upon the bridge to look,
    And would have toppled down without being pushed,
    Had I not taken hold of a great rock.
My leader, seeing how I was concerned,
    Then told me: "There are souls inside those flames,
    Each one involved in that by which it's burned."
"My master," I replied, "now I can hear
    You saying that, I'm certain, but I thought   50
    That it was so; I wanted to enquire:
Who's coming in that flame which we see sever
    Itself on top, as coming from the pyre
    On which Eteocles burnt with his brother?"[6]

---

1   God's grace.
2   The sun. The season is summer.
3   The evening.
4   Some children teased the prophet Elisha for his baldness; he cursed them, and two bears came and killed them.
5   Elisha saw his master, the prophet Elijah, ascend into heaven in a chariot of fire.
6   Eteocles and his brother Polynices, sons of King Oedipus of Thebes, killed each other in battle. When their bodies were burnt on the same pyre, the flames divided into two, which was taken as a sign of their continuing enmity.

He made this answer: "There, within that flame,
   Diomed and Ulysses go together,
   As once in guilt, now in avenging pain;
And burning in that flame, they both regret
   Their trickery and the horse that made the breach
   Through which the noble Roman seed came out.[1]   60
Now they regret that guile which makes the dead
   Deidamia mourn Achilles still; now also
   The price for the Palladium is paid."[2]
"If they, inside the flashing of those flames,
   Can speak," I said, "my master, I request,
   Repeating the request a thousand times,
That you do not forbid my waiting here
   Until that flame that has two horns arrives:
   You see me lean towards it in desire!"
He answered: "Your request is laudable,   70
   And so I grant it willingly – however,
   Take care to hold your tongue a little while.
I'll do the talking, for I understand
   What you would like to ask – and they, being Greeks,
   Might think your speech was something to be scorned."[3]
So, when the flame had come to where my guide
   Judged that both time and place were opportune,
   I heard him speak, and this is what he said:
"O you, who share one flame and yet are two,
   If I earned honour from you while I lived,   80
   If great or small the honour I earned from you
When in the world I wrote my tragedy,[4]
   Do not move off, but one of you recount
   Where, when he went astray, he came to die."
That ancient fire's great horn[5] began to bend
   And straighten, shake itself about and murmur,
   Like a flame that's troubled by the wind;
And as it waved its tip from side to side,
   As though it were the tongue itself that spoke,
   It managed to emit a voice, which said: 90
"When I left Circe's charms, strong to detain
   Me near Gaeta more than one whole year

---

1   Diomed and Ulysses, Greek commanders at the siege of Troy, devised the stratagem
   of the wooden horse, by means of which Greek soldiers managed to enter the city. As
   Troy was falling, Aeneas and his companions escaped and eventually reached Italy, where
   their descendants founded the city of Rome.
2   Diomed and Ulysses persuaded Achilles to go with them to Troy: his lover Deidamia
   died of her grief. They also stole from Troy the Palladium, a statue of Pallas Athena on
   which the safety of Troy was believed to depend.
3   The Greeks were proverbially an arrogant race.
4   The *Aeneid*.
5   Ulysses's flame rises higher than Diomed's.

(Before Aeneas called it by that name),[1]
Neither paternal fondness,[2] nor the duty
   I owed to my old father,[3] nor the love
   I owed Penelope, to make her happy,[4]
Could overcome the great desire I had
   To widen my experience of the world,
   Of human wickedness and human good;
And so I set out on the open sea   100
   With one ship only and that tiny band
   Of men who never had deserted me.
I saw the shores that stretch on either hand
   To Spain and to Morocco; and Sardinia
   And other countries with that Sea[5] all round.
My companions and I were old and weak
   When we came to those straits where Hercules
   Set up on either side a great landmark[6] –
His warning that nobody should go further:[7]
   Upon the right I left Seville behind,   110
   Having upon the left abandoned Ceuta.
'O brothers who have reached the west,' I cried,
   'With a hundred thousand dangers overcome,
   You will not let yourselves now be denied –
Now your brief lives have little time to run –
   Experience at first hand of the unpeopled
   World we shall find by following the sun.
Consider well your origin, your birth:
   You were not made to live like animals,
   But to pursue and gain wisdom and worth.'   120
Now I had made my company so keen,
   With this oration, to be on their way,
   I would have found them difficult to restrain;
So, having turned our stern towards the east,
   We used our oars like wings in our mad flight,
   Making continual headway west-south-west.
And now at night we could see every star

---

1   Circe bewitched Ulysses on his way home from Troy and kept him with her for a year.
    A little later Aeneas, on his voyage from Troy to Italy, founded a city on Circe's island
    and named it after his nurse.
2   Ulysses had a son, Telemachus.
3   When Ulysses returned from Troy, his father Laertes was still alive.
4   Ulysses's wife Penelope remained faithful to him throughout the years he was away at
    Troy.
5   The Mediterranean.
6   The Straits of Gibraltar. There is a mountain on each side, and together they were known
    as the Pillars of Hercules. There was a common belief that the Pillars were there to
    indicate that men should not sail beyond them.
7   The Pillars of Hercules were taken as marking the boundary of the known world, and
    often of the knowable world.

Of the south hemisphere: ours were so low
  They did not rise above the ocean floor.[1]
The light beneath the moon had been five times   130
  Rekindled, and as many times extinguished,[2]
  Since we began on this hard enterprise,
When up in front there rose a mountain,[3] dark
  In the distance, and it seemed to me to be
  Higher than any northern mountain peak.
Then we were glad, but soon began to weep;
  For out of that new world a whirlwind rose
  And struck against the forepart of the ship.
It turned us round three times with all the water:
  And at the fourth it lifted up the stern   140
  So that the prow sank down, as pleased Another,[4]
Until the sea closed over us again.

---

1   The voyagers have crossed the equator.
2   Five lunar months had passed.
3   This, although naturally Ulysses does not know it, is Mount Purgatory.
4   God.

CANTO XXVII

The shade of Ulysses stops talking and moves away. Its place is taken by another soul hidden in a flame, which seems to be trying to speak. This, as we learn later, is Guido da Montefeltro, another counsellor of fraud. He asks whether Romagna is at peace or war. Dante replies that there is at present no open warfare, but that war is always in the hearts of the rulers there: he emphasizes this by referring to the various rulers not by name, but by their coats of arms, which all bear creatures of prey. Dante then asks the shade to reveal his identity.

Guido replies that he would not say who he was if he thought that there was any chance of this information reaching the world of the living: he assumes that Dante and Virgil are shades who have recently arrived in the Inferno.

After a lifetime of fighting and deceit, Guido explains, he decided to retire, and he entered the Order of St Francis as a way of atoning for his sins. Pope Boniface VIII, however, called him out of retirement to get his advice on how to subdue his enemies and destroy Palestrina. Guido was at first unwilling but, encouraged by the Pope's assertion that his sins were forgiven in advance, he suggested that large promises should be made and then broken. By following this advice, the Pope succeeded in his object, but Guido himself, when he died, was damned: the Pope's advance absolution proves to be invalid.

Dante and Virgil go further along the rocky ridge until they come to where they can see into the next ditch of the eighth circle, where the sowers of discord are punished.

In keeping with the theme of fraud or deception, this canto is full of dramatic irony. Guido thinks that his secret is safe with Dante, who will in fact give a public account of it; Guido, the great deceiver, is himself deceived by Pope Boniface; the outward forms of religion (for which Dante always shows a great respect) prove in this instance to be valueless, since the right intention is ultimately what matters.

That flame, now standing upright, had gone quiet
    With nothing more to say, and was departing
    With the permission of the kindly poet,
When one more flame, that came right after it,
    Forced us to turn our eyes up to its crest
    Because of those strange noises coming out.
As the Sicilian bull – bellowing first
    With his wild cries who filed it into shape
    (An outcome that was only right and just) –
Would bellow with men's voices under torture,   10
    So that, although it was a brazen image,
    It seemed as though the bull itself must suffer[1] –
Just so, because there was no way for them
    To issue at the start, the grieving words
    Were changed into the language of the flame.

---

1   A Sicilian tyrant had a brass bull made, in which he roasted his victims, whose shrieks came out as though the bull was bellowing. The tyrant used it first on the man who made it for him.

But once they had discovered how to go
  To the flame's tip, and given it that flicker
  Given them by the tongue as they went through,
We heard them: "You, who just this moment were
  Talking like one from Lombardy and saying,   20
  'You may go now; I'm urging you no more',[1]
Although I am a little late arriving,
  Don't be displeased, but stay and talk with me:
  You see I'm not displeased, and I am burning!
Say – if you've fallen only recently
  Into this blind world from that Latin land,[2]
  So lovely, whence I bring my guilt with me –
Whether Romagna lives in war or peace:
  I'm from those hills between Urbino and
  That ridge from which the Tiber is unleashed."   30
While I was still intently gazing down,
  My leader nudged me lightly on the side
  And said: "He is a Latin: you begin."
I had the answer on my lips unbidden,
  And so began to speak with no delay:
  "O soul down there, so well and truly hidden,
Your Romagna is not, nor was it ever,
  Quite free of war within its tyrants' hearts,
  But when I left there was no open rupture.
Ravenna stands as it has stood for years: 40
  The Eagle of Polenta[3] broods above it,
  And covers Cervia[4] with its wings and claws.
That city, under siege more than a year,
  That raised a bloody mountain of dead Frenchmen,[5]
  Finds itself under the Green Paws[6] once more.
Both bulldogs of Verrucchio, old and new,[7]
  Who used Montagna with such cruelty,[8]
  Still use their teeth as they're accustomed to.
The Lion Cub in White Lair[9] has his claws on
  The cities on Lamone and Santerno:[10]   50

---

1   The shade is addressing Virgil (born near Mantua in Lombardy) and referring to Virgil's
    dismissal of Ulysses in ll. 2–3 above.
2   Italy. The shade presumes that Virgil has only recently been damned.
3   The coat of arms of the da Polenta family bore an eagle.
4   A town on the Adriatic, south of Ravenna.
5   The shade to whom Dante is speaking shone in the defence of Forlì against French
    troops (1281–83).
6   The coat of arms of the Ordelaffi family bore a green lion.
7   The father and son Malatesta and Malatestino da Verrucchio.
8   Montagna, a Ghibelline lord of Rimini, was imprisoned by Malatesta and killed by
    Malatestino.
9   The coat of arms of Maghinardo Pagani da Susinana bore a blue lion on a white field.
10 Faenza on the River Lamone, and Imola on the River Santerno.

He changes sides according to the season.[1]
That city which the Savio ripples by,[2]
    Just as it lies between low land and mountain
    Lives between tyranny and being free.
And now, I beg you, tell us who you are;
    Be no more taciturn than I have been;
    So may your fame throughout the world endure."
After the flame had been roaring somewhat
    In its own way, it moved its pointed end
    From side to side, and finally breathed out: 60
"If I believed the words I'm saying were
    To somebody returning to the world,
    This flame of mine would not move any more;
But since no one has ever made his way
    Alive from this abyss, or so I'm told,
    I'll answer with no fear of infamy.
I was a soldier, then a Cordelier,
    Hoping, thus girdled, to make full amends;[3]
    And so my conscience would have been quite clear,
Had not the High Priest[4] – may he rot in hell! –   70
    Plunged me right back into my former guilt:
    And how and why is what I wish to tell.
While I was living, with the flesh and blood
    My mother gave me, then not lion-like
    But vulpine rather were the things I did.
Every underhand trick and stratagem
    Was at my beck and call; I had such skill
    That the wide world resounded with my fame.
When finally I saw myself attain
    That stage of life when everybody ought to   80
    Lower his sails and take the rigging in,
What had one time so pleased me, now so irked
    Me I repented and confessed and entered;[5]
    And – oh, I am a wretch! – it should have worked.
The ruler of the modern Pharisees[6] –
    Engaged in warfare near the Lateran,[7]
    And not with Saracens, and not with Jews,
For all his enemies were Christians, and

---

1   Inclining sometimes to the Ghibellines, and sometimes to the Guelfs.
2   Cesena.
3   The speaker is Guido da Montefeltro (c.1220–98), leader of the Ghibellines in Romagna.
4   Pope Boniface VIII.
5   Entered the Franciscan Order.
6   Pope Boniface VIII.
7   In Rome itself: the Lateran Palace was the Pope's residence. The Pope's quarrel was with the Colonna family, who did not recognize the abdication of his predecessor Celestine V and Boniface's election.

Not one of them had been besieging Acre[1]
   Or merchandising in the Sultan's land[2] –   90
Abused his office and those vows of mine –
   His priestly orders, and my knotted cord
   Which one time made its wearers good and thin.[3]
And just as Constantine called Pope Sylvester
   Down from Soratte, to cure leprosy,[4]
   So this man chose me out to be his master
And cure him of the fever of his pride:
   He asked for my advice, and I was silent,
   Because his words seemed wandering and wild.
But he insisted: 'Set your mind at rest;   100
   I absolve you from now on; so just advise me
   How to lay Palestrina in the dust.[5]
I can lock heaven's gates, as you're aware,
   And unlock heaven's gates:[6] I hold both keys
   My predecessor did not hold so dear.'[7]
I, influenced by those weighty arguments,
   And thinking silence a worse fault than speech,
   Said: 'Father, since you cleanse me in advance
Of that sin which I'm going to commit –
   Large promises, but minimally kept,   110
   Will make you triumph in the Holy Seat.'[8]
When I was dead, and Francis came to bear
   Me off to heaven, one of the black angels
   Cried out: 'Don't take him: that would be unfair.
Servitude under me is this man's doom:
   The counsel that he gave was fraudulent,
   And since that time I've had my eye on him;
Without repentance there's no absolution,
   And no one can repent while willing sin,
   For that would be an obvious contradiction.'   120
Oh, wretched me! I realized my position
   When he grabbed hold of me and said: 'Perhaps
   You did not know I was a strict logician!'
He took me off to Minos; Minos twisted

---

1   Acre, in the Holy Land, had fallen to the Saracens in 1291.
2   Egypt. The Church banned trade with Muslim countries.
3   The Franciscans' rope girdle was a sign of their poverty and asceticism.
4   According to legend, the Roman Emperor Constantine was cured of his leprosy by Pope
   Sylvester I.
5   Boniface was at the time besieging the Colonnas in their fortress of Palestrina, near
   Rome.
6   "And I will give unto thee the keys of the kingdom of heaven" (Matt. 16:19).
7   A sneer at Pope Celestine V, who relinquished the Papacy.
8   Boniface promised an amnesty to the Colonnas and then, once they had surrendered,
   destroyed Palestrina.

His tail around his scaly back eight times,[1]
And then announced in anger as he bit it:
'Another sinner for the thieving fire!'
  So that is why, as you can see, I'm lost,
  And walk in bitterness and strange attire."[2]
When all his talking was completely done,   130
  The miserable flame departed, mourning,
  Still wriggling and still writhing its sharp horn.
And so we carried on, the two of us,
  Along the ridge to reach an arch which led
  Over the ditch where sinners pay the price
For all the seeds of discord that they sowed.[3]

---

1 See *Inf.* v, 4–12.
2 He is clothed in fire.
3 This is the ninth ditch of the eighth circle.

CANTO XXVIII

The ninth ditch of the eighth circle reveals a sight which, Dante says, no one could describe adequately. Here are innumerable sowers of religious and political discord, and they are dreadfully and disgustingly mutilated.

Mahomet is here; he was regarded in the Middle Ages as a Christian schismatic and, if it does not seem quite so natural today to look at him in that light, we can still see how he represents in this canto the greatest religious, political and cultural schism in the smaller world which Dante knew. Mahomet's body is cut open from his chin to his belly, while his son-in-law Ali has his face cut open from his chin to the top of his head.

Also present are Pier da Medicina, who has, amongst other mutilations, his throat slit and speaks through the gash; Curio, whose tongue is slit because he advised Caesar to take the action which led to civil war in the Roman Empire; Mosca de' Lamberti, the originator of the feud between the Guelfs and Ghibellines, who has both his hands cut off so that, as he lifts them in the air, the blood falls down to drench his face; and Bertran de Born, who sowed dissension among the children of Henry II of England, and who carries his own severed head in front of him like a lantern.

Dante does not in any way attempt to mitigate our natural reaction of physical disgust. It would, however, be a mistake to see this canto as a mere chamber of horrors: here, as elsewhere in the Inferno, the punishment fits the sin, and those who tore society apart are themselves torn apart. The disgust we feel at such physical horrors is a disgust which Dante makes us feel also at the sin which caused them.

W ho could describe, even in words set free
From rhyme and metre, all the wounds and blood
I now saw, though he tried to, tirelessly?
There is no doubt that every tongue would fail,
   Together with the words and memory:
   They cannot hope to comprehend it all.
If we could reunite the multitude
   That fought one time upon your fatal earth,
   Apulia,[1] and lamented all their blood
Shed by the Trojans[2] or in that long war   10
   That culminated in a mound of rings[3]
   (As Livy[4] tells us, and he does not err),
With all of those who suffered heavy blows
   In their engagements with Robert Guiscard;[5]

---

1   Apulia is used here to indicate southern Italy in general.
2   Aeneas and his descendants who, refugees from Troy, gradually took possession of all Italy.
3   The reference is to the Second Punic War (219–202 BC) and the Battle of Cannae, after which the Carthaginians were said to have collected three bushels of rings from the fingers of dead Romans.
4   Roman historian (59 BC–17 AD).
5   A Norman invader of the eleventh century.

And all those others who are heaps of bones
   There at Ceprano, there where turn by turn
   Apulians broke their faith,[1] or Tagliacozzo,
   Where old Alardo did not fight but won,[2]
And some showed wounded limbs, and some limbs which
   Had been hacked off – that would not give a notion   20
   Of how things were within that foul ninth ditch.
I never saw a barrel gape apart,
   Through loss of hoop or stave, as I saw one
   Ripped from his chin right down to where we fart;
His guts between his legs, his inside out,
   Intestines on display, with that foul pouch
   That changes what we swallow into shit.
While I was all intent upon this sight,
   He looked, tore his breast open with his hands
   And said: "See how I pull myself apart!   30
See how Mahomet is discomfited![3]
   Ali[4] is walking off in front and weeping,
   His face split open – chin to top of head.
And all these other shades here whom you see –
   Because, while still alive, they sowed dissension
   And scandal – have been riven in this way.
A hidden fiend back there renews our trouble
   Continually, by putting to the sword
   All of the shades included in this rabble,
Each time we travel round this road of pain,   40
   Because each time we come to face that devil
   Our open wounds have all healed up again.
But who are you, standing up there and gaping?
   Perhaps you're trying to postpone the torment
   Which after your confession you are facing?"[5]
"Death has not reached him yet, nor does guilt bring
   This man," my master said, "to be tormented;
   But, that he may experience everything,
I, who am dead, act as his leader here,
   Down through the Inferno, circle after circle: 50
   This is as true as that I'm standing here."
Souls by the hundred stopped to stare at me,
   And stood and wondered, when they heard this said,
   For once oblivious of their agony.

---

1   This treachery led to the defeat of King Manfred at Benevento in 1266.
2   In 1268 Alardo, although he did not himself take part in the fighting, devised a winning
    strategy by which Charles of Anjou defeated Manfred's nephew Conradin.
3   In the Middle Ages Mahomet was often regarded as a Christian schismatic.
4   Mahomet's son-in-law and his eventual successor. He came to represent a schism within
    Islam itself.
5   Mahomet assumes that Dante is a soul who has confessed to Minos (*Inf.* v, 4–12) and
    been damned.

IT HELD ITS SEVERED HEAD UP BY THE HAIR,
SWINGING IT IN ONE HAND JUST LIKE A LANTERN...

INFERNO XXVIII, 121–22

...I SAW TWO, FROZEN WITHIN ONE HOLE,
WHERE ONE HEAD WORE THE OTHER LIKE A HOOD...

INFERNO XXXII, 125–26

"You who, shortly perhaps, will see the sun,
　　Tell Fra Dolcino to provide himself –
　　Unless he wants to join me very soon –
With victuals; or the snow, blocking him in,
　　Will bring a victory to the Novarese,
　　Which otherwise he would find hard to win."[1]　　60
With one foot in the air, with half a mind
　　To go away, Mahomet said these words;
　　Then moved off, as he put it to the ground.
Another – with his throat slit open wide,
　　His nose cut off right up to his eyebrows,
　　And only one ear left upon his head,
And who, in his surprise at us, had stood
　　Still like the others – was the first to clear
　　His windpipe's fissure, all blood-red outside,
To speak through: "You, who do not stand condemned,　　70
　　Are one, unless the likeness is deceptive,
　　I've seen before above on Latin ground.
I'm Pier da Medicina.[2] If you go
　　Back ever to revisit that dear plain
　　That from Vercelli slopes to Marcabò,
Remember me.[3] Tell Fano's two best men,
　　Guido I mean, and also Angiolello:
　　If our apparent foresight here's not vain,
They will be weighted down, drowned in the sea,
　　Thrown overboard close by Cattolica,　　80
　　Through a brute tyrant and his treachery.[4]
Neptune has never witnessed such a crime
　　Between the isles of Cyprus and Majorca,
　　By pirates now or Greeks in ancient time.
That one-eyed traitor,[5] wielding power within
　　The city which somebody here with me
　　Heartily wishes he had never seen,[6]
Will make them meet with him and talk together,
　　Then so arrange it that they'll need no prayers
　　To shield them from Focara's wind and weather."[7]　　90
　　I said: "Explain that – point him out to me

1　Dolcino Tornielli was the leader of a heretical sect who, with his followers, was block-aded in the hills between Novara and Vercelli, then forced by starvation to surrender and burnt alive in 1307. The "Novarese" is the Bishop of Novara who led the crusade against Dolcino.

2　Nothing is known of him apart from what Dante tells us here.

3　Many of the damned share this anxiety to be remembered in the land of the living.

4　This murder was committed on the orders of Malatestino, lord of Rimini, in 1312.

5　Malatestino da Rimini.

6　Because it was there that he committed the sin for which he is damned.

7　The implication is that they will be drowned before their ship reaches the proverbially dangerous weather off the headland of Focara on Italy's Adriatic coast.

(If you want news of you spread up above)
   That man who hates the sight of Rimini."
He laid his hand on a companion's cheek,
   And prised his jaws apart for him and shouted:
   "This is the fellow, and he does not speak!
This man, an exile, managed to allay
   All Caesar's doubts: 'The man who's good and ready
   Will only suffer harm if he delay.'"[1]
Oh how aghast, dismayed that man appeared,   100
   His tongue slit in his gullet – Curio –
   Always so ready to put in a word!
And one who had his hands docked, both of them,
   Lifted his stumps in that dark atmosphere
   So that his face was fouled as blood dripped down,
And cried: "Remember Mosca too, who said –
   With what result! – 'A thing once done is done',
   Which for the Tuscans sowed such evil seed."[2]
I added: "And sowed death to all your race!"[3]
   And at these words, which piled grief onto grief,   110
   He went like someone maddened by distress.
But I remained to gaze upon that crowd,
   And I saw what I'd hardly dare to mention
   Without someone supporting what was said,
If conscience did not now encourage me,
   The good companion that emboldens men
   Under their breastplate of integrity.
I really saw, and still I seem to see,
   A trunk without a head, moving along
   With all the others in that company;   120
It held its severed head up by the hair,
   Swinging it in one hand just like a lantern;
   The head saw us and moaned in its despair.
It made itself a lamp of its own head,
   And they were two in one and one in two:
   But how, He only knows who so decreed.
When it arrived just under where we were,
   It lifted up both arm and head together,
   To bring the words it had to say more near.
Those words were: "Now you see outrageous pain,   130
   You who, still breathing, visit all the dead:
   Tell me, is any grief as great as mine?
So that you may take up some news of me,
   You must know I'm Bertran de Born, the man

1   The sinner is Curio, the Roman who in 49 BC urged Julius Caesar to cross the Rubicon,
   an action which precipitated civil war.
2   In 1215 Mosca de' Lamberti urged the killing of Buondelmonte de' Buondelmonti,
   which started the feud in Florence between Guelfs and Ghibellines.
3   The Lamberti family were expelled from Florence in 1258.

Who led the Young King into treachery,
Setting the father and the son at odds:[1]
   Achitophel did not do worse to David
   And Absalom, with his contentious words.[2]
Because I severed people joined like this,
   I carry here my brain, which has been severed   140
   From where it drew its life – this trunk, alas!
And thus fit retribution is delivered."

---

1   The famous troubadour Bertran de Born encouraged Prince Henry, the son of Henry II
     of England, to rebel against his father.
2   Achitophel persuaded Absalom to rebel against his father King David (2 Samuel 15–18).

CANTO XXIX

Dante finds it difficult to tear himself away from the sowers of discord, and it becomes apparent that his anguish is for one in particular of those mutilated shades. This is Geri del Bello, a relative of Dante, who is angry that his murder has not been avenged. Dante shows some sympathy with his relative's plight, but Virgil has already insisted that he should turn his attention elsewhere: such sympathy is out of place, and also time is pressing.

The travellers then come to where they can look down into the last ditch of Eviltiers, reserved for falsifiers of all kinds. The description of this ditch, like an enormous hospital where all the sinners are punished with illness, will continue into the next canto. The falsifiers of metal, the alchemists, are punished with a sort of leprosy or scabies; the falsifiers of people, the impersonators, with hydrophobia; the falsifiers of money, the coiners, with dropsy; and the falsifiers of words, who use them for deception, with a burning fever.

We see in this canto two members of the first group, the alchemists, whose lives are revealed as not only sinful, but absurd. This absurdity provokes some comments on the pretentiousness of the Sienese, and particularly on their tendency to indulge in wildly extravagant living.

Dante and Virgil, here as everywhere in the Inferno, have time to speak with only a few of those who represent the sins which are being punished. It is, however, not difficult for the reader to provide his own, perhaps contemporary instances. This is strikingly the case with the big spenders of Siena, the mention of whom may seem at first to give us merely an insight into a quaint, and repulsive, thirteenth-century fad, but which, after a moment's thought, is very likely to strike home to the reader. And this is, of course, the intention behind the whole of *The Divine Comedy*.

Such crowds, such frightful wounds! My eyes filled up –
    I found myself with a compelling urge
    Simply to linger there, and stand and weep,
But Virgil said: "Why do you stand and gaze?
    Why do you pause and let your vision linger
    Among the sad and mutilated shades?
Think, if you mean to number all these souls –
    Something you did not do in other ditches –
    This valley runs for two-and-twenty miles.
By now the moon is underneath our feet:[1]   10
    Not much of our allotted time is left,
    And there's much more to see than you've seen yet."
"If you had known," I answered straight away,
    "The reason why I wished to go on looking,
    I think perhaps you would have let me stay."
My leader simply went ahead meanwhile;

---

1   The moon is in the southern hemisphere. In the northern hemisphere the time is about noon.

But as I followed him I went on talking,
Explaining what I meant: "Within that hole
On which I was intent, I think I saw
   A spirit, one of my own blood, regretting   20
The guilt for which they pay so dearly there."
At this my master said: "Henceforth refrain
   From thoughts of him, for more important things;
And where that sinner is, let him remain;
I saw him pointing at you, from the hollow
   Beneath our bridge, and threaten, with his finger,
And heard him being called Geri del Bello.[1]
And then you had your eyes so fixed upon
   The shade which was the ruler of Hautefort[2]
You did not look that way till he was gone."   30
"O my good lord, the violent death he died,
   Which up to now is unavenged," I answered,
"By anyone who shares his shame and blood,
Made him disdainful – that is why he parted
   Without a word to me, or so I think;
And that has made me feel more tender-hearted."[3]
We went on talking till we were in sight
   Of the next valley and its lowest parts,
Or would have been if there had been more light.
And when we'd finished walking and we stood   40
   Above the last cloister of Eviltiers,
And could distinguish all the brotherhood,[4]
Such lamentation struck me, sharp and fierce
   As arrowheads, and barbed with sympathy,
I had to clap my hands upon my ears.
There'd be such pain, if all the hospitals
   Of Val di Chiana, in the summer months,
Sardinia and Maremma, and all their ills,[5]
Were thrown into a single ditch together,
   As there was here; and such a stench arose   50
As we expect from limbs that rot and fester.
We climbed right down onto the final ridge
   That runs across our pathway, keeping left,
And there I found at last my sight could reach
Down where the handmaid of the highest lord,

---

1   He was a cousin of Dante's father.
2   Bertran de Born, seen in the previous canto in the ditch reserved for the sowers of
    discord.
3   Dante is sensitive to the custom of blood revenge, and even feels the obligation emotion-
    ally, but he clearly does not believe in honouring it.
4   The religious terms "cloister" and "brotherhood" are ironical. Virgil and Dante are now
    looking down into the ditch reserved for the falsifiers of metals and money, people and
    words.
5   These regions were all notoriously marshy and malarial.

Justice that is unerring, punishes
 The falsifiers she has registered.
I do not think they made a sorrier sight,
 The sickly population of Aegina –
 Whose atmosphere was so infected that   60
All creatures, even to the little worm,
 Had to succumb, until that ancient race,
 Or so the poets strenuously affirm,
Was recreated, now with ants as seed[1] –
 Than those we saw along the sombre valley,
 Spirits languishing and diversified,
Some on their bellies and some on the back
 Of someone else, and some upon all fours
 Dragging themselves along the gloomy track.
We went on step by step without a sound,   70
 But listening to and watching those sick souls,
 Who could not raise their bodies from the ground:
Two propped against each other where they sat,
 Like pans propped against pans to be warmed up,
 And both covered with scabs from head to foot;
And I have never ever seen a curry-
 Comb being plied for an impatient master,
 Or plied by one up late and in a hurry,
As I saw both of them go scratch, scratch, scratch,
 Their own nails scratching them in all the fury 80
 Of endless itching to relieve the itch;
And so they scraped their scabs off with their nails,
 Just as a knife does when it strips a carp
 Or any other fish with largish scales.
"O you who scale yourself with your own fingers,"
 My leader chose to speak to one of them,
 "And sometimes have to turn them into pincers,
Tell us if any Latin[2] is within
 That group of yours, so may your scaling nails
 Last out to do that work that's never done."[3] 90
"The two of us are Latins you see here
 So dreadfully disfigured," was the answer
 That came with tears, "but tell us who you are."
My leader answered: "I am going down
 From terrace to terrace, for I must reveal
 The whole Inferno to this living man."
Those sinners broke apart as he replied;
 Then, as they turned to look at me, they trembled,

1 According to the myth, ants were changed into human beings in order to repopulate
 the Greek island of Aegina.
2 Italian.
3 Frequently, to persuade the shades to answer questions, Virgil or Dante expresses a wish
 to please them. Here the wish is a backhanded one.

With others who by chance had overheard.
My master came up close to me and told   100
  Me then: "Say what it is you want of them."
  And I began, since that was what he willed:
"So that you may not fade from minds of men
  In the first world above, but your names live
  Through many revolutions of the sun,
Disclose your stock and your identity;
  And do not let your loathsome punishment
  Deter you from revealing this to me."
"I was an Aretine," the first[1] replied.
  "Alberto da Siena[2] had me burnt.   110
  I was not brought here for the way I died;[3]
The truth is, when I told him, jokingly,
  'I could rise up and fly into the air,'
  He, with less sense than curiosity,
Desired to see this feat; for this alone –
  Failing to make him Daedalus[4] – he had
  Me burnt by one who held him as a son.[5]
But never-erring Minos had me hurled
  Into the final ditch of all the ten
  For the alchemy I practised in the world."   120
I asked the poet: "Were there ever folk
  As hoity-toity as the Sienese?
  Certainly not the French, by a long chalk!"
To which the other leper, who'd heard me,
  Replied: "Exceptions to all this are Stricca,[6]
  Who knew the art of living frugally,
And Niccolò,[7] who first revealed to men
  Habitual usage of the costly clove
  In the city where such fashions soon catch on;[8]
And also Caccia d'Asciano's[9] company,   130
  With whom he wasted vineyards and whole woods,
  While Muddlehead[10] showed his sagacity.
But, if you wish to know who's backing you
  Against the Sienese, look hard at me,

---

1   Griffolino d'Arezzo, an alchemist, who died before 1272.
2   A favourite of a bishop of Siena.
3   He was burnt alive for annoying Alberto da Siena, but damned for his alchemy.
4   Famous in myth as the first man to fly successfully.
5   The bishop who favoured Alberto da Siena.
6   A notorious spendthrift of Siena in the second half of the thirteenth century. The word "exceptions" is ironical.
7   Niccolò dei Salimbeni, still alive in 1311.
8   The city is Siena. Cloves were imported from the Far East and were therefore expensive.
9   Caccia was contemporary with Stricca and Niccolò, and like them devoted to extravagant spending.
10   A nickname, and another member of the band of spendthrifts.

And once you have my visage in full view,
You'll know the shade of old Capocchio,[1] who
    Falsified metals with his alchemy;
    And you'll recall, if I remember you,
How I aped nature most successfully."

1   A Florentine and an acquaintance of Dante, burnt alive for alchemy in Siena in 1293.

CANTO XXX

This canto begins with two accounts of madness, drawn from myth and Trojan history, which lead into a description of two shades running about wildly and savagely attacking the other shades – Gianni Schicchi, who impersonated someone in order to draw up a false will in his own favour, and Myrrha, who impersonated another woman in order to commit incest with her own father.

Then Dante notices a sinner lying there, who is so deformed that he has, if one ignores his legs, the appearance of a lute – his face is shrunken like the neck of the lute and his body bloated like its body. This is Master Adam, damned for coining. He says how he had all he wanted while he was alive, but now is desperately craving a drop of water. He gives a lyrical description of the little streams which run down from the Casentino to join the Arno: this image is always in his mind and forms a great part of his punishment. With a dramatic reversal of tone, any sympathy we might have for Adam is destroyed however when he says that, if he could only see in the Inferno the shades of the three brothers who persuaded him to sin, he would prefer that sight to all the water in Fonte Branda. Adam believes that one of the brothers is already dead and damned, but he cannot move to look for him because of the weight of his dropsical body.

Adam identifies for Dante two sinners huddled together, so hot with fever that steam is rising from their bodies as from "warm wet hands in winter". They are Sinon, who lied to persuade the Trojans to take the wooden horse into Troy, and Potiphar's wife, who falsely accused Joseph of attempted rape.

A quarrel breaks out between Sinon and Master Adam, one which is both disgusting and amusing. When Virgil reproves him for his baseness in listening to such bickering, Dante's shame is such that he is quickly forgiven.

O
f old, when Juno was infuriated
    Through Semele against the Theban blood,
    As time and time again she demonstrated,[1]
Then Athamas was driven so insane
    That, when he saw his wife go passing by,
    Bearing upon each arm a little son,
He cried: "Let's spread the nets and let me catch
    The lioness and both her cubs at once."
    And then he stretched his talons out to snatch
The child known as Learchus, whirled him round   10
    And dashed him on a rock – at which his wife
    Leapt in the sea with the other, and they drowned.
And when on Fortune's wheel the Trojan pride,
    Which had been full of daring, was brought low,
    So that both King and kingdom were destroyed,

---

1   Juno, to avenge herself on her husband Jupiter when he was unfaithful to her with Semele, contrived Semele's death. She also took a wider revenge by driving Semele's brother-in-law Athamas mad.

Hecuba, now a wretched prisoner,
    When she had seen Polyxena lie dead,
    And she, in all her mourning, was aware
That it was Polydorus by the sea,
    Then she went howling madly like a dog,   20
    So far had grief driven her wits astray.[1]
But never was Theban fury ever seen,
    Or Trojan either, running so amok,
    Ripping up beasts, and even limbs of men,
As two pale naked shades I saw come by,
    Running and biting everybody like
    A hog that's just been let loose from the sty.
The one got to Capocchio, and in the nape
    Of the neck he stuck his tusks and, dragging him
    On the hard ground, he made his belly scrape.   30
The one shade left, the trembling Aretine,[2]
    Told me: "That imp of hell is Gianni Schicchi:[3]
    He rages, and does this to everyone."
I answered him: "Oh! That the other may
    Not sink its teeth in you, be not displeased
    To say its name before it gets away."
And he replied: "That is the ancient soul
    Of Myrrha the accursed, who loved her father,
    But in a way that's not permissible.[4]
And this is how that sinner came to sin: 40
    She took upon herself another's figure.
    The other,[5] who goes there, took it on him –
He so desired the queen of all the herd –
    To make believe he was Buoso Donati,
    And made a will in due form, word for word."
And when the two, still raging, had passed on,
    Whom I'd been looking at so fixedly,
    I turned to other shades of the ill-born.
I saw one who'd be fashioned like a lute
    If only at the groin, where human beings   50
    Divide up into two, he'd been cut short.
Ponderous dropsy, working to confound
    The limbs with liquid that will not digest,

---

1   After the sack of Troy, the ex-queen Hecuba, by now herself a slave, witnessed the
    sacrifice of her daughter Polyxena. She also saw the body of her son Polydorus when
    it was washed up by the sea.
2   Griffolino. See the previous canto.
3   A Florentine (died c.1280) who impersonated Buoso Donati in order to dictate a false
    will by which he was to inherit a valuable mare.
4   The mythical Myrrha disguised herself as another woman in order to commit incest
    with her father.
5   Gianni Schicchi. See l. 32 and note.

Till face and belly fail to correspond,[1]
Forced him to hold his lips asunder, like
   Consumptives who, dried up and thirsting, turn
   One to the chin and one lip up and back.
"O you who seem to pay no penalty,
   I don't know why, in this bleak world of ours,"
   He said to us, "now look this way and see   60
The heartache Master Adam[2] has to suffer:
   Alive, I'd everything I ever wanted,
   And now, alas, I crave a drop of water.
The little streams of the green hills which fall
   From Casentino[3] down into the Arno,
   In channels that are always moist and cool,
Are never out of mind, and not in vain,
   Because their image parches me much more
   Than this illness which makes my face so lean.
The rigid justice that is racking me   70
   Uses the very region where I sinned
   To make my sighs come faster as they flee.
There is Romena,[4] there is where I coined
   Metal that bore the image of the Baptist[5] –
   And there it was I left my body, burned.
But, could I see the soul of Alexander
   Being punished here, or Guido's, or their brother's,
   I would not swap that sight for Fonte Branda.[6]
One's here already,[7] if shades running round,
   In such a fury, are to be believed.
   But what good's that to me, whose limbs are bound?[8]   80
If I were still endowed with such great speed
   That I could inch one inch each hundred years,
   I would already be upon the road,
To find him in this crooked crowd, for all
   The ditch's circuit is eleven miles,
   And side to side is more than half a mile.
It is their fault I'm here with folk like this:
   They were the ones persuading me to strike
   Florins containing such a deal of dross."   90

---

1 Dropsy has the effect of swelling the belly while shrinking the flesh of the head.
2 Burnt alive in 1281 for coining.
3 A district in Tuscany which includes the upper Arno valley.
4 A castle in Casentino.
5 Florentine gold florins bore the image of the city's patron, John the Baptist.
6 Guido da Romena and his brothers, Alessandro and Aghinolfo, persuaded Master Adam
   to counterfeit the Florentine florin. There is a famous fountain, Fonte Branda, in Siena;
   but it seems more likely from the context that Adam is referring to Fonte Branda near
   Romena. Either way the significance is obvious.
7 Guido da Romena had died in 1292.
8 Bound figuratively by the weight of his swollen body.

I asked: "Who are those two in such a plight
    They send up steam like warm wet hands in winter,
    Lying there close to you upon your right?"
"I found them when I came," he said, "and they
    Have not stirred ever since and, I believe,
    They will not stir to all eternity.
One is Sinon of Troy, the lying Greek[1] –
    The other's she who cited Joseph falsely[2] –
    It is their raging fever makes them reek."
And one of them, who seemed perhaps to blench   100
    At being named and spoken of so badly,
    Landed a punch on Adam's tightened paunch.
The paunch resounded like a beaten drum,
    And Master Adam struck him on the face
    With something that was just as hard – his arm –
And said to him: "Although my body loses
    The ability to move, with its great weight,
    I have my arm free when the need arises."
To which he answered: "When you went to burn,
    Your arms were not unbound – and yet they were   110
    Quite free and easy when you went to coin."
The one with dropsy then: "What you now say
    Is true: but you were not a truthful witness
    When you were asked to tell the truth at Troy."
"If I spoke lies, you faked your coins as well,"
    Said Sinon. "I am here for one fault only,
    And you for more than any devil in hell!"
"Perjurer, bear in mind the horse," was how
    The one with bloated belly answered him,
    "And be dismayed the whole world knows it now!"[3]   120
"And may your thirst," the Greek said, "sicken you,
    Cracking your tongue, while all the filthy water
    Distends your belly, blocking out your view!"[4]
At this the coiner: "Your mouth has to burst
    Apart with fever as it always does!
    For if I'm bloated and I have a thirst,
You have your fever and your aching head –
    To get you to lap up Narcissus' mirror[5]
    There'd be no need to press you very hard."
I was wholly intent upon these two,   130
    When my guide said to me: "Just go on looking,
    And soon there'll be a clash between us too!"

---

1   Sinon pretended he had changed sides and persuaded the Trojans to take the wooden
    horse (secretly filled with armed Greeks) into their city.
2   Potiphar's wife falsely accused Joseph of trying to rape her (Gen. 39: 7–20).
3   The incident of the wooden horse is dealt with in detail by Virgil in his *Aeneid*.
4   Adam is supine.
5   Water. The mythical Narcissus fell in love with his own reflection in a pool.

When I heard him address me angrily,
   I turned towards him and I felt such shame
   That even now it haunts my memory.
Like someone who is having a bad dream
   And, dreaming, wishes he were dreaming, therefore
   Wishing what is were happening to him,
Just so was I: I could not say a word –
   I longed to excuse myself, and did excuse   140
   Myself in fact, and did not think I did.
"Less shame would wash away a greater fault,"
   My master said to me, "than yours has been:
   So do away with any sense of guilt.
Always remember I am still about,
   If chance again should bring you to a place
   Where there is such another falling-out;
The wish to listen to such things is base."

CANTO XXXI

When the canto opens, Dante is still thinking of his shame at Virgil's rebuke for his vulgar curiosity. Then the two companions start to make their way through half-light across the parapet which bounds the final circle of the Inferno. Suddenly they hear a horn, so loud that it outdoes even the sound of Roland's at Roncesvalles. Dante looks round him and sees what appear to be many towers. To forearm Dante, Virgil explains that they are really giants, those giants who tried to seize power from the Olympian gods. They are ranged all round the central lake or well of this final circle. Again and again their overwhelming size, much greater than that of any unmythical giant, is emphasized.

The first whom Dante sees clearly is the biblical Nimrod, "the mighty hunter before the Lord". It was he who blew the horn. He speaks briefly in a strange babble which reminds us of his responsibility for the Tower of Babel, whose construction led to the multiplication and confusion of human tongues. The few words which Virgil addresses to him are reproving and scornful: this sets the tone for Dante's similar attitude towards the people he will meet in the following canto.

As the pilgrims go on their way, they see Ephialtes, bound five times round with chains. When they come to Antaeus, who did not take part in the revolt against the Olympian gods, Virgil speaks to him politely and asks him to lift them down onto the frozen lake of Cocytus. Virgil grasps Dante to him, and this double burden is lifted by Antaeus and put down in the first zone of this circle, Caïna (named after Cain), where those who betrayed relatives are punished.

It was the same tongue giving me the wound,
    Tinging with red first one cheek then the other,
    Which then made sure that I was medicined:[1]
Just as, so I have heard, Achilles' lance,
    Which was his father's lance before, delivered
    Agony first and afterwards redress.[2]
Turning our backs upon that wretched ditch,[3]
    We went up on the bank surrounding it
    And made our way across without more speech.
It was not night, but certainly not dawn: 10
    I could but see a little way ahead –
    And then I heard a loud blast on a horn
That would have made a thunderclap seem light,
    And as I traced that sound back to its source,
    I fixed my eyes upon one single spot.
After the dire defeat when Charlemagne
    Lost all his holy band of paladins,

---

1   See the previous canto, ll. 130–48.
2   Rust from Achilles's spear could heal the wounds the spear had inflicted.
3   The tenth and last ditch of Eviltiers.

Not such a shock arrived from Roland's horn.[1]
Not long I tried to pierce the gloom before
　　I saw, or so it seemed, many high towers. 20
　　"Master," I asked, "what city is this here?"
And he replied: "You'll find, now that you fix
　　Your eyes on something far off in the shadows,
　　That your imagination's playing tricks.
Once you get there, then you will clearly see
　　How much the distance has deceived your sight:
　　So let that knowledge urge you on your way."
Then tenderly he took me by the hand
　　And said: "Before we go on any further,
　　And so that you may not get too alarmed, 30
Know now you are not seeing towers at all,
　　But giants[2] round this rampart, who are buried
　　Up to their navels in the central well."
As when a mist begins to dissipate,
　　And bit by bit we start to make some sense
　　Of what the foggy air hid from our sight,
So, as I pierced the murky atmosphere
　　And kept on coming closer to the brink,[3]
　　My error vanished, giving way to fear;
For just as round the circle of its wall 40
　　Monteriggioni crowns itself with towers,[4]
　　Just so, above the bank around the well,
The giants tower, half shown, half hidden under,
　　So tall, so terrible, but such as still
　　Jove threatens out of heaven with his thunder.
Already I could see the face of one,
　　His shoulders, breast, a great part of his belly
　　And his high sides by which his arms hung down.
Nature did well to leave off making these
　　Creatures and other creatures like them, taking 50
　　Such monstrous ministers away from Mars.[5]
And though she still continues with the whale
　　And elephant, if one considers subtly,
　　That turns out to be well advised as well:
It's where the reasoning of a man of sense

1　When Charlemagne's army, in the year 778, was withdrawing from Spain, his rearguard
of select warriors under the command of Roland was wiped out at Roncesvalles. Char-
lemagne learnt of this when he heard Roland blow his horn from eight miles away to
summon help.
2　Dante conflates the giants mentioned in Gen. 6:4–5 with the giants of Greek mythol-
ogy who tried to storm Mount Olympus but were foiled by the Olympian gods and
particularly by Jove's thunderbolts.
3　The parapet round the lowest circle of the Inferno.
4　There were originally fourteen high towers round the walls of this fortress near Siena.
5　The Roman god of war.

Combines with evil will and such great power
    That mankind has no adequate defence.
His face seemed every bit as long and round
    As the huge pine cone standing in St Peter's,[1]
    And all his body equally big-boned;   60
Indeed the bank, which served him as a screen
    Down from his waist, revealed so much above
    That three Frieslanders[2] would have hoped in vain
That they might boast of reaching to his hair,
    For downward from the spot where cloaks are buckled[3]
    I could see thirty spans at least laid bare.
"Raphèl maì amècche zabì almi,"[4]
    Such were the words which came from that brute mouth
    (Sweeter psalms would have come less suitably).
My leader said to him: "You babbling fool,   70
    Stick to your horn, and with that vent your feelings
    When ire or other passion stirs your soul!
Feel round your neck, and you will find the strap
    That holds it fast, you poor bewildered creature:
    It lies across your great chest like a stripe."
Virgil went on: "By himself he stands revealed –
    For this is Nimrod, through whose evil notion
    One single tongue no longer serves the world.[5]
Let's leave him, let's not talk with him in vain,
    For every other language is to him   80
    As his to others – understood by none."
So, turning to the left, we went on further,
    Until we found, a crossbow-shot away,
    Another giant, more fierce and even larger.
And whosoever was the master hand
    That tied him I can't tell you, but he had
    His left arm in the front, his right behind,
Both pinioned by a chain that held him bound
    From the neck down, and what was visible
    Was circumvented fully five times round.   90
"This was a giant who wanted, in his pride,
    To pitch his strength against almighty Jove,"
    My guide went on, "and this is his reward.

---

1   This is the old basilica of St Peter in Rome: the present building was made long after
     Dante's day. However, the giant bronze pine cone is still to be seen in the Vatican Museum.
2   Noted for their stature.
3   The throat.
4   As Dante makes clear in ll. 79–81, this is meaningless babble.
5   "And Cush begat Nimrod: he began to be a mighty one in the earth. He was a mighty
     hunter before the Lord… And the beginning of his kingdom was Babel…" (Gen. 10:8–10).
     It is appropriate for Nimrod, as a hunter, to have a horn. There is also a tradition that he
     was chiefly responsible for the building of the Tower of Babel, which led to the confu-
     sion of tongues (Gen. 11:1–9).

He's Ephialtes, strong in that endeavour
    When gods were terror-stricken by the giants:
    The arms he moved then have been stilled for ever."
To this I answered: "I am curious,
    If possible, to see with my own eyes
    One above all – the huge Briareus."
And he replied: "Antaeus is the one   100
    We'll find nearby, who speaks and is unfettered:[1]
    He'll place us at the centre of all sin.
He whom you want to see's much further on,
    And he is bound and built like Ephialtes,
    Except his face looks even more malign."
No earthquake ever gave so great a shock,
    So sudden, to a tower to make it tremble,
    As Ephialtes, when he heard this, shook.
Oh, then I feared to die, so great my fright:
    The fear itself seemed great enough to kill me,   110
    Had I not seen the chains that held him tight.
And so we carried on and went ahead,
    And reached Antaeus, rising up five ells
    Above the rock, not reckoning his head.
"O you who once, within the fateful vale
    Where Scipio inherited such glory
    When Hannibal and all his troops turned tail,[2]
Seized on a thousand lions for your prey,[3]
    And who, if you'd accompanied your brothers
    In their great war, some reckon to this day   120
The sons of earth might well have gained the field,
    Do not disdain to set us down below you,
    Where the Cocytus[4] is locked in with cold.
Must we ask Tityus, Typhon, and so on?
    This man can give you what you all crave here;
    So do not curl your lip, but just bend down.
He can reward you with fresh worldly fame,
    For he's alive, and he expects long life,
    Unless grace summons him before his time."
So said my master; the other, like a shot,   130
    Reached down and took my leader in that grasp
    Which had one time held Hercules so tight.[5]

---

1   Antaeus is unfettered because he did not take part in the rebellion of the giants against
    the gods.
2   In North Africa at the Battle of Zama in 202 BC the Roman general Scipio decisively
    defeated Hannibal.
3   The number is hyperbolic, but lions were his usual diet.
4   One of the rivers of the underworld which has here spread to a lake and frozen over.
5   When he wrestled with Antaeus, Hercules found that every time he threw him he rose
    up stronger than ever. This was because Antaeus was born from the earth and drew his
    strength from it. When Hercules realized this, he held Antaeus above his head and won.

And Virgil, when he felt those fingers, said:
  "Come over here, let me hold on to you."
  And so the two of us became one load.
The way the Garisenda[1] looks, below
  The side it leans on, when a cloud goes over
  So that it seems to topple – that is how
Antaeus, as he leant down, looked to me
  Who stood in apprehension: at that instant   140
  I would have much preferred some other way.
But down he set us gently in the abyss
  Where Lucifer and Judas are held fast;[2]
  Nor did he lean down long: straight after this
He straightened up again, like a ship's mast.

---

1   A leaning tower in Bologna.
2   The lowest part of the Inferno, where the sinners are locked in ice.

CANTO XXXII

Dante stresses the difficulty of describing the ninth and lowest circle of the Inferno – the frozen lake of Cocytus, divided, as it slopes towards the centre, into four concentric zones: Caïna, for betrayers of their relatives; Antenora, for betrayers of their country; Ptolomea, for betrayers of guests; and finally Judecca, for betrayers of benefactors.

This is the cruellest canto so far: in the sinners' punishments, in their attitude to each other, in Dante's own actions, and in the harsh, at times blackly humorous tone of the canto as a whole. Two brothers who committed mutual fratricide are locked together; they weep, but their tears congeal as they issue: they butt each other like goats. Their names are revealed by another shade, who insists that his own sins pale into insignificance in comparison with those of a cousin whom he is expecting to join him. The shades here are not so quick to name themselves as others are in the Inferno, but they are very quick to name each other: the habit of betrayal sticks. As Dante moves down from Caïna into Antenora, he "happens" to kick a sinner's head. Dante is anxious to know who this shade is; the shade is anxious he should not know. Dante seizes him by the scruff of his neck and threatens to tear all his hair out if he does not reveal his name; the sinner remains adamant, but of course another shade gives the game away: this is Bocca degli Abati, who betrayed the Guelfs at Montaperti. Dante adds to this sinner's suffering by promising to report the truth about him to the world above. Other sinners, who with nice understatement are said to be "laid out to cool", are dealt with more summarily.

Finally, Dante and Virgil reach two shades engaged in eating and being eaten, and Dante promises the eater that, if he tells his story, it shall be related in the world above.

I   f I could conjure up such raucous, rasping
  Rhymes as would suit the melancholy hole
  Where all the other rocks converge, then grasping
My theme more firmly, I would press the juice
  More fully from it: since I have none such,
  I am, here at the outset, timorous;
This is no May game for just anybody –
  To sound the depth of all the universe –
  Nor for a tongue that still says "mummy", "daddy":
But may those learnèd ladies[1] now help me   10
  Who once helped Amphion throw a wall round Thebes,[2]
  That style and substance may not disagree.
Oh, misbegotten brood, down in this deep
  So hard to talk about, it had been better
  By far had you been born as goats or sheep![3]
As we were standing, down in that dark well,

---

1 The Muses.
2 The myth has it that Amphion, with the music of his lyre, attracted stones down from the mountains to build the walls of Thebes.
3 They would not then be responsible for, and punished for, their actions.

Under the giant's feet and much much lower,
   With me still gazing up at the high wall,[1]
I heard this said to me: "Look how you go!
   And take good care you do not trample over   20
   The heads of the sad brotherhood of woe!"
At this I turned and saw in front there was –
   And underfoot – a lake so frozen over
   It did not look like water, but like glass.
The Austrian Danube's never ever veiled
   Itself to such a depth in winter, nor
   The River Don, for all the northern cold.
This sheet of ice would not – if Tambernic
   Were to crash down on it, or Pietrapana[2] –
   Not even at the edge, so much as creak.   30
Like frogs that keep their muzzles out of water
   To croak, that season[3] when the peasant girl
   So often dreams of what she'll glean and gather,
So, livid, sunken up to where the face
   Can show its shame, and where the teeth can chatter
   In time with storks,[4] shades suffer in the ice.
They were all looking down – their eyes revealed
   Their inner sadness as they wept – their teeth
   Bore chattering witness to the outer cold.
And after a short time of looking round,   40
   I, glancing down, saw two so close together
   The hairs upon their heads were intertwined.
"You who are locked in such a strong embrace,"
   I said, "who are you?" They bent back their necks,
   And as they both looked up and in my face,
Their eyes, which had been only moist within,
   Gushed over at the lids, until the cold
   Congealed those tears and locked the lids again.
No clamp has ever clamped two beams of wood
   So tight as they were held – whereat they butted   50
   Each other like two billy goats gone mad.
Another who, in this perpetual winter,
   Had lost both ears, kept looking down and said:
   "Why do you stare at us, as in a mirror?[5]
You want to know who these two are together?
   The Vale of the Bisenzio was theirs,

---

1   The parapet around this lowest part of the Inferno.
2   Mount Tambura (Tambernic) and Pietrapana are mountains in the Apuan Alps, in the
    north-west of Tuscany.
3   Early summer.
4   When they rattle their bills.
5   The image conveys primarily the intensity of Dante's gaze. Also, the ice acts as a
    mirror.

After Alberto, and he was their father.[1]
They issued from one body – and when you've seen
  All of Caïna you'll have found no shade
  More suitable to set in gelatine;   60
Not even him whose breast and shadow were
  Pierced by a single blow from Arthur's hand,[2]
  Not Focaccia,[3] and not this fellow here,
Whose head's so in the way I can't see through;
  Sassolo Mascheroni[4] was his name –
  If you're a Tuscan, he'll be known to you.
So that I need not say another word,
  I'll say my name: Camicione de' Pazzi;[5]
  And when Carlino[6] comes, I'll not seem bad."
And then I saw a thousand faces, pale   70
  And blue in all that cold – which makes me shudder
  Now to see ice on pools, and always will.
As we continued downwards and towards
  The centre where all weight and woe converges,
  And shivered in the eternal too-cool shade,
Whether by my intention, or by fate,
  Or chance, I do not know, with all those heads,
  I knocked against a face there with my foot.
He wept, and shouted out complainingly:
  "Unless you're here to add to all the vengeance   80
  For Montaperti,[7] why d'you tread on me?"
Then I said: "Let me linger here, my master,
  Until I have resolved a doubt about him,
  And then I'll hurry up – I'll go much faster."
My leader did stop, and I asked the one
  I'd kicked, who kept on cursing all the while:
  "Now who are you, to grunt like this and groan?"
"Now who are you, to walk through Antenora,[8]
  Kicking us in the cheek?" he asked in turn.

---

1   Napoleone and Alessandro, the sons of Alberto degli Alberti, quarrelled over their inheritance and for political reasons, and in 1286 killed each other.
2   When Mordred, who had rebelled against his uncle King Arthur, was killed, the lance made such a great hole in his body that even his shadow had a hole in it.
3   A citizen of Pistoia, he treacherously killed a cousin, which led to such disturbances that the Florentines were called in to help. This created a feud between the Black and White Guelfs in Florence.
4   A Florentine who murdered a relative for his inheritance.
5   A Tuscan who killed a relative.
6   Carlino de' Pazzi, a relative of Camicione, took a bribe to deliver a castle he was holding for the White Guelfs into the hands of the Black Guelfs.
7   A battle in 1260 at which the Tuscan Ghibellines defeated the Florentine Guelfs.
8   The second zone of the ninth circle, reserved for betrayers of their country, is named after the Trojan Antenor, who was said to have betrayed Troy to the Greeks.

"That's something which, alive, I would not suffer!"[1]   90
"Now I, I am alive. If you want fame,"
   I said, "I know the way to make you grateful,
   Setting down, with the other names, your name."
Then he to me: "I want the opposite;
   Get on your way – stop causing all this trouble –
   Your flattery is pointless in this pit!"
I grabbed him by his scruffy scruff and said:
   "It is essential that you give your name,
   If you want any hairs left on your head!"
He only answered: "Though you make me bald,   100
   I'll never say my name, or let it slip,
   However much I'm hauled about and mauled."
I had by now his hair wrapped round my hand,
   And had already torn some clumps away,
   And he, head down, was howling like a hound,
When someone else cried out: "What is it, Bocca?[2]
   Can't you be satisfied with rattling jaws,
   But you must bark? Now what the devil's the matter?"
"Well now," I said, "you need not speak again,[3]
   You wicked traitor – now I'll tell the truth   110
   In spite of you and to your grief and shame."
"Then go," he said, "and say whatever you like –
   But don't be silent, if you do get out,
   About that fellow there, so quick to speak.
He's here atoning for French silver: you'll
   Find time to say, 'I saw him of Duera,[4]
   There where the sinners are laid out to cool.'
And if you're asked about the other dead,
   You have just there beside you Beccaria,[5]
   Legate to Florence, where he lost his head.   120
Gianni de' Soldanieri,[6] if I'm right,
   Is there with Ganelon[7] and Tebaldello,
   Who unlocked Faenza in the dead of night."[8]
We had already gone beyond this shade,

---

1   He means he would take vengeance.
2   Bocca degli Abati, whose treachery was largely responsible for the Guelf defeat at Montaperti.
3   From the mention of Montaperti, Dante had probably guessed his name.
4   Buoso da Duera, bribed by the French to allow free passage to the troops of Charles of Anjou when they invaded Lombardy in 1265.
5   Tesauro dei Beccaria was charged with conspiring with the Ghibellines, who were banished from Florence.
6   A Florentine Ghibelline who, in 1266, betrayed his own party by allying himself with the Guelfs.
7   After Judas, probably the most famous traitor of all.
8   Tebaldello de' Zambrasi, a citizen of Faenza who, to avenge a private grudge, in 1280 opened the gates of the city to the Bolognese.

When I saw two, frozen within one hole,
  Where one head wore the other like a hood;
Like someone who is famished, he on top
  Was digging with his teeth into the other,
  Just where the brain's connected to the nape:
As ancient Tydeus, in a fit of spite,   130
  Gnawed Melanippus' temples,[1] so this shade
  Chewed skin and bone and brain up, every bit.
"O you who show by such a bestial act
  How much you hate him whom you're eating up,"
  I said, "say why, and we will make a pact:
If you can show good cause for this bad blood,
  I will, when I'm above, return the favour,
  Once I know who you are and what he did,
So long as what I speak with does not wither."[2]

---

1   Tydeus, one of the Seven against Thebes, was mortally wounded by Melanippus as he
    was killing him. He had the head of Melanippus brought to him and ate it.
2   Dante is referring to his tongue. He is using an accepted formula to emphasize the
    firmness of his promise.

CANTO XXXIII

The shade mentioned at the end of the previous canto lifts his face from the skull he is gnawing, wipes his mouth on his victim's hair and tells his own story. He is Ugolino della Gherardesca of Pisa who, damned for treachery, was himself betrayed on the orders of Archbishop Ruggieri and imprisoned with his sons in a tower, where they were all starved to death. At the end of his account he goes back to gnawing the head of his betrayer.

This account is famous for its pathos, yet it is framed by a bestial action: the horror of Ugolino's earthly punishment is not allowed to obscure his guilt. Dante shows his anger at the cruelty of the Pisans, and pity for the unmerited suffering of Ugolino's sons, but no sympathy for Ugolino. Our sympathy is aroused by Ugolino's account, but so too is our disgust at his revenge upon Ruggieri. The result is to stress the strictness of divine judgement, which is concerned solely with human merit or demerit, and which is not deflected by other considerations.

Dante and Virgil then move down to the next zone of Cocytus, Ptolomea, where those who betrayed their guests lie supine in the ice, with their eyes frozen over so that they cannot vent their grief in tears. Dante makes what seems to be a solemn promise to clear the ice from the face of one of them, Friar Alberigo, in return for his name, but he does not carry out his promise: to do so would be an attempt to interfere with the operation of divine justice.

Alberigo has given much more than his name: he has explained that, for sins as serious as his, it often happens that a soul descends into Antenora while the body is still alive in the world above: he himself is one example of this, and Branca Doria is another.

The canto concludes with an invective against Genoa, the city of which Branca Doria was, in fact still is bodily, a citizen.

He raised his mouth from his barbaric feed,
    That sinner,[1] and he wiped it on what hair
    There still remained on the half-eaten head.
And then began: "You ask me to revive
    Death and despair, a weight upon my heart
    Even to think of, never mind describe.
But since my words may bear this bitter fruit –
    Infamy for the traitor I am chewing –
    Then, though I weep, yet will I speak of it.
I don't know you, nor by what ways and means   10
    You've come down here – but certainly I think
    Your way of speaking is a Florentine's.
You must know Ugolino is my name,
    And this man is Ruggieri,[2] the archbishop:

---

1   See ll. 124–39 of the previous canto. This is Ugolino della Gherardesca, born in Pisa *c.*1230. Although a member of a Guelf family, he conspired to bring the Ghibellines to power in Pisa. This may be the betrayal for which he is damned in Antenora. He was later himself betrayed by the Ghibellines and imprisoned with two sons and two grandsons in a tower, where all were starved to death in 1289.

2   Archbishop of Pisa 1278–95.

I'll tell you why I am so close to him.
That he had all my trust, and that I fell
  Into the snare he laid, and was imprisoned
  Until I died, there is no need to tell;
But what you can't have heard of, you'll now hear –
  That is, the agonizing death I died –   20
  And know the rightness of the grudge I bear.
A tiny aperture inside the Mew,[1]
  Called now, on my account, the Tower of Hunger,
  Where others after me will be locked too,
Had let me have a glimpse already through
  Its slit of several moons,[2] before my dream
  In which the future's veil was torn in two.
This man appeared,[3] the master of the hunt
  Of wolf and wolf cubs on that Mount which means
  That Pisans looking to see Lucca can't.[4]   30
With lean and hungry hounds this man had sent
  Gualandi and Sismondi and Lanfranchi[5]
  Up there before him and way out in front.
And then it seemed to me that all too soon
  Father and sons started to tire; sharp fangs
  Invaded them – I saw their bodies torn.
When I awoke, before the dawn, I heard
  My sons,[6] who were imprisoned with me, weeping
  While still asleep, and crying out for bread.
You must be hard of heart if you can keep   40
  Your tears back, as you guess what I foresaw.
  Oh, if you don't weep now, when would you weep?
They were awake, and it was near the time
  When it was customary to bring us food –
  We were all frightened by the selfsame dream –
When down below I heard the key being turned
  To lock that tower – and it was then I looked
  My children in the face, without a word.
I could not weep, being turned to stone inside:
  They wept; and my poor little Anselm asked: 50
  'Father, why look like that? Are you afraid?'
I did not weep and I did not reply
  All of that day and all the following night,
  Until another sun rose in the sky.

---

1 Tower belonging to the Gualandi family, which stood in what is now the Piazza dei
   Cavalieri in Pisa.
2 Months.
3 Ruggieri, in Ugolino's dream.
4 This is Monte di San Giuliano. The periphrastic mention of it here suggests subtly an
   unfulfilled longing for Lucca, a Guelf stronghold.
5 All members of powerful Ghibelline families in Pisa.
6 Ugolino refers to all those with him, sons and grandsons, simply as his sons or children.

The moment that some light managed to make
    Its way into our jail, and I could see
    Four faces looking as my own must look,
I chewed my two hands in my agony;
    And they, thinking I did this out of hunger,
    Struggled onto their feet immediately,   60
And said: 'Father, we'd be in much less pain
    If you were eating us: you clothed us with
    This wretched flesh, so strip it off again.'
I calmed myself, not to make them feel worse;
    That day, the next day, no one spoke. Why did
    You, earth, not open up and swallow us?
When our starvation came to its fourth day,
    Gaddo threw himself at my feet and cried:
    'Father, why can't you do something for me?'
With that he died – and clear as you see me,   70
    I saw the other three fall one by one
    Between the fifth day and the sixth day; I
Was blind[1] by now, and called and fumbled over
    Their bodies two days after they were dead –
    Then what grief could not do was done by hunger."[2]
He said this, rolled his eyes, and once again
    He got the wretched skull[3] between his teeth,
    As savage as a dog is with a bone.
Pisa! Dishonoured city, dreadful blot
    On that dear country where the word is *sì*,[4]   80
    Whom your neighbours seem slow to castigate,
Could but Capraia move – Gorgona too[5] –
    And make a dam across the Arno's mouth,
    Until it drowned all living souls in you!
Even with Ugolino said to be
    Betrayer of your castles, was it right
    To put his children to such agony?
New Thebes![6] They were too young to share his blame,
    Brigata and Uguccione, and those others,
    The two[7] already mentioned in my rhyme.   90
We went on further,[8] where the frozen zone

---

1   Through starvation.
2   He did not die from grief, but hunger.
3   Of Archbishop Ruggieri.
4   Italy is distinguished from some other countries with Romance languages by its use of *sì* for yes.
5   Two islands just off the mouth of the Arno, which runs through Pisa.
6   Ancient Thebes had a reputation for cruelty.
7   Anselmo (l. 50) and Gaddo (l. 68).
8   Into Ptolomea, the third zone of Cocytus, reserved for those who betrayed guests or other associates. The name is derived either from Ptolemy, King of Egypt 51–47 BC, or from Ptolemy, governor of Jericho (1 Macc. 16:11–17): they both murdered guests.

Has other people wrapped up cruelly,
Not looking down now: all of them supine.
Their very weeping will not let them weep:
   Their pain, finding obstruction in their eyes,
   Turns back inside them to augment their grief;
Their first tears form a cluster, as they freeze,
   Which like a sort of visor made of crystal
   Fills up the cavities below their brows.
And even though, being in a land of ice   100
   Where everything is harder than a callus,
   I had no feeling in my frozen face,
I felt that I could feel some wind blow there,
   And asked my master: "What's the cause of this?
   Isn't it true there are no vapours here?"[1]
And he replied: "You'll find yourself quite soon
   Where your own eyes will come up with the answer,
   And see the reason why this wind blows down."
One of the sinners of the frozen crust[2]
   Cried out to us: "O souls who are so cruel   110
   The zone that you're assigned to is the last,[3]
Remove these heavy veils from off my face,
   That I may briefly vent heart-swelling grief,
   Before my tears, as always, turn to ice."
"Tell me your name," I said: "that is my price;
   And if I do not liberate you after,
   May I go to the bottom of the ice."
"Friar Alberigo," he said straight away,
   "The man whose fruits grew in an evil orchard.[4]
   Here dates for figs are given back to me."[5]   120
"Oh then!" I burst out. "You're already dead?"[6]
   "What's happened to my body in the world
   Is something I've no news of," he replied.
"We have one privilege in Ptolomea:
   Many a soul falls down into this place
   Well before Atropos has sent it here.[7]
And so that you may scrape with better will
   This glazing tears have made from off my face,
   I shall explain: as soon as any soul

---

1   The belief was that winds were caused by vapours drawn out of the earth by the sun.
2   Those whose eyes are blocked with ice.
3   Judecca, the fourth and last zone of Cocytus.
4   Friar Alberigo in 1285 invited his brother and a nephew to a banquet. When Alberigo called for the fruit course, hidden assassins killed the guests.
5   Dates were more expensive than figs, and the expression means to pay dearly for a misdeed.
6   Alberigo was still alive at the time of Dante's vision (1300).
7   Before death. The mythical Atropos was one of the three Fates: she cut the thread of life which had been spun and measured out by her sisters.

Betrays as foully as I did, a fiend   130
   Captures the body and controls its actions
   Until its time on earth comes to an end,
While into this cold well the soul drops down.
   Perhaps the world above still sees the body
   Of the shade that winters here behind my own?
You must know him, if you have only just
   Come here: he's Branca Doria,[1] and some years
   Have now gone by since he was so embraced."[2]
"I think," I said, "you're trying to abuse
   My trust, for Branca Doria has not died: 140
   He eats and drinks and sleeps and puts on clothes."
"Before Michele Zanche reached the hole
   Above, where Clawboys play their games," he said,
   "Where sticky pitch is always on the boil,[3]
This soul here left a demon in his stead
   Inside the body – as a relative,
   Who helped in the betrayal, also did.
But now stretch out your hand – this is the time
   To clear my eyes." But that I did not do:
   Courtesy here meant being rough with him.[4]   150
You, Genoese, so utterly devoid
   Of all good customs, full of every vice,
   Why have you not been driven from the world?
For, with Romagna's foulest shade of all,[5]
   I found a Genoese[6] with sins so grave
   That he bathes in Cocytus in his soul,
And seems in body still alive above.

---

1   A Genoese who murdered his father-in-law, Michele Zanche, at a banquet to which he
    had invited him.
2   So closed in ice.
3   In the fifth ditch of the eighth circle, that of the barrators.
4   It would have been discourteous (to God) to try to interfere with His justice.
5   Friar Alberigo.
6   Branca Doria.

CANTO XXXIV

Virgil and Dante are now in Judecca. This is the lowest zone of Cocytus, the lowest part of the Inferno: the sinners here (who betrayed their benefactors) are, with a few notable exceptions, covered entirely by the ice.

An atmosphere of mystery and menace pervades this canto. Where does the wind come from? What is the strange building or contrivance, rather like a windmill with turning sails, which Dante glimpses in the distance?

Both of those questions are answered when Dante at last sees Lucifer or Dis or Beelzebub, the source of all the evil in the world. He is a shaggy giant set, up to mid-chest, in the ice. He has three heads and three mouths, and each mouth is furiously chewing a sinner. These sinners are Judas Iscariot (who gives his name to this region), and Brutus and Cassius, who betrayed Julius Caesar.

Virgil and Dante make their way down the body of Lucifer. There is another mystery (startling at first to Dante and his reader, but soon explained) when Virgil suddenly turns upside down and begins to climb up Lucifer's body, so that, when the pilgrims detach themselves from the body to rest in a cleft in the surrounding rock, Dante finds that Lucifer's legs are upside down.

The atmosphere changes when we learn of a little stream which flows into this cleft from the world outside. Dante and Virgil follow the course of this stream, and eventually they emerge from a hole in the rock and see the stars once more. They are now in the southern hemisphere, and Dante has been told that he will there see some rising land which, although he does not yet know it, is Mount Purgatory, which will be explored in the second part of *The Divine Comedy*.

For all the physical horror, perhaps the most striking feature of this canto is that none of the sinners communicates with Dante or Virgil in any way. All human feelings are frozen, and all sense of community is lost.

"_Vexilla regis prodeunt inferni_[1]
     Towards us. And so, looking straight ahead,"
     My master told me, "see if you discern him."
It looked most like, as when mist gathers round,
     Or night begins to cloak our hemisphere,
     A distant mill, sails whirling in the wind –
At least I thought I saw something like that.
     I shrank out of the wind, behind my guide,
     There being no other rock or safe retreat.
I fear to set it down: I found I was   10
     Somewhere where all the sinners were iced over,
     Yet seen distinctly, like straws under glass.[2]

---

1   "The banners of the King of hell advance." This, with the parodic addition of _inferni_ (of hell), is the first line of a sixth-century hymn by Venantius Fortunatus in honour of the Cross.
2   Virgil and Dante are now in Judecca (named after Judas Iscariot), where they see the shades of those who betrayed their benefactors.

Some of them lie there; others are upright,
   Standing apparently, or on their heads;
   Some bowed like bows, face bent towards the feet.
We carried on until, after a while,
   My guide considered it was time to show me
   That creature who had been so beautiful:[1]
He stepped aside and stopped me, and he said:
   "Look upon Dis! And look upon the region   20
   Where you'll have need of all your fortitude."
Then how I shuddered, how my blood ran cold!
   Don't ask me, Reader, how: I cannot write it –
   There is no tongue in which it could be told.
I did not suffer death, or live on either:
   Try to imagine, if you have the wit,
   My state, bereft of one and of the other.
The emperor of the empire of despair
   Rose from mid-chest above the ice all round;
   I bear comparison to giants more   30
Readily than giants do to this one's arms:
   So now consider what the whole is like,
   Imagined in proportion to those limbs!
If he was once so beautiful as he
   Is ugly now, yet flouted his Creator,
   No wonder he's the fount of misery.
I found he had three faces on his head,
   Which was not something I had seen before!
   One was in front, and that one was bright-red;
The other two were joined onto the first   40
   At just about the mid-point of each shoulder;
   And all were joined together at the crest:
That on the right was white to yellow, while
   The one upon the left had the complexion
   Of those who live along the Upper Nile.[2]
Under each face two monstrous wings were spread,
   Proportionate to such a monstrous bird:
   I never saw sails on the sea so broad.
They were not feathered, but of such a kind
   As bats have – and the fiend was beating them   50
   So that he blew at once three blasts of wind:
And hence Cocytus is all frozen over.

---

1   Satan (aka Dis, Lucifer, Beelzebub) was reputedly the most beautiful of the angels before
    his fall.
2   The three faces are a parody of the three persons of the Holy Trinity. The symbolism is
    complex and disputed: the different colours seem to cover the whole human race – the
    red indicating Europeans, the yellowish the Asiatic races and the black the Africans; also
    different colours suggest qualities in opposition to those God personifies – red indicating
    hatred (as against love), yellow impotence (as against power) and black ignorance (as
    against omniscience).

With six eyes he was weeping; down three chins
    The tears were dripping, mixed with bloody slaver.
In every mouth, as with a rake or comb,
    The teeth were scraping, grinding up a sinner:
    There were three simultaneously in pain.
And yet to him in front being so gnawn
    Seemed nothing to the clawing: very often
    This sinner's back was bare down to the bone.   60
"That soul up there that is worst scarified,"
    My master said, "is Judas Iscariot,[1]
    His head within, his wriggling legs outside.
Of the other two, dangling with swinging head,
    The one who's hanging from the black snout's Brutus:[2]
    Look how he writhes and does not say a word;
That other's Cassius,[3] who looks strong and tall.
    But night is coming on – now is the time
    To go from here, since now we've seen it all."
Just as he told me to, I held him tight   70
    Around the neck; he looked for time and place,
    And when the wings were wide enough apart,
He grabbed tight hold upon the shaggy sides
    And made his way down slowly, tuft to tuft,
    Between thick fur and the encrusting ice.[4]
When we had reached the point at which the thigh
    Curves round, just on the swelling of the haunch,[5]
    My leader, struggling, breathing heavily,
Turned his head round to where his legs had been,
    And grasped the fur as though to climb: I thought   80
    That we were going back to Hell again.
"Now hold on tight, for it is by such ladders,"
    My master said, panting in his exhaustion,
    "That we must say goodbye to so much badness."
At last he issued by a rocky vent,
    And set me on the edge of it to rest;
    Then placed himself there, minding how he went.
I raised my eyes, believing I'd be faced
    With Lucifer once more, as I had left him;
    And saw his legs stick up, feet uppermost!   90
Now how I was bewildered and aghast
    Slow-witted people may imagine, they
    Who do not realize what point I'd passed.[6]
"Get up," my master said to me, "stand steady:

---

1   Who betrayed Christ.
2   The leader of the conspirators who murdered Julius Caesar.
3   Another of the murderers of Caesar.
4   The ice encasing the hole in which Dis is fixed.
5   The broadest part of the hips, regarded as the centre of the body.
6   Virgil and Dante have passed through the centre of the earth.

The way is long, the road is difficult;
    The sun has gone halfway through terce¹ already."
It was no palace chamber where we were,
    But simply a rough tunnel made by nature,
    With little light on the uneven floor.
"Even before I'm out of this abyss,   100
    Master," I asked, once I was on my feet,
    "Settle the problems that come out of this:
Where has the ice gone? Why's he upside down?
    And how has evening been transformed to morning
    By such a rapid journey of the sun?"
He answered: "Do you think you're still withheld
    North of the centre, where I grasped the fur
    Of this damned grub that hollows out the world?
You were still there while I was climbing down;
    When I turned over, we went past the point   110
    To which all weights from every part are drawn.²
Now you're beneath the hemisphere of sky³
    Antipodal to that⁴ which arches over
    The great dry land,⁵ under whose zenith⁶ He⁷
Was killed who lived, as He was born, sinless:
    You're standing on a little circular
    Region⁸ which forms Judecca's other face.
Here it is morning, when it's evening there;
    And he whose fur was useful as a ladder
    Is still fixed firmly as he was before.   120
When he fell down from heaven, he fell here;
    And all the land which had before protruded
    Veiled itself under water out of fear,
And fled until it reached our hemisphere;⁹
    And, fleeing him perhaps, this hollow space
    Was left by land which you'll see rising here."¹⁰
There is a place down there, far underground,
    Far from Beelzebub as his tomb reaches,¹¹

---

1   The first of the four canonical hours (set hours for prayers) of the daytime.
2   Virgil is referring to the force of gravity.
3   The southern celestial hemisphere.
4   The northern celestial hemisphere.
5   It was a common medieval belief that the northern hemisphere contained all the land
    in the world.
6   Jerusalem was believed to lie at the mid-point of the habitable world.
7   Christ.
8   One facet of a small sphere at the centre of the earth, an opposite facet of which is
    Judecca.
9   This is the origin of the land in the northern hemisphere.
10 Mount Purgatory, which Dante will see in the second part of *The Divine Comedy*.
11 Beelzebub's "tomb" is the "rough tunnel made by nature" of l. 98, and Dante and Virgil
    are now at the far end of it from Beelzebub.

And not perceived by sight, but by the sound
Of a small stream which makes its trickling way   130
   Through the hollow of a rock it has eroded
   In its winding course which slowly slopes away.
My guide and I followed that hidden route
   To bring us once more to the light of day;
   And, with no rest from the fatigue of it,
We clambered up, he first, till finally
   I saw the glory of the heavenly spheres,
   Through a round hole, the aperture whence we
Emerged to look once more upon the stars.[1]

---

1   All three books of *The Divine Comedy* end with the same word – *"stelle"* ("stars").

PURGATORY

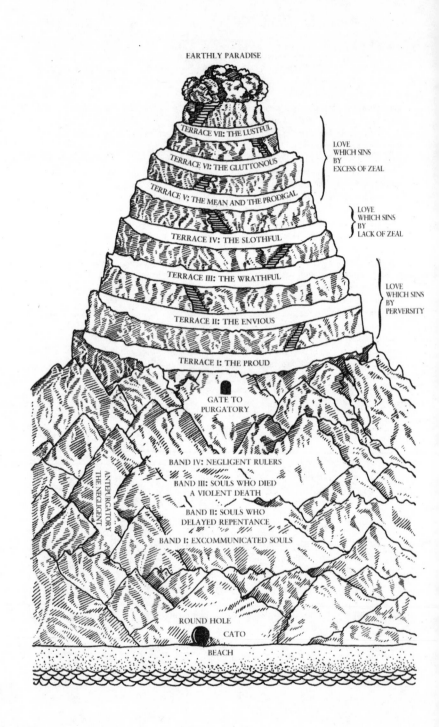

EARTHLY PARADISE

TERRACE VII: THE LUSTFUL

TERRACE VI: THE GLUTTONOUS

TERRACE V: THE MEAN AND THE PRODIGAL

TERRACE IV: THE SLOTHFUL

TERRACE III: THE WRATHFUL

TERRACE II: THE ENVIOUS

TERRACE I: THE PROUD

LOVE WHICH SINS BY EXCESS OF ZEAL

LOVE WHICH SINS BY LACK OF ZEAL

LOVE WHICH SINS BY PERVERSITY

GATE TO PURGATORY

BAND IV: NEGLIGENT RULERS

BAND III: SOULS WHO DIED A VIOLENT DEATH

BAND II: SOULS WHO DELAYED REPENTANCE

BAND I: EXCOMMUNICATED SOULS

ANTEPURGATORY THE NEGLIGENT

ROUND HOLE

CATO

BEACH

CANTO I

Dante prays to the Muses to inspire him as he describes the second, and "more propitious", stage of his journey.

The pilgrims have now climbed out of the Inferno and find themselves in the southern hemisphere, on the island of Mount Purgatory. The geography of this place will become clear to them gradually in this and later cantos: on the lower slopes are souls waiting to be admitted to their purgation; above are the seven terraces on which the seven deadly sins are purged; and at the top is the Earthly Paradise, the place of innocence and happiness from which Adam and Eve were expelled after their Fall. The souls in Purgatory suffer severely, but not as in the Inferno, since their suffering has a purpose: to purify them from their last traces of sin and enable them to go to heaven.

For the moment all that Dante notices, and conveys to us, is a strong sense of relief and hope after his experience of the Inferno. He conveys this largely by his descriptions of the sky as day is breaking. The atmosphere is strange, but not frightening: in the sky in this southern hemisphere there are, for instance, stars not seen by anyone since Adam and Eve.

These stars are so bright that they illuminate the face of a venerable old man who seems to appear from nowhere. This is Cato of Utica, the champion of freedom, and the guardian of the entrance to this realm. He is a problematic figure, one who is clearly saved although he was a pagan and a suicide; he is shown as worthy of all honour: even Virgil has to accept a rebuke from him. After questioning, he accepts Virgil's explanation of how he and Dante come to be there, and says that Dante must be girded with a rush (a sign of humility) and have his face washed in dew before he can begin the ascent of the Mountain. Then Cato disappears as mysteriously as he came.

Dante and Virgil descend to the seashore, Cato's commands are obeyed, and Dante is ready for the next stage of his journey.

And now the little vessel of my mind
   Sets sail across these more propitious waters,
   Leaving a sea of cruelty[1] behind;
And now I sing in rhyme that second reign,[2]
   There where the human spirit is made worthy
   To soar to Heaven, being purged of sin.
Here raise my inspiration from the dead,
   O sacred Muses, since I am all yours;
   And here, Calliope,[3] come to my aid,
And lend my utterance that more lofty tone   10
   Which struck the wretched magpies, and so hard
   They knew all hope of pardon was in vain.[4]

---

1   The Inferno.
2   Purgatory.
3   The muse of epic poetry.
4   According to the myth, the nine daughters of King Pierus challenged the nine Muses to a singing contest, and were turned into magpies for their presumption.

Soft hue of oriental sapphire,[1] clear
  Up to the very circle of the moon,[2]
  Suffusing all the intervening air,
Restored my joy in seeing, once I'd passed
  Clearly beyond the lifeless atmosphere
  Which was so troublesome to eyes and breast.
The radiant planet,[3] love's encourager,
  Occasioned happy laughter through the East,   20
  Veiling the Fishes[4] that escorted her.
Then, turning right, I fixed my mind upon
  The other pole,[5] and I observed four stars[6]
  Not seen before but by the world's firstborn.[7]
The sky appeared delighted with their light:
  Oh, northern regions, well and truly widowed,
  Because you are excluded from their sight!
When I could tear my eyes away from them,
  Turning somewhat towards the other pole,[8]
  There where the Wain[9] already had gone down,   30
I saw a solitary ancient man,[10]
  Worthy, by how he looked, of such respect
  No father is owed more by any son.
His beard was long, and it contained a mix
  Of white, as did the hair upon his head,
  Which fell down to his breast in two long locks.
The rays of those four stars shone down upon
  His face, adorning it with such a glow
  He looked like one who looks into the sun.
"Who are you who, against the underground   40
  River,[11] have fled the everlasting gaol?"
  He asked, and shook his grizzled hair and beard.
"Who guided you, what lamp was at your back,
  As you came out of that abysmal night
  Which keeps the infernal valley in the dark?
The laws of hell are broken, does this mean?

---

1   Eastern sapphire is of very high quality.
2   The moon is the nearest planet to the earth.
3   Venus, the morning star.
4   Outshining the stars of the constellation Pisces.
5   The southern celestial pole.
6   Symbolic of the four cardinal virtues – prudence, justice, fortitude and moderation –
     known to the pagan philosophers.
7   Adam and Eve, who were created in the Earthly Paradise on the top of what is now
     Mount Purgatory.
8   The northern celestial pole.
9   The seven bright stars of the Great Bear or the Plough.
10   Cato of Utica (95–46 BC), known for his integrity, opposed Julius Caesar and committed
     suicide to avoid submitting to his tyranny.
11 See *Inf.* XXXIV, 127–34.

Or has a new decree come out of Heaven,
That you, though damned, approach these rocks of mine?"
So then my leader took a hold of me,
  And with his words and hands and other gestures   50
  He made me lower my eyes and bend the knee.
And then he answered him: "I did not come
  Unbidden, but a lady[1] came from Heaven,
  And through her prayers I came to succour him.
But, since it is your will to have expressed
  At greater length exactly how we stand,
  I feel no need to shrink from your request.
This man has not yet seen his final hour;
  But through his sinfulness it came so close
  That there was very little time to spare.   60
As I have said to you, I have been sent
  To save him; and there was no other way
  To save him but this one on which I'm bent.
I've shown him all the infernal guilty nation;
  And now I mean to show him all those spirits
  Who, under your control, work their purgation.
How I have managed with this man so far
  Would take too long to tell – strength from above
  Helps me bring him to you, to see and hear.
Be pleased to make him welcome at this spot: 70
  He comes in search of freedom, which is precious,
  As he must know who gave his life for it.
You know – for you, not thinking death was bitter
  For freedom's sake, in Utica discarded
  The clothes that on the great day will shine brighter.[2]
We have not broken the eternal laws;
  For this man lives, and Minos[3] does not bind me,
  But I am from that circle[4] where the eyes
Of your chaste Marcia[5] are; she seems to pray,
  O holy man, that you still think her yours: 80
  For love of her receive us favourably.
Allow us through your seven kingdoms,[6] so
  That I may tell her of your kindness here,
  If you'll accept being talked of there below."
"Marcia was pleasing in my sight," he said,
  "While I was yonder in the living world,

---

1   Beatrice. See *Inf.* II.
2   Cato's "clothes" (his body) will be glorified on the Day of Judgement. It is clear that Cato, an unbaptized pagan who committed suicide, is saved.
3   Minos is the judge of the underworld (*Inf.* v, 1–12). Virgil, being in Limbo, is beyond his jurisdiction.
4   Limbo.
5   Cato's wife.
6   The seven terraces on Mount Purgatory, on which the seven deadly sins are purged.

And any kindness she required, I did.
Now that she is beyond the evil river,
   She cannot move me longer, by that law[1]
   Laid down when I went out from there for ever.[2]   90
But if a heavenly lady is your guide,
   As you declare, there is no need to flatter:
   Ask for her sake, you will not be denied.
Go now, and take this man, and round him wind
   A smooth and supple rush,[3] and wash his face
   Till there is nothing of it left uncleaned.
For it would not be fitting, with his eyes
   Still clouded over, to approach the First
   Custodian, one of those from Paradise.[4]
Upon this little island, and all round   100
   Its base where waves are beating on the shore,
   Rushes are growing in the muddy ground;
No other plant, not such as puts out leaves
   Or grows more stiff and hard, could flourish there,
   Not bending to the blows that it receives.
And afterwards, do not return this way;
   The sun, which now is rising, will reveal
   How you may climb the Mount more easily."
He disappeared; I got up from my knees
   Without a word and drew close to my guide,   110
   And now it was on him I fixed my eyes.
He said: "I shall go on; you follow after;
   We must turn back, for if we go that way,
   The land keeps sloping down right to the water."
The hour of matins[5] had begun to flee
   Before the breaking dawn, and in the distance
   I recognized the ripple of the sea.
We made our way across the lonely plain,
   Like one returning to the road he'd lost,
   Who till that moment seemed to walk in vain.   120
And when we came to where the dew had made
   A stand against the sun, a region where
   It thins out slowly, being in the shade,
My gentle master spread out either hand,
   Taking great care, upon the tender grass;
   And I, who gathered what was in his mind,
Lifted my face to him – it was still smeared
   With weeping, but my master rediscovered

1   The decree which separates the saved from the damned.
2   When, after the Crucifixion, Christ harrowed hell and released the souls of the virtuous.
3   A symbol of humility, the pliability of the soul to the will of God.
4   The angel at the gate of Mount Purgatory.
5   The first of the canonical hours (times for prayer) of the Church, usually observed just
before daybreak.

That colour the Inferno had obscured.[1]
We came then to that solitary shore   130
   Which never saw its waters navigated
   By men who made their way back home once more.[2]
And there he girded me, as pleased Another.[3]
   And what a miracle! Where he had torn
   The humble plant up that he chose to gather,
It was straightway, identically, reborn.

---

1   Dante's normal complexion had been hidden by the filth of the Inferno.
2   Ulysses made his way there, but did not survive. See *Inf.* xxvi, especially ll. 127–42.
3   See *Inf.* xxvi, 141.

CANTO II

Dante and Virgil are uncertain where to go next. Suddenly they notice a white light on the horizon, which rapidly grows brighter and more distinct. Virgil tells Dante to kneel down in respect: this is one of God's angels, in a boat borne over the sea by no human means, and bringing the souls of the saved to Purgatory. As they land, the angel blesses them, they all spill out onto the beach, and the angel departs as quickly as he had come.

The new arrivals are bewildered by their new surroundings, and they ask Virgil and Dante the way to the Mountain. Virgil explains that they also are strangers there. Then the others notice that Dante is breathing, and they crowd around him in wonder.

One of these spirits, the singer and composer Casella, comes forward to embrace Dante who, recognizing him as an old friend, tries to return the embrace; but his arms meet empty air, for this is an incorporeal spirit. Dante learns that Casella's crossing to the island of Purgatory was delayed for some time after his death, but that he is one of those who have benefited from the plenary indulgences available in the Church's Jubilee Year of 1300. In response to Dante's request, Casella sings one of Dante's own poems. Everyone is enraptured by the singing, but Cato interrupts this apparently harmless amusement to warn them that their duty now is to go to the Mountain and purify themselves of the last traces of their sin. The souls of the saved flee towards the Mountain, and Dante and Virgil move as quickly as any of them.

The poet shows here, as so often, his humanity and at the same time his sense of duty. It is natural that the newly dead should continue to be attracted by what pleased them in their old lives, but they must learn to forsake their old ways, even their most noble and refined ones, in order to fulfil their eternal destiny: Cato is acting as the voice of conscience.

> The sun had made his journey by this time
>   To the horizon, whose meridian covers,
>   At its most lofty point, Jerusalem –
> And night, wheeling as always opposite,
>   Was rising from the Ganges with the Scales,
>   Which she lets drop when she is dominant;
> So that Aurora's cheeks, first white and then
>   Tinged with vermilion, where I stood and watched,
>   Were glowing golden as old age drew on.[1]
> We were still lingering beside the ocean,   10

---

1   Lines 1–9: with the sun at the western horizon of the northern hemisphere, it is now
     sunset at Jerusalem (the centre of the inhabited world, as it was then known), while night
     is rising from the Ganges at the eastern limit of this world. Therefore the sun is now
     rising in Purgatory, which is in the southern hemisphere, directly opposite Jerusalem.
     The constellation Libra ("the Scales") dominates the night sky in spring (the time of
     Dante's journey), until after the autumn equinox, when the nights are longer than the
     days. Dawn is personified as the goddess Aurora, ageing as the day breaks. This complex
     description is not merely a piece of bravura: by means of it Dante reminds us of how
     his universe is arranged.

Like men uncertain of the way to take,
Themselves immobile but their hearts in motion.
Then just as, overtaken by the day,
    Mars reddens through dense vapours in the west
    Scarcely above the surface of the sea,
So I saw what I hope to see at last[1] –
    A light that came across the sea so swiftly
    No bird in flight could ever be so fast.
I looked again, when I had glanced from it
    One instant only, questioning my guide,   20
    And found that it had grown more broad and bright.
Then suddenly I saw on either side
    A something that was white, while underneath
    Another whiteness gradually appeared.
And still my master did not say a word,
    Till the first whitenesses were clearly wings;
    Then, seeing who the pilot was, he cried:
"Down, down, immediately, and bend your knees!
    This is God's angel! Join your hands in prayer:
    From now on you will see such ministers.   30
See how he scorns human contrivances,
    And needs no oar, nor any other sail
    Than his own wings between such distant shores.
See how he holds them pointing to the skies,
    Fanning the air with those eternal pinions,
    Which do not moult as mortal plumage does."
And then, as he came near, and yet more near,
    That bird of God, he grew more luminous,
    And brighter than my eyes could now endure,
So that I lowered my gaze – the boat meanwhile   40
    Swept into shore: it was so light and swift
    It sank into the water not at all.
The sailor sent from heaven stood astern,
    Sealed, so it seemed, with his beatitude.
    More than a hundred spirits sat therein,
And as they sat they sang in unison:
    "*In exitu Israel de Ægypto*",[2]
    With all that's written after in that psalm.
He made the sign of Holy Cross, and they
    Flung themselves down as one upon the shore,   50
    And quickly as he'd come, he went away.
It looked as though the crowd who'd landed there
    Were strangers in that place, all gazing round

---

1   Dante hopes to return to Purgatory after his death, in order to go eventually to heaven.
2   "When Israel went out of Egypt": the beginning of Psalm 114, a celebration of the
    release of the children of Israel from slavery, and here with the allegorical sense of the
    release of souls from sin.

Like people seeing things not seen before.
Now on all sides the sun was shooting day,
    Having with his unfailing arrows hunted
    Capricorn from the centre of the sky,[1]
When the newcomers turned to us and said:
    "Point out the way to take us to the mountain –
    That is, if you're familiar with the road."   60
And Virgil said: "Perhaps you think we are
    At home here, well acquainted with this place;
    But we are wandering strangers, as you are.
We came here just before you did, but by
    Another road,[2] a road so rough and hard
    That this climb facing us[3] will seem child's play."
The spirits, who had gathered what it meant
    That I was breathing – I was still alive –
    Had turned quite pale in their astonishment.
As people, hungry for good tidings, rush   70
    Around an olive-bearing messenger,[4]
    And no one hesitates to shove and push,
So everybody there, each happy soul,
    Stood gazing at my face, as though forgetting
    To go and make themselves more beautiful.[5]
And then I noticed one of them, who came
    Up to embrace me, and with such affection
    That he moved me to do the very same.
Oh shades, in all but your appearance, vain!
    Three times I clasped my hands behind him, and   80
    Three times I brought them to my breast again.
Wonder, I think, was what my face displayed,
    So that the shade drew back a little, smiling,
    And I pressed forward, following his lead.
He told me gently that I should hold back:
    And then I realized who he was, and begged him
    To pause a moment so that we might talk.
He answered me: "Because you had my love
    While bound in flesh, and have it now I'm freed,
    I'll pause; but why do you walk here, alive?"   90
"Casella,[6] friend, to come another time
    To where I am," I said, "I make this journey;[7]

---

1   The risen sun, which is in Aries, has made the constellation Capricorn move down from
    the zenith, where it was at sunrise. The sun is personified as the archer god Apollo.
2   Through the Inferno.
3   The ascent of Mount Purgatory.
4   An olive branch was a sign that the news was good.
5   To purify themselves from the last traces of sin.
6   A man of whom little is known, except that he sang and set words to music.
7   Dante knows that the purpose of his journey is to make him worthy of salvation.

But why are you deprived of so much time?"[1]
He said: "I have been done no injury,
   Though he who carries whom and when he pleases[2]
   Had several times refused to carry me,
Since his is fashioned by a will that's fair.[3]
   Nevertheless, for three months he has taken
   All wishing to embark, without demur.[4]
So he, when I'd arrived upon the shore,   100
   There where the River Tiber meets salt water,[5]
   Kindly received me as a passenger.
He is now winging to that mouth again,
   For it is there that all souls always gather,
   Unless they sink down to the Acheron."[6]
I answered: "If no legislation here
   Bans use or memory of those loving songs
   Which always fully solaced my desire,
I beg you sing them, and refresh somewhat
   My soul which, since it travelled with my body   110
   To reach this place, is utterly tired out!"
"Love who is talking with me in my mind…"[7]
   So he began to sing, and sang so sweetly
   That I still hear the sweetness of that sound.
My master then, and I, and all that band
   Around the singer seemed so well contented
   As nothing else could ever come to mind.
All of us were entranced, intent upon
   The notes, when, "What is this, you idle spirits?"
   It was that venerable aged man,[8]   120
Who cried: "What negligence! And what a waste
   Of time! Run to the mountain; cast the slough[9]
   That will not let you see God manifest."
As pigeons that have gathered for their feed,
   And peck and pick up grains of wheat or tares,
   Calmly, with none of their accustomed pride,[10]

---

1   Time to complete his purgation. Dante, who must have known that Casella had been
   dead for a while, is surprised to find him arriving only now at the island of Purgatory.
   All those in Purgatory feel the need to complete their purgation as quickly as possible.
2   The angel who ferries the souls to Purgatory.
3   His will is conformed to God's. No reason is given for the angel's previous refusals.
4   Since the Christmas of 1299, when the Pope declared the start of the Jubilee Year of
   1300, with the possibility of gaining plenary indulgences for the dead.
5   Where the Tiber flows into the Tyrrhenian Sea.
6   The souls of the saved assemble at the mouth of the Tiber, and the damned on the bank
   of Acheron.
7   The first line of a *canzone* by Dante which is discussed in the third section of his *Convivio*.
8   Cato.
9   Their covering of sin.
10 An allusion to the way a pigeon struts with pouting breast.

Should something happen to provoke their fear,
    Straight away leave their victuals where they are,
    Being concerned with some much greater care –
Just so I saw that group who'd just come there   130
    Desert the singing for the mountainside,
    Like men who rush away and don't know where:
Nor was our own departure with less speed.

CANTO III

The souls of those destined for Purgatory are running towards the Mountain. So are Dante and Virgil. But Dante clings to Virgil, while Virgil himself seems shamefaced, regretting their dilatoriness which earned Cato's rebuke. As Virgil slows to a walk, Dante looks up at the Mountain rising so far above the sea.

Dante is frightened when he sees that only one shadow, his own, is visible on the ground in front of him, and suspects that he has been abandoned. Virgil is still there, however; but his mortal body was buried in Italy, and his present one is diaphanous and therefore casts no shadow, although he still feels pain and cold and heat. As Virgil explains, the human mind cannot conceive how this may be, and must be contented with the fact itself.

Meanwhile the pilgrims have come to the foot of the Mountain where it rises sheer. While they are wondering what to do next, they see another group of souls approaching them and moving very slowly. Virgil and Dante make towards them and, when the souls notice this, they huddle together against the rock in their uncertainty. Those in front see that Dante is casting a shadow – behind him now and stretching out to the edge of the mountain, since the sun is low on the horizon – and they are baffled. Virgil explains the reason for this and says that Dante's journey is sanctioned by God. The souls tell them the way to go and courteously ask them to walk in front.

One of the souls explains that he is Manfred, once the ruler of Sicily, who was killed in battle and was refused Christian burial because he was excommunicate. Since he repented only at the instant of death, his entry into Purgatory, like that of the other souls with him, is delayed for a period thirty times the length of his contumacy. This period can, however, be shortened by the prayers of the living.

B ut while those spirits, put to sudden flight,
    Were scattering pell-mell towards that Mountain
    Where we are goaded on by what is right,
I drew much closer to my trusty guide.
    For how could I have carried on without him?
    Who could have led me up the mountainside?
It seemed to me that he felt culpable:[1]
    Oh, what a fine, discriminating conscience,
    To whom each petty fault's a bitter pill!
Now, when his feet had given up that speed   10
    Which robs all actions of their dignity,
    My mind, which had been too preoccupied,
Widened its scope in curiosity,
    And saw the Mountain rising from the water
    Up to the sky, as far as eye could see.
The sun's rays, which were flaming red behind,
    Were broken by the obstruction of my body,
    And formed my shape before me on the ground.

---

1   After Cato's rebuke in the previous canto.

I turned and looked beside me, now afraid
   That I had been abandoned, since I saw,   20
   In front of me alone, the earth in shade;
But then my comforter: "Still terrified?"
   He questioned, and he turned around to face me.
   "Can't you believe I'm with you as your guide?
It is now evening where they buried me[1] –
   My flesh and blood which used to cast a shadow –
   In Naples, carried there from Brindisi.[2]
Therefore, if there's no shadow made by me,
   You should not wonder more than at the heavens,
   Since none of them obstructs another's ray.[3]   30
The heavenly Power creates bodies like those,[4]
   Except they suffer and feel cold and heat,
   But will not have us know just how He does.
One would be mad to think a human brain
   Could make its way along that endless road
   One Substance in three Persons[5] travels on.
Be happy with the *quia*,[6] men of earth;
   For if you had been able to see all,
   Mary had never needed to give birth;
And you have seen those men who longed in vain,[7]   40
   Who could, if any could, have stilled that longing
   Which now is given them for eternal pain –
Aristotle, Plato and all the rest –
   So many others." And he bowed his head
   And said no more, but clearly was distressed.[8]
We came upon the Mountain's base meanwhile;
   And there we found the rock face was so sheer
   The nimblest legs would be of no avail.
The loneliest broken cliff between Turbia
   And Lerici's a broad and easy stairway[9]   50
   Compared to the ascent we're faced with here.
"Now, who knows where there is some gentler slope,"
   My master wondered, and he paused a while,
   "Where men who have no wings can clamber up?"

---

1   As the sun is rising in Purgatory it is evening in Italy.
2   Virgil died in Brindisi, and he was taken to Naples for burial.
3   The heavens were thought to be concentric transparent spheres, on which the stars and
    planets revolved.
4   Like the heavenly spheres.
5   The Blessed Trinity.
6   A medieval scholastic term, indicating what is, as opposed to how or why it is.
7   In Limbo (*Inf.* IV). Their longing is for knowledge and understanding.
8   Virgil is himself one of those condemned to Limbo, because he was not baptized, and
    suffering the pain of unsatisfied longing, since he is separated from God.
9   These places, where in Dante's day the cliffs fell sheer into the sea, are at the western
    and eastern limits of the Italian Riviera.

THE RADIANT PLANET, LOVE'S ENCOURAGER,
OCCASIONED HAPPY LAUGHTER THROUGH THE EAST...

PURGATORY I, 19–20

"DOWN, DOWN, IMMEDIATELY, AND BEND YOUR KNEES!
THIS IS GOD'S ANGEL! JOIN YOUR HANDS IN PRAYER"...

PURGATORY II, 28–29

And while he pondered which way we might take,
   Keeping his eyes still fixed upon the ground,
   And I looked up, examining the rock,
A band of souls came shuffling into view
   Upon the left, and moved their feet our way,
   But hardly seemed to, since they were so slow.   60
"Lift up your eyes from off the ground, my master.
   You see these people here: they will advise us,
   If you yourself cannot provide the answer."
Then he looked up, seemed to be more serene,
   And said: "We'll go to them, since they come slowly;
   Meanwhile you can be full of hope, my son."
And still that band of people was as far –
   Even when we had gone a thousand paces –
   As a good stone's throw by a mighty thrower,
When they flattened themselves against the rock   70
   Which stood so high, and huddled up, like people
   Who don't know where to go, but stop and look.
"O you who've ended well, you the elect,"
   Said Virgil, "by the virtue of that peace
   Which I am certain all of you expect,
Inform us where the mountainside slopes least
   And where it's possible to make the ascent:
   Wise men are most annoyed when time is lost."
Even as sheep that come out of the fold
   By one, by two, by three, while others stand   80
   And timidly keep eyes and muzzles lowered –
And what the first sheep does the others do,
   Crowding upon it should it chance to stop,
   All meek and mild, not knowing why they do –
So I saw then the leaders of that flock,
   So happy in their fortune,[1] coming forward
   With humble faces at a steady walk.
When those in front noticed on my right side
   That the sun's light upon the ground was broken,
   My shadow stretching to the mountainside,   90
They stopped walking, and then stepped back a bit,
   And all the others coming up behind them,
   Without knowing the reason, did just that.
"Before you ask, I want to make it plain:
   This is a human body that you see,
   Which causes the occlusion of the sun.
Don't be surprised, however wonderful
   This seems: not without strength derived from Heaven
   Does he intend to scale this obstacle."
So said my master; to which "Turn around,"   100

---

1   Because they are destined for heaven.

Those worthy people said, "and go before us,"
And showed the way with gestures of the hand.
One of them said: "Whoever you may be,
  Look back as you are walking, and consider
  If ever, back there,¹ you set eyes on me."
I turned and looked at him with steady eyes:
  Though he was fair and handsome and looked noble,
  A blow had cloven one of his eyebrows.
When I in all humility confessed
  I'd never seen him, he replied: "But look!"   110
  And pointed to a wound high on his chest.
"I am Manfred,"² he told me, and he smiled,
  "The grandson of the Empress Constance; and
  I beg you, when you're once more in the world,
To go and see my lovely daughter, mother
  Of kings of Sicily and Aragon;
  Tell her the truth,³ if she's heard something other.
After I'd had my body riven by
  Two mortal wounds, I wept, and I repented
  To Him Who gives His pardon readily.   120
My sins were dreadful, but the infinite
  Goodness has arms which it keeps open wide,
  Embracing all of those who turn to it.
And had the Bishop of Cosenza known
  And understood that aspect of the Lord,
  When Clement sent him out to hunt me down,
My body's bones, still buried, would have lain
  Against the bridge's head by Benevento,
  Under the shelter of the heavy cairn.⁴
Now they are scattered by the wind and drenched   130
  With rain, outside the Kingdom,⁵ near the Verde,⁶
  Where he transported them with candles quenched.⁷
For all their maledictions there's not one
  So lost eternal love may not return,

---

1   In the world of the living.
2   Born in Sicily c.1231, the natural son of the Emperor Frederick II. He was appointed
    regent of Sicily in 1250 and became King in 1258. He was a Ghibelline, and was excom-
    municated by two Popes. Defeated by Charles of Anjou (who was supported by Pope
    Clement IV) at Benevento in 1266, he was killed in the battle.
3   That, although excommunicate, he has been saved.
4   Manfred could not be laid in consecrated ground, because he had been excommunicated.
    Charles of Anjou, however, had him buried with honour under a cairn to which each
    of Charles's soldiers contributed a stone.
5   Outside the lands of the Church.
6   The river known now as the Garigliano.
7   It was the custom to take the bodies of heretics and excommunicates to the grave with
    candles inverted and extinguished. It would seem that Manfred's remains were not
    buried, or at least not buried very well, after their removal from the cairn.

As long as hope still shows a touch of green.
The truth is, he who dies unreconciled
  With Holy Church, repenting *in extremis*,
  Has to be dilatory too outside
This threshold, thirty years for every year
  He lived in his presumption, if that time   140
  Be not abbreviated by true prayer.
So now you know the way to gladden me,
  If you tell Constance, my beloved daughter,[1]
  How you have found me here, and that decree:
Those over there[2] can make our time here shorter."

---

1   See ll. 115–17.
2   People who are still alive.

CANTO IV

Much of this canto consists in explanations – of the make-up of the human soul, of the reason for the sun's apparently erratic course, and of the nature of Mount Purgatory.

Dante's insistence on the oneness of the human person allows him to indicate how much time has passed since he and Virgil arrived on the island. It also, by implication, stresses an essential assumption behind the *Comedy* – that each human being is an indivisible whole and responsible for his actions.

Dante and Virgil begin their ascent through a gap in the rock. Its narrowness may bring to mind Christ's saying: "Strait is the gate, and narrow is the way, which leadeth unto life…" (Matt. 7:14). The track they take has to be "flown" rather than trodden: this metaphor is first a hyperbolic way of conveying the steepness of the track, and then indicative of the eagerness which alone can scale these heights. This movement between the concrete and the abstract, and the literal and the figurative, exemplifies in a few lines the modus operandi of the poem as a whole.

When the two reach at last a level terrace, Virgil explains how normal astronomical assumptions are reversed in the southern hemisphere. He also encourages Dante by telling him that the ascent becomes easier as one goes on.

The pilgrims are surprised by a voice coming from behind a large boulder. This is Belacqua, languidly awaiting his time to enter Purgatory proper. He, with the other souls there, delayed his repentance until the time of death, and so he has to wait outside for a time equal to that which he spent on earth. The conversation between Dante and Belacqua is on a low key, intimate and teasing as befits old friends.

Virgil, as so often, reminds Dante that they have no time to waste, since it is now midday where they are and – as follows from what has been said previously – night time in the northern hemisphere, where the living are.

W hen, for the pleasure it affords, or hurt,
    Something attracts one of our faculties,
    And our soul's focused utterly on that,
It heeds no other faculty at all;
    And this disproves that error which maintains
    That there is kindled in us soul on soul.[1]
Therefore, when there is something seen or heard
    Engaging utterly the soul's attention,
    Time passes by us and we pay no heed;
There is one faculty to watch time pass,   10
    Another one which occupies the soul:
    This one's engaged, while that one's not in use.
I had experience of precisely that,

---

1   The "error" of l. 5 is Plato's: that there are, in each human being, several souls, each with a separate function. Dante maintains that there is one soul which contains different faculties: one faculty, when it is operating intensely, can impede the operation of the others.

Hearing that spirit[1] speak and marvelling;
    Because the sun had now ascended quite
Fifty degrees,[2] without my noting it,
    When we came where those spirits with one voice
    Told us: "This is the place you asked about."
With the few thorns he has on his pitchfork,
    The farmer often blocks a wider gap,[3]   20
    Then when his grapes are starting to turn dark,
Than that space up through which my guide, with me
    Behind, began to climb, we two alone,
    After that band of souls had gone away.
Men climb up to San Leo, or climb down
    To Noli, or surmount Bismantova[4] –
    And all on foot; but this path must be flown;
I mean with swift wings feathered for their flight
    With strong desire, and following that guide
    Who gave me hope and acted as my light.   30
We went up through a broken rocky fissure,
    Whose sides were pressing closely in on us,
    On ground demanding feet and hands together.
When we had climbed across the topmost brow
    Of that high bank, onto the open slope,
    I had to ask my master: "Which way now?"
He said: "You must not take one step aside;
    But keep on climbing up straight after me,
    Until we come across some expert guide."
The peak was distant; it was out of sight –   40
    The slope fell much more steeply than a line
    Drawn from mid-quadrant to the centre point.[5]
From utter weariness I made this plea:
    "O kindly father, turn around and look:
    I'm left alone, unless you wait for me."
"Drag yourself till you get to that," he said,
    Showing a terrace somewhat higher up,
    Which went around the Mountain on that side.
His words spurred me to such an effort that
    I crawled to him on hands and knees, until   50
    The curving terrace lay beneath my feet.
There we sat down, the two of us together,
    Both looking east, towards the way we'd come:

---

1   Manfred (*Purg.* III, 103–45).
2   Three hours and twenty minutes had passed since the sun's rising.
3   In a hedge, to guard the ripening grapes against thieves or animals.
4   San Leo is a town on a steep hill, not far from San Marino, accessible in Dante's day
    only by a narrow path cut into the rock; Noli is on the Gulf of Genoa, accessible at
    that time only by sea or by a difficult climb down the mountain behind it; the Rock of
    Bismantova, located in the Apennines, is accessible only by one difficult track.
5   The gradient was much greater than 45°.

To look back thus can often be a pleasure!
I fixed my eyes first on the lowest shores,
   Then raised them to the sun, and was astonished,
   For it was from the left it sent its rays![1]
The poet saw just how it was with me –
   Dumbfounded by the chariot of light
   Between us and the north upon its way.   60
"If Castor and Pollux,"[2] he explained to me,
   "Were travelling together with that mirror[3]
   Which takes light up and down,[4] then you would see
The reddish section of the Zodiac[5]
   Revolving even closer to the Bears,[6]
   Unless it had abandoned its old track.[7]
If you would understand how that can be,
   Then pull yourself together: think of Zion[8]
   And this Mount placed on earth in such a way
There's one horizon for the two of them,   70
   But different hemispheres;[9] so that the road[10]
   Which Phaethon badly drove his chariot on[11]
Passes this Mountain here upon one side,
   And Zion on the other, as you see
   If you have listened and have understood."
"My master," I replied, "I certainly,
   When it appeared that I was baffled, never
   Saw anything as clearly as I see
That the celestial motion's median,
   Known to one branch of learning as the equator,[12]   80
   Always between the winter and the sun,[13]
For the reason you give, from here is quite
   As far towards the north, as to the Hebrews

---

1   In the northern hemisphere, to which Dante is accustomed, anyone looking east sees
     the sun rising on his right, between him and the south.
2   The constellation Gemini, the Twins.
3   The sun, presumably because it receives its light from God and reflects it down to earth.
     When the sun is in the constellation Gemini, the summer solstice is approaching.
4   North and south, between the tropics of Cancer and Capricorn.
5   Glowing red from the presence of the sun.
6   To the north, represented by the constellations of the Great Bear (Ursa Major) and the
     Little Bear (Ursa Minor).
7   Regarded as an impossibility.
8   One of the hills of Jerusalem, and used by synecdoche for the city itself.
9   Jerusalem and Purgatory are directly opposite each other, in the northern and southern
     hemispheres respectively.
10 The course taken by the sun.
11 The mythical Phaethon was permitted to guide the chariot of the sun, but proved
     unequal to the task.
12 The celestial equator.
13 When the sun is north of this line, it is winter in the southern hemisphere, and summer
     in the northern hemisphere, and vice versa when the sun is south of this line.

It was towards the region which is hot.[1]
But if it pleases you, I'd like to know
  How far we have to travel, for the Mountain
  Goes up much farther than my eyes can go."
He said: "The nature of our Mountain's this:
  Beginning from the base is always hard,
  And yet the higher one goes, the less distress.   90
And therefore, when it seems the slope's become
  So gentle going further up's as easy
  As gliding on a ship and with the stream,
You've come to where this track goes on no more,
  And where you may expect to have some rest.
  That's all I'll say, but that I know for sure."
And when he'd finished telling me all that,
  A voice was heard nearby: "It's possible,
  Before you reach that stage, you'll want to sit!"
And at that sound we both turned round and saw   100
  There was on our left hand a massive boulder
  Neither of us had chanced to see before.
And there were people, once we got to this,
  Stock-still behind that boulder in the shade,
  In attitudes betraying negligence.
One of them, such it seemed his lassitude,
  Was sitting with his arms around his knees,
  Looking between them, and with lowered head.
"My kindly lord," I said, "just look at this
  One here! He seems to be more negligent[2]   110
  Than if his sister's name were Laziness."
Then turning to us more attentively,
  Raising his gaze somewhat above his thighs,
  He said: "You climb! You've got the energy!"
Then I knew who he was, and all that pain
  Which made my breathing rather rapid still
  Did not prevent my reaching him; and when
I did reach him, he hardly raised his head
  To ask: "Now do you fathom how the sun
  Can drive his chariot on our left side?"   120
His negligent behaviour and his brief
  Words moved my lips to hazard a slow smile;
  I said: "Belacqua,[3] I no longer grieve
For you – but tell me: why do you sit down
  Just on this spot? You're waiting for a guide?
  Or fallen into your old ways again?"

---

1 Towards the south. In his reference to the Hebrews, Dante is thinking of the time before
    the Diaspora.
2 Neglectful of his secular and religious duties.
3 A Florentine lute-maker and a friend of Dante. Dante is glad to find that he is one of
    the saved.

"Brother," he said, "and if I were to climb,
   God's angel who is sitting by the threshold
   Would not allow me through to martyrdom.[1]
First it's essential that the heavens turn round   130
   Me here outside,[2] as often as in life,
   Since I put off repenting till the end,
Unless to bring me aid there are some prayers,
   Arising from a heart that lives in grace:
   What use are other kinds, which Heaven ignores?"
Now Virgil was before me and in motion,
   Saying: "Come now: the sun is at its height
   Here, while already by the shore of Ocean[3]
Night covers up Morocco with her foot."[4]

---

1   The torments by which the souls in Purgatory are purified.
2   Outside the gate of Purgatory. Belacqua's entry to Purgatory is delayed for the length
     of his time on earth.
3   The sea beyond the Pillars of Hercules, which themselves marked the western limit of
     the known world.
4   It is midday in Purgatory, in the southern hemisphere, and night time in the northern
     hemisphere.

CANTO V

Dante pauses by souls who are staring at him because he casts a shadow. Virgil reproves him for wasting time, and Dante reddens in shame.

Meanwhile a band of souls singing a penitential psalm crosses the slope above the pilgrims. They also are amazed that Dante casts a shadow, and they send two of their band to find the reason for this. Virgil tells them that Dante is still alive and can be of service to them.

Virgil warns Dante to keep on walking, although so many souls are crowding round. These are, as they explain, people who died violently and did not repent of their sins until the last. Dante does not recognize any of them, but swears that he will help in any way he can.

Three of these souls (contemporaries of Dante, whose violent deaths were notorious) come forward to beg for prayers. The first is Jacopo del Cassero, who was assassinated in a region where he thought he was quite safe. With that courtesy typical of the souls here, he tells Dante that he need not swear to help, since everyone believes in his good intentions. Then he explains, briefly and without self-pity, how he came to die, and he asks Dante to ask for prayers for him in his birthplace, Fano.

The second soul is Buonconte da Montefeltro, killed in the Battle of Campaldino, whose body was never recovered. He died repentant, invoking the name of the Virgin Mary. His fate contrasts with that of his father, Guido, whose fate was described in *Inferno* xxvii. Good and evil angels quarrel over his soul also, but on this occasion the good angel wins, and the evil angel is allowed only to wreak his ill will on Buonconte's body.

The third soul, Pia, shows concern for Dante's welfare, before she asks him to pray for her. This concern, together with the quiet way she alludes to her own violent death, ends the canto on a note of calm resignation.

I'd left those shades, and I was on my way
    Already, in the footsteps of my leader,
    When one of them exclaimed, pointing at me:
"It looks as though the sun's rays do not shine
    On the left side of him who follows after,[1]
    Who seems to move like someone who's alive!"
I turned towards them once these words were spoken,
    And saw them staring in bewilderment
    At me, at me and where the light was broken.
"Why is your mind caught up in such a snare,"   10
    My master asked, "that you are slowing down?
    What's it to you what they are murmuring there?
Come after me, and let those people talk:
    Stand like a sturdy tower, whose utmost height,
    Whatever winds may blow, will never shake.
For he in whom a fresh thought starts to sprout
    After his first thought, weakens his intention:

---

1   This is the same surprise at Dante's shadow which was shown in *Purg.* iii, 88–96 and will be seen again in ll. 25–36 of this canto.

The new thought's impulse saps the former thought."
I said: "I'm coming." What else could I say?
   I said it, shaded somewhat with that colour   20
   Which may procure us pardon possibly.[1]
Meanwhile, across the slope that we were on,
   People came but a little way above us,
   Chanting "*Miserere*"[2] in antiphon.
When they had noticed I permitted no
   Way for the rays of light to pierce my body,
   They changed their song into a long hoarse "Oh!"
And two of them, acting as messengers,
   Hurried to meet us and made this request:
   "Explain to us what your condition is."   30
My master answered: "Go back to the ones
   Who sent you to us, and inform them truly
   That this man's body's made of blood and bones.
If but to see his shadow made them waver,
   As I believe, they have their answer: let them
   Do him honour: he can return the favour."[3]
I have not ever seen the open sky
   At nightfall rent by fiery vapours,[4] nor
   At sunset August clouds, as rapidly
As those two envoys went back up again;   40
   And, having got there, turned round with the others
   Like horsemen speeding without drawing rein.
"There are so many crowding in upon
   Us, and requesting help," the poet said.
   "Don't stop, but listen as you carry on."
"O soul making your way to happiness,
   Still with those limbs you had when you were born,"
   They shouted on arrival, "stay with us.
See if there's anybody here you know,
   So that you may take news of him back there.[5]   50
   Please won't you stop? Why do you have to go?
We died by violence; till our final hour
   All of us lived as unrepentant sinners;
   Then light from heaven made us so aware
That, penitent, forgiving and at peace
   With God, we left that life behind us, with
   Our hearts pierced with the urge to see His face."
"However hard I gaze at you like this,"

---

1   Only "possibly", since one may blush for reasons other than repentance.
2   "Have mercy" (Latin). This occurs at the beginning of Psalm 51, a penitential psalm.
3   Dante can revive knowledge of them in the world of the living, and also pray for their souls.
4   Shooting stars when they rend the open sky, and lightning flashes when they rend the August clouds.
5   Into the world of the living.

I said, "there's none I recognize; yet if
   There's something in my power, souls born for bliss,   60
Say it, and I shall do it, by that peace
   Which makes me seek itself from world to world,
   In the footsteps of such a guide as this."
One of them[1] spoke: "Don't swear it:[2] we can all
   Rely on your good offices, provided
   You find the task is not impossible.
So I, who speak before these others do,
   Beg – if you ever see the lands between
   Romagna and the realm of Charles[3] – that you
Show me such kindness as to ask that they   70
   In Fano offer prayers in grace[4] that my
   Heavy offences may be purged away.
That was where I was born; but the deep wounds
   From which my lifeblood issued were inflicted
   On me in Antenor's descendants' lands,[5]
There where I thought that I was most secure:
   He of Este[6] arranged it, hating me
   Beyond what justice gave him warrant for.
But had I only fled to Mira,[7] when
   I found them at my heels at Oriago,[8]   80
   I'd still be in the world of living men.
I ran into the marsh, where reeds and mud
   Entangled me; I fell – and there I saw
   My veins pour out into a lake of blood."
Another said: "So you be granted your
   Desire which draws you up the lofty Mountain,
   Be kind and helpful too to my desire!
From Montefeltro once, Buonconte now:[9]

---

1   Jacopo del Cassero, a Guelf leader, assassinated in 1298 on the orders of Azzo VIII of
   Este.
2   Dante has already sworn (in ll. 61–62) to keep his promise.
3   He is indicating the region of Marche, between Romagna to the north and the Kingdom
   of Naples, ruled by Charles of Anjou, to the south.
4   The only efficacious prayers are those of someone free from mortal sin.
5   The territory ruled by Padua, whose mythical founder was Antenor. According to some
   accounts, Antenor betrayed his own city, Troy, to the Greeks. The region of the Inferno
   reserved for such traitors is Antenora. Possibly Dante is hinting at some Paduan collusion
   in Jacopo's assassination.
6   Azzo VIII, lord of Ferrara 1293–1308. It is striking, but typical of the souls in Purgatory,
   that Jacopo tacitly agrees that he himself gave some reason to be hated.
7   A small town between Padua and Venice.
8   A village about nine miles from Venice, near the lagoons.
9   Buonconte da Montefeltro (a Ghibelline leader who fell in the Battle of Campaldino
   in 1298) is implying that the glory of his family name is no longer relevant to him. He
   is the son of Guido da Montefeltro (*Inf.* XXVII, 4–132), and it is illuminating to compare
   and contrast the fates of father and son.

Since no one, not Giovanna,[1] cares about me,
  I walk among these here with lowered brow."   90
I answered him: "What chance or forceful hand
  Took you so far away from Campaldino[2]
  Your place of burial was never found?"
"Across the Casentino's foothills[3] runs,"
  He said, "a river, the Archiano, born
  Above the convent[4] in the Apennines.
Where that river abandons its own name[5]
  I found my way at last, pierced through the throat,
  Fleeing on foot and bloodying the plain.
There both my sight and speech came to an end   100
  Saying the name of Mary;[6] there I fell,
  And on that spot my flesh alone remained.
This is the truth – repeat it to the living.
  God's angel took me, and the infernal one
  Shouted: "Oh, why are you from heaven depriving
Me of my rights? You carry him away –
  What is eternal of him – for one teardrop;
  But I shall treat the rest quite differently!"
You know how humid vapour in the air
  Condenses and is turned back into water   110
  When it reaches the colder atmosphere?
The always ill-intentioned will[7] is knit
  To intellect, and raises mist and wind
  By that power which is to him innate.[8]
He cloaked the valley, once the day was spent,
  From Pratomagno to the mighty ridge,[9]
  With cloud; and made the sky above more dense;
The saturated air turned into rain,
  Which as it fell flowed over so that gullies
  Took what the earth itself could not contain;   120
Then water gathered into torrents, and
  Rushed headlong down towards the royal river[10]
  At such a speed as nothing could withstand.
The turbulent Archiano came across
  My cold corpse, where it flows into the Arno,

---

1   His widow.
2   A small plain in the upper Arno valley.
3   The Casentino is a district in Tuscany which includes the upper Arno valley.
4   Known as the Camaldoli hermitage.
5   As it flows into the Arno.
6   His invocation of the Virgin Mary signifies his repentance.
7   The Devil.
8   It is an old tradition that the Devil has great power over matter.
9   From the Tuscan mountain ridge which marks the western end of the Casentino to the
    main ridge of the Apennines in the east.
10 This is the Arno, called "royal" because, unlike its tributaries, it flows directly into the sea.

And swept it in, breaking apart the cross
Made on my breast in my death agony,[1]
   Rolled me along the banks and riverbed,
   Then wrapped me in its booty and its prey."[2]
"When you are in the world of living men   130
   Once more, and fully rested from your journey,"
   A third soul followed on the second, "then
"Do please remember me – my name is Pia;
   Siena made, Maremma unmade me:
   And he knows all about that, who before
Had given ring and gem to marry me.[3]

---

1   He had made the sign of the cross with his arms folded across his breast.
2   The detritus which a river in spate sweeps along.
3   Almost all that is known about Pia is what Dante tells us – that she was born in Siena and died in Maremma (the notoriously unhealthy marshland on the Tuscan coast). The tradition is that her husband had her killed, but whether because he wished to remarry, or in revenge for some fault of hers, is uncertain. She seems to have died shortly before 1300.

CANTO VI

The two poets manage, with some difficulty, to continue their journey: they are delayed by the crowds of souls, some of whom Dante recognizes and names, who are all fervently asking for prayers to shorten the time before they enter Purgatory proper.

Once he has left the crowds behind, Dante asks Virgil to resolve a problem. He understands, correctly, that in his *Aeneid* Virgil has denied the possibility of prayers altering the decrees of Heaven, which is precisely what those souls have been begging for. Virgil explains that there is a difference between the prayers of pagans and those of Christians, the former being utterly inefficacious. Moreover, Dante is not being asked to pray for Heaven's decree to be altered, but merely for its accomplishment to come more quickly. Virgil adds that these matters are difficult, and says that Dante should keep the problem in mind until he meets Beatrice, who will explain further.

As they move on, making the most of the remaining daylight, they come across a solitary silent soul couched like a lion, and Virgil asks him the way. Once this soul, who turns out to be Sordello, a famous thirteenth-century poet and statesman, realizes that Virgil is a fellow Mantuan, the two embrace, and this gives Dante the opportunity to praise them for their affection as fellow citizens. This, he says, is in contrast to most of Italy where, since the imperial power is not being exercised properly, the country is the prey to conflicting and unscrupulous interests. Meanwhile, ignoring Christ's injunction of "Render unto Caesar…", the clergy attempt to wield secular power, and this makes matters worse. The Emperor, too concerned with increasing his power in Germany, should intervene to save Italy, "the garden of the Empire", from itself.

Dante singles out Florence for ironic praise: he sees his own city as typifying the worst tendencies of these Italian states, full of unrest and corruption.

When men are breaking up a dicing session,
    The loser stays behind unhappily,
    Repeats the throws, and learns a bitter lesson;
The winner goes surrounded by the crowd;
    One walks in front, one tugs him from the rear,
    One struggles to be noticed by his side:
He does not pause, but heeds that one and this;
    And those his hand goes out to, then move off;
    And so he travels safely through the press.
With all of them around, that's how I was –   10
    Turning my face on this side and on that,
    Freeing myself by making promises.[1]
The Aretine[2] Ghino di Tacco[3] sent
    To death so brutally was there, and also

---

1   Promising to pray for the curtailment of the souls' time outside Purgatory.
2   Benincasa da Laterina, a thirteenth-century Aretine judge, who sentenced to death a relative of Ghino di Tacco.
3   An infamous bandit who murdered Benincasa da Laterina in revenge.

The other who was drowned during the hunt.[1]
I noted too, hands stretching out to plead,
    Federigo Novello,[2] and the Pisan[3]
    Who made Marzucco show such fortitude.
I saw Count Orso,[4] and that soul which was
    Split from the body out of spite and envy,   20
    As he said, not for any fault of his –
Pierre de la Brosse[5] I mean. Because of this,
    The living Lady of Brabant must change,
    Or she'll be numbered in a herd that's worse.[6]
When I was free at last from every shade
    That prayed continually for men to pray
    To shorten time till they were sanctified,
I questioned: "O my light, it seems to me
    That you deny expressly in one passage
    That prayer can ever alter Heaven's decree;[7]   30
Yet that is what these souls are praying for.
    Could it be that this hope of theirs is vain?
    Or are you, as I read you, not quite clear?"
"My meaning is apparent," he replied,
    "And yet that hope of theirs is not deceptive,
    If one considers with an open mind:
Celestial judgement's not impaired, although
    The fire of love accomplishes instanter
    The expiation which these souls here owe;
And, where I made my point clear when I said   40
    That prayer could not make up for what was lacking,
    That was because such prayers could not reach God.[8]
However, in a matter of such doubt
    Do not desist till she, who'll be a light
    Between the truth and intellect, speaks out.
Make no mistake, for I mean Beatrice:
    You will see her above, upon this Mountain's
    Summit, and see her smile in happiness."
I said: "My lord, let us increase our speed:

---

1   Guccio dei Tarlati da Pietramala, a thirteenth-century Aretine Ghibelline, who drowned
    in the Arno while pursuing, or being pursued by, Guelf exiles from Arezzo.
2   Killed c.1290, son of Count Guido Novello.
3   A son of Marzucco degli Scornigiani, probably the one killed in 1287 on the orders of
    Ugolino della Gherardesca (*Inf.* XXXII, 125*ff*; XXXIII, 1–90).
4   Orso degli Alberti, killed in 1286 by his cousin.
5   Chamberlain of Philip III of France. On the death of Louis, Philip's son by his first wife,
    Pierre accused the second wife, Mary of Brabant, of poisoning Louis to secure the suc-
    cession of her own son. Pierre was executed in 1278. The charge against him was not
    revealed, and Dante clearly regards him as an innocent victim of Mary of Brabant.
6   Unless she repents, she will be damned.
7   *Aeneid* VI, 376: "Do not hope to change the decrees of the gods by prayer".
8   Since they were the prayers of pagans.

I'm not so weary as I was before,   50
  And look, the slope already casts a shade!"
"We shall go forward with the light of day,"
  He answered then, "as far as possible;
  But things are not as you would have them be.
He[1] will return, before you reach the height,
  Who is already covered by the slope
  So that you fail to interrupt his light.
But see that soul who's sitting all alone
  And looking over here in our direction?
  He'll teach us the best road to travel on."   60
We went to him. O soul of Lombardy,
  What pride and what disdain was in your stance,
  And in your glance what truth and gravity!
He uttered nothing while we were approaching,
  But let us come, and kept his eyes upon us,
  Just as a lion does when it is couching.
Yet Virgil went right up to him, and pressed
  Him to point out the easiest ascent;
  And he made no reply to that request,
But asked about our city and our way   70
  Of life; and my dear lord was just beginning
  "*Mantua*..." when that shadow, previously
So self-absorbed, spoke to him as he raised
  Himself: "O Mantuan, I am Sordello,[2]
  Of your own city!" and the two embraced.
O abject Italy, O seat of sorrow,
  Vessel without a pilot in a storm,
  No queen of provinces, but a bordello!
That noble soul was eager, merely when
  He heard his city mentioned, even there,[3]   80
  To make friends with a fellow citizen;
But now nobody lives in you without
  War, where they go on gnawing at each other,
  Even encircled by one wall, one moat.
O squalid Italy, search all your seas
  And coasts around, then look inland, and see
  If any part of you delights in peace.
What is the use, although Justinian came
  With a new bridle,[4] if the saddle's empty?
  There would indeed without it be less shame.   90
You who should concentrate on being devout,[5]
  Acknowledging that Caesar's in the saddle,

---

1   The sun.
2   Born *c.*1200, famous as a poet (writing in Provençal) and as a politician.
3   In Purgatory.
4   Justinian, Emperor 527–65, reorganized Roman law.
5   The clergy, especially the Popes.

Obedient to the rule which God sets out,[1]
See how this beast, which nobody restrains,
  Grows wicked, uncorrected by the spur,
  Since you have laid your hands upon the reins.
O Albert, son of Germany,[2] who take
  No care at all of this unmastered brute,
  Yet should bestride the saddle on its back,
May rightful judgement fall upon your blood   100
  Out of the stars; let it be strange and plain,
  To make the one who follows you afraid!
Because you and your father, both possessed
  By greed for what is near you, have allowed
  The garden of the Empire[3] to lie waste.
See the Montecchi and the Cappelletti,[4]
  Monaldi and Filippeschi,[5] heedless man:
  The former ruined, and the latter shaky!
See, stony-hearted, see the tribulation
  Of your nobility, and heal their wounds;   110
  You will see Santa Fiora's sad condition![6]
See your own Rome, now weeping and widowed,
  And all alone, day and night crying out:
  "My Caesar, why are you not by my side?"
See all the love there is within this nation!
  And if no pity for us moves your heart,
  Be moved by shame for your bad reputation.
And if, Almighty God, I am allowed
  To ask it: You were crucified for us
  On earth: are Your just eyes now turned aside?   120
Or is there looming in the vast abyss
  Of all Your wisdom some great happiness
  As yet unnoticed and remote from us?
For every town in Italy's a den
  Of tyrants; every peasant is Marcellus[7]
  Once he decides to be a partisan.
My Florence,[8] you must be well satisfied
  That this digression does not bear on you,
  Thanks to your citizens, who try so hard.
Many love justice, but let time elapse   130

---

1   "And he said unto them, 'Render therefore unto Caesar the things which be Caesar's, and unto God the things which be God's'" (Luke 20:25).
2   Emperor 1298–1308. Like his father and predecessor, Rudolf, he was preoccupied with Germany and neglected Italy.
3   Italy.
4   Rival factions in Lombardy.
5   Rival factions in Orvieto.
6   Santa Fiora, at this time under Sienese rule, had been an imperial fief.
7   Probably the Marcellus who opposed Julius Caesar and was Consul in 51 BC.
8   What follows, up to the last four lines of this canto, is heavy irony.

In thought before they loose it from the bow;
  But your folk have it always on their lips.
Many think office is too burdensome;
  But your folk always eagerly respond,
  Without being asked, and shout: "I'll take it on!"
You should rejoice, for you have every reason,
  Being so wealthy, peaceful, well advised!
  Isn't this true? The facts are hardly hidden.
Athens and Lacedaemon, known for giving
  Laws in the past and good administration,   140
  Made but a gesture towards upright living
Compared to you, who spin so many clever
  Provisions and provisos those October
  Provided do not last till mid-November.
How many times, in living memory,
  Have you revised your laws, coins, offices
  And customs – and revised your citizenry![1]
If you consider, with enlightened eyes,
  You'll see your image in an invalid
  Who finds, though feather-bedded, no repose,   150
Tossing, to ease his pain, from side to side.

---

1   This refers to the Florentine habit of exiling some citizens while recalling others, according to the party in power.

CANTO VII

After the two famous poets and fellow citizens, Virgil and Sordello, have greeted each other enthusiastically, Sordello draws back a little and asks Virgil who he is. When Virgil answers, making it clear that he is not bound for heaven, Sordello is overwhelmed with the honour of seeing him, and greets him again, no less enthusiastically now, but much more humbly. The contrast between earthly fame, in which Virgil exceeds all others, and his exclusion from heaven, while the lesser poet Sordello is saved, is very marked.

Virgil asks Sordello to guide Dante and himself to the entrance to Purgatory, and Sordello explains that, although he may wander where he will in daytime, it is forbidden to him and the other souls in waiting to ascend the Mountain after sunset. However, he takes them to a place where they may spend the night, and spend it with some pleasure. This is a small valley in the side of the mountain, adorned with colourful flowers and fresh grass and sweetly scented, where the souls of neglectful princes are resting.

In the fading daylight, Sordello takes the opportunity, while he points out the various rulers, to illustrate the serious consequences of their negligence. He also shows, with examples, that human virtue is not passed on automatically from parent to child: it is a gift of God, and the apparently random way in which it is bestowed emphasizes its dependence on Him.

Despite the anguish some of these rulers still feel for the condition of their former realms, the main impression this canto leaves us with is one of calm after a storm, as the rulers, some of whom were deadly enemies in life, sit on the grass in unity, and sing the evening hymn '*Salve, Regina*'.

W hen these kind greetings had been given, more
  Than once or twice, and joyfully, Sordello
  Drew back somewhat and said, "Say who you are."
"Before a single soul had ever gone,
  Being fit to climb to God, towards this Mountain,[1]
  My bones were buried by Octavian.[2]
I am Virgil; and for no other sin
  Than lack of faith I failed to get to heaven."
  Such was the answer my guide gave him then.
Like somebody accosted suddenly   10
  By what astonishes, which he believes
  And doubts, and says, "It is… it cannot be" –
That's how Sordello looked: he lowered his eyes,
  Going back to him in all humility,
  Embracing him as an inferior does.[3]
"O glory of the Latin race, through whom

---

1 Before the Incarnation and Redemption.
2 Caesar Augustus. He ordered Virgil's body to be removed from Brindisi, where he died, to Naples, where he was buried. See *Purg.* III, 25–27.
3 Around the knees or feet.

Our tongue revealed its power,[1] O everlasting
Distinction of that place from which I come,[2]
What merit or what grace brings me this sight?
  If I am worthy but to hear your words,   20
  Say if you're from the Inferno, and what part."
"Through all the circles of the realm of gloom,"
  He answered, "I have journeyed and come here:
  It was celestial power that made me come.
Not what I did, but what I failed to do
  Cost me the sight of that Sun you desire,
  Which when it was too late I came to know.
There is a place down there, not sad with pain
  But only with the darkness, where laments
  Do not emerge as groans, but sighs alone.   30
I'm there with little ones who had no fault,
  And who were bitten by the teeth of death
  Before they could be freed from human guilt;[3]
I'm there with people who did not put on
  Theological virtues[4] and, unerring,
  Practised the other virtues, every one.
But, if you know and are allowed to, say
  What is the quickest route for us to come
  To the real entrance to Mount Purgatory."
He answered: "We have no fixed place assigned;   40
  I may go up and I may walk about;
  As far as I'm allowed, I'll be your guide.
But see the day's already drawing in,
  And climbing up at night is not permitted;
  We need to find some place to settle down.
There are souls set apart here on our right:
  If you agree, I'll take you there, and you
  Will get to know them, not without delight."
"How is that?" Virgil asked. "Whoever wanted
  To climb by night, would he be stopped by others?   50
  Would his own incapacity prevent it?"
Then good Sordello's finger drew a line
  Upon the ground; he said: "See? Even this
  Cannot be crossed after the sun goes down:
Not that anything else is in the way
  Of climbing on and up, but shades of night
  Tangle the will in incapacity.
One could of course at nightfall turn back down

---

1 Italian and Provençal are regarded here as part of the Latin language, which by derivation they are.
2 Mantua.
3 Before they were baptized and cleansed from original sin.
4 Faith, hope and charity, knowledge of which depends on God's revelation, not human intelligence.

And move along the shore and wander round,
    While the horizon still secretes the sun."   60
At which my lord, like someone full of wonder,
    Said: "Lead on then, and bring us where you say
    It will be a delight for us to linger."
We had not travelled very far before
    I saw there was a hollow in the Mountain,
    As valleys hollow out the mountains here.[1]
"We shall go there," that shade said, "where the slope
    Is broken by a sort of lap or ledge,
    And there we'll wait until the sun comes up."
There was a winding way, not steep, not flat,   70
    Which took us to a place along that chasm,
    Where the side drops to less than half its height.[2]
Pure gold and silver, cochineal and white
    Lead, wood of India[3] and unclouded skies,
    Fresh emerald at the instant it is split,
Matched with the grass and flowers in that place,
    Would find that they were all surpassed in colour:
    The greater gets the better of the less.
And nature had not only painted there,
    But from a thousand sweet scents she had blended   80
    One, indefinable, not known before.
I saw, among the flowers upon the green,
    Souls sitting, singing out *"Salve, Regina"*,[4]
    Whom the valley till now had kept unseen.
That Mantuan who'd taken us so far
    Said then: "Do not, before the sun has nested,
    Ask me to guide you down among them there.
From this bank you'll more easily make out
    The faces and the gestures of them all,
    Than if received by them down on the flat.   90
He who is seated highest and who looks
    Like someone who has failed to do his duty,
    And does not, while the rest sing, move his lips,
Was Emperor Rudolf,[5] one who had the power
    To heal the mortal wounds of Italy,
    That land it is too late now to restore.
The other, soothing him apparently,
    Ruled the land[6] where the water's born which Moldau
    Bears to the Elbe, Elbe to the sea:

---

1   In the world of the living.
2   The sides of this cavity naturally decrease in height as the mountain slopes down.
3   Ebony, which takes a high polish.
4   "Hail, Queen" (the usual English translation is "Hail, holy queen"), a prayer to the Virgin
    which describes those who say it as "mourning and weeping in this vale of tears".
5   Reigned 1273–91, the father of Emperor Albert (*Purg.* vi, 97 and note).
6   Bohemia.

He was Ottocar;[1] in his infancy   100
   A better man than Wenceslas[2] when bearded –
   His son, who feeds on ease and lechery.
And the snub-nose[3] who seems in such close parley
   With that one whose demeanour's so benign,[4]
   Died in full flight, deflowering the lily[5] –
Look over there, and see him beat his breast!
   And see his neighbour who has made his palm
   The bed on which his sighing cheek may rest.
They are the father[6] of the plague of France[7]
   And father-in-law:[8] they know his filthy vices,   110
   And hence their grief that pierces like a lance.
He who looks so robust,[9] in harmony,
   Singing, with that one with the manly nose,[10]
   Was girded round with all integrity;
And if he had been followed on the throne
   By that youngster who's sitting there behind him,[11]
   His worth would have been duly handed down,
Which can't be said of his two other sons;
   His kingdoms are now ruled by James and Frederick:[12]
   No one received the best inheritance.   120
It's seldom we see human honour come
   Up through the branches,[13] since the One who plants it
   Wants it to be attributed to Him.
My words concern that large-nosed one[14] no less
   Than they concern King Peter, singing with him,
   Whence Apulia and Provence are in distress.
The plant is as inferior to its seed
   As, more than Beatrice and Margaret,

---

1   Ottocar II of Bohemia (r.1253–78). He refused to recognize Rudolf as Emperor, and was defeated and killed by him.
2   Wenceslas IV of Bohemia (r.1278–1305).
3   Philip III (the Bold) of France (r.1270–85). He made war on Peter III of Aragon and was defeated.
4   Henry the Fat of Navarre (r.1270–74).
5   The fleur-de-lis, the French royal coat of arms.
6   Philip III.
7   Philip IV (the Fair) of France (r.1285–1314). He is strongly criticized elsewhere in the *Comedy* (*Inf.* XIX, 87; *Purg.* XX, 85–93, XXXII, 152–53; *Par.* XIX, 118–20).
8   Henry the Fat.
9   Peter III of Aragon (r.1276–85).
10   Charles I of Anjou (r.1266–85), King of Naples and Sicily and Count of Provence. In life he was an enemy of Peter III of Aragon.
11   Peter III's youngest son, Peter, who predeceased his father.
12   James II, King of Sicily from 1286, succeeded to the throne of Aragon in 1291, and died in 1327. Frederick II became King of Sicily in 1296, and died in 1337.
13   Of the family tree.
14   See note 10 above.

Constance can glory in her married lord.[1]
See him who lived in all simplicity   130
   Sitting there all alone, Henry of England:[2]
   He is more fortunate in his progeny.[3]
That marquis on the ground among them there,
   Lower than all the others, looking up,
   Makes, through his war with Alessandria,
Monferrato and Canavese weep.[4]

---

1   Charles II is as much inferior to his father, Charles I, as Charles I was to Peter III; Constance has more reason to glory in her husband, Peter III, than Beatrice and Margaret have to glory in theirs, Charles I (who married both).

2   Henry III (r. 1216–72).

3   Edward I (r. 1272–1307).

4   William VII, Marquis of Monferrato and Canavese 1254–92. He attacked Alessandria to put down a rising, but was imprisoned by the Alessandrians and died in prison. His son tried to avenge his death, and Alessandria responded by invading Monferrato.

CANTO VIII

It is now evening, that time of day when church bells ring for compline and travellers think longingly of what they have left behind. This famous passage – often imitated by later poets, notably Thomas Gray – hints at the attachment which the newly arrived souls, destined for heaven, still have to their former lives on earth.

After the souls in the valley have sung their evening hymn, two beautiful angels descend and stand on guard.

Dante and Virgil go with Sordello down into the valley, where Dante meets an old and honoured acquaintance – Judge Nino. He and Sordello are amazed when Dante explains how he comes to be there while still alive. Nino is anxious that his daughter Giovanna should pray for him: he has no such hopes from his wife, who has married again. Nino is still interested in earthly affairs, but it is clear from his tone of voice that he now views them with serenity.

Dante looks up to the south celestial pole, where previously he had seen four stars representing the four cardinal virtues: now those stars have set and three others, representing the three theological virtues, are circling close to the pole: virtues which can be understood by the light of human reason alone have given way to higher virtues dependent on the grace of God.

Suddenly a snake, reminiscent of the tempter in the garden of Eden, appears, but is immediately put to flight when the two guardian angels move towards it. The angels then return to their previous posts.

Another shade introduces himself to Dante. He is Corrado Malaspina, whose love while he lived was directed too exclusively towards his family: this love is now being refined. Dante praises the Malaspina family, famous for their generosity and their ability in war. Corrado says that, within the space of seven years, Dante will have reason to appreciate the virtues of that family from his own experience. This is a prophecy of Dante's coming exile.

T hat time of day had now arrived which sends
    Sailors' desires back homewards, makes them fonder,
    The very day they've parted from dear friends –
The hour the traveller starting on his way
    Is pierced with love, hearing a distant chime
    That seems to mourn the dying of the day[1] –
When I, now hardly listening any more,
    Was gazing at a soul who stood upright
    And gestured with his hand for us to hear.
He joined his palms and raised them, fixedly   10
    Looking towards the east, as if he were
    Saying to God: "Nothing else interests me."
"*Te lucis ante*"[2] came with such devotion
    Out of his mouth, and with a sound so sweet,
    That I forgot myself in delectation;
And then the rest, with sweet sounds and devotion,

---

1   Bells are ringing for compline, the last canonical hour of the day.
2   A traditional night-time prayer, "Before the ending of the daylight".

Joined in and sang the hymn right through together,
  Eyeing the spheres in their supernal motion.
Sharpen your eyes here, reader, see the truth,
  Because the veil at this point is so thin   20
  It's all too easy to look through the cloth.[1]
I saw that company of noble people
  Gaze up in utter silence at the sky,
  As if in expectation, pale and humble;
And saw two angels making their descent
  Out of the sky, each with a flaming sword
  Which was truncated and without its point.
These angels' garments had the tender green
  Of newborn leaves, and billowed out behind them,
  Fanned by green feathers as they fluttered down.[2]   30
One came down just above; the other one
  Came down to rest on the opposing bank,
  So that the people were contained between.
Quite clearly I could see their heads were blond;
  But my eyesight was dazzled by their faces,
  Like any sense excess comes to confound.
"From Mary's bosom[3] both of them come here,"
  Sordello said, "as guardians of the valley,
  Against the serpent which will soon appear."
And I, who was uncertain by what road,   40
  Turned round and pressed myself, in frozen fear,
  Against the trusty shoulders of my guide.
Sordello said: "Let us go down there now
  Among the shades of these great men, and talk:
  They will be very pleased to welcome you."
I think I'd only gone three paces down,
  And was within the valley, when I noticed
  One stare at me, and recognition dawn.
Already there was darkness in the air,
  But not such darkness that his eyes and mine   50
  Did not make obvious what had not been clear.
He made towards me, and I too advanced:
  Noble Judge Nino,[4] I was so delighted
  To see you there, and not among the lost!
No courteous words of welcome were left out;

---

1   The metaphor here is of the narrative as something which conceals, at the same time as
    it expresses, some truth: when this truth is obvious, the reader may not read carefully
    enough.
2   Green is a traditional symbol of hope.
3   From heaven, where the mother of God lives.
4   Nino Visconti of Pisa, judge of the district of Gallura in Sardinia (see *Inf.* XXII, 81–82
    and note). Chief of the Guelf party in Pisa, he was expelled in 1288 by his grandfather
    Count Ugolino (see *Inf.*: XXXII, 125*ff*; XXXIII, 1–90). He visited Florence several times, and
    Dante had obviously met him. He died in 1296.

And then he asked me: "When did you come over
    The distant waters to the Mountain's foot?"[1]
"They were," I said, "sad places[2] I came from,
    This very morning, still in my first life,
    Though, journeying, I gain the life to come."   60
The instant that they'd gathered my reply,
    Sordello and Judge Nino both drew back,
    As people do when awestruck suddenly.
One[3] turned to Virgil, and the other one[4]
    To a shade seated there, and cried: "Corrado,
    Come here! See what the grace of God has done."
He turned to me: "By that great gratitude
    You owe to Him whose motives are so hidden
    They're inaccessible by any ford,
When you are back beyond the boundless sea,[5]   70
    Ask my Giovanna,[6] where the innocents
    Are heard and answered, to cry out for me.
I doubt her mother loves me any more:
    She gave up the white fillets,[7] which – poor woman! –
    She will have reason to be longing for.[8]
We can with ease, through her example, note
    How long the fire of love in females lasts,
    If sight or touch do not rekindle it.
The viper will not ornament her tomb,
    Though under it the Milanese pitch camp,   80
    As the cock of Gallura would have done."[9]
So Nino said to me, and he expressed,
    In his appearance, all that righteous zeal
    Which glows with moderation in the breast.
My greedy eyes gazed up at heaven still,
    Especially where the slowest stars are circling,
    Like motion at the centre of a wheel.[10]
My leader asked: "What do you see up there?

---

1   To Purgatory from the mouth of the Tiber: Nino assumes that Dante is dead.
2   The Inferno.
3   Sordello.
4   Judge Nino.
5   The "distant waters" of l. 57.
6   Nino's daughter, who in 1300 was nine years old.
7   Worn as a sign of widowhood.
8   Nino's widow, Beatrice d'Este, married Galeazzo Visconti, lord of Milan. He was exiled
    from that city and died impoverished, and his wife suffered with him.
9   The arms of the Visconti family of Milan, which took precedence over the arms of other
    families in that city when they made war, are contrasted unfavourably with the arms of
    the Visconti family of Pisa and Gallura. The significance is probably that it would have
    been regarded as more honourable for her to remain a widow.
10   Dante is looking towards the south celestial pole.

And I replied: "I see three tiny torches[1]
   With which this southern pole is all on fire."   90
He said: "Those four bright stars you used to see
   This morning have descended over there,
   And these have risen where those used to be."
And even as he talked Sordello took
   Him closer, saying: "There's our enemy!"
   And with his finger showed him where to look.
At that edge, where there was no barricade
   Defending the small valley, was a serpent,
   Such as gave Eve perhaps the bitter food.[2]
Through grass and flowers slithered the evil streak,   100
   Turning its head from time to time and licking
   Its back like beasts that make themselves more sleek.
I did not see, and therefore cannot say
   How these two hawks of heaven were set in motion,
   But saw them clearly as they went their way.
Hearing their green wings as they cleaved the air,
   The serpent fled: the angels turned as one
   And went back up to where they were before.
The shade[3] who had approached the judge when he
   Called out to him, had never for one instant   110
   During that raid taken his eyes off me.
"So may that lamp which leads you up and up
   Discover in your will sufficient wax
   To take you to the Mount's enamelled top,"[4]
He said; "if you have tidings to declare
   Of Val di Magra or the parts nearby,
   Tell me: I used to count for something there –
Corrado Malaspina,[5] not the old
   Corrado – his grandson: I gave my own
   The love that in this place is purified."[6]   120
"Oh!" then I answered him, "I've never been
   Over your lands – but where, in all of Europe,
   Lives anyone to whom they are not known?
The reputation of your family
   Exalts your lords so, and exalts your land,
   He knows of them who never went that way.
So may I climb this mountain, be assured

---

1   Symbolic of the three theological virtues (i.e. those which depend upon the grace of
   God) – faith, hope and charity. See *Purg.* 1, 23 and note, and ll. 91–93 of this canto.
2   The forbidden fruit in the garden of Eden.
3   See l. 65.
4   The lamp is God's grace, and the (candle)wax Dante's cooperation with it.
5   Lord of Lunigiana, the land around the valley of the Magra in north-west Tuscany, and
   grandson of the founder of the family. He died *c.*1294.
6   Corrado's love was too limited, being directed mainly to his family, and so must be
   purified and made more disinterested.

Your honourable family has not lost
The glory of the purse and of the sword.
Custom and blood favour that family;   130
  So, while the evil head[1] misleads all others,
   It walks upright and scorns the wicked way."
Then he: "Enough – the sun won't sink to rest
  On seven occasions in the bed the Ram
  Covers with all four feet and grips so fast,[2]
Before that good opinion you display
  Is hammered squarely home into your head
  With more effective nails than mere hearsay,
Unless the course of God's intent is stayed."[3]

---

1   Probably Rome, including therefore both the Pope and Emperor.
2   The sun will not enter the spring sign of Aries seven times, i.e. "seven years will not pass, before…"
3   This line expresses an impossibility. Corrado is hinting at Dante's future exile and the kindness he will receive from the Malaspina family.

CANTO IX

In the first light of dawn Dante dreams that he is taken up by an eagle to the sphere of fire, where the heat awakens him. Then he discovers that the dream has come true: in his sleep St Lucy has carried him up to a point near the gate of Purgatory.

Above the three steps leading up to the gate sits an angel, sword in hand, with a face of dazzling brightness. The angel questions them closely and, once he is satisfied by Virgil's answers, he tells them to approach. The lowest step is made of pure-white marble, the second of black broken rock, and the third of porphyry.

The angel with the point of his sword inscribes on Dante's forehead seven Ps, signifying the seven capital sins, and says that Dante must wash these marks away when he is inside the gate. The angel then uses two keys to unlock the gate, which opens with a loud roar. Dante hears voices inside singing the traditional hymn of thanksgiving, '*Te Deum laudamus*'.

This canto is remarkable for its elaborate descriptions: for instance, of the light which precedes the dawn (ll. 1–9 and 13–15); of Dante's dream (ll. 19–33); and even of the mere act of wakening (ll. 34–40). Partly this is a way of marking the importance of this stage of Dante's journey. It also allows Dante to include symbols of many different kinds to illuminate much that might otherwise be ineffable. There are references to pagan classical myth (e.g. the rape of Ganymede), biblical references (e.g. "the keys of the kingdom of heaven") and traditional Judaeo-Christian symbols (e.g. the colour of the angel's robe). There is also what might be called "natural" symbolism mixed in: that there are steps to be climbed to reach the gate of Purgatory hardly requires interpretation.

Dante himself draws attention to the complexity of his style in this canto (ll. 70–72): he enjoys presenting us with a tour de force.

A ncient Tithonus' bedfellow was white
　　Already on the eastern balcony,
　　Beyond the loving arms of her sweetheart;[1]
Her forehead was lit up with many a jewel
　　Set in the shape of that cold-blooded creature[2]
　　That strikes at human beings with its tail;
And night had gone two stages further on
　　And upward, in the valley where we were,
　　And the third stage was folding its wings down,[3]
When I, in whom old Adam played a part,[4]   10
　　Conquered by sleep, lay down upon the grass,
　　There where all five of us already sat.
In that hour when the swallow starts to sing
　　Her sad songs, when the morning's very near,

1　It is dawn. The mythical Aurora, goddess of the dawn, fell in love with a mortal, Tithonus. She managed to obtain immortality for him, but forgot to ask for eternal youth.
2　The zodiacal sign of Scorpio, the scorpion.
3　Nearly three hours ("stages") of the night have passed.
4　Unlike his companions, Dante has a body and needs sleep.

Mindful perhaps of her old suffering,[1]
And when our intellect is peregrine,
   Out of the flesh and less weighed down by thought,
   And in its visions is almost divine,[2]
I seemed to see an eagle in my dream,
   Hovering in the sky, its feathers golden,   20
   Its wings wide open, ready to swoop down;
I seemed to be where his own family
   Were left behind by Ganymede when he
   Was snatched up to the high consistory.[3]
I was thinking: "Perhaps it's only here
   It strikes its prey; perhaps its claws disdain
   To carry up its victims from elsewhere."
And then it seemed that eagle wheeling there
   Swooped down on me as terrible as lightning,
   And snatched me up into the fiery sphere.[4]   30
Once there it seemed that both of us blazed up;
   And the imagined fire burned me so badly
   That I was roused perforce out of my sleep.
Achilles shook himself no otherwise –
   Casting his eyes around him as he wakened,
   With no idea at all of where he was,
That time his mother took him stealthily,
   A child in arms, from Chiron and to Skyros,
   Whence afterwards the Greeks lured him away[5] –
Than I then shook myself: sleep fled my face,   40
   And I went deathly pale as people do
   When they're so terrified they turn to ice.
Only my comfort now was there with me.[6]
   The sun had climbed above two hours already –
   And I, my eyes were turned towards the sea.
My lord told me: "There's no cause for alarm.
   Be confident: we're well upon our way;
   Do not draw back, but give your strength free rein.

---

1   Tereus, husband of Procne, raped her sister Philomela. Procne, in revenge, killed the
     son she herself had borne to Tereus, and served him up to Tereus, who ate him. When
     Tereus discovered what he had done, he tried to kill both sisters, but all three were
     changed into birds – Tereus into a hoopoe, Procne into a nightingale and Philomela
     into a swallow.

2   As mentioned before, there was a common belief that dreams dreamt at dawn came
     true.

3   Jove, in the form of an eagle, snatched the beautiful youth Ganymede from Mount Ida
     up to heaven to be a cup-bearer to the gods.

4   This is the sphere above the sphere of air round the earth and below the sphere of the
     moon.

5   The goddess Thetis hid her son Achilles on the island of Skyros, away from his tutor, the
     centaur Chiron. He was discovered and was persuaded to take part in the war against Troy.

6   Virgil: Sordello, Nino and Corrado have disappeared during Dante's sleep.

At last you have arrived at Purgatory:
    See there the rampart that encloses it –   50
    See there the entrance where it falls away.
Just now, in the first light, before day dawned,
    And while your soul was still absorbed in sleep,
    Upon the flowers with which down there's adorned,
A lady came. "I am Lucy,"[1] she said:
    "Let me take up this man who's sleeping here,
    And I shall help to speed him on his road."
Sordello and the other souls remained;
    She lifted you and, once the day was bright,[2]
    She came up here, and I came on behind.   60
She set you down, but first her lovely eyes
    Showed me that open way; then she and sleep
    Went that same instant on their separate ways."
Like one who felt uncertain but grows sure,
    And finds his fear turn into confidence
    The moment that he sees the truth is clear,
That's how I changed; and when he saw me quite
    Unhesitant, my leader moved and climbed
    The rampart, and I followed towards the height.
Reader, you clearly see me elevate   70
    My subject matter: do not be surprised
    If now I buttress it with greater art.
As we approached we came upon a spot
    From which, where first I'd merely seen a breach,
    Just like a crack by which a wall is split,
I saw a gateway, and three steps below
    Going up to it, of different colours, and
    A porter who'd not spoken up to now.
And as my eyes grew wide and still more wide,
    I saw him seated on the topmost step,   80
    His face a radiance I could not abide;
And in his hand he held a naked blade,
    From which the sun's beams were reflected so
    However much I looked my eyes were blurred.
And then he said: "Speak out from where you are.
    What are you looking for? Where is your escort?
    You may be harmed by climbing up: beware!"
"A lady out of Heaven, who is expert
    In things like this," my master said, "just now
    Told us: 'Go there: that's where you'll find the gate.'"   90
"And may she lead your steps in righteousness,"
    The courteous porter spoke to us again,
    "And so come forward and approach our stairs."

---

1   St Lucy (see *Inf.* II, 100 and note) embodies the illuminating grace of God.
2   Climbing is forbidden in Purgatory during the hours of darkness (see *Purg.* VII, 44).

We went there, and the first step was of white
  Marble, so smoothly polished and so clear
  That I was mirrored in it to the life.
The second, more than murky, was pitch-black,
  Dry crumbling rugged rock, and right across,
  In all its length and breadth, there ran a crack.
The third, which seemed to weigh the others down,   100
  Was, so it seemed, of flaming porphyry,
  As bright as blood that's spurting from a vein.[1]
God's angel kept his feet both planted on
  This last step, while he sat upon the threshold,
  Which seemed to me to be of diamond stone.
My leader led me up the steps, with my
  Complete consent, and said: "Ask for the lock
  To be undone, in all humility."
I fell down at the sacred feet; then first,
  Before I begged for mercy's open door,   110
  I struck myself three times upon the breast.
Then he inscribed seven Ps[2] on my forehead
  With his sword's point, and "Once you are within,
  Be sure to wash away these wounds," he said.
Ashes or recently dug-up dry earth
  Would be a match in colour for his robe;[3]
  And he drew out two keys[4] he kept beneath.
One key was gold, silver the other key;[5]
  First with the white key, after with the yellow,
  He worked upon the door, which gladdened me.   120
"Whenever one of these does not succeed
  In turning as it ought to in the lock,
  This entrance can't be opened up," he said.
"One is more precious,[6] but much mother wit
  And skill are used to make the other work,
  Because that is the one to loose the knot.[7]
They are from Peter, and he said I ought

1   The precise allegorical interpretation of these steps is much discussed. In general terms,
     it may be suggested that the first step signifies the clear-sighted self-knowledge which
     leads to the admission of sin, the second step signifies remorse, and the third step signi-
     fies the desire to expiate sin by penance.
2   P stands for the Latin *peccatum* (sin). The seven capital sins, i.e. the sins, or sinful disposi-
     tions rather, from which all other sins derive, are (in the order of the importance which
     Dante ascribes to them) pride, envy, wrath, sloth, avarice, gluttony and lust.
3   This subfusc shade is reminiscent of the habits of some religious orders, and also of the
     sackcloth and ashes traditionally associated with penitence.
4   "The keys of the kingdom of heaven" (Matt. 16:19).
5   Traditionally the gold key symbolizes the power of the Church to forgive sins, and the
     silver key the wisdom and discretion needed to exercise this power justly.
6   The gold key.
7   The entanglement of sin.

To err in opening, not in keeping closed,
    If people throw themselves down at my feet."
Then he pushed back the sacred gates. "Be warned,"   130
    He told us, "when you enter: anyone
    Must go back out again who looks behind."
And then the pivots of that sacred portal
    Were turning ponderously in their sockets,
    Being made of mighty and resounding metal:
The doors of old Tarpeia did not roar
    So loudly, hard to turn, when good Metellus
    Was taken, for Tarpeia to be bare.[1]
I turned, attentive once that sound began,
    And seemed to hear the singing of '*Te Deum*   140
    Laudamus'[2] to sweet music from within.
The impression made on me by what I heard
    Was that precisely which we always get
    When we hear singing while an organ's played:
The words are sometimes clear, and sometimes not.

---

1   Ancient Rome's public treasury was kept in a temple on the Tarpeian Rock. The tribune
    Metellus tried to prevent Julius Caesar from plundering it, but was removed and so was
    unsuccessful.

2   "We praise you, O God", the traditional hymn of thanksgiving.

CANTO X

Mount Purgatory contains seven terraces, placed one above the other, and connected by difficult ascents. On each terrace there are souls being punished for, and purified from, one of the seven capital sins. In addition to this punishment, which is always appropriate to the sin, there are prayers for the penitents, and also examples of the opposing virtue and of the sin itself. The sins are dealt with in order of importance: the sinful disposition to pride, the root of all the others and therefore the most heinous, comes first.

In this canto Dante and Virgil have to thread a narrow, winding cleft in the mountain. This brings them to the first terrace, which is rather less than eighteen feet across. On the side of the mountain, which is of white marble, is a series of carvings, so skilfully executed as to be beyond human art. Among the scenes Dante sees represented here are the Annunciation (which reveals Mary's humility), King David dancing before the Ark of the Covenant, without regard for his kingly dignity since he is excited by his joy in the Lord, and the pagan Emperor Trajan who, according to the legend, was redeemed by his humility in listening to the petition of a poor widow and granting her justice. We have, therefore, examples drawn from the New Testament, the Old Testament and legend.

A crowd approaches, whose composition is at first difficult to make out, since the people in it do not look like human beings. This is because they are bowed down under the weight of heavy stones. Their punishment, although it is fitting, is clearly very severe. Dante has, however, been careful to emphasize to us, his readers, that this punishment (unlike those in the Inferno) will have an end: all the sinners Dante meets in Purgatory are ultimately destined for heaven.

When we had crossed the threshold of the gate –
So very seldom used, since love perverted
Can make the crooked path appear the straight –
I realized by the sound that it had closed;
    And if my eyes had turned towards the gateway,
    How could that fault of mine have been excused?[1]
We went up by a cleft cut in the rock,
    Which swayed about on one side and the other,
    Just like a wave that goes and then comes back.[2]
"Now here a little artifice is needed,"   10
    My leader said to me, "in keeping close
    To this side and to that once it's receded."
This made us travel slowly with great care,
    So that the moon, now waning, had already
    Gone back to bed to rest again, before
We'd quite contrived to thread that needle's eye.[3]

---

1   See *Purg.* IX, 130–32.
2   The meaning is probably simply that the cleft is winding, although some commentators take it that the rock moves literally.
3   The phrase is biblical (see e.g. Mark 10:25).

But once we were released into the open,
Up where the mountain is set back some way –
I very weary, both of us nonplussed
   About our road – we halted on a ledge   20
   More lonely than a pathway through a waste.
From that side where it borders on blank space
   To the base of the slope which goes on rising
   It was three human bodies' lengths across;
As far as I could measure with my eyes,
   Now on the left side, now upon the right,
   This terrace seemed to stay that selfsame size.
We had not moved at all up there as yet
   When I saw that the Mountain's inner slope –
   Which, being steep, permitted no ascent –   30
Was of white marble and was decorated
   With scenes so fine not merely Polycletus
   But even nature's self would feel defeated.[1]
The angel who came down with the decree
   Announcing the long-wept-for reign of peace
   Which opened heaven after long delay,[2]
Appeared before us there, and so lifelike,
   The sculpture showing all his gracious bearing,
   It seemed impossible he did not speak.
That he was saying *"Ave!"*[3] you'd have sworn;   40
   For she was pictured there who held the key
   To open the high Love, and made it turn;[4]
And she was pictured there like one who speaks:
   "Ecce ancilla Dei",[5] as precisely
   And clearly as a figure sealed in wax.[6]
"You must not concentrate on just one part,"
   Said my kind guide, who had me now upon
   That side of him where people have their heart.
And so I moved my eyes about and found,
   Behind where Mary was, and on that side   50
   Where he was standing who led me around,
Another story carved upon the rock;

---

1 Polycletus (*fl.* 450–420 BC) was a celebrated Greek sculptor. Art is regarded here as an
   imitation of nature, and both art and nature are outdone by these reliefs, the product
   of supernatural artistry.
2 An allusion to the Annunciation.
3 "Hail!" See note 5 below.
4 Mary's acceptance of the angel's message was essential for the way to the Incarnation
   to be opened.
5 "Behold the handmaid of God." "And the angel came in unto her, and said, 'Hail, thou
   that art highly favoured, the Lord is with thee: blessed art thou among women...' And
   Mary said, 'Behold the handmaid of the Lord; be it unto me according to thy word.'"
   (Luke 1:28 and 38).
6 To the Divine Artificer it is as easy to work in hard stone as in malleable wax.

Therefore I crossed past Virgil and drew near it
   In order to obtain a clearer look.
There I saw, cut in that same marble stone,
   Wagon and oxen draw the sacred Ark
   Which makes men shun what God does not enjoin.[1]
In seven choirs people went on ahead;
   They made two of my senses speak and say,
   One, "No", the other, "Yes, they sing indeed".[2]   60
The incense rising from the censers too,
   As it was imaged there, made eyes and nose
   Discordant likewise as to yes and no.
Before the sacred vessel, capering
   And with his robes girt up, the humble Psalmist[3]
   Was in this act both more and less a king.
But, pictured in the window opposite
   Of a great palace, Michal, stupefied,
   Looked like a lady full of scorn and spite.[4]
I stirred myself again and moved my feet   70
   To look more closely where another story,
   Behind where Michal was, was gleaming white.
I saw an act of true nobility
   Set forth there, where the Roman prince's virtue
   Moved Gregory to his great victory;[5]
It's Trajan whom I mean, the Emperor,
   Who had a widow clinging to his bridle,
   Portrayed in floods of tears and full of care.
There seemed to be a trample all around
   Of horsemen, and the banners' golden eagles   80
   Above them seemed to flutter in the wind.
The wretched woman, mixed up with all these,
   Seemed to be begging him: "My lord, avenge
   The murder of my son, for whom I grieve."
And he seemed to reply: "Till I return
   You'll have to wait." Then she once more: "My lord,"
   Speaking like someone whom grief urges on,
"If you do not return?" He said: "The one
   Who follows me will do it." She: "What good
   To you is others' virtue, not your own?"   90
To this he said: "Take comfort; it is right

---

1   Uzzah touched the Ark to steady it, and was struck dead for his officiousness (2 Samuel 6:6–7). This is seen here as a warning to others.
2   The two senses are sight and hearing: the carving is so lifelike that the sight of it gives the illusion that the singing can be heard.
3   King David.
4   Michal, daughter of David's predecessor, King Saul, reproached David for the indignity, as she saw it, of his dancing before the Ark (2 Samuel 6:14–16, 20–23).
5   The legend is that Pope Gregory the Great, by his prayers, saved the soul of the pagan Emperor Trajan.

That I perform my duty here and now:
   Justice, mercy hold back my horse's feet."
He[1] in whose sight nothing is new or rare
   Produced this dialogue made visible,
   Novel to us – there's nothing like it here.
While I was still absorbed in my delight
   With images of such humility
   And, for their Maker, precious in our sight,
"See these whose coming seems somewhat constrained,"   100
   The poet murmured, "such a crowd of people;
   And they will show us where the stairs ascend."
These eyes of mine, which took such delectation
   To see such novelties, of which they're fond,
   Were hardly slow to turn in his direction.
Reader, I would not have you be deterred
   From all your good intentions when you hear
   How God requires the debt to be repaid.
Ignore the nature of the penalty,
   And think of what ensues[2] – think, at the worst,   110
   It cannot last beyond the Judgement Day.
I said: "There's something coming I can see,
   But what it is – it does not look like people –
   My sight is so confused, I cannot say."
And he replied: "What all their miseries
   Are caused by makes them bow down to the ground,
   So that at first I could not trust my eyes.
But concentrate, distinguish, fix your gaze
   On what is moving underneath those stones:
   Now you can see their breasts struck by their knees."   120
O you proud Christians, exhausted, sad,
   Who, undiscerning in your inward vision,
   Have placed your hopes in going retrograde,
Do you not see that we are worms and bred
   To turn into the angelic butterfly,
   Flying to justice and without a shield?
Why do your spirits strive to flutter up,
   Since you are undeveloped insects rather,
   Or worms that have not reached their final shape?
As, for a corbel holding roof or ceiling,   130
   We sometimes see a sculptured human figure
   Whose knees adjoin its breast, since it is kneeling,
And from what is unreal there is created
   Real anguish in the observer,[3] so I saw

---

1 God.

2 Heaven. The souls in Purgatory are being purified, but they are not on trial: their ultimate
    blessedness is assured.

3 The observer empathizes with the suffering depicted in the sculptured figure.

Those people crouching, once I concentrated.
The truth is they were more or less contracted
  According to the weight that their backs bore;[1]
  And the most patient in the way he acted
Seemed to say weeping: "I can bear no more."

---

1   It is appropriate that the proud should be forced to bow down. The weight they bear
    varies according to the degree of pride which has to be purged.

CANTO XI

The canto opens with a paraphrase of the 'Our Father', spoken in chorus by the souls suffering on this terrace. Appropriately, this most famous of all Christian prayers is amplified to stress human weakness and the need for humility.

Virgil asks for directions to climb the mountain. He is answered helpfully, but at first it is not clear by whom: all the shades have their faces to the ground. The shade who answered turns out to be Umberto Aldobrandeschi, a member of a powerful Tuscan family, brought down by pride.

Dante too has to bend down to listen to the suffering souls. Another of them twists his head in an attempt to look at Dante. This is Oderisi da Gubbio, once famous as an illuminator of manuscripts. He represents the pride of the artist; but now he says that the work of his successor, Franco of Bologna, is superior to his – an admission he would never have made while alive. To exemplify further the vanity of artistic pride, he mentions how Cimabue's place in painting has been taken by Giotto, and how Guido Guinizzelli's poetry is now less valued than that of Guido Cavalcanti, while a third poet – presumably Dante himself – will eclipse them both.

Oderisi indicates another shade, Provenzano Salvani of Siena, who was once so proud as to hope to subdue all Tuscany. His entrance into Purgatory proper might have been delayed by his late repentance; but he performed one act of outstanding humility: he humbled himself to stand as a beggar in the main square of Siena, asking for money to ransom a friend who was in danger of death. Oderisi says that Dante will himself soon experience such humiliation – a hint of his imminent exile from Florence. Abruptly, Oderisi returns to the subject of Provenzano, and says that this one supreme act of charity and humility gave him immediate access to the Mountain.

"Our Father, You Who dwell in heaven above,
    Not circumscribed there, but because Your first
    Creations[1] there elicit such great love,
Praised be Your name and Your omnipotence
    By every creature, since it is but fitting
    To render thanks to Your bright effluence.
May the peace of Your kingdom come to us,
    Since we can never find it by ourselves,
    Although we summon up our utmost force.
As every angel offers up his will   10
    In sacrifice to You, singing hosanna,
    So may we humans offer ours as well.
Give all of us this day our daily bread:
    Without that manna in this wilderness
    He moves backward who strives to move ahead.
And as we pardon each and every one
    For evil done to us, so may You pardon,

---

1   The angels, created before mankind.

Without considering merit, but benign.
Do not allow our strength, so soon subdued,
   To face the test of our old enemy:[1]   20
   Free it from him who always tries us hard.
That final prayer, O Lord Who are so kind,
   Is not for us, who have no need of it,[2]
   But for all those whom we have left behind."
So, offering prayers for their and our success,
   Those shades went walking underneath such weights
   As sometimes in a nightmare weigh on us –
Around, around, and variously oppressed,[3]
   And all exhausted, up on this first terrace,
   Purging themselves of our world's murky mist.   30
Now if up there they always pray for us,
   What can be said or done down here for them
   By those whose wills take root in righteousness?
We ought to help them wash those stains of theirs
   They carried hence, so that, now pure and light,
   They may ascend into the starry spheres.
"May justice and compassion lighten you
   Soon, and enable you to spread your wings,
   To lift yourselves to where you wish to go!
Now show us whereabouts a stair goes up,   40
   The nearest way; and if there's more than one,
   Direct us to the one that is less steep,
For my companion, with that heavy load
   Of Adam's flesh he wears as he wears clothes,
   Despite all his good will, finds climbing hard."
Words came in answer to those words, addressed
   To them by him whom I was following after –
   But whom they came from was not manifest.
And yet words came: "Along the rocky wall,
   And to the right: come with us, and you'll find   50
   A pass a living human being can scale.
And were I not prevented by this stone
   Which subjugates my neck so stiff with pride,
   So that I have to keep my gaze bent down,
I'd look at him who's still alive, whose name
   I've not yet heard, to see if we're acquainted,
   And move his pity for my heavy doom.[4]
I was Italian, Tuscan, and well born:
   Guglielmo Aldobrandeschi[5] was my father;

---

1   The Devil.
2   The souls in Purgatory are no longer subject to temptation.
3   Their burdens vary according to the degree of their pride.
4   It is not emotional sympathy which the shade desires, but prayers.
5   A famous member of an ancient and powerful Ghibelline family in the Tuscan Maremma.
    He died in the 1250s. The speaker is his son Umberto.

WE WENT UP THROUGH A BROKEN ROCKY FISSURE,
WHOSE SIDES WERE PRESSING CLOSELY IN ON US...

PURGATORY IV, 31–32

[IT] SWOOPED DOWN ON ME AS TERRIBLE AS LIGHTNING,
AND SNATCHED ME UP INTO THE FIERY SPHERE...

PURGATORY IX, 29–30

I don't know if you've ever heard that name.[1]   60
My ancient lineage and the deeds of honour
   Done by my ancestors made me so proud
   That, quite forgetful of our common mother,[2]
I held all other men in such despite
   It brought me death – and every Sienese
   And child in Campagnatico knows that.[3]
I am Umberto, and not me alone
   Has pride done harm to: all my relatives
   Have been by that same dreadful sin brought down.
And here I have to bear this heavy load   70
   Because of it, till God is satisfied:
   Living, I did not, so I now must, dead."[4]
As I listened I held my head bent down,
   And one of them, and not the person speaking,
   Twisted beneath the weight that weighs them down
And saw me, recognized me, started calling,
   And with some effort kept his eyes on me,
   Who went, bent down, the way that they were walking.
"Surely you're Oderisi!" I cried out,
   "Glory of Gubbio and illumination,   80
   As the Parisians like to call your art!"[5]
"Brother," he said, "those leaves laugh more and shine
   Painted by Franco of Bologna's brush:[6]
   The honour's his now, very little mine.
I hardly would have been so generous
   While I was still alive, because my heart
   Was goaded by the urge for excellence.
We suffer here for overweening pride –
   And I'd not yet be here, if I had not,
   While still alive to sinning, turned to God.[7]   90
Vanity of vanities is man's renown!
   How short a time it flourishes at best,
   Unless an age of dulness follows on!
In painting Cimabue[8] was so sure

---

1   It is uncertain whether this line indicates a new-found humility in the speaker, or simply
    the survival of his old pride: the uncertainty fits the context beautifully.
2   Eve.
3   He was killed in 1259 by the Sienese in his fortress of Campagnatico.
4   Umberto is undergoing this penance now, because he did not curb his pride while he
    lived.
5   Oderisi da Gubbio, a famous illuminator of manuscripts, died c.1299.
6   Franco of Bologna is said to have been a pupil of Oderisi. He was still alive in 1300.
7   Presumably Oderisi repented of his sins some time before his death, otherwise he would
    have had to wait for a period outside Purgatory proper.
8   Cimabue (born c.1240 and still alive in 1300) was a famous Florentine painter known
    for his arrogance.

He held the field, while Giotto's now acclaimed,[1]
And all that former glory is obscure.
Guido from Guido has contrived to wrest
    The glory of our tongue,[2] and now perhaps
    There's one who'll drive them both out of the nest.[3]
A changing gust of wind is worldly fame,   100
    Now here, now there – and what we call it varies
    According to the quarter it blows from.
What greater glory will you have, if you
    Relinquish aged flesh, than if you'd died
    While still content with bow-wow and boo-hoo,
After the passage of a thousand years?
    (Less to eternity than one eye blink
    Is to the slowest of the heavenly spheres).[4]
His name, whose steps in front of me are slow,[5]
    Resounded through the whole of Tuscany,   110
    Though scarcely whispered in Siena now,
Where he was lord of lords when they frustrated
    The fury of the Florentines,[6] who were
    Then arrogant, though now they're prostituted.[7]
Your name and fame are like the grass in colour,
    Which comes and goes, and that which makes it grow
    Out of the earth when tender makes it wither."[8]
And I to him: "Your words, which are so true,
    Fill me with meekness, and deflate my pride.
    But who is he of whom you spoke just now?"   120
"Provenzano Salvani," answer came.
    "And he is here because of his presumption,
    Getting Siena underneath his thumb.
He's walked in that way ever since he died,
    With no repose: such is the reparation
    They make who over there[9] were overproud."
I said: "If spirits who delay until –

---

1   Giotto di Bondone (c.1266–1337), a very famous painter and a friend of Dante.
2   The fame of the poet Guido Guinizzelli (c.1230–76) has been overshadowed by that of
    Guido Cavalcanti (c.1258–1300; see Inf. x, 60–63).
3   Probably Dante is alluding to himself – not such a proud boast, in this context of the
    vanity of all worldly fame.
4   This is the sphere of the fixed stars.
5   Provenzano Salvani, leader of the Sienese at the time of the Battle of Montaperti (1260),
    when the Florentine Guelfs were defeated. He advocated the destruction of Florence
    (see Inf. x, 91–93 and note). He was beheaded after being captured by the Florentines in
    1269. Here he is walking slowly because of the weight he carries.
6   At Montaperti.
7   The Florentines were once so proud that they wished to dominate Tuscany. Now, Oderisi
    says, they are concerned solely with making money.
8   "The sun is no sooner risen with a burning heat, but it withereth the grass" (James 1:11).
9   In the world of the living.

Before repenting – the far end of life
Must wait below and not ascend the hill
(Unless right-minded prayer comes to their aid)   130
   For the whole length of time that they have lived,
   How is it that his entry was allowed?"
"When his renown was greatest," he replied,
   "Unconstrained, in the Campo of Siena,
   He took his stand, with all shame laid aside;
There, to alleviate his friend's heartache –
   Unransomed as he was in Charles's prison –
   He forced himself to quiver and to quake.[1]
I know my words are dark, but just hear this:
   Not long from now your neighbours will take action   140
   Such that you will yourself provide the gloss.[2]
This act of his freed him from that restriction."

1   In humiliation. Provenzano begged in public for the money to ransom a friend impris-
    oned by Charles of Anjou. The money had to be raised quickly, before the friend was
    put to death.
2   A hint of Dante's coming exile from Florence, after which he would himself have to
    beg for a living.

CANTO XII

Identifying himself with the souls suffering on this terrace, Dante moves along with Oderisi, both of them bent down like a pair of oxen under the yoke. Soon, however, Virgil reminds Dante that he must hurry, since it is already midday.

To balance the examples of humility in the previous canto, there are here many examples of pride and its punishment – narrative carvings on the ground, rather like those on flat tombstones. Dante must bend to see them, and that is part of their purpose. There are thirteen carvings, beginning with the fall of Lucifer, continuing with a number of mythical and biblical characters and incidents, and ending with the fall of Troy. The first letters of the tercets which describe them (lines 25–63) form an acrostic: MAN. This is not a mere jeu d'esprit, since it connects mankind with the first sin of all, pride, and the misery it entails.

An angel appears and leads them to the steps which go up to the next terrace. He strikes Dante on the forehead with his wings: the significance of this action is explained later by Virgil. Dante says these steps are like those in Florence which lead up to the Church of San Miniato, except that the ones in Purgatory are, significantly, much narrower. This comparison includes an attack on the present corruption of Florence.

Now the pilgrims hear a voice singing one of the Beatitudes, '*Beati pauperes spiritu!*', in praise of humility. The climb seems easier, and Dante feels as though a weight has been lifted from him. Then Virgil explains that the first of the seven Ps which were cut on Dante's forehead when he entered Purgatory has been erased: when eventually they are all erased, he will enjoy the climb. Somewhat embarrassed, Dante feels his forehead and finds that one P has indeed disappeared. Virgil smiles to see all this.

❋

Like oxen who are yoked, so side by side
    I went along there with that burdened soul,
    As far as my kind schoolmaster allowed.
But when he said: "Leave him, and carry on:
    Here it is right to use both sails and oars
    And urge the boat as quickly as we can,"
As walkers should, I raised myself once more –
    I mean I raised my body, for my thoughts
    Were stooping in submission as before.
Now I was moving, glad to follow where   10
    My master led me, and we two already
    Showing just how swift and how erect we were,
When Virgil said to me: "Cast your eyes down,
    For it will help you and will ease your journey
    To see the bed your feet are treading on."
As, to preserve the dead in memory,
    The lids of tombs laid flat upon the ground
    Are carved to show them as they used to be –
Which means we often have to weep again
    Because of recollection's poignant sting,   20

Which only strikes truly devoted men –
So I saw there, more accurately done
   By better workmanship, a set of carvings
   Across the mountain ledge we travelled on.
My eyes made out the creature[1] who was made
   More noble than all other creatures, falling
   Like lightning out of heaven, on one side.
My eyes made out Briareus[2] – the bolt
   From heaven still transfixed him – opposite,
   Heavy upon the ground, and deadly cold.   30
My eyes made out Thymbraeus,[3] still in arms
   With Mars and Pallas, gathered round their father,[4]
   Gazing upon the Giants' scattered limbs.
My eyes made out dazed Nimrod,[5] by the side
   Of the great work, and gazed at by the others
   Who on the plain of Shinar shared his pride.
Ah Niobe, how very tearfully
   I saw you on this road sculptured between
   Seven and seven of your dead progeny![6]
Ah Saul, how on your own sword you were slain!   40
   I saw you lying dead on Mount Gilboa,
   Which afterwards felt neither dew nor rain![7]
Ah mad Arachne, how I saw you caught,
   Half turned into a spider, in sad remnants
   Of work produced by you to your own hurt![8]
Ah Rehoboam, hardly menacing
   Now in this effigy, you flee in fear
   By chariot, with no one following![9]
Now also our hard marble road reveals
   Alcmaeon, how he makes his mother pay   50

---

1   Lucifer, aka Dis or Beelzebub. See *Inf.* xxxiv passim.

2   One of the Giants who tried to storm Olympus, but were destroyed by the Olympian
    gods.

3   Apollo. With Mars and Pallas Athena he was foremost in defeating the Giants.

4   Zeus.

5   The builder of the Tower of Babel. God destroyed it and confused men's language, to
    curb their pride (Gen. 10:8–10 and 11:1–9).

6   Niobe boasted that she was superior to Latona, because she had seven sons and seven
    daughters, while Latona had only Apollo and Diana. As a punishment, her children were
    killed and she was turned into a weeping stone statue.

7   When Saul was defeated by the Philistines, he killed himself by falling on his sword.
    Thereupon David cursed the battlefield: "Ye mountains of Gilboa, let there be no dew,
    neither let there be rain, upon you" (2 Samuel 1:21).

8   Arachne arrogantly challenged Athena to a weaving contest. Athena destroyed Arachne's
    tapestry and then, as Arachne in despair tried to hang herself, transformed her into a
    spider.

9   Rehoboam, Solomon's successor as King of Israel, threatened to rule even more tyran-
    nically than his father. When the people rebelled, he fled in panic to Jerusalem.

A heavy price for those accursèd jewels.[1]
Now it showed how his children fell upon
 Sennacherib while he was in the temple,
 And then how he was dead and they were gone.[2]
Now it showed all the devastation made
 By Tomyris, and how she said to Cyrus:
 "You thirsted for our blood: I'll give you blood."[3]
Now it revealed Assyrians in a rout
 With Holofernes dead, and showed moreover
 The relics of the slaughter after that.[4]   60
My eyes made out a cavernous ruin:
 Ah Ilium, how humble you appeared,
 Now dust and ashes in the sculptured stone![5]
What master of the brush or of the pen
 Delineated here such shades and outlines
 As would amaze the minds of subtlest men?
The living seemed alive, the dead seemed dead:
 Who saw the real events saw no more clearly
 Than all, head bent, I saw beneath my tread.
Walk on in pride, walk on with heads held high, 70
 Children of Eve, and do not lower your glance,
 Or you may find you walk an evil way!
We'd gone already further on the road
 Around the mountain, and used up more daylight
 Than I had thought, being so preoccupied,
When he, who was ahead and looking out,
 As always, told me: "You must raise your eyes:
 The time has gone for being lost in thought.
See, over there, an angel on his way
 To meet us, and the sixth handmaid returning, 80
 Having performed her duty to the day.[6]
Show reverence in your actions and your mien,
 So that it pleases him to send us higher:
 Think that this day will never dawn again!"
I was so used by now to what he said

---

1 Alcmaeon killed his mother: she had been bribed with a necklace to betray her husband's
  hiding place, and so he had to fight at Thebes, where he died.
2 Sennacherib was King of Assyria. The destruction of his army outside Jerusalem led
  ultimately to his murder.
3 Cyrus, Emperor of Persia, had murdered the son of Tomyris. She captured Cyrus, and
  had his head cut off and placed inside a bladder full of blood.
4 Holofernes, an Assyrian general, moved against the Jews. Judith, the Jewish widow
  whom he had hoped to seduce, cut off his head and took it away. When the Assyrians
  found the headless body, they fled in panic and were defeated.
5 The carving shows the destruction of Troy, described by Virgil (*Aeneid* III, 2–3) as "proud
  Ilium".
6 The mythical Hours were represented as maidservants attending the chariot of the sun.
  The meaning is that six hours of daylight have passed, i.e. it is midday.

About not wasting time that he could hardly,
    On such a matter, be misunderstood.
Meanwhile that glorious creature came more near:
    He was in white, his countenance resembled
    The apparent trembling of the morning star.   90
He spread his arms wide and those wings of his,
    And said: "Come here: the steps are close at hand,
    And from now on they can be climbed with ease."
To such solicitations few respond:
    O humankind, born to fly up and up,
    Why do you drop down at a breath of wind?
He led us where the mountainside divided:
    Once there, he struck my forehead with his wings,
    Then promised me I would be unimpeded.
As on the right, when one ascends the hill   100
    Towards the church[1] which, over Rubaconte,[2]
    Commands that city which is governed well,[3]
The hillside's upward thrust is interrupted
    And eased by steps constructed in those times
    When records, weights and measures were respected[4] –
In the same way the slope which tumbles down
    From the next terrace is made easier, but
    On both sides now we're grazed by the high stone.[5]
Then, as we turned, we heard a voice sing out
    "Beati pauperes spiritu!"[6] so sweetly   110
    That human speech could never rise to it.
How different is such an opening
    From the way down to hell! For here one enters
    To songs, but there to savage yammering.
We were already on the sacred stair
    And climbing, but I felt myself much lighter
    Than, when on level ground, I was before.
And so I asked: "Master, what heavy load
    Is lifted from me, that I find it almost
    No effort now to travel on this road?"   120
He answered: "When the Ps that still remain
    Upon your forehead, not yet quite extinguished,
    Are utterly erased, like this first one,
Your feet will be so governed by good will
    That they not only will not feel the effort,
    But will delight in being urged uphill."

---

1 San Miniato al Monte.
2 The old name for a bridge on the site of the present Ponte alle Grazie.
3 Florence: the praise is ironical. See the similar sarcasm in ll. 70–72 above.
4 Dante has in mind the recent abstraction of part of the public records to hide a crime,
   and also a notorious instance of giving short measure.
5 The steps up to San Miniato are, on the contrary, very wide.
6 "Blessed are the poor in spirit", the first of the Beatitudes (Matt. 5:3).

Then I behaved like someone walking on
  Who's unaware there's something on his head,
  While people's gestures fill him with concern,
So he employs his hand to find it out: 130
  His hand feels round, and touch performs that office
  Which could not be accomplished by his sight.
My right hand with its fingering verifies
  Those letters down to six which had been cut
  On my forehead by him who bears the keys:
My leader was amused to see all that.

CANTO XIII

At the top of the stairs leading from the terrace of the proud there is a second terrace cut into the Mountain. This is similar to the one below, except that there are no carvings or marble here, but simply smooth, bare livid rock.

About a mile farther on the travellers hear voices in the air, moving past them and fading in the distance. The speakers are the Virgin Mary, Orestes and his friend who speak as one, and Christ Himself. These voices incite the penitent shades to the virtue of generosity – the virtue which is most opposed to the vice of envy which is here being purified.

More voices are heard, praying the Litany of the Saints. Those praying are the penitent souls themselves, sitting slumped along the rock face, cloaked in haircloth and leaning upon each other. Their eyelids are sewn up, like the eyes of savage hawks being tamed, and tears make their way through the sutures.

When Dante asks if there is any Italian there, he is rebuked: he should have asked if there was anyone there who used to live in Italy as an exile from his true home which is heaven.

The shade who answered is that of a noble Sienese lady, Sapia, notorious while she lived for her envious disposition. She admits her sin frankly and supplies a particularly bad instance of it. This was when she prayed for the defeat of her fellow citizens in a battle with the Florentines, and rejoiced when what she hoped for came about, although she realizes now that this was not as a result of her prayers.

At the end of her life Sapia repented, and the prayers of the humble saint Pier Pettinaio saved her from a long wait outside Purgatory. She asks Dante to reassure her relatives, if he ever returns to Tuscany, that she is saved, and also to pray for her. Her last words to Dante are a sad comment on the vainglorious stupidity of the Sienese.

W e had ascended to the topmost stair,
    There where the mountain, cleansing those who climb it,
    Is cut into and levelled out once more:
For there another terrace runs around
    The mountainside, just as the first one does,
    Except that this describes a sharper bend.
No effigies or signs are to be seen –
    The cliff seems and the road seems smooth and bare –
    The only colour is the livid stone.
"If we wait here to ask someone the way,"   10
    The poet said to me, "I am afraid
    Our choice will be too subject to delay."
He turned his eyes to gaze up at the sun;
    Then, with his right side as a sort of pivot,
    He made the left side of his body turn.
"Sweet light, trusting in whom I go on this
    So unaccustomed road," said Virgil, "give us
    The guidance that we need in such a place.
You warm this world of ours and shine on it:

If other reasons do not contradict,   20
  We should be guided always by your light."
What we would reckon here to be a mile,
  That was the distance we had travelled there,
  And not been long about it, such our zeal,
When flying through the air to us we heard,
  And yet we could not see them, spirits proffer
  Kind invitations to love's festive board.
The first one that came past us on the wing
  Cried out in a loud voice: *"Vinum non habent,"*[1]
  Which it repeated as it went along.   30
And then, before that voice was heard no longer
  In the distance, another passed and cried:
  "I am Orestes"[2] – and it did not linger.
"Oh, father!" I exclaimed. "What cries are these?"
  And even as I asked, there came a third one,
  One of persuasion: "Love your enemies."[3]
My kind lord said: "This terrace is the whip
  Against the sin of envy, and therefore
  The cords are drawn from love that make this whip.
The bridle[4] must be contrary in sound: 40
  And I believe that you will hear that sound
  Before the pass of pardon[5] is attained.
But send your gaze intently through the air,
  And you'll see folk who sit in front of us,
  All ranged along the rock that rises there.
Then I opened my eyes, wider than ever,
  And looked ahead, and saw shades wrapped in cloaks
  Which did not differ from the rock in colour.
And then, a little nearer to that place,
  I heard a cry of "Mary, pray for us!",   50
  Then cries of "Michael!", "Peter!" and "All saints!"
I think that nowadays there is no one
  On earth so callous that he would not be
  Full of pity for what I lighted on;
For, once I'd reached them and I was so near
  That I could see their bearing quite distinctly,
  My eyes were wrung with many a bitter tear.
They seemed to be in haircloth, coarse and stiff,

1   "They have no wine": the words with which Mary persuaded Christ, at the wedding
    feast of Cana, to change water into wine (John 2:1–10).
2   In a Roman play, when Orestes was condemned to death, his friend Pylades pretended
    to be Orestes, and Orestes asserted his own identity, each trying to save the other.
3   Matt. 5:44.
4   As on the other terraces, examples of the punishment of the relevant sin (here envy),
    which are a "bridle" to restrain human beings, balance examples of the opposite virtue
    (here generosity), a "whip" to encourage them.
5   The steps leading up to the next terrace.

And each one propped the next one on his shoulder,
   And all of them were propped up by the cliff: 60
Just as the blind and needy come together
   In the church porch on feast days, mendicant,
   And each one rests his head upon the other,
In order to arouse our pity quickly,
   Not merely by the sound of what they say,
   But by the sight which cries out just as loudly.
And like the blind, neglected by the sun,
   So the shades here, which I am speaking of,
   Find heaven's light is nowhere to be seen;
For their eyelids are threaded through and sewn   70
   With iron wire, like savage sparrow hawks
   Treated that way to help to make them tame.
I thought it was a grave discourtesy,
   As I walked on, to see and not be seen,
   So I turned to him I knew could counsel me.
He saw what I would say, though I was mute,
   And therefore did not wait to hear the question,
   But said: "Speak. Make it brief and to the point."
Virgil was on the outside, to my right,
   Along the terrace edge whence one might fall,   80
   Being unprovided with a parapet;
Upon my other side sat the devout
   Shades: they were squeezing through their horrible
   Sutures such tears as made their cheeks all wet.
I turned to them. "You people who are sure,"
   I said, "to see the light that shines on high,
   The one and only thing that you desire,
May, in your consciousness, all filth and scum
   Soon be dissolved, so that your memory
   May flow clear through it in a lucid stream,   90
Tell me – what I'd find welcome and most dear –
   If there's a soul among you who's Italian:
   It might help him if I could meet him here."[1]
"All of these souls are citizens, my brother,
   Of one true city[2] – and you meant to say,
   'Who used to live in Italy, a stranger'."
It seemed to me that this reply had come
   From somewhere up ahead of where I was,
   And so I made myself heard further on.
I saw one shade, among the others, was   100
   Waiting apparently. Should one ask "How?",
   It raised its chin just as a blind man does.
And so I said: "Spirit now growing tame

---

1   By renewing his memory on earth and so perhaps persuading people to pray for him.
2   The City of God.

For soaring flight, if you're the one who answered,
　Make yourself known to me by place or name."
"Siena," was the answer. "And with this
　Group here I purify my wicked life,
　Weeping to Him to show Himself to us.
I was not sapient, although my name,
　Sapia,[1] might suggest it; I rejoiced　　　　　　110
　Less at my own good luck than others' harm.
And lest you think that I exaggerate,
　Judge if I was, as I say, crazy, with
　The sands of life already running out.
My fellow citizens were in the field
　At Colle, up against their enemies,
　And I prayed God would grant what He had willed.[2]
There was a rout: they turned in hugger-mugger
　Flight from the field. I, seeing the pursuit,
　Was seized with gladness unlike any other,　　　120
And therefore raised my brazen face to God,
　Shouting: 'Now I don't fear you any more!'
　Like the blackbird for one fine period.[3]
I wished to make my peace with God at last,
　Near my life's end; and even now my debt,
　Paid with this penance, would not be reduced,[4]
If I had not been kept in memory,
　And prayed for duly, by Pier Pettinaio,[5]
　Who grieved for me in his great charity.
But who are you, who ask about our state　　　　130
　As you walk round, whose eyes are not sealed up,
　Who breathe as well as speak, if I am right?"[6]
"My eyes," I said, "will be deprived of sight,
　But not for long: such sins as they committed
　By looking on in envy were but slight.
A fear that's greater holds me in its own
　Suspense: I mean the torment that's below;[7]
　The burden there already weighs me down."

1　A noble lady of Siena, aunt of Provenzano Salvani (see *Purg.* XI, 109–42). She died before
　1289.
2　She prayed for her fellow citizens' defeat at Colle di Valdelsa in 1269: they were defeated
　because God willed it.
3　This refers to the fable in which a blackbird imagines, simply for one fine spell of weather,
　that winter has gone.
4　As a late penitent, Sapia would normally have been kept out of Purgatory proper for a
　period as long as her time on earth. See *Purg.* IV, 130–35.
5　A comb-seller in Siena who was renowned for his honesty and revered as a saint. He
　died in 1289.
6　Sapia must have heard Dante approach, and so realized that he was able to see where
　he was going, and she must also have heard him breathing.
7　The penance of the proud on the terrace beneath.

And she to me: "By whom have you been led
   Up here to us, thinking you'll go back down?"   140
   And I: "By this man who's not said a word.
And, since I'm still alive, just tell me if,
   Elected soul, you wish me, once back there,
   To take some mortal steps on your behalf."
"For such a thing to happen is so rare,"
   She said, "it demonstrates how God must love you;
   So succour me from time to time with prayer.
And I beg you, by what you long to win,[1]
   If ever you return to Tuscany,
   Restore my name among my kith and kin.[2]   150
You'll find them with those harebrains hoping in a
   Port pitched at Talamone, wasting there
   More effort than they'll waste on the Diana;
But there the admirals will lose much more."[3]

---

1   Eternal salvation.

2   She wishes Dante to tell them that, despite her great failings, she is saved.

3   The reference is to two fiascos for which the proverbially foolish Sienese were responsible: the purchase of a malarial town with a silted-up harbour, Talamone, for use as a port, and the futile search for an underground stream (named in advance the Diana) to supplement the city's inadequate water supply. The word "admirals" is most probably a sarcastic allusion to unfulfilled naval ambitions.

CANTO XIV

Dante hears two shades talking: they wonder about this man who is allowed to walk around the mountain and who is able to open his eyes. One of these shades, Guido del Duca, asks Dante for his name and origin.

Dante's reply is vague: he was born beside a river he does not name, and his own name is not yet important enough to be mentioned. Guido realizes that the river is the Arno, and the other shade, Rinieri da Calboli, assumes that it is shame which prevents Dante from naming his native city. For Guido it is only right that the river's name should be forgotten: he traces its course from Falterona, through the Casentino, whose inhabitants are like swine, near to Arezzo from whose doglike citizens it turns away scornfully, and through Florence with its wolfish citizens, until it flows into the sea near to the foxlike citizens of Pisa. This diatribe ends with a denunciation of Fulcieri da Calboli, grandson of Rinieri who is being addressed.

Guido then turns to his native Romagna, lamenting its present decadence, which he contrasts with its past glory. He laments that some families have died out, and that some others have not died out. Eventually he is in such anguish that he asks Dante to leave him to weep in silence.

As Dante and Virgil walk on, they hear a voice like thunder: this is Cain lamenting, after his murder of his brother Abel, that all men will try to kill him. There is a slight pause, and another thunderous voice is heard: this is Aglauros, who was turned to stone by Mercury because she envied his love for her sister. In the silence that follows, Virgil explains that those two voices are examples of the punishment of the sin of envy. He laments the tendency of human beings to be seduced by the Devil: instead of looking up to the heavens, they keep their eyes on the ground. That, he says, is why God has to chastise them into a better frame of mind.

"Who is this walking round this Mount of ours
    Before his death has set him free for flight,
    Who opens, when he wants, and shuts his eyes?"
"He's not alone; I don't know who he is:
    You ask him, since you're nearer him than I,
    And ask politely, so that he replies."
These were two spirits, leaning cheek to cheek,
    Discussing me, somewhere upon my right;
    And as they tilted back their heads to speak,
One of them asked: "O soul who, while being still   10
    Bound to your body, make your way to heaven,
    Comfort us out of charity and tell
Us where you come from, tell us who you are;
    We wonder at the grace which you receive,
    Such grace as there has never been before."
And I: "Through central Tuscany there ranges
    A brooklet that is born in Falterona;[1]
    Nor does a hundred-mile-long course contain it.

---

1   A peak in the Apennines, north-east of Florence.

From that river I bring this body of mine:
   To say my name would be a waste of breath,   20
   Since up to now it's not earned much renown."
"If I have had the skill to penetrate
   Your meaning with my mind," said the first speaker,
   "It is the Arno that you adumbrate."
The other asked him then: "Why did he hide
   The name that river goes by, like some horror
   Men find too awful to be specified?"
The shade to whom that question had been put
   Replied: "I don't know; but I know it's fitting
   The name of that whole valley should die out,   30
For from its source – there where that mountain mass[1]
   (From which Pelorus[2] broke off) teems with water
   Whose amplitude few places can surpass –
To where the river once again restores
   All that the sky has soaked up from the ocean,
   All which provides a river with its course,
They flee from virtue like an enemy,
   Or like a snake, being goaded by the place's
   Ill customs or its evil destiny.
The inhabitants have so transformed their nature   40
   In that unhappy valley that it seems
   As if Circe herself drives them to pasture.[3]
First among filthy swine,[4] more fit to feed
   On acorns than on human nourishment,
   That river starts upon its meagre road.[5]
And then it comes on dogs[6] as it goes down,
   Whose snarl and bark are fiercer than their bite,
   And turns its snout away from them in scorn.[7]
And, as it flows on down, this river, which
   Swells constantly, finds dogs becoming wolves[8]   50
   Beside its cursèd and unhappy ditch.
Descending through abyss upon abyss,
   It comes on foxes,[9] cunning, unafraid
   Of being trapped by any artifice.
Nor will I stop because I'm overheard:
   It will be well if this man here remembers
   All that, through me, the spirit of truth has said.

---

1   The Apennines.
2   Now Cape Faro, a promontory in the north-east of Sicily.
3   Circe had the power to change men into beasts.
4   The inhabitants of the Casentino, known for their sensuality.
5   The Arno at this point has little water in it.
6   The inhabitants of Arezzo.
7   The Arno passes near, but not through, Arezzo.
8   The Florentines.
9   The Pisans.

I see your grandson:[1] he's become a hunter
   Of wolves, those wolves inhabiting the banks
   Of the cruel stream,[2] and fills them all with terror.   60
He sells their flesh while they're still living; then
   He has them slaughtered like decrepit cattle;
   They lose their lives: he loses his good name.
He comes all bloody from the wasted wood,[3]
   Leaving it such that in a thousand years
   The devastation will not be made good."
As at the news of some appalling harm
   The face of one who hears the news is clouded,
   No matter whence the danger threatens him,
So I noticed that other soul, alert   70
   To what was said, become disquieted,
   Once he had taken all the words to heart.
The words of one, the other full of care,
   Made me so anxious to be told their names
   That I begged them to tell me who they were;
At this the shade who'd spoken previously
   Began again: "You would have me persuaded
   To do for you what you won't do for me.
But, since God wishes that His grace should shine
   Through you so brightly, I will not be chary: 80
   Know that Guido del Duca[4] was my name.
Envy had made my blood so boiling hot
   That if I noticed someone being happy
   You'd find me livid at the thought of it.
From what I sowed I'm reaping now this straw:[5]
   O humankind, why do you give your hearts
   To things it is impossible to share?
This is Rinieri, the honour and the praise
   Of the house of Calboli,[6] where there's nobody
   Who has inherited his qualities.   90
And his is not the one and only race,
   Between the Po, sea, mountain and the Reno,[7]
   Stripped of integrity and gentleness;
For all within those bounds is so replete
   With poison stumps and thorns that cultivation
   Would now arrive too late to root them out.

---

1   Fulcieri da Calboli, a member of a famous Black Guelf family. He was Podestà of Florence
     in 1303, and was a ruthless enemy of the White Guelfs. This shade is speaking to his
     fellow shade, and not directly to Dante.
2   The Florentines.
3   Florence.
4   One of the Onesti family of Ravenna. He is known to have been still alive in 1249.
5   His purgation on the terrace of the envious.
6   Rinieri da Calboli (d.1296) was a member of a famous Guelf family.
7   The region of Romagna.

Where is Arrigo Mainardi,[1] Lizio,[2] Piero
   Traversaro[3] and Guido di Carpigna?[4]
   O men born bastards in Romagna, where?
When will a Bolognese Fabbro[5] take root   100
   Again? Faenza grow a Bernardino
   Di Fosco,[6] noble branch from humble shoot?
Now do not wonder, Tuscan, if you find
   Me weeping to recall Guido da Prata,[7]
   And Ugolino d'Azzo[8] in our land,
Federigo Tignoso's[9] company,
   The Traversaro stock,[10] the Anastagi[11]
   (Both houses now without male progeny),
Ladies and knights, the exploits and the fine
   Living that love and courtesy inspire,   110
   There where men's hearts have now turned so malign.
O Bertinoro,[12] why not fade away,
   Since your best family has gone, with many
   Others who would avoid depravity?
Bagnacavallo[13] does well to breed no heirs;
   Castrocaro does ill, and Conio[14] worse,
   Striving to breed such counts as now it does.
The Pagani will do well, once they're bereft
   Of their own demon,[15] and yet not so well
   That an unclouded record will be left.   120
O Ugolino de' Fantolini,[16] your name
   Is safe, since nobody is now expected

---

1   A great friend of Guido del Duca. He was still alive in 1228.
2   Lizio di Valbona, an ally of Rinieri da Calboli. He was still alive in 1279.
3   A powerful member of a famous family in Ravenna who died in 1225.
4   Of the family of the Counts of Montefeltro. Podestà of Ravenna in 1251. He died before 1289.
5   Fabbro de' Lambertazzi. Podestà of many Italian cities. Died in 1259.
6   Born in the thirteenth century of humble stock in Faenza, he became a distinguished statesman.
7   A native of Romagna who flourished 1184–1228.
8   A member of the Ubaldini family who lived in his castles in Romagna. Died in 1293.
9   Lived probably in the first half of the thirteenth century. Famous for his hospitality.
10   A very old family with no male members surviving.
11   A family from Ravenna which had long ago died out. Piero Traversaro (ll. 97–98) was a famous member.
12   A small town in Romagna, the birthplace of Guido del Duca (l. 81) and Arrigo Mainardi (l. 97).
13   A town in Romagna.
14   Castrocaro and Conio are castles in Romagna whose counts are blamed by Guido del Duca for not dying out.
15   The "demon" of the Pagani family, lords of Faenza, is their last survivor, Maghinardo Pagani da Susinana (*Inf.* xxvii, 49–51).
16   A worthy of Romagna who died in 1278, leaving two childless sons who were dead before 1291.

Who, being degenerate, would bring you shame.
Go on your way now, Tuscan: there's more joy
  By far for me in weeping than in speech,
  Our conversation so depresses me."
We knew that those well-meaning souls had heard
  Us moving off; and so their silence now
  Assured us we were taking the right road.
When we had gone so far we were alone,   130
  Then like a lightning flash that splits the air,
  A voice flew out to meet us: "Anyone
Who finds me now will kill me!"[1] And it fled,
  Like thunder rumbling as it rolls away
  After its sudden rupture of a cloud.
Another voice with a resounding crash
  Came when that first voice gave a breathing space,
  Like thunder following a lightning flash:
"I am Aglauros, who was turned to stone."[2]
  Then I, to huddle closer to my poet,   140
  Moved to the right instead of moving on.
And now the air was silent all around,
  And he explained: "That was the bit and bridle
  To keep all human beings duty-bound.
But still you take the bait, so that the hook
  Of the old adversary draws you in;
  And neither bit nor lure[3] can hold you back.
The heavens call you as they circle round
  And show eternal beauties to delight you,
  And yet you keep your eyes upon the ground: 150
And that is why the All-seeing has to smite you."

---

1   The voice of Cain, after he had killed his brother Abel out of envy (Gen. 4:14).
2   Aglauros envied her sister because she was loved by Mercury. The latter turned Aglauros
    into stone.
3   A bunch of feathers used to recall a hawk.

CANTO XV

It is now time for vespers, and the pilgrims have gone so far round the Mountain that they are facing the setting sun. Suddenly Dante is dazzled, and he lowers his head; but the light is refracted from the ground and still dazzles him. Virgil explains that this is an angel who will help them on their way, and he tells Dante that he will get accustomed to such sights. The angel invites them to ascend a stairway he indicates, one less steep than previous ones. As they leave the terrace of the envious they hear the blessing of the merciful, whose virtue is opposed to envy.

As they ascend, Dante asks Virgil to explain a remark made by Guido del Duca, and he is told that love differs from other things we desire in that the more we give the more we get. Beatrice will explain this truth in more detail, Virgil says. Meanwhile Dante must be sure to heal the five remaining wounds, signs of the capital sins, on his forehead: the second was healed when they left the terrace of the envious.

Dante now has a vision which shows him three examples of meekness, the virtue most opposed to the vice of anger which is being purged on the next terrace.

First he sees the finding of the Child Jesus in the temple and hears how gently the Virgin Mary remonstrates with her Son. Then he sees and hears how Pisistratus, ruler of Athens, used a gentle answer to turn away wrath. Finally he sees the murder of the first Christian martyr, Stephen, and hears him forgive his murderers.

Dante is so affected by these sights that he staggers like a drunken man or like someone just roused from sleep, and Virgil tells him to pull himself together, since there is no time to lose.

The pilgrims continue walking into the light of the setting sun until they are met by a cloud of smoke which envelops them and deprives them of fresh air and of their ability to see. This smoke is from the terrace of the wrathful.

That length of time we see the circling sphere[1]
    That always frolics like a child[2] – between
    Day breaking and the end of the third hour –
Such time the sun had left until it set,
    Apparently, on its diurnal course;
    There it was time for vespers, here midnight.[3]
The rays were striking us full on the face,
    Because we'd gone so far around the Mountain
    That we were heading for their resting place;[4]
Then I was forced to keep my eyes cast down   10
    By light much brighter than I'd seen before,
    And I felt stupefied by the unknown;
At that I raised my hands to my eyebrows
    And formed them in the fashion of a shade,

---

1   The sun.
2   This seems to allude to the sun's apparently oblique course in relation to the celestial
    equator.
3   "There" is Purgatory, and "here" is Italy.
4   The west.

To impose some limit on the dazzling rays.
  As when, from water or a looking glass,
    A ray of light leaps in the opposed direction,
    And so ascends at the same angle as
It first descends, diverging from the line
  A stone makes when it drops, at equal distance,   20
    As knowledge and experiment have shown –
Just so it seemed that I was struck by light
  Refracted there in front of me, so that
  My vision was not slow to take to flight.
"What is this, my dear father, from which I
  Cannot protect my eyes sufficiently,"
  I asked, "moving this way apparently?"
"No marvel that the servants of the skies
  Still dazzle you: this is a messenger,"
  He said, "who comes inviting us to rise.   30
Very soon seeing things of this kind will
  No more be burdensome, but a delight
  As great as nature fashioned you to feel."
When we had reached the angelic messenger,
  He said invitingly, "Go in this way."
  It was less steep than any previous stair.
We heard, as we went forward on our climb,
  "*Beati misericordes!*"[1] sung behind us,
  And then "Rejoice, all you who overcome!"
My guide and I alone went on ahead,   40
  Always climbing – and as we went I thought
  I'd get some benefit from what he said.
I turned to him and asked him then and there:
  "What did the spirit from Romagna[2] mean
  By 'things it is impossible to share'?"[3]
The answer was: "He knows by now the cost
  Incurred by his great flaw; so naturally
  He's warning you, lest you end up distressed.[4]
It is because your longing tends to be
  For things which, once shared out, leave less for each,   50
  That envy works the bellows and you sigh.
If love inhabiting the highest sphere,[5]
  However, were to lift up your desires,
  Your breast would not be troubled with that fear;
For there the more there are who can say 'our',
  The more each individual possesses,
  And in that cloister charity burns more."

1   "Blessed are the merciful" (Matt. 5:7).
2   Guido del Duca.
3   See *Purg.* XIV, 87.
4   Lest you have to suffer for the same fault in Purgatory.
5   The Empyrean, heaven.

"I'm now more hungry and less satisfied,"
 I said, "than if I had not raised the question,
 And greater doubts have come into my mind.   60
How can a good, a good distributed
 Among more people, make each one more rich
 Than if possessed by few and never shared?"
And he replied: "It is because you set
 Such store persistently on earthly things
 That you pluck darkness even from true light.
That Good, ineffable and infinite,
 That is up there, runs to a loving soul
 Like sunbeams to a mass reflecting light.[1]
It gives itself wherever it finds ardour;   70
 So that, wherever charity extends,
 It but augments the everlasting vigour.
And the more souls above who love each other,
 The more there is to love and love the more,
 And each reflects the others like a mirror.
And if my speech has failed to fill you full,[2]
 You will see Beatrice, and she will fully
 Fill this and every longing that you feel.
Therefore take care that you heal very soon
 (Two are already healed) the five wounds left,[3]   80
 Which can be healed by feeling so much pain."[4]
I was about to say, "You fill me full,"
 When I saw that I'd reached the other terrace,
 And there my greedy eyes kept my tongue still.
And there it seemed that I was suddenly
 Caught up in an ecstatic vision showing
 A temple filled with a great company;
And in the doorway, with that mild demeanour
 That mothers have, I saw a woman saying:
 "My son, why do you treat us in this manner?   90
Your father and myself have looked for you
 With sorrow in our hearts."[5] And when she finished,
 All that appeared had disappeared from view.
I saw a second woman, and saw water
 Run down her cheeks, distilled there by the grief
 Brought on by sheer resentment of another,

---

1 The image is of the sun providing light to the stars, just as those who are worthy receive
   grace from God.
2 A reminiscence of the image of hunger in l. 58.
3 Refers to the Ps cut into Dante's forehead (*Purg.* IX, 112–14 and XII, 121–36). The second
   P was erased when Dante started to climb this stairway.
4 Penitential pain.
5 The Finding in the Temple (Luke 2:41–50). This and the following two visions are
   "whips", examples of the virtue (meekness) opposed to the sin (anger) which is purged
   on the third terrace.

Who said: "If you do rule that city, about
   Whose name gods even found themselves at strife,
   That city whence all wisdom flashes out,
Take vengeance on those arms which were so wild   100
   As to embrace our daughter, Pisistratus."
   That lord himself appeared, kindly and mild,
And with a calm demeanour answered thus:
   "What shall we do to those intending harm,
   If we condemn someone who's fond of us?"[1]
Then I saw people blaze with anger while
   They stoned a youth to death, and heard them shouting
   Out loudly to each other: "Kill! Kill! Kill!"
I saw him underneath those heavy blows
   Fall down upon the ground and to his death,   110
   Still making gates to heaven with his eyes,
Begging the Lord, in all this great dissension,
   To pardon those who persecuted him,
   With such a look as must unlock compassion.[2]
When my soul turned again to things outside
   Myself and true, I recognized the error,
   A not misleading one, that I had made.[3]
My guide, who saw that I was in a state,
   Like somebody who is still half asleep,
   Said: "What is wrong with you? You can't walk straight,   120
But you have gone for half a league or more
   With your eyes closed, unsteady on your legs,
   Like a drunk man or stubborn slumberer."
"O my kind father, if you hear me out,"
   I said, "I'll tell you what I seemed to see
   When I was so unsteady on my feet."
He said: "If you'd a hundred masks upon
   Your face, all of your thoughts would be revealed
   To me, down to the very slightest one.
All that you saw was to make sure you don't   130
   Keep your heart shut against the peaceful waters
   Which flow and spread from the eternal fount.
I did not ask 'What's wrong?' as someone does
   Who only looks with eyes that cannot see,
   Finding somebody lying in a daze;
I asked that question to inspire your feet:
   The sluggish must be goaded, if they're slow,
   When consciousness returns, to gain by it."

---

1   The daughter of Pisistratus, ruler of Athens, was embraced in public by the man who
    loved her. Her mother was outraged, but Pisistratus gave a gentle answer, and their
    daughter and her suitor were married. The strife of the gods mentioned in l. 98 was
    between Poseidon and Athena.

2   The martyrdom of Stephen (Acts 6 and 7, especially 7:54–60).

3   Dante realizes that he has been "seeing things", visions which reveal the truth.

We went on walking through the evening light,
   Looking as far ahead as eyes could reach,   140
   Into the sun which, setting, was still bright.
Then gradually there came a cloud of smoke
   Coming towards us like the gathering night;
   There was no way to avoid it, and it took
The fresh air from us, and it took our sight.

CANTO XVI

The smoke surrounding the pilgrims is now so dense, almost palpable, that Dante, like a blind man, has to rely on Virgil to guide him. This physical blindness is like the mental blindness caused by anger.

They hear voices singing the 'Agnus Dei', a prayer for mercy and peace. The harmony of the singing contrasts with the disharmony of anger.

No one is to be seen, but a voice is heard asking how Dante is able to cut through the smoke, an action impossible for a mere shade, and why he speaks like a living person. Dante promises to explain, if the spirit keeps him company. After this explanation, and the giving of directions, the spirit says he is Marco Lombardo.

Dante asks Marco to explain why the present world is so corrupt. He is told that it is a mistake to attribute our faults to the stars. The heavens give us our first impulses, but we are provided also with the ability to distinguish good from evil, and the free will to choose between them.

Laws are needed to guide people along the right path. Two institutions have been provided for this purpose – the temporal power, the Holy Roman Empire, and the spiritual power, the Papacy; the first should guide men's actions in this world, and the second should lead them to heaven. These two powers ought to be kept separate, but the struggle between Emperor and Pope has led to the victory of the Pope, who now has temporal as well as spiritual power. The lack of any restraint upon these combined powers means that they are abused. The Popes act badly, and their flock imitates them.

Since dawn is breaking, and Marco must not be seen by the angel of this terrace, whom they are approaching, he ends the conversation and leaves.

*

Infernal darkness, or a night devoid
   Of all its stars, beneath a barren sky,
   One overshadowed utterly by cloud,
Had never drawn such a thick veil across
   My sight, one so repulsive to the touch,
   As that thick smoke which there enveloped us;
And so my eyes could not stay open, which
   Obliged my faithful, understanding guide
   To offer me his shoulder as a crutch.
And as a blind man goes behind his guide   10
   Lest he be lost, or strike against something
   By which he might be hurt or even killed,
So I went through the acrid, dirty air,
   And listened to my guide, who kept on saying:
   "Make sure we stay together. Do take care."
I could hear voices, and it seemed each one
   Was offering prayers for peace and mercy to
   The Lamb of God Who takes away our sin.

"*Agnus Dei*"[1] was the exordium
  Of what they always sang, and sang together,   20
  So that all seemed harmonious with them.
"Can those be spirits I am hearing, master?"
  I asked. And he said: "You have hit the mark;
  And they are loosening the knot of anger."[2]
"Now who are you, who cut through our smoke here,[3]
  And speak about us like somebody still
  Dividing time up by the calendar?"
Those were the words from one voice which we heard;
  And so my master ordered: "Answer him,
  And ask if we can go up on this side."   30
I said: "O creature here to purify
  Yourself, and go back clean to your Creator,
  You'll hear a marvel if you come with me."
"I'll follow you as far as I'm allowed,"
  The voice replied. "If smoke obscures our sight,
  Hearing will serve to keep us linked instead."
I said: "I am still swaddled in those bands[4]
  Which death unbinds, and I am travelling up;
  I came here through the Inferno and its pangs.
And since God has so wrapped me in His grace   40
  That He intends to let me see his court
  In a manner beyond our modern ways,[5]
Then tell me who you were before you died,
  And tell us if we're going to the pass:
  We'll make our way there with your words as guide."
"I was from Lombardy, Marco by name;[6]
  I knew the way the world goes, and I loved
  That worth which no one now seems to esteem.
Go straight ahead to climb the Mount." Thus he
  Replied, and then he added: "I implore   50
  You, once you are above, to pray for me."
And I replied to him: "I give my word
  To do that, but inside I'm simply seething:
  There is a doubt from which I must be freed.
First it was one thing, now you make it two
  With your remarks, and make me doubly certain

1 "Lamb of God." The full prayer, which is taken from the Mass, is "Lamb of God, Who take away the sins of the world, have mercy on us" (sung twice), and "Lamb of God, Who take away the sins of the world, grant us peace" (sung once).
2 This is the third terrace, where the sin of anger is purged.
3 Something a disembodied soul could not do.
4 His body.
5 St Paul had been "caught up into paradise" long ago (2 Cor. 12:2–4).
6 Little is known about this thirteenth-century figure, except that he was an honest counsellor.

What I'm told here,[1] and there,[2] is really true.
This world of ours is utterly without
  Goodness, as you remark, and overspread
  With ill intent, and pregnant too with it;   60
But I beg you to show the cause, that so
  I may both see and point it out to others:
  Some place it in the stars, some down below."
A sigh becoming "Ah!" was what he wailed
  First in reply, and then he said: "My brother,
  The world is blind, and you come from the world.
You who are living always place causation
  Up in the heavens above, as though all things
  Had to be moved by them and by their motion.
If that were so, free will were null and void,   70
  And there would be no justice in dispensing
  Joy for goodness, sorrow for being bad.
The heavens give your first tendencies – not all
  Of them, but even if I did say all,
  Light is given to know both good and ill.
Free choice is yours, and can it only pull
  Through its first battles with the sky, it conquers
  All things at last, if it is nourished well.
You're subject to a greater strength, a more
  Benign nature[3] – and this creates in you   80
  A mind that's uncontrolled by any star.
So, if the present world has gone astray,
  The reason lies, and should be sought, in you;
  Which I intend to make as clear as day.
There issues from the hand of God, Who's filled
  With love for it before it's made, there issues,
  Weeping and giggling like a little child,
The simple soul that's utterly untaught,
  Except that, tutored by its happy Maker,
  It turns towards whatever gives delight.   90
It has at first a taste for trivial good,
  Which so beguiles it that it chases after,
  If not restricted by some rein or guide.
So as a rein there had to be the law;
  There had to be a monarch to distinguish
  The towers of God's true city from afar.
The laws are there: who puts them to the proof?
  No one, for those by whom the flock is guided

---

1   See l. 48 above.

2   Guido del Duca, on the terrace below, has lamented the moral decadence of
     mankind.

3   God.

Can chew the cud, but do not cleave the hoof;[1]
And so the people, when they see their pastor   100
    Snatching at that for which themselves are greedy,
    Feed on it too, and ask for nothing other.
So you can see how evil government
    Is what has made the world become so wicked:
    Your nature's not corrupt and decadent.[2]
Old Rome, that used to turn the world to good,[3]
    Had two suns to illuminate two roads,
    The road the world takes, and the road to God.
Now one's eclipsed the other – now the sword
    Has joined the crozier,[4] and the two together,   110
    And linked by force, lead only to what's bad;
Since they're united, neither is afraid:
    If you doubt this is true, think of the harvest,
    For every plant's known only by its seed.[5]
In the lands watered by the Adige
    And Po,[6] valour and openhandedness
    Flourished, till Frederick met with rivalry:[7]
Now anyone can go there, unafraid
    Of coming on good people to his shame,
    Whose speech or whose mere presence would upbraid.   120
There are, indeed, three old men still alive
    In whom the old times chide the new, who find
    God slow to call them to a better life:
Corrado da Palazzolo,[8] and the good
    Gherardo[9] – Guido da Castello,[10] much better
    Called, in the French phrase, "the sincere Lombard".
And so the Church of Rome, we may conclude,
    By merging these two powers, lands in the mire,

---

1   The allusion is to Jewish dietary laws, by which clean animals are those that chew the
    cud and have cloven hooves (Lev. 11:3). Allegorically the chewing is interpreted as ru-
    mination on Scripture, and the division of the hoof as the ability to distinguish between
    good and evil.
2   That is, not made so by the stars.
3   Rome was traditionally seen as having civilized the world in preparation for the coming
    of Christ.
4   The sword represents the temporal power, the Holy Roman Empire, and the crozier
    the spiritual power, the Papacy.
5   An adaptation of Matt. 7:16–17: "You shall know them by their fruits. Do men gather
    grapes of thorns, or figs of thistles? Even so every good tree bringeth forth good fruit;
    but a corrupt tree bringeth forth evil fruit."
6   Northern Italy.
7   The Holy Roman Emperor Frederick II (r.1220–50) engaged in a long political struggle
    with the Papacy.
8   A Guelf ruler from Brescia in the second half of the thirteenth century.
9   Gherardo da Camino, lord of Treviso from 1283 until his death in 1306.
10 A Lombard (d.1315) whom even the French thought honest.

And with that fouls herself and her great load."¹
"Oh Marco," I replied, "you talk much sense;   130
  And now I realize why the sons of Levi
  Could have no share in the inheritance.²
But who is that Gherardo you allege
  Is left us of a dying generation
  In reprehension of a savage age?"
"Your words deceive me, or they lead me on,"
  He said to me, "when you, whose speech is Tuscan,
  Imply the good Gherardo is unknown!
There is no other name that I can give you,
  Unless I were to call him Gaia's father.³   140
  God bless you now: I go no further with you.
Piercing the smoke you see the rays of dawn
  Already growing whiter, and before
  That angel there sees me, I must be gone."
He turned away, and spoke with me no more.

---

1   Her function and responsibilities.
2   The tribe of Levi, appointed to be priests of the temple, were not to possess any part of the Promised Land (Num. 18:20–24).
3   Gherardo da Camino's daughter Gaia was famous, according to some accounts, for her virtue, and according to others for her vice.

CANTO XVII

Dante and Virgil emerge from the dense smoke on the terrace of the wrathful and glimpse once more the sun, which is now setting.

Dante sees in his mind's eye examples of the sin of wrath – the mythical Procne, the biblical Haman, and Lavinia's mother from the *Aeneid*. Dante is roused from these visions by a bright light. He hears a voice telling them this is where they must climb, and is dazzled by the light veiling the speaker, an angel. The longing to see into this brightness will haunt Dante all his days.

Virgil insists that they start to climb immediately: during the night no movement is possible on Mount Purgatory. As Dante sets foot on the first step up he feels a wing brush his face with a breath of wind, and he hears a voice reminding him of the blessing upon peacemakers. The angel's wing has removed the third P from Dante's forehead.

As darkness falls, Dante finds his strength is failing. At the top of the stairway they halt: they are now on the terrace of the slothful. Virgil explains the nature of the sins, or rather sinful dispositions, that are purged in Purgatory.

No creature is without love, and this love is of two kinds – innate and chosen. The first cannot err, but the second can. It can err in three ways – when it is directed to evil; when it is directed to the true Good, that is God, with too little determination (the sin of acedia); or when it is directed too much to finite things (the sins of avarice, gluttony and lust).

Love is therefore the source of all good and all evil. People sin against their neighbour – by pride, by envy or by wrath. This triple love is purged on the three terraces below. Defective love of God, the sin of sloth or acedia, is purged on this fourth terrace. Other love, which abandons itself to finite satisfactions, is purged on the terraces above them.

    I f, reader, you were ever caught within
      A mountain mist which let you see no better
      Than a mole sees through eye-enclosing skin,[1]
Recall how, when such damp dense fogs begin
    To thin out and disperse, the sun's great globe
    Is visible but feebly in between,
And your imagination will soon get
    A mental picture of the way I saw
    The sun again as it began to set.
Now, walking step by step with those true steps   10
    My master took, I issued from such cloud
    To rays now dead upon the lower slopes.[2]
Imagination! From the world at hand
    You sometimes steal us till we notice nothing,
    Although a thousand trumpets sound around!
What moves us when our senses play no part?
    A light moves us that takes its form in heaven,

---

1   It was believed that moles had skin over their eyes, which made them purblind.
2   Only the higher ground can still catch the rays of the setting sun.

Self-sent or by a will directing it.[1]
The wickedness of her who was transformed
  Into that bird which most delights in singing[2]   20
  Appeared as an impression in my mind:
Imagination was so self-contained
  That it was now unable to receive
  Anything that arrived there from around.
Then into my deep fantasy like rain
  Dropped one being crucified, who as he died
  Kept his ferocity and his disdain:[3]
The great Ahasuerus and his bride
  Esther were there, and also Mordecai,
  Who was so just in all he said and did.   30
And then, the instant that this image burst,
  Shattering like a bubble when the water
  By which it has been fashioned is displaced,
There rose into my vision a young girl[4]
  Weeping loudly and saying: "O my queen,
  Why did you choose to perish in your gall?
Rather than see Lavinia lost you kill
  Yourself: now you have lost me! Now I mourn
  Yours, mother, more than anybody's fall."
As sleep is broken when occluded eyes   40
  Are stricken by daylight and, being broken,
  Twitches a little till it wholly dies,
Just so my vision broke and went away
  The instant that my face was struck by light
  Much brighter than the usual light of day.
Wondering where I might be, I looked around
  And heard a voice say: "Here's the place to climb."
  This drove all other objects from my mind,
And filled my will with such desire to place
  The person who was speaking in that way –   50
  Such that it cannot rest till face to face.
But, as before the sun which dazzles us,
  Veiling its aspect with excess of light,
  What powers I brought to bear were of no use.
"This spirit is divine, one who, without
  Any request of ours, directs us upward;

---

1 Sent either directly by God or by the natural operation of the planets.

2 Procne. See *Purg.* IX, 13–15 and note.

3 Haman. The Jew Mordecai refused to do reverence to Haman, the first minister of King
    Ahasuerus. Haman planned therefore to have all the Jews in Persia killed. Esther, wife
    of the King and cousin to Mordecai, intervened and Haman was executed. These events
    are commemorated by the feast of Purim. See the book of Esther.

4 In the *Aeneid* (XII, 595–607) Amata of Latium is determined not to see her daughter
    Lavinia (the "young girl") married to Aeneas rather than Turnus. When she thinks
    Turnus is dead, she hangs herself in despair.

And he conceals himself in his own light.
He does to us as we would be done by;
   For one who must be asked, in time of need,
   Is predisposed wickedly to deny.   60
Let's further this proposal with our feet
   And try to make the climb before it's dark,
   For then, until the daybreak, we cannot."
So said my leader, and so I with him
   Turned my feet, making for a set of steps;
   And once my foot was on the first of them,
I sensed what seemed the brushing of a wing, a
   Breath of wind in my face, a voice: "*Beati
   Pacifici*, who shun unrighteous anger!"[1]
The sun's last rays had risen to such a height   70
   Above us, for the dark to follow after,
   That on all sides the stars were coming out.
"This strength of mine, why does it fade away?"
   I had to ask myself, since I was feeling
   My legs were losing all their energy.[2]
We'd come to where the stairway rose no more,
   And there we stood and made no further motion,
   Just like a vessel that has come to shore.
I paused awhile to hear what might be heard,
   If anything, upon this latest circle,   80
   And then turned to my master, and I said:
"My gentle father, clarify: what fault
   Is purged here on this terrace where we're standing?
   Although our feet stand still, your words need not."
And he replied: "The love of what is good,
   Which yet falls short, pays here its compensation:
   The oar which slackened off is doubly plied.
To make this situation still more clear,
   Give me your full attention, and you'll gain
   Some profit from this pause we're making here."   90
"Neither what is created," he began,
   "Nor the Creator, ever lacked for love,
   Innate or chosen, as you know, my son.
While innate love is always free from error,
   This other love[3] can err with evil objects,
   Or with too great or else too little fervour.
When it's directed to the Primal Good,
   And lesser good things in due moderation,
   The pleasure that it gives cannot be bad;
But when it turns to ill, or else with greater   100

---

1   "Blessed are the peacemakers" (Matt. 5:9).
2   See ll. 62–63.
3   The mental or rational love, which can choose how to act.

Or less care than it ought, to what is good,
The creature then opposes his Creator.
So you can comprehend, by definition,
Love is in you the seed of every virtue
And every deed that merits retribution.
Now since love never turns aside its face
From what is beneficial for the lover,
All things are safely shielded from self-hate;
Since nothing can be seen to self-exist,
Or be divided from the Primal Being,   110
No creature can abhor Him Who comes First.[1]
Therefore, if what I say distinguishes
Aright, the evil wished for is our neighbour's,
Which in your dust[2] arises in three ways.
There's one who lives in hopes he will excel
If others are kept down, and so desires
Nothing so much as his great neighbour's fall;[3]
There's one who fears to lose honour and favour
And fame and power if others rise, and therefore
Bitterly craves the converse for his neighbour;[4]   120
And lastly there are those whose feelings seem
So injured that they hunger for revenge,
And so they have to do their neighbour harm.[5]
This triple love is expiated here
Beneath us; now I'd have you know the other
Love which seeks good in ways that are impure.
All men conceive, confusedly, some good
To satisfy the mind, and they desire it;
And all men struggle that it be secured;
When love that draws you is inadequate   130
To see it or to gain it, on this terrace,
After repentance, you must pay for that.[6]
There's other good, which does not make men glad;
It is not happiness, and not Essential
Goodness, the fruit and root of all that's good.
The love pursuing that excessively
Is wept above us on three terraces;[7]
But how it is divided into three
I do not say: you work out how it is."

---

1 Since the creature's very existence depends on Him.
2 The "dust of the ground" from which man was created (Gen. 2:7).
3 The sin of pride.
4 The sin of envy.
5 The sin of wrath.
6 The sinful disposition to sloth is purged on this terrace.
7 The terraces of the avaricious or prodigal, of the gluttonous and of the lustful, the three highest circles of Mount Purgatory.

CANTO XVIII

If we are creatures born to love, how can our love of anything incur either praise or blame? Virgil explains that man has been given reason or understanding, which enables him, indeed requires him, to choose what he does. Ancient philosophers founded their notion of morality (the very existence of right and wrong) on man's ability to choose. Virgil admits that he has now gone as far as human reason can take him, and suggests that Dante should raise any questions he may still have with Beatrice when he meets her. She is enlightened by divine revelation, which goes beyond human reason.

It is now almost midnight, and Dante is feeling drowsy, but he is startled by a crowd of shades rushing up from behind. They are those who in life were guilty of sloth, and now they are punished for this, and expiating it by moving at great speed. Two of them mention encouraging examples of zeal, the opposite of sloth: the Virgin Mary, who after the Annunciation hurried to see her cousin Elizabeth; Julius Caesar's rapid defeat of Pompey.

When Virgil asks if someone will direct Dante and himself to the gap in the mountainside through which they may ascend, he is answered by the shade of a former Abbot of San Zeno, who says they will find the place if they follow the rushing crowd. He apologizes for not pausing, but explains that these shades are impelled to rush to fulfil their penance.

Two of the shades are heard giving warning examples of sloth and its punishment: the Hebrews who perished before they saw the Promised Land, in punishment for their truculence and lack of zeal; those followers of Aeneas who settled down in Sicily instead of following him to fulfil his destiny.

These shades are now so far ahead that Dante can no longer see them. His mind is full of various confusing thoughts; he falls asleep and has a dream.

T hat seemed to end the subtle argument
    My teacher had presented: he was searching
    My face to see if I appeared content;
While I, provoked by yet another thirst,[1]
    Was silent outwardly, but said within:
    "He may find all my questioning a pest."
But my true father, well aware of what
    I wished and hesitated to express,
    Emboldened me, by speaking, to speak out.
So I said: "Master, you uncloud my vision   10
    With that bright light you shed, till I see clearly
    All your distinctions and each firm conclusion.
And so I hope, my dear good father, that
    You'll clarify the love to which you trace
    Every good action and its opposite."
He said: "Direct the bright eyes of your mind
    To what I say, and you will realize
    The error of the blind who lead the blind.

---

1   His desire for further knowledge.

The soul, which is created apt for loving,
   Is drawn to anything which gives it pleasure   20
   The very instant pleasure sets it moving.
Your apprehension of reality
   Takes in an image it displays within you
   Until the soul is made to turn that way;
And if, once turned, it feels an inclination,
   Then that is love: that is the work of nature
   Who binds herself to you by this attraction.
And like that tendency to rise which fire
   Exhibits, since its essence is to rise
   To its own matter where it can endure,[1]   30
So the enamoured soul desires: it moves
   In spirit only – and it never rests
   Till it rejoices in the thing it loves.
Now you can see the truth, and how it is
   Hidden from all those people who affirm
   That every kind of love deserves our praise.
Perhaps that is because love's matter makes
   It seem a good – and yet not all impressions
   Are always good, however good the wax."[2]
"Your words and my attentive mother wit,"   40
   I answered him, "have shown me what love is,
   Only to leave me open to more doubt:
If love is proffered to us from outside,
   And if our soul can only walk one way,
   Then straight or crooked's neither good nor bad."[3]
Then he to me: "I can reveal such truth
   As human reason sees: you must await
   Beatrice for all beyond – the work of faith.[4]
Every substantial form, which is combined
   With matter,[5] though they are to be distinguished,   50
   Contains a disposition of a kind
Which cannot be perceived or ever shown
   Except by its effects in operation,
   As we know plants are living when they're green.
And so nobody comprehends where our
   First grasp of notions comes from, or our first
   Attraction to first objects of desire,

---

1   Fire's "own matter" is the sphere of fire between the air round the earth and the sphere of the moon, a place where fire can flourish.

2   The predisposition to love (i.e. the "wax") is good, but any particular use of it (i.e. the "impression" or seal) may be either good or bad.

3   If we are predisposed to love, how can we be responsible for our actions?

4   Knowledge acquired by human reason (philosophy, represented by Virgil) is inferior to the truth of divine revelation (theology, represented by Beatrice).

5   This "substantial form" is the essence of a thing, what makes it itself and nothing else; "matter" is what the "substantial form" is given to act upon.

Which are innate in you as in the bees
    Their urge for making honey; and this yearning
    Is not susceptible to blame or praise.   60
Now, so that every other wish be bent
    To this first will, you have the power of reason,
    Which ought to guard the threshold of assent.
This is the principle from which derives
    The basis of your merit, as it garners
    And winnows all your good and evil loves.
They whose thoughts reached into profundity
    Came to awareness of this innate freedom,
    And therefore taught the world morality.[1]
Assuming it as automatic then   70
    That many various loves arise in you,
    The power to curb those loves is all your own.
That noble power is called by Beatrice
    Free will, so you should keep it well in mind
    If she has cause to speak to you of this."
The moon, delayed almost until midnight,
    Had made the stars appear more widely scattered,
    Being like a massive bucket burning bright;[2]
It ran against the sky along those lanes
    The sun inflames when men in Rome observe it   80
    Mid Corsicans and Sards as it declines.[3]
And that most noble shade because of whom
    Pietole's more renowned than Mantua[4]
    Had shed the burden I had laid on him;
And I, who'd harvested such clear and deep
    Discussion of the questions I had raised,
    Was there like someone wandering in his sleep.
But sleep was driven from me out of hand
    By people who by now were up to us,
    Having come round upon us from behind.   90
Ismenus and Asopus[5] saw a crowd
    Hurtle by night along their ancient banks
    When Thebans called on Bacchus in their need;
Just so around that terrace in a curve
    Come at a gallop people who are driven
    By good will, so it seems, and righteous love.
And then they were upon us, that great crowd,

---

1   Ancient philosophers based morality on the freedom of man's will to choose between
    right and wrong.
2   It is a half-moon.
3   The moon is moving in the opposite direction to the sun's apparent course. It appears,
    when it rises, in that constellation where the sun is when Romans see the sun set between
    Corsica and Sardinia.
4   Because Virgil was born in Pietole, that village is more famous than the city of Mantua.
5   Rivers in Boeotia, the home of the wine god's bacchanalian rites.

And all arriving at a rapid run,[1]
And two in front in tears cried out aloud:
"Mary made haste into the hills,"[2] and then,   100
   "Caesar, who wished to subjugate Lérida,
   Struck at Marseille, and thence rushed into Spain."[3]
"Hurry! Hurry! Now there must be no waste
   Of time through lack of love," was shouted back.
   "Zeal to do good increases God's good grace."
"You people whose enthusiasm makes
   Up for your previous dawdling and neglect,
   Which came from being lukewarm in good works,
This man, who's living still – I tell no lies –
   Is keen to climb up once the sun is shining: 110
   So tell us where the gap or passage is."
Those were my leader's words, and then a call
   Came from one spirit in that scurry: "Follow
   Behind us quickly, and you'll find the hole.
We are so anxious to move rapidly
   We cannot stop, and therefore pardon us
   If this, our penance, seems discourtesy.
San Zeno's abbot in Verona once,[4]
   I lived beneath the worthy Barbarossa,
   Whom they still mention in Milan with groans.[5]   120
And there is one with one foot in the grave[6]
   Who will soon learn to mourn that monastery,
   Made wretched by the very power it gave:
It is his son, a physical disgrace,
   And mentally much worse, his bastard son,
   Whom he has put in the true pastor's place."
I do not know if he went any further
   In what he said, he'd run so far beyond us –
   But I heard that, which I like to remember.
And he who in my need was nothing loth   130
   To help me said: "Turn round and see two others
   Who as they run are reprehending sloth."

---

1   They are making up for, and thereby purging, their former sloth.
2   The Virgin Mary's visit to her cousin Elizabeth: "And Mary arose in those days, and went
    into the hill country with haste" (Luke 1:39). This is an encouragement to zeal for those
    who sinned by sloth.
3   Julius Caesar's legendary speed of action, here a further encouragement to zeal, was
    shown when he left Brutus to continue the siege of Marseille and rushed to defeat
    Pompey at Lérida in Spain.
4   Gherardo II, who left a reputation for sloth.
5   The Emperor Barbarossa (r.1155–90) destroyed Milan after it rebelled against him.
6   Alberto della Scala, Lord of Verona, who appointed his lame, depraved and illegitimate
    son Giuseppe to the abbacy of San Zeno, against the law and authority of the Church.
    Alberto died in 1301 and, since Dante places the action of his *Comedy* in 1300, he "will
    mourn that monastery" very soon in either Inferno or Purgatory.

Behind the rest what they were saying was:
  "They were all dead for whom the Red Sea opened,
  Before the River Jordan saw its heirs"[1]
And: "Those who could not stomach all the strife
  Up to the end with great Anchises' son
  Gave themselves up to an inglorious life."[2]
And when those shades had gone so far away
  From us that they were nowhere to be seen,   140
  I felt another thought arise in me,
From which yet other various thoughts arose.
  And as from one to the other I rambled on
  And wandered in my mind, I shut my eyes,
Translating those vague thoughts into a dream.

---

1   All the Hebrews who passed safely through the Red Sea in their escape from Egypt, with the exception of Joshua and Caleb, perished before they could see the Promised Land. This, mentioned here as a warning against sloth, was their punishment for being unenthusiastic in following Moses (Num. 14:22–23).
2   Companions of Aeneas who preferred to settle in Sicily rather than follow him to the accomplishment of his mission (*Aeneid* v, 604–718), another warning against sloth.

CANTO XIX

Dante's dream is described. In it he sees a cross-eyed, crippled, stuttering woman; but, as he gazes at her, she seems to regain her health and lose her stutter. She sings a song revealing that she is a seductive siren who misleads sailors. Then a holy lady appears who indignantly interrupts the song. Virgil tears the siren's clothes to bare the front of her body, and such a stench comes from her that Dante is roused from sleep. Later Virgil explains that the crippled woman represents earthly attractions. The holy lady apparently stands for reason and good sense.

Meanwhile Virgil and Dante continue their journey in broad daylight, with Dante bowed in thought, pondering his dream. They hear a gentle voice directing them to the next circle, and the speaker, an angel, fans Dante with his wing to remove another P from his forehead, and quotes one of the Beatitudes: this is the release from the sin of sloth.

Through a narrow crevice in the rock the pilgrims come out onto the fifth circle, where the covetous and the prodigal are purged. They are face down on the ground, bound hand and foot. One of the shades gives them directions. With Virgil's permission Dante questions the shade, who explains he was Pope Adrian V; he was Pope for only a brief period, but long enough for him to realize the vanity of his greed. These sinners are prone, because while they were alive they did not look up to heaven, and shackled because their sin prevented them from acting as they should have done. Out of respect for Adrian's high office Dante genuflects to him, and is about to speak when the former Pope forbids him to kneel, declaring that in death all such distinctions are void.

Adrian asks Dante to leave him to go on with his penance; he mentions his niece Alagia, who he hopes will not be corrupted by the example of the rest of their family.

I t was that hour at which the heat of day
 No longer warms the coldness of the moon,
 Quelled by the earth, or Saturn it may be,[1]
When geomancers see before the dawn
 Their Greater Fortune[2] rising in the east
 Along a road to be enlightened soon,
And in a dream I saw a woman stutter,
 Cross-eyed, unsteady on her twisted feet,
 With crippled hands, her face without much colour.
I gazed at her; and just as sunlight rouses   10
 The chilly limbs that night has made lethargic,
 My simply looking at her now releases
Her shackled tongue, and makes her body straight
 In next to no time, flushing her pale face

---

1   That time of night when the sun's residual warmth has been cooled by the earth, and by the cold planet Saturn when it is on the horizon. Special importance was attached to dreams which occurred shortly before dawn. See *Purg.* IX, 13–33 and XXVII, 94–108.

2   A pattern formed by stars of the constellations Pisces and Aquarius, regarded by geomancers as a favourable sign.

With that fresh colour love finds requisite.[1]
And she, her tongue being loosened in this way,
  Began to sing, sing such a song that only
  With stress and strain could I have turned away.
"I am," she sang, "a siren whose sweet air
  Distracts the sailors on the open sea –   20
  I give such pleasure to the listening ear.
My song sent Ulysses off course,[2] although
  Intent upon his voyage: he who lingers
  Seldom departs, I gratify him so!"
Her singing lips had come to no conclusion
  When there appeared a holy lady,[3] eager,
  Alongside me, to put her to confusion.
"O Virgil, say, who can this person be?"
  She asked in indignation, and he came
  And gazed at her in all her honesty.   30
He seized the other, made her front all bare,
  Tearing her clothes and showing me her belly,
  And roused me with the stench that came from there.
I rolled my eyes around; my master said:
  "I've called three times at least! Get up and walk,
  And let us find the opening that you need."
I rose to find the fully risen day
  Filling the circles of the sacred mountain,
  Shining behind us as we made our way.
I bend my brow, as after him I trudge,   40
  Like one so overburdened with his thoughts
  He makes himself the half arch of a bridge.
And then I heard: "Here one may go beyond,"[4]
  Spoken in such a gentle, kindly tone
  As never heard in this our mortal land.
With outspread wings, like those which grace the swan,
  He who had spoken signed us to move upwards
  Between two walls of adamantine stone.
Fluttering his feathers to fan us[5] he declared
  That all of those *"qui lugent"*[6] are *"beati"*:[7]   50
  Their souls will be completely comforted.
"What's bothering you? You keep on looking down,"
  My guide began to ask once we had travelled

---

1   Needed in order to arouse love in those who see it.
2   Dante knew only indirectly of the Homeric episode of the sirens in which the Greek
    hero remains unseduced.
3   Symbolic of reason.
4   Showing the way up to the fifth circle.
5   The angel is erasing the fourth P from Dante's forehead.
6   "Who mourn."
7   "Blessed." The angel is quoting Matt. 5:4: "Blessed are they that mourn: for they shall
    be comforted."

A short way past the angel in our climb.
And I: "What puts me in perplexity
  Is a strange vision and one so compulsive
  The thought of it will never let me be."
"You saw that age-old witch, who is up there,"
  He said, "the only thing to be lamented[1] –
  You saw how man can free himself from her.   60
Let that suffice you. And now shake the dust.
  Look up and see the lure[2] which the Eternal
  King whirls above you as the spheres roll past."
Now like the falcon which at first looks down,
  Then turning to the call flies after it
  In yearning for the food which draws it on,
Just so I moved: through that long crevice in
  The mountain's rock for those who mount on high
  I went to where the circling starts again.
Where the fifth circle[3] opens out I found   70
  People scattered about it who were weeping
  And lying down, their faces to the ground.
"Adhæsit pavimento anima mea"[4]
  I heard them say, and say with such deep sighs
  The words themselves were difficult to hear.
"Elect of God, whose painful punishment
  Is made less harsh by justice and by hope,
  Direct us to the stair for our ascent."
"If you have come with no need to prostrate
  Yourselves, and want to find the shortest way,   80
  Then keep the outside always on your right."
That was the poet's request; it was replied
  To by someone some way in front; I gathered
  Some implication that was left unsaid;[5]
I turned to look into my master's eyes,
  And he assented with a kindly gesture
  To the desire he noted in my gaze.
Now that my guide had granted my request,
  I moved towards and stood above that creature
  Whose words had made me notice him at first,   90
And said: "Spirit whose tears serve to mature
  That without which no one returns to God,[6]

<hr>

1 The immoderate use of earthly goods remains to be purified on the last three circles: other sins are purged below.
2 A device to bring a falcon back to its master.
3 Where the covetous and prodigal are punished.
4 "My soul has cleaved to the ground" (Psalms 119:25).
5 The shade is probably uncertain of the status of the pilgrims, one of whom he may suspect to be alive.
6 Penitence.

LIKE OXEN WHO ARE YOKED, SO SIDE BY SIDE
I WENT ALONG THERE WITH THAT BURDENED SOUL...

PURGATORY XII, 1–2

AND WE'RE ARRIVING NOW WHERE THE GREAT TREE
REJECTS THEIR CONSTANT WEEPING AND THEIR PRAYERS...

PURGATORY XXIV, 113–14

For me defer awhile your greater care.[1]
Who were you all? Tell me. Why do you have
   Your backs up-reared? And is there anything
   You need from there whence I have come alive?"[2]
His answer to me was: "Why Heaven has set the
   Backsides towards itself I'll tell you – first
   Scias quod ego fui successor Petri.[3]
Between Sestri and Chiavari flows down   100
   A lovely river, and my noble house
   Derives its title from that river's name.[4]
One month or so I knew the heavy weight
   Of the great mantle raised above the mire,[5]
   To which all other cares are feather-light.
My change of heart came very late, alas!
   But when I was elected Roman Pastor,
   Then I discerned how fraudulent life was.
I realized there the heart could never rest,
   Nor in that life could I rise any higher;   110
   And so my love of this life was aroused.
Up to that point I was a soul apart
   From God, and wretched, given up to greed:
   Here, as you see, I pay the price for it.
What avarice achieves is here made plain
   In the purgation of converted souls;
   For us the mountain holds no greater pain.
As hitherto our eyes had never scanned
   The heavens above, intent on earthly things,
   So justice sinks them here down to the ground.   120
Since avarice quenched the love of all true good
   In us, and every action was in vain,
   So justice has us here within its hold,
Held in strict custody, bound hand and foot;
   And for as long as pleases the just Lord,
   We shall remain immobile and stretched out."
I was upon one knee and in the act
   Of speaking to him – he became aware
   (Through listening) of my gesture of respect.
"Why," he enquired, "do you crouch down like that?"   130
   And I replied: "Because of your great office
   My conscience smote me when I stood upright."
"Straighten your legs, get up, my brother!" he
   Replied. "Make no mistake. I serve, like you

---

1   All the shades in Purgatory are anxious to hasten their purification.
2   A tactful offer of prayers.
3   "Know that I was a successor of St Peter", i.e. Pope.
4   The speaker is Adrian V (r.1276), a member of the de' Fieschi family, Counts of Lavagna, which is the Ligurian river referred to.
5   The Papacy is a particularly heavy burden for a Pope who tries to remain uncorrupted.

And others, but the one Authority.
  If you have ever really understood
    The Gospel's holy utterance *'Neque nubent'*,[1]
  You will perceive there's sense in what I've said.
If you have ever really understood
  You interrupt my weeping, which matures   140
    My penitence, as you have said before.[2]
Beyond[3] I have a niece, Alagia, good
  Within herself, if but our family
    By its example does not make her bad.[4]
And she is all beyond that's left to me."

---

1   "They neither marry", from Matt. 22:30: "In the resurrection they neither marry nor
    are given in marriage, but are as the angels of God in heaven." This is quoted to indicate
    the absence of all earthly ties and obligations in the afterlife.
2   See ll. 91–92.
3   In the world of the living.
4   Alagia de' Fieschi, wife of one of Dante's patrons, Moroello Malaspina. The condemna-
    tion of her family refers only to her blood relations.

CANTO XX

Dante and Virgil go on, through the sounds of lamentation, hugging the side of the Mountain on the narrow space left by the shades lying prone close to the cliff's edge. Dante apostrophizes and condemns avarice as a she-wolf – a reminder of that beast in the first canto of *Inferno*.

Dante hears the Virgin Mary invoked by a voice up ahead. This is followed by references to three examples of poverty willingly accepted – the virtue opposite to avarice: the Virgin Mary, the Roman consul Fabricius and St Nicholas. The shade who has spoken is Hugh Capet. He condemns the rapacity of his own dynasty, and particularly the assault on Pope Boniface VIII arranged by Philip the Fair, an incident so outrageous that it is compared to a second Crucifixion.

Hugh Capet explains that his invocation of the Virgin is the usual prayer on this terrace during the hours of daylight, while during the night the shades recite examples of avarice: Pygmalion, who murdered his brother-in-law; Midas, who asked that all he touched might be turned to gold; Achan, who kept some of the spoils of Jericho for himself; Sapphira and her husband Ananias, who lied to St Peter; Heliodorus, whose intention was to sack the Temple in Jerusalem; Polymnestor, the murderer of Priam's son, who had been entrusted to him; the wealthy Roman Crassus, into whose dead mouth gold was poured.

Suddenly the whole Mountain trembles, and there is a great shout which Dante identifies as the Gloria, first sung by the angels who announced the Nativity to the shepherds. Dante moves on with Virgil, wondering what all this can mean.

*

One's will cannot oppose a better will,
  So I withdrew – for his and not my pleasure –
  My sponge from water, although far from full.[1]
I went on, and my leader also went
  On through the vacant space along the cliff,
  As on a strait way by a battlement,
For all the people straining, drip by drip,
  The evil of the whole world through their eyes,
  On the other side, were too close to the drop.
Curses upon you, ancient she-wolf,[2] finding   10
  More prey than all the other beasts together
  To feed your hunger that is never-ending!
O heaven, whose revolutions, so men say,
  Make changes in our earthly circumstances,
  When will he come who'll drive this beast away?[3]
We went on at a slow deliberate pace,
  And I went on attentive to the shades,
  Whose weeping and laments were piteous;
And then I heard "Sweet Mary!" shouted out

---

1   Reluctantly Dante stops questioning Pope Adrian V.
2   Avarice. See *Inf.* 1, 49*ff.*
3   Probably alludes to the hound of *Inf.* 1, 100*ff.*

By someone wailing up ahead of us,   20
  As women in their labour pains cry out.
And then straight after: "You were poor indeed,
  As evident by what accommodation
  You had when you laid down your sacred load."[1]
And following that I heard: "O good Fabricius,
  You wished to keep your virtue and be poor
  Rather than gather riches and be vicious."[2]
That sentence gave me such immense delight
  That I walked on to gain some knowledge of
  Whatever shade it seemed had uttered it.   30
It went on, speaking of that generous donor,
  St Nicholas, whose gifts enabled maidens
  To live their lives out married and with honour.[3]
"O soul by whom such goodness is made known,
  Say who you were," I begged, "and tell me why
  These praises are renewed by you alone.
Your answer shall not lack for a reward,
  If ever I return for that short distance
  My life has yet to run along its road."[4]
He answered: "I shall tell you, not for aid   40
  Expected from beyond, but for the grace
  That's shining out of you before you've died.[5]
I was the root of that pernicious tree[6]
  Overshadowing all the Christian lands,
  From which good fruit is plucked infrequently.
If only Douai, Lille and Ghent and Bruges[7]
  Were able, then the vengeance would be swift:
  I beg for that from Him Who is our judge.
I was known as Hugh Capet in the world:
  From me were born those Philips and those Louis 50
  By whom our France has recently been ruled.
I was a Paris butcher's son: when all
  The offspring of the ancient kings had died,
  But one, who entered, putting on grey wool,[8]
I found the kingdom's reins clutched in my hands,

---

1   "And she brought forth her firstborn son… and laid him in a manger, because there was
     no room for them in the inn" (Luke 2:7). First example of acceptance of poverty, the
     virtue opposed to avarice.
2   Fabricius, a Roman consul in 282 BC, refused bribes offered to him to betray his country
     and died in poverty.
3   According to legend, this fourth-century bishop in Asia Minor gave gold to three poor
     maidens as dowries: this allowed them to marry and avoid prostitution.
4   An offer of prayers for his salvation.
5   Dante is favoured by God in being allowed to see Purgatory while still alive.
6   Founder of the French Capetian dynasty.
7   Conquered by Philip the Fair, King of France 1285–1314.
8   The last of the Carolingian kings entered a monastery.

And its whole government, and so much power
   So recently acquired, so many friends,
The widowed crown was placed on my own son's
   Head, and thereby he was the origin
   Of all the others and their sacred bones.[1]   60
Before the dowry of Provence[2] had come
   To drive out from my race all sense of shame
   It was worth little, but did little harm.
Then with brute force and sheer chicanery
   They started looting; then, to make amends,
   Seized Ponthieu, Normandy and Gascony.
Charles came to Italy, to make amends,
   And murdered Conradin;[3] and afterwards
   Shoved Thomas back in heaven,[4] to make amends.
I see, and not in some far distant time,   70
   Another Charles[5] attracted out of France
   To make him and his family better known.
He comes alone and quite unarmed, with just
   The lance that Judas jousted with, and aims it
   To strike the belly of Florence and make it burst.[6]
He'll gain by this no land, but sin and shame
   To call his own, a heavier[7] acquisition
   The lighter all that ruin seems to him.
The other Charles, once captured on the waves,
   I see selling his daughter, see him haggle   80
   As Barbary corsairs do over their slaves.[8]
O avarice, what worse awaits our brood,
   Now that we have become so close to you
   We have no care for our own flesh and blood?
To make the past and future look less dire,
   I see the fleur-de-lis enter Anagni
   And, in His vicar, Christ made prisoner.[9]
I see Him once again Whom men deride,

---

1   The Capetians were anointed at Rheims. Here "sacred" is used sardonically.
2   By the marriage of Charles of Anjou to Beatrice of Provence that county came under
     the French crown.
3   Charles of Anjou invaded Italy in 1265, and in 1268 he had Conradin, the rightful heir
     to the crown of Sicily and Naples, beheaded.
4   A false rumour had it that Thomas Aquinas's death was caused by poison.
5   Charles of Valois, brother of Philip the Fair.
6   Charles of Valois, with the connivance of Pope Boniface VIII, used fraud and treachery
     to favour the Black Guelfs in Florence, which resulted in the expulsion of the Whites,
     including Dante.
7   Morally.
8   Charles II of Anjou ("the Lame", r.1285–1309, was defeated at sea by the Aragonese. He
     married his daughter off, for a large sum, to the murderous Azzo VIII d'Este.
9   In 1303 Philip the Fair sent agents to arrest Pope Boniface VIII in his palace at Anagni.
     Boniface was rescued, but died of shock.

I see again the vinegar and gall,
  With two thieves by who are not crucified.[1]   90
I see the second Pilate, who is still
  So far from satisfied that lawlessly
  He raids the Temple with rapacious sail.[2]
O Lord, when shall it be that I rejoice
  To see Your vengeance which, though hidden now,
  Still makes Your anger taste so sweet to us?
What I was saying of that only bride
  Of the Holy Ghost,[3] which made you turn to me
  To ask for some explanatory word,
Is the response[4] we all make when we pray   100
  While daylight lasts; but when the night descends
  We cite examples that are contrary.[5]
And then Pygmalion's tale is told again,
  Turned into traitor, thief and parricide
  By his ungovernable love of gain.[6]
And greedy Midas, with his lust for gold
  Whose consequence was that unhappiness
  For which he always must be ridiculed.[7]
Then we remember Achan, him who stole
  The spoils of Jericho, so that the anger   110
  Of Joshua seems here to sting him still.[8]
Then we accuse Sapphira and her spouse;[9]
  We praise the kicks Heliodorus had;[10]
  Then round the Mount resounds the infamous

---

1   The likening of Boniface's ill treatment to the Passion and Crucifixion of Christ expresses
     Dante's revulsion at the offence to the Pope's sacred office, despite his often expressed
     disapproval of Boniface himself. The "two thieves" are the leaders of the attack on the
     Pope; they are described as "not crucified" to distinguish them from the thieves at either
     side of Christ on the cross.

2   Philip the Fair is likened to Pontius Pilate because he washed his hands of the respon-
     sibility for the attack on Boniface. He destroyed the Order of the Knights Templar, by
     false accusations of heresy and ill conduct, in order to seize their property.

3   The Virgin Mary.

4   In the sense of a response in the liturgy, a prayer spoken by the congregation in reply
     to the priest.

5   After the encouraging examples of virtue come warning examples of the vice of avarice.

6   The legendary Pygmalion, King of Tyre, murdered his brother-in-law to acquire his
     wealth. See *Aeneid* I, 340ff.

7   This legendary king obtained from Bacchus the power to turn all he touched into gold;
     if he had not managed to get the gift revoked he would have died of hunger and thirst.

8   He was stoned to death. See Josh. 6:17–19, 7:1–26.

9   Ananias and his wife Sapphira, members of the early Christian community, kept back
     some of the money gained by selling land; both fell dead when denounced by St Peter
     for lying about the price.

10   When about to sack the Temple in Jerusalem he was attacked by a mysterious rider
     whose horse's hooves kicked him into abandoning his intention. See 2 Macc. 3:1–40.

Polymnestor, who murdered Polydorus.[1]
   And finally we shout: 'Crassus, you know
   How gold tastes in the mouth, so please inform us!'[2]
At times one speaks aloud, another low,
   According to the impulse which is spurring
   Us on to be more swift or be more slow: 120
So I, evoking goodness praised by us
   While daylight lasts, was not alone – no, simply
   Nobody else nearby had raised his voice."[3]
We had already left that shade behind,
   And we were struggling up the narrow way
   With all the speed our feeble power could find,
And then I felt – just like some object falling –
   The Mountain tremble, and a coldness clutched
   Me, as it clutches one whose life is failing:
No, Delos never shook so violently   130
   Before Latona built in it the nest
   In which she bore the twin eyes of the sky.[4]
Then all around a shout arose, so loud
   My master drew up closer to me, saying:
   "You need not fear, so long as I'm your guide."
"*Gloria in excelsis*", they all said,
   And "*Deo*",[5] as I gathered from those nearest
   Whose shouting could be heard and understood.
We stopped and waited; motion was suspended,
   As with those shepherds who first heard that hymn,   140
   Until the quake ceased, and the hymn had ended.
Then on our sacred way once more we went,
   Still gazing at the shades upon the ground,
   Who had gone back to their accustomed plaint.
Ignorance never launched such an assault
   To give me such desire to understand,
   Unless in this my memory's at fault,
As it did then, while I was pondering.
   I dared not ask, we moved at such a rate,
   Nor by myself could I see anything: 150
I walked on timidly and lost in thought.[6]

---

1   Priam of Troy entrusted his son Polydorus, together with much gold, to King Polymnestor of Thrace, who killed him and took the gold. See *Aeneid* III, 19–68.

2   The wealthy Roman Crassus was defeated by the Parthians and decapitated. When the Parthian King received the head, he ordered gold to be poured into its mouth and said: "You thirsted for gold: drink gold."

3   This is in answer to Dante's second question in ll. 35–36.

4   The Isle of Delos was believed to have been floating about haphazardly before Latona fled there to give birth to the twins Apollo and Diana (the sun and moon).

5   "Glory to God in the highest", from the song of the angels at the Nativity (Luke 2:14).

6   Dante is wondering why the Mountain shook and why the Gloria was sung.

CANTO XXI

Dante and Virgil move on quickly, picking their way among the prostrate shades. Dante is still perplexed by the earthquake and the Gloria.

Suddenly a shade appears who, unlike the others suffering on this terrace, is upright. He comes from behind and greets them. Virgil tells the shade that Dante, who is still a living man, is journeying through the realms of death with him as a guide – so far as a pagan unenlightened by faith can be a guide. Then, in reply to Virgil's questions, the shade explains that no earthly disorders, such as rain or hail or snow or earth tremors – the result of physical causes on earth – can affect the Mountain above the entrance to Purgatory. The shaking of the Mountain was a supernatural phenomenon. The quake, and the Gloria which accompanied it, were to celebrate the moment when a soul in Purgatory was ready to ascend to heaven; this time it was his own soul which was purged, after having lain there for more than five hundred years. He reveals he was the famous poet Statius, who lived in the first century AD. He owed all his poetic skill to Virgil's *Aeneid*. He has such reverence for Virgil that, if he could only have been alive when Virgil lived, he would gladly accept another year's purgation.

The dramatic irony is clear. Virgil gives Dante a look to dissuade him from saying anything, and Dante does not speak; but he cannot suppress a fleeting smile. Statius notices this, and so Dante, with Virgil's permission, has to explain that the shade with them is Virgil himself. Overcome by the news, Statius throws himself down to clasp Virgil's feet. However, since they are both shades, contact is impossible. The canto ends with Statius standing up and declaring that the strength of his love for Virgil is shown by his forgetting their insubstantiality.

✳

The natural thirst, always unsatisfied
   Without that water the Samaritan
   Woman wanted and for which she prayed,
Was troubling me,[1] while I went pricked by haste
  Along the obstructed way behind my master,
   Grieving over the vengeance that is just.
Then suddenly, just as Luke's words affirm
  That Christ appeared to two upon the road,
   Already risen from the empty tomb,[2]
A shade, appearing there, began to walk   10
  Behind, as we steered clear of prostrate people –
   Nor did we notice it until it spoke.
It said: "My brothers, may God give you peace."
  We turned around immediately, and Virgil
   Gave in return the appropriate response.
Then Virgil said to him: "May you be sent

---

1   The innate human thirst for knowledge can only be satisfied by the truths of Christianity. See John 4:6–15.

2   Luke 24:13–16.

To lasting peace by that unerring justice
Which sends me to eternal banishment."
"What?" he replied, while we were rushing there,
   "If you are shades God will not have above,   20
   Then who has led you so far up His stair?"
My teacher answered: "See this man's forehead
   With signs upon it that an angel traced?[1]
   Now you can see he must reign with the good.
Since she who labours night and day to spin
   Had not extracted for him all the fibre
   Clotho accumulates for everyone,[2]
His soul, the sister soul to you and me,
   Coming up here could not have come unguided,
   Because it does not see the way we see.   30
So I was drawn out from the gaping throat
   Of Hell[3] to guide him, and I'll go on guiding
   As long as my discernment guides him right.[4]
But, if you can, explain why, just before,
   The Mountain shook and cried out altogether
   Down to its base, it seems, upon the shore."
His question threaded with such great success
   The needle of my desire that hope alone[5]
   Meant that immediately I thirsted less.
That shade began: "This Mountain's sanctity   40
   Permits no incident that is disordered
   Or else outside of what is customary.
This place is free from any alteration:
   What heaven receives into itself and issues
   Out of itself provides the sole causation.[6]
And therefore neither rain, nor hail, nor snow,
   Nor dew, nor frost can ever fall beyond
   The stairs with three steps only, down below.[7]
Clouds, whether dense or thin, do not appear,
   Or lightning flashes – nor does Thaumas' daughter,[8]   50
   Who often shifts her whereabouts down there:[9]
Dry vapour does not ever rise and get
   Above the top step of those three I mentioned,

---

1   Dante is still bearing the last three Ps on his forehead.
2   He is not dead. Lachesis spins the thread of each human life from material provided by
    Clotho, and the third Fate, Atropos, cuts it off at death.
3   Virgil is from Limbo, at the top of the inverted hollow cone of the Inferno.
4   Virgil is limited throughout by his lack of faith, and eventually he must give up his role:
    see *Purg.* xxx, 40–57.
5   The hope of an answer.
6   Only supernatural causes, which never change, can operate.
7   At the entrance to Purgatory. See *Purg.* ix, 76–78.
8   Iris, the rainbow.
9   Visible in various parts of the sky, according to the position of the sun.

Where Peter's delegate[1] has set his feet.
Down there this Mount has tremors, huge or slight,
  Perhaps; but here winds hiding in the earth,
  I don't know why, have never shaken it.[2]
Here there's a tremor when some soul feels clean
  Enough to ascend, or to bestir itself
  To climb up higher – and shouting follows on.   60
The will alone attests this cleanliness
  When, free to change its place and company,
  It shocks the soul, which is rejoiced by this.
It willed to rise before, but was checked then
  By that strong yearning which transcendent justice
  Directs to penance and away from sin.
So I, who've lain tormented on this floor
  More than five centuries, felt only now
  The will to travel through a better door:
Therefore you felt the earthquake and you heard   70
  Good souls throughout the Mountain as they honoured
  That Lord we pray to send them up with speed."
Those were his words, and just as we enjoy
  A drink the more, the deeper is our thirst,
  I can't express what good he did to me.
Then my wise master said: "I see the net
  In which you are caught up, how you escape,
  Why the Mount quakes, and why you celebrate.
Now tell me who you once were, tell me please,
  And as you answer help me understand   80
  Why you've lain here so many centuries."
"In that age when good Titus (as was willed
  By the Almighty King) avenged the wounds
  From which the blood flowed out which Judas sold,[3]
That title which endures and brings renown[4]
  Was mine back there," the spirit said. "I was
  Famous indeed, but faith was not yet mine.[5]
The spirit of my poems was so gentle
  That men drew me from Toulouse out to Rome,
  And there I merited a crown of myrtle.[6]   90
Back there men call me Statius to this day;
  I sang of Thebes, then of the great Achilles;

---

1   The angel at the entrance to Purgatory. See *Purg.* IX, 76–84.

2   It was believed that earthquakes were caused by dry vapours underground, and winds by those vapours when they escaped.

3   In 70 AD Jerusalem was sacked by the Romans under Titus, an event seen by Dante as the Jews' punishment for having, especially in the person of Judas, betrayed Christ to His death.

4   The title of poet.

5   He was still pagan. The details of his imagined conversion are given at *Purg.* XXII, 55–93.

6   He won a prize for poetry.

But under that last load fell by the way.[1]
The seeds which kindled all my ardour were
    Sparkles emitted from that holy flame
    By which a thousand have been set on fire.
I speak of the *Aeneid*: when I wrote
    It was both midwife and wet nurse to me:
    I would not else have weighed a pennyweight.[2]
And I, to live there in that epoch when   100
    Virgil was living, would accept a further
    Year's penance till the lifting of my ban."
These words made Virgil turn to me and give
    The sort of look that silently says "Silence",
    But wills may often try and not achieve,
For tears and laughter come so hard upon
    The heels of what arouses them they least
    Obey the will of the most honest man.
I merely smiled, like one who drops a hint –
    At that the shade fell silent, and he stared   110
    Me in the eyes, where truth seems evident.
And "May your arduous journey finish well,"
    He said, "but say – why did your face just now
    Show me the semblance of a fleeting smile?"
Now I am caught whichever way I turn:
    One keeps me silent, with the other anxious
    To hear me speak – and so I sigh, and then
My master understands, and "Have no fear,"
    He said, "of speaking – tell him: simply answer
    The question he has posed with such desire."   120
And I replied: "You seem to be amazed,
    O ancient shade, to see that I was smiling,
    But now I'll make you even more surprised.
This guide, who leads aloft these eyes of mine,
    Is that same Virgil who provided you
    With all your power to sing of gods and men.
If you imagine my amusement came
    From any other cause, dismiss the thought:
    The reason was those words you said of him."
He was already bending as he made   130
    To clasp my teacher's feet, but Virgil: "Brother,
    Do not: you're but a shade that sees a shade."
Statius rose and said: "Now you can guess
    The depth of all the affection which I feel,
    When I, oblivious of our nothingness,
Find myself treating shades as they were real."

---

1   The poet Statius (*c.*40–*c.*96) wrote one epic, the *Thebaid*, and started another, the *Achilleid*, left unfinished at his death.

2   Reminiscent of Dante's own praise of Virgil in *Inf.* I, 79–87.

CANTO XXII

The angel of the fifth circle has directed the three poets upwards and, in his blessing, intro-
duced the image of thirst, which runs throughout this canto. Thirst represents the human
desires which must be curbed. Dante now finds the ascent less difficult, because the angel
has effaced another P (the sin of avarice).

Virgil expresses his affection for Statius: in Limbo he has heard him praised by the poet
Juvenal. What puzzles Virgil is how Statius could be guilty of avarice. Statius explains that
Virgil has been misled by meeting him on the terrace of the avaricious. He was guilty of the
opposite sin, prodigality: the two faults – avarice and prodigality – are punished in the same
place, since they both offend the virtue of temperance.

When Virgil says that he has found no evidence of Statius's Christianity in his *Thebaid*,
Statius explains that light dawned on him when he read the apparent prophecy of the Incarna-
tion in Virgil's fourth Eclogue. Impressed by the sanctity of the early Christians, Statius took
to frequenting them, and he shared their sufferings in the persecution under the Emperor
Domitian. He was baptized, but out of fear he kept his Christianity secret: for this he suffered
for four centuries in the fourth circle of Purgatory, that of the slothful. Statius asks about the
fate of other writers, and Virgil mentions some who are with him in Limbo.

The three poets go to the next circle, with Virgil and Statius in front discussing poetry,
and Dante following them attentive to their words. Suddenly they come across a tree on
their path, shaped like an inverted fir, with its branches lengthening as it rises from its roots,
and watered by a cascade. Its attractive fruit cannot be plucked, because its shape makes it
impossible to climb. A voice from the foliage states that this food cannot be eaten, and it
mentions several examples of temperance, the virtue opposed to the fault – gluttony – which
will be purged on this sixth terrace.

T he angel had been left behind us now,
    After he'd shown us to the following circle,
    The sixth, and cleared one blemish from my brow,[1]
And said that those directing their desire
    To justice are the blessèd, and his words
    Had got as far as thirst with nothing more.[2]
And I was moving lighter than I had
    On any of the other passageways,
    And following the spirits in their speed
Effortlessly, when "Love," Virgil began,   10
    "Kindled by virtue kindles further love,
    Provided that love's flame is clearly shown;
So from that very hour when Juvenal[3]

---

1   Erased the fifth P.
2 .   Matt. 5–6: "Blessed are they which do hunger and thirst after righteousness: for they
    shall be filled." The angel omits here any mention of hunger; but it will be referred to
    by the angel of the following circle in relation to the gluttonous. The image of thirst
    runs throughout this canto.
3   Roman satirical poet (*c.*47–*c.*130).

Descended into Hell, to us in Limbo,
    And told me how he always loved you well,
My feelings in response have been so great,
    Greater than any for an unseen person,
    That now these stairways will seem all too short.
But tell me, and forgive me as a friend
    If too much candour makes my reins go slack,   20
    And talk with me as you would with a friend:
How was there room for avarice to dwell
    Inside that breast of yours, despite the wisdom
    With which your studious care had filled you full?"
These words moved Statius to a momentary
    Half-smile at first, and then he made this answer:
    "Your words are dear signs of your love for me.
Often a situation can occur
    Which gives misleading cause to be uncertain,
    Because the genuine reason is not clear.   30
Your question shows me your opinion is
    I sinned through avarice in the other life,
    Your reason being the circle where I was.
Know then that I was far from avarice –
    Too far away from it indeed, and many
    Thousands of moons have punished my excess.[1]
And had I never changed my disposition
    By giving heed to lines where you exclaim,
    As human nature roused your indignation:
'Why is there no control, O cursèd lust   40
    For gold, upon the appetites of mortals?',[2]
    I would be rolling stones in the grim joust.[3]
Then I perceived that hands can spread like wings
    Too wide in spending: therefore I repented
    Of that as much as of my other sins.
How many will arise with heads quite bare[4]
    Through ignorance which takes away repentance
    Of this sin during life and at death's door!
And know that any sin of ours, whenever
    It butts another sin in opposition,   50
    Must here like that one see its foliage wither:
If I have been with people who regret
    Their avarice, to further my purgation,
    What brought me there was the opposing fault."
"Now when you sang about the cruel wrongs

---

1   The sin of prodigality.
2   A paraphrase of *Aeneid* III, 56–57.
3   Like those punished for their avarice or prodigality. See *Inf.* VII, 25–35.
4   The spendthrifts, so wasteful that they have thrown away even the hair from their heads.
    See *Inf.* VII, 57.

Done by the double sorrow of Jocasta,"[1]
Said then the singer of the pastoral songs,[2]
"From strings you touched with Clio[3] in that place
    It does not seem that you'd yet found that faith[4]
    Without which righteous deeds do not suffice.   60
If this be so, what candles or what sun
    Dispersed your darkness and reset your sails
    To follow on behind the Fisherman?"[5]
He answered then: "You were the first to guide
    Me to Parnassus to imbibe its springs,
    The first to light the way for me to God.
You acted then like one who walks by night,
    Who holds the lamp behind, which does not help him,
    But gives the after-comers all the light,
When you declared: 'The world begins again;   70
    Justice returns and the first human era;
    A heaven-sent generation is new-born.'[6]
You made me poet, made me Christian:
    Now I shall, for your better understanding,
    Take that brief sketch and fill the details in.
The whole world was already travailing
    With true belief, which had been propagated
    By messengers from the Eternal King;[7]
And words of yours, which I've just quoted from,
    Were in such harmony with those new preachers   80
    I formed the habit of frequenting them.
To me they came at last to seem such saints
    That in Domitian's reign[8] and persecution
    Their weeping did not go without my plaints;
While I was with the living, I did all
    I could to help them, and their righteous conduct
    Made every other sect contemptible.
Before I, in my epic poem, had led
    The Greeks to Theban streams,[9] I was baptized;
    But stayed a secret Christian, out of dread,   90
And made protracted show of pagan ways;
    That lack of zeal it was which made me circle

---

1   In his *Thebaid* Statius narrates the war between Jocasta's twin sons.
2   Virgil, who wrote ten *Eclogues* (pastoral poems).
3   Muse of history.
4   Christianity.
5   St Peter.
6   A paraphrase of *Eclogues* IV, 5–7. Virgil's celebration of Rome under Augustus has often been taken as a prophecy, however unconscious, of the Incarnation.
7   The Apostles.
8   81–96 AD.
9   Either before he began writing his *Thebaid*, or before he described (in Book IX) the Greeks' arrival at the rivers Ismenus and Asopus.

Round the fourth circle[1] for four centuries.
Now you, who lifted up the lid for me
    From hidden good which I have been describing,
    Now while we have the opportunity,
Tell me where Terence is, our ancient author,
    Caecilius, Plautus, Varro, if you know:[2]
    Tell me if they are damned, and to what quarter."
"All of them, Persius,[3] I, and many a one,"   100
    My leader answered him, "are with that Greek
    The Muses suckled more than any man,[4]
In the first circle of the sightless gaol.[5]
    Many a time we talk about that mountain
    On which our foster-mothers always dwell.[6]
Euripides is there and Antiphon,
    Simonides and Agathon,[7] and other
    Greeks who were honoured with the laurel crown.
Some of your characters are there together –
    Antigone, Deiphyle, Argia;   110
    Ismene also, still as sad as ever.[8]
She can be seen who pointed out Langia:[9]
    The daughter of Tiresias too, with Thetis,
    And Deidamia[10] and her sisters there."
Both poets were silent now, and now again
    They were intent on looking all around them,
    Clear of the climb and of the wall of stone.
By now the first four handmaids of the dawn
    Had gone; the fifth was at the chariot pole,
    And still directing up its blazing horn;[11]   120
My master said: "I think it's time that we
    Turned our right shoulders to the terrace edge,
    Circling the Mountain in the usual way."
So custom now became our banderole,[12]
    And we continued with less trepidation

---

1   Where the slothful are purified.
2   The first three are Roman dramatists of the second century BC. The identity of Varro
    (or, possibly, Vario) is uncertain.
3   Roman satirical poet of the first century AD.
4   Homer.
5   In Limbo. See *Inf.* IV, 88.
6   Mount Parnassus, sacred to the Muses.
7   Except for the Greek lyric poet Simonides (556–467 BC), all Greek dramatists of the fifth
    century BC.
8   Antigone and Ismene are daughters of King Oedipus, Deiphyle is the wife of King
    Tydeus, and Argia his sister-in-law.
9   Hypsipyle, who led the thirsty Greek army to the fountain of Langia.
10   Respectively the sorceress Manto (*Inf.* X, 59–93), Achilles's mother, and Achilles's wife.
11   Four hours of the day are past, and the fifth hour is guiding the chariot of the rising sun.
12   The flag to be followed.

With the agreement of that worthy soul.[1]
The two went on ahead; after them I
    Went on alone, hanging on their discussion,
    Which gave such insights into poetry.
But their delightful colloquy was brought   130
    To a sudden end: we found upon the road
    A tree that bore sweet-smelling, wholesome fruit.
And as a fir tree tapers to the top
    From bough to bough, so did this tree, but downwards,
    Lest anyone, I think, should clamber up.
Clear liquid from the high rock tumbled down,
    At that side where our pathway was blocked off,
    And spread itself throughout the inverted crown.
As the two neared the tree there came a shout
    From a voice hidden in the greenery: 140
    "This food is something you must do without."
It then said: "Mary gave more thought to how
    The wedding might be honourably accomplished
    Than to her mouth, which answers for you now.[2]
Women in ancient Rome were satisfied
    With water for their drink; the prophet Daniel
    Grew great in wisdom while despising food.[3]
The first age was the Golden Age: a zest
    Was added to the acorns by our hunger,
    And streams were filled with nectar by our thirst.   150
Honey and locusts were the foodstuffs that
    Nourished the Baptist in the desert waste;
    And therefore he is glorious and great,
As in the Gospel is made manifest."[4]

---

1   Statius, who is now worthy of heaven.
2   This first example of temperance, the virtue opposed to gluttony, refers to Mary's concern
    when the wine ran out at the wedding feast of Cana (John 2:1–11). See also *Purg.* XIII,
    28–30.
3   Dan. 1:3–20.
4   Luke 7:28.

CANTO XXIII

Dante is gazing at the tree's foliage, wondering at the voice which issues from it, when Virgil exhorts him to hurry.

Weeping is heard, mingled with a joyful singing of the penitential Psalm 51. This is the terrace of the gluttonous. Many shades suffering intensely from starvation pass by: Dante is reminded of the mythical Erysichthon, whose hunger led him to eat himself, and also of the siege of Jerusalem in 70 AD, when starvation led one mother to eat her son. Dante cannot understand how bodiless shades can suffer from hunger.

One of the shades turns his sunken eyes upon Dante and expresses his joy at meeting him again. Dante, who could not have recognized him from his appearance, completely altered by his unsatisfied hunger, immediately recognizes the voice of his old friend Forese Donati. Dante asks for an explanation of the shades' starvation and extreme emaciation. Forese explains that, after being gluttons in life, they are now tormented with hunger, and glad to be tormented, to accomplish their purgation: the fruit of the inverted tree and the water which irrigates it cause their craving. Forese would, because of his late repentance, have had to spend many years before climbing the Mountain, if it had not been for the assiduous prayers of his widow Nella. His praise of her leads him, by contrast, to inveigh against the immodest dress of Florentine women.

Now Dante answers Forese's questions. He casts a shadow, he says, because he is still alive in his earthly body. He has been saved from his misguided way of life by Virgil, who has led him through the Inferno and up the slopes of Mount Purgatory: eventually, however, Virgil's guidance will be insufficient, and then Beatrice will guide him. Dante points out Virgil as one of the two shades with him, and says the other is Statius, whose liberation from Purgatory has recently been celebrated by the earthquake which shook the Mountain.

W hile I was gazing at the greenery
    To see inside it, like the serious hunter
    Of little birds, idling his life away,
"My son," my more than father said to me,
    "Come on now, for the time that is allowed us
    Ought to be used in a more useful way."
I turned my face and feet with equal speed
    Towards those sages whose fine conversation
    Made it no effort for me to proceed.
And all at once we heard this wept and sung: 10
    "*Labia mea, Domine*",[1] its manner
    Producing both delight and suffering.
"O gentle father, what is that?" I said.
    And he replied: "It is perhaps some shades
    Now paying off the debt they have incurred."
As pilgrims do, when they are lost in thought

---

1   "My lips, Lord" from Psalms 51:5: "O Lord, open thou my lips; and my mouth shall shew forth thy praise."

And overtaking strangers on their road –
   They turn to them but don't slow down one bit –
So after us, but moving with more speed,
   And overtaking us and full of wonder,   20
   There came a silent and devoted crowd.
The eyes of all were dark-ringed, sunken in,
   Their faces colourless, their flesh so wasted
   The bones controlled the contours of the skin:
Not Erysichthon was, I think, so dried
   Out by his hunger, down to skin and bone,
   When worse to come made him still more afraid.[1]
And I was thinking to myself: "Behold
   The very folk who lost Jerusalem,
   When Mary stuck her beak in her own child!"[2]   30
Each eye pit seemed a ring without a gem:
   All those who in men's faces can read "OMO"
   Would have distinguished easily the M.[3]
Who would believe the fragrance of a fruit
   And of water could generate such craving,
   Unless he understood the cause of it?
It puzzled me, this hunger and this thirst,
   Because the cause of their emaciation
   And scurviness was not yet manifest:
And then from hollow caverns in his head   40
   One shade turned his eyes round to stare at me
   And then "What grace is shown me!" cried aloud.
I never would have known him from his face;
   But all that had been purged from his appearance
   Was soon apparent to me from his voice.
That was the one clue needed to induce
   My recollection of the altered features:
   I realized it was Forese's face.[4]
"Pay no attention to the scurf and scab
   Discolouring my dried-out skin," he begged,   50
   "Nor yet to any lack of flesh I have.
Tell me about yourself: who are those two
   Shades with you there and acting as your escort –
   Let me not be begrudged one word from you!"
"That face of yours, which at your death I mourned,

---

1   A Thessalian, punished by Ceres with hunger for felling an oak in her sacred grove, he
    ended up gnawing his own flesh.
2   In the siege of 70 AD, when Jerusalem was starving, a certain Mary killed and ate her
    own son.
3   A current conceit was that the word OMO (man) could be traced on the human face,
    with the cheekbones, eyebrows and nose forming the M.
4   Forese Donati (d.1296), friend of Dante, and companion in dissipation apparently;
    Dante's Rime includes six sonnets (XXVI–XXVIIIa) which compose a flyting between the
    two.

Is giving now no lesser cause of weeping,"
I answered, "now I see it so deformed.
So tell me, in God's name: how are you flayed?
    Don't make me speak while I am full of wonder:
    No one speaks well with other thoughts inside."   60
He answered: "By perpetual decree
    There's virtue in that water and that tree;
    And this it is which makes me waste away.
All of these people here who sing and mourn,
    Because they loved their bellies to excess,
    In thirst and hunger cleanse themselves again.[1]
Our lust for food and drink is kindled by
    The fragrance of the fruit and of the spray
    Which spreads itself throughout the greenery.[2]
And not once only, for our circulation   70
    Around this stretch of ground renews our pain –
    I say pain, but I should say consolation:[3]
We're led to the trees by that desire which led
    Christ to exclaim in his exuberance,
    "*Eli*", when he redeemed us with his blood."[4]
I said to him: "Forese, from that day
    When you exchanged our world for somewhere better,
    Not even five years have yet passed away.
If all your power to persevere in sin
    Failed you before the coming of that hour   80
    When holy grief weds us to God again,
How do you come to be up here so soon?
    I thought that I would find you down below
    Where wasted time must be paid back again."[5]
He answered me: "By Nella I was led
    To drink so soon the bittersweet of torment,
    Nella my widow: with her constant flood
Of tears and ardent prayers and heartfelt sighs
    She brought me from the lower slopes of waiting
    And freed me from the other terraces.   90
So much more precious and beloved of God
    Is my dear widow, whom I loved so much,
    The lonelier she is in doing good;
For the Barbagia in Sardinia's far
    More modest in its women and their ways

---

1   This is the circle of the gluttonous.
2   See *Purg.* XXII, 130–38.
3   The pain is accepted joyfully, because it purifies.
4   "Eli" (God) is from Christ's last words on the cross: "My God, my God, why hast
    thou forsaken me?" (Matt. 27–46). To redeem mankind Christ accepted His suffering
    joyfully.
5   Dante expected that Forese's late repentance would have doomed him to a long wait
    before ascending Mount Purgatory. See *Purg.* IV, 127–35.

Than that Barbagia is where I left her.[1]
What, my dear brother, would you have me say?
   I have a vision of a future time,
   But one which is not distant from today,
When from the pulpit it will be forbidden   100
   To brazen women of the Florentines
   To walk abroad without their breasts being hidden.
And what barbarian, or what Saracen,
   Ever needed, to make her dress discreetly,
   Some spiritual or other discipline?
But did these wantons only know full well
   What the swift heavens have in store for them,
   They'd have their mouths wide open in a howl:
If my foresight is not deceiving me,
   They shall be grieved before down clothes the cheeks   110
   Of him who's now consoled with lullaby.[2]
But now, my brother, clear this doubt of mine!
   You see not only I, but all these people
   Are gazing at you where you veil the sun."[3]
And so I answered him: "If you recall
   What life we led together, you and I,
   That memory must be a burden still.
But from that way of living I was turned
   By him who's up ahead, some days ago,
   When his sister appeared to you quite round,"[4]   120
(I pointed to the sun). "Through the profound
   Darkness he led me, through the truly dead,[5]
   In this true flesh which follows on behind.
From there his help and comfort have escorted
   Me up and up, to circle round this Mountain
   Which rectifies you whom the world distorted.
Indeed he has assured me he will be
   My guide until I am where Beatrice is:
   And then I must forgo his company.
And it is Virgil who has told me this" –   130
   I pointed to him – "and this other shade
   Is he for whom on every precipice
Your kingdom shook just now, when he was freed."

---

1 The literal Barbagia in Sardinia was notorious for its barbarity: the figurative Barbagia is Florence.
2 See ll. 100–102 above.
3 Dante is casting a shadow, and therefore must be alive in flesh and blood.
4 The moon (Diana) is mythically the sister of the sun (Apollo).
5 The Inferno.

CANTO XXIV

Forese says that his sister, Piccarda Donati, is already in heaven. He points out the shades of the poet Bonagiunta da Lucca, Pope Martin IV, Ubaldino dalla Pila, Archbishop Boniface of Ravenna and the Marchese degli Orgogliosi.

Bonagiunta can hardly believe he is in the presence of the writer of the *canzone* beginning "Ladies who have intelligence of love". Dante admits his authorship, and says that he was simply writing down what was dictated to him by Love. Bonagiunta accepts this as the explanation of the "sweet new style" (*dolce stil novo*) which distinguishes Dante's poems from those of his predecessors, including Bonagiunta himself.

Most of the shades rush away to hasten their penance, while Forese asks Dante when he will see him again. Dante says that he is so distressed by the ruin which he sees overtaking Florence that his death cannot come too soon. Forese prophesies the damnation of the man whom they both see as most responsible for the evil in Florence – Forese's own brother, Corso Donati.

Suddenly Dante sees a tree, similar to the one found earlier on this cornice. People stand beneath it, grasping for its fruit which hangs out of reach. A voice from this tree warns Dante and his companions to keep well away from it: it is an offshoot of the Tree of the Knowledge of Good and Evil. This voice reminds them of two examples of gluttony – the mythical centaurs who drunkenly attacked the women at the wedding of Pirithous, and those Hebrews who, because they did not restrain their thirst, were not chosen by Gideon for his attack on Midian.

A mile or so farther on the three companions hear another voice, this time of an angel directing them. The angel appears as a dazzling light. Dante feels a fragrant breath of wind and the touch of a wing, as the sixth P is removed from his forehead. The angel blesses those who are temperate in their desires.

✳

S peech did not slow us, nor were we restrained
    From speaking by our speed, but we went on,
    Swift as a ship before a following wind.
The shades, that looked far worse than dead, meanwhile
    Drew in through hollows of their eyes great wonder
    At me, from seeing I was living still.
And I, as I went further in my talk,
    Said: "His ascent perhaps is more delayed
    Than it might be, for other people's sake.[1]
But, if you know, say where Piccarda is: 10
    Say if I'm seeing some noteworthy person
    Among this throng staring at me like this."
"My sister, she of whom I cannot say
    Whether she was more fair or good, already
    Triumphs on high Olympus in her joy."[2]

---

1 Dante is speaking to Forese and referring to Statius, who is delaying for the pleasure of being with Virgil and out of courtesy to Dante.

2 Dante will meet Piccarda Donati in the Heaven of the Moon (*Par.* III, 34*ff*).

Then he explained to me: "We are allowed
   To name each shade here, since our lineaments
   Are drained so drastically by lack of food.
This shade is Bonagiunta," and he gestured,
   "Bonagiunta da Lucca¹ – and that face   20
   Beyond him, the most shrivelled and disfigured,
Is his who once made Holy Church his own.
   He was from Tours, and fasting now he purges
   Eels from Bolsena and Vernaccia wine."²
Then he named many others one by one –
   And all of them seemed happy to be named,
   So that I saw no face that wore a frown.
I did see, biting nothing in their hunger,
   Ubaldino dalla Pila³ and Boniface,
   Who with his rook led many out to pasture.⁴   30
I saw Messer Marchese,⁵ who once had
   More scope to drink, with less thirst, at Forlì,
   Yet even there was never satisfied.
Yet as, when looking round, we often see
   One more noteworthy, so with him of Lucca,
   Who seemed to want a word or two with me.
He muttered low: "Gentucca"⁶ – so I heard,
   Or something like, from where he felt that wound,
   So justly dealt, by which they are so gnawed.⁷
"O soul," I said, "so keen to talk with me,   40
   It seems, speak up and let me understand you,
   And satisfy us both with what you say."
"A maiden's born who wears no wimple yet,"
   So he began, "and she will make my city
   Please you, however men may censure it.⁸
You will go forward with this prophecy:
   And if my muttering led you into error,
   Events will speak with greater clarity.
But do I see before me him who gave
   The start and impulse to new rhymes, beginning   50

---

1   A poet active in the second half of the thirteenth century.
2   Pope Martin IV (r.1281–85) was said to have died from a surfeit of eels stewed in wine.
3   Died 1291. Member of a powerful Ghibelline family, who voted for the destruction of
   Florence after the Battle of Montaperti in 1260. See Dante's meeting with Farinata degli
   Uberti in *Inf.* x, 37–93.
4   Archbishop of Ravenna 1274–95. His pastoral staff was surmounted by the image of a
   rook in chess.
5   Marchese degli Orgogliosi, of Forlì, Podestà of Faenza in 1296.
6   See ll. 43–45 below and note.
7   His mouth feels most acutely his hunger and thirst.
8   Probably an unmarried lady named Gentucca, to whom Dante was to be attracted.
   Dante had himself denounced Lucca (*Inf.* xxi, 37–49). Other commentators interpret
   Gentucca as *gentuccia*: "rabble", "riff-raff".

'Ladies who have intelligence of love'?[1]
And I replied: "I'm simply one who, when
   Love breathes, takes note of it, and in Love's fashion
   Articulates what he dictates within."
"O brother, now I see the obstacle,"
   He said, "that held the Notary, Guittone,[2]
   And me from mastering the sweet new style![3]
Now I see clearly how your pens keep close
   Behind Love as they follow his dictation,
   Which certainly was not the case with us;   60
And deeper delving with the same intent
   Would find no other gap between the styles."
   Then he fell silent, and he seemed content.
Now, as those birds that winter on the Nile
   Form in a flock and float upon the air
   And then increase their speed and fly in file,
So all the people who were with us there
   Turned their eyes round and moved away much faster,
   Made lighter both by leanness and desire.
And as one tired of moving at a trot,   70
   Who lets his friends go on, while he slows down
   Until the panting in his chest dies out,
So then Forese let the holy flock
   Pass by, and came along behind with me,
   And asked me: "When will I see you come back?"
"I do not know how long my life may last;
   And yet, however soon is my return,
   Desire to reach the shore[4] will move more fast,"
I answered, "for the place where I was born[5]
   Divests itself of good from day to day,   80
   And seems ordained to be a dismal ruin."
"Indeed," he said, "the one who's most at fault[6]
   I see dragged by a beast towards that valley

---

1   The first poem written by Dante after saying: "I decided that ever after I would take as
   my theme the praise of my most gracious lady." See *Vita Nuova* 17–18.
2   The two poets Bonagiunta refers to are Jacopo da Lentini, "the Notary" (*d*.1250), tradi-
   tionally the inventor of the sonnet form, poet at the court of Frederick II in Sicily, and
   the Tuscan poet Guittone d'Arezzo (*d*.1294) who is always disparaged by Dante.
3   The *dolce stil novo* has become the accepted name for the innovative poetry, with its
   emphasis on the psychology of love and its technical skill, written by Guido Cavalcanti
   and Dante and influenced by Guido Guinizzelli. See *Purg.* XI, 94–99 and notes, and *Purg.*
   XXVI.
4   Of Purgatory.
5   Florence.
6   The brother of Forese and Piccarda, Corso Donati, head of the Black Guelfs, seized power
   in Florence in 1301 with an orgy of killing and destruction. In 1308 he was killed after
   falling from his horse. The image Dante uses to express his damnation is derived from the
   statutory punishment for treason – to be dragged through the streets tied to a horse's tail.

Where there is no discharging of men's guilt.[1]
That beast at every stride is going faster,
    Faster and faster, till it batters him
    And leaves his body but a foul disaster.
Those wheels,"[2] he raised his eyes up to the sky,
    "Will not turn long before you understand
    What now I cannot say with clarity.   90
Now drop behind me: time is precious to
    Us in this realm, and I am wasting it
    Walking along here side by side with you."
As you may see a knight come at a canter
    Out of a band of horsemen off to war,
    To have the honour of the first encounter,
So he went faster, leaving us behind,
    And I went on my way with those two shades
    Who in this world were men of such command.
And when he'd gone, and gone so far ahead   100
    My eyes had to strain hard to follow him,
    As did my mind to follow what he said,
There suddenly appeared the laden, green
    Boughs of another tree:[3] it was not distant,
    But I had only just come round the turn.
People were under it raising their hands,
    And shouting who knows what into the foliage,
    Like greedy children making their demands,
Who pray with no response from him who's bidden,
    Except he makes their longing more acute   110
    By dangling what they want, on high not hidden.
Then, being disappointed, they disperse.
    And we're arriving now where the great tree
    Rejects their constant weeping and their prayers.
"Keep well away from here as you pass on:
    Above there is a tree from which Eve ate,[4]
    And this tree is an offshoot of that one."
So from among the branches someone spoke;
    Virgil, Statius and I kept close together
    And picked our way beside the rising rock.[5]   120
"Recall," the voice continued, "those accursed
    Creatures conceived in clouds who, being gorged,

---

1   The Inferno.
2   The celestial spheres.
3   Compare the tree in *Purg.* xxii, 130–54.
4   The Tree of the Knowledge of Good and Evil. Gen. 3:3: "The fruit of the tree which is
    in the midst of the garden, God hath said, 'Ye shall not eat of it, neither shall ye touch
    it, lest ye die.'"
5   The side of the Mountain.

Fought against Theseus with twofold breast;[1]
Those Hebrews drinking with no discipline,
  So Gideon refused their company
  When he moved down the hills on Midian."[2]
Thus, keeping close to one of the two verges,[3]
  We went along, and heard of guilty greed
  And how it was requited with harsh wages.
Then, spreading out along the lonely road,   130
  A thousand paces took us farther on,
  Each of us deep in thought without a word.
"What are you pondering, you three, who walk
  Alone?" a sudden voice asked, and I, startled,
  Like a young animal began to shake.
To see who it might be I raised my head,
  And never was there seen in any furnace
  Glass or metal so glowing and so red
As someone I saw saying: "If you please
  To climb on farther up, you must turn here: 140
  This is the way towards eternal peace."
His dazzling look deprived me of my sight,
  So I turned back to follow my two teachers,
  Like one who goes by what his ears make out.
And as the breeze in May, which harbingers
  The dawn, stirs and exhales its balmy fragrance,
  Suffused with all the grasses and the flowers,
Just such a wind it was I felt respire
  Upon my forehead, as I felt the feathers[4]
  Breathing the fragrance of ambrosia.   150
And then I heard one saying: "They are blessed
  Whom grace enlightens and whose love of taste
  Breathes not too much desire within their breast,
Who hunger always but for what is just."

---

1   The mythical centaurs, who were half man, half horse ("twofold breast"), became drunk
    at the wedding of Pirithous and tried to kidnap the women. Theseus helped his friend
    Pirithous to defeat them.
2   Gideon chose for his attack on Midian only those men who "lapped, putting their hand
    to their mouth", rejecting those who "bowed down upon their knees to drink water"
    (Judg. 7:1–7), that is, excluding those who drank too greedily.
3   The edges of the terrace.
4   An angel (who was speaking at ll. 139–41 and will speak again at ll. 151–54) brushes
    Dante with his wing and removes the sixth P.

CANTO XXV

It is now early afternoon. Dante, Virgil and Statius hurry, forced by the narrowness of the track to go in single file.

Dante wishes to know how the shades of the gluttonous can be emaciated when, being immaterial, they do not need food. Virgil's short answer is to remind Dante of the mythical Meleager, the continuance of whose life depended on a burning brand: this shows a mysterious connection between things apparently unrelated. He mentions also how a mirror reflects things outside itself. Virgil knows this answer is insufficient, and so begs Statius to give a lengthier explanation.

Statius first explains how a human being is generated physically, when the male semen meets the female element. The soul thus created is first vegetative (that is, its nature is to grow, as plants do, insensibly), then sensitive (a being with feelings, such as animals have), and then it spreads and develops human faculties, until finally its Creator instils into it a spirit which is self-aware and the soul becomes a rational human one. As soon as the soul arrives at its destination after death, either for eternal punishment or for salvation, it acts upon the space around it to form an impalpable body which is able to suffer and to experience joy, and to take on the appearance of what it is feeling.

The travellers have now reached the place on the seventh and last terrace, where the lustful are purged. The Mountain is blasting out fire, while a wind from the outside of the Mountain is blowing the flames back, leaving only a narrow space between for a path. Dante hears the shades of the lustful singing their hymn, a prayer for chastity. Then they shout out, one by one in the intervals of their hymn-singing, examples which encourage chastity. The shades of the lustful have, Dante concludes, the fire for their therapy, and they are fed by the examples of chastity and by their special hymn.

This was the hour to climb and not go slow:
 The sun had ceded the meridian
 To Taurus, as night had to Scorpio;[1]
And so, like someone who'll not brook delay,
 But travels on no matter what he sees,
 Being sharply goaded by necessity,
Just so we entered that constricted pass,[2]
 And one by one we started up the stairway
 Which severs climbers with its narrowness.
And as a fledgling stork lifts its wings up   10
 And feels the urge to fly, yet does not dare
 To leave the nest, and down it lets them drop,
So my desire was roused and quenched to seek
 Some answers, and it ended with that action
 Performed by one who is about to speak.[3]

---

1 It is 2 p.m. in Purgatory, which is in the southern hemisphere, and 2 a.m. at the point opposite in the northern hemisphere.
2 The way up to the seventh terrace.
3 He opens his mouth.

My gentle father, despite all our speed,
    Did not forbear to say: "Release your bow
    Of speech, now drawn up to the arrowhead."
So now that I was made more confident,
    I moved my lips and asked: "Who can grow lean   20
    Where nobody has need of nourishment?"
"Remember Meleager, how he was
    Consumed at the consumption of a brand,"[1]
    He said, "and you'll not find this arduous.
Consider that, the slightest move you make,
    Your image makes that motion in a mirror,
    And you'll not find this reasoning hard to take.
But so that all your wishes may be met,
    Statius is here: I call on him and beg him
    To heal the wounds inflicted by your doubt."   30
"If I disclose to him the eternal view,"
    Statius answered Virgil, "in your presence,
    Please pardon me: I can't say no to you."
And he began: "My son, if what I say is
    Taken into and kept within your mind,
    It will shed light upon the 'how' you raise.[2]
The purest blood, that which the thirsty veins
    Do not drink up, is like the nourishment
    Which after all have feasted still remains,
And in the heart receives the power to inform   40
    Our human limbs, just like that blood which runs
    Throughout our veins to shape each human limb.
Further refined, it sinks to where it's well
    That we be mute,[3] and then it drops upon
    Another's blood, in the right receptacle.[4]
They run together there, the one disposed
    To passiveness, the other to be active
    Thanks to the perfect place from which it rose.[5]
Arriving there, it is the operator,
    Coagulating first, then livening   50
    What it solidified to be its matter.
This active virtue – now become a soul,
    Like a plant's soul, but different in that
    It's moving, while the latter's reached its goal[6] –
Then operates till it can move and feel,

1 At Meleager's birth the Fates threw a log onto a fire and said his life would last as long
   as that burning brand – a mythical example of the unexpected influence of one thing
   on another. The mirror mentioned below is another example.
2 How mere shades can be affected by hunger and thirst.
3 The male genitalia.
4 The womb.
5 The male principle, originating from the heart, is active.
6 The soul of the plant cannot develop further.

Like a sea mollusc, and thereafter forms
Organs for powers of which it is the seed.[1]
That virtue from the heart of the begetter
Unfolds, my child, and then it spreads itself
Where nature destines it for every member.   60
But how that animal turns into one
Gifted with speech[2] is still beyond your grasp –
A point which once misled a wiser man,[3]
Who argued that the intellectual
Faculty was divided from the soul,
Because he found no organ for its role.
Open your mind up to the truth, and know
The instant that the brain's articulation
Has been perfected in the embryo,
The Primal Mover turns there, in delight   70
At such a work of nature, and infuses
A new and powerful spirit into it,
Strong to attract all that is active there
Into itself, to form a single soul
That lives, that feels and that is self-aware.[4]
And if you wonder at these words of mine,
Think of the sun's heat turning into wine
When it joins liquid flowing from the vine.[5]
When Lachesis has no more thread to spin,[6]
The soul, freed from the flesh, takes with itself,   80
Potentially, the human and divine;
With all the other potencies now mute,
The memory, the intelligence, the will
Are in their operation more acute.[7]
Forthwith, and of itself, the soul falls down,
Mysteriously, on one shore or the other,
And then first knows what road it travels on.[8]
And when space manages to circumscribe
The spirit, its forming virtue radiates

---

1   The soul now has feelings, like even the lowest forms of animal life. It is also developing
    human members.
2   Speech is regarded as a distinctively human characteristic.
3   Averroës, a twelfth-century Arab philosopher, famous for his commentary on Aristotle.
    Finding no corporeal organ for the operation of the human rational intellect, he pos-
    ited two souls, one in the brain (a feature we share with animals) and one which is not
    individual but universal.
4   Human beings have the unique ability, not only to think, but to reflect on what they are
    thinking: they therefore have not only consciousness, but consciences.
5   Two things combine to form a third thing distinct from either of them.
6   At death. Lachesis is the Fate who spins the thread of human life.
7   The immaterial soul is not affected adversely by physical decay: indeed it grows stronger.
8   It lands either on the shore of Acheron for damnation, or on the shore of the Tiber for
    salvation.

As once it did in limbs that were alive;   90
And as the air, when it is full of water,
   With the sun's rays outside reflected in it,
   Is beautified by such a range of colour,[1]
Just so, imprinted on the neighbouring air,
   The form remains which the soul seals upon it
   With all its potency while resting there;
And in the same way as the little flame
   Follows the fire wherever it may go,
   The soul's accompanied by its new form.[2]
And since made visible in this way, it   100
   Is called a shade, and hence it organizes
   All of our senses, even that of sight.
Hence we can speak, hence we can laugh and hence
   We form the tears and sighs which you perhaps
   Have heard around the Mount on your ascent.
According as we're seized by our desires
   And other feelings, so this shade takes shape[3] –
   And this is what occasions your surprise."
Now we had reached the final turn and torture,
   And we had swung around towards the right,   110
   And we had other things to worry over.
On one side here the Mountain blazes out,
   While from the Mountain's edge a blast blows up
   Which bends the flames and keeps them back from it;
And we were forced to travel one by one
   Along the space left free, so that I feared
   On this side fire, on that side falling down.
"Along this passageway," my leader said,
   "You have to keep your eyes under control:
   It's easy here to slip down at the side."   120
"*Summæ Deus clementiæ*"[4] I heard
   As it was sung within the intensive burning,
   Which made me no less keen to turn aside.[5]
And I saw spirits walking through the flame,
   And stared at them while staring at my steps,
   Switching my eyes about from time to time.
When they had reached the last word of that hymn,
   They shouted loudly: "*Virum non cognosco*",[6]
   Then re-began the hymn in softer tone.
That ended, they cried out once more: "Diana   130
   Stayed in the woods and banished Helice,

---

1 A rainbow, formed by the sun's rays.
2 The new, impalpable body remains with the immaterial soul.
3 Hence the emaciation of the gluttonous.
4 "God of supreme mercy" – the first words of a prayer for chastity.
5 No less keen to look into the flames than to watch where he treads.
6 "I know not a man" (Luke 1:34), Mary's reply to the angel at the Annunciation.

Who had the wound which Venus deals upon her."[1]
Then back to singing. Then they shout in praise
　　Of all those wives and husbands who were chaste
　　As probity requires, and marriage vows.
The spirits must continue in this mode,
　　It seems, for all the length of time they burn:
　　It's by such therapy and with such food
That the last wound must be healed up again.[2]

1　The goddess of chastity, Diana, lived apart from men. Her nymph Helice had been
　　seduced by Jupiter.
2　The wound inflicted by the sin of lust, and more specifically the mark of the seventh
　　and last P on the forehead.

CANTO XXVI

Dante follows Virgil and Statius along the narrow track between the fire and the cliff. The setting sun now casts Dante's shadow on the flames and deepens their colour. This astonishes the shades, and some of them ask him why he seems to have a material body. Dante is about to answer, when he sees another group of shades coming from the opposite direction. The sinners on both sides give each other a rapid kiss in greeting. Then each group raises a great shout: one group shouts out "Sodom and Gomorrha!", while the other tells of the unnatural sin of Pasiphaë. Then both groups repeat the hymn and the examples of chastity mentioned previously.

When those who had questioned Dante come round the Mountain again, he explains how he comes to be there in the flesh, and asks them who they are. One of them says that there are two sins purged on this terrace: homosexual lust, the sin of those shades coming in the opposite direction, and heterosexual lust. He himself is guilty of the second sin. Dante is delighted to find that this shade is Guido Guinizzelli, an early exponent of the lyrical style which Dante favours. Dante declares his admiration for Guinizzelli's vernacular poetry, but Guinizzelli points out a shade ahead of him who, he says, was a better craftsman.

Dante addresses the shade mentioned by Guinizzelli, who is the Provençal poet Arnaut Daniel, from the second half of the twelfth century, one of the forerunners of the Italian poets of Dante's day. He speaks in his native language and, after revealing his name, says he is weeping and singing at once, sorry for his past sin and joyful at the thought of the blessedness which awaits him. After telling Dante to remember his example and repent of his sins in time, he hides himself once more in the refining fire.

W hile thus along the ledge we made our way
    In single file, with my kind guide repeating:
    "Take note: you may be helped by what I say,"
I was aware of how the sunshine beat
    On my right shoulder, while its rays already
    Changed the whole western sky from blue to white.
My shadow made the flames appear more red,
    And I saw how, at this slight indication,
    So many shades, as they went by, paid heed.
This started them discussing me, and gave   10
    Them every reason to begin by saying:
    "His body does not look like make-believe."[1]
Then some of them approached, but as they turned
    Towards me, took considerable care
    Not to come out to where they'd not be burned.[2]
"O you who go, and not for lack of haste,

---

1   As happens several times in the Inferno and in Purgatory, Dante's shadow reveals that
    his body is a living one.
2   The shades accept their purgation enthusiastically.

But out of reverence, behind the others,
    Respond to me who burn in fire and thirst.
Your answer would not be for me alone:
    All these thirst for it more than Indian   20
    Or Ethiopian for a cooling stream.
Why do you make yourself a parapet
    Against the sunlight, just as though you were
    Somebody still at large outside death's net?"
So one said, and immediately I would
    Have told him who I was, but my attention
    Was caught by something else strange which occurred:
For through the middle of the blazing fire
    Came people in the opposite direction,
    Which made me wonder, pause a while and stare.   30
I saw the shades on both sides give a fleeting
    Kiss to each other as they hurried past
    Without a pause, content with that brief greeting:
Just so do ants in black battalions greet
    Each other, just by touching nose to nose,
    To find their way or ascertain their fate.
 Immediately that friendly welcome's over,
    Before they take one step to separate,
    Each company tries hard to shout the louder.
One: "Sodom and Gomorrha!"¹ while the first   40
    Crowd shouts: "Pasiphaë invades the cow
    For the young bull to satisfy her lust!"²
As if two flocks of cranes were flying, some
    To northern heights, and others to the desert,
    These shy of frost, the former of the sun,
One group moves off from us, while others come;
    Then, weeping, they repeat their earlier songs
    With the loud shouts most suitable for them.³
And those who had been questioning me before
    Came back, drew close to me, and by their looks   50
    Were all attentive and prepared to hear.
And I, who now had seen them question twice,
    Began: "O souls who have the certainty,
    Sooner or later, of eternal peace,
I have not left my limbs, whether as green
    Or ripe fruit, yonder: they are here with me
    With all their ligaments and blood and bone.
I climb up here to be no longer blind:

---

1   Cities notorious for homosexual lust (Gen. 19).
2   The mythical Pasiphaë had a wooden cow made for her, and went into it to receive the
    bull for which she lusted.
3   See *Purg.* xxv, 121–39.

A lady up above[1] wins grace for me
  To bear my mortal body through your land.   60
But – may your great desire be satisfied
  In a short space, and you be housed in heaven,
  Which is replete with love and spreads most wide –
Say who you are, that I may write it out.
  And who are all that crowd behind your backs,
  Who move in the direction opposite?"
No peasant from the hills shows more alarm,
  Struck dumb and gazing all about in wonder,
  When, rough, uncivilized, he sees the town,
Than did those shades appear to be astonished;   70
  But when they'd shaken off that stupefaction,
  Which in exalted hearts is soon diminished,
"Blessèd are you who, in this borderland,"
  That shade began to speak who spoke at first,
  "Store up experience for a better end![2]
All those who do not come with us have been
  Stained with that sin for which triumphant Caesar
  Heard himself taunted with the name of 'Queen':[3]
So they shout 'Sodom!' as they travel on,
  And reprimand themselves, as you have heard,   80
  And with their shame they help the fire to burn.[4]
Our own transgression was hermaphrodite,[5]
  And since we did not live as humans should,
  But like brute beasts indulged our appetite,
To our opprobrium we shout aloud,
  As we go moving off, the name of her
  Who made herself a beast in bestial wood.[6]
Now you know what we did and know our guilt,
  Perhaps you'd like to know us name by name?
  But there's no time to tell, and I could not.   90
I can at least provide you with my name:
  I'm Guido Guinizzelli,[7] being purged
  Since I repented fully and in time."
Such as in King Lycurgus' grief and ire
  The twin sons were on finding their lost mother,

---

1 See *Inf.* II, 94–105, where the Virgin Mary asks St Lucy to help Dante, and St Lucy transmits the request to Beatrice.

2 I.e. to die well.

3 It was customary, during a Roman general's triumph, for his soldiers to mock him, as a reminder that he was only human. Julius Caesar was accused of homosexuality by his troops in their bawdy songs.

4 See note to l. 15 above.

5 Involving both sexes.

6 See note to ll. 41–42 above.

7 A Bolognese (*c.*1230–76), the most famous poet in Italian before Dante. See *Purg.* XI, 97–98 and note.

Just so was I (without going quite so far)[1]
To hear him name himself, the father of
  Me and those better poets, all who ever
  Constructed sweet and graceful rhymes of love.
Thoughtful, with nothing heard and nothing said,   100
  I stared at him a while but, for the fire,
  I did not dare move closer to his shade.
When finally I'd looked at him enough,
  I placed myself entirely at his service
  With such avowals as compel belief.
And he to me: "You leave a deep impression,
  A clear one too, with what you've said to me,
  Which Lethe cannot take away or lessen.
But if that is the truth to which you swore,
  Tell me the reason why you seem, from all   110
  Your words and from your looks, to hold me dear."
"Those graceful rhymes of yours," so I replied,
  "Which will, as long as our new language lasts,
  Ensure their very ink will be adored."
He said: "O brother, that shade whom I bring
  To your attention up in front there was
  A better craftsman in his mother tongue.[2]
In love rhymes and romantic tales in prose
  He overcame all others, though some dolts
  Prefer that other writer from Limoges:[3]   120
They turn their faces rather to repute
  Than to the truth, and harden their opinion
  With no attention paid to sense or art.
So with Guittone[4] many did of old,
  Passing his praise about from mouth to mouth,
  Until eventually the truth prevailed.
Now if you are so blessed you are allowed
  To make your way at last into the cloister[5]
  Where Christ is abbot and the only lord,
Say me a Paternoster once you're in,   130
  Or rather say as much of one as needed
  Where we no longer have the power to sin."[6]

---

1 Queen Hypsipyle was sold into slavery to King Lycurgus. When his infant son, whom
he had entrusted to her, died, he ordered her execution. She was recognized by her twin
sons, Thoas and Euneus, from whom she had long been parted, and they rushed to
embrace her and save her. Dante is similarly delighted to meet Guido Guinizzelli, but
does not embrace him for fear of the fire.

2 See ll. 136–48 below and note.

3 The Provençal poet Giraut de Bornelh (c.1160–1210).

4 Guittone d'Arezzo. See *Purg.* XXIV, 55–57 and note.

5 Heaven.

6 The last verse of the Our Father ("And lead us not into temptation, but deliver us from
evil") is not relevant to souls in Purgatory. See *Purg.* XI, 22–24.

Then, possibly to make way for another,
   He vanished in the burning, like a fish
   Which flashes to the bottom of the water.
I made towards that shade he'd pointed out
 -   And said how much I longed to know his name,
   And so provide an honoured place for it.
Without the least demur his answer came:
   "Tan m'abellis vostre cortes deman,   140
   qu'ieu no me puesc ni voill a vos cobrire.
Ieu sui Arnaut, que plor e vau cantan;
   consiros vei la passada folor,
   e vei jausen lo jorn qu'esper, denan.
Ara vos prec, per aquella valor
   que vos condus al som de l'escalina,
   sovenha vos a temps de ma dolor!"[1]
With that he hid in the refining fire.

---

1   "So pleseth me your words of curtesye / That I nill kepe it hidden who I am. / I am
   Arnaut, who walke and wepe and syng; / I se to my distress olde tymes of follie, / And se
   the joy I hope for beckoning. / I pray yow, by that vertu and heigh power / That guideth
   to the topmost of the stair, / Be mindful, whil time is, of my doloùr!" This speech of
   Arnaut Daniel (poet who flourished *c.*1180–1200) is written by Dante in Arnaut's native
   Provençal, as a tribute to him and other Provençal poets who had such an influence on
   later writers in Italian.

CANTO XXVII

As the sun sets, Dante sees an angel and hears him singing of the blessedness of the pure in heart. The angel says that the three travellers must go through the fire. Dante is terrified, but Virgil reminds him how he has always helped him, even in the Inferno. Virgil insists that the fire will torment Dante, but not injure him.

Dante is encouraged when Virgil tells him that Beatrice is beyond the wall of fire. So he walks into it, with Virgil ahead and Statius behind. The fire is almost indescribably hot. As they come out of the fire and reach the stairway, Dante hears a voice from within a dazzling light, welcoming them and urging them to climb quickly while the light lasts.

The disappearance of Dante's shadow shows that the sun has set. The travellers then lie down to rest. Dante feels that, with Virgil and Statius, he is well protected. He notices that the stars are bigger and brighter. He falls asleep and dreams, and in his dream he sees a beautiful lady walking over a meadow at dawn and gathering flowers. She explains that she is Leah, one of Jacob's wives. She symbolizes the active life, while her sister Rachel, Jacob's other wife, symbolizes the life of contemplation.

When Dante awakens, Virgil explains to him that he is about to experience the happiness which all mortals seek. This encourages Dante to climb so fast that he seems to fly.

Virgil speaks his final words to Dante. He can no longer help and guide him. Beatrice will take his place and, until she does, Dante may sit or walk at his leisure and enjoy the sunshine, flowers and shrubs here where plants grow of their own accord, without any need for sowing or cultivation. Dante is now so purified that his will is in complete conformity with the will of God, and consequently he may, indeed should, simply follow his own inclinations.

W hen the daylight is shooting its first rays
    There where the sun's Creator shed His blood,[1]
    While Ebro flows beneath the lofty Scales,[2]
And Ganges' waves are being scorched at noon,
    So stood the sun, and so the day was passing.[3]
    Then God's bright angel made his presence known.
Beyond the flames, beside the precipice,
    He stood and sang: *"Beati mundo corde!"*[4]
    In a melodious, more than human voice.
And then: "You sacred souls cannot proceed   10
    But through the cruel fire. So you must enter,
    Not deaf to singing on the other side."
That, as we came up close, was what we heard.
    And when I understood him, I became

---

1   Jerusalem.
2   The constellation Libra.
3   It is sunrise at Jerusalem, midnight on the River Ebro in Spain, noon in India, and sunset on Mount Purgatory.
4   "Blessed are the pure in heart", the sixth Beatitude (Matt. 5:8).

Like somebody about to be interred.[1]
With hands held up to shield my face, and staring
  Into the flames, I saw in my mind's eye
  All of the human bodies I'd seen burning.[2]
Both of my kindly guides turned to me, with
  These helpful words from Virgil: "My poor child,   20
  There may be torment here, but never death.
Remember, just remember! I'm the guide
  Who guided you so well on Geryon's shoulders:[3]
  So what will I do now, closer to God?
One thing is certain: even if you were
  To stay within these flames a thousand years,
  They would not make you balder by one hair.[4]
You think that I deceive you? If you doubt
  My word, simply approach the flames and hold
  Your robe's hem in both hands and try it out.   30
By now you should have cast off fear: so turn
  To me and come uninjured through the flames!"
  Against my better judgement I stood firm.
When he saw I was stubborn and stood still,
  He was somewhat perturbed and said: "My child,
  All that keeps you from Beatrice is this wall."
As dying Pyramus, when he but heard
  The name of Thisbe, raised his eyes to her,
  Then when the mulberry was turning red,[5]
So I, my stubbornness being softened, turned   40
  To my wise leader as I heard once more
  That name that's never distant from my mind.
At that he shook his head at me and smiled:
  "We really want to stay here?" as one might,
  In winning over an unwilling child.
He went, before I did, into the fire,
  While begging Statius to come behind,
  Who had so long divided us before.
Once I was in I would have gladly thrown
  Myself in molten glass to cool me down,   50
  So beyond measure did the flames there burn.
My sympathetic guide, to keep me steady,
  Walked on and talked of Beatrice all the while,

---

1 Dante probably has in mind the punishment for hired assassins – to be placed upside
  down in a hole which was then filled with earth (see *Inf.* XIX, 49–51). The emphasis is on
  horror and terror.
2 Dante would have seen criminals burnt alive.
3 When Dante was terrified (*Inf.* XVII, 79–136).
4 See Luke 21:18: "But there shall not an hair of your head perish".
5 Pyramus, believing that Thisbe had been killed, stabbed himself. His blood dyed red the
  berries of the mulberry beneath which the lovers had arranged to meet. Thisbe returned
  unharmed to find him dying, and he roused himself to look at her before his death.

Saying: "I think I see her eyes already."
And a voice guided us, singing beyond
    The flames, till we, intent on that, came out
    Of fire at last to where we could ascend.
"*Venite, benedicti Patris mei*"[1]
    Sounded within a light that was so splendid
    I could not look at it: it dazzled me.   60
"The sun is setting: it will soon be night,"
    The voice went on. "Don't pause, quicken your pace –
    Now, while the western sky has still some light."
The pathway went straight up, cut in the rock,
    While I, ahead of me, blocked out the sun,
    Which was already sinking at my back.
We three made trial of a few steps, but
    We knew, the instant that my shadow vanished,
    The sun behind us had already set.
Before the sky through all its vast extent   70
    On the horizon had become one colour,
    And night had reassumed its government,
Each of us made his bed upon one step:
    The nature of the Mountain took away,
    Not the desire, the power of climbing up.
Like she-goats standing still to ruminate
    Tamely, though they were restless on the hills
    Before they had been given enough to eat,
Silent in shade, beyond the blazing sun
    And guarded by the goatherd, who is leaning   80
    Upon his staff and taking care of them,
And like the shepherd living out-of-doors,
    Who spends the night in silence by his flock
    To keep them safe and sound from predators,
Such were we then all three – I like a goat,
    And they like shepherds, all of us protected
    By the high rock on this side and on that.
Little beyond those walls was visible,
    But in that little I could see the stars,
    Larger, more luminous than usual.   90
Gazing up thus and ruminating there,
    I was subdued by sleep – sleep that so often,
    Before it happens, shows what will occur.[2]
It was, I think, that hour when Cytherea[3]
    Is shining on the Mountain from the East,
    She who is always flaming with love's fire,
When in my dream I seemed to see a young

---

1   "Come, ye blessed of my Father" (Matt. 25–34).
2   Dreams at dawn were believed to be prophetic. See *Inf.* xxvi, 7 and *Purg.* ix, 13–19.
3   The morning star, the planet Venus (goddess of love).

And lovely lady walking through a meadow
And gathering flowers, and saying as she sang:
"Whoever wonders who I am may know   100
   That I am Leah, and to weave a garland
   My lovely hands are working to and fro.
I deck myself to please my looking glass;
   But sister Rachel cannot be distracted
   From gazing at her image in the glass.
She is as keen to see her lovely eyes
   As I to deck myself: it's contemplation
   With her, with me it's work which satisfies."[1]
Already with the brightness before dawn –
   All the more welcome in the eyes of pilgrims   110
   The nearer home they lodge on their return –
The shadows all around were taking flight,
   And my sleep with them: I arose to find
   My masters were already on their feet.
"That tempting fruit which mortals with such zest
   Go searching for among so many branches
   Today will set your hungry mind at rest."
Virgil addressed these words, or words like these,
   To me – and there were never any gifts
   Which did as much as these words did to please.   120
Longing added to longing grew so great
   To be above that at each step I took
   I felt that I was growing wings for flight.
When all the stairs beneath us had flown by
   And we were standing on the topmost step,
   Then Virgil turned and fixed his eyes on me
And said to me: "My child, now you have seen
   The temporal and eternal fires,[2] and come
   Where, of myself, there's no more I discern.
I've led you here with sense and expertise,   130
   And now you must take pleasure for your guide:
   You are beyond the steep and narrow ways.
Look at the sun that shines on your forehead –
   Look at these grasses and these flowers, these shrubs
   This earth produces of its own accord.
Until the advent of those lovely eyes[3]
   Which once, with weeping, made me come to you,[4]
   You may sit down or wander through all these.
Expect no further word or sign from me:

---

1   Leah and Rachel were both wives of Jacob (see Gen. 29), and they came to be regarded
    as symbols of, respectively, the active and contemplative lives.
2   In Purgatory and in the Inferno respectively.
3   Beatrice's.
4   See *Inf.* II, 115–17.

Your will is now upright and free and proper.   140
Did you not follow it, you'd go astray:
Over yourself I grant you crown and mitre."[1]

---

1   Dante has now been so purified that his will is in complete conformity with the will of
God. These are the last words spoken by Virgil in the poem.

CANTO XXVIII

Dante moves into the sacred forest, walking slowly in order to appreciate the beauty of this earthly paradise.

Deep in the forest Dante finds his way blocked by a little stream, purer and clearer than any other, even though it is coloured brown by the shade of the trees. He sees across the stream a lady singing and plucking flowers. This makes Dante think of the mythical Proserpine, who was seized by Dis and taken into his realm, with the loss of eternal spring on earth and the coming of the seasons as we now know them. Dante begs the lady to come closer so that he may understand the words of her song.

The lady does draw near; she raises her bright eyes and smiles. Dante is angry with the stream, which prevents their coming closer. She says that the psalm '*Delectasti*' will explain her pleasure in being where she is: it reveals a delight in God's creation. She will answer all Dante's questions. She says that this is the place ordained by God for the human race and lost through man's sin. Dante is anxious to know how there can be wind here and moving water, for Statius has already told him that none of the atmospheric disturbances which are usual in the world of the living have any place on the Mountain above the entrance to Purgatory. The lady says the gentle invariable breeze here is caused by the turning of the heavenly spheres, while the water, like the wind invariable, flows from a spring generated directly by God. Seeds from the plants here are taken by this wind and deposited in the northern hemisphere. The spring feeds two streams: Lethe, which gives forgetfulness of sins, and Eunoë, which brings the remembrance of good deeds: both must be tasted by the purified soul. She says that it is probable that this place, Eden or the Earthly Paradise, is what ancient poets meant when they spoke of the primeval Age of Gold.

✳

E ager to search through all its spacious ways
    The sacred forest, dense and evergreen,
    Which filtered the fresh daylight to my eyes,
I left the Mountain's edge with no delay
    And took unhurried steps across the plain
    On ground that breathed out fragrance all the way.
A soft invariable breeze was there,
    Touching me ceaselessly upon my brow
    With no more pressure than a breath of air.
The trembling boughs, compliant with its sway,   10
    Inclined towards that quarter where the Mountain
    Casts its first shadow at the break of day.[1]
Yet their deflection was not very great,
    And not a single bird upon the treetops
    Left off the exercise of all its art,
But with hearts full of joyfulness they sang
    To welcome the first daybreak among leaves
    Contributing the bass notes to their song:

---

1   Towards the west.

Just such as gathers through the greenery
   In the pine forest on the shore by Classe[1]   20
   When Aeolus sets the sirocco free.[2]
Unhurried footsteps had already borne
   Me deep into the ancient forest, and
   I could not see the way I had come in,
When suddenly a little stream denied
   Me headway as it rippled to the left,
   Bending the grass that grew along its side.
The purest of all waters in our world
   Would look as though they were contaminated
   Compared to that, where nothing is concealed,   30
Even though as it flows it's dark and brown
   Under the everlasting shade which never
   Gives access to the rays of sun or moon.
I stayed my feet, but travelled with my eyes
   Beyond the little rivulet to wonder
   At all the various blooms upon the boughs;
And over there appeared – as suddenly
   As something can at times to drive, in sheer
   Amazement, every other thought away –
A lady who was walking quite alone,[3]   40
   Singing and choosing flowers from all the flowers
   Enamelling the path she paced upon.
"Oh, lovely lady, warmed in gentle heat
   Of love – if I may trust in outward signs,
   Which usually bear witness to the heart –
I pray that you'll indulge me, if you're willing,"
   I said to her. "Come closer to the river,
   That I may understand what you are singing.
With you I find I am remembering
   Where Proserpine was walking that same instant   50
   Her mother lost her, and she lost the spring."[4]
Then – as a lady keeps both feet together
   And on the ground, pivoting in the dance,
   And scarcely puts one foot before the other –
She, on the yellow and vermilion
   Flowers turned towards me, and not otherwise
   Than a shy virgin with her eyes cast down.
And so my prayers received full recompense
   As she came near and the delightful sound

1   The ancient harbour of Ravenna.
2   Aeolus is the classical god of the winds. The sirocco is a south-east wind.
3   She is not named until *Purg.* XXXIII, 119.
4   Proserpine, the daughter of Ceres the goddess of fertility, was seized by Dis while she
   was gathering flowers, and taken into the Underworld. Her mother's grief caused the
   earth to lose its fruitfulness, which later was restored for part of the year: perpetual
   spring gave way to our seasons.

AND I SAW SPIRITS WALKING THROUGH THE FLAME,
AND STARED AT THEM WHILE STARING AT MY STEPS...

PURGATORY XXV, 124–25

I SAW A GIANT STANDING AT HER SIDE,
AND THEY EMBRACED AND KISSED FROM TIME TO TIME...

PURGATORY XXXII, 152–53

Came borne to me together with the sense.   60
The instant she was where the herbage grows
   So near the rivulet its ripples bathe it,
   She favoured me so much she raised her eyes:
I scarcely can believe such clear light shone
   From under Venus' lids when she was stricken,
   However accidentally, by her son.[1]
She stood and smiled upon the other side,
   Her hands arranging all the many colours
   That bloom in that high country without seed.
The stream between us was three paces wide,   70
   Yet Hellespont, which was traversed by Xerxes –
   To this day still a curb on human pride –
Had from Leander less hostility
   Because it swelled mid Sestos and Abydos,
   Than this because it did not part for me.[2]
"You are new here. Perhaps it is my laughter,"
   She said, "in this place which has been selected
   To be the fostering ground of human nature,[3]
That makes you wonder what you may expect;
   But there is light for you from 'Delectasti',[4]   80
   That psalm which will uncloud your intellect.
And you who stand in front there, you who prayed
   For my approach, please question me: I'm ready
   To answer you until you're satisfied."
"The water?" I replied. "The sounding wood?
   Both of them seem to me to contradict
   Something I've just been told and understood."[5]
She answered me: "I shall explain just how
   There is a cause for all which makes you marvel,
   And dissipate the cloud that troubles you.   90
The highest Good, alone self-pleasing, made
   Man good and for the good, and gave this place
   To be a pledge of peace that would not fade.
Through his own fault his time here was but short;
   Through his own fault he changed to grief and trouble

---

1   Cupid wounded his mother unintentionally with one of his arrows, which caused her
    tragic love for Adonis.
2   Across the Hellespont (the Dardanelles) King Xerxes of Persia built a bridge of boats
    for his ill-fated invasion of Greece. The mythical Leander swam the same straits to visit
    his lover Hero at Sestos, and one stormy night he was drowned.
3   A strong hint that this Earthly Paradise is the Garden of Eden. The identity is made
    explicit at ll. 91–93 below.
4   Psalms 92:4 ("For thou, Lord, hast made me glad through thy work"), referred to here
    mainly because of the delight it shows in God's creation.
5   The presence here of wind and moving water appears to be at odds with the statement
    by Statius (Purg. xxi, 40–54) that there is no rain or wind or any atmospheric disturbance
    above the entrance to Mount Purgatory.

His honest laughter and his harmless sport.[1]
So that the storms created down below
  By exhalations from the earth and water,
  Rising towards heat as far as they can go,
Might wage no war upon humanity,   100
  This Mountain rose till it was safe beyond
  The gate where it is under lock and key.[2]
Since, with the turning of the Primal Sphere,[3]
  All air is always turning round and round,
  Unless its circuit is blocked anywhere,
This motion strikes the Mountain, unconfined
  By earthly currents as it is, and makes
  The forest in its density resound;
And the plants struck by this revolving air
  Have vigour to suffuse it with their seeds   110
  Which, as it turns, it scatters here and there.
The earth elsewhere,[4] according to its worth
  And its particular climate, then produces
  From diverse seeds diversity of growth.
It should not seem, once this is understood,
  A wonder over there whenever plants
  Take root and grow without apparent seed.
And you should be aware this sacred ground
  Where you are standing has all kinds of seeds
  And bears fruit which back there is never found.   120
The water you see here flows from no vein
  Restored by vapours which the cold condenses,
  Like streams back there which rise and fall again,
But issues from a sure unvarying fount
  Which by the will of God regains as much
  As, on two separate courses, it pours out.[5]
Here it flows with the power to take away
  All memory of sin – beyond, it brings
  All good deeds back into the memory.
It is called Lethe[6] here, and Eunoë[7]   130
  Beyond, and both of them need to be tasted
  Or it will not reveal its potency:
Its savour is more sweet than any other.

---

1   The Fall of Man (Gen. 3).

2   The entrance to Purgatory (*Purg.* IX, 73–129).

3   The Primum Mobile, which sets in motion all the other heavenly spheres around the static earth, with a consequent movement of air.

4   The land in the northern hemisphere, believed in Dante's day to be the only inhabited part of the globe.

5   The water here has no natural cause, such as it has in the fallen world.

6   "Oblivion" (in Greek). This river of forgetfulness is found in classical descriptions of the Underworld.

7   "Kindly, benevolent", a coinage by Dante from the Greek.

Your thirst for knowledge would be satisfied
   Even if I enlarged on this no further,
But there's one inference which I must add.
   I do not think my words will seem less precious
   If I exceed the promise that I made:[1]
Perhaps those poets in the olden days
   Who sang the Age of Gold and utter bliss   140
   Were dreaming on Parnassus of this place.[2]
The human race's root was without fault –
   All fruits were here and everlasting spring:
   This is the nectar all men talk about."
At that I turned right round with my whole body
   To face my poets, and they smiled, I saw,
   At that last comment from the lovely lady.[3]
Then I turned back to gaze on her once more.

---

1   See ll. 83–84 above.
2   See *Purg.* XXII, 148–50. The pagan poets, especially Ovid in Book I of his *Metamorphoses*,
   describing the mythical Age of Gold, were unconsciously testifying to a Christian truth.
3   Virgil and Statius are naturally delighted, as is Dante when he turns to them, by the
   lady's appreciation of ancient poetry.

CANTO XXIX

The lady and Dante continue to walk on opposite sides of the stream, until the lady tells Dante to look and listen. Suddenly a light, as bright as lightning but not as ephemeral, shines throughout the forest. This, combined with a sweet melody, leads Dante to reflect how happy life would have been if Eve had not sinned and human beings had been allowed to stay in the Garden of Eden until they attained the joys of heaven. Then what at first seem to be seven golden trees appear – which, as they come closer, are revealed as seven lit candlesticks. Meanwhile the sweet music resolves itself into a chant of "Hosanna!" Dante looks round, to see that Virgil is no less astonished than he is.

The lady calls Dante's attention away from the lights to the procession of white-clad people which follows them. The candle flames move on, leaving in the air behind them seven bands of coloured light. The procession consists of twenty-four elders, representing the twenty-four books of the Old Testament (according to St Jerome's grouping); four animals representing the Evangelists; a chariot, in the space between the Evangelists, representing the Church and drawn by a gryphon representing Christ; three ladies representing the theological virtues and four representing the cardinal virtues, who dance by the sides of the chariot; two aged men representing St Luke and St Paul; four men representing the writers of the Catholic Epistles; and a solitary man representing the book of Revelation. When the chariot is opposite Dante, there is a clap of thunder, and the whole procession halts.

The interest of this canto lies in the complex symbolism of the procession. It reveals the unity of the Old and New Testaments and the all-embracing nature of Christian faith, but in true apocalyptic tradition its details are not always easy to decipher.

*

The lady, like a lover in her rapture,
    Chanted once she had said those last few words:
    "Beati quorum tecta sunt peccata!"[1]
And like those nymphs who used to stray alone
    Through forest shades, when some of them were longing
    To contemplate, some to escape, the sun,[2]
She moved against the river in its course,
    Along the bank – and I along with her,
    Shortening my steps to make them short as hers.
With not a hundred steps between us paced,   10
    Both of the river's banks turned at an angle,
    And turned so far that I was facing east.
And then, when we had still not travelled far,
    The lady turned herself right round to me,
    Saying: "My brother, you must look and hear."
Then all at once an instantaneous brightening
    Coursed through all corners of the massive forest,
    Such that it made me think it might be lightning.

1   "Blessed are they whose sins are covered" (i.e. "forgiven"), an adaptation of Psalms 32:1.
2   A reminiscence of pagan classical pastoral poetry. See *Purg.* XXVIII, 139–41.

But since the lightning, once it is, is not,
    While this was lasting and indeed grew brighter,   20
    "What can be happening here?" was my next thought.
Also, a most mellifluous melody
    Ran through the luminous air, and righteous zeal
    Led me to censure Eve's audacity,
Since she, when all of heaven and earth obeyed,
    One woman only, only just created,
    Could not endure to be the least bit veiled[1] –
Had Eve had the humility to linger,
    I would have tasted those ineffable
    Delights much sooner, tasted them for longer.[2]   30
As I was walking rapt among such sweet
    First fruits of everlasting joy, and yearning
    For what was still to come – still more delight –
The air in front of us turned brilliant
    With what seemed blazing fire beneath green boughs,
    And the sweet sound turned out to be a chant.
O hallowed Virgins, if I have endured
    Hunger and cold and vigils for you ever,
    Now is the time to beg for my reward.
From Helicon my stream must take its course,   40
    And all Urania's choir must help me put
    Things difficult to think of into verse.[3]
Seven trees of gold, a little farther on
    From us, appeared to be but were not – an
    Illusion fostered by the space between;
But when I came up close, and so much nearer
    That the main sight, which could deceive the senses,
    Became in all its circumstances clearer,
Perception, which feeds reason with the manna
    For discourse, showed that they were candlesticks,[4]   50
    And in the singing voices heard "Hosanna!"
Above, the glorious pageant was ablaze,
    Far brighter than a moon in cloudless sky,
    At darkest midnight, in its central phase.
I turned around, so great was my surprise,
    To honest Virgil, and he answered me
    With no less wonder obvious in his eyes.

---

1   The veil was a sign of humility and obedience: Eve chose to disobey the divine prohibi-
    tion against the knowledge of good and evil (Gen. 2:16–17).
2   If Eve had not sinned, then she, Dante and all mankind would eventually have progressed,
    presumably by death, from a state of natural to one of supernatural happiness.
3   The invocation of the Muses is to prepare us for an important scene (see *Inf.* XXXII, 10–12
    and *Purg.* I, 7–12). Helicon is a mountain range sacred to the Muses, and Urania is the
    Muse of heavenly things.
4   Representing the seven gifts of the Holy Spirit (wisdom, understanding, right judgement,
    fortitude, knowledge, piety and fear of the Lord).

Again I turned to the exalted vista:
    It moved towards us, but it was so slow
    That newly wedded brides would walk much faster.[1]   60
The lady chided me: "Why do you burn
    In such devotion to the living lights,
    While still ignoring what comes in its turn?"
And then, behind the leaders, came in sight
    A white-clothed company; nothing on earth
    With us has ever been so white and bright.
Upon the left I saw the water glitter,
    And it reflected my left side to me,
    If I looked in it, as it were a mirror.
When I had reached that place beside the river   70
    Where it was all that kept me at a distance,
    I paused a while in order to see better,
And saw the candle flames go moving on,
    Leaving the air they left behind them coloured
    With brushstrokes, as a painter might have done;
And so the air above the candles shone
    With seven bands, displaying all the colours
    Of rainbows, or a halo round the moon.
These pennants stretched behind till they were lost
    To sight; also, as far as eye could tell,   80
    Ten paces were between the outermost.
Under this lovely sky which I portray,
    Twenty-four elders,[2] walking two by two,
    Came wearing coronets of fleurs-de-lis,
Singing: "*Benedicta* are you before
    All of the daughters born of Adam, and
    May your beàuties be blessed for evermore!"[3]
After the flowers and the fresh greenery
    Opposite and along the other bank
    Were, after these elect had gone, left free,   90
As starlight follows upon starlight in
    The sky, there followed on four animals,
    And each of them was crowned with leaves of green.
Each of them had six wings, covered with eyes
    Through all the feathers, and the eyes of Argus,[4]
    Were he alive, would be as sharp as these.[5]
Reader, I cannot squander any more
    Rhymes in describing them: further impending

---

1   Such homely imagery helps to keep even this elaborately symbolic canto in touch with
    mundane matters. See ll. 73–75.

2   The books of the Old Testament as they were grouped by St Jerome.

3   This hymn to the Virgin Mary is adapted from the Annunciation (Luke 1:28).

4   A mythical creature with a hundred eyes.

5   The four animals represent the four Evangelists: Matthew (man), Mark (lion), Luke
    (bull) and John (eagle).

Expense prevents my being lavish here;
But read Ezekiel: as he has said,   100
   He saw them coming from the frozen north
   In a whirlwind, a ball of fire and cloud.
And as you find them in his pages they
   Were here as I describe, but for the wings
   Where St John differs and agrees with me.[1]
The space between the four was occupied
   By a triumphal chariot on two wheels
   Drawn by a gryphon harnessed at the head.[2]
He held on high one and the other wing
   Between the middle band and each of three,   110
   Not striking and not harming anything.
The wings rose till their tips were out of sight;
   His limbs were gold so far as he was birdlike;
   The rest, with crimson mixed in it, was white.[3]
Rome never celebrated with so fine
   A chariot Africanus or Augustus:[4]
   The sun's is paltry in comparison –
That of the sun which, straying, was combust
   In answer to the pious prayers from earth,
   When Jove, in his mysterious way, was just.[5]   120
Three ladies by the right wheel in a round
   Came dancing, with the one of them so red
   In blazing fire she'd hardly be discerned;
The second looked as though her bones and flesh
   Had all been fashioned out of emerald;
   The third appeared like snow when it is fresh;
The white one seemed to lead the dance along,
   And then the red one: whether quick or slow,
   The others took their measure from her song.[6]
Four other ladies on the left-hand side   130

---

1   The four beasts of Revelation 4:4–8 are identified with the four "living creatures" of
    Ezekiel 1:1–14. In St John's Revelation the creatures have six wings each, and in Ezekiel
    only four. Why Dante should draw attention to the discrepancy is unclear, but it does
    have the effect of emphasizing the identification.
2   The chariot is the Church. The dual nature of the mythical gryphon (head and wings
    of an eagle, body of a lion) represents the dual nature (divine and human) of Christ.
3   White represents purity, and crimson Christ's blood sacrifice of Himself.
4   Refers to the triumphal processions the ancient Romans awarded to successful generals
    (here Scipio Africanus, who defeated Hannibal decisively at Zama in North Africa, and
    Caesar Augustus, the first Roman Emperor).
5   The mythical Phaethon obtained from his father permission to guide the chariot of
    the sun. He lost control of it and, when the sun came ruinously close to the earth, Jove
    struck Phaethon with a thunderbolt. Line 120 hints at the inscrutability of God's actions.
    See also *Inf.* XVII, 107–8.
6   The ladies represent the three theological virtues: faith (white), hope (green) and charity
    (red).

Danced, dressed in purple, following the lead
Of one of them with three eyes in her head.[1]
And after this whole group I have described
I saw two agèd men, unlike in clothing,
But like in bearing, honest, dignified.
One of them seemed to be a follower
Of that Hippocrates whom nature made
To help those creatures whom she holds most dear.
The other showed an opposite regard,
Holding a sword that was so bright and sharp   140
That this side of the stream I felt afraid.[2]
Next I saw four men with a humble mien,[3]
And then, behind, a solitary old man
Came in a sort of trance: his face was keen.[4]
And this last company of seven had
White clothes like the first twenty-four, except
They had no lily garlands, but instead
Roses mingled with other crimson flowers:
From a short distance anyone would swear
That there was blazing fire on all their brows.[5]   150
The chariot was now facing where I stood.
A clap of thunder, and that noble band
Appeared to have its further progress barred,
And came with the first ensigns[6] to a stand.

---

1   These ladies represent the four cardinal virtues: prudence (her three eyes indicating
knowledge of the past, understanding of the present and provision for the future),
justice, fortitude and moderation. See *Purg.* I, 22–27).

2   The first aged man is St Luke, a doctor and follower of Hippocrates, the most famous
physician of antiquity, and the second is St Paul, frequently shown with "the sword of
the Spirit" (Eph. 6:17) and known for his sharp, sometimes disturbing discrimination.

3   The four "Catholic" Epistles (i.e. addressed to the Church as a whole) of Peter, James,
John and Jude.

4   The final book of the Bible, Revelation, notable for its mystical nature and esoteric
symbolism.

5   The red flowers represent charity.

6   The candlesticks of ll. 43–51 above.

CANTO XXX

As the chariot comes to a halt, one of the twenty-four elders welcomes the Bride of Christ, singing an extract from the Song of Solomon, then the other elders repeat it. This is followed by a hundred people singing from within the chariot, using the words which welcomed Christ into Jerusalem: they scatter lilies in abundance.

Inside this cloud of flowers a woman appears, wearing a white veil, a green mantle and a dress of bright red. The veil prevents Dante from seeing her properly, but he trembles because she reminds him of his earliest love. In his confusion he turns round to Virgil for reassurance and sees that Virgil has disappeared. Now Dante's cheeks, which were cleansed in dew before his ascent of Mount Purgatory began, are stained with tears.

The lady addresses him by name, saying that his tears should not be for Virgil, but for another reason. She reveals that she is Beatrice. At this Dante is stricken with shame. The angels sing, rejoicing in God, and it seems to Dante that they sympathize with him, but Beatrice continues to reprove him. She says that he has been greatly gifted by nature and the grace of God, and yet he has not used his gifts well. When she died, at the age of twenty-four, he looked to others for solace and fell so far from grace that nothing could save him but to see, in his journey through the afterlife, the results of sin. And that is why Beatrice asked Virgil to guide him through the Inferno and Purgatory. Now Dante must have true contrition for his sins before he may taste of the water of Lethe.

Dante's name is used only here in the *Comedy*. He is holding himself up as an example of sinfulness, and exposing himself to Beatrice's reproof. As always in this poem, man's duty to God takes precedence over everything else.

> N ow when the Primal Heaven's Septentrion[1] –
> Those stars that never rise and never set,
> And know no veil except the cloud of sin,
> Those stars by which the people there were taught
> Their duty, as our lower seven[2] guide
> The man who turns the tiller safe to port –
> Came to a halt, then those men worth our trust,[3]
> Standing between the gryphon and his charge,
> Turned to the chariot as their place of rest.
> And one of them, a heavenly messenger,   10
> Sang *"Veni, sponsa, de Libano"*[4] thrice,
> As all the others did in sequence there.
> As at the Last Trump, when the blessed arise
> Each from his cavern[5] with alacrity

---

1 The seven candlesticks, representing the seven gifts of the Holy Spirit (see *Purg.* XXIX, 50 and note). The Primal Heaven is the Empyrean.
2 The stars of the Great Bear, used in navigation.
3 The twenty-four elders of *Purg.* XXIX, 83.
4 "Come from Lebanon, my bride" (Song of Songs 4:8): the Church is the bride of Christ.
5 Tomb.

And alleluia from each new-clothed voice,[1]
So on the godly chariot arose
    A hundred men, *ad vocem tanti senis*,[2]
    Eternal life's servants and messengers.
All of them cried: *"Benedictus qui venis"*,[3]
    Scattering flowers up above them and around,   20
    "Manibus, oh, date lilia plenis!"[4]
Before now I have seen at break of day
    The eastern heavens glowing rosy-red
    And all the rest one blue serenity,
And seen the sun's face at its birth, but shaded,
    So that with all the intervening vapour
    The eye for long was able to sustain it:
Just so, within a flower-engendered cloud
    Rising and falling from the hands of angels
    To drift within the chariot and outside,   30
In a white veil, and olive-garlanded,
    A lady appeared to me, mantled in green,
    Her dress beneath the mantle flaming-red.[5]
My spirit now – for all the length of time
    Which had gone by since merely in her presence
    I shook with awe till I was overcome,
Without more knowledge which the eyes can give,
    Through hidden virtue coming out of her –
    Felt the great potency of ancient love.[6]
The instant that my eyes were stricken by   40
    That mighty power which had already pierced me
    Before my early boyhood had gone by,
I turned round to the left with all the trust
    A child has running up towards his mother
    When he's afraid or otherwise distressed,
To say to Virgil: "There is not one dram
    Of blood now left in me that does not tremble:
    I know the tokens of the ancient flame";[7]
But Virgil had left us. Oh, the deprivation

---

1   The voices are now, with the resurrection of the body, "clothed" in flesh.

2   "At the voice of so great an elder", in Latin for greater solemnity.

3   "Blessed is he that cometh [in the name of the Lord]" (Matt. 21:9), Christ's welcome into Jerusalem.

4   "Scatter lilies from full hands" (*Aeneid* VI, 883). This lament for Marcellus, nephew of Augustus, who died young, is used here to express rejoicing.

5   The colours of the veil, the mantle and the dress allude respectively to faith, hope and charity. The olive garland is a sign of peace; also the olive was sacred to Minerva (Pallas Athena), goddess of wisdom (see l. 68 below).

6   "Since my birth the sun had already returned nine times to the same point in its revolution, when there first appeared to me the glorious lady of my memory" (*Vita Nuova*, 1). See l. 115 below.

7   *Aeneid* IV, 22

Of Virgil, dearest father, and that Virgil   50
     To whom I gave myself for my salvation!
All our first mother lost out of her keeping[1]
     Was insufficient now to keep my cheeks,
     Though washed in dew,[2] from being streaked with weeping.
"Dante, though Virgil has just disappeared,
     You must not weep yet, you must not weep yet,
     For you must weep beneath another sword."[3]
Now, like an admiral on prow or stern
     Who moves along the decks to check the sailors
     Serving on other ships and cheer them on: 60
So on the left side of the chariot,
     When I turned round at hearing my name spoken
     (Which here, here only I'm obliged to note),[4]
I saw the lady who first appeared to me
     Under the veil of the angelic welcome
     Direct across the stream her eyes to me.
Although the veil which came down from her head,
     Encircled by the foliage of Minerva,
     Would not allow her to be quite descried,
Regal of bearing, rigorous, steadfast,   70
     She recommenced like someone who, when speaking,
     Has kept her warmest words until the last:
"Look at me well! For I am Beatrice.
     How did you ever come to climb the Mountain?
     Did you not know here is man's happiness?"
I let my eyes sink to the limpid stream,
     But when I saw myself, looked at the grass,
     My forehead was weighed down with so much shame.
Just as a mother seems towards her child,
     So did she seem to me: the taste is bitter   80
     When someone is being cruel to be kind.
She fell silent; the angels all at once
     Sang: *"In te, Domine, speravi"*,[5] but
     From *"pedes meos"* they did not advance.
Just as the snow upon the living joists[6]
     Along the spine of Italy congeals,
     Piled up, compacted by Slavonian gusts,

---

1   All the pleasures of the Garden of Eden, lost by Eve.
2   At the foot of Mount Purgatory (see *Purg.* I, 121–29).
3   The knowledge of his sins.
4   This, an apology for what might be construed as vanity, has also the effect of stressing
     that Dante is recording facts accurately.
5   "In thee, Lord, have it put my trust" (Psalms 31:1). In the following line *pedes meos* ("my
     feet") is from verse 8 of the same psalm: "Thou hast not shut me up into the hand of
     my enemy: thou hast set my feet in a large room." The angels do not sing beyond this
     point because the psalm becomes one of lamentation.
6   Trees in the Apennines, which have not yet been cut and shaped into beams.

Then through itself it melts and trickles down –
   If but the land where shadows shrink should breathe[1] –
   Rather like wax beneath the candle flame: 90
Just so was I bereft of sighs and tears
   Before I heard that singing which is always
   Tuned to the music of the eternal spheres.
But when I realized from their melodies
   They sympathized with me, as if they said:
   "Why must you, lady, force him to his knees?"
Then what had tightened round my heart like ice
   Was breath and water issuing from my breast
   In anguish through my lips and through my eyes.
But she, still standing motionless beside   100
   The chariot on its left, spoke to those beings,
   Those angels who were pitying me, and said:
"You keep your vigil in the eternal day,[2]
   Where neither night nor slumber steals from you
   One single step the world takes on its way;
Therefore my answer must show more concern
   For him who's weeping there beyond the river,
   So that his grief may keep pace with his sin.
Not only by the turning of the spheres
   Directing every seed to its own end   110
   According to the influence of the stars,
But through the plenitude of heavenly grace,
   Which rains upon us from such lofty clouds
   Our mortal vision cannot reach that place,
This man was so endowed in his new life,[3]
   Potentially, that all his natural powers
   Should have shone out in coming to the proof.
But ground grows all the weedier and wilder
   When badly seeded and uncultivated,
   The more the soil is blessed with natural vigour.   120
My countenance sustained him for a while:
   Turning my youthful eyes in his direction,
   I guided him towards a righteous goal.
But soon as I was standing at the door
   Into my second age and changed my life,
   He turned from me and gave himself elsewhere.[4]
When I had risen out of flesh to spirit,
   And so had grown in beauty and in virtue,
   To him I was less dear and had less merit.

---

1   When a warm wind blows from the African deserts, where the sun at midday casts no
    shadow since it is directly overhead.
2   In the presence of God.
3   His early life; but see note to l.39 above.
4   When Beatrice was about to enter into full adulthood, at the age of twenty-four, she
    died, and Dante turned to other studies and loves.

He made his way on a misleading road 130
   After deceitful semblances of virtue
   Which never keep their promise as they should.
Nor did it help to pray for inspiration,
   By which in dreams and various other ways
   I called him back: he paid them slight attention!
He fell so far I could not place my trust
   In any way of saving him, except
   By showing him the people who are lost.[1]
For this I visited the truly dead,
   And to the one who guided him up here[2] 140
   My weeping and my prayers were forwarded.
It would do violence to God's decree
   If Lethe could be crossed and such nutrition[3]
   Tasted without the payment of a fee
Composed of penitence and true contrition."

---

1   In the Inferno.
2   Virgil. How Beatrice gave him this task is described in *Inf.* II, 49–74.
3   To drink the water of Lethe gives forgetfulness of sin (see *Purg.* XXVIII, 127–28).

CANTO XXXI

Beatrice continues to reprove Dante for his sins, insisting that he must confess them. He is too disturbed to talk coherently. Beatrice now speaks more harshly, saying that he cannot have forgotten his wrongdoing. At this, Dante appears to agree and breaks into sighs and tears. Beatrice does not relent, but says that, even after her death, he should not have allowed himself to be distracted from loving her. Dante admits he was attracted by what was near at hand. His repentance is accepted and he is forgiven, but Beatrice continues to upbraid him in order to make him more steadfast in future. She indicates, with some asperity, that he is old enough to know better.

The angels have now stopped scattering flowers. Beatrice, although veiled and separated from Dante by the river, still seems to him to be surpassingly beautiful. He is so stricken with remorse that he faints. When he recovers, the lady whom he had seen walking alone through the Earthly Paradise plunges him forcibly in the Lethe, and he drinks of it and loses the memory of his sins. Then she leads him inside the dance of the four ladies (the cardinal virtues). They take him to where Beatrice is looking at the gryphon and tell him to look into her eyes. He does so and sees there the gryphon's reflection, which alternates between the human and the divine – the two natures of Christ whom the gryphon represents.

The group of three ladies (the theological virtues) sing during their dance and ask Beatrice to unveil. When she does so, Dante says that no poet, however accomplished, could convey her beauty.

"You, on the far side of the sacred river,"
    She brought her censure sharply to the point,
    After its edge had struck me as most bitter,
And recommenced without procrastination,
    "Say, say if this is true: such a great charge[1]
    Must be accompanied by your confession."
My faculties were lacking – when my voice
    Began to move, it found itself exhausted
    Before its usual organs let it loose.
She bore this briefly, then: "What's to consider?   10
    Answer me, you, with your bad memories
    Not yet obliterated in the water!"[2]
Fear and confusion intermingled said
    Something from me that seemed to be a "Yes",
    Which needed seeing to be understood.[3]
As a crossbow will break if it's let loose
    When cord and bow are drawn with too much tension,

---

1 Beatrice is referring to the account of Dante's misdeeds which she gave to the angels at the end of the previous canto.
2 Dante has not yet drunk the water of Lethe.
3 Dante's reply is so muffled that his meaning is more clearly understood from his contrite expression.

And the bolt strikes its target with less force –
I broke beneath my burden of confusion,
   Pouring a torrent out of sighs and tears,   20
   And my voice faded out in its emission.
And so she said to me: "In your desire
   For me, which made you hungry for the good
   That leaves us nothing to be hungered for,[1]
What ditches did you find across your road,
   What chains which led you to divest yourself
   Of any hope of going on ahead?
And what allurements, what advantages
   Did you observe displayed in other people
   That you should struggle to attract their eyes?"   30
After a sigh, bitter and long-drawn-out,
   I hardly had the breath to give an answer,
   And my lips struggled hard to fashion it.
Weeping I said: "Things right in front of me
   Turned me aside with their delusive pleasures,
   The moment that your face was hid away."[2]
And she: "Had you kept silent or denied
   What you confess, your guilt would still be known:
   Such is the judge from Whom nothing is hid![3]
But when the accusation has been made   40
   To burst from one's own mouth, then in our court
   The grindstone turns itself to blunt the blade.[4]
However, so that you may feel more shame
   For going wrong, and therefore in the future,
   Hearing the Sirens,[5] you may be more firm,
Dismiss your cause of weeping and attend:
   Hear how this body of mine, when it was buried,
   Ought to have led you to a different end.
Never did art or nature glad you with
   Beauty to match the lovely limbs wherein   50
   I was enclosed, now scattered in the earth;
And when this beauty was no longer there
   But failed you when I died, what mortal thing
   Should have been able to provoke desire?
At the first arrow shot, at the first touch
   Of perishable things, you should have risen
   After myself who no longer such.[6]
Your wings should not have been deprived of motion,

---

1   Dante's love for Beatrice led him to love God.
2   When she died.
3   A reference to God's omniscience.
4   Acknowledgement of a fault, with repentance, is met by immediate forgiveness. A
    metaphor of the sword of justice is understood.
5   The deceptive allurement of earthly goods. See *Purg.* xix, 19–24 and note.
6   No longer perishable, since her soul has risen to Heaven.

To wait for further shafts, by a young girl
　　Or other vanity of short duration.　　　　　　　　　　60
The fledgling waits about for two or three,[1]
　　While in the eyesight of the fully fledged
　　Nets may be spread, bolts shot, but uselessly."
As children put to shame make not a sound,
　　But listen, see their guilt and show their sorrow,
　　Keeping their eyes cast down upon the ground,
So did I stand there; and she went on: "If
　　You're grieving just to hear it, raise your beard,
　　And what you see will give you further grief."
With less resistance than our northern wind　　　　　　70
　　Encounters to uproot some sturdy oak,
　　Or wind encounters from Iarbas' land, [2]
I lifted up my chin as she required.
　　And when by "beard" she signified my face,
　　I understood the venom in that word.[3]
Then as I raised my countenance my eyes
　　Alighted on those first-created creatures[4]
　　And saw that they had finished scattering flowers.
And, still unsure and hesitant, my vision
　　Came towards Beatrice, who faced the beast　　　80
　　Who is, with his two natures, but one person.[5]
Under her veil, beyond the waterway,
　　I thought she still surpassed her former self
　　More than she did all others in her day.
Now feelings of regret so nettled me
　　That every other thing I'd found alluring
　　Became at once my greatest enemy.
My heart was bitten by such deep remorse
　　I fell into a faint – and how I was
　　She knows who had administered the cause.　　　　90
Then as the blood coursed through my veins again,
　　I found that lady whom I'd found alone[6]
　　Saying to me: "Hold on to me! Hold on!"
She'd plunged me in the stream up to my throat
　　And, pulling me behind her moved across,
　　Skimming the surface like a little boat.
When I was near the other sacred side
　　I heard "*Asperges me*",[7] pronounced more sweetly

1　Shots. The young bird does not realize immediately that it is being attacked.
2　Libya. Iarbas was a king in love with Dido, Queen of Carthage (*Aeneid* IV, 196*ff*).
3　She is implying that Dante ought to act his age.
4　Angels. See *Purg.* XXX, 22–33.
5　See *Purg.* XXIX, 108 and note.
6　See *Purg.* XXVIII, 40.
7　"You will sprinkle me [with hyssop, Lord, and I shall be cleansed]" – intoned at the
　sprinkling of holy water before Mass.

Than I can now recall, much less describe.
That lovely lady brought her arms together   100
  Around my head and plunged me so far under
  I could not help but swallow down some water.[1]
She drew me out, now newly cleansed, and led
  Me right inside the dance of the four ladies,[2]
  And they all held their arms above my head.
"Here we are nymphs and in the sky we're stars,[3]
  And before Beatrice was in the world
  We were ordained, as handmaids, to be hers.
We'll lead you to her eyes – to their glad light
  Your eyes must be habituated by   110
  The three beyond with their more sharp insight."[4]
So they began by singing. After this
  They took me with them to the gryphon's breast,
  Where Beatrice was standing facing us.
They said: "Do not be chary with your gaze:
  We have brought you to face those emeralds[5]
  Whence Love once shot his shafts into your eyes."
A thousand longings more intense than flame
  Held my eyes fixed upon those shining eyes,
  Which stayed upon the gryphon all that time.   120
Exactly as the sun shines in a mirror,
  The double beast was shining in her eyes,
  Showing now one, and now the other nature.[6]
Imagine, reader, if I was delighted
  To see how in itself it was unchanging,
  As the reflection of it alternated.[7]
While, full of wonderment, my soul rejoiced
  In tasting of that nourishment which, while
  It satisfies, yet still arouses thirst,
That other trio,[8] who were obviously   130
  Ladies of greater eminence, advanced
  And danced in their angelic roundelay.
"Turn, Beatrice, and direct your holy gaze,"
  So ran their song, "upon your faithful one
  Who, to see you, has come by such hard ways![9]

---

1 Having drunk the water of Lethe, Dante no longer remembers his sins.
2 The four cardinal virtues. See *Purg.* xxix, 130–32 and note.
3 See *Purg.* i, 22–24.
4 The three theological virtues. See *Purg.* xxix, 121–29 and note.
5 Beatrice's eyes, described thus because they are shining, although not necessarily green.
6 The human nature and the divine nature of Christ. See ll. 80–81 above, and *Purg.* xxix,
   108 and note.
7 In the person of Christ the two natures (human and divine) are one being: in the human
   reflection they are seen as distinct.
8 The theological virtues.
9 Dante's descent into the Inferno and his ascent of Mount Purgatory.

Graciously of your graciousness unveil
    Your smile to him, so that he may discern
    Your second beauty, which you still conceal."[1]
Reflection of the light that does not fail![2]
    Anyone who'd grown pallid in the shade   140
    Of Mount Parnassus, or drunk from its well,
And deeply, would still find it far too hard
    To represent you as you issued there[3]
    By nothing but heaven's harmony obscured,[4]
When you unveiled your beauty to the air.

---

1   Her smile: her first beauty is her eyes.
2   God.
3   Any poet, however hard-working and however inspired, would find the task beyond him.
4   A much discussed line. Another interpretation of this difficult passage is: "There [in
    Eden] where the sky, in harmony with the land of innocents, adumbrates your divine
    beauties with its beauty". There is probably an allusion to the music of the spheres, and
    also a more general implication that Beatrice's beauty is subordinate to that of Heaven.

CANTO XXXII

Dante's contemplation of Beatrice is interrupted by the ladies who represent the theological virtues. The procession now wheels to the right. Dante, Statius and the lady who had pulled Dante through Lethe follow the inner wheel of the chariot. For a distance of about three arrow flights they travel on, accompanied by angelic music, until Beatrice descends from the chariot.

Then all arrange themselves around a very tall barren tree. The gryphon draws the pole of the chariot to the base of the tree and leaves it tied there. The tree bursts into leaf. Dante falls asleep to the sound of an unearthly hymn. A voice is heard telling him to rouse himself, and he does so, just as the disciples did after the Transfiguration.

Dante looks for Beatrice and sees her seated on the root of the tree, surrounded by the seven virtues. Beatrice tells him that he will eventually get to heaven, but in the meantime he must write down everything he now sees, for the benefit of the sinful world.

An eagle descends and despoils the tree. A starving vixen gets inside the chariot, but is put to flight. The eagle descends again and covers the chariot with its feathers. A voice is heard deploring this last event. A dragon damages the chariot, which then becomes over-grown with grass. The chariot sprouts seven heads with ten horns. A harlot is sitting on the chariot. A giant embraces her and then, when she turns her glance away from him, beats her savagely. Then the giant drags the now disfigured chariot so far into the woods that Dante can no longer see it.

The sights and actions in this canto are presented as prophetic: they are speaking of divine matters and they foretell one event, the removal of the Papacy to Avignon, which happened after the date Dante assigns to his poetic journey. The imagery is dense, detailed, fantastic and, in accordance with the traditions of apocalyptic writing, deliberately oblique.

M y eyes were fixed so firmly, so intent
    On slaking, satisfying ten-years' thirst,[1]
    That every other sense of mine was spent.
On this side and on that they[2] had great walls
    Of total unconcern (so her blessed smile
    Drew me towards her in her ancient toils!),
When my attention was drawn forcibly
    Towards my left by those three goddesses,[3]
    Hearing them say: "You stare too fixedly!"
And that condition which we often find   10
    In eyes that have been dazzled by the sun
    Left me, for a brief period, quite blind.
But, with my sight inured to what was less
    (I say "was less" in contrast with the greater
    Splendour[4] from which it was removed by force),

---

1   The ten years since the death of Beatrice.
2   Dante's senses.
3   The theological virtues.
4   The sight of Beatrice, which surpasses the lights in the procession.

I saw the glorious host had wheeled upon
   Its right hand and was now returning, facing,
   Together with the seven flames,[1] the sun.
As, covered by their shields in their retreat,
   An army turns, wheeling upon its standard,   20
   Until the total action is complete,
Just so the troops of the celestial land,
   Those of the vanguard, passed in front of us
   Before the chariot swung its pole around.
The ladies[2] then went back up to the wheels;
   The gryphon pulled along its hallowed burden
   Without one feather fluttering in the least.
The lady who had pulled me through the water[3]
   And Statius and myself followed that wheel,
   Whose arc, as it was turning, was the shorter.[4]   30
 So through the dense wood, uninhabited
   Through her misdeed[5] who trusted in the serpent,
   Angelic music paced us as we trod.
When we had travelled in this way about
   Three times the distance of a loosened arrow,
   Beatrice descended from the chariot.
I heard a murmuring of Adam's name,
   Then they stood round a tree that was divested,
   Each single bough, of leaf and bud and bloom.[6]
Its crest, which spreads wider and wider out   40
   The higher it rises, would have been admired
   By Indians in their forests for its height.
"Blessèd are you, O gryphon, since your beak
   Tears nothing from this tree, so sweet to taste,
   Which tasted makes the belly writhe and ache."
So cried the others standing all around
   The sturdy tree. Then the two-natured beast:[7]
   "Thus is the seed of righteousness sustained."
Then, turning to the pole which he had drawn,
   He dragged it to the base of the bare tree   50
   And left it bound to that from which it came.[8]
As trees in our world – when they're beamed upon
   By the great light commingled with that other

---

1   The candles (*Purg.* XXIX, 43–54).
2   The theological virtues.
3   See *Purg.* XXXI, 100–105.
4   As the chariot turns, the inside wheel moves less than the outer wheel.
5   Eve's.
6   The tree of the knowledge of good and evil (Gen. 2:16–17).
7   The gryphon.
8   The pole of the chariot (the Church) is the Cross, which is itself, according to legend, made from the wood of the tree of the knowledge of good and evil.

Which shines when the celestial Fish have gone[1] –
Burgeon and spread and blossom out again,
   Each in its own bright hue, before the sun
   Can yoke his team beneath another sign,
So, opening out into a colour more
   Of violets than roses, did the tree
   Renew its branches which were bare before.   60
A hymn was sung I failed to understand –
   It was a hymn not sung here in our world –
   I could not bear to hear it to the end.[2]
Could I describe how the relentless eyes
   Grew drowsy when they heard the tale of Syrinx,
   Those eyes which stayed awake at such a price,[3]
Then like a painter painting what he sees
   I would portray the way I fell asleep –
   But who can fathom his own drowsiness?
I pass therefore to my awakening: 70
   A splendour rent the veil of sleep, a voice
   Was heard: "Arise! Why all this dithering?"
As when – to view the flowering apple tree
   Which makes the angels greedy for its fruit,
   With marriage feasts in heaven eternally –
Peter and John and James were all three taken
   And overcome, and wakened at the word
   By which much deeper slumbers had been broken,
And found their gathering had now grown less,
   With Moses and Elias having left it,   80
   And their Lord altered in His mien and dress:[4]
Just so I roused, and saw that kindly lady
   Standing above me, she who had conducted
   My steps along the riverside already.[5]
Perplexed I asked her: "Beatrice? Where is she?
   She answered: "See her seated on its root
   Under the new-sprung foliage on the tree,
And see the company she has around her.
   The others are ascending with the gryphon,
   And to a song that's sweeter and profounder."   90

---

1 The "great light" is the sun; "that other" light is from the constellation Aries (March to
   April), which follows Pisces ("the celestial Fish").
2 Presumably overcome by the sweetness of the sound.
3 Argus, who had a hundred eyes, was ordered to keep watch on Io, of whom Juno was
   jealous. Mercury lulled him to sleep by singing of the metamorphosis of the nymph
   Syrinx, and then cut off his head.
4 The "flowering apple tree" (l. 73) symbolizes the Transfiguration of Christ: see Matt.
   1:1–9 ("his face did shine as the sun... there appeared unto them Moses and Elias... Jesus
   came and touched them and said, 'Arise, and be not afraid...'"). Lines 77–78 allude to
   the resurrection of Lazarus (John 11:43–44).
5 See note to l. 28 above.

And if she went on speaking any further
   I do not know, for I could see already
   Her who kept me from heeding any other.
She was sitting alone on the bare ground,
   Left there as guardian of the chariot
   Which I had seen the two-formed beast fast bind.
The seven nymphs made a circle round about
   Her, holding in their hands those seven lights[1]
   Not Aquilo nor Auster could blow out.
"You will live in this wood a little time,   100
   Then be with me perpetual citizen
   Where Christ Himself is citizen of Rome.[2]
So, for the bad world and its benefit,
   Gaze at the chariot, and what you see
   Make sure, when you return back there, you write."
So Beatrice said – and I, who was fast bound
   To obey all her commands with true devotion,
   Whither she ordered turned my eyes and mind.
Never did fire descend so rapidly,
   When dropping out of concentrated cloud   110
   From the far limits of the moving sky,
As did the bird of Jove[3] drop through the tree,
   Tearing the bark off it, and even tearing
   Its blossoms and its recent greenery:
It struck the chariot with all its might
   And rocked it like a ship caught in a storm
   Tilting to starboard now and now to port.
Then I saw, as it hurled itself inside
   That chariot of victory, a vixen[4]
   That seemed to have been starved of all good food.   120
But, reprimanding it for its foul sins,
   My lady put it to a flight as rapid
   As could be managed by those fleshless bones.
Then once again, and by the selfsame route,
   The eagle swooped into the chariot,
   And left its eagle's plumes all over it;[5]
And like the sound of an afflicted heart,
   I heard a voice from heaven cry aloud:
   "O my poor vessel! Fraught with evil freight!"[6]

---

1   The candlelights representing the virtues.
2   Paradise, the heavenly Rome.
3   An eagle, representing the Roman Empire in its persecution of the early Christians.
4   The heresies which afflicted the early Church.
5   This symbolizes the Emperor Constantine favouring the Church.
6   It was believed that the Emperor Constantine, when he moved his capital to Byzantium,
    gave all temporal power in the West to the Pope, by the so-called Donation of Constan-
    tine. For Dante the Church's temporal power is the source of great evil. See *Inf.* XIX,
    100–17.

And then it seemed to me earth opened out 130
  Between the wheels – I saw a dragon issue
  And send its tail up through the chariot;
Then, like a wasp when it retracts its sting,
  Drawing its evil tail back, taking with it
  Part of the base, resume its wandering.
All that was left of it, like fertile land
  Now overgrown, was by those feathers (offered
  Perhaps with an intent both good and kind)
Covered, and wheels and pole were covered by
  Them also, in less time than should be needed 140
  To keep the mouth wide open for a sigh.
The sacred chariot, so transfigured, then
  Sprouted with heads on every part of it,
  Three on the pole, at every corner one:
The first were horned like oxen, but the four
  Had each a single horn upon its forehead:
  No monster such as this was seen before.
Then, brazen as a fortress on a mound,
  I saw a woman seated there, a harlot,
  In loose disordered dress, eyes rolling round.[1] 150
And there, to keep her always close to him,
  I saw a giant[2] standing at her side,
  And they embraced and kissed from time to time.
And then, the instant that she turned her hot
  And wandering eyes on me, that brutal lover
  Beat her and battered her from head to foot.
Then, full of jealousy and cruelty,
  He dragged off the monstrosity, unloosed,
  So far into the trees I could not see
Either the harlot or the freakish beast. 160

---

1 The imagery, taken from Rev. 17:1–5, is appropriate to an attack on the corruption of
  the Papacy.
2 Generally interpreted as Philip the Fair of France, who in 1309 had the Papacy trans-
  ferred from Rome to Avignon, where it remained until 1377 – a blatant instance of the
  subjugation of religion to politics.

CANTO XXXIII

The ladies representing the seven virtues sing a psalm lamenting the destruction of Jerusalem. Beatrice responds to the psalm by quoting some words of Christ which foretell, again obliquely, His own death and resurrection. Using terms taken from the obscure book of Revelation, she promises retribution on those who have degraded the Church. The Church will be saved by a mysterious figure, alluded to only by a number. Dante, Beatrice says, must remember all that is said and report it faithfully for the benefit of the wicked world.

A procession of the seven virtues, Beatrice, the mysterious lady who had taken Dante through the Lethe, Dante and Statius halts by the common source of Lethe and Eunoë. Dante asks what water this is. Beatrice directs him for an answer to Matelda, who has already helped him so much, and who is now named for the first time. Matelda takes Dante and Statius to drink from Eunoë to ensure the memory of their good deeds.

Dante says that his state of being purified and prepared to rise to Heaven cannot be further described, because he has already used up all the pages allotted to Purgatory. This low-key, almost comic way of putting it fits the general tone of this canto, where Beatrice is comparatively relaxed in her treatment of her pupil and even teases him a little. The stress and strain of the Inferno and Purgatory are now over. At the end of the Inferno Dante was relieved "to look once more upon the stars"; here he is ready "to rise up to the stars", as he is about to do in the *Paradise*.

"*D*eus, venerunt gentes*",[1] alternating
   By three by four their dulcet psalmody,
   The seven ladies[2] sang between their weeping.
Sighing and full of pity, Beatrice
   Listened, her features stricken little less
   Than Mary's when she wept below the Cross.
But when the choir had given place to her
   To let her speak, she rose and stood upright
   And answered, with a face as red as fire:[3]
"*Modicum, et non videbitis me;*   10
   Et iterum, dearly belovèd sisters,
   Modicum, et vos videbitis me."[4]
She placed the seven virgins up ahead
   And, with a nod, she signed to follow her
   Me and the lady and the sage who'd stayed.[5]
So she went forward, and had hardly gone

---

1   "The heathen are come [into thine inheritance; thy holy temple have they defiled; they have laid Jerusalem on heaps]" (Psalms 79:1).
2   The four cardinal virtues and the three theological virtues.
3   A sign of religious zeal and righteous anger as Beatrice makes her prophecy.
4   Lines 10–12: "A little while, and ye shall not see me: and again, a little while, and ye shall see me" (John 16:16): Christ's prophecy of His death and resurrection.
5   Statius, who remained when Virgil left.

Ten paces on the earth, so I believe,
 When with her shining eyes she dazzled mine.
And gazing tranquilly, "Be quick, come near,"
 She said to me, "so, if I speak with you,   20
 You will be rather better placed to hear."
When I was there where I'd been told to be,
 She asked me: "Brother, why have you no questions
 Now that you are at long last here with me?"
Like those who, speaking to superiors,
 Adopt a tone that's over-reverential
 And cannot get the words out through their jaws,
Just so I was: scarcely articulate,
 I said: "My lady, everything I need
 You know already, and can furnish it."   30
Then she replied: "Both fearfulness and shame
 Should have been left behind you by this stage:
 Now speak no more like someone in a dream.
Know that the vessel which the snake broke up[1]
 Was and is not[2] – but they whose guilt it is
 Can be quite sure God's vengeance fears no sop.[3]
And not for ever shall the eagle be
 Heirless that cloaked the chariot with his plumage
 Till it became a monster, then a prey;[4]
For I see clearly what I have to tell: 40
 The stars are close to bringing on the time,
 Secure from every bar and obstacle,
When he who is five hundred five and ten,[5]
 A messenger from God, shall kill the thief,
 And the giant with her joining in her sin.[6]
Perhaps my narrative, being indirect,
 Like Sphinx and Themis dark,[7] is less persuasive
 Because like them it fools the intellect;
But things will soon occur that will unlock
 This dark enigma like the Naiads,   50

---

1 The chariot which the dragon damaged (*Purg.* XXXII, 130–35).
2 "The beast that thou sawest was, and is not; and shall ascend out of the bottomless pit, and go into perdition" (Rev. 17:8).
3 God's vengeance is inevitable. By ancient custom, if a murderer could eat a sop on the grave of his victim, he could escape vengeance.
4 See *Purg.* XXXII, 124–26.
5 In roman numerals this is DVX, which is also the Latin for leader. This enigma, which probably alludes to a secular ruler, can be compared to the mysterious hound (*veltro*) in *Inf.* I, 100–11.
6 See *Purg.* XXXII, 148–60.
7 The Sphinx was a monster on the road to Thebes which killed travellers who could not solve its riddle. The prophesying goddess Themis was associated with the notoriously ambiguous Delphic Oracle.

And with no damage done to crop or flock.[1]
Take note: and as they issue with my breath,
   Communicate these words of mine to those
   Who live that life which is a race to death.
And bear in mind: you must not keep concealed,
   When you are writing, how you saw this tree
   Grow here and how you saw it twice despoiled.[2]
Whoever robs or otherwise offends
   That tree commits offence to God, Who made it
   Sacred and sacrosanct to His own ends.   60
In pain and longing, after eating it,
   The first soul[3] yearned five thousand years or more
   For One[4] who punished in Himself that bite.
Your wits have left you if you have not guessed
   That for a special cause the tree is growing
   So tall and so expansive at its crest.[5]
And if vain thoughts did not engulf your mind,
   As in the Elsa,[6] and obscure it, as
   By Pyramus the mulberry was stained,[7]
You would be driven to the recognition,   70
   By shape and height alone, seen morally,
   Of God's clear justice in the prohibition.
But since I see your mind is petrified
   And, worse than petrified, so overcast
   That you are dazzled by the words I've said,
I'd have you bear away my words within,
   Not clearly written out but shaded, as
   Palms wreathe a pilgrim's staff on his return."[8]
I answered her: "As wax beneath the seal,
   Taking a true unmodified impression,   80
   My brain has stamped on it what you reveal.
But why does your long longed-for meaning fly
   So far beyond my sight as to diminish
   More rapidly the harder that I try?"

---

1   Dante believed erroneously, from a corrupt passage in Ovid, that the Naiads (fresh-water nymphs) solved the riddle of the Sphinx. Annoyed when her own riddle was solved, Themis sent a monster against Thebes to destroy animals and crops.

2   The tree of the knowledge of good and evil, first despoiled by Adam when he ate the forbidden fruit (*Purg.* XXXII, 37–39), and then by the eagle representing the imperial persecution of the early Church (*Purg.* XXXII, 109–14).

3   Adam.

4   Christ in His redeeming Passion.

5   High and broadening instead of narrowing at its crest, to show that mortal minds cannot ascend to the knowledge of God and His providence.

6   A tributary of the Arno, whose water calcifies objects left in it.

7   See *Purg.* XXVII, 37–39 and note.

8   Pilgrims returning from the Holy Land were recognized by their staffs wreathed in palm leaves.

"It is to help you know that school,"[1] she said,
  "Which you have followed, and to see how far
  It's in accordance with what I have said –
To help you see your ways and see how far
  They are from God's ways, as the earthly globe
  Is distant from the fastest-turning sphere."[2]   90
At that I answered her: "I can't recall
  That I was ever once estranged from you:
  My conscience is not stung by that at all."
She smiled. "If that has slipped your memory,"
  She answered, "there's one thing you may remember:
  That you drank Lethe water just today.
And if from smoke we may conclude there's fire,
  Then this forgetfulness of yours proves clearly
  Your guilt, directing your desire elsewhere.[3]
But from henceforth, as more appropriate,   100
  The words I use to you will be quite naked,
  To make them obvious to your feeble sight."
And now, more blazing and with slower paces,
  The sun was holding the meridian circle,[4]
  Which shifts about as seen from different places,[5]
When, just as anyone who to escort
  Some travellers goes ahead, but stops on finding
  Something that's novel or some trace of it,
Those seven ladies halted at the brim
  Of a pale shadow such as mountains cast   110
  Through green leaves and black boughs on a cold stream.
In front of where they stood I seemed to see
  The Tigris and Euphrates rise together,
  Then separate, like friends, unwillingly.[6]
"O light, O glory of the human race,
  What water is this, branching from itself
  So very far, though rising in one place?"
That was my question; and the answer: "Call
  Upon Matelda[7] to explain." At which,
  As keen to show she was not culpable,[8]   120

1 School of philosophy, i.e. of purely human reason.
2 The Primum Mobile, the celestial sphere farthest from the earth.
3 A slightly fallacious argument: that he cannot remember his sin does not prove that it once existed.
4 At noon the sun appears to linger.
5 The imaginary circle which cuts the observer's horizon at north and south, which the sun crosses at local noon, is imagined as being at different places according to where the observers are.
6 Lethe and Eunoë are compared to the Tigris and Euphrates.
7 It is puzzling that this is the first and only time this lady, with her important role in these final cantos, is named. Her historical identity (if she has one) remains a puzzle also.
8 I.e. remiss in not explaining everything to Dante.

That lovely lady answered: "Many a matter
  Like that I have explained, and I am sure
  It's not concealed from him by Lethe's water."
And Beatrice: "Perhaps some greater care,
  Such as may often cloud the memory,
  Has made his mental vision turn obscure.
But see where Eunoë pours from its source:
  Lead him there and, according to your custom,
  Instil fresh life into his drooping powers."
A noble spirit does not seek excuses,   130
  But makes its own will merge into another's
  Will which the merest word or sign discloses:
Just so the lady took me by the hand
  And, as she moved, she turned to Statius.
  "Come with him," was her courteous command.
If, reader, I had but the space to write,
  Then I would sing, as far as I was able,
  The sweet draught that would never satiate[1] –
But now, since every single page is full
  Of those ordained for this my second book,   140
  Art's laws demand nothing additional.
I rose and came back from that sacred spring
  Renewed like new-sprung plants and opening flowers
  Newly invigorated in the spring,
Pure and prepared to rise up to the stars.

---

1   The water of Eunoë preserves the memory of good deeds.

328

PARADISE

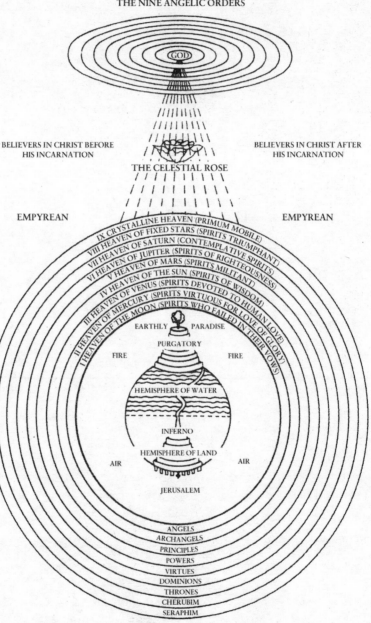

THE NINE ANGELIC ORDERS

GOD

BELIEVERS IN CHRIST BEFORE
HIS INCARNATION

BELIEVERS IN CHRIST AFTER
HIS INCARNATION

THE CELESTIAL ROSE

EMPYREAN

EMPYREAN

IX CRYSTALLINE HEAVEN (PRIMUM MOBILE)
VIII HEAVEN OF FIXED STARS (SPIRITS TRIUMPHANT)
VII HEAVEN OF SATURN (CONTEMPLATIVE SPIRITS)
VI HEAVEN OF JUPITER (SPIRITS OF RIGHTEOUSNESS)
V HEAVEN OF MARS (SPIRITS MILITANT)
IV HEAVEN OF THE SUN (SPIRITS OF WISDOM)
III HEAVEN OF VENUS (SPIRITS DEVOTED TO HUMAN LOVE)
II HEAVEN OF MERCURY (SPIRITS VIRTUOUS FOR LOVE OF GLORY)
I HEAVEN OF THE MOON (SPIRITS WHO FAILED IN THEIR VOWS)

EARTHLY   PARADISE

PURGATORY

FIRE   FIRE

HEMISPHERE OF WATER

INFERNO

HEMISPHERE OF LAND

AIR   AIR

JERUSALEM

ANGELS
ARCHANGELS
PRINCIPLES
POWERS
VIRTUES
DOMINIONS
THRONES
CHERUBIM
SERAPHIM

CANTO I

At the end of *Purgatory* Dante was standing with Beatrice in the Earthly Paradise, "prepared to rise up to the stars" (xxxiii, 145). We are now to experience that ascent with him. According to the Ptolemaic model of the universe, which Dante and his contemporaries accepted, nine hollow and transparent concentric heavens or spheres are revolving, at differing rates, around the earth, which is the physical centre of the universe. Within each of the seven spheres nearest the earth is a shining body which gives the sphere its name: moving outwards from the earth, these are the Moon, Mercury, Venus, the Sun, Mars, Jupiter and Saturn. Beyond them is the sphere of the fixed stars, and beyond that is the Primum Mobile, whose movement causes the other spheres to move. Finally there is the Empyrean, pure light, the abode of God, Who sets everything in motion. The souls of the blessed are, of course, in the Empyrean, but Dante speaks of meeting them, or rather their semblances, on the various planets.

Dante cannot fully recall his ascent to Heaven. To describe it as best he can, he invokes not simply the Muses, as he had in the first two books of *The Divine Comedy*, but Apollo, the god of poetry himself. Dante hopes that his efforts will win him the poet's crown of laurel.

Beatrice, who has taken Virgil's place as Dante's guide, is looking directly into the sun. When Dante fixes his eyes on her, the light of the sun grows more intense, and he is changed in a way that is indescribable. Beatrice explains that he is no longer on earth, but moving towards the Empyrean. This is the natural tendency of human beings – to desire to be with God – but it is often thwarted because we do have the power to turn away from God. Dante's ascent is, in his now sin-free state, as natural as a stream running downhill. Then Beatrice turns her eyes from him to gaze once more on Heaven.

His glory, through Whom everything that is
 Is moving, fills the universe, resplendent
 In one part more and in another less.
Now in that heaven which most receives His light[1]
 I was, with things nobody could recall,
 Or can describe, who comes down from that height,
Because, as it draws near to its desire,
 The mind sinks into such profundity
 That memory cannot pursue it there.
And yet, despite such losses, everything   10
 My mind did treasure up from that blessed realm
 Shall now become the matter of my song.
O good Apollo, for this crowning task
 Make me just such a vessel of your worth
 As you, when granting your loved laurel, ask.[2]
One of Parnassus' peaks has been enough

---

1 The Empyrean, the highest (or, in relation to the earth, the outermost) heaven, pure
 light.
2 Dante now has to invoke not merely the Muses, as he did in *Inferno* and *Purgatory*, but
 the god of poetry himself. On his wish for the laurel crown see *Par.* xxv, 1–12.

Up to this point, but in this ultimate
Arena where I struggle I need both.[1]
Enter my breast with your inspiring breath,
    Just as you did when you drew Marsyas   20
    Out of his fleshly limbs as from a sheath.[2]
Virtue divine, if you vouchsafe to me
    Yourself, till I make manifest the image
    Of the blessed realm lodged in my memory,
You shall behold me coming to the foot
    Of your loved tree[3] to crown myself with leaves
    For which the theme and you have made me fit.
So seldom are they plucked to celebrate
    The triumph of a Caesar or a poet –
    In which the shameful human will's at fault –   30
That the Peneian frond[4] must breed delight
    Within the joyful Delphic deity[5]
    When he sees anybody thirst for it.
A spark can be the prelude to a fire:
    And so some better voices after mine
    May find that Cyrrha[6] answers to their prayer.
For mortal men the world's great lamp arises
    At various points, but from its outlet, where
    Four circles are united with three crosses,
It issues on a better course and joined   40
    To better stars, and it can mould and stamp
    The worldly wax most after its own kind.[7]
It had brought morning yonder,[8] evening here,[9]
    When rising at that point, till almost all
    Yonder was white,[10] and black our hemisphere,[11]
And I saw Beatrice turn to her left side
    And gaze unflinchingly into the sun

---

1   Mount Parnassus has two peaks, one sacred to the Muses, the other (Cyrrha) to Apollo
    himself.
2   The satyr Marsyas challenged Apollo to a singing contest, and when he lost he was
    punished by being skinned alive.
3   See "your loved laurel" (l. 15 above): the nymph Daphne, pursued by Apollo, was changed
    into a laurel.
4   Daphne was the daughter of the river-god Peneus.
5   Apollo, whose oracle was at Delphi.
6   A metonym for Apollo: see note 1 above.
7   Lines 37–42: the sun appears to rise in different places according to where one is in the
    world. When the circles of the celestial equator, the ecliptic and the equinoctial colure
    cross the circle of the horizon at the same spot, the sun (now, at the spring equinox, in
    Aries) is most favourable to the earth ("worldly wax").
8   In Purgatory.
9   In Italy.
10   The southern hemisphere, believed to be composed entirely of water except for the
    island of Mount Purgatory.
11   The northern hemisphere.

As never any eagle ever could.
And, as a second ray flies up again,
    Out of the first one, like a peregrine   50
    That, having stooped, is eager to return,[1]
Just so her action, piercing through my eyes
    Into my fantasy, caused my reaction:
    I looked into the sun as no one does.
Much is allowed there which on earth is banned
    To human faculties, because that place[2]
    Was formed expressly for all humankind.
I could not bear the sun for long, but not
    So short a time I failed to see it sparkle
    Like iron emerging from the fire red-hot.   60
And daylight suddenly seemed added on
    To daylight, as if He Who has the power
    Adorned the heavens with another sun.[3]
Beatrice stood with her eyes fixed upon
    The eternal wheels,[4] while I was fixing mine
    On her, once they had shifted from the sun.
By gazing at her I was changed inside
    As Glaucus changed on tasting of the herb
    Which made of him an oceanic god.[5]
Transhumanition[6] cannot be expressed   70
    In words – so this example must suffice
    For those who will experience it at last.[7]
And whether I was nothing then but what
    You fashioned last,[8] O Ruler of the heavens,
    You know, O Love Who raised me with Your light.
When the wheeling,[9] which You eternalize
    Through its desire for You, drew my attention
    With varied melody You harmonize,[10]
The blazing of the sunlight seemed to make
    The sky so far enflamed no rain or river   80
    Ever resulted in so broad a lake.
The newness of the sound and the great light

---

1   Other commentators interpret Dante's *pellegrin* as meaning "pilgrim" – therefore, like
    a homesick pilgrim wishing to return.
2   The Earthly Paradise, created for Adam and Eve and their descendants.
3   Dante is approaching the sphere of fire (between the earth and the moon).
4   The heavenly spheres.
5   The mythical Greek fisherman Glaucus, noticing that the fish he caught revived on
    contact with a certain herb, tasted it himself and was transformed into a sea-god.
6   Going beyond human limitations.
7   When they go to heaven.
8   His soul.
9   The turning of the heavenly spheres.
10 The music thought to be caused by the friction between the various spheres revolving
    at different speeds.

Kindled in me such longing for their cause
  That I had never known desire like that.
So she, who saw within me as I do,
  Parted her lips to calm my troubled mind,
  Before I parted mine to ask her to,
And she began: "You make yourself obtuse
  With false imaginings, and do not see
  What you would see if you could shake them loose.   90
You're not on earth, though you suppose you are,
  But lightning, flying from its proper place,
  Flies not so fast as you returning there."[1]
Divested as I was of my first wonder
  By those few words she said and by her smile,
  I found myself entangled even further,
And said: "Before you spoke I was contented
  To rest in wonder – now I wonder more
  How these light bodies are by mine transcended."
Then Beatrice, with a sigh of pity mild,   100
  Turned her eyes onto me and, with that look
  A mother casts on her delirious child,
Began to speak: "All things there are are made
  Cognate with one another: this it is
  Which makes the universe most like to God.
Here all the higher creatures show the hand
  Of the Eternal Excellence, the end
  For which the aforesaid order was designed.
Into this selfsame ordinance are drawn
  All natures in their varying degrees,   110
  Some near, some nearer to their origin;
And so they sail, each to a different haven,
  Over the ocean of all being, each
  Drawn onward by the instinct it was given.
This is what draws fire up towards the moon –
  This is the motive force in human creatures –
  This makes the earth compact itself in one:
Not only those created things which have
  No intellect are driven by this bowstring,
  But those who have intelligence and love.[2]   120
The providence by which all this is made
  Keeps by its light one heaven[3] motionless,
  Within which whirls that heaven that has most speed.[4]
To that still heaven, as to the place designed,
  We are impelled by virtue of that bowstring

---

1   To Heaven.
2   Angels and men.
3   The Empyrean.
4   The Primum Mobile, the outermost and fastest of the revolving spheres.

Which shoots its shafts towards a happy end.
Now it is true we all too often find
  His finished work belies an artist's purpose,
  When his matter is deaf and won't respond;
Just so the creature may be seen to stray   130
  From the right path at times, having the power,
  Though urged aright, to go another way
(As we at times may actually see fire
  Descending from a cloud)[1] with the first impulse
  Diverted down to earth by false desire.
You should not be amazed, if I judge right,
  By your ascending, more than by a river
  Which courses down a mountain to its foot.
The miracle would be if you, now clear
  Of all impediment,[2] had failed to rise,   140
  Like immobility in flames of fire."
Then back to Heaven once more she turned her eyes.

---

1   The natural tendency of fire (except for lightning) is to rise.
2   Freed from all trace of sin.

CANTO II

Dante warns his readers that, unless they fervently desire to know God, they should stop reading: he is sailing over uncharted waters, and those who follow him may easily be lost.

Dante finds himself, inexplicably, within the moon. He is anxious to know the reason for the moon's dark spots. He suggests that the moon may be made of matter which is partly dense and partly rarefied. Beatrice destroys his argument by pointing out that he is presuming that only one virtue or power is active, whereas in the sphere of the fixed stars, the stars differ not only in magnitude but also in their brightness and influence, and must therefore be informed by differing virtues. Beatrice explains further that the rarefied substance must either go right through the moon or be in layers. In the first case, light would shine right through during solar eclipses – but this does not happen. In the second case, there would have to be some point at which density resulted in the sun's rays being thrown back as from a mirror, although more dimly than from other parts. Beatrice outlines a simple experiment to show how lights at different distances vary in size but not in brightness. So this second possibility is ruled out.

Beatrice explains the true reason for the dark and light spots. All virtue comes from God, and is distributed throughout the various spheres, sending different powers to each (see *Par.* I, 1–3). There is a different blend in each of the heavenly bodies, hence "the difference from light to light", and from one part of the moon to another.

This canto fully justifies Dante's initial warning: it is the most difficult in the poem for a modern reader to understand and appreciate. But the physical / metaphysical discussion is not included to satisfy idle curiosity: it shows how everything in existence depends on God and shares in His virtue or power in its own peculiar way.

Y ou who have followed in your tiny skiff,
   Eager to listen to the song I sing,
   And sailed behind my ocean-going ship,
Turn back and seek again your native coast –
   Do not attempt to cross the open water:
   If you lose sight of me, you will be lost.
No one has ever ventured on this sea:
   Minerva[1] swells my sail, Apollo steers –
   The Muses all point out the Bears[2] to me.
But you, you few still hungry for the bread   10
   Of angels,[3] now as in your earliest years,
   Bread which you live on, never surfeited,
You may commit your vessel to the main,
   Up close within the furrow which I make,
   Ahead of water settling down again.
Those heroes who reached Colchis did not find

---

1   Goddess of wisdom.
2   The constellations Ursa Major and Ursa Minor, essential for navigation by night.
3   Wisdom.

As much to astonish them as you will see,
  When they saw Jason ploughing up the land.[1]
The inborn thirst, thirsting perpetually
  For the most godlike realm,[2] transported us   20
  At a speed equal to the heaven men see.[3]
Beatrice was gazing up, and I at her –
  And at the speed at which a crossbow bolt
  Strikes home, let loose and flying through the air,
I came to where a wonder was revealed
  Which turned my gaze to it. And she from whom
  Nothing I had at heart could be concealed,
Turned and, joyful as she was beautiful,
  Said to me: "Turn in gratitude to God,
  Who merges us with the first star of all."[4]   30
It seemed to me that we were held within
  A thick cloud, luminous, dense, solid, polished,
  And like a diamond smitten by the sun.
Into itself this pearl that lasts for ever
  Accepted us, the way a stretch of water
  Accepts a ray of light and does not shiver.
If I was flesh – given we cannot guess
  How any substance can endure another,
  Though it must be so, if mass flows into mass –
Our longing is perforce intensified   40
  To see Him in Whose being we discern
  Our human nature coalesce with God.[5]
What here we hold by faith shall there[6] be seen,
  Not demonstrated, but an axiom,
  Self-evidently true and simply known.
I answered her: "My lady, I am filled
  With true devotion, giving thanks to Him
  Who has removed me from the mortal world.
But tell me: what are those dark spots upon
  This planet, which down there upon the earth   50
  Start people spinning stories about Cain?"[7]
She smiled, then answered: "If the comprehension

---

1   Jason, leader of the Argonauts, who sailed in quest of the Golden Fleece, had to harness two fire-breathing oxen, plough a field with them and sow dragons' teeth, which sprang up as armed men.
2   The Empyrean.
3   The eighth sphere, that of the fixed stars.
4   The moon, nearest planet to the earth.
5   Lines 37–42: the fact that Dante still has his body, and one substance cannot penetrate another and remain unchanged (which appears to have happened with Dante and the moon), must make us all the more eager to see Christ, Who is fully God and man.
6   In Heaven.
7   A popular belief had it that the first murderer was banished by God to the moon, and could be distinguished there in its dark spots.

Of mortals may be baffled over things
   Which cannot be unlocked by sense perception,
Then certainly you should not feel the dart
   Of wonder now, since even when the senses
   Are all behind it, reason may fall short.
But say what you yourself have in your mind."
   I said: "What here appears diverse is caused
   By matter being dense or rarefied."   60
She answered: "You will see now how your thought
   Is floundering in error, if you listen
   To my clear reasons as I counter it.
You know the eighth sphere[1] from your world displays
   A host of lights, which in their size and brightness,
   As you observe, show various visages.
If this were caused by dense and rarefied
   Alone, there'd be one power within them all,
   More, less, or equally distributed.
Virtues that are diverse must be deployed   70
   By diverse formal causes, and all these,
   But one, would by your reasoning be destroyed.[2]
Again, if rareness makes these spots which you
   Speak of, there'd be two possibilities:
   Either the substance[3] has been skimped right through
This planet[4] or, as flesh has lean and fat
   In layers, so throughout this planet's volume
   The thick leaves and the thin would alternate.
Were the first true, that would be obvious
   In the eclipses of the sun, since light   80
   Shines right through matter that is tenuous.
Not so: therefore what's left to be disputed
   Now is the second case,[5] which if I shatter,
   Your whole hypothesis remains confuted.
If your thin substance does not run throughout
   The moon, there has to be a point at which
   Density gives no passage to the light;
And from that point the sun's rays would not pass,
   But be thrown back again as coloured objects
   Are thrown, when it has lead behind, by glass.   90

---

1   That of the fixed stars.
2   Lines 67–72: Dante's suggestion presupposed one virtue in all the stars (with them dif-
     fering only in the amount they received), whereas they differ not only quantitatively but
     also qualitatively, since they have differing influences on the earth. Dante takes astral
     influence for granted: see ll. 112–23 below.
3   The *rarefied* substance.
4   The moon.
5   The possibility that the moon is composed of alternating layers of dense and rarefied
     substance.

"WHAT YOU ARE SEEING ARE REAL SUBSTANCES,
PLACED HERE BECAUSE THEIR VOWS WERE NOT FULFILLED"...

PARADISE III, 29–30

"MY SHINING FOREHEAD WAS ALREADY CROWNED
AS MONARCH OF THAT EARTH THE DANUBE WATERS"...

PARADISE VIII, 64–65

Now you will say such rays will show more dark
   Than rays reflected from the other parts,
   Since they're reflections sent from farther back.
This further argument be can ruled out,
   If you are willing, by experiment –
   The root of every branch of human art.
So take three mirrors, set the first two down
   At the same distance, and the third one farther,
   Where it will strike your eyes from in between.
Now face them, having fixed a light to blaze   100
   Behind your back and light up all three mirrors,
   And so send light reflected to your eyes.
Although in magnitude the farther light
   Is no match for the others, you will find
   That of necessity it is as bright.
Just as the matter[1] which makes snow is spoiled –
   Once it's subjected to the sun's warm rays –
   Of both its former colour and its cold,
So your intelligence has been stripped bare,
   To be informed by me with light so vivid   110
   That it will sparkle to you like a star.
Within the heaven of peace that is divine,
   A body circles in whose power resides
   The being of everything it has within.[2]
That heaven below, which many stars make bright,
   Imparts that being to those essences
   Distinct from it and yet contained in it.[3]
These other spheres, each with its difference,
   Distribute all of those distinctive powers
   To have their due effects and influence.   120
These organs of the universe go on
   From step to step, as now you understand,
   Receiving from above, delivering down.
Consider now how I advance upon
   This road towards the truth which you desire,
   That you may learn to cross the ford alone.
The influential movement of the spheres –
   As the hammer depends upon the smith –
   Must act inspired by sacred engineers.
That heaven so many stars make beautiful   130
   Takes from the unfathomed Mind which keeps it turning

---

1   Water.
2   The Empyrean sets in motion the Primum Mobile, which in turn influences all the other
    spheres.
3   The sphere of the fixed stars influences all the spheres within it, and thence everything
    on earth.

That stamp from which it makes a further seal.[1]
And as the soul that animates your dust –
  And thence, throughout your organs, each of which
  Differs in potency – becomes diffused,
So does the Mind deploy its multiplied
  Beneficence throughout the various stars,
  While still revolving and still unified.
Each different virtue makes a different blend
  Within the cherished mass it animates,   140
  With which, like life with you, it is combined.
True to the nature whence it comes to be,
  The virtue mingled with the body shines
  As joy shines through the pupil of the eye.
Hence comes the difference from light to light,
  Or part to part, and not from dense and rare:
  The informing principle produces what,
From its goodness, is either dark or clear."[2]

---

1   Lines 127–32: the stars influence all below them, but only because they are controlled
     by intelligent beings (angels), as a hammer in a forge has its effect only because it is con-
     trolled by an intelligent being (the smith). All is the effect of the Supreme Intelligence,
     God. The metaphor in l. 132 is of sealing wax.
2   Lines 133–48: God's goodness is in everything, but in differing ways and to different
     degrees: the stars differ from each other, and the moon differs within itself.

CANTO III

Dante is ready to accept the cogency of what Beatrice has said about the dark spots in the moon, but he is distracted by what appears to be vague reflections of people. He turns to see who they are, but is told by Beatrice that they are real, and that he should speak with them and believe whatever they say.

One of these souls says that she is Piccarda Donati, and she is in heaven, but in the lowest part of it, because she did not fulfil the vows she made as a religious. She was forced by her brother, to whom she alludes obliquely, to leave her convent and marry. Dante, who had known her in life, recognizes her now: at first the intensification of her beauty, which comes from her being in Heaven, had prevented this recognition.

Dante asks her if she does not wish she had a higher place in Heaven, and Piccarda explains that all the blessed are happy where they are, because their wills are now fully in accord with God's will. There is a hierarchy in Heaven, but no dissatisfaction.

Piccarda points out to Dante another soul who had, like herself, been a Poor Clare and was prevented from adhering to her vows. This is Constance, wife of the Emperor Henry VI and mother of the Emperor Frederick II.

Piccarda disappears, singing the 'Ave Maria', and Dante follows her with his eyes as long as he is able. He then turns to Beatrice once more, but he is so dazzled by her light that he is slow to question her further.

T hat sun[1] who warmed my bosom at the first
    With love, had made, by proving and reproving,
    Truth and its lovely aspect manifest –
And I, admitting now that I was quite
    Persuaded and corrected, raised my head
    To speak to her, no higher than was right[2] –
When a vision appeared, and my attention
    Was fixed so firmly on it as I looked
    That I quite failed to utter my confession.
As through a sheet of smooth transparent glass,   10
    Or water that is glittering and peaceful
    And not so deep none knows how deep it is,
The outline of our features is reflected,
    So faint that pearls upon a pearl-pale brow
    Are not more difficult to be detected –
So I saw faces all about to utter,
    Which made me make the opposite mistake
    To what stirred love between one man and water.[3]
The moment that I looked and saw them there,

---

1   Beatrice.
2   Showing his respect for Beatrice.
3   The mythical Narcissus fell in love with his reflection, thinking it was someone else: Dante is seeing real people but thinks they are reflections.

341

Imagining that they were but reflections,   20
  I turned around to find out whose they were –
And I saw nothing, so I turned my gaze
  Back to the light which came from my dear guide,
  And saw the smiling in her holy eyes.
"You must not be surprised I smile at you,"
  She said. "The reason is your childish notions
  Which still do not stand firm on what is true,
But always send you spinning in a void:
  What you are seeing are real substances,
  Placed here because their vows were not fulfilled.[1]   30
So speak to them, and trust to what they say,
  Since the true light in which they find their peace
  Never permits their feet to go astray."
Then, to that shade who seemed most to require
  Some speech with me, I turned and I began,
  Like somebody bewildered by desire:
"O spirit born to bliss, who in the light
  Of everlasting life enjoy that sweetness
  Uncomprehended till we taste of it,
I should be grateful if you would apprise   40
  Me simply of your name and of your lot."
  To which with ready voice and smiling eyes:
"Our charity will never bar the gate
  To righteous longing, any more than His
  Whose Will is in all wills within His court.
I was a virgin sister in the world,
  Whom if you delve into your memory,
  This greater beauty cannot keep concealed.
But you will see I am Piccarda[2] who,
  Placed here among these other blessèd spirits,   50
  Am blessèd in the sphere that is most slow.[3]
All our affectionate desires, whose ardour
  Is kindled solely by the Holy Spirit,
  Rejoice to be contained within His order.
This lot of ours which must appear so lowly
  Is what we have been given, since we neglected
  The vows we made, or failed to keep them wholly."
Then I replied: "Your marvellous semblances
  Shine out with something strange that is divine,
  Transfiguring our old remembrances: 60

---

1   The reference is to religious vows.
2   The beautiful Florentine Piccarda Donati entered a convent as a Poor Clare. Her brother
    Corso, leader of the Black Guelfs, removed her and forced her into marriage (see *Purg.*
    xxiv, where Dante speaks with Piccarda's other brother, Forese).
3   The sphere of the moon which, being nearest the earth, has the shortest orbit and
    therefore does not need to move as fast as those beyond it.

That made me slow in bringing you to mind,[1]
    But what you have just told me now is helpful:
    I recognize you and I understand.
But tell me: you, whose happiness is here,
    Are you not ardent for a higher region,
    To see God better, see Him friendlier?"
She and the others smiled at first, and then
    She gave her answer with such great delight
    That she seemed burning in love's primal flame:
"Brother, these wills of ours are set at peace   70
    By charity, which makes us only wish
    For what we have, and thirst for nothing else.
If we were anxious for a higher sphere,
    Then our desire would be at variance with
    The will of Him Who has assigned us here –
Which in these circles simply cannot be,
    Since being in charity is here essential,
    If you consider what is charity.
And at the heart of being beatified
    Is life within the Will that is divine,   80
    So that our various wills are unified;
Therefore this being ranged from stair to stair
    Throughout this realm rejoices all the realm
    And the King too Whose Will involves us here.
Within His Will at last we find our peace:
    That is the ocean into which there flows
    All He creates or nature adds to this."[2]
Then it was plain to me how everywhere
    In Heaven is Paradise, although God's grace
    Does not rain down invariably there.[3]   90
But as it happens when our appetite,
    Sated with one food, hungers for another –
    We ask for this while giving thanks for that –
Just so with signs and words I tried to find
    From her the nature of the web through which
    She had not drawn the shuttle to the end.
"A lady[4] is enskied high on the scale
    For worth, under whose holy rule," she told me,
    "Down in your world they're clothed and take the veil,
So that, sleeping or waking, they may be   100
    With that Spouse who accepts each solemn vow

---

1   Dante had known Piccarda, and was distantly related to her by marriage.
2   The distinction is between what God creates out of nothing – e.g. angels and human
    souls – and what is produced by procreation and propagation.
3   God's grace permeates Heaven, but not without variation between the different parts
    of Heaven.
4   St Clare of Assisi (c.1194–1253), friend of St Francis, under whose aegis she founded the
    Order of Poor Clares.

Conforming to His Will by charity.
I fled the world in all my youthful ardour
    To follow her, and clothed me in her habit,
    And promised to obey her holy Order.
Then men prone more to evil than to good[1]
    Seized me and took me from my cherished cloister:
    And after that God knows what life I led.
This other splendour you distinguish here
    On my right side, and who is incandescent   110
    With all the light that's shining in our sphere,
Could say about herself what I have said:
    She was a sister, and that sacred cover,
    Her veil, was snatched by force from off her head.
But since she was brought back into the world
    Against her wishes and against fair usage,
    Her heart continued as it had been, veiled.
This is the light of the great Constance: she
    Gave birth, by the second gust of Swabia,
    To the third and ultimate authority."[2]   120
She spoke, and then she sang, "*Ave Maria*,"[3]
    And went on with her singing as she vanished
    Like something heavy sinking in deep water.
My eyes, which had been following her as long
    As possible, soon as she disappeared
    Turned to the object of desire more strong,
To concentrate on Beatrice once more;
    But she was shining in my face and shone
    So dazzlingly I hardly could endure,
Which made me slow to question her again.   130

---

1 A gentle allusion to Piccarda's brother Corso, or to those who acted on his orders.
2 The three "gusts" are the Dukes of Swabia (of the Hohenstaufen dynasty), all in turn
   Holy Roman Emperors – Frederick Barbarossa, his son Henry VI and his grandson
   Frederick II. The Empress Constance (1154–98) was the wife of Henry VI and mother
   of Frederick II (see *Inf.* x, 119).
3 The first words of the prayer to the Virgin, "Hail, Mary".

CANTO IV

This is a doctrinal canto, in which Beatrice resolves certain theological difficulties for Dante's always enquiring mind. Also we are shown incidentally how the whole poem has been arranged.

Dante has two questions, both so urgent that he does not know which to ask first. Beatrice can read Dante's mind, and she expresses the two problems for him. How could Piccarda and Constance be blamed for failing to fulfil their vows when they were under duress? Is not the appearance of their souls in the moon in line with a theory of Plato's?

Beatrice treats the second problem first, as an incorrect solution is likely to be more misleading. All the blessed, she says, are in the Empyrean, but with greater or less enjoyment according to their degree of holiness. Souls such as Piccarda and Constance have appeared to Dante on the moon (the planet farthest away from the Empyrean) as a figurative way of showing their lowly position in Paradise. Figurative forms of expression are those best adapted to human understanding, as Scripture and the Church's iconography show. Plato's theory, that the human soul returns to the planet on which it was born is not relevant here, because he probably meant it literally.

In resolving the first problem, Beatrice says that we must distinguish between the will which is free and the will which is constrained by others. The wills of Piccarda and Constance were constrained, but they must have assented to some extent, as otherwise they would have refused to leave their convents, or at least returned to them later, whatever the cost to themselves. In contrast, St Lawrence and Mucius Scaevola, who showed contempt for the force to which they were subjected, exhibited a rare heroic virtue.

The canto ends with Dante unable to express his gratitude fully. He has a further question. Can we make up for broken vows with other works of merit? Under Beatrice's loving gaze he casts down his eyes and almost faints.

*

B
efore two equidistant dishes, both
Tasty, one free to choose might die of hunger
Before he lifted either to his mouth;
So would a timid lamb come to a stand
Between two ravenous wolves, afraid of both;
So, held between two hinds, would be a hound.
And that is why I take no blame whatever
For staying silent, being tugged two ways
Perforce – yet give myself no plaudits either.
I held my tongue, whose longing was portrayed   10
Upon my face, together with my questions,
More keen and clear than if they had been said.[1]
Then Beatrice acted as did Daniel once,
Who calmed and mollified Nebuchadnezzar

---

1 Dante does not know which question to ask first.

When wrath made him unjustly merciless;[1]
She said: "I see how this desire and that
   Are tugging at you till your eagerness
   Is tangled in itself and can't speak out.
You argue: 'If good will survives duress
   Imposed by others,[2] then for what good reason   20
   Can what we are entitled to be less?'[3]
A further cause of your perplexity
   Is all these souls returning to the stars,
   Which seems in line with Plato's theory.[4]
These are the doubts which weigh upon your will,
   Demanding answers equally: so first
   I shall treat that which has in it more gall.
Neither that seraph who is placed most near
   To God, nor Moses, nor whichever John
   You are inclined to choose,[5] I tell you, nor   30
Mary herself, is in a different zone
   Of Heaven from these spirits who've appeared,
   Or lasts more years or fewer years therein:
The First Sphere[6] with them all is full of grace,
   And all enjoy sweet life, as all of them
   Sense the eternal breath, some more some less.
Some were apparent here, not that this star
   Is their allotted place, but as a sign
   That in the Empyrean their place is lower.
To speak to men in this way is correct,   40
   Since only what is gathered by the senses
   Becomes fit matter for the intellect.
This is why Holy Scripture condescends
   To you, assigning hands and feet to God,
   When there is something else which it intends;
So Holy Church provides a human mien
   For Gabriel and Michael, and that other
   Archangel who made Tobit sound again.[7]
And what Timaeus[8] says about the soul

---

1   King Nebuchadnezzar of Babylon intended to execute his magicians for being unable
    to reveal to him and interpret a dream of his which he himself could not recall. The
    prophet Daniel did what the King required, and saved the magicians' lives (Dan. 2).

2   As Piccarda has said of Constance (*Par.* III, 109–17).

3   Piccarda and Constance are in the lowest part of Heaven.

4   Plato's dialogue *Timaeus* mentions human souls returning to the various stars from
    which they came. This is at odds with the belief that all the blessed are in the one place,
    Heaven.

5   John the Baptist or the Apostle John.

6   The Empyrean.

7   The archangel Raphael enabled Tobias to cure the blindness of his father Tobit (Tobit
    3:16).

8   The eponymous main speaker in Plato's dialogue. See note 4 above.

Is nothing like what you were seeing here,   50
  Since his intended sense is literal.
He says the soul returns to its own star,
  Believing that was whence it was abstracted
  To be embodied as an avatar.[1]
And it could be his reasoning is worded
  In one way while his sense runs in another,
  And his intention should not be derided.
If he intends to give these spheres the honour
  And blame for what they influence, perhaps
  He does in fact hit on some truth or other.[2]   60
This principle, ill-comprehended, was
  What once misled the whole wide world almost,
  Invoking Jove and Mercury and Mars.[3]
Your other harassing perplexity
  Has much less poison in it, for its malice
  Could not lead you elsewhere, away from me,
For when our justice here at times looks less
  Than just in mortal eyes, this argues faith,
  Not heresy and downright wickedness.[4]
But since it's possible for human wit   70
  To find its way into this other truth,
  I will enable you to come to it.
If genuine violence is when the abused
  Contributes nothing to the one who forces,
  These souls were not on that account excused,
For the unwilling will can't be constrained,
  But acts like fire according to its nature,[5]
  However often it is held and bound.
However much or little it gives way,
  It aids the force – and that is what these did,   80
  Who could have fled back to their sanctuary.
So if their wills had been entirely sound,
  Like that which kept St Lawrence on his grill,[6]
  Or made Scaevola cruel to his hand,[7]
It would have sent them on that road once more
  Whence they were drawn, the instant they were free –
  But such unflinching wills are all too rare.

1 To take on a corporeal human form.
2 Dante accepts the belief that the stars influence human beings, within limits which are
   explained in *Purg.* XVI, 73–78.
3 Treating them not simply as the names of planets, but as gods.
4 See ll. 130–32 below.
5 The natural tendency of fire is to rise.
6 He was martyred by being roasted on a gridiron and accepted the torture cheerfully.
7 The Roman Mucius Scaevola tried to kill the Etruscan king Lars Porsena, but was cap-
   tured. As a show of his valour, he thrust the hand that had failed into a camp fire, and
   Lars Porsena, impressed, decided to free him.

So by these words of mine, if you have taken
   Their import as you should, that reasoning
   Which would have gone on troubling you is broken.   90
But now another mountain to be crossed
   Confronts your eyes, and such as by yourself
   You could not scale: you would be wearied first.
I have already made it very clear
   To you that souls in bliss can never lie:
   With them the source of truth is always near.
Yet you recall Piccarda, who declared
   That Constance always had the veil at heart –
   Which seems to contradict what I have said.
Now, brother, often in times past have men,   100
   In their great fear of falling into danger,
   Done what they should not do, against the grain:
Just as Alcmaeon once, under duress,
   Urged to it by his father, killed his mother,
   And out of piety was pitiless.[1]
You must see that, by this stage, violence
   Is mingled with the victim's will: together
   They mean there's no excuse for the offence.
The will does not quite sanction the abuse,
   But only in so far as it is fearful,   110
   If it does not, to suffer something worse.
It is the will which is not forced Piccarda
   Has in her mind: I mean the will that's forced –
   And therefore we agree with one another."
Such was the rippling of the sacred river,
   Arising from the fountainhead of truth,
   That put my two desires to rest together.
"Belovèd of the Primal Love, divine
   Being," I said at once, "whose speech flows over
   Me, warming me, refreshing me again,   120
Although my sense of gratitude's profound
   It cannot render to you grace for grace:
   So may the One Who sees and can, respond.
I see we'll never satisfy the mind
   Unless it be illumined by that Truth,
   Such that there is no truth at all beyond.
It rests there like a wild beast in its den
   When it has reached it – as it's able to.
   If not, all our desires would be in vain.
From these there rises, like a springing shoot,   130
   Doubt at the foot of truth: this natural urge
   Is always lifting us from height to height.
And this invites me, makes me feel secure

---

1   The mythical Alcmaeon is shown as right to obey his father, but wrong to kill his mother.

In asking you, with all respect, my lady,
  About another truth I find obscure.
I wish to know if we can add some weight
  To broken vows with other works of merit,
  And therefore in the balance not be light?"
Beatrice looked at me with her eyes full
  Of sparkling love, a radiance so divine   140
  That I felt all my faculties must fail
And almost fainted, with my eyes cast down.

CANTO V

Beatrice explains why Dante is dazzled by the light emanating from her. Then she replies to his question as to whether there can be an acceptable alternative for a vow once made. He is now, she says, in a fit state to understand her explanation.

God's greatest gift, she says, is free will. This is surrendered when a vow is made, and nothing can replace it – the vow must stand. However, the Church does sometimes grant dispensations from vows: a substitute for what was originally offered may be acceptable, but only if the compensation is authorized by the Church, and is much greater than the original. Where it is impossible to find something greater – as in religious vows – no substitution is possible. Mortals should therefore be very cautious in making vows, and not be tempted to do so by the hope of gain. The biblical Jephthah and the legendary Greek Agamemnon are presented as examples of men who fulfilled vows which were evil: it would have been better for them to break their vows, which should not have been made.

Then Beatrice and Dante speed in an instant to Mercury, where Beatrice adds to that planet's light with her presence. As fish in a pond move towards something dropped in the water, believing it may be food, so now many shining semblances move towards Dante and Beatrice, and all of them are praising her.

Dante is anxious to question the semblances. When one of them offers to answer him, Beatrice encourages Dante to do so and says he may trust the answers. Dante asks who this semblance is, and why he is assigned to this planet, Mercury, which is so often hidden from observers on earth by its nearness to the sun's brightness. At this the semblance glows even more brightly, until it is hidden in its own light, and then it answers Dante's questions in a way that will be revealed in the canto which follows this one.

"If in my warmth of love to you I flame
    Beyond the measure that is seen on earth,
    So that your sense of sight is overcome,
You must not be amazed: my light derives
    From my perfected vision, which becomes
    More and more like the Good to which it moves.
I clearly see your intellect is live
    And gleams already with the Eternal Brightness,
    Which seen, alone and always kindles love;
Should love by something other be misled,   10
    That other's nothing but a trace of this,
    Which filters through, and is ill understood.
You wonder if good works may compensate
    For vows that are not kept, sufficiently
    To keep the soul secure from all dispute."
So Beatrice began this canto's theme,
    And barely with a pause to take a breath
    Took up her sacred discourse once again:
"The greatest gift that God in His largess
    Gave to creation, and the one most near   20

To His own goodness, what He prizes most,
Is free will, will completely unconstrained,
   With which the creatures that have intellect,[1]
   And they alone, all were and are endowed.
Now you will see, following this argument,
   The importance of a vow, when it's so made
   That God consents to it when you consent;
Because, when God and man conclude this pact,
   A sacrifice is made of this same treasure
   I have described, offered by its own act.[2]   30
So what amends are possible, what pains?
   Thinking to use what you have given away
   Is seeking goodness with ill-gotten gains.
By now you are certain of the matter's core;
   But seeing Holy Church grants dispensations,
   Which seems against the truth I have laid bare,
You must not rise up from the table yet,
   Because the food is tough[3] which you have eaten
   And you need further aid digesting it.
Open your eyes to what I shall expound,   40
   And keep it well in mind: there is no knowledge
   Unless what's comprehended is retained.
Two things are needed for this sacrifice:
   First the material of which it's made,
   And then there is the vow donating this.
The latter fact is never abrogated
   Until it is fulfilled – and that is why
   My words above are so precise about it.
The Hebrews therefore always had to offer
   Some sacrifice, even though what it was,   50
   As you must be aware, could sometimes differ.[4]
So what I have defined here as the matter
   May well be such that there is no offence
   If it be altered into something other.
But let nobody ever think to ease
   One weight off for another weight, without
   The turning of the white and yellow keys[5] –
And waste of time is any alteration
   Unless the lost weight's smaller than the weight
   Assumed,[6] and four to six is the proportion.   60

---

1   Angels and men.
2   Free will sacrifices itself.
3   Literally: the doctrine is a hard one.
4   For the requirement of sacrifice under the Law, see Lev. 27:1–33.
5   "The keys of the kingdom of heaven" (Matt. 16:19), the authority of the Church. The gold key symbolizes the power to forgive sins, and the silver key the discretion needed to exercise this power. See *Purg.* IX, 117–29.
6   The weight of obligation offered in compensation.

Therefore when any vow is of such weight –
    Such value I would say – it tips the scales,[1]
    Nothing can ever be a substitute.
Mortals must never take a vow in jest:
    But keep their vows, and yet not be wrong-headed
    Like Jephthah with the gift he promised first:[2]
He had done better owning his mistake
    Than keeping to his vow – and just as stupid,
    If you consider, was that famous Greek,[3]
Whose Iphigenia rued her lovely face,   70
    And who made all and sundry weep for her
    When they heard such a rite had taken place.
Christians, be more aware what you take on,
    And do not be a leaf for every wind,
    Nor think that every water washes clean.
You have both Testaments, the Old and New –
    You have the shepherd of the Church as guide –
    So let these things suffice for saving you.
Should you be tempted by your evil greed,[4]
    Be men, not like a flock of silly sheep,   80
    Not such as Jews among you must deride![5]
Do not be like the lamb that runs away
    From his own mother's milk, a foolish creature
    Who makes himself his own worst enemy!"
So Beatrice spoke, exactly as I write,
    And then she turned, in plenitude of longing,
    To where the world is liveliest and most bright.[6]
Her silence now and that great change I found
    In her appearance struck dumb my desire
    To pose the further questions in my mind.   90
And like an arrow when it has hit home
    Before the bowstring has stopped quivering,
    So we both sped into the second realm.[7]
I saw my lady there so rapturous,
    When she had entered in that heaven's light,
    The orb itself became more luminous.
And if that star could change and laugh and smile,

---

1   Such as vows made by priests, nuns and members of religious orders.
2   Jephthah, a judge in Israel, vowed that, if he was victorious over the Ammonites, he
    would sacrifice whatever came first to meet him on his return home. This happened to
    be his daughter (Judg. 11:30–40).
3   Agamemnon, who sacrificed his daughter Iphigenia to secure a favourable wind for the
    expedition to Troy.
4   Both Jephthah and Agamemnon offered sacrifice in return for a desired advantage.
5   The Jews are mentioned here with approval as a people whose sacrifices are precisely
    regulated.
6   Upwards, towards the planet Mercury, and then beyond to the sun and the Empyrean.
7   The sphere of Mercury.

Imagine how I was who am by nature[1]
Subject to sudden moods and variable!
As in a fishpond that is still and clear   100
   The fishes move towards what is dropped in
   As though it might be food for them, so here
I saw a thousand or more splendours move
   Towards us, and from each of them was heard:
   "She has arrived who will increase our love."
And always, as each one of them drew near,
   It could be seen the shade was full of joy,
   Because that joy shone from it, bright and clear.
Consider, reader, if what's starting here
   Did not continue, how much you would suffer   110
   In your anxiety to know some more,
And you will soon appreciate how from these
   I longed to hear their names and their condition,
   The instant they appeared before my eyes.
"O born for bliss, who are allowed by grace
   To see the thrones of the eternal triumph[2]
   While yet your worldly warfare does not cease,[3]
The brightness spreading through all Heaven gives light
   To us, and therefore if you have such longing
   To know us, satisfy your appetite."   120
One of the sacred spirits spoke those words
   To me, then Beatrice urged me: "Ask, and ask
   With confidence: trust them as they were gods."
"I can see quite distinctly how you nestle
   In your own light, drawing it from your eyes,
   For when you're smiling, I can see it sparkle,
But do not know you, spirit worthy praise,
   Or why you are appointed to this sphere
   Veiled from us mortals by another's rays."[4]
I said this to the light which had before   130
   Spoken to me, which at these words became
   Far brighter than it had been earlier.
Then like the sun whose overplus of light
   Occludes it, when its warmth has dissipated
   Heavy vapours that made it temperate:
Just so its ever-expanding gladness hid
   That sacred semblance in its own bright light,
   And once quite hidden from my eyes replied
With what the following canto's lines repeat.

---

1   His human nature.
2   The saints in Heaven.
3   The speaker realizes that Dante is still a member of the Church Militant, i.e. the Church
   on earth.
4   Because Mercury is so near the dazzling sun it is often not visible from the earth.

CANTO VI

Dante has asked one of the lights on Mercury to say who he is and why he is there, and the reply occupies the whole of this canto. First Constantine's transfer of the capital of the Empire from Rome to Byzantium, "against the course of Heaven" (which implies much more than simply "eastwards") is mentioned. Then the light identifies himself as the Emperor Justinian, who reformed Roman Law. The theme of this canto is the need to establish the secular power, the Roman Empire (symbolized throughout by its eagle standard), in order to create the conditions in which Christianity can flourish.

Justinian gives a brief and partly mythical history of the Empire from before the foundation of Rome to Dante's day. The most important event is the Crucifixion, humanity's just punishment for the sin of Adam and Eve. The destruction of Jerusalem in 70 AD is mentioned as just retribution for the wrong done by the Crucifixion.

Justinian moves from Charlemagne (who was crowned Emperor in 800) to Dante's day, a leap of some five hundred years. Justinian speaks for Dante in attacking both the Guelfs, who oppose the Empire on behalf of the Papacy, and the Ghibellines, who fight under the eagle banner as a way of achieving their own selfish ends.

Justinian now answers Dante's second question from the previous canto. He has been placed in Mercury, the next-to-lowest part of Heaven, because he acted righteously, but out of ambition, and not for pure love of God. Like the souls on the moon he rejoices in his lot, and its justice, and does not wish for a higher place.

Justinian finishes with the example of another soul, one much less exalted on earth than himself, but who is in the same part of Heaven. This is Romée, a minister of the Count of Provence, who served his master well, also out of ambition. He was ill rewarded on earth, but now has his just reward in Heaven.

"When Constantine had turned the eagle's flight
    Against the course of Heaven[1] – which it had followed
    With him who took Lavinia for his wife[2] –
Two hundred years or more the bird of God
    Remained at that extremity of Europe
    Close to the mountains whence it rose of old,
And in the shadow of its sacred vans
    Governed the world from there, changing its rulers,
    Till at the last it came into my hands.[3]
Caesar I was, and am Justinian[4] –   10
    Who, urged by Love I now feel, purged the laws

---

1   In 324 AD the Emperor Constantine the Great moved the capital of the Empire (symbolized throughout this canto by its eagle standard) eastwards from Rome to Byzantium, which then became Constantinople.

2   After the fall of Troy, Aeneas had moved west from Asia Minor to Italy, and founded the race which eventually founded Rome. Lavinia was the daughter of Latinus, King of Latium.

3   The Emperor Justinian reigned 527–65 AD.

4   Earthly titles have no force in heaven.

Of everything superfluous or vain.[1]
Before I concentrated on that stint,
   I held there was one nature in Our Lord,[2]
   No more, and in that faith I was content,
But blessed Agapetus, at the head
   Of all the pastors, had the skill to draw me
   To the authentic faith with what he said.[3]
I trusted him, and what he said was due
   To faith I now see clearly, as you see   20
   Two contradictories are not both true.[4]
In step with the True Church I moved my feet:
   God's grace inspired the noble venture,[5] and
   I gave myself exclusively to that.
I trusted war to Belisarius,[6]
   To whose right hand the Lord was so benign
   It was a signal I might work in peace.
You have the answer now to your first question,[7]
   And yet the very nature of that answer
   Implies I must say something in addition,   30
If you're to ascertain with how much right
   They act who move against the sacred standard –
   Both those who own it and those fighting it.[8]
See by what feats of valour it became
   Worthy of reverence, starting from that hour
   When Pallas died for its imperium.[9]
You know it made its home in Alba[10] for
   Over three hundred years, until at last
   Three fought another three for it once more.[11]
You know what feats it did, from when they sinned   40
   Against the Sabines to Lucretia's woe,[12]
   In seven reigns, and conquered all around.

1   Justinian ordered a complete reorganization of Roman Law.
2   He was a Monophysite, believing only in the divine nature of Christ.
3   Pope Agapetus (r.533–36) convinced Justinian that Christ was fully human as well as
     divine.
4   What he took on faith while he was on earth is now obvious to him in Heaven, a self-
     evident truth.
5   The reform of Roman Law.
6   Justinian's successful general.
7   See *Par.* v, 127–29.
8   Both the Ghibellines, who appropriate this standard for their own ends, and the Guelfs,
     who oppose it, are acting against the best interests of the Empire.
9   While fighting for Aeneas, Pallas was killed by Turnus (who had been engaged to La-
     vinia, see note to l. 3 above). His death provoked Aeneas to kill Turnus and take over
     the kingdom of Latium.
10   Alba Longa, town in Latium built by Ascanius, son of Aeneas.
11   The three Alban Curiatii were defeated by the three Roman Horatii.
12   From the rape of the Sabine women, during the reign of Romulus, the first King of
     Rome, to the suicide of Lucretia, which led to the expulsion of Tarquin, the last King.

You know what feats it did, whenever it was
    Borne by famed Romans over Brennus,[1] Pyrrhus[2]
    And other princes and communities.
With it Torquatus,[3] Quintius – whose name
    Came from his unkempt hair[4] – the Decii[5]
    And Fabii[6] won the glory I embalm.
It laid the arrogance of those Arabs low
    Who followed Hannibal[7] across the Alpine   50
    Rocks, whence your waters glide, O River Po.
Under it Scipio[8] and Pompey[9] won
    While they were still young men. It acted harshly
    Towards that hill beneath which you were born.[10]
When Heaven judged the time had almost come
    To make the whole world like itself serene,
    Caesar received it by the will of Rome.[11]
What feats it did between the Var and Rhine
    Were witnessed by the Seine, Isère and Loire,
    And every valley which supplies the Rhône.[12]   60
What then it did, crossing the Rubicon
    On issuing from Ravenna, was so swift
    A flight it leaves behind both tongue and pen.[13]
That standard led the legions on to Spain,
    Thence to Durazzo, and then struck Pharsalus[14]
    So hard the hot Nile even felt the pain.[15]
It saw once more the Simois, whence it came,
    Antandros, and the place where Hector lies,

1   Leader of the Gauls, defeated in 390 BC.
2   King of Epirus, defeated in 275 BC.
3   He defeated the Gauls and the Latins.
4   Better known as Cincinnatus ("with curly locks", but erroneously understood as "shaggy-haired"), taken from the plough to defeat Rome's enemies.
5   A father, son and grandson who sacrificed their lives for Rome.
6   A patrician family with many distinguished members.
7   The Carthaginian general who came perilously close to conquering Rome.
8   A successful general in his youth, he eventually defeated Hannibal at Zama.
9   A Roman general, so successful he was granted a triumph at the age of twenty-five.
10   Fiesole, on a hill above Florence, was said to have been destroyed by loyal Romans during the Catiline rebellion.
11   Julius Caesar is regarded by Dante as the first Emperor of Rome, and the establishment of the Empire (with its state of comparative peace throughout the known world) as part of the preparation of the world for the Incarnation.
12   Caesar's victories in Gaul.
13   Caesar's crossing of the River Rubicon was in effect a declaration of war on the Roman Republic. Dante regards the war, however deplorable in itself, as necessary for the establishment of the Empire.
14   At Durazzo, in modern Albania, Caesar was repulsed by Pompey's army, but he moved to Pharsalus in Greece and defeated him.
15   Pompey was treacherously killed in Egypt, where he had fled after the Battle of Pharsalus.

Then – woe to Ptolemy! – it roused again.[1]
Thence fell on Juba like a stroke of lightning,[2]   70
   And then it wheeled towards the west of you,
   Where the Pompeyan trumpet was still sounding.[3]
For what it did through him who followed on[4]
   Brutus and Cassius bay in the Inferno,[5]
   And Modena[6] and Perugia[7] had to mourn.
Through him sad Cleopatra has to make
   Her endless moan, who fleeing from that standard,
   Was swiftly killed by the atrocious snake.[8]
With him it reached the very Red Sea shore[9] –
   With him it brought the world such lasting peace   80
   The bolts were shot on Janus' temple door.[10]
But what the standard which has made me say
   All this had done or would in future do,
   Throughout the mortal realms beneath its sway,
Comes to seem insignificant, obscure,
   Once one looks at the hands of the third Caesar,[11]
   Looks with clear eye and with a heart that's pure:
Because the Living Justice, by Whose breath
   I speak, committed to that Caesar's hands
   The glory of wreaking vengeance for His wrath.[12]   90
You'll be astonished at what follows on:
   That eagle hurried afterwards with Titus
   To avenge the avenging of the ancient sin![13]
And when the Lombard fangs were fastening on
   Holy Church, help arrived beneath this eagle,

---

1 Caesar visited the ruins of Troy, the city from whose port, Antandros, Aeneas came to
   Italy; the River Simois and the tomb of the Trojan hero Hector are nearby. Ptolemy, the
   King of Egypt who had Pompey murdered, was defeated by Caesar.
2 Juba, King of Numidia and an ally of Pompey, committed suicide after his defeat by
   Caesar.
3 Caesar defeated Pompey's sons in Spain.
4 Octavian, Caesar's adopted son and heir, later the Emperor Augustus.
5 Caesar's assassins who were defeated at Philippi, traitors to their benefactor and now
   in Judecca, the lowest region of the Inferno (see *Inf.* xxxiv, 64–67).
6 Where Octavian defeated his rival, Mark Antony.
7 Where Octavian defeated Mark Antony's brother.
8 Cleopatra, Queen of Egypt and mistress of Mark Antony, fled from Octavian's fleet at
   the Battle of Actium and committed suicide by snake bite.
9 Octavian conquered Egypt.
10 The doors of the temple of Janus in Rome were closed in time of peace.
11 Tiberius.
12 At the Crucifixion (carried out by the Roman authorities in Palestine), humanity,
   represented by Christ's human nature, was punished for the original sin of Adam
   and Eve.
13 Titus, a Roman general and later Emperor, captured and destroyed Jerusalem in 70 AD,
   thus punishing the Jews for their part in Christ's death.

Which flew above victorious Charlemagne.[1]
Now you can be the judge of such as those
   Whom I accused but now,[2] and of their errors,
   Which are the origin of all your woes.
One sets against this universal sign   100
   His yellow lilies,[3] and one commandeers it:[4]
   It's hard to tell who sins the greater sin.
The Ghibellines may play their tricks, but under
   Another sign, for evil always comes
   From putting justice and this sign asunder.
Nor should young Charles[5] oppose it with his Guelfs:
   Rather he ought to stand in awe of talons
   Which stripped much stronger lions of their pelts.[6]
Sons have already wept, and frequently,
   Their fathers' sins: let no one think the Lord   110
   Will swap His standard for the fleurs-de-lis!
This little star of ours[7] is beautified
   With righteous souls who lived industriously,
   Hoping for fame and honour as reward,
And when desires have such an inclination,
   The rays of the true love, being so deflected,
   Mount up indeed, but with less animation.
But part of our delight is to compare
   This our reward with what we merited,
   And see that it is neither less nor more.[8]   120
And so the Living Justice mellows us
   And our affections, so that we can never
   Be turned aside to any wickedness.
As diverse voices make the sweetest sound,
   So diverse ranks among the blessèd make
   Sweet music where these spheres are wheeling round.
This very diamond within is lighted
   By light shed from Romée,[9] from him whose labours,
   Though great and righteous, were but ill requited.
And yet those Provençals opposing him   130

---

1   Charlemagne (r.800–14) defended the Church against the Lombard King Desiderius, whom he dethroned in 774. In 800 Charlemagne was crowned Roman Emperor.

2   See ll. 31–33 above.

3   The Guelf faction opposes the Empire under the aegis of the golden lilies of the French Kings of Sicily and Naples.

4   The Ghibelline faction acts under the eagle standard as a cover for its own ambitions.

5   Charles II of Anjou, King of Naples (r.1285–1309).

6   Humbled much greater kings.

7   Mercury.

8   See *Par.* III, 64–84.

9   Romée de Villeneuve (1170–1250). A minister of Raymond Berengar, Count of Provence, he served faithfully, particularly by arranging advantageous marriages for the Count's daughters, and was unjustly disgraced.

   Did not have the last laugh: they take wrong ways
     Who see another's good as their own harm.
All four daughters of Raymond Berengar
     Were queens – and it was he who made them so,
     Romée, although a stranger there and poor.
But then the Count was moved by vicious men
     To ask a reckoning of his just steward
     Who'd given him returns of twelve for ten.
He left the court, impoverished now and old,
     And if the world could know what heart he bore,   140
     Having to beg for every crust of bread,
Much as they praise him, they would praise him more."

CANTO VII

Justinian, singing a hymn of praise, disappears from view. Dante is left with problems he dare not mention to Beatrice, since he is too much in awe of her. She reads his mind and answers his unspoken questions.

Adam's sin led to his condemnation, which has been inherited by his descendants. When Christ, human as well as divine, was crucified, the sin of humanity was punished, Adam's sin was expiated and justice was done. But Christ's divine and wholly sin-free nature was crucified unjustly, and this injustice was avenged by the destruction of Jerusalem in 70 AD. Why did God choose this method to redeem mankind? There might have seemed to be only two possibilities: either God should simply pardon mankind, or man should so humble himself as to make up for his original sin of pride. The second method would seem to be impossible, since man's finite nature cannot humble itself enough to make up for such an outrageous sin against the Infinite. God chose both ways: He was merciful and, in the human nature of Christ, man humbled himself sufficiently to redeem himself.

Finally Beatrice explains that everything created directly by God – the angels, the heavens, man's rational soul – is not subject to destruction. So mankind may look forward to resurrection and, if we consider how Adam and Eve's bodies were created directly by God, to the resurrection of the body.

" "O sanna, sanctus Deus sabaòth,
    Superillustrans claritate tua
    Felices ignes horum malacòth!"[1]
Thus, as he turned in time to his own notes,
    I looked upon that soul[2] as he went singing,
    With over him the coupled double lights.[3]
He moved in measure, and the others too,
    Till faster than the fastest sparks can sparkle,
    The sudden distance veiled them from my view.
"Tell her!" I told myself – I was nonplussed –   10
    "Tell her!" I told myself – I meant my lady,
    Who with her gentle dew quenches my thirst.[4]
But that great reverence which possesses me
    Merely to hear the sound of *Bea* or *ice*,[5]
    Kept my head bowed as in a lethargy.
Beatrice suffered me to stay like this
    A short time only, then began, while smiling

---

1   "Hosanna, holy God of hosts, Who with Your brightness pour down light upon the blessed flames in these realms." This prayer is based on the *Sanctus* of the Mass.
2   Justinian.
3   Probably the light of the soul illuminated by God's light, as in the prayer which opens this canto.
4   I.e. who answers my questions.
5   The first and last syllables of Beatrice's name.

A smile to bring a burning man to bliss:
"In my opinion, which cannot be wrong,
   How a just punishment can possibly   20
   Be justly punished sets you wondering.[1]
But I shall leave you with an easier mind
   If you but hang upon these words of mine,
   In which a precious doctrine is contained.
Because he scorned the curb so helpfully
   Placed on his will, that one man never born[2]
   Condemned himself and his posterity –
Which meant the human race was left unsound,
   Cast down for centuries in grievous error,[3]
   Until God's Word decided to descend   30
To where that nature, which had wandered off
   From its Maker, united with Himself
   By the sole act of His eternal Love.[4]
Now fix your mind on what is being said:
   This nature, now united with its Maker,
   Was as at its creation pure and good,
Though now it was exiled from Paradise
   By its own act, because it wandered from
   The way of truth and from its real life.
The penalty inflicted on the Cross,   40
   If it be measured by the adopted nature,[5]
   Was much more just than any ever was,
And likewise never such an act of horror,
   If we regard the Person Who endured it,
   He Who had taken to Himself that nature.
So two results come from a single deed:
   One death pleased God and also pleased the Jews –
   It made earth quake and Heaven was revealed.
By now you should not find the saying hard:
   When you are told of vengeance that was just[6]   50
   Being avenged with justice[7] afterward.
But I see how your intellect, being thrust
   From thought to thought, has tied itself in knots,
   From all of which it longs to be released.
You say: 'I understand what I have heard,
   But still I find it strange why God should wish
   To accomplish our redemption in this mode.'
Brother, this choice lies buried, hidden from

1   See *Par.* VI, 88–93 and notes.
2   Adam, created directly by God without human parents.
3   Original sin.
4   The Incarnation.
5   The human nature of Christ.
6   The punishment of humanity, in the Crucifixion, for the sin of Adam.
7   The punishment of humanity for assaulting the divinity of Christ in the Crucifixion.

The eyes of anyone whose intellect
Has not been fed and ripened in love's flame.   60
Nevertheless, since there are many shooting
And few of them can ever hit the mark,
I shall say why this method was most fitting.
God's generosity, never allured
By envy, burns inside and sends out sparks,
And so the eternal beauties spread abroad.
That which without a medium is distilled[1]
Is everlasting: no one can remove
God's imprint from it once it has been sealed.
That which without a medium is so meted   70
Out is quite free, because it is not subject
To the influence of anything created.
Most like to God, it pleases Him the more:
The sacred glow that shines from everything
Shines brightest in what is most similar.
All of these gifts[2] have been bestowed upon
The human creature, and if one is lacking
His nobleness must naturally decline.
Sin is the only thing enslaving him,
Making him differ from the Highest Good,   80
So that God's light in him is little seen.
And man cannot regain his dignity,
Unless he fills again what sin left empty,
False pleasure balanced by just penalty.
Your nature, by the total fall from grace
Of its progenitors, was banished far
From those endowments[3] as from Paradise –
Not to be won back, if you scrutinize
The matter carefully, by any method,
Except by taking one of these two ways: 90
Either that God, and by His mercy solely,
Should pardon man, or man by his own efforts
Should make full satisfaction for his folly.
Now turn your gaze down into the abyss
Of the Eternal Counsel – fix your mind
As closely as you can on my discourse.
Man could not ever make full recompense:
Given his limits, he could not bow down,
However humbly, in obedience,
As far as, disobeying, he'd have risen.   100
Man was, simply by what he was, excluded

---

1   The angels, the heavens and the souls of human beings, all created directly by God.
2   Immortality, free will and likeness to God.
3   See l. 76 above.

From making satisfaction, for this reason.[1]
So of necessity God by His own
   Methods must bring man back to his full life,
   By one way or by both of them,[2] I mean.
But just as anybody's action shows
   His graciousness the more that it discloses
   The goodness of his heart from which it flows,
The Good that puts His seal upon the world
   Was pleased to operate by both His ways   110
   To raise you up and have you reinstalled.
Between the final night and the first day[3]
   There has not been such a superb proceeding
   By either method, or will ever be:
Giving Himself, God was more bounteous,
   By thus enabling man to raise himself,
   Than if He simply had forgiven us –
And every other means to accomplish this
   Would have lacked justice, if the Son of God
   Had not humbled Himself in human flesh.   120
Now, to grant all your wishes through and through,
   I shall go back and clarify one point,
   To help you see as clearly as I do.
You say: 'I see how water, see how fire,
   The air, the earth and all their combinations
   Come to corruption, after their brief hour –
And these were all created, so that they,
   If what has been already said is true,
   Should never have been subject to decay.'
The angels, brother, and with them this pure   130
   Space where you're standing, were indeed created
   In all their fullness, and as they still are,
Whereas the elements which you have cited,
   And all the things resulting from their mixture,
   Receive their forms from power that is created.
Created was the matter which is theirs,
   Created was the influence which forms them,
   Which comes to them from these encircling stars.
The lives of all the animals and plants
   Are drawn from compounds which have potency,   140
   By the light and motion of the sacred lamps,[4]
But your souls are immediately inspired
   By the Supreme Benevolence, Who makes
   You love Him so He is always desired.

1   Man's sin of pride was so heinous that his finite humanity could not atone for it by any
     act of humility.
2   See ll. 91–93 above.
3   Between the Creation and the Last Day.
4   The stars.

And thinking of all this you may infer
   Your resurrection, if you call to mind
   How human flesh was first created for
The two progenitors of humankind."[1]

---

1   Adam and Eve.

CANTO VIII

Dante now finds himself on the planet Venus, where he sees the souls of those who were devoted to human love and friendship, which may include, but does not have to, sexual passion. He does not know how he comes to be on this planet, but he does know he has risen in the heavens, because he sees that Beatrice has now become even more beautiful.

Within the great light of Venus, Dante is able to distinguish many lesser lights wheeling like sparks in a fire. One of them is willing, even anxious, to speak to him. With Beatrice's approval Dante listens to this soul, who speaks modestly and only gradually and allusively reveals that he is Charles Martel of Anjou, the first-born son of Charles II of Anjou: Dante was on very friendly terms with him during Charles's short life. He lived long enough to be crowned King of Hungary, but died before he could come into his inheritance in Provence and the Kingdom of Naples. He did not have the opportunity to show his full worth as a ruler. He laments the bad effects of the ill-government imposed by some members of his family.

Dante asks how it is that capable and well-meaning forebears can have degenerate offspring. Charles explains that God gives the angelic intelligences who rule the heavens the power to influence things on earth, including the individual dispositions of human beings. This they do efficiently, but they take no account of the circumstances, the environments in which these individuals find themselves, which are often at odds with their natural capabilities. So for example, Daedalus was a gifted inventor, but his son could not even make sensible use of his father's finest invention.

An important corollary to this is that if each member of society did the work for which he was most suited, then the world and the individuals in it would all be better.

T he world believed, while it was still in peril,[1]
   The lovely Cyprian Queen[2] rayed sensual love
   As she whirled round in the third epicycle,[3]
So that they did not only render honour
   To her, with sacrifice and votive vows –
   Those ancient people in their ancient error –
But to Dione and Cupid offered up
   Their prayers, to her as mother, him as son,
   And fabled how he sat on Dido's lap.[4]
And after her, with whom I have begun   10
   My canto, they have named this brilliant star
   Courted, at dawn and evening, by the sun.[5]
I had no sense of the ascent, until

---

1   Unredeemed, before the Incarnation.
2   Venus, said to have been born in the sea off Cyprus.
3   The revolution of Venus, the third planet from the earth, on its axle while revolving in its sphere.
4   Cupid took on the form of Aeneas's son, Ascanius; Dido fondled him in her lap, and he inspired her with love for Aeneas (*Aeneid* 1, 683–90).
5   Venus is the morning star at dawn and the evening star after sunset.

I knew we were upon that planet[1] when
I saw my lady grow more beautiful.
And as in flames we see a spark arise,
    Or as in singing voices are distinguished –
    While one holds firm another comes and goes –
So I saw other lamps within that light,
    Which wheeled, some more and some less swift, according,   20
    As I imagine, to their inner sight.[2]
No blasts ever descended from cold cloud –
    Seen blasts or unseen blasts[3] – so rapidly
    As not to look unhurried and delayed
To anyone who'd watched those lustres come
    Towards us, turning from that gyre which first
    Began with the exalted Seraphim.[4]
And then there sounded from those in the fore
    "Hosanna!" so that since I've never been
    Without desire to hear that sound once more.   30
Then one of them drew nearer, and he thus
    Began to speak alone:[5] "We are all ready
    To please you, so you may rejoice in us.
With the celestial Princes we are whirled,
    In the same orb and with a single thirst,
    Princes whom you addressed once from the world:
'You, moving the third heaven by sheer thought'.[6]
    We are so full of love that, to delight you,
    A little stillness shall be no less sweet."
After my eyes in reverence had been bent   40
    Upon my lady, and she graciously
    Had given them assurance and consent,
They turned back swiftly to the generous
    Light and "Tell me. Who are you all?" I begged
    In tones that were imbued with tenderness.
Oh, how much brighter, greater grew that light
    Through all the fresh delight which was being added,
    As I spoke, to its previous delight!
So changed, he said: "Your world did not detain

1   Venus.
2   Their individual vision of God.
3   Lightning or wind.
4   The souls, which come from the Empyrean to meet Dante, pass first through the Primum Mobile, which sets all the other spheres in motion and is itself moved by the angelic order of the Seraphim.
5   A well-informed contemporary of Dante would have had the pleasure of seeing the speaker's identity becoming gradually clearer, although he does not name himself. He is Charles Martel of Anjou (1271–95), who was crowned King of Hungary in 1292 but died before he could inherit Provence and the Kingdom of Naples.
6   The beginning of Dante's *canzone* 'Voi che 'ntendendo il terzo ciel movete', addressed to the angels which keep the planet Venus in motion.

Me very long, but if my life had lasted,   50
   Much evil that will come would not have been.
I'm hidden from you by this joy of mine
   Which rays around me, hiding me away
   Like any insect in its silk cocoon.
You were my friend, and had good cause to be,
   For had I stayed below, I would have shown you
   More of my friendship than mere greenery.
The left bank watered by the Rhône, when Sorgue
   Has mingled all its waters with that river,[1]
   Expected me to be in time its lord,   60
As did Ausonia's horn – its boundary
   Marked by Bari, Gaeta, Catona – where
   Tronto and Verde drop into the sea.[2]
My shining forehead was already crowned
   As monarch of that earth the Danube waters
   When it has left its German banks behind.[3]
And beautiful Trinacria[4] – overcast
   Between Pachino and Pelorus,[5] over
   The gulf which Eurus irritates the most,[6]
Dark not through Typhon but through rising sulphur[7] –   70
   Would still have looked to have its rulers, born
   Through me to Charles[8] and Rudolf,[9] in the future,
If evil governance, bound to annoy
   Its subject population, had not moved
   Those of Palermo to shout out: "Die! Die!"[10]
And could my brother see this in good time,
   He would avoid the grasping poverty
   Of Catalans, before it does him harm.[11]
And certainly provision should be made,
   By him or others, that his loaded vessel   80
   Be not worse burdened with an overload.

---

1   He is alluding to Provence.
2   The Kingdom of Naples.
3   Hungary.
4   Sicily.
5   Respectively, present-day Cape Passaro and Cape Faro.
6   The Gulf of Catania, where the prevailing wind is the stormy south-east, the sirocco.
7   The eruptions of Mount Etna are caused not by the struggles of the monster said to be buried beneath it, but by the ignition of underground sulphur.
8   Charles I of Anjou, Charles Martel's grandfather.
9   Charles Martel's father-in-law.
10   If it had not been for the misgovernment of Charles's grandfather, which provoked the massacre of the French known as the Sicilian Vespers (1282), his descendants would have succeeded to the throne of Sicily.
11   Charles's younger brother Robert employed avaricious retainers from Catalonia in his Kingdom of Naples.

His niggard nature, offspring of a past[1]
   That was more bountiful, needs officers
   Who are not bent on feathering the nest."
"Since I believe the deep joy that descends
   Within me from the words you speak, my lord,
   Is, where all good begins and all good ends,
Seen as clearly by you as ever I could,
   It pleases me the more – and is more dear –
   Because you see it in the sight of God.   90
You gladden me, so please clear up one doubt:
   What you have said has driven me to wonder:
   How can sweet seed result in bitter fruit?"[2]
Thus I to him. He answered: "If I can
   But demonstrate one truth to you, you will
   Face up to what you've turned your back upon.
The Goodness which revolves and fills with joy
   The realm you're climbing, turns Its providence
   In these great bodies into energy.[3]
Not just their natures are provided for   100
   Within the Mind that is Itself perfection,
   But their well-being also is His care:
And so whatever this bow shoots must come
   Perforce to somewhere that is preordained,
   Like arrows shot with an unerring aim.
Were this not so, the heavens through which you travel
   Would still produce their own effects, but they
   Would not be works of art, but so much rubble –
Which cannot be, unless the minds are flawed
   Which keep these stars in motion, and the Primal   110
   Mover also who made them so impaired.
Do you require this truth to be made clearer?"
   And I replied: "No, it's impossible
   That Nature in her works should ever falter."
Then he again: "Would man not be worse off
   Below if he were not a social being?"
   "Yes," I replied, "and here I need no proof."
"And how could that be so, if men on earth
   Did not live diversely with diverse functions?
   It cannot, if your master[4] writes the truth."   120
So he continued logically like this,
   Then he concluded: "Now it follows that
   The roots of your effects must be diverse:
So one is born a Solon, Xerxes one,

1   His forebears.
2   Why do parents sometimes have degenerate children?
3   God not only sets the planets in motion, but gives them power to influence life upon earth.
4   Aristotle.

And one Melchizedek, another he
  Who, when he took to flying, lost his son.[1]
Whirling nature, who puts her seal upon
  The mortal wax, does her work well, but favours
  One lodging no more than another one.[2]
And so it comes about that Esau is   130
  Estranged from Jacob in the womb,[3] Quirinus,
  Although base-born, is thought to come from Mars.[4]
Those engendered would have to take the road
  Taken by those who had engendered them,
  Did not divine provision override.
Now that's before your eyes which was behind,[5]
  And so that you may know how you delight me,
  Here's a corollary to wrap you round.
Face any nature with discordant fate,
  And like a plant outside its proper climate   140
  It cannot fail to yield a poor result.
And if the world down there only paid heed
  To the foundations which are laid by nature,
  And built on them, then people would be good.
But you're perverting to religion such
  As are born fitter to gird on the sword,
  And fashion kings from men who ought to preach:
And so you wander off from the right road."

---

1 Respectively, a legislator, a ruler, a priest and an inventor (Daedalus), whose son (Icarus)
    misused the wings his father had made for him and fell to his death.
2 Nature, operating through the heavenly spheres, gives individuals their dispositions, but
    takes no account of the circumstances into which anyone is born.
3 Even twins can differ greatly: see Gen. 25:21–34.
4 Romulus, the mythical founder of Rome, was so successful that people could not believe
    in his low birth. Quirinus was the name given to him when he was apotheosized after
    death.
5 See l. 96.

CANTO IX

Dante apostrophizes Clemence, Charles Martel's widow. He tells her that Charles has made a veiled prophecy that his son will not, as he should, inherit the Kingdom of Naples: he will be the victim of deceit. Charles had advised Dante not to comment on this, but Dante cannot resist saying that the treachery will be punished.

Another light moves towards Dante and, with Beatrice's permission, he asks it to speak. This is Cunizza, sister of the bloodthirsty tyrant Ezzelino III da Romano. She had indulged her lustful temperament before repenting, and that is why she is in this, one of the lower states of blessedness; but she is completely happy. After briefly mentioning another light near her, the soul of someone famous, she prophesies disaster for the March of Treviso as punishment for the vicious acts committed there.

Dante now asks the other light, the one mentioned by Cunizza, to speak. The spirit says that he was born in Marseille. His name was Folquet. He does not mention that he was a famous troubadour. Until the onset of old age, he says, he burned in love as much as anybody ever did. Like Cunizza, he marvels at the good which has been brought out of this.

Folquet points out to Dante the light that was Rahab, the harlot of Jericho who protected the spies sent into that city by Joshua as a preliminary to his conquest of the Holy Land. As a reward Rahab was taken up into Heaven at Christ's Harrowing of Hell, the first person to be so taken up, and she is now the brightest light on Venus.

Folquet ends with a fierce denunciation of Florence and its obsession with money, and an even fiercer denunciation of the avarice of the higher clergy. He suggests cryptically that an end to this corruption is near.

A simple summary takes no account of Cunizza's and Folquet's allusive and periphrastic eloquence, so suited to their prophecies of disaster, and to the seriousness of the sins which they condemn.

B eautiful Clemence,[1] once your Charles had said
    All this to me, he prophesied the scheming
    Which would be detrimental to his seed,[2]
But added: "Silence! Let the years roll by" –
    And so what can I say? Except to tell you
    Just punishment succeeds your injury.[3]
And now the splendour of that sacred soul
    Had turned back to the Sun with which it's filled –
    That loving kindness which can never fail.
Deluded creatures, souls gone so awry   10
    As to avert your hearts from such well-being
    And give your countenance to vanity!
And then another of those splendours turned
    Towards me, signifying its desire

---

1   The widow of Charles Martel.
2   Charles Martel's son, Charles Robert, was heir to the Kingdom of Naples, but it went to Charles Martel's brother Robert.
3   The usurper's brother and nephew were killed at Montecatini in 1315.

To please me by the glow with which it burned.
The eyes of Beatrice, which she kept bent
  Upon me, as they were before, assured
  Me my desire met with her dear consent.
"Oh, blessèd spirit, may my longings meet
  With rapid recompense," I said, "and show me   20
  You are a glass in which I see my thought!"[1]
At this the light – one still not known to me –
  Out of the depth from which it had been singing
  Spoke in its urge to be of help to me:
"In the degenerate Italian land,
  Between Rialto and the highlands whence
  The Brenta and the Piave streams descend,[2]
A hill arises, though to no great height,
  From which a firebrand[3] once descended, bringing
  Havoc to all the land that lies about.   30
And he and I were born out of one root:
  Cunizza was my name – I sparkle here
  Since I was mastered by this planet's light.[4]
I grant myself forgiveness – and I'm glad
  To do so – for the reason for my fate,[5]
  Which would be baffling to your common herd.
This precious jewel shining in our star,
  This soul which is most near to me, has left
  Great fame on earth, which will not die before
This hundredth year of ours is reproduced   40
  Five times.[6] So should not men seek excellence
  Until a second life[7] succeeds the first?
All this means nothing to the rabblement
  Between the Adige and Tagliamento,[8]
  And though chastised, they still do not repent.
Not long but Paduans at the marshy pool
  Shall stain with blood the stream that bathes Vicenza,[9]
  For being restive and undutiful –
And where the Sile and Cagnano meet
  Someone is lording it with head held high,   50

---

1   Dante wishes the spirit to understand his questions without their needing to be expressed.
2   The March of Treviso, with Venice (indicated by its principal island, Rialto) to the south, and the Trentino Alps to the north.
3   Ezzelino III da Romano (1194–1259), a bloodthirsty tyrant: see *Inf.* XII, 109–10.
4   Cunizza, sister of Ezzelino, was notorious for her love affairs, under the influence of the planet Venus.
5   Having been influenced too much by the planet Venus, she is in one of the lower states of blessedness, but utterly happy with her lot.
6   Dante's vision is set in the year 1300: Cunizza sees the fame as lasting five centuries.
7   Posthumous fame.
8   The inhabitants of the March of Treviso.
9   The bloody defeat of the Paduan Guelfs at the River Bacchiglione in 1314.

For whom already people spread the net.[1]
While Feltre shall have reason to bewail
    Her impious pastor's treachery,[2] so dreadful
    That for its like none ever went to jail.
It would indeed require a mighty vat
    To take the blood of all those Ferrarese
    (A tiring task to try to weigh it out!)
Which this obliging cleric will provide
    To show his party zeal: such gifts as his
    Will suit the kind of life these people lead.   60
Above are mirrors – Thrones to you – whose light
    Is God in judgement shining down on us,[3]
    And so this way of speaking seems but right."
Here she fell silent; and she seemed to me
    To turn elsewhere, going back into the round
    To dance where she'd been dancing previously.
The other joy, which I'd already seen
    Was something to be treasured,[4] had the semblance
    Of a fine ruby smitten by the sun.
Up there rejoicing is expressed in brightness,   70
    As on the earth in smiles – but shadows darken
    The shades below us[5] overcome by sadness.
"God sees all things, and all your seeing too,"
    I said, "sinks into Him. Since no desire,
    Blessed spirit, hides itself away from you,
Why does your voice – delighting Heaven with songs
    In constant concert with those holy fires
    Who make themselves a cowl with their six wings[6] –
Not answer my desires? I certainly
    Would not delay to deal with your request,   80
    If I were sunk in you as you in me."
"The greatest vale of water[7] which is filled,"
    So he began in words to frame an answer,
    "From that wide sea encompassing the world,[8]
Between discordant banks[9] extends so far
    Against the sun's course that it makes its zenith

---

1   Rizzardo da Camino, Ghibelline lord of Treviso (indicated here by its two rivers) was
    assassinated in 1312.
2   The pro-Guelf Bishop of Feltre, Alessandro Novello, betrayed to their death thirteen
    Ghibellines from Ferrara who had taken refuge with him.
3   The angels reflect the judgement of God.
4   See l. 37.
5   In the Inferno.
6   The highest angels, the Seraphim (see Isaiah 6:2).
7   The Mediterranean.
8   Oceanus, the sea which was believed to surround all the dry land on our globe.
9   Europe and Africa, whose inhabitants differ in race and religion.

Where the horizon used to be before.[1]
Now I was one who lived along those shores
   Between the Ebro and the little Magra
   Which parts the Tuscans and the Genoese.[2]   90
Sunrise and sunset are as far apart,
   Almost, from Bougie as from my own city,[3]
   Whose blood once warmed the water in its port.[4]
I was called Folquet[5] by those people who
   Had heard my name – and now this heaven bears
   My print, as I once bore its imprint too.
For even Belus' daughter did not burn,
   When she wronged both Sichaeus and Creusa,[6]
   More than I, till my hair began to turn;[7]
Nor did that Rhodopean girl beguiled   100
   By her Demophoon,[8] nor Hercules
   When Iole inside his heart was sealed.[9]
It's not that we repent here: no, we smile –
   Not at the sin, which never comes to mind,
   But at the Power that has arranged all well.
We marvel at the art by which such love
   Is beautified, and see the good which brings
   The world below up to the world above.
That you may go away well satisfied
   On all the questions rising in this sphere,   110
   It is incumbent on me to proceed.
You wish to know who is beside me here
   Within this luminosity, and sparkling
   As sunbeams sparkle in a limpid mere.
Know then that she is Rahab,[10] now at rest,
   And she has so much honour in our order
   You see it signed with her light more than most.
Into this sphere, where your world's shade at last

---

1 The Mediterranean extends so far that the celestial meridian at one end has its horizon at the other end.
2 I.e. in Marseille, halfway between the mouth of the Ebro in Spain and the mouth of the Magra.
3 Bougie, in what is now Algeria, is more or less on the same line of longitude as Marseille.
4 A reference to the bloodshed involved in the Roman capture of Marseille in 49 BC.
5 Folquet of Marseille (d.1231), a noted troubadour who became a monk.
6 Dido of Carthage had sworn to remain faithful to her murdered husband Sichaeus, but loved Aeneas. Creusa was the wife of Aeneas.
7 To turn grey.
8 Phyllis, daughter of the King of Thrace (indicated by its Mount Rhodope), loved Demophoon, the son of Theseus, and was betrayed by him.
9 Hercules's love for Iole was indirectly the cause of his death.
10 The harlot of Jericho, who protected the men sent by Joshua to spy out the city before his attack on it (Josh. 2).

Comes to a point,[1] she was assumed, like others
    After Christ's triumph,[2] and she was the first.   120
It was but right to leave her as a palm,[3]
    Somewhere in heaven, witnessing the lofty
    Conquest that was achieved by palm and palm,[4]
Because she aided the first glory gained
    By Joshua in the Holy Land our Pope
    Only infrequently can bring to mind.[5]
And your own city, which was planted by
    The first to turn his back upon his Maker,[6]
    When envy brought about such misery,
Produces and distributes that cursed flower[7]   130
    Which leads both sheep and lambs astray, now shepherds
    No longer guard the flock which wolves devour.
For love of this the Gospel and the Church's
    Doctors are done with, but decretals pondered,[8]
    As witnessed by their pages' crumpled edges.
On this the Pope and cardinals are set:
    They do not give a thought to Nazareth,
    Which Gabriel visited with wings apart.[9]
But Vatican, and all of the revered
    Places in Rome which are the cemetery   140
    Where those who fought for Peter[10] are interred,
Shall soon be freed from prelates' treachery."[11]

---

1 Venus is here regarded as the farthest planet reached by the earth's conical shadow.
2 She was taken into Heaven at Christ's Harrowing of Hell.
3 A palm branch as a sign of victory.
4 The Crucifixion, at which both of Christ's hands were pierced by nails.
5 The Pope appears indifferent to the fact that Christians have no foothold in the Holy Land.
6 Florence, founded by Satan.
7 The golden florin, stamped on one side with the Florentine lily.
8 The study of Canon Law takes precedence because it is financially profitable.
9 In depictions of the Annunciation, Gabriel is shown with his wings spread in homage to Mary.
10 The early martyrs of the Church.
11 In this prophecy of the end of financial corruption in the Church there may be an allusion to the death of Boniface VIII in 1303.

CANTO X

Dante asks his readers to lift up their eyes to the heavens and see the harmony of creation, which reflects the mutual love of the three persons of the Holy Trinity. It is now the spring equinox, a point at which the celestial equator is crossed obliquely by the zodiac. This leads Dante to say that if the planets were to veer even a little from their courses, then their influence on our world would be less beneficial.

Dante does not go into this in more detail, since he is now concerned with describing his own situation – in the sphere of the sun, with no idea how he got there. The souls in this sphere are so bright that they stand out against the light of the sun itself. Urged by Beatrice, Dante concentrates his attention on God, so that he loses sight even of Beatrice. When she smiles at this, Dante's attention becomes divided.

Dante and Beatrice are surrounded by the lights of souls who were famed for their wisdom and religious understanding. One of these lights speaks, says that he is St Thomas Aquinas and names the other souls there.

Just as the canto opens stressing the harmony in creation, so the unspoken theme which binds these souls together is harmony and reconciliation. A foremost philosophical question in Dante's day, and for some hundreds of years before, was the relation of pagan philosophy to Christian revelation. This is why Aquinas, who spent his life on an attempt to reconcile these approaches to the truth, is the leading character here. So Aquinas introduces and praises not only Dominic, the founder of his order, and Albertus Magnus, his own master, but also Boethius, whose chief work is one of pagan philosophy, and even Siger of Brabant, whose ideas Aquinas opposed so strongly in his lifetime.

It is appropriate that the canto should end with these spirits in the sun wheeling and singing in a harmony that is apprehensible nowhere but in Heaven itself.

G azing upon His Son, and with that Love[1]
    Which One and the Other breathe eternally,
    The primal and unutterable Worth[2]
Made whatsoever spins through space and mind
    Exist in such coherence nobody
    Can look thereon and not discern His hand.
And therefore, reader, raise with me your sight
    To the exalted wheels, and to that place
    At which one motion and the other meet,[3]
And start to adore and contemplate the art   10
    The Master uses with such ardent love
    He never ever takes His eyes from it.
Observe how from that very point proceeds
    The slanting circle carrying the planets[4]

---

1   The Holy Spirit.
2   God the Father.
3   The point where the daily movement of the planets round the earth (the celestial equator) crosses obliquely the movement of the sun through the zodiac.
4   The zodiac.

To satisfy the world with all it needs.
For if the planets' course were not aslant,
    Much virtue in the heavens would be vain,
    And everything on earth be impotent;
And if the zodiac's orbit were to veer
    From the straight course a little more or less,   20
    Much would be lost to either hemisphere.
Now, reader, for a little while stay seated,
    Chewing over this foretaste you are given,
    For long before you tire you'll be delighted.
I've set it out for you – now you must:
    All my solicitude is taken up
    With this matter of which I have to write.
The greatest minister of nature,[1] that
    Imprints the worth of Heaven on our world,
    And with its light measures our seasons out,   30
Reaching that point which I touched on before,[2]
    Was turning round and round along the spiral
    On which he keeps appearing earlier,[3]
And I was with him, but no more aware
    Of how I came to rise than anybody
    Is conscious of a thought before it's there.[4]
And I have Beatrice guiding me so well
    From what is good to what is better, with
    Such speed her action takes no time at all.
They must have been inordinately bright,   40
    Those souls within the sun as I arrived there,
    To stand out, not by colour, but by light!
Were I to call on genius, practice, art,
    I could not make that apprehensible:
    You can believe it, and should long for it!
If our imaginations cannot come
    To this great height, that is no cause for wonder:
    No eye has ever pierced beyond the sun.
There on that planet the High Father sets
    His fourth household, which He is always pleasing,   50
    Showing them how He breathes, how He begets.
And Beatrice began: "Give thanks for this,
    Thanks to the Sun of all the angels, Who
    Lifts you to His material sun by grace."
No mortal heart was ever so prepared
    To give itself to God in true devotion,
    With utter readiness and gratitude,

---

1   The sun.
2   See ll. 7–9.
3   It is the spring equinox and days are lengthening.
4   Dante is now in the sphere of the sun, where he meets the semblances of those known
    for their wisdom.

IN JUST THAT WAY THE SEMPITERNAL ROSES
WERE TURNING ROUND ABOUT US IN TWO GARLANDS...

PARADISE XII, 19–20

I SAW ANOTHER MOVING AND REVOLVING:
GLAD RAPTURE WAS THE WHIP WHICH SPUN THAT TOP...

PARADISE XVIII, 41–42

As I the instant that those words were said –
   And I directed all my love to Him,
   Until all thought of Beatrice was obscured.   60
She did not mind – no, but she smiled at that,
   And with the splendour of her smiling eyes
   The whole attention of my mind was split.
And I saw many a living dazzling light
   Make us the centre and themselves a garland,
   One even sweeter-voiced than shining-bright:
Just so we see the daughter of Latona[1]
   Encircled sometimes when the atmosphere
   Is dense with rays that fashion her corona.
In Heaven's court, from which I now return,   70
   Are many beautiful and precious jewels:[2]
   One tries to bring them down to earth in vain.
The song sung by those lights was such a gem:
   Who does not wing himself for flight up there
   May as well hope for tidings from the dumb.
When, singing thus, I'd seen those bright suns wheel
   Three times around the two of us, like stars
   Rotating near to an unmoving pole,
They looked like dancers, with their dance not ended,
   But pausing silently, waiting to hear   80
   Till they could catch the new notes being sounded.
Then from within one of those lights I heard:
   "Because the ray of grace, by which true love
   Is kindled at the first, then magnified
By loving, shines so greatly in you and
   Conducts you upwards on that flight of stairs[3]
   Where none goes down who will not reascend,
Anyone who denied his flask of wine
   To quench your thirst would have to be as hindered
   As a river that is not flowing down.[4]   90
You wish to know what flowering souls enliven
   This garland which encircles with devotion
   The lovely lady fitting you for Heaven.
I was a lamb, one of that holy flock
   Dominic[5] shepherds through green pastures feeding
   All those who do not turn aside or back.
The nearest on my right was from Cologne.
   He was my brother and my master: his name

---

1   The moon.
2   The souls which Dante sees shining.
3   The ascent to the vision of God. The next line means that those who have had this vision
    during their lives will certainly be saved.
4   It is natural for those in Heaven to be eager to satisfy Dante's longing for knowledge.
5   St Dominic (1170–1221), founder of the preaching order which goes by his name.

Was Albert,[1] Thomas of Aquino mine.[2]
If you would be informed about them all,   100
   Then follow with your eyes as I am speaking
   And move them round the blessèd coronal.
That other blaze is coming from the smile
   Of Gratian,[3] who served both courts of law,
   And pleases Paradise, he served so well.
The other one along who decks our band
   Was Peter, he who, like the humble widow,
   Offered to Holy Church all that he owned.[4]
The fifth,[5] which is among us the most bright,
   Breathes out such love that all the world below   110
   Hungers and thirsts to have some news of it:
Within it is the soul in whom profound
   Wisdom was placed, such that, if truth be true,
   No second paralleled his piercing mind.
Next see the radiance of that luminary
   Who down there, in the flesh, saw best of any
   The angels' nature and their ministry.[6]
There smiles inside that other little light
   The champion of Christian times,[7] whose Latin
   Made sure Augustine was well fortified.   120
If you have moved your mind's eye on from light
   To light, and always following my praises,
   You must be at the eighth, and keen for it.
Therein, seeing all good, a sacred soul[8]
   Is full of joy: he lays the lying world
   Open to all of those who read him well.
The body out of which that soul was chased

1   Albert of Cologne (1193–1280), also known as Albertus Magnus, a Dominican friar
    whose encyclopedic works included a commentary on Aristotle.
2   Thomas Aquinas (1225–74), a pupil of Albert. He attempted a reconciliation between
    Aristotle (regarded as the acme of pagan philosophy) and Christian revelation.
3   Gratian was born in Italy c.1090. He brought order to the laws of ecclesiastical and civil
    courts and set them in relation with each other.
4   Peter Lombard (c.1100–64) collected and discussed the pronouncements of the Christian
    Fathers in his *Sentences*. He offered his work to the Church as the poor widow offered
    her mite (Luke 21:1–4).
5   Solomon, King of Israel, and traditionally author of the books of Proverbs, Ecclesiastes,
    Song of Songs and Wisdom.
6   Dionysius the Areopagite, who was converted to Christianity by St Paul (Acts 17:34), and
    who was wrongly believed to be the author of *Celestial Hierarchies*, the most authoritative
    work on angels.
7   Paulus Orosius (early fifth century AD) whose main work was intended to show that the
    Roman Empire had not deteriorated since the acceptance of Christianity.
8   Boethius (c.475–525), whose *Consolation of Philosophy*, written while he was in prison
    under sentence of death, maintains (without recourse to Christian revelation or faith)
    that virtue is preferable to vice.

Lies now down in Ciel d'Oro;[1] and he came
Through martyrdom and exile to this rest.[2]
Beyond, you see the glowing spirits burn   130
   Of Isidore,[3] of Bede,[4] of Richard[5] who
   In meditation was much more than man.
This soul from whom your gaze turns back to me
   Was one so burdened with his weighty thought
   It seemed to him that death was dilatory:
This is Siger's imperishable light –
   He, when he lectured in the Street of Straw,[6]
   Syllogized certain truths that brought him hate."[7]
Then, like the clock that calls us at the hour
   The Bride of God[8] arises to sing matins   140
   To keep her Bridegroom[9] still in love with her,
While each part of the clock is pulling, driving,
   In such attractive tintinnabulations
   The well-intentioned spirit swells with loving –
Just so I now perceived the glorious wheel[10]
   Revolving, joining voice to voice in chime,
   With sweetness that's inapprehensible
But there where joy is not decreased by time.

---

1   The Basilica of San Pietro in Ciel d'Oro in Pavia.
2   It is generally accepted that the charges which led to Boethius's execution (when his
     soul was "exiled" from his body) were spurious.
3   Isidore of Seville (c.560–636), author of an influential encyclopedia.
4   The Venerable Bede (c.673–735), the father of English history.
5   Richard of St Victor (d.1173), author of De contemplatione.
6   The street in Paris where the schools of philosophy were located.
7   Siger of Brabant (c.1225–c.1283) tended to divorce the truths of reason from those of
     faith. He was strongly opposed by Aquinas.
8   The Church.
9   Christ.
10   The circle of spirits in the sphere of the sun.

CANTO XI

Dante is amazed to find himself in Heaven with Beatrice, and contrasts this joyous fulfilment with the many pointless pursuits of people on earth.

The souls in the sun have been singing and circling round Dante and Beatrice. Now they stop, and St Thomas speaks. He knows already what Dante would like to ask, and he will answer questions arising from his own previous speech.

Providence, he says, has given two guides to keep the barque of St Peter, the Church, on its right course. One was renowned for the ardour of his love, and the other for the intellectual light he shed. St Thomas will speak only of one, since their purpose was the same. The identity of this guide is revealed gradually by a brief account of his life. Here we have St Thomas, a Dominican, praising Francis of Assisi, the founder of the Franciscan Order. The approaches of these two orders were so different, and their interests so often clashed, that they were often at odds, but here in Heaven all such disagreements have disappeared and harmony prevails.

St Thomas describes Francis's early days and that devotion to the Lady Poverty which influenced others to join him in his way of life. He mentions how Pope Innocent III approved the Franciscan Rule, and how this approval was later confirmed by Pope Honorius III. St Thomas describes Francis's mission to the Sultan of Egypt and Palestine, and how he returned home to Italy when he found his time among the Muslims was fruitless. The climax came when, on La Verna, Francis received the stigmata which he bore until his death two years later. A devotee of poverty to the last, he requested that his body should be laid upon the bare earth.

St Thomas mentions St Dominic, but not by name, describing him only as "our patriarch", and he takes the opportunity to criticize those Dominicans who have fallen short of the high ideals of the Dominican Order, leaving very few of them faithful to their calling.

S enseless anxieties of human kind!
　　Oh, how inadequate that reasoning
　　Which makes you beat your wings so near the ground!
One gives himself to the law, one to prescriptions,
　　One to the hunt for priestly offices,
　　And one to reign by force or by deceptions,
And one to thieve, and one to politics,
　　One toils in the pursuit of carnal pleasure,
　　Another drudges simply to relax,
While I, released from all such frippery,　　　　　　　　　　10
　　Am up above, with Beatrice, in Heaven,
　　Where I receive a welcome, gloriously.
Each light, the instant that it had come back
　　To that point on the circle where it started,
　　Paused, like a candle in its candlestick.[1]
And from within that light which had before
　　Been speaking to me, I perceived a smile

1　The twelve souls in the sun have been circling round Dante and Beatrice (*Par.* x, 145–48).

Begin to spread, and grow more bright and clear:[1]
"As I am growing brighter in its rays,
   So, as I look into the Eternal Light,   20
   I apprehend your thoughts and see their cause.
You are in doubt, and wish me to expand
   And clarify in more explicit language
   My words, that you may better understand
What I meant, saying 'through green pastures feeding',[2]
   And where I said, 'No second paralleled'.[3]
   Now here some sharp distinctions are worth making.
That Providence by which the world is ruled –
   Whose counsels no created scrutiny
   Can fathom, being always unrevealed –   30
In order to delight His chosen Bride[4] –
   Her whom He wedded when He cried out loudly,[5]
   Sealing their union with His precious blood,
Making her self-assured and faithfuller –
   Ordained two princes for her benefit,
   On this side and on that as guides for her.
The one was like a seraph in his ardour;[6]
   The other, with the wisdom he displayed,
   Shone out on earth in a cherubic splendour.[7]
I shall speak but of one, since both of them   40
   Are praised when either one of them is praised:
   Their double labour had a single aim.
Between Topino's stream and that which drops
   Down from the hill the blessed Ubaldo chose[8]
   There is a lofty rock[9] whose fertile slopes
Mean that Perugia feels both cold and heat
   Through Porta Sole[10] – Nocera behind
   And Gualdo[11] must lament their heavier lot.
From this steep slope, and where its sharp decline
   Eases, a sun once came into the world,[12]   50

---

1   The light is St Thomas Aquinas.
2   *Par.* x, 95.
3   *Par.* x, 114.
4   The Church.
5   On the cross. "Jesus, when he had cried again with a loud voice, yielded up the ghost" (Matt. 27:50).
6   The angelic order of the Seraphim is characterized mainly by love.
7   The main characteristic of the Cherubim is intellectual light.
8   Bishop Ubaldo (1084–1160) chose for a hermitage the hill where the River Chiascio rises.
9   Mount Subasio in Umbria.
10 The eastern gate of Perugia, which receives from Mount Subasio the reflection of heat in the summer and cold blasts in the winter.
11 Two towns north-east of Mount Subasio, which does not protect them from north winds and takes their sunlight in the summer.
12 This sun's identity is made explicit only in l. 74.

As ours does from the Ganges now and then.[1]
Nobody therefore, when this place is meant,
   Should say 'Ascesi', which means much too little,
   But name it more correctly 'Orient'.[2]
That sun was not so distant from his birth
   When he began to make the world conceive
   A certain strength and comfort from his worth;
For even as a youth he went to war
   Against his father, all for her[3] for whom,
   Like death, none wishes to unlock the door.   60
In spiritual jurisdiction, and before
   His father, he espoused himself to her;
   Then day by day he loved her more and more.
She, losing her first Husband[4] long before,
   Remained eleven hundred years – until
   That sun arose – neglected and obscure;
To no avail she stayed unterrified,
   We gather, with Amyclas, at the voice
   Of him who made the whole wide world afraid.[5]
To no avail, faithful and undismayed,   70
   While even Mother Mary stayed below,
   She climbed with Christ upon the cross and cried.
But, lest my meaning should remain opaque,
   Francis and Poverty, you understand,
   Are the two lovers in this lengthy talk.
Their harmony, their obvious happiness,
   Their love and wonder and their tender glances
   Made them the cause of others' holiness.
They made the Venerable Bernard[6] go
   Barefoot, the first to seek this utter peace –   80
   And though he ran, he felt he was too slow.
O undiscovered wealth! O fertile good!
   Egidius goes barefoot, as does Sylvester,[7]
   Behind the groom, since they adore the bride.
He goes his way, this father and kind lord,
   Together with his lady and the household
   Already tying on the humble cord.[8]

---

1   At the spring equinox the sun rises in what was regarded as the true east (with respect
     to the meridian of Jerusalem), and more brightly than usual.
2   "Ascesi", the Tuscan form of Assisi, merely suggests ascent, while "Orient" suggests the
     place where the sun rises.
3   See ll. 74–75.
4   Christ.
5   The fisherman Amyclas felt so secure in his poverty that he was not afraid even of Julius
     Caesar.
6   Bernard of Quintavalle, the first follower of Francis.
7   Two of the earliest followers of Francis.
8   The simple cord worn by Franciscan friars instead of an elaborate belt.

Nor did his modest heart cast his eyes down,
　　Though but the son of Pietro Bernardone,
　　And though he met with marvellous disdain,　　　　　90
But like a king set out his stringent rule
　　Before the Pope – and that was when his Order
　　Received from Innocent its primal seal.[1]
And then the increase of the humble poor,
　　Who followed after him whose life of wonder
　　Were better sung in glory by Heaven's choir,
Was circled with a second coronal,
　　Through Pope Honorius by the Holy Spirit,
　　Upon this archimandrite's sacred will.[2]
And then, when in his thirst for martyrdom　　　　　100
　　And in the presence of the haughty Sultan,[3]
　　He had preached Christ and those who followed him –
And he, finding the people there unripe
　　To be converted, would not work in vain,
　　But had gone back to Italy to reap –
There, on a rock[4] between the Tiber and
　　The Arno, Christ bestowed His final seal,[5]
　　For two years borne on side and foot and hand.[6]
When it pleased Him, Who for outstanding good
　　Favoured this man who made himself so humble,　　110
　　To raise him up to his well-earned reward,
Then to his brethren as his rightful heirs
　　He left his dearest lady, and he told them
　　To love her faithfully now she was theirs.
And this illustrious soul went from his lady,
　　And went back to its kingdom up above,
　　No bier but naked earth for his dead body.[7]
Imagine now somebody fit to be
　　His counterpart to keep the barque of Peter[8]
　　On its right course across the open sea!　　　　　120
And such a person was our patriarch[9] –
　　So you can see, who follows his commands
　　Is bearing precious burdens in his barque.
But now his flock has worked up such a greed
　　For novel pasturing,[10] it cannot be

1　Pope Innocent III approved the Franciscan Rule in 1209.
2　Pope Honorius III confirmed the Franciscan Rule in 1223.
3　Of Egypt and Palestine.
4　La Verna, a retreat on Mount Penna in the Apennines.
5　The stigmata.
6　Francis died in 1226.
7　Francis, when near to death, asked for his body to be laid naked on bare earth.
8　The Church.
9　St Dominic.
10　Worldly pursuits not fitting for a Dominican friar.

But they must stray through many a far-flung field,
And in their wanderings they grow remoter
  From him, and when they backtrack to the fold
  Their need for nourishment is ever greater.
True, there are those who in their fear of dearth   130
  Cling to the shepherd, but so few one might
  Make cowls for all of them from little cloth.
Now if my meaning is not too obscure,
  If you have listened with all due attention,
  If you remember what I said before,
Your wishes will be partly granted, seeing
  What plant I mean[1] from which some branches break –
  And you will see what I implied by saying
'All those who do not turn aside or back'."[2]

---

1   The Dominican Order.
2   At *Par.* x, 96.

CANTO XII

As St Thomas Aquinas stops speaking, the circle of saints moves round once more. A similar circle of lights is now turning outside the first one and in tune with it. The appearance is of a double rainbow, and the biblical significance of the rainbow as a mark of God's goodwill to men is recalled. As the motion stops, a voice is heard from one of the lights in the outer circle.

Eventually he tells us he is St Bonaventura, but not before he – a former General of the Franciscan Order – has delivered a eulogy of St Dominic. This balances the eulogy of St Francis by a leading Dominican, St Thomas Aquinas, in the previous canto. St Bonaventura mentions Dominic's birth in Spain. He recalls the good omens which accompanied his mother's pregnancy and his baptism, and the auspicious significance of his name and those of his parents.

Emphasis is laid not simply on Dominic's great learning, but more especially on his use of that learning in order to fight energetically, defending the Faith against heresy. He is "the holy athlete".

As St Thomas has lamented the corruption of his own order, the Dominicans, so now St Bonaventura laments the corruption of so many in his own Franciscan Order. His main concern is the harm caused by the rift between those Franciscans who wish to relax their Rule and those who wish to interpret it even more strictly.

After naming several other saints in the outer circle – all known for devoting their learning to God – St Bonaventura says that he has been moved to praise the founder of the Dominican Order by the praise accorded to the founder of his own order by the Dominican St Thomas. The two orders, so often regarded in this life as rivals, are seen in this and the previous canto to be complementary in their defence of the purity of the Christian faith.

✳

T he instant that the sacred flame¹ began
    Pronouncing the last word it had to say,
    The blessed millstone² was on the move again,
And it had not revolved completely round
    Before a second circle had embraced it
    And matched it both in motion and in sound –
Such singing as excels, it is so sweet,
    Our Muses and our Sirens, by as much
    As direct light outshines reflected light.
And like two arches curving in thin cloud,   10
    Concentric, corresponding in their colours,
    When Juno gives the word to her handmaid,³
The outer one being born from that within,
    Like what was spoken by the errant nymph
    Consumed by love as mist is by the sun,⁴

---

1   Representing St Thomas Aquinas.
2   The circle of lights representing souls in the sun.
3   Iris, the messenger of Juno, used to leave a rainbow behind when she came to earth.
4   The nymph Echo was so consumed by her unrequited love for Narcissus that she wasted away until nothing was left of her but her voice, an echo.

Making it certain for the people here,
    According to the pact God made with Noah,
    This world will not be flooded any more[1] –
In just that way the sempiternal roses
    Were turning round about us in two garlands,   20
    The outer answering what it encloses.
When all that dancing and festivity,
    The singing and the constant flashing-out
    Of light on light in glad benignity,
In the same instant with one will was over,
    Just as our eyes, reacting to delight,
    Are thrown wide open or shut tight together,
From the profundity of one of those
    New lights a voice was heard and, like the needle[2]
    Towards the north, I turned to where it was,   30
And it began: "The love which makes me shine
    Leads me to celebrate that other leader[3]
    Because of whom I hear such good of mine.[4]
It is but right that, where one is, the other
    Be introduced since, as they fought as one
    They ought to gleam in gloriousness together.
The army led by Christ, which cost so dear
    To re-equip, was following His standard
    Slowly, and in small numbers, full of fear,
When the Emperor, Whose rule is limitless,   40
    Aided His troops in all their doubt and danger,
    And not for their desert but from His grace.
And, as we've heard, He sent to help his Bride[5]
    Two champions, by whose actions and whose preaching
    The people reassembled who had strayed.
In that part of the world[6] where gentle Zephyr
    Arises to disclose the greenery
    Which Europe welcomes as her novel vesture,[7]
Not distant from the pounding of that sea[8]
    Wherein, grown weary of the lengthening days,   50
    The sun in season[9] hides itself away,
The favoured town of Caleruega sits
    Under protection of that mighty shield

---

1   Gen. 9:12–15.
2   Magnetic needle.
3   St Dominic.
4   St Francis.
5   The Church.
6   Western Europe, the Spanish peninsula in particular.
7   In springtime.
8   The Atlantic.
9   The summer solstice.

In which the subject lion subjugates.[1]
And there it was that champion arose
    Who loved the Christian faith – the holy athlete,[2]
    Kind to his own, and cruel to his foes.
His mind at its creation was so full
    Of energy and force that in the womb
    He made his mother's dreams prophetical.[3]   60
And when the nuptial promises were made
    Over the font by him and by the faith,
    Where mutual salvation was bestowed,[4]
The lady giving his agreement[5] was
    Shown in her sleep the wonderful results
    To come from him and his inheritors.[6]
To show his very essence by his name,
    A spirit went from here to have them call him
    After his Lord in the possessive form.[7]
So he was Dominic: as I have said,   70
    He was the husbandman elect of Christ
    To labour in His garden and give aid.
As servant and as messenger of Christ,
    The first affection that he ever showed
    Was to the first instruction given by Christ.[8]
He was found by his nurse so many a time
    Silent and wide-awake upon the floor,[9]
    As if he said: 'It was for this I came.'
Félix was his father, and named truly![10]
    Juana was his mother, just as truly,[11]   80
    If names mean what they say, translated duly!
Not for the sake of worldly wealth and honour,
    As men ape Taddeo[12] or the Ostian,[13]
    But simply for the love of the true manna,

---

1   Caleruega, St Dominic's birthplace, is in Castile. Its arms bore a castle in two of the quarterings and a lion in the other two, so that in one place the lion was below the castle and in another above it.

2   St Dominic.

3   According to legend, his mother dreamt that she gave birth to a dog which was black and white (the colours of the Dominican Order) holding in its mouth a torch with which it set fire to the world. The Dominicans were known as *Domini canes* (the hounds of the Lord).

4   At his baptism, when he and faith were married.

5   His godmother (one who at baptism makes the responses on behalf of the baby).

6   She was said to have dreamt of him with a star on his forehead to light up the world.

7   *Dominicus* ("belonging to the Lord") in Latin.

8   It is uncertain whether this alludes to poverty or humility.

9   When he might have been expected to be in bed.

10   Félix, from the Latin *félix*, meaning "happy".

11   The name Juana (derived from Hebrew) was understood as meaning "grace of God".

12   Probably Taddeo d'Alderotto, a writer on medical matters (*d*.1295).

13   Henry of Segusio, Bishop of Ostia (*d*.1271), a canon lawyer.

He was, in no great time, a learned teacher,
　　Such that he came to oversee the vineyard
　　Which soon turns grey, ill-tended by its keeper.
And of that Seat[1] which used to be more kind
　　To the deserving poor (now too corrupted
　　By him who sits on it) he made demand,　　　　　　90
Not to give two or three for six,[2] or for
　　The blessing of a vacant benefice,[3]
　　Or for the tithes belonging to God's poor,
But rather for the right to make a stand
　　Against the erring world, and for that seed[4]
　　Whence grew those four-and-twenty plants around.[5]
Then with his learning and his zeal combined,
　　With apostolic sanction he swept down,
　　A torrent tumbling from the highest ground,
Among the scrubs of heresy, and smote　　　　　　100
　　With greatest impetus and energy
　　Where the resistance was most obstinate.
And then from him the various rivulets sprang
　　To water and sustain the Catholic garden
　　And make its saplings grow more straight and strong.
If that was one wheel of the chariot
　　That Holy Church guided in her defence
　　To win the civil war she had to fight,
To you the other's excellence must be plain –
　　I mean that other wheel[6] about whom Thomas　　　110
　　Spoke with such courtesy before I came.
And yet the furrow where that wheel once rolled
　　Is now abandoned, like a cask of wine
　　Neglected till the crust has turned to mould.
His household, which was once so strictly bound
　　Upon his footprints, has now turned about,
　　And those in front walk into those behind.
Soon we shall see, when the harvest's gathered in,
　　How poor the cultivation, as the tares[7]
　　Complain at being banished from the barn.　　　　120
I do admit that if we rummaged in
　　Our volume leaf by leaf, we might discover
　　One page which read 'I am what I have been' –

1　The Papacy.
2　Distribute only a part of what was meant for the poor, keeping the rest for himself.
3　With a revenue but no responsibility.
4　The Christian faith.
5　The two circles of souls on Mars.
6　St Francis.
7　Those friars who have not persevered in their calling. See Matt. 13:24–30.

Not from Casale,[1] though, or Acquasparta,[2]
   Who, in interpreting our holy rule,
   Make it more loose, or pull it even tighter.
I am Bonaventura's soul.[3] I was
   From Bagnoregio: in high offices
   I always gave less thought to worldly cares.
Illuminato and Augustine[4] here   130
   Were of the first poor friars to go unshod
   And gain God's friendship with the cord they wore.[5]
Hugh of St Victor's[6] shining here with them,
   Petrus Comestor,[7] and the Spanish Peter,[8]
   Who shines down there in many a weighty tome;
Nathan prophet,[9] the Metropolitan
   Chrysostom,[10] Anselm,[11] and that Donatus[12]
   Who treated the first art with no disdain.
Rabanus[13] is here, and shining at my side
   The abbot of Calabria, Joachim,[14]   140
   Whose spirit was prophetically endowed.
In giving this great paladin[15] such praise
   I was moved by the warmth and courtesy
   Of Brother Thomas and his lucid phrase,[16]
As were indeed all of this company.

1   Followers of Ubertino da Casale (1259–1338), who interpreted the Franciscan Rule very
    strictly.
2   Followers of Matteo d'Acquasparta (d.1302), who favoured a relaxation of the Franciscan
    Rule.
3   As General of the Franciscans he worked for a compromise between the two extreme
    interpretations of their Rule.
4   Two of the earliest followers of St Francis.
5   See *Par.* XI, 87 and note.
6   Theologian (c.1097–1141).
7   Author of a paraphrase of the Scriptures (d.1179).
8   Wrote *inter alia* a treatise on logic. He became Pope John XXI. Died 1277.
9   Jewish prophet at the time of King David.
10 St John Chrysostom (c.345–407), one of the greatest Fathers of the Greek Church.
11 Archbishop of Canterbury 1093–1109.
12 Roman author (fourth century AD) of a standard work on grammar, the first of the
    Seven Liberal Arts.
13 Theologian (c.776–856).
14 The Cistercian Joachim of Fiore (c.1132–1202), author of many prophecies.
15 St Dominic.
16 In his praise of St Francis in the previous canto.

CANTO XIII

Dante sees the souls in the sun as two concentric circles of lights revolving in opposite directions. Imagining these circles as formed from the brightest stars in our sky gives an idea – but only a vague and inadequate idea – of their appearance. As they move they sing hymns to the Trinity.

Once the movement and singing have stopped, St Thomas Aquinas speaks once more. Having already explained some words of his own about those who fall away from the true vocation of the Dominican Order, he will now clear up another problem that is perplexing Dante. How can it be true, as St Thomas has said, that no one was ever as wise as Solomon?

St Thomas's explanation is based on a detailed exposition of creation. Angels and men's souls are created immediately by God and are therefore immortal, while all that is formed rather than created (including plants and animals and the human body) through the angels as intermediaries is imperfect and short-lived. Adam's understanding before the Fall must have been as great as it was possible for a human being to have, since he was created directly by God – and Christ, since He is God as well as man, must understand everything. St Thomas explains that the contradiction between those certainties and what he has previously said about Solomon is only apparent, since the wisdom which Solomon asked for and received was merely the practical wisdom necessary for his work as king. He was not concerned with anything beyond that.

This leads St Thomas to emphasize what is implicit in his explanation – that no human being should dare to seek for theological understanding unless he is skilled in such matters, and he must be slow to come to conclusions. Many theologians have gone astray because they lacked those qualities. In more mundane matters also we should be aware that we may easily deceive ourselves, since we cannot see as God sees.

Now let him picture, who would truly seek
    To grasp what I now saw – and while I'm talking
    Hold on to what he pictures like a rock –
Those fifteen stars[1] that, scattered here and there
    About the heavens, light them up so brightly
    They overcome the cloudy atmosphere;
Imagine too that Wain[2] which day and night
    Is bound within the limits of our sky,
    So that, revolving, it remains in sight;
Imagine too the wide mouth of that horn,[3]   10
    Whose narrow end is seated at the axle
    The Primum Mobile is turning on;
Think that these stars form two signs in the sky,
    Most like the constellation that was fashioned

---

1   Stars of the first magnitude visible in the northern hemisphere.

2   The constellation also known as Ursa Major (the Great Bear), seven stars which never set in the northern hemisphere.

3   Ursa Minor, a constellation in the shape of a horn, with two stars at its mouth, and with the Pole Star (the axis on which the Primum Mobile revolves) at its narrow end.

By Minos' daughter when she came to die;[1]
And think their rays reach to a common centre,
  While they are turning, and in such a fashion
  That one goes one way and one goes the other[2] –
Then you will have some shadow, a mere taste
  Of the real constellation and the double   20
  Dancing around the spot where I was placed.
All this is far beyond our grasp, as far
  As is, above the motion of the Chiana,[3]
  The motion of the fastest-turning sphere.[4]
Bacchus they did not sing, or Paean[5] either:
  They hymned three Persons in one God, and hymned
  In One of Them[6] both God and human nature.
The singing and the dance had run their measure,
  And then those holy torches turned to us,
  Happy to move from one care to another.   30
The silence of those souls in harmony
  Was broken by that light[7] by whom the wondrous
  Life of God's pauper had been told to me.
He said: "When one sheaf has been threshed, and when
  Its grain is stored inside the barn already,
  Sweet love leads me to thresh the other one.
You think that in that side,[8] from which was drawn
  The rib which formed the lovely face[9] whose greedy
  Palate has cost the whole world such great pain,
And into His which, wounded by the lance,   40
  Made satisfaction both for past and future,[10]
  Tipping the scale against the whole offence,
Such understanding as our human nature
  Is fitted for has been implanted by
  That Power which made the one and made the other;
And so you wonder whether I was right
  When I affirmed 'no second paralleled'
  The wisdom which was found in the fifth light.[11]
So open up your mind now as I answer:

---

1 The garland worn by Ariadne (daughter of Minos, King of Crete) was changed into a circular constellation known as Ariadne's Crown.

2 The souls are represented as forming two circular constellations on the same axis, revolving in opposite directions.

3 A very sluggish Tuscan river.

4 The Primum Mobile.

5 Apollo.

6 Christ.

7 St Thomas Aquinas.

8 Adam's.

9 Eve's.

10 At the Crucifixion.

11 Solomon (*Par.* x, 109-14).

You'll see that what you think and what I said   50
   Meet in the truth, the target's very centre.
All things which die and those which cannot die
   Are only the reflection of that Word
   Our loving Lord begets eternally,
Because that living Light that so goes from
   Its Source it never separates from It,
   Or from the Love which makes up three with them,
Of Its own goodness focuses Its rays
   As in a mirror – still remaining one
   Eternally – in nine existences.[1]   60
Thence It descends to the last potencies
   From heaven to heaven, till at the last It's such
   That all It makes are brief contingencies[2] –
And these contingencies, by definition,
   Are those things generated, those produced
   With or without seed by the heavens in motion.
Neither the wax they're made of nor the force
   That moulds them is unvaried – so the Light
   Divine shines through them either more or less.
Just so it happens the same kind of trees   70
   Bear some good fruit and others rather worse –
   And you are born with differing tendencies.
Now if the wax were moulded at its best,
   And if the heavenly powers were at their finest,
   The seal's full brilliance would be manifest,
But nature's working never is quite sound:
   In operation she is like the artist
   Who shows his skill, but with a shaky hand.
Yet if the ardent Love conveys the clear
   Vision of the original Worth, and seals it,   80
   Perfection is achieved, and only there.
In this way dust was dignified and filled
   With the perfection of a living being[3] –
   In this way was the Virgin brought with Child.
I say therefore that what you say is true,
   That human nature never ever was,
   Or shall be, what it was within those two.[4]
Should I proceed no further in this way,
   'How can you think he was unparalleled
   Therefore?' is what you would begin to say.   90
To make what's far from obvious manifest,
   Think who he[5] was, and think what reason moved him,

---

1   The orders of angels who move the spheres.
2   Transient things.
3   The creation of Adam, perfect before the Fall.
4   Adam and Christ.
5   Solomon.

When told to ask, to make such a request.
I am not so obscure that you cannot
   Perceive he was a king, who asked for wisdom
   That as a king he might be adequate,
And not to number all the stars in motion,
   Or know if necessary with contingent
   Premises ever give a sound conclusion,[1]
Whether a *primum motum*[2] is a must,   100
   Or if a triangle, with no right angle
   And in a semicircle, can exist.
So, if you think of what I said and say,
   Then royal prudence is the unparalleled
   Vision I aimed at speaking previously.
'No second paralleled' should now be clear:
   It was meant only with regard to kings,
   Who are so many, while good kings are rare.
And this distinction serves to clarify
   How what I said concurs with your idea   110
   Of the first father[3] and of our great Joy.[4]
And may this always make you feel you're shod
   With lead, and make you plod on like one weary
   Towards the yes or no when vision's blurred;
For he must be of all men stupidest
   Who goes about affirming or denying
   When relevant distinctions have been missed:
Opinions formed too rapidly distract
   The mind and lead it on to false conclusions,
   Or else emotion clogs the intellect.   120
It is far worse than ineffectual –
   Since no one ever ends up as he started –
   To angle for the truth, but with no skill.
Parmenides, Melissus, Bryson[5] are
   Obvious examples in the world, and others
   Who went on walking without knowing where –
Sabellius,[6] Arius,[7] many an idiot,
   Acting like polished swords towards the Scripture,
   Strangely distorting the straight face of it.[8]
Again, men should not ever feel too sure   130

---

1   Whether, in a syllogism, an uncertainty in one of the premises can give a valid conclu-
    sion: e.g. A=B, and B *may* equal C, therefore A=C.
2   Something which, itself unmoved, produces motion.
3   Adam.
4   Christ.
5   Three pagan Greek philosophers.
6   A third-century theologian who denied the doctrine of the Trinity.
7   A fourth-century theologian who denied the divinity of Christ.
8   Probably we are meant to think of Scripture reflected in a distorted form, as in curved
    metal, but there is also a suggestion of Scripture being hacked about.

Of their own judgement, like a farmer counting
　His ears of corn before they are mature.
For I have seen the brier, which always shows
　Itself as stiff and bristling through the winter,
　Bear afterwards upon its crest the rose –
And I have seen a ship go sailing straight
　And speedily throughout its lengthy voyage,
　And finally be wrecked outside the port.
Nor should Tom, Dick or Harry ever hold,
　Because he sees one give, another steal,　　　　　　　140
　That he is looking with the eye of God:
For one may rise up and the other fall."

CANTO XIV

When St Thomas has spoken from the circle of lights and is answered by Beatrice in the centre of the circle, Dante is reminded of how water moves when struck in different ways. Beatrice speaks for Dante (understanding his unspoken thoughts, just as Virgil always did). She asks St Thomas whether the glorified souls will be dazzled, after the Day of Judgement, by the light surrounding them, which they will then be seeing with the eyes of their resurrected bodies.

The soul of Solomon answers Beatrice, saying that the joy of Heaven will be continually increased when souls are reunited with their bodies, and since all the organs of the resurrected bodies will be enhanced, their eyes will be able to bear that light. Indeed, just as coal can produce flame, and yet continue to glow brighter than that flame, so the risen bodies will be brighter than the light which now surrounds them.

Now lights, like stars gradually becoming visible at twilight, appear beyond the circle of the souls. Dante realizes that he has risen to another planet, one glowing red, the planet Mars. He sees two rays forming a cross on which Christ appears as a shining light. Lights are moving up and down the upright of the cross, and back and forth along the crossbeam. These are like motes in a ray of sunlight. From these lights comes a subtle music, joyful but ineffable.

Dante, fearing that he may seem to be slighting the delight inspired by Beatrice's eyes, explains how the joy they give grows more intense as they ascend through the spheres.

It is striking how Dante, in his efforts to express what is for a mortal inexpressible, returns again and again to the primal elements of fire and water, and appeals to what are perhaps the most important of our human senses – sight and hearing.

From brim to centre, from centre to the brim
   Of a round bowl the water is displaced,
   As it is struck outside or struck within.
That very notion I have just expressed
   Occurred the instant that the explanation
   Launched by the shining soul of Thomas[1] ceased,
Because a similarity was born
   Between his speech and that of Beatrice,[2]
   Who after he had spoken thus began:
"This man here has a need, one he has not   10
   Expressed in words or even mentally,
   To trace another truth down to its root.
That light which makes you blossom, tell him whether
   Or not it will remain to shine around you
   Exactly as it now is and for ever,
And then explain how, if it does remain,

---

1   At *Par.* XIII, 34–142.
2   St Thomas has spoken from his place on the circle of lights to Dante in its centre, and Beatrice is about to speak from the centre to St Thomas on the circle, as hinted in ll. 1–3.

Once you yourselves are remade visible,[1]
    It will not harm your eyesight when it's seen."
As, animated by increasing joy,
    Sometimes the dancers dancing in a ring   20
    Lift their voices and dance more happily,
So, at this eager and devout appeal,
    The sacred circles showed intensifying
    Joy in their whirling and their canticle.
Whoever mourns that we, to live again
    Up there, must die here, has not comprehended
    The cool refreshment of the eternal rain.
The One and Two and Three, perpetual,
    Living and reigning Three and Two and One,
    Not circumscribed, but circumscribing all,   30
Was thrice hymned by those spirits, every one,
    And hymned with such a melody as would
    For any merit make a just return.
Then I heard, from within the most intense
    Light of the lesser ring,[2] some modest words,
    Soft as the angel's voice to Mary once,[3]
Answering: "While the feast of Paradise
    Endures, for such a length of time our love
    Will radiate around us like a dress.
Its brightness follows from our eagerness,   40
    Eagerness from our vision, which is such
    As grace abounds beyond our worthiness.
When our flesh is transfigured, and we wear
    It, glorious and holy, once again,
    We shall, perfected now, please all the more,
With hence an increase in that light of grace
    The Highest Good bestows upon us freely,
    Light which enables us to see His Face –
By means of which the vision grows more great,
    More great the eagerness which that enkindles,   50
    More great the radiance coming out of it.
But, just as coal may generate a flame
    And by its incandescence still outshine it,
    So that it is itself not overcome –
So will this brilliance shining all around
    Us be outshone by resurrected flesh,
    Which all this while lies hidden in the ground.
Nor will we be offended by that light:
    The organs of our bodies will be strengthened
    To welcome all that gives us such delight."   60

---

1   When, after the Last Judgement, souls are reunited with their bodies.
2   Solomon (see *Par.* x, 109).
3   At the Annunciation.

They seemed to me so quick to cry "Amen",
    Both of these choruses, that just how much
    They longed for their dead bodies was made plain:
And not just for themselves, but for their mothers
    And for their fathers, all they loved before
    They were eternal flames – so many others.
And suddenly a gleam, lustrous throughout,
    Appeared around the one already there,
    As when the skyline gently grows more light.
And just as, with the evening drawing near,   70
    The sky begins to show new semblances,[1]
    Such that it seems they are and are not there,
It seemed I saw some new existences
    Beginning to be visible, a circle
    Beyond the other two circumferences.
Oh true effulgence of the Holy Breath!
    So sudden, so candescent that my eyes,
    Unable to endure it, sank beneath!
But Beatrice was now revealed to me,
    So smiling-lovely she is left among   80
    Those visions that escape the memory.
My eyes regained their usual strength at that:
    I looked up, and I found myself transported
    Alone with Beatrice to a higher state.
I was assured that I had gone up higher
    By the enkindled smiling of the star
    Which more than usual glowed more red than fire.
With all my heart, and in that wordless manner
    Common to all, I gave myself entirely
    To God, as fitting for this further favour.   90
The blaze of sacrifice within my breast
    Had not died down before I realized
    My offering was accepted and was blessed;
For with such gleaming and such fiery glow
    Splendours appeared to me within two rays
    That I cried: "Helios,[2] you deck them so!"
Just as, tricked out with bright stars and more bright,
    The Galaxy gleams white from pole to pole,
    Bewildering even the most erudite,[3]
So, constellated in the depth of Mars,[4]   100
    Those two rays formed the venerable sign
    A circle parcelled out in quadrants does.
My memory here has overcome my wit:

---

1   Stars.
2   The Greek word for the sun, here used for God.
3   As to the origin, nature and purpose of the Galaxy.
4   This is the planet (already suggested in l. 87 by its redness) to which Dante and Beatrice
have now risen.

For radiating from that cross was Christ,
   And I can find no simile for that –
But who takes up his cross and follows Christ
   Will surely pardon me for my omission,
   When he sees whiteness which is blazing Christ.[1]
From arm to arm, and from the head and base,
   Lights were moving and throwing out great sparkles   110
   When they were meeting, when they came to pass:
Just as on earth we see – twisting and straight,
   Rapid and slow, and always shifting shape –
   The tiniest particles, some long, some short,
Moving around throughout the ray of light
   Streaking the shade which, for their own protection,
   People contrive to find or fabricate.
And as a harp or viol, strung and tuned,
   Sends from so many strings a subtle music
   To one who cannot separate each sound,   120
So from the lights that I was seeing there
   A melody was mustered on the cross
   Which thrilled me, though its meaning was not clear.
I recognized it as a song of praise,
   Because there came to me *"Resurgi"*, *"Vinci"*,[2]
   As to someone who can't tell what he hears.
And I was so enamoured of that sound
   That up until that time there had been nothing
   Holding me quite so tightly, sweetly bound.
Perhaps I seem too bold, speaking like this,   130
   And seem to slight the pleasure of those eyes[3]
   Which bring me when I look in them such peace.
But he who sees that the insignia
   Of beauty[4] have more power the higher we go,
   And that I'd not yet turned to where they were,
Will certainly deny the accusation
   I bring for my excuse – my words are clear:
   That holy pleasure suffers no exclusion,
But grows, in its ascending, more and more.

---

1   When he goes to Heaven. Christ's name in Dante's *Comedy* only ever rhymes with itself, and does so in *Paradise* three times, in three places. See also *Par.* XII, 71–75 and XXXII, 83–87.
2   "Arise" and "Conquer" (presumably from an Easter hymn).
3   Beatrice's.
4   Eyes.

CANTO XV

The music coming from the cross stops. One of the lights on the cross moves swiftly along an arm of it and down to its foot. Then the light speaks – in Latin, surprisingly – to reveal that he is one of Dante's own family. He speaks at first in Latin not only to emphasize that this is an important moment, but also to relate the meeting more closely to an analogous one – the meeting of Aeneas in the Underworld with the shade of his dead father Anchises, as related in the *Aeneid*. Dante leaves the implications of this to be understood by the reader who knows his Virgil: Anchises provides an account of the future of Rome, and this leaves us to expect some prophecies from this shade to Dante.

After those first few words the light speaks in Italian, but expresses thoughts which Dante does not understand, because they are beyond any mortal's comprehension. Then he says things which Dante does comprehend: he praises the Holy Trinity, and says how blessed he is in his descendants.

This soul has waited for a long time for Dante to arrive. He knows Dante's wishes before they are spoken, and yet he asks Dante to express them, a courteous action which will make his joy complete. Dante does this, and the soul reveals with considerable detail that he is Dante's great-great-grandfather. Then he launches into praise of Florence as it was when he was born, in contrast with how it has become in Dante's day. Its citizens were, he says, frugal in their habits and simple in their dress, and honest in their dealings. It is an idealized picture – one that could hardly be seen as other than idealized – whose purpose is not to teach history but to attack the current state of Florence and its citizens.

Eventually the soul reveals precisely who he is: Cacciaguida, who died fighting against Saracens in the Holy Land, and is now therefore in Heaven.

✳

The will to good, which is always distilled
  Out of the love which longs for righteousness
  (Just as greed leads to what is wrongly willed),
Imposed now quietude upon that sweet
  Lyre,[1] and immobilized those sacred strings
  Made by Heaven's hand melodious or mute.
Can they be deaf to prayers made in good will,
  Those beings who, in urging me to pray
  To them, agreed to be inaudible?
It is but right he suffers endlessly   10
  Who, in desire for things that do not last,
  Strips himself of this love eternally.
As through the clear and tranquil evening skies
  A sudden fire will shoot from time to time,
  Such as to activate incurious eyes,
And seem to be a star shifting its station –
  Except that from the place where it was kindled
  Nothing is lost, and it has no duration –

---

1   The cross formed by the souls on Mars.

So, from the right arm of the cross one star
    Passed rapidly, and so down to the foot   20
    Of the whole constellation shining there –
Nor did that gem desert its ribbon[1] after,
    But ran along the radials of the cross,[2]
    Which looked like fire glimpsed under alabaster.
Anchises' shade with like affection ran –
    If faith is given to our greatest poet –
    When in Elysium he saw his son.[3]
"O sanguis meus, o superinfusa
    Gratia Dei, sicut tibi cui
    Bis unquam cœli ianua reclusa?"[4]   30
Those words came from that light; I turned to him,
    And then turned my attention to my lady,
    And then by both of them was overcome –
For such a smile was blazing in her eyes
    I thought my eyes had reached the utmost bound
    Of my being blessed and of my paradise.
And then – and what a joy to hear and see –
    That spirit added things to his first greeting
    I could not understand, too deep for me;
Nor did he hide himself deliberately   40
    But from necessity, for his conceptions
    Went far beyond a man's capacity.
And when his bow of burning love had slacked
    So much that his discourse was comprehended
    Within the range of human intellect,
The first expression that I understood
    Was this: "Blessèd be You, both Three and One,
    Who are so generous to me in my seed!"
And then: "A pleasurable, long-standing hunger –
    Drawn from my reading of that mighty volume[5]   50
    In which the black and white can never alter –
Has been assuaged by you, son, in this light
    In which I speak to you, and thanks to her[6]
    Who gave you feathers for the lofty flight.
You think your thoughts flow into me from Him
    Who is the First, as digits five and six,

---

1   As the light moves it resembles a jewel strung on a ribbon.
2   It is a Greek cross, i.e. its arms are of equal length (as are the radii of a circle): see *Par.* XIV,
    100–2.
3   *Aeneid* VI, 684*ff*.
4   "O you who share my blood! O God's good grace / Which overflows! Was ever for
    another, / As thus to you, heaven's gate thrown open twice?" The use of Latin stresses
    the importance of the occasion. The word "twice" alludes to Dante's present journey
    and his salvation after death.
5   God's knowledge of the future.
6   Beatrice.

Say, come from the number one when that is known,
And therefore fail to ask who I may be,
    And why I seem to you to be more joyful
    Than others in this happy company.   60
You are not wrong: the lesser and the great
    Spirits in this life gaze into that Mirror[1]
    Which shows your thought before you think of it;
But, that the sacred love in which I've waited
    And watched so long – which rouses such a thirst
    Of sweet desire – be the more fully sated,
Let your assured, bold, happy voice be heard
    Expressing all the will and the desire
    To which my answer has been long decreed!"
I turned to Beatrice – she heard before   70
    I spoke – and then she smiled at me, a gesture
    Which magnified the wings of my desire.
Then I began to speak: "Love and insight,
    Once you beheld the Prime Equality,
    Became for both of you of equal weight,
Because the sun which warmed you with its light
    Has heat and brightness so unvariable
    That any simile perforce falls short.
But in mankind will and capacity,
    For reasons which are obvious to you,   80
    Are feathered for the flight unequally:
So I, a mortal and all too aware
    Of this disparity, render no thanks,
    But in my heart, for your paternal care.
I beg of you, you living topaz, gem
    Adorning this inestimable necklace,[2]
    To satisfy me, giving me your name."
"O my dear branch, in which I took such pleasure
    Merely expecting you, I am your root."
Such was the way that he began his answer,   90
Then said: "The man[3] who gave your family
    Its name, who for a hundred years and more
    Rounds the first terrace of Mount Purgatory,
Was son to me and your grandfather's father:
    It is appropriate that you should shorten
    With your good works his long-protracted labour.
Florence, within those walls which were built first[4]
    And where she still receives both terce and nones,[5]

---

1   God, in Whom all thoughts are reflected.
2   The shining cross.
3   Alighiero, Dante's great-grandfather, whom Dante speaks of as dead for over one hundred
    years in 1300 (the date given to Dante's journey).
4   Said to have been built in the age of Charlemagne.
5   The hours for prayer sounded from the Badia, a church close to the old walls of Florence.

Lived long ago in peace, sober and chaste.
There was no fancy chain, no coronet,   100
   No fine embroidered skirt, no belt or sash
   More striking than the person wearing it.
No daughter at her birth dismayed her father,
   When neither marriageable age nor dowry,
   Too soon, too much, exceeded the right measure.
There were no houses larger than men need,
   For Sardanapalus[1] had not yet come
   To show what can be done at home in bed.[2]
Then your Uccellatoio'd[3] not outdone
   Rome's Monte Mario,[4] which, as in its splendour,   110
   Will be exceeded too in its decline.
Bellincion Berti[5] – I have seen him pass
   With belt of bone and leather, and his lady
   Come from her mirror with unpainted face;
The lords de' Nerli and del Vecchio,[6] all
   Wearing but simple leather, with their ladies
   Content to tend the spindle and the spool.[7]
Happy ladies! Each of them still assured
   Of her own burial place, and none for France[8]
   Was left to lie in a deserted bed.   120
One watched above the cradle,[9] and she used,
   To soothe her child, that childish idiom
   Which always keeps the parents well amused;
One, drawing thread from distaff, in her home
   With all her household gathered round her, told
   Tales of the Trojans, Fiesole and Rome.[10]
A Lapo Salterello,[11] a Cianghella[12]
   Would have been then just such a prodigy
   As Cincinnatus[13] now would or Cornelia.[14]
To such a settled life, to such well-bred   130

1   Ancient King of Assyria, proverbial for effeminate luxury.
2   A deliberately vague statement, to convey horror and disgust.
3   A hill which affords the first sight of Florence to travellers from the north.
4   A hill which affords the first sight of Rome to travellers from the north.
5   A twelfth-century Florentine of the ancient Ravignani family, known for his simple
   clothing.
6   Ancient noble Florentine families.
7   Intended literally, and also by metonymy for all honourable household duties.
8   One of the countries to which Florentine merchants of Dante's day made long trips on
   business.
9   She did not, that is, leave it to the servants.
10 According to legend, Rome was founded by refugees from Troy, and Florence by Romans
   and Fiesolans.
11 A corrupt contemporary of Dante.
12 A Florentine woman of ill repute, contemporary with Dante.
13 A Roman of the fifth century BC, known for his frugality and integrity. See *Par.* VI, 47.
14 A virtuous woman of Republican Rome, mentioned in contrast to Cianghella.

Citizens' lives, to such an uncorrupted
Citizenship, to such a sweet abode
Our Lady gave me when my mother prayed her[1] –
And I within your ancient Baptistery[2]
Became a Christian[3] and Cacciaguida.
Moronto and Eliseo were brothers of mine:
My bride was from the Valley of the Po –
From her forebears your surname[4] is handed down.
Later I followed and I served Conrad
The Emperor;[5] he girded me his knight,   140
Being well satisfied with all I did.
With him I marched against that evil, that
Religion[6] which deprives you and your people,
Because your pastors fail you, of your right.[7]
And there I was disburdened, by that foul
Race, of this world,[8] which is so treacherous
That love of it has ruined many a soul,
And came by martyrdom[9] into this peace."

---

1   When his mother was giving birth.
2   The Baptistery of San Giovanni.
3   Was baptized.
4   Aldighieri, and then Alighieri.
5   Emperor Conrad III of Swabia (r. 1138–52).
6   Islam.
7   The Holy Land.
8   I.e. killed.
9   Death incurred while fighting for the Faith.

CANTO XVI

Dante is both pleased and a little surprised to find that respect for nobility of blood is found even in Heaven. In great awe, and rather to Beatrice's amusement, Dante asks Cacciaguida about their common ancestors and the Florence that he knew. Cacciaguida is delighted to be asked. He will not talk about their ancestors, but rather about the state of Florence in his day, to make clear the contrast between that and the city Dante knows.

Cacciaguida was born in the most ancient part of the city, at a time when its adult male population was a fifth of what it had since become. This was a city where everyone, from the highest by blood and office down to the most humble workman, was of pure Florentine descent. The moral corruption of the city is, according to Cacciaguida, the result of the pollution of this blood by families from outside the city. He mentions numerous families whose actions are reprehensible, and also some which have since his day simply disappeared. The climax of his lament is his reference to Buondelmonte de' Buondelmonti's grave fault in jilting a member of the Amidei family, an action which led to his murder and hence to the feuds which still bedevil Florence a century later.

The attempt of the Catholic priesthood to usurp temporal power, which Dante believes should belong to the Emperor, does not escape blame for civil disruption and moral decline. But the main theme here is Cacciaguida's belief in high birth and the purity of blood: he is strongly against miscegenation (which in his account includes the acceptance of relations with people from only a few miles away). Cacciaguida's – and we must assume also Dante's – lament for "the good old days" and his blame of "outsiders" for whatever is wrong give his speech a powerful emotional (if not intellectual) appeal, even though the names of many of the families he mentions mean little or nothing now.

> O h, our petty nobility of blood!
>   That you can make men take a pride in you,
>   On earth where there is little love of good,
> No longer seems to me a miracle,
>   For there, where appetite is uncorrupted,
>   In Heaven, I gloried in you to the full.
> Nobility's a cloak that quickly wears:
>   We have to patch and mend it day by day –
>   Time travels swiftly round it with his shears.
> Then with that plural "you" first used in Rome,   10
>   But which her people now use less and less,
>   As I spoke up again, I honoured him.[1]
> And Beatrice, who stood somewhat apart,
>   Smiled, rather like that lady who discreetly
>   Coughed, hearing Guinevere's first noted fault.[2]

---

1   This respectful form of address is used by Dante only to Brunetto Latini, Farinata and Cavalcante (all in *Inferno*), and to Beatrice.

2   Her fault was a declaration of love for Lancelot. Beatrice is gently smiling at Dante's pride in his ancestry.

And I began to address him: "You are my
   Father, and you encourage me to speak:
   You lift me up till I am more than I.
So many channels feed and fill my heart
   With happiness, it joys in its own joy   20
   That it can bear this and not burst apart.
So tell me, O dear root from which I spring:
   Who were your ancestors, what were the years
   The records registered when you were young?
Tell me about the sheepfold of St John:[1]
   How many lived in it, and who they were
   Who merited the highest place therein."[2]
As a coal rouses at a passing breeze
   And bursts into a flame, just so that light[3]
   Glowed and grew brighter at my loving speech.   30
And as it grew more glorious in my eyes,
   So in a sweeter and more gentle tone,
   Not in the idiom of these modern days,
He said: "From that day 'Ave' was first spoken[4]
   Until my mother, who is now a saint,
   Delivered me, with whom she had been laden,
Five hundred and eighty times this fire of Mars
   Had come back to its own familiar Lion[5]
   To be rekindled underneath its paws.
My ancestors and I were all born where   40
   The riders in your city's annual race
   Enter the last of all the districts there.[6]
Let that suffice as to my ancestors:
   Who they might be, and whence, it would be better
   To leave unsaid than hold a long discourse.
All capable of bearing arms who were
   Between Mars and the Baptist[7] at that time
   Numbered a fifth of those now living there.
But the community, now mixed with men
   From Campi, from Certaldo, from Figline,[8]   50
   Was pure down to the lowliest artisan.
Oh, how much better if they were your neighbours,[9]

---

1   Florence, whose patron saint was John the Baptist.
2   Referring not only to noble blood but to high office.
3   Cacciaguida.
4   At the Annunciation.
5   The constellation Leo. Cacciaguida was born in 1091. The influence of Mars and Leo
    was propitious for one who was to be a brave soldier.
6   The district of Porta San Piero, the most ancient part of the City.
7   Between the statue of Mars at the Ponte Vecchio and the Baptistery of San Giovanni,
    i.e. in Florence.
8   Areas in Florentine territory.
9   Rather than citizens.

Those coming from outside, while at Galluzzo
And at Trespiano[1] you preserved your borders,
Than to endure the stench of them inside,
 That scum from Aguglione and that from Signa[2]
 Already with their eyes well-skinned for fraud!
If those who, in the world, have most declined
 Had not been like a stepmother to Caesar,
 But, as a mother to her son, been kind,   60
Then one, a Florentine engaged in trade,
 Would have been left instead in Semifonte,[3]
 Where his grandfather had to beg his bread;[4]
Montemurlo would still be ruled by Conti
 Guidi;[5] the Cerchi still be in Acone;[6]
 Val di Greve contain the Buondelmonti.[7]
Mingling of populations meant always
 More evil in the city: undigested
 Food gives a body many maladies –
A blind bull's fall is swifter, heavier than   70
 A blind lamb's, and a solitary blade
 May well cut better than five others can.
If you but think of Luni, Urbisaglia,[8]
 And how they are no more, and how they're closely
 Followed by Chiusi and by Sinigaglia,[9]
Then when you hear how families disband
 It will not strike you as a strange occurrence,
 Since even cities have their natural end.
All your possessions, when it comes to it,
 Die, as you must – but some, that are long-lasting, 80
 Conceal this fact, since human life is short.
And like the moon's, in regular recurrence
 Concealing shores and then revealing them,[10]
 Are Fortune's actions with regard to Florence:
And so there's nothing startling in the theme
 I shall develop of great Florentines

---

1 Small villages on the outskirts of Florence.
2 A reference to the Black Guelfs Baldo di Guglielmo da Aguglione and Fazio dei Moru-
 baldini, the first of whom was one of those responsible for Dante's exile in 1302.
3 Fortress near Florence.
4 Lines 58–63: If the corrupt Catholic priesthood ("those who… have most declined") had
 not tried to usurp secular power, represented particularly by the Emperor ("Caesar"),
 then much civil discord and disruption would have been avoided.
5 In 1254 the Counts Guidi ceded this fortress to Florence.
6 Village near Florence, original home of the Cerchi, powerful heads of the White Guelfs.
7 The removal of this family from their fortress at Val di Greve into Florence is the climax
 of Cacciaguida's lament. See ll. 136–44 below.
8 Two once powerful Roman towns.
9 Towns in decline.
10 By the action of the tide.

Whose eminence is now obscured by time.
I've seen the Ughi, the Catellini, seen
   Filippi, Greci, Ormanni and Alberichi,
   Famed citizens already in decline;   90
And I have seen, both great and venerable,
   Men of Sannella, Arca, Soldanieri,
   Of the Ardinghi and Bostichi as well.[1]
Above that gate[2] which is now loaded down
   With recent treachery of such great weight
   That it will wreck the vessel very soon,
The Ravignani[3] lived, from whom there came
   Conte Guido[4] and all who since have taken
   The most illustrious Bellincione's name.[5]
The della Pressa family[6] were expert   100
   In governing already; Galigaio
   Already had the gilded pommel and hilt.[7]
By then the pale of vair[8] was glorified,
   Sacchetti,[9] Giuochi,[10] Fifanti[11] and Barucci,[12]
   Galli,[13] and those the bushel turns bright red.[14]
That stock[15] from which there issued the Calfucci[16]
   Was great already, and the curule chairs
   Possessed by the Sizii and Arrigucci.[17]
Oh I have seen them great who're now destroyed
   Through their own pride! I've seen the gleaming bezants   110
   Adorning Florence in her every deed!
Such lustre from the ancestors of these
   Who now, whenever the bishopric falls vacant,
   Sit growing fat in their consistories![18]

---

1   Lines 88–93: families either extinct or insignificant by Dante's day.
2   The Porta San Piero, the district inhabited by the Cerchi family, White Guelfs who were among those instrumental in Dante's exile.
3   Ancient noble family, extinct in Dante's day.
4   See ll. 64–65 above.
5   See *Par.* xv, 112–14.
6   Ancient Ghibelline family expelled from Florence in 1258.
7   Symbols of knighthood. The Galigai, who were knighted, were another Ghibelline family.
8   Heraldic arms of the Pigli family.
9   Enemies of the Alighieri family.
10   Originally noble, decayed in Dante's day.
11   Ghibellines expelled from Florence in 1258.
12   Extinct in Dante's day.
13   Ancient family, of no account in Dante's day.
14   The Chiaramontesi, blushing for a fraud involving the falsification of measures, already alluded to in *Purg.* xii, 105.
15   The ancient Donati family, Black Guelfs.
16   Extinct in Dante's day.
17   Ancient Guelf families.
18   The Visdomini and Tosinghi families had the right to administer the See of Florence and enjoy its revenue whenever it was vacant.

That race[1] which is so dragonish to him
  Who's fleeing, but when someone shows his teeth,
  Or purse, becomes as quiet as a lamb,
Was on the rise, but from such humble stock
  That Ubertin Donati,[2] when by marriage
  He was made kin to them, was taken aback.   120
And Caponsacco had come down by then
  From Fiesole[3] to the Market;[4] Infangato,[5]
  With Giuda,[6] was a worthy citizen.
Hard to believe, but this is truth I say:
  The gateway in the inner walls was named
  After the della Pera family![7]
All those entitled to the blazonry
  Of that great baron whose prestige and name
  Are celebrated on St Thomas' day,[8]
Had knighthood from him and that privilege[9] –   130
  Although there is one siding with the riff-raff[10]
  Who gives that coat of arms a golden edge.
Gualterotti and Importuni were
  Already there:[11] the Borgo would be much
  More peaceful if new neighbours were more rare.
That house,[12] the origin of all your grief,
  Whose righteous anger has become your ruin,
  And put an end to your contented life,
Was honoured then, and so were its allies.
  O Buondelmonte, wickedly renouncing   140
  Your marriage with them after bad advice!
Many would joy who now have broken hearts,
  If God had but consigned you to the Ema[13]
  That day you first approached our city's gates!
But Florence was a destined sacrifice

---

1   The Adimari family.
2   Married a daughter of Bellincione Berti; his wife's sister married one of the Adimari, a family of inferior status (see ll. 98–99).
3   The Ghibelline family of Caponsacchi arrived in Florence from Fiesole in 1125.
4   The old market place, Mercato Vecchio, in Florence.
5   Member of an ancient Florentine Ghibelline family expelled in 1258.
6   Member of an ancient Florentine family, in decline by Dante's day.
7   A family which had declined by Dante's day.
8   Ugo, Marquis of Tuscany, 961–1001.
9   Of displaying his arms.
10 Giano della Bella, who tried to exclude the nobility from public office in Florence.
11 Two Guelf families living in the Borgo Santi Apostoli.
12 The Amidei, whose vengeance in 1215 on Buondelmonte de' Buondelmonti (ll. 140ff) began the feud between Guelfs and Ghibellines.
13 A stream running between Florence and the country estates of the Buondelmonti.

To that disfigured stone which guards the bridge,[1]
  A victim in her final days of peace.
With these men and with other suchlike men
  I witnessed Florence in such deep repose
  She never had a reason to repine: 150
With these men I saw people who were just
  And so renowned the city's lily on
  Its staff had never ever been reversed,[2]
Nor yet by faction dyed vermilion."[3]

---

1 The mutilated statue of Mars at the Ponte Vecchio (see l. 47 and note). There was a superstition that bad luck had come to Florence as a result of forsaking their former patron Mars for John the Baptist.
2 As a sign of defeat.
3 In 1251 the Guelfs changed Florence's white lily on a red field to a red lily on white.

CANTO XVII

As so often, Dante is anxious to question those he meets, but hesitant to do so. Beatrice encourages him to ask, while stressing that Cacciaguida and she know already what is in his mind. Dante is concerned by the enigmatic prophecies of future trouble made to him during his journey.

Cacciaguida replies affectionately, and tells Dante bluntly that he will soon be exiled from Florence as a result of false accusations. He will feel all the worst effects of exile – the bitterness of homelessness, the having to depend on others for his daily bread and his disillusionment with those who were exiled with him.

Dante is told he will benefit from the patronage and spontaneous generosity of Bartolomeo della Scala. He will, while staying at Bartolomeo's court in Verona, become acquainted with Bartolomeo's nine-year-old brother, Cangrande, who is destined for great things. Dante tell us that finally Cacciaguida informed him of other matters which he must keep hidden.

Dante now worries that he has learnt, and reported, many unfavourable things about many prominent people, and this may lose him friends when he needs them most – and yet, if he does not speak the truth, his future reputation will suffer. Again Cacciaguida speaks bluntly, and tells him to tell the whole truth. Dante will offend most those in some of the highest places, but this is essential to one purpose of the *Comedy*, which is to provide eminent examples of moral evil and of good that will strike home to the reader's heart.

This canto is central in two ways: it is the middle one of the thirty-three cantos of *Paradise*, and it is also where, after Cacciaguida has elucidated the previous hints of a life-changing disaster awaiting Dante, he gives the clearest explanation of the moral purpose of the whole *Comedy*. Dante devotes more than three cantos to his meeting with his famous ancestor, not simply from familial piety but because Cacciaguida was a fighter for the Faith, and it is implied that Dante himself is too.

> I was like him who asked Clymene once
>   If what he'd heard against himself was true,
>   Who still makes fathers cautious with their sons[1] –
> So anxious was I, and so known to be
>   By Beatrice and by the sacred lamp
>   Who had already changed his place for me.[2]
> Therefore my lady said: "Send out in full
>   The heat of your desire, so that it issues
>   Stamped strongly with the intensity you feel –
> Not that we do not understand without   10
>   Your telling us, but that you get accustomed
>   To express your thirst, that drink may be poured out."
> "Dear ground in which I'm rooted, you're so high
>   That, as we see two angles (both obtuse)

---

1   Phaethon asked his mother Clymene to reassure him that Apollo was his father. Apollo allowed Phaethon to drive the chariot of the sun, with disastrous consequences (see *Inf.* XVII, 106–8).

2   Cacciaguida. See *Par.* XV, 19–21.

In one triangle simply cannot be,
You see contingent things before the event,[1]
   Having your eyes still fixed upon the Mind
   Where every time is present at one point –
While I was climbing, Virgil at my side,
   Up round the Mountain where the souls are purged,[2]   20
   After descending to the world that's dead,[3]
I was told things about my future state
   Which were most grievous,[4] though I feel myself
   Firm and four-square against the blows of fate.
I would be therefore happier to know
   What stroke of fate is coming close to me:
   A sighted arrow strikes a lighter blow."
Thus I addressed that same light which before
   Had spoken to me, and as Beatrice
   Required, articulated my desire.   30
In no dark sayings,[5] such as once ensnared
   Men's foolish minds before the Lamb of God,
   Who takes away our sins, was crucified,
But with plain words in a straightforward style,
   That fatherly affection answered me,
   Hidden and yet revealed by his own smile:
"Contingency, outside the written sheet
   Of mortal comprehension, is depicted
   Fully and clearly in the Eternal Sight:
Necessity is not implied by that,   40
   Any more than the ship which sails downstream
   Depends upon the eye observing it.[6]
And in that vision, like sweet harmony
   Of organ music to the ear, all that
   Time has in store for you appears to me.
Just as Hippolytus was driven out
   From Athens by his faithless, fierce stepmother,
   So you and Florence are about to part.[7]
It is already plotted and so willed,
   Soon to be engineered by him who plans it[8]   50

---

1 Souls in Heaven see our future, and even chance happenings in it, as clearly as we see
    axioms.
2 Mount Purgatory.
3 Inferno.
4 E.g. by Brunetto Latini (*Inf.* xv, 61–72) and, more obliquely, by Corrado Malaspina (*Purg.*
    VIII, 133–39).
5 Such as were delivered by the pagan oracles.
6 God's foreknowledge of events does not bring them about.
7 As Hippolytus had to leave Athens because of false accusations (his stepmother Phaedra
    claimed that he had raped her), so Dante will have to leave Florence.
8 Pope Boniface VIII, responsible for the exile of the White Guelfs from Florence.

There where Christ every day is bought and sold.¹
Rumour, of course, will blame the injured part
  As it does always, but the vengeance will
  Witness the Truth by Whom it's carried out.
You shall leave every single thing behind
  You hold most dear: and this is but the first
  Arrow shot by your exile – your first wound.
You shall experience the bitterness
  Of eating strangers' bread, and feel how hard
  Going up and down another's staircase is.   60
The burden on your back will weigh most heavy
  With that ill-natured, evil company
  Of those with whom you fall into this valley;
For they will be ungrateful, and turn out
  To be engaged against you; but soon after
  Their heads, not yours, will bleed in their defeat.²
Their progress will provide all needed proof
  Of brutishness; it will be to your honour
  That you have formed a party of yourself.
Your first refuge, first where you will have stayed,   70
  Will come by kindness of the great Lombard³
  Who on the ladder bears the sacred bird.⁴
So generous the glance which he will cast
  Upon you that, in giving and in asking,
  What is most often slower will come first.
There you shall be acquainted with that one⁵
  Whose birth was moulded so by this strong star⁶
  That all his deeds will win him great renown.
People have not yet realized this because
  He is so very young – these wheels of ours⁷   80
  Have only wheeled around him for nine years.
And yet before the Gascon can beguile
  Great Henry,⁸ sparks of virtue will be shown by
  His disregard of silver, his hard toil.
The greatness of his generous soul shall yet
  Be so well known even his enemies,
  When they consider it, will not stay mute.

1   Rome, city of simony.
2   Dante quarrelled with the other exiled White Guelfs. Their attempts to regain power
     in Florence failed disastrously.
3   Bartolomeo della Scala, Lord of Verona.
4   The punning emblem of the della Scala family was a ladder ("scala") surmounted by an
     eagle as a sign of allegiance to the Empire.
5   Cangrande, younger brother of Bartolomeo.
6   He was born under Mars.
7   The planets.
8   The French Pope Clement V at first supported the Emperor Henry VII, and invited him
     into Italy, and then withdrew his support.

Have trust in him and in his benefits:
    Through him shall many peoples be transformed,
    With rich and poor exchanging their estates.   90
You shall bear well in mind, but never tell,
    What I say now..." The things he then said will
    To those who see them seem incredible.
He added: "Son, these are the explanations,
    Of what you have been told – you see the pitfalls
    Lying in wait behind but few gyrations.[1]
You should not hold your neighbours in despite,
    Because your life will last out well beyond
    Their punishment for treason and deceit."
After that holy soul by silence showed   100
    He had completed his design of weaving
    His woof across the warp which I had laid,
Then I began, like somebody who craves,
    In his great doubt, counsel from someone else
    Who sees the good and wills it, and who loves:
"I see quite clearly now, my father, that
    Time spurs towards me, ready with the blow
    Which hits him hardest who sinks under it.
I must be armed with foresight, or I may,
    After the dearest place of all's denied me,   110
    Lose all the others through my poetry.
Down through the world of endless misery,[2]
    Up round the Mountain[3] to whose lofty height
    My lady's eyes raised and attracted me,
And afterwards through heavens from light to light,
    I have learnt things which, if I should repeat them,
    Would be the cause to many of despite –
And if, though friend to truth, I am not bold,
    I fear that I shall lose my reputation
    With those who'll see these as the days of old."   120
The light in which there smiled the precious gem
    I'd found within it, firstly coruscated,
    Most like a golden mirror in the sun,
And then replied: "A conscience that is dark,
    Through its own fault or by another's shame,
    Will certainly consider your words harsh.
Nevertheless, no lies! Be sure your speech
    Makes manifest the wholeness of your vision:
    Then let them scratch themselves who feel the itch.
For, if your words at first, when they're but tasted,   130
    Seem bitter and repugnant, they provide

---

1   Of the planets. Dante was exiled two years after the date (1300) he gives to his vision.
2   Inferno.
3   Purgatory.

Much vital nutriment once they're digested.
This cry of yours will do as does the wind,
  Which strikes most hard upon the mountain tops –
  Which is one reason it should be renowned.
Therefore within these spheres you have been shown –
  And on the Mount, and in the doleful valley –
  Only those souls whose standing is well known.
Because the soul who listens will not put
  His doubts to rest, or trust, if you present   140
  Examples springing from some hidden root,[1]
Or any enigmatic argument.[2]

---

1   Well-known people will have more force as examples.
2   Dante is enigmatic at times, but his moral judgements are unambiguous.

CANTO XVIII

Dante ponders the prophecies made by Cacciaguida: in his mind he balances the suffering they foretell against their promise of punishment for those who will wrong him and the encouragement he has been given to describe his vision with utter and fearless truthfulness. Beatrice insists that now he turn his thoughts instead to God, and as Dante looks at Beatrice his worries fall away. Then she tells him to listen once more to Cacciaguida. Cacciaguida explains that all the souls revealed on this planet were famous fighters for God. He names Joshua, Judas Maccabeus, Roland, Charlemagne and others. Then Cacciaguida returns to join the other lights in their singing.

Dante turns to Beatrice, sees that she is more beautiful than ever, and notices at the same instant that the planet he is on is moving in a wider orbit. This is because he is actually now on a different planet – the sixth, Jupiter. It is shining with silvery light.

The lights denoting the souls on this planet begin to move about like a flock of birds organizing the formation for their flight. They shape letters which spell out the first words of The Book of Wisdom, indicating that this is the planet dedicated to justice. Then little by little the lights convert the final M of the Latin words into the shape of an imperial eagle, the symbol of earthly power and justice.

The canto concludes with a strong attack on what Dante sees as the greatest stumbling block to justice on this earth – a corrupt Papacy, guilty of simony and of using spiritual power for gain and as a weapon for its own secular ends. He addresses directly one self-seeking Pope who is devoted to money.

N ow, while that blessèd mirror[1] took delight
　　In his unspoken thoughts, I tasted mine,
　　Softening their bitterness with what was sweet.[2]
And she who was conducting me to God
　　Told me: "Think rather I am close to Him
　　Who takes the weight of every evil load."
That made me turn to the affectionate voice
　　Of my dear comfort, but the love I saw
　　In those dear eyes I shall not now express:
Not only since I cannot trust my speech,　　　　　　　　　10
　　But since my memory cannot go back
　　Upon itself without Another's touch.
This much at least of it I can aver:
　　That, gazing at her eyes, I was quite free
　　From every other longing or desire:
While the Eternal Joy on Beatrice
　　Was shining straight, then I was well contented
　　With the reflected light from her fair face.
But, with a smile which left me in a daze,

1　Cacciaguida, reflecting the light of God.
2　Dante is considering the prophecies made by Cacciaguida.

She said: "You must turn round to him[1] and listen: 20
  Paradise is not solely in my eyes."
As we read here on earth from time to time
  Men's feelings in their faces, if they're such
  That all the soul is taken up with them,
So in the flaming of that sacred light
  To which I turned, I recognized his wish
  To have more conversation with me yet.
He said: "In this fifth level of the tree[2]
  Which draws all life and being from its crest,
  Never sheds leaves and fruits eternally,   30
Are blessèd spirits, of such name and fame,
  On earth, before they entered into Heaven,
  That any Muse would be enriched by them.[3]
Look therefore at the cross, along its horns:[4]
  He whom I name will run there just as swiftly
  As, in a cloud, a flash of lightning runs."
Along the cross I saw a light being drawn
  The very instant Joshua[5] was named:
  To me it seemed no sooner said than done.
Then when great Maccabeus[6] was called up,   40
  I saw another moving and revolving:
  Glad rapture was the whip which spun that top.
So for Roland[7] and Charlemagne:[8] my sight
  Followed the two of them attentively,
  As does the falconer the falcon's flight.
Afterwards Rainouart[9] and William[10] drew
  My eyes as rapidly along the cross,
  Godfrey the Duke[11] and Robert Guiscard[12] too.
Then, moved and mingling with them all, that light
  Which had been speaking to me demonstrated,   50
  Among the singers of the sky, his art.[13]

---

1 Cacciaguida.
2 Mars, fifth planet from the earth, in a metaphorical conception of Paradise as a tree nourished not from its roots but by God.
3 They are an ideal theme for poetry.
4 The crossbeam of the cross.
5 Successor to Moses, he led the Chosen People into the Promised Land, with much fighting along the way.
6 Judas Maccabeus, who defended the Jews against the King of Syria and restored the Temple in Jerusalem (163 BC).
7 Christian champion who died fighting the Saracens. See *Inf.* XXXI, 16–18.
8 King of the Franks, crowned Emperor of the West in 800 AD.
9 Rainouart was one of the heroes of a cycle of medieval legends.
10 Count of Orange and one of Charlemagne's generals. Like Rainouart, he was the hero of a cycle of medieval legends.
11 Godfrey de Bouillon (*d.*1100), a leader of the First Crusade.
12 A Norman who fought against Saracens in Sicily and southern Italy (*d.*1085).
13 Cacciaguida joined in singing with the other souls.

I SAW, COLOURED IN GOLD, SHOT THROUGH WITH LIGHT,
A LADDER WHICH WAS REACHING SO FAR UPWARDS...

PARADISE XXI, 28–29

"GLORY TO FATHER, SON AND HOLY GHOST!"
SO SANG THE WHOLE OF PARADISE...

PARADISE XXVII, 1–2

And I swung round towards my right-hand side
    To see from Beatrice where my duty lay,
    As shown by gestures or by what she said,
And saw her eyes were shining with such light,
    And with such happiness, her form outshone
    Even that time when I last looked at it.[1]
And as, in sensing an increased delight
    In doing good, a man from day to day
    Perceives his virtue as it gathers weight,   60
So I detected that my circling round
    Upon that heaven had increased its arc,[2]
    Because that miracle[3] was more adorned.
Such change as happens in so short a time
    To a pale lady, when we find her face
    Unburdened of the burden brought by shame,[4]
Appeared now as I turned myself away
    To the bright whiteness of the temperate star
    Which had become the sixth to welcome me.
And I discovered in that Jovial light[5]   70
    The sparkling of the love which was within it
    Delineating language to my sight;
For, as birds when they're rising from a river,
    As if rejoicing that their thirst is quenched,
    Shape the flock into one form or another –
But all clear-cut – so in those lights blessed creatures
    Sang as they went on flying here and there,
    And fashioned D, I, L out of those figures.
They moved first to the rhythm of their song;
    Then, as they were transformed into each letter,   80
    They stopped, and they were mute, but not for long.
O Pegasean goddess,[6] who make great minds
    Illustrious, and render them immortal,
    As they with you do cities and whole lands,
Light me up with yourself, as I rehearse
    Their figures as they're in my understanding:
    Reveal your potency in this poor verse!
Eventually they showed themselves to be
    Thirty-five vowels and consonants: I noted
    The letters well as they appeared to me.   90
    "Diligite iustitiam"[7] were the first

---

1   Lines 7–11.
2   Dante has moved to another planet, beyond Mars and therefore with a wider orbit.
3   Beatrice.
4   I.e. a blush.
5   The planet Jupiter, containing the souls of those who dispensed justice. Its influence
     was thought to be benign and joyful.
6   Probably a reference to Calliope, the muse of poetry.
7   "Love justice" (an imperative).

Verb and noun to appear in that display;
    "Qui iudicatis terram"[1] were the last.
Then, once the M of the fifth word was told,
    The lights had settled, so that Jupiter
    Appeared in silver,[2] there inlaid with gold.
And I saw lights descending on the M
    And, coming to its apex,[3] settle there,
    Singing, I think, the Goodness drawing them.
Then, as innumerable sparks arise   100
    Out of a burning log when it is struck –
    From which some foolish folk draw auguries –
From that M seemed to surge light upon light,
    More than a thousand, and some high, some low,
    As fated by the Sun by Whom they're lit.
And when each, in its place, had quieted,
    I could make out an eagle's head and neck
    Presented by the fire that was inlaid.[4]
He Who paints there has none to guide or trust,
    But guides Himself, and from Him is transmitted   110
    The bird's ability to build a nest.
The other souls, who were at first content,
    Apparently, to twine the M with lilies,
    With one slight move completed the imprint.[5]
O kindly star, thus many a gleaming gem
    Revealed to me how justice here on earth
    Is ordered by the Heaven which you begem![6]
Therefore I pray the Mind from Which there flows
    Your motion and your power that you regard
    The source of all the smoke that clouds your rays,   120
So that anger be stirred up once again
    Against the merchandising in that temple[7]
    Built up by miracles and martyrdom.[8]
O warrior hosts of Heaven whom I survey,
    Pray for all those who here upon this earth
    By such examples have been led astray!
Men would wage war with swords in times long gone,

---

1   "You who rule the earth." The Latin in ll. 91 and 93 quotes the first words of *Liber
    Sapientiæ* (The Book of Wisdom), a book omitted from Protestant Bibles.
2   The colour of Jupiter.
3   The central vertical stroke of the M elongated upwards.
4   See ll. 94–98.
5   Finished fashioning the eagle. Dante has in mind a Gothic or uncial M (◖), with the
    central stroke elongated and shaped into the eagle's neck and head, and the side strokes
    curving outwards like wings.
6   The eagle is the Imperial Eagle, symbolic of just rule.
7   The Church.
8   Lines 120–23 are an attack on the Papacy, not as an institution, but for its corruption,
    especially simony.

But now war means withholding here or there
Bread God the Father would deny to none.[1]
But you, who only write to cancel out,[2]   130
Remember Paul and Peter – who both died
For that vine[3] you despoil – are living yet.
You may well say: "I'm so intent on him
Whom I admire, who longed to live alone,
And was by dancing drawn to martyrdom,[4]
That I know neither Paul nor Fisherman."[5]

---

1   Spiritual help, especially the sacraments, whose denial was used by some Popes as a
    weapon.
2   Dante is addressing Pope John XXII (r. 1316–34), accused of imposing excommunications
    which could then be lifted in return for money.
3   The Church.
4   John the Baptist, who lived alone in the desert, and who was decapitated when Salome,
    the daughter of Herodias, requested his death as a reward for her dance (Matt. 14:1–11).
5   St Peter. The devotion expressed in ll. 133–36 is for the Florentine gold florin, which
    bore the image of John the Baptist, the city's patron.

CANTO XIX

The Imperial Eagle spreads its wings. Dante is about to describe something never described before. The Eagle, formed of many souls, speaks with one voice as if one person, saying that models of the true and indivisible justice have been left on earth in the lives of just men.

Dante says that the Eagle knows, without being told, the doubt which has troubled him for so long: the Eagle can resolve it. The Eagle replies with a long speech emphasizing the power of God, Who is the source of justice and cannot therefore be challenged by someone created by Him. Eventually the Eagle expresses Dante's doubt plainly. How can someone who lived and died without hearing of Christ, and who lived a good life, be damned for his lack of faith? The Eagle's answer is to stress again that the creature cannot hope to understand his Creator. Justice consists in conforming to the Creator's will.

The Eagle repeats the teaching of the Church, that no one was ever saved who did not believe in Christ. But, he says, there are many calling upon the Lord in this life who, on the Day of Judgement, will be farther from Him than some pagans.

The Eagle concludes with a list of kings who are to be condemned for their evil rule, their lack of justice.

This canto makes explicit a doubt which has troubled Dante throughout his journey. There is for instance the figure of Virgil, Dante's revered guide through Inferno and Purgatory, known for his piety and goodness, who is nevertheless condemned to spend eternity in Limbo, a part of Hell. The answer which Dante gets is the same as that given in the book of Job: who are you to challenge the God Who created you? This is a coherent answer, but not one likely to resolve all speculation, particularly in such a curious mind as Dante's – and indeed in the following canto he is still wondering.

There now appeared to me with wings outspread
    That lovely image[1] which, in sweet fruition,
    The happy souls united there had made:
Each one appeared a ruby where the rays
    Of the sun burned, and were so strongly kindled
    The whole sun seemed reflected to my eyes.
And what is now my duty to report
    No voice has ever said, no ink has written,
    Nor wildest fantasy has ever thought:
I saw the beak discoursing, and I heard   10
    A sound which issued saying "I" and "my"
    When "we" and "our" had to be understood.[2]
"Through justice and through mercy I am here,"
    It said, "exalted, and to this great glory
    Never achieved, or outpaced, by desire –
And on the earth I've left my memory
    So fashioned that the wicked people there

---

1   The Imperial Eagle.
2   The souls who compose the Eagle speak with one voice, united in their love of justice.

Commend, but never heed the history."
Thus, as from many coals there comes but one
  Sole warmth, so from the many loving souls   20
  Forming that image came one voice alone.
"O everlasting flowers," I then began,
  "Of everlasting joy, who make to me
  Your various fragrances appear as one,
Free me, as you exhale, from that great dearth
  Which has so long imprisoned me in hunger,
  Since I could find no food for it on earth.[1]
I do know that, though in another realm[2]
  God's justice fashions for itself a mirror,
  You here perceive it with no veil between.   30
You know I am already listening
  Attentively – you know exactly what
  Doubt has kept me so hungry for so long."
Like a falcon emerging from its hood,
  Moving its head around, clapping its wings,
  Showing its willingness and looking proud,
So I observed that sign enact, criss-crossed
  By praises of God's heavenly grace, such songs
  As only they can know who are so blessed.
Then it began to speak: "He Who has wheeled   40
  His compass round the world's confines, and in it
  Arranged so much that's hidden, much revealed,
Could not with all His Power so much impress
  The whole wide universe, but that His Word
  Had to remain in infinite excess.[3]
Of that the first proud being makes us sure –
  For he, who was the summit of creation,
  Impatient for the light, fell immature.[4]
Hence it is clear that every lesser nature
  Is a vessel too tiny for that Goodness   50
  Which knows no end, and is Its own sole measure.
It follows that that sight of yours, which must
  Be but one ray of the Intelligence
  Which into everything has been infused,
Could not of its own nature have the power
  To see its own beginnings much beyond
  The way they are presented or appear.
Therefore the sight your world receives can see
  No farther into the Eternal Justice

1 What is troubling Dante, which the Eagle understands without being told, becomes clear to the reader only gradually.
2 That of the Thrones, angels reflecting God's justice.
3 Creation demonstrates God's power, without ever revealing the full extent of it.
4 The angel Lucifer, the finest created being, rebelled because he was unwilling to accept his inferiority to God.

Than any eye can penetrate the sea: 60
We can observe the seabed near the shore,
  But cannot when far out at sea, and yet,
  Although the depth conceals it, it is there.
There is no light but from that cloudless Light
  Which never is perturbed – all else is darkness
  Shadowed by flesh, or that which poisons it.[1]
By now you have a glimpse inside that maze
  In which the living Justice has been hidden,
  Which you've called into question all your days.[2]
For you would say: 'Beside the Indus River   70
  A man is born, where there is nobody
  To speak of Christ or write of Him whatever –
And all his wishes and his acts are good,
  So far as can be judged by human reason,
  Sinless in every deed and every word.
Faithless and unbaptized he meets his death:
  Where is the justice in his condemnation?
  Is it his fault, if he does not have faith?'
Now, who are you to sit upon the seat
  Of judgement and adjudicate in cases   80
  A million miles away, with your short sight?[3]
For you who'd like to bandy words with me,
  Were there no Sacred Scriptures for instruction,
  There'd be a case for doubt, admittedly.
Oh, earthbound creatures! Minds as dull as mud!
  The primal Will, which is Itself all goodness,
  Cannot forsake Itself, the highest Good.
Justice is simply what fits in with that:[4]
  No creature ever draws good to itself,
  Since it is goodness which created it."   90
Just as a stork will circle in the air
  Above her nest when she has fed her brood,
  And as one she has fed looks up to her,
So did, as I was lifting up my eyes,
  That blessèd image – and its wings were moved
  By many wills, but all unanimous.
It turned and sang and spoke: "My notes outrun
  Your understanding: thus eternal judgement
  Runs far beyond the wit of mortal men."
Soon as the Holy Spirit's flames were stilled,   100
  Though shaping yet that ensign[5] which once made

---

1   Mortal understanding is obscured by the doubtful evidence of our senses and by the
     temptations to which we are prone.
2   Dante's problem is about to be made clear.
3   An obvious Scriptural analogue is Job 38, where God answers Job out of the whirlwind.
4   See *Par.* III, 85 above.
5   The Imperial Eagle.

The Romans so revered throughout the world,
It spoke again: "No one was sanctified
   Ever, if he did not believe in Christ,
   Before or after Christ was crucified.
But see how many shout aloud: 'Christ! Christ!'
   Who on the Day of Judgement will be farther
   From Him than those who never heard of Christ.
The Ethiopian[1] will condemn such, there
   Where the two companies are separated,   110
   One to eternal wealth, and one left bare.
What will the Persians[2] have to tell your kings,
   On that Day[3] when they see the open volume
   In which are written all their wrongdoings?
There they shall see, when Albert's reign is told,
   That deed which soon will set the pen in motion,
   Through which the realm of Prague will be despoiled.[4]
There they shall see the grief brought on the shore
   Of the Seine, through debasement of the coinage
   By him whose death comes from a bristling boar.[5]   120
There they shall see abounding greedy pride
   Driving the Scot and Englishman insane
   Till neither of them keeps to his own side.[6]
They'll see life lived in lechery and ease
   By him of Spain,[7] by him too of Bohemia,[8]
   Who never knew nor wished for worthiness.
They'll see the Cripple of Ierusalem,
   Whose virtue is denoted by the I,
   Whereas his vice necessitates the M.[9]
They'll see the avarice and cowardice   130
   Of the protector of that isle of fire
   Where old Anchises ended his long days[10] –
And, just to emphasize his paltriness,
   The words recording him shall be contracted,

---

1   Standing for all pagans.
2   Like the Ethiopian in l. 109 above.
3   The Day of Judgement.
4   Emperor Albert of Habsburg (r.1298–1308), invaded Bohemia in 1304.
5   Philip the Fair of France, killed by a wild boar in 1314.
6   Conflict across the English-Scottish border was almost incessant. Dante may be allud-
   ing to Edward I of England (d.1307), although the Eagle (prophesying in 1300) may be
   alluding to Edward II and his conflict with Robert the Bruce.
7   Ferdinand IV, King of Castile 1295–1312.
8   Wenceslas IV (r.1278–1305).
9   The lame Charles II of Anjou, King of Naples 1285–1309, and King of Jerusalem (an
   empty title). I, the first letter of Jerusalem in Dante's version, is the Roman numeral for
   1, and M (the last letter) is the Roman numeral for 1,000.
10 Frederick II of Aragon (r.1296–1337) ruled the volcanic island of Sicily, where the father
   of Aeneas had died (*Aeneid* III, 707*ff*).

To note much pettiness in little space.
And everyone will see the dirty work
  Of uncle and of brother,[1] who have dragged
  An honoured race and two crowns through the muck.
The Kings of Norway[2] and of Portugal[3]
  Will be recorded there, and him of Rascia   140
  Who made sound coinage unreliable.[4]
Oh blessèd Hungary, would she but bear
  Ill treatment now no longer![5] Blessed Navarre,
  If she would arm her rocky frontier![6]
Take it already as a grim forecast
  How Nicosia and Famagusta[7] suffer,
  Howling in sorrow under their own beast,
Who is no different from any other."

---

1   Frederick's uncle is James, King of Majorca, and his brother is James, King of Aragon.
2   King Haakon V (r.1299–1319).
3   King Denis (r.1279–1325).
4   King Stephen Uroš II Milutin of Serbia (r.1282–1321) counterfeited the Venetian coinage. Rascia was the main province of the Serbian realm.
5   Hungary was ruled in 1300 by Andrew III, the last king of the family of St Stephen. In 1301 he was succeeded by Charles Robert, son of Charles Martel. It is uncertain whether Dante is warning of disasters to come or hinting at the possibility of good government.
6   The Pyrenees. Navarre was annexed to France in 1305.
7   Cyprus, indicated by its two main cities, was governed in 1300 by a French king, Henry II of Lusignan.

CANTO XX

As the Eagle stops speaking, the lights in it shine more brightly than ever, and they sing a hymn, one which has slipped from Dante's memory. Then there is a sound, like a stream running over rocks, which issues from the Eagle's beak as speech. The Eagle tells Dante to look at its eye. In the pupil is the soul of King David, and along the eyebrow (in order from the part nearest the beak) are Trajan, Hezekiah, Constantine, William II of Naples and Sicily and Ripheus.

The Eagle explains why each of these souls is there: Trajan because he answered the prayers of a widow, Hezekiah because he was granted fifteen more years of life, which led to true penitence, Constantine because his intentions were good when he transferred the capital of the Empire to the East, William II because he ruled justly, and Ripheus because he was righteous.

Dante is amazed at the inclusion of two of these souls. He cannot understand how the two pagans could be in Heaven. Trajan, the Eagle says, is there by reason of his own good works and the prayers of Pope Gregory the Great, which freed him from Limbo. Ripheus is there by his own merit and the special grace of God, so that his faith and hope and charity served as a baptism for him. Trajan came to believe in the crucified Christ, and Ripheus (who lived before the Incarnation) believed in the Christ who would suffer in the future.

Dante is comforted to have God's inscrutability emphasized once more. And the two lights representing Trajan and Ripheus twinkle in time to the Eagle's words.

This canto continues the main theme of the previous one. Having been told that God's judgements are inscrutable (and therefore to be accepted even if, to human thought, they seem unfair), Dante is now shown two souls in Heaven whose presence there is hard to understand but undeniable. His doubts are put to rest.

W hen he[1] whose rays light up the universe
    Descends so far beneath our hemisphere
    That every speck of daylight disappears,
The sky, which was first lit by him alone,
    Becomes straightway perceptible once more
    Through many lights reflected from that one.[2]
Now this celestial process came to mind
    The instant our world's emblem[3] and the rulers
    Inside its sacred beak made no more sound,
Since all those living lights, increasingly   10
    Shone out in splendour, while the songs they sang,
    Being hard to grasp, slip from my memory.
O sweetest love forever wreathed in smiles,
    The love of spirits breathing holy thoughts,
    How ardent was your breath through those flute holes![4]

1   The sun.
2   Stars were believed to reflect the sun's light.
3   The Imperial Eagle.
4   The souls which compose the Eagle.

The instant that the dear and gleaming gems
　　With which I saw the sixth light[1] was bejewelled
　　Ended in silence their angelic chimes,
I seemed to hear a murmuring watercourse
　　Descending limpidly from rock to rock,　　　　　　20
　　Revealing the abundance of its source.
And just as at the gittern's neck[2] a sound
　　Is shaped to music, or the bagpipes' music
　　Is fashioned from the penetrating wind,
So, with no waiting period to follow,
　　The murmuring of the Eagle came ascending
　　Up through its neck, as though that neck were hollow.
There it became a voice, and thence came out,
　　As the beak opened, in the form of words,
　　Awaited, and remembered, in my heart.　　　　　　30
"That part of me[3] which can endure the sun
　　In mortal eagles," it began by saying,
　　"Must now unflinchingly be gazed upon;
For, of the fires that serve to fashion me,
　　Those where the eye is sparkling in my head
　　Are all the highest in their own degree.
He who, midmost, as pupil seems to glitter,
　　Was once the singer for the Holy Spirit,
　　Who took the Ark from one town to another:[4]
Now he sees what deserving psalms he made –　　　　　40
　　So far at least as they were of his making[5] –
　　Measured by the extent of his reward.
Of those five who trace out the eyebrow's turn,
　　He who is placed the nearest to my beak
　　Consoled the widow grieving for her son:[6]
Now he sees all the heavy price to pay
　　Not following Christ, through his experience
　　Of this sweet life and of its contrary.[7]
And he who's next on the circumference
　　I'm speaking of, along the upward arc,　　　　　　50
　　Delayed his death by his true penitence:[8]
Now he sees how the imperishable decree

1　The planet Jupiter.
2　The place on this instrument where the player has his left hand on the strings.
3　This heraldic eagle is shown with its head in profile, with only one eye visible.
4　King David, who took the Ark of the Covenant to Jerusalem . See also *Purg.* x, 55–69.
5　The Holy Spirit inspired him.
6　The pagan Emperor Trajan (r.98–117 AD), who was moved by a widow's prayers to avenge her murdered son, and who was himself saved by the prayers of Pope Gregory the Great (*Purg.* x, 70–93).
7　He spent some five hundred years in Limbo before his translation to Heaven.
8　King Hezekiah of Judah was, during an apparently fatal illness, granted fifteen more years of life (2 Kings 20:1–11).

Is not transmuted, when true prayer on earth
   Gives to tomorrow what was for today.
He who, with me and with the laws, comes after,
   With good intentions which bore evil fruit,
   Became a Greek to give way to the Pastor:[1]
Now he sees how the evil which ensued
   From his good deed can never harm himself,
   Though through it the whole world should be destroyed. 60
He whom you see upon the downward curve
   Was William,[2] much lamented in that land
   Which weeps that Charles and Frederick[3] are alive:
Now he sees how the heavens are always full
   Of love for the just ruler, and the splendour
   Of his appearance makes that obvious still.
Who in the erring world could have supposed
   The Trojan Ripheus[4] would appear the fifth
   Of the blessed lights of which this eye's composed?
Now he sees much which is still undiscerned   70
   By the wide world about the grace of God,
   But which his vision cannot ever sound."
Like the skylark which soars into the air,
   Singing at first, then silent and content
   With the last sweetness which has sated her,
Such seemed to me the sign[5] which images
   His everlasting pleasure, at Whose bidding
   Each thing becomes the thing it really is.
And though I was, with reference to my doubt,
   Like clear glass to the colour which it covers,   80
   I was impatient to articulate,
And from my mouth I heard: "How can this be?"
   Come with the force of all my weighty wonder –
   At which the ensign sparkled in its glee.
Then straightway, with the eye glittering brighter,
   The blessèd ensign answered my amazement,
   That it might hold me in suspense no longer:
"I see that you believe what you are told
   Because I tell you, but not how it happens:
   So, though believed, it still remains concealed.   90
You are like somebody who knows the name
   Which something goes by, not its very essence –
   Unless somebody else makes it quite plain.

---

1   The Emperor Constantine (r.306–37 AD) moved his capital from Rome to Byzantium,
    leaving the sovereignty of the West to the Pope. Dante sees the political power of the
    Church as a great evil (see *Inf.* XIX, 115–17 and *Par.* VI, 1–6).

2   King of Naples and Sicily (r.1166–89).

3   Denounced by the Eagle in *Par.* XIX, 127–29 and 130–32.

4   A pagan mentioned by Virgil as the most just of the Trojans (*Aeneid* II, 426–27).

5   The Eagle.

Regnum cælorum[1] suffers violence from
   Intensity of love and living hope,
   By which the Will Divine is overcome –
Not as a man breaks through a man's defence,
   But simply since It wishes to be conquered
   And, conquered, conquers by benevolence.
The first light and the fifth[2] above my eye   100
   Fill you with wonder, simply since you see them
   Adorn what is the angels' territory.
They did not leave this earth, as you've conjectured,
   As pagans, but as Christians, and believed
   In feet[3] that were to suffer or had suffered.
One[4] from the Inferno, whence no one comes up
   And back to good, came back to flesh and blood.
   And that was the reward of living hope –
Of living hope, which made more powerful
   The prayers which had been offered up to God   110
   To resurrect him and convert his will.
The glorious soul whom I am speaking of,
   Once back to life, though but for a short time,
   Believed in Him Who has the power to save
And, in belief, burst into such great flame
   Of true love that he was considered worthy
   Of this rejoicing when he died again.[5]
The other[6] – through grace springing from such deep
   Recesses no created being ever
   Sees down into the place whence it wells up –   120
Set all his love below on what was right,
   So that God made redemption in the future,
   Through grace upon grace, apparent to his sight:
So he believed, and would not tolerate
   The stench of paganism, and rebuked
   Perverse people who persevered in it.
Those ladies were for him a baptism,
   Whom you saw by the right wheel in a dance,[7]
   Predating that rite one millennium.
Predestination, how remote you are   130
   From those whose vision does not see your root
   In the First Cause and see it all entire!
And you, mortals, do not be swift and strict

---

1   "The Kingdom of Heaven" (Latin).
2   The souls of Trajan and Ripheus.
3   Christ's.
4   Trajan.
5   See ll. 43–48 above.
6   Ripheus.
7   The three theological virtues (faith, hope and charity), which Dante saw by the chariot representing the Church (*Purg.* XXIX, 121–29).

In making judgements: we, who can see God,
  Do not yet know the number of the elect.
To us this falling-short is wonderful,
  For in this good our own good is refined,
  Since what is willed by God, we also will."
In this way the divine imagining,
  To make me see my own short-sightedness,   140
  Gave me sweet medicine for my comforting.
And like the playing of a lutanist –
  Whose trembling strings accompany the singer,
  And pleasure from the singing is increased –
So, while the Eagle spoke, as I recall,
  Were the two lights[1] who, being overjoyed,
  As eyelids both together rise and fall,
Twinkled their flames to accompany his word.

---

1   Trajan and Ripheus.

CANTO XXI

Dante has his eyes fixed on Beatrice, but she does not smile. This is, she says, because her smile grows in intensity as they ascend through the heavens, and at this stage would be too much for Dante to bear.

They are now in the seventh heaven, the planet Saturn. Beatrice tells Dante to concentrate on what this planet shows him. This is a ladder which rises so far that it goes out of sight. Lights are descending the ladder and, once they reach a certain rung, they move about in various ways like birds at break of day. Dante is encouraged by Beatrice to question the light which is nearest to him. He has two questions. Why is this particular spirit so near to him and ready to be questioned? And why is there no music on this planet?

The spirit answers that Dante's hearing could not endure the music at this level of Heaven, any more than his eyes could have endured Beatrice's smile. He tells Dante also that no one could possibly understand why one soul rather than another has been predestined by God to speak to him: some things are beyond any created being's comprehension. The spirit says that he lived once at a hermitage below Monte Catria, near Florence, a monastery which was devoted to prayer and which brought many mortals into Heaven, but is now so corrupt that soon its uselessness will be revealed. He is Peter Damian, who called himself "Peter the Sinner". He lived frugally and became a cardinal with great reluctance.

St Peter Damian concludes with a violent attack on the wealth and self-indulgence of the higher clergy of Dante's day, contrasting them with the poverty and plain living of the Apostles Peter and Paul. The other lights greet this denunciation with a cry so deep that it leaves Dante thunderstruck and unable to make out what the cry means.

B y now my eyes were fixed once more upon
    My lady's face, and with them went my mind,
    Remote from all extraneous concern.
She was not smiling, but "Were I to smile,"
    She told me, "you would be like Semele,
    Burnt to a cinder in a little while,[1]
Because my beauty, which upon the stairs
    Of the eternal palace glows more brightly,
    As you have seen, the higher that we rise,
Were it not tempered, would shine in such splendour,   10
    That at its flashing all your mortal strength
    Would be like foliage shattered by the thunder.
We're lifted to the seventh glory,[2] which –
    Beneath the breast of the perfervid Lion[3] –
    Beams down its rays with which his force is mixed.

---

1   Jove appeared to Semele in his full splendour as a god, attended by lightning and thunderbolts, and she was burned to ashes.
2   The planet Saturn.
3   The constellation Leo.

And now your eyes and mind must work together,
    Making your eyes a mirror for the symbol
    Which will appear to you within this mirror."[1]
Whoever understood the nourishment
    My eyes were taking from her lovely sight,   20
    As I transferred them to a fresh intent,
Would realize I must be overjoyed
    To be obedient to my heavenly mentor,
    Weighing the one against the other side.[2]
Within that crystal sphere which bears the name,
    As it goes round the world, of its dear ruler,
    Beneath whom wickedness was all unknown,[3]
I saw, coloured in gold, shot through with light,
    A ladder which was reaching so far upwards
    That where it ended was beyond my sight.   30
And I saw too descending, round by round,
    So many splendours I thought every light
    That shines distinct in Heaven had been combined.
And as jackdaws, as habit has instilled,
    Act all together, at the break of day,
    And move to warm their wings which have grown chilled –
Then some fly off, not to return, and some
    Fly off, but then come back to where they started,
    While others, wheeling round, remain at home –
Such was the fashion of the glittering,   40
    It seemed to me, as they came down together,
    Once they arrived upon a certain rung.
And one which, once it halted, was nearby,
    Became so bright that in my mind I said:
    "I see the love which you convey to me.
But she, from whom I usually take
    My cue to talk or not, is pausing; so,
    Against my wish, I do well not to speak."
Then she, who saw my silence in the sight
    Of Him Who sees all things, encouraged me: 50
    "Cool down your longing by expressing it."
And I began: "No merit has sufficed
    To earn me your reply, but for the sake
    Of her who has allowed me this request,
O blessèd spirit, who are hidden away
    Within your happiness, please let me know
    The reason you are placed so near to me.
And tell me why, within this heaven of yours,

---

1   The planet Saturn, which reflects the Divine Mind, as Dante's eyes reflect what he sees
    on the planet.
2   Dante's desire to obey Beatrice is even greater than his desire to look at her.
3   Saturn's reign was the fabled Age of Gold, a time of happiness and innocence.

The symphony of Paradise is silent,
   Which rings devoutly through the lower spheres."   60
"You hearing's mortal, and your sight is too,"
   He answered me, "so here there is no singing,
   And likewise Beatrice did not smile at you.[1]
Through each grade of the ladder I've descended
   Purely to make you happy by my speech
   And by the light with which I am surrounded.
It was not greater love that urged me on:
   For just as great, and greater, love is burning
   Above, as all these blazing souls make plain.
But the deep charity which makes us serve   70
   Promptly the Providence that rules the world
   Arranges all things here, as you perceive."
"I see," I said, "O sacred brilliance,
   How in this court unfettered love suffices
   To make you serve Eternal Providence,
But this is what is hard to understand:
   Why you alone were, out of your companions,
   Predestined to this work you have in hand."
Before I finished what I had to say,
   The light, making a pivot of its centre,   80
   Was turning like a millstone rapidly,
And then the love that was within replied:
   "The Light that is divine descends on me,
   And penetrates the love in which I hide.[2]
Its power, united with my understanding,
   Lifts me so far above myself I see
   The Highest Essence whence it is descending.
Hence comes the happiness with which I flame,
   Because my sight, so far as it is clear,
   Is equalled by the flame with which I shine.   90
But even that soul in Heaven who is most clear,[3]
   Or Seraph[4] with his eye most fixed on God,
   Could not give you the answer you desire;
For what you ask lies down in the abyss
   Of the eternal statutes, at a depth
   Where no created sight could ever pierce.
When you go back to earth, report all this,
   So that nobody ever dares again
   To try to penetrate such mysteries.
The intellect, which shines here, is but smoke   100
   On earth: what could it possibly see there

---

1   The implication is that, in this seventh heaven, both the singing and Beatrice's smile
   would be more than Dante could bear.
2   The spirit's love can be seen by Dante only as a light.
3   The Virgin Mary.
4   The Seraphim are, of all the angelic orders, nearest to God.

That it cannot see at its very peak?"
His words imposed such a constraint on me
   I dropped my questioning, and limited
   Myself to asking him who he might be.
"Rocks rise in Italy between two shores,[1]
   And not far from your birthplace,[2] and so high
   That they are far above where thunder roars,
And these rocks form a hump called Catria,
   Above a consecrated hermitage[3]   110
   Which was devoted once solely to prayer."
So he began to address me the third time,
   And then, continuing, he told me: "There,
   In the service of God, I was so firm
That, on food seasoned but with olive oil,
   I lightly made my way through heat and cold,[4]
   Content, for contemplation was my all.
That cloister did provide a copious yield
   To Heaven, but has since become so barren
   That very soon the truth will be revealed.   120
In that place I was Peter Damian:[5]
   On the Adriatic in Our Lady's house
   As Peter the Sinner[6] I was better known.
But, when my life had almost run its course,
   I was compelled to wear that hat[7] which always
   Goes down from one bad wearer to a worse.
When Cephas[8] came, and also the great vessel
   Of the Holy Spirit,[9] they were lean, unshod,
   And glad to take their food at any hostel.
Now modern pastors need, on either side,   130
   Strong buttresses, and one in front to lead them –
   Being men of weight – and one to lift behind.
Their mantles cover their palfreys when they ride
   (O patience, how can you endure all this?)
   So that two beasts move on beneath one hide!"
At this I saw more flames begin to whirl,
   And they moved down from step to step still whirling,

---

1   The Apennines between the Adriatic and the Tyrrhenian Sea.
2   Florence.
3   The Benedictine monastery of Santa Croce di Fonte Avellana.
4   Summer and winter.
5   Theologian and zealous reformer (1107–72), born in Ravenna.
6   He signed himself "Petrus Peccator".
7   The red hat of a cardinal.
8   St Peter. "And when Jesus beheld him, he said, 'Thou art Simon the son of Jonah: thou shalt be called Cephas, which is by interpretation, a stone.'" (John 1:42). Peter, the first Pope, is the rock on which the Church is built.
9   St Paul. "The Lord said... he is a chosen vessel unto me, to bear my name before the Gentiles..." (Acts 9:15).

And every whirl made them more beautiful.
They gathered round this light, and there they stayed,
    And they cried out with such a depth of sound   140
    The earth provides no fit similitude –
Nor could I understand it, thunder-stunned.

CANTO XXII

Confused by the cry raised by the spirits and unable to grasp its meaning, Dante turns to Beatrice. She comforts him by reminding him that, since he is in Heaven, all that is said and done is the result of holy zeal and not to be feared. If he had understood that cry, he would know that vengeance will fall upon corrupt prelates.

Dante looks towards other spirits on this planet. One of them comes forward and, when Dante hesitates to speak, explains that he will answer Dante's unspoken question. He is St Benedict, the founder of Western monasticism. All the souls with him were in their mortal lives contemplatives. He praises St Macarius and St Romualdus as two monks who kept their vows.

Dante asks if he may be allowed to see St Benedict in the flesh, and not hidden, as are all these souls, in light. Benedict tells him that this will only be possible in the Empyrean, where all desires will be gratified.

Benedict laments the degeneration of the Benedictine Order, especially their misappropriation of money intended for the poor, and their use of it to enrich relatives and concubines. Benedict says that the Church began with St Peter in poverty, his own order began with prayer and fasting, and the Franciscans began with humility; but now they all fall short of these ideals. Nevertheless, a miracle of transformation is still possible. With that, Benedict rejoins his fellow souls, and they all sweep away upwards.

Obedient to a gesture from Beatrice, Dante follows Benedict, and in an instant finds himself in the sphere of the fixed stars, in the zodiacal sign of Gemini, under which he was born. He prays for help to continue his poem.

Beatrice tells Dante to look down. He sees all the spheres he has been through and, in the centre, our earth, which seems so insignificant. Dante recalls briefly all the sin and trouble which takes place on earth, and then he turns his eyes back to Beatrice.

Half-stunned,[1] in my bewilderment I bent
    Towards my guide, just as an infant does
    Who runs to where he feels most confident –
And then she, motherlike, quick to support
    Her pale and panting baby with the sound
    Of mother's voice and put him in good heart,
Asked me: "Have you not realized yet you are
    In Heaven now, where everything is holy?
    And all is done for good that is done here?
And how the singing would have altered you,   10
    And how my smiling would, you may imagine,
    Now that the sound alone has moved you so.[2]
If you had heard the prayer within that cry,
    You would already understand the vengeance[3]
    Which you will see before you come to die.

---

1   See *Par.* xxi, 140–42.
2   See *Par.* xxi, 4–12.
3   Upon corrupt and avaricious prelates.

The sword which strikes from up here does not cut
  Too early or too late but in their view
  Who long or tremble as they wait for it.
But now turn where the other spirits are:
  You shall see many who are notable,   20
  If you but look – I shall instruct you where."
According to her wish, I turned my eyes
  To where a hundred little suns together
  Were made more beautiful by mutual rays.
I stood like one who stifles his desire,
  Although it stings, and does not dare to question,
  Because he is afraid he'll go too far.
And then the largest, most illustrious
  Of all those jewels came up to the front
  To grant my wish by saying who he was.   30
And from within I heard: "Could you but see,
  As I, the charity that burns in us,
  Your thoughts would be expressed without delay.
But, lest by such delay you should be late
  Arriving at your goal,[1] I shall now answer
  The thought itself, since you so hesitate.
That mount which has Cassino on its slopes
  Was long ago frequented on its summit
  By folk who were deluded, ill-disposed,[2]
And I am he[3] who introduced the name   40
  Up there of Him who had brought down to earth
  That Truth enabling men to be sublime.
And such the splendour of the grace which filled
  Me I drew all the places round about
  From that foul cult which so corrupts the world.
These other lights were all contemplative
  Christians, and kindled by that warmth which brings
  The flowers and fruits of holiness to birth.
Macarius[4] and Romualdus[5] are both here –
  Here are my brothers too who kept their feet   50
  Inside the cloisters, keeping their hearts pure."
And I replied: "The love you demonstrate
  In speaking, and the kindly countenance
  Which shines in you, of which I take good note,
Make me enormously more confident,

---

1 The vision of God in the Empyrean.
2 A reference to Mount Cairo, on which there was an ancient temple of Apollo.
3 St Benedict (c.480-c.547), patriarch of western monasticism, who founded the famous
   monastery of Monte Cassino and established the Benedictine Order.
4 Probably St Macarius of Alexandria (d.405), credited with having established monasti-
   cism in the East.
5 St Romualdus (c.960-c.1027), founder of the Order of Camaldoli or Reformed
   Benedictines.

Just like the sun, which opens up the rose
    Until it blossoms to its full extent.
Therefore I beg, and ask you if such grace,
    My father, can be granted me that I
    May have the sight of your uncovered face."   60
And he replied: "Your high desire, my brother,
    Will find fulfilment in the highest sphere,[1]
    As will my own desire and every other.
There is perfection, ripeness, wholeness in
    That highest sphere of all desiring, where
    Each part remains where it has always been.[2]
It has no poles, and it is not in space:
    Our ladder reaches up to it, and that
    Is why it flies away beyond your gaze.
Once by the patriarch Jacob it was seen   70
    To lift its highest rungs from earth to heaven,
    When he saw angels moving up and down.[3]
But now, in order to get there, no one
    Will lift his feet up off the earth: my rule
    But spoils the parchment it is written on.
The walls which formed a house of holy zeal
    Are now dens of iniquity, the cowls
    Are now sacks overflowing with foul meal.
Excessive usury is not so bad,
    Not such a slight to God, as is that harvest   80
    Which makes the greedy hearts of monks run mad,
Since what the Church is keeping in her purse
    Belongs to those who ask it in God's name,[4]
    And not to relatives or someone worse.
The flesh of mortals is so soft and weak
    That a good start on earth does not endure
    The time it takes for acorns from an oak.[5]
Peter began with no gold and no silver,
    And I began with prayer and fasting – Francis
    In all humility began his Order.   90
If you look at the start of every one,
    And then you look to see where they have travelled,
    You will discover white becoming brown.
Yet Jordan turning back,[6] and the Red Sea
    Fleeing at God's command,[7] were more amazing

---

1   The Empyrean.
2   The Empyrean is motionless.
3   Gen. 28:12.
4   The poor.
5   The brief period from the planting of an oak to its fructifying.
6   Josh. 3:14–17.
7   Exod. 14:21–29. Lines 94–95 suggest how it would take a miracle, but not an exceptional
    one, to remedy this state of affairs.

Than any remedy for this would be."
So he explained to me, and then he turned
    Back to his company. They reassembled,
    Then all swept up as in a whirling wind.
My dearest lady thrust me up that ladder   100
    Behind them, just by making one small sign,
    So far her power had overcome my nature:
Down here on earth, where rising, plummeting
    Must always follow nature's laws, was never
    Motion as swift as mine upon the wing.
So, reader, as I hope to see the blessed
    Triumphal souls again – for which I often
    Bewail my sins and beat my sinful breast –
You would not in so short a time pull out
    Your finger from a flame as I perceived   110
    The sign that seeks the Bull and entered it.[1]
O glorious stars, crammed to capacity
    With mighty power, to which I am indebted
    For all my talents, such as they may be[2] –
Rising with you, and hiding himself there,
    Was he, the father of all mortal life,[3]
    When I breathed my first breath of Tuscan air:
And now, when I was granted that great grace
    Of entering the high sphere that moves you round,
    It was your region that became my place.   120
My soul is sighing now in heartfelt prayer
    In hope of gaining the ability
    To take the hard road that awaits me here.[4]
"You are so near the final blessedness,"
    So Beatrice began, "that both your eyes
    Are open now and more acute – and thus,
Before you enter further into that,[5]
    You should look down upon the universe
    I have already put beneath your feet,
So that your heart, rejoicing more than ever,   130
    May be presented to the crowds in triumph
    Who come rejoicing through this curving ether."[6]
So, turning back my eyes, I looked through all
    The seven spheres below, and saw this globe,[7]

1   Dante has risen to the eighth sphere, that of the fixed stars, and entered it at the zodiacal
     sign of Gemini, which follows that of Taurus.
2   Dante was born under Gemini (c.21st May to 21st June) which was believed to predispose
     the soul to study and letters.
3   The sun.
4   Probably referring to the artistic difficulties which Dante still faces as a poet.
5   The "final blessedness" of l. 124.
6   This heavenly sphere.
7   The earth, immobile at the centre of the universe.

And had to smile at the sad spectacle.
And I approve the man who thinks of it
   As but the least of things: who looks elsewhere
   May justly be considered in the right.
I saw Latona's daughter's radiance[1]
  - Without that shade in her which previously   140
   Had made me think of her as rare and dense.[2]
I saw how your son[3] looks, Hyperion,
   And stayed undazzled, and I looked at Dione
   And Maia,[4] both circling near to him.
And then I looked at temperate Jupiter[5]
   Between the father and the son – and how
   These vary their positions was quite clear.
And all the seven planets could be seen,
   How vast they are, how rapidly they move,
   And what great distances there are between.   150
The tiny threshing floor on which we're vicious[6] –
   As I wheeled with the Twins – came to my gaze,
   Entire, from mountain peaks to mouths of rivers.
I turned my eyes back to her lovely eyes.

---

1   The brightness of the moon.
2   See the discussion at *Par.* II, 46–148 (esp. ll. 59–60) of the dark patches on the moon.
3   Apollo, the sun.
4   The planets Venus and Mercury are referred to here by the names of their mythological parents: Dione and Maia respectively.
5   The planet Jupiter was thought to be temperate: it revolved between the cold planet Saturn (Jupiter's father) and the hot planet Mars (Jupiter's son).
6   Our world.

CANTO XXIII

Dante looks at Beatrice, who stands in keen expectation, like a mother bird waiting for dawn when she will be able to feed her little ones.

Then Christ appears in triumph with His saints, but Dante's sight cannot endure the vision of Christ's resurrected body. Beatrice comforts him by explaining that this is a vision which conquers everyone.

Dante is now able to look at Beatrice's smile, which gives him a joy that he cannot express – some things in Heaven are ineffable – and cannot indeed quite recall, although the joy the sight gave remains with him and will always do so. Dante emphasizes to the reader the difficulties of his task of conveying a vision of Heaven.

Beatrice draws Dante's attention to the Mystical Rose, which is the Virgin Mary, and the lilies with her, which represent the Apostles. Dante can see crowds of spirits, but he cannot see their source in Christ. There is a circle of light around the Virgin, which is also a circle of music: the Archangel Gabriel is singing in praise of the Virgin. Then, as the singing finishes, all the other lights or spirits make the name of Mary resound.

The Primum Mobile, or Crystalline Sphere, which causes all the other spheres to revolve, is so far distant from Dante that he cannot see it, and his eyes cannot follow the Virgin as she follows Christ into the Empyrean. All the sainted spirits stretch out their flames in adoration of the Virgin, but remain where Dante can see them and hear them singing the *"Regina cœli"* in her honour.

Dante expresses his joy in the great heavenly wealth the saints have won by despising wealth on earth. He ends by speaking of St Peter, now triumphant and holding the keys of the Kingdom of Heaven. As often happens, these last few lines of the canto hint at important matters to follow.

M ost like that bird – close by the leaves of home,
    Perched near the nest which holds her little ones,
    Throughout the night which hides all things in
gloom –
Who, anxious to behold their longed-for faces
    And find the usual food to nourish them
    (A hard labour indeed, but one which pleases),
On a bare branch wishes the time away
    And ardently desires the well-loved sun,
    Waiting intently for the break of day:
That was the way in which my lady stood,   10
    Upright and eager, looking to that region[1]
    Beneath whose arc the sun slackens its speed.
And I, seeing her there and so caught up,
    Became like one who, while he longs for what
    He does not have, is satisfied with hope.
But time was short between each instant there,
    Between expectancy, I mean, and seeing

---

1   The meridian, where the sun "stands" at noon.

The sky becoming radiant more and more.
And Beatrice said: "Behold the hosts of those
  Who triumph in Christ's Triumph, all the fruit   20
  Harvested by the turning of these spheres!"[1]
Her face was glowing, and so ardently,
  And her eyes overflowing with such joy,
  That all words fail me, and I pass it by.
As, when the moon is full and all's at peace,
  Trivia[2] smiles, while her attendant nymphs[3]
  Colour the sky unto its last recess,
Putting a thousand lights into the shade,
  There was one Sun[4] enkindling all of them,
  As our sun does the lustres overhead.   30
And through the living brilliance, bright and clear,
  The Substance[5] pierced, with an intensity
  Such as these mortal eyes could not endure.
O Beatrice, my sweet and loving guide!
  She said to me: "What overcomes you is
  A strength against which nothing can provide.
Here is the wisdom and here is the power
  Which opened up the road from earth to Heaven
  For which there had so long been such desire."
And just as from a cloud a fire[6] breaks forth,   40
  Expanding till it cannot be contained,
  And quite against its nature[7] strikes the earth:
Just so my mind, within that festival,
  Expanded till it issued from itself,
  And what it then became I can't recall.
"Open your eyes – see me more beautiful:
  You have seen such things as enable you
  To gaze unflinchingly into my smile."
I was like one who knows he has come round
  From a forgotten vision, and is striving   50
  In vain to bring it back into his mind,
When I was made this offer, which was one
  So gladdening as never to be stricken
  Out of the book of what is past and gone.
If all those tongues were now to sound aloud
  Which Polyhymnia[8] with all her sisters
  Had fortified with their nutritious food,

---

1   The result of heavenly influences upon mankind.
2   The moon, personified as Diana with her nymphs.
3   Stars.
4   Christ.
5   Christ in His resurrected body.
6   Lightning.
7   The natural tendency of fire is to rise.
8   The Muse of singing and rhetoric.

They would not even reach a thousandth part
    Of what is true about her sacred smile,
    And how it made her sacred face so bright –   60
And so, in symbolizing Paradise,
    The sacred poem has to leap at times,
    Like walkers who find obstacles to cross.
But no one who regards the weighty theme,
    And sees the mortal shoulders which must bear it,
    And sees them tremble, will find cause to blame:
This is no voyage for a little vessel,
    These waters my audacious prow is cleaving,
    Nor for a boatman who would spare his muscle.
"Why are you so enamoured of my face   70
    You do not contemplate the lovely garden
    Which blossoms in the splendour of Christ's rays?
Here is the Rose[1] in which the Holy Word
    Became incarnate – here are all the lilies[2]
    Whose fragrance manifested the right road."
Thus Beatrice – and I, eager to submit
    To her good counsels, once again surrendered
    To the bewilderment of my weak sight.
As I have seen the sun through fractured cloud
    Irradiate a meadow full of flowers,   80
    With both my eyes protected in the shade,
So I saw crowds of spirits, glorious
    Under the rays which burned down from above,
    Yet could not trace the shining to its source.
O kindly Power, You who imprint them so,
    You raised Yourself, withdrew to give me space,
    And spared my sight not strong enough for You!
The name of that fair flower,[3] to which my prayer
    Rises each morning and each evening, drew me
    To concentrate upon the greatest fire.   90
And when on both my eyes the living star,
    Its magnitude and nature, was depicted,
    Conquering all up there and all down here,
Then from within the sky a torch came down
    And girdled her and circled round about her,
    Shaped like a ring in likeness of a crown.
Whatever tune is most enrapturing
    Down here, and draws the soul towards itself,
    Would seem a broken cloud that's thundering,
When weighed against the music of that lyre   100
    With which I saw the lovely sapphire crowned
    By whom the brightest heaven becomes sapphire.

---

1   The Virgin Mary.
2   The Apostles.
3   Mary, the Mystical Rose. See ll. 73–75 above.

"I am the angelic love:[1] I always gyre
    About the gladness breathing from the womb
    Which was the dwelling place of our Desire –
And, Lady of Heaven, I shall always turn,
    Until you, following your Son, have entered
    The highest sphere[2] and made it more divine."
Immediately the circumscribing hymn
    Had sealed itself, all of the other lights   110
    Resounded with the sound of Mary's name.
The royal cloak[3] of all the turning spheres
    Within the universe, which is most ardent
    And quickening in God's breath and in His laws,
Had high above us its internal shore,[4]
    Which was so distant not a glimpse of it,
    From where I was positioned, could appear:
And so these eyes of mine did not succeed
    In following the lady crowned with flame
    As she ascended after her own Seed.   120
And as a little baby lifts his arms
    Towards the mother who has suckled him,
    So that his love in outward gesture flames,
Each of those incandescent lights stretched out
    Its rising flame, so that the deep affection
    They had for Mary was without a doubt.
Then they remained there, still within my sight,
    Singing *"Regina cœli"*[5] – and so sweetly
    That I have never lost that first delight.
Oh what abundance is there crammed within   130
    Those fecund vessels[6] which down here on earth
    Were in their sowing such good husbandmen!
Now they live there, delighting in untold
    Riches acquired in their lamented exile
    In Babylon,[7] where they rejected gold.
Now here he[8] triumphs in his victory,
    Under the Son of God and Mary, and
    With both the old and new consistory,[9]
Who has the keys of glory in his hand.[10]

1   The Archangel Gabriel.
2   The Empyrean.
3   The Primum Mobile, which keeps all the other spheres in motion.
4   Its concave surface.
5   'Queen of Heaven', a hymn to the Virgin, sung at Easter.
6   The saints.
7   The exile of the Jews in Babylon (597-c.538 BC) was a common image for mortals on
    earth exiled from their true home in Heaven.
8   St Peter.
9   The saints from the Old and New Dispensations.
10   Matt. 16:18–19: "Thou art Peter, and upon this rock I will build my church... And I will
    give unto thee the keys of the kingdom of heaven."

CANTO XXIV

Beatrice asks the souls in the sphere of the fixed stars to satisfy Dante's curiosity about the things of Heaven. The lights representing the souls form themselves into spheres which revolve and flash, differently but in concord. From the brightest of these spheres a fire issues and, singing a hymn, revolves three times round Beatrice. Dante cannot describe this hymn, since neither his language nor his imagination is subtle enough.

Beatrice asks the fire which encircled her, who we now find is St Peter, to catechize Dante on his faith. When asked what faith is, Dante replies by quoting St Paul: "The substance of things hoped for, the evidence of things not seen". He then has to explain why he says faith is a substance, and how it can be evidence, and his replies are so satisfactory that St Peter praises him. He is asked whether he has this faith, and he replies that he has. Asked where it comes from, Dante says from the Scriptures which, as the miracles described in them show, are the word of God. St Peter objects that this sounds like a circular argument, since the miracles are described in the very works whose inspiration they are said to attest. Dante replies with an age-old argument: the spread of Christianity, from such unlikely beginnings, is a greater miracle than any other. His reply ends with a glancing blow at the corruption of the Church in his day. The 'Te Deum' is heard, sounding in approval of Dante's answers. Asked by St Peter how he comes to have faith, Dante replies that there are various proofs, physical and metaphysical ones, and also the words of the Holy Spirit as it comes to us through the Scriptures. This leads him to speak of the Holy Trinity as the source of all enlightenment. St Peter is so pleased with these replies that he, or rather the light which represents him, embraces Dante three times.

"O fellowship invited to the feast
    Of the blessed Lamb of God, Who nurtures you
    So your desires are always set at rest,
Since by God's will this man has a foretaste
    Of fragments that keep falling from your table,
    Even before his time on earth is past,
Direct your minds to his immense desire,
    And so bedew him somewhat: you are always
    Tasting that fount[1] he has such longing for."
Thus Beatrice – and those delighted souls,   10
    Blazing and flashing like so many comets,
    Made themselves spheres revolving on fixed poles.
And as wheels in a clock, in harmony,
    Revolve so that the large one, when observed,
    Seems static, and the smallest one to fly;[2]
So those revolving dancing spheres, by go-
    ing variously, made me realize

---

1   The truth, which is "a well of water springing up into everlasting life" (John 4:14).
2   These are toothed wheels, the largest one, which is turned by a weight, governing the smaller ones, which then move faster.

What wealth is theirs, as they were swift or slow.
From one sphere, of a beauty even greater
   Than all the others, issued fire, so gladly   20
   It left behind it nothing that was brighter.
And it revolved three times round Beatrice,
   Singing meanwhile an anthem so sublime
   Imagination cannot cope with this.
My pen must leap, and leave it all unsaid:
   To paint such folds and shades imagination's,
   Not merely speech's, palette is too loud.[1]
"O holy sister, your devoted prayer
   To us, inspired by such intense affection,
   Has separated me from that bright sphere."   30
Thus, having stopped revolving, the blessed fire
   Breathed out its loving breath towards my lady,
   And said those words which I've repeated here.
Then she: "Eternal light of that great man[2]
   To whom on earth Our Lord bequeathed the keys
   Of this amazing joy, which He brought down,
Test this man here on all points, grave or slighter,
   As it seems right to you to do, concerning
   The faith by which you once walked on the water.[3]
His love, his hope, his faith are not unknown   40
   To you, and if they're strong or weak: you see
   Where everything that happens can be seen.
But since this realm is citizened throughout
   By the true faith, then to express the glory
   It's right that he should have to speak of it."
Now, as the bachelor prepares, tongue-tied,
   Until the master has proposed the matter
   That he must argue over, not decide,[4]
So I prepared myself with every reason
   While she was speaking, wishing to be ready   50
   For such a questioner, such a profession.
"Good Christian, speak – make yourself manifest:
   Say what faith is." I raised my face towards
   The light by which this question was expressed,
Then turned to Beatrice, and Beatrice made
   A sign immediately that I should open
   The waters of the source I have inside.[5]
"Now may the Grace that sanctions my confession

---

1   The metaphor is of folds in clothing, which are reproduced in a painting in shades more
    subdued than the rest of the material.
2   St Peter. See *Par.* XXIII, 136–39.
3   Matt. 14:25–31.
4   A procedure in medieval universities: the master proposed the matter for discussion,
    the bachelor/student discussed it, and then the master settled it.
5   The ideas which well up in his mind.

In presence of the Chief Centurion,"[1]
I prayed, "allow my thoughts their full expression."   60
I carried on: "As he who wrote the truth
    Said to us, father – and I mean your brother,[2]
    He who, with you, set Rome on the right path,
Faith is the substance of things hoped for, with
    The evidence of things not seen[3] – and this
    Appears to me its essence and its pith."
And then he said: "Your answer shows good sense,
    If you know why he says faith is a substance,
    And then defines it as the evidence."
I said: "Those things which are profound, and show   70
    Themselves to me in these appearances,
    Are hidden from the eyes of men below,
Where their existence lives in faith alone,
    Which is the very groundwork of high hope:
    Faith is the substance hope is based upon.
Now from this faith, without more proof of it,
    We syllogize – and of all argument
    Evidence is a necessary part."
And then I heard: "If all that we are taught,
    Down there on earth, were understood so well,   80
    There'd be no place for sophists and their wit."
It was that kindled love[4] which breathed that out,
    And then it added: "You have tried and tested
    The alloy in this money and its weight,
But tell me if you have it in your purse."
    And I replied: "I have – so round, so bright
    It could not possibly be spurious."
Next from the depth of light which there rejoiced
    These words issued: "Tell me: this precious gem,
    Bedrock on which the virtues are all based,   90
Where is it from?" Then I: "The heavy dew,
    Shed by the Holy Spirit and diffused
    Throughout both Testaments, the Old and New,
Presents a syllogism[5] with such point
    That it concludes the matter in my mind,
    While other arguments seem dull and blunt."
And then I heard: "These premises which lead,
    The Old, the New, up to this firm conclusion –
    Why do you think they are the word of God?"
Then I: "The proof which brings the truth to light   100

---

1   St Peter, leading the Church Militant.
2   St Paul.
3   Heb. 11:1.
4   St Peter.
5   I.e. an argument, which in medieval universities had to be in syllogistic form.

Lies in the works[1] that followed, for which nature
  Never beat anvil or made iron hot."[2]
Then the reply came: "Why do you believe
  That these things happened, when attested by
  The book whose truth is what you have to prove?"[3]
"Had the world turned to Christianity,"
  I said, "not needing miracles, that were
  A miracle greater than all could be;
For you yourself were poor and hungry once,
  And came into the field to sow the plant   110
  Which grew into a vine now turned to thorns."[4]
This done, the high and holy chorus sang
  "*Te Deum*",[5] sounding through the spheres in such
  A melody as only there is sung.
And then that spirit who, from test to test,
  Had led me on and up through all the branches
  Until we neared the foliage on the crest,
Began again: "Grace, which so loves to woo
  Your intellect, has opened up your mouth
  And helped you speak as it behoves you to,   120
So I approve all that has left your mouth:
  But now you must explain what you believe,
  And how it was you came to have that faith."
"O Holy Father, spirit who have come
  To see at last what you believed so firmly
  You outran younger feet to reach the tomb,"[6]
So I began, "You wish me to make plain
  The essence of my confident belief,
  And also to declare its origin.
And I reply: my faith is in one sole   130
  God, Who has made the heavens in love, and Who,
  Eternally unmoving, moves them all.
For this I have not only many a proof,
  Physical and metaphysical, but also,
  Descending like the rain from heaven, the truth
Through Moses, Psalms and prophets and, not least,
  The Gospel narratives, and you Apostles
  When you were quickened by the Holy Ghost.
Three persons I believe in also: this
  Eternal essence, truly one and trine,   140

---

1 Miracles.
2 I.e. could not have natural causes.
3 St Peter suggests Dante is arguing in a circle.
4 The spread of Christianity by poor men such as St Peter is a miracle greater than any other. The "vine" is the Church, and the "thorns" represent its corruption by self-indulgent prelates.
5 The hymn 'Te Deum laudamus' ('Thee, Lord, We Praise'), always sung at times of rejoicing.
6 John 20:3–9, where Peter reaches the tomb of Christ later than John, but enters it first.

Is written equally with 'are' or 'is'.[1]
The Gospel more than once has left its mark
  Upon my mind, concerning this profound
  Mysterious circumstance of which I speak.
This is the principle, this is the spark
  Spreading until it bursts into a flame
  Which like a star illuminates the dark."
Like the master who hears what gives delight,
  And throws his arms around the messenger,
  The instant that the messenger is mute,   150
So, as he blessed me and he sang, I found
  Myself thrice circled, at my final word,
  By the apostle's light at whose command
I spoke – he was so pleased with what I said!

---

1   The Holy Trinity is singular and plural at once.

CANTO XXV

Dante expresses his fervent wish that his sacred poem may help to end his exile from his native Florence, and that he may be crowned with laurel in the Baptistery there, his beloved San Giovanni.

    The sphere out of which St Peter emerged now releases a second light, and Beatrice identifies this as St James the Greater. The two lights greet each other with joy, and Dante is dazzled by them. St James encourages Dante to speak, and asks him to say what hope is and how he comes to have it. After Beatrice has emphasized the strength of the hope that is in Dante, he answers the questions. The hope is for future glory, and it is the result of the grace of God and the soul's own merit. It has come to Dante from many sources, and especially from the Psalms and then from the Epistle of St James himself. St James is pleased with this answer, and he asks for more detail on what is being hoped for. Dante replies that it is the hope of a life in Heaven for both body and soul. All the revolving spheres are delighted with this answer.

    Dante has supported his last answer with a reference to St John's Revelation. At this, a third light, as bright as the sun, comes from the same sphere as St Peter and St James, and all three lights dance in harmony. Beatrice introduces this new light as St John the Apostle. He explains that he cannot be seen by Dante, because his body has not yet been resurrected. Only Christ Himself and the Virgin have been assumed body and soul into Heaven: other saved souls must wait for the Last Day to be reunited with their bodies.

    Suddenly the dancing and music stop. Dante is left in some confusion, since he is still blinded by the light of St John, and therefore he cannot look at Beatrice, even though he is close to her and they are in Heaven.

If it should happen that the sacred verse,
   In which both heaven and earth have played their part,
   And which has kept me haggard all these years,
Should overcome the hate which bars me out
   Of my own fold,[1] where I slept as a lamb,
   An enemy to wolves[2] that war on it,
Then with an altered voice,[3] an altered fleece[4]
   I shall return, a poet, to receive
   The laurels where my baptism took place[5] –
Because into the faith which makes souls known   10
   To God I entered there, and afterwards
   For that faith Peter circled thus my crown.[6]
What happened next was that a light came forth
   From that same sphere, after the first[7] of those

---

1   His native Florence, which had exiled him.
2   Malignant Florentines.
3   More mature poetry.
4   Grey hair.
5   The Baptistery, "my beloved San Giovanni" of *Inf.* XIX, 17.
6   See *Par.* XXIV, 151–54.
7   St Peter, the first Pope.

Whom Christ left as His vicars upon earth.
And then my lady, full of gladness, said:
  "Look, look! This is the saint because of whom
  On earth Galicia is visited."[1]
As when a turtle dove flies to his mate,
  And they make manifest their mutual   20
  Affection, as they murmur and gyrate –
In that way I saw each of those august
  And glorious princes welcomed by the other,
  Praising the food[2] on which up there they feast.
When their felicitations were complete,
  They both paused silently in front of me,
  So dazzling that they overcame my sight.
Beatrice smiled, rejoicing, and she said:
  "Famed life, by whom the generosity
  Of our basilica has been displayed,[3]   30
Send hope re-echoing through this heavenly height:
  You know how often you became its symbol,
  When Christ showed in the three his great delight."[4]
"Lift up your head – you may be well assured –
  Whatever comes here from the mortal world,
  It is in rays of ours it is matured."
This comfort reached me from the second blaze,[5]
  And so I raised my eyes up to those hills[6]
  Which had before so overwhelmed my eyes.
"Since through His grace it is our Emperor's will   40
  That you come face to face, before your death,
  With His attendants in His inmost hall,
In order that, once you have seen this court,
  You reinforce, both in yourself and others,
  Hope which makes us enamoured of the right –
Say what it is, say how it blossoms in
  Your mind, and from what source you have derived it."
  It was the second light who spoke again.
That tender lady, who had been my guide
  And feathered me for such a lofty flight,   50
  Gave the reply for me before I could:
"Church Militant has no son more possessed
  Of hope than he, as we can see it written
  Within the Sun Who shines throughout our host:

---

1   St James the Greater, whose shrine at Santiago de Compostela is still a place of pilgrimage.
2   The spiritual nourishment of seeing God.
3   Beatrice is addressing St James, and referring particularly to James 1:5.
4   St Peter, St James and St John, Christ's most favoured disciples, symbolizing respectively faith, hope and charity.
5   St James.
6   The two apostles. This image of enlightenment and assistance is biblical, e.g. Psalms 121:1: "I will lift up mine eyes unto the hills, from whence cometh my help."

Therefore it has been granted him to come
    From Egypt to Jerusalem,[1] to see it
    Before his days of soldiering are done.
And those two other questions, which you do
    Not ask for information, but that he
    May tell how much this virtue pleases you,   60
I leave to him: he will not find them hard,
    Nor will they make him boast – so let him answer,
    And may the grace of God come to his aid."
Like students with their master, well-prepared
    And eager in so far as they are able,
    So that their competence may be displayed,
I said: "Hope is the certain expectation
    Of glory in the future, and produced
    By grace and merit in anticipation.
From many stars this light comes as my guide: 70
    But he who poured it in my heart first was
    The supreme singer[2] of the supreme Lord.
'And may they hope in You,' so says one Psalm,
    'Who know Your name'[3] – and is there anybody,
    With faith like mine, who does not know God's name?
From his distilling you poured hope again
    From your epistle,[4] till I overflow,
    And now I rain on others with your rain."
While I was speaking, from the living breast
    Of that great blazing came a trembling flame,   80
    Quick as repeated lightning, burst on burst.
And then it breathed: "The love with which I flame
    Towards that virtue which pursued me till
    I quit the field once I had won the palm,[5]
Wills that I breathe on you who live and long
    In this great hope – and now it is my pleasure
    That you explain what hope is promising."
I said: "The Scriptures, Old and New, set up
    The target for those souls whom God befriends,
    And this is what is promised me by hope.   90
Isaiah says each of the chosen wears
    A double vesture in his native land[6] –

---

1   From the earth, a place of exile, to Heaven, man's true home.
2   King David, author of the Psalms.
3   Dante translates from the Vulgate Psalms 9:11. The Authorised Version, where it is
    Psalms 9:10, gives a slightly different sense.
4   The General Epistle of James.
5   Died, having won his place in Heaven.
6   Isaiah 61:7: "In their land they shall possess the double: everlasting joy shall be unto
    them." Dante relates this to verse 10: "He hath clothed me with the garments of salva-
    tion." The "double vesture" signifies body and soul.

His native land being this sweet land of ours.[1]
And by your brother[2] it has been expressed
   In detail: when he talks of the white robes[3]
   He makes this revelation manifest."
And first, the instant that these words were said,
   "*Sperent in te*"[4] above us all resounded,
   To which all the revolving spheres replied.
Then from them blazed out such a brilliant ray   100
   That, if a star like this were seen in Cancer,
   Winter would boast a month of endless day.[5]
And, as a virgin rises up to tread
   The dance, not vainly or for some worse motive,
   But by her action honouring the bride,
Just so I saw that brightening splendour move
   Towards the other two, who danced in rhythm,
   As was most fitting for their ardent love.
He entered in the singing and the dance –
   Meanwhile my lady held her eyes upon them,   110
   Like a new bride, silent and motionless.
"This is the one who lay upon the breast
   Of Christ our pelican,[6] the one in whom,
   Upon the cross, the greatest trust was placed."[7]
So said my lady – and she did no more
   Remove her eyes from their steadfast intent
   After her words were spoken than before.
Like someone who has squinnied and has strained
   To see the sun when partially eclipsed,
   And who with looking hard has ended blind,   120
So I became in front of this last fire,
   Until these words were said: "Why do you dazzle
   In your attempts to see what is not there?
My body is earth in earth, and shall remain

---

1   Heaven.

2   St John.

3   Rev. 7:9: "After this I beheld, and lo, a great multitude... stood before the throne, and before the Lamb, clothed with white robes."

4   "May they hope in You" (Latin), as in l. 73 above.

5   Between 21st December and 21st January the constellation Cancer rises in the east as the sun is setting in the west: if Cancer contained a star as bright as this light which represents St John, then there would be continuous daylight during that month.

6   John 13:23: "Now there was leaning on Jesus's bosom one of his disciples, whom Jesus loved." The disciple is St John. The pelican, reputed to tear open its own breast to feed its young with its blood, is a common symbol for Christ, Who sacrificed Himself for sinners.

7   John 19:25–27: "Now there stood by the cross of Jesus his mother... when Jesus... saw his mother, and the disciple standing by, whom he loved, he saith unto his mother, 'Woman, behold thy son!' Then saith he to the disciple, 'Behold thy mother!' And from that hour the disciple took her unto his own home."

With all the others, till our number equals
    All those envisaged in the eternal plan.[1]
In the blessed cloister with the double robe[2]
    Are only those two lights who have ascended[3] –
    And this you must report in your own globe."
With this the scintillating circle ended   130
    The dancing and the mellow harmony
    Made by the sound of their three voices[4] blended,
As when, forestalling weariness or peril,
    The oars, which have been striking on the water,
    Pause all together at the helmsman's whistle.
Then, oh what turbulence was troubling me,
    When I turned round to look at Beatrice,
    And could not look at her, albeit I
Was close to her, and in the world of bliss![5]

---

1   His body will be reunited with his soul on the Last Day, when all those who are to be
    saved will have been saved.
2   With the "double vesture" of l. 92, i.e. in body and soul.
3   Christ and the Virgin. See *Par.* XXIII, 118–20.
4   Peter, James and John.
5   Dante has been blinded by the light of St John (ll. 118–23).

CANTO XXVI

St John reassures Dante that his blindness is temporary: Beatrice will restore it as Ananias did for St Paul. Meanwhile Dante should compensate for the loss of his sight by putting his thoughts into words.

St John says that it is not sufficient for Dante to say his aim is the knowledge of God: he must also say how he knows that God is the Supreme Love to which all should aspire. Dante replies that sources for this belief are philosophy, which is the exercise of human reason, and the Sacred Scriptures. Dante mentions particularly some words of God to Moses and St John's own introduction to his Gospel, which is a salient piece of theology. The nature of the world, Dante's own nature as a human being, Christ's Passion in His love for mankind and even some of the ordinary things of life (if they are loved in the right way) all point in the same direction.

Heaven resounds with the cry of "Holy, holy, holy!" in approval of Dante's answers, and Beatrice rewards him by enabling him to see again, indeed see better than before.

Dante can now see a fourth light, in company with St Peter, St James and St John, and he asks who this is. He is told that this is Adam, the first man, the only one created as an adult, and the progenitor of all humankind. Adam answers Dante's unspoken questions. The fault which led to the loss of Eden lay not essentially in the eating of forbidden fruit, but in the transgression against God's command. Adam gives the time he spent in Limbo after his death as 4,302 years, the length of his life as 930 years, and the time he spent in Eden, both as an innocent man and after the Fall, as a mere six hours. He explains that the language he spoke was already extinct by the time that men began to build the Tower of Babel: language, like all human inventions, changes continually.

W hile I was standing full of apprehension
  Because of my lost sight, the flame that quenched it[1]
  Sent out a breath that caught all my attention,
Saying: "Until you have your vision back,
  Which you exhausted as you gazed at me,
  It would be well to compensate with talk.
Begin therefore, and tell me to what end
  Your soul aspires – remember that you are
  But dazzled, and not permanently blind:
The lady who conducts you through this land   10
  Of God possesses in her eyes the power
  That Ananias wielded with his hand."[2]
I said: "At her good pleasure, late or soon,
  May comfort reach these eyes, these gates she entered
  Bringing the fire in which I always burn.[3]
The Good which keeps this court so satisfied

---

1 St John.
2 Ananias, an early follower of Christ, restored St Paul's sight (Acts 9:17).
3 His love for Beatrice, not negated by his experiences in Heaven, came with his first sight of her.

Is Alpha and Omega of all the writings
Love reads to me, with low voice or with loud."[1]
The very voice[2] which had dispelled that fear
   Of mine at such a sudden dazzlement   20
   Now turned my mind towards discourse once more.
He said to me: "You certainly must work
   With a much finer sieve – you must declare
   What made you aim your bow at such a mark."
I answered: "Reason and philosophy,
   And the authority sent down from here
   In Scripture, have imprinted love in me,
For goodness – in so far as understood
   As goodness – kindles love and kindles love
   The more, the more that it contains of good.   30
Hence, to the Essence with such potency
   That any good which may be found outside It
   Is but a light reflected from Its ray,
More than to any other essence must
   That mind be moved, in loving, which discerns
   The truth on which this argument is based.
My mind is helped to grasp what this truth is
   By him[3] who demonstrates the primal love
   Of all the everlasting substances.[4]
And the true Author makes this patent for me,   40
   Saying to Moses, speaking of Himself:
   'I will make all my goodness pass before thee.'[5]
You too express it in your introduction[6]
   When you proclaim these mysteries, which are here,
   Down there beyond all other proclamation."
Then I heard: "Human intellects conclude,
   And all authorities agree with them,
   The highest of your loves is fixed on God.
But say if you feel other cables too
   Drawing you unto Him, that you may blazon   50
   How many teeth this love has into you."
The meaning of Christ's eagle[7] was not hidden:
   I easily perceived his sacred purpose,
   And where he wished to go with my profession.
I said: "All of those teeth which bite on me

1   The personification of Love is in the manner of Dante's early poetry. The phrase "with low voice or with loud" suggests that some writings on love manifest God more clearly than others.
2   Of St John.
3   Aristotle, standing for philosophy in general.
4   Angels and men.
5   Exod. 33:19.
6   The theological verses which introduce St John's Gospel (John 1:1–14).
7   The eagle is a common symbol for St John.

And have the power to turn the heart to God,
  Combine to stimulate my charity,
Because the nature of the world, and mine,
  The death which He endured that I might live,[1]
  The hope of all believers, and my own,   60
With the aforesaid lively consciousness,[2]
  Have dragged me from the sea of twisted love[3]
  And placed me on the shore of righteousness.
The leaves[4] enleavening the garden of
  The eternal Gardener attract my love
  According to the goodness which He gave."
As I fell silent, all the heavens duly
  Re-echoed with a hymn, and with the others
  My lady chanted: "Holy, holy, holy!"
And as sharp light can make a sleeper rouse –   70
  The visual spirit running to the splendour
  Which comes through all the membranes of the eyes[5] –
And he who is aroused remains quite dazed,
  Because his sudden eyesight knows so little
  Until his judgement rushes to his aid:
So Beatrice got rid of all the scales
  Upon my eyes with rays that came from hers,
  Whose radiance reached beyond a thousand miles.
This made me see much better than before –
  And then, still somewhat stupefied, I asked   80
  About a fourth light that I could see there.
My lady answered me: "Within that lustre,
  And loving his Creator, is the first
  Of all the souls that God created ever."
Then, like the tree which in obedience bows
  Its crest beneath the passing wind, then lifts it
  From its own natural tendency to rise,
So did I in amazement while she spoke,
  Until I found my confidence restored
  By the burning desire I had to speak.   90
I said: "O only fruit produced mature,[6]
  O ancient father, to whom every bride
  Is both a daughter and a daughter-in-law,[7]
In my most deep devotion I request
  You speak to me: you know my wishes – I,

1   Christ's Passion.
2   That God is the Supreme Love.
3   The various kinds of human love are detailed by Virgil in *Purg.* XVII, 91–139.
4   The things of this life.
5   It was thought that a spirit moved from the brain to the eye to apprehend the sight
    coming to meet it.
6   Adam was created as an adult.
7   A descendant of his and married to a descendant.

...THE RINGS BEGAN TO SEND OUT SPARKS,
EXACTLY AS SPARKS FLY FROM MOLTEN METAL...

PARADISE XXVIII, 89–90

IT WAS IN SEMBLANCE OF A PURE-WHITE ROSE
THAT I PERCEIVED THE SACRED SOLDIERY...

PARADISE XXXI, 1–2

To hear you sooner, leave them unexpressed."
A covered animal at times will quiver,
   Till all its impulses are evident,
   Its motions duplicated by its cover –
Likewise, beneath his covering of light,   100
   The primal soul made obvious his elation
   At coming there to give me such delight.
And then he breathed: "Without their being expressed
   By you, I understand your wishes better
   Than you do what you're conscious of the most,
Because I see them in the Truthful Mirror
   Which in Itself reflects all things, while they
   Cannot reflect His own perfection ever.
You wish to know the vast expanse of time
   From when God placed me in the lofty garden[1]   110
   Till she[2] disposed you for the lengthy climb;[3]
How long inside that garden I delighted;
   The exact occasion of the mighty anger;
   What idiom I used and I created.
It was not, son, the tasting of the fruit
   That was itself the cause of this long exile,
   But trespassing beyond the limit set.
The sun – while I desired these loving sessions[4]
   (With Virgil until Beatrice came)[5] – described
   Forty-three hundred and two revolutions.[6]   120
I saw the sun returning on his path
   And passing through the zodiac nine hundred
   And thirty times while I was on the earth.[7]
The language that I spoke was quite exhausted
   Before the men of Nimrod undertook
   That work which could not ever be completed.[8]
For nothing that mere reason has produced,
   Since all our human likings chop and change
   According to the stars,[9] could ever last.
It is a natural thing for man to speak;   130
   But whether in this language or in that,
   Nature leaves you to do whatever you like.

---

1   The Earthly Paradise, or Eden, which Dante has imagined at the summit of Mount
    Purgatory (*Purg.* XXVIII).
2   Beatrice.
3   Through all the spheres of Heaven.
4   In Heaven, but desired by Adam while he was in Limbo.
5   Beatrice took Virgil from Limbo to guide Dante through the Inferno and Purgatory.
6   Adam was in Limbo for 4,302 years.
7   Adam lived on earth for 930 years.
8   The building of the Tower of Babel (Gen. 11:1–9), with which Nimrod (see *Inf.* XXXI,
    40–81) was traditionally associated.
9   According to their temperaments, which are influenced by the stars.

Before I went down into misery,[1]
    Jah was the name on earth of the great Goodness
    Who with this gladness now envelops me.
Later He was called *El*: and that beseems,
    Because men's customs are most like the leaves
    On branches: when one goes another comes.[2]
On the high mount[3] which rises from the billows
    I lived a life unspotted and impure,[4]   140
    From the first hour of all to that which follows,
As the sun changes quadrant,[5] the sixth hour."[6]

---

1   Into Limbo, at his death.
2   Both *Jah* and *El* are used in the Hebrew Scriptures for God.
3   In the Earthly Paradise on Mount Purgatory.
4   First before and then after the Fall.
5   Having completed 90 degrees of its course of 360 degrees.
6   Adam lived in Eden for six hours.

CANTO XXVII

All Paradise sings the Gloria, and Dante is enraptured by this feast for his ears and his eyes.

The light representing St Peter approaches Dante: the light grows in intensity and then, as it nears, is seen to be red. Everyone is silent while St Peter attacks the venality of the Papacy. All the other lights redden, and Beatrice too blushes to hear of such corruption.

St Peter speaks again to lament and condemn once more the Papacy's venality, and its meddling with secular politics, and its warfare upon others who are Christians. He is particularly angry at a representation of the Pope's keys of Heaven and Hell being displayed on a military standard, and the Pope's own image reproduced on seals to documents recording venal ecclesiastical transactions. He believes that Providence will save the Church, and he tells Dante to let everyone know what he has been told.

All the souls float up into the Empyrean, as gently as snow when it falls. Beatrice tells Dante to look down and see how far he has travelled with the motion of the sphere of the fixed stars.

When Dante turns back to look again at Beatrice, he finds her smile gives him the power to rise to the ninth sphere, the Primum Mobile or Crystalline Sphere. Beatrice explains that this sphere keeps all the others in motion and provides times and seasons for human beings. It has no physical location, but it exists in the mind of God, Whose love keeps it in being.

Dante laments men's cupidity, which he says is not kept in check by any effective secular ruler. He prophesies, in the figurative and cryptic terms usual for prophecies, a moral regeneration.

    "**G**lory to Father, Son and Holy Ghost!"
      So sang the whole of Paradise, so that
      The sweetness of the song held me engrossed.
  And what I saw appeared to me most like
    A smile of all the universe, because
    This rapture entered both by ears and sight.
  Elation! Oh ineffable happiness!
    Oh perfect life compact of love and peace!
    Oh steadfast wealth where longing has no place!
  Before my eyes are the four torches[1] lit,   10
    That one which came towards me at the first[2]
    Starting to shine with an increasing light,
  Until in its appearance it assumes
    The look of Jupiter, if he and Mars
    Were birds and had agreed to swap their plumes.[3]
  Now Providence, by which there are assigned
    All offices and times in Heaven, imposed
    Silence on the blessed chorus all around,
  When I heard said: "That I have changed my hue

---

1   The three apostles and Adam.
2   St Peter.
3   If Jupiter exchanged its white light for the red light of Mars.

Is not amazing: for when I am speaking,   20
   You will see all of these changing theirs too.
Now he by whom my place on earth[1] is taken –
   My place on earth, my place on earth, which therefore
   Now in the sight of God's own Son lies vacant[2] –
Has made a cesspit of my cemetery,[3]
   Brimming with blood and filth – which the arch-rebel,[4]
   Who fell from here, is pleased down there to see."
At this that colour which the facing sun
   Paints on the clouds at evening and at dawn
   Coloured the lights in Heaven, every one.[5]   30
And like a lady who, herself though chaste
   And self-assured, must at another's fault,
   Merely to hear it, find herself abashed,
Just so the look of Beatrice was altered:
   Such an eclipse there must have been in Heaven
   That very day when the Almighty suffered.[6]
His words continued, but not as before,
   Because that voice of his was so transmuted
   Even his semblance had not altered more:
"The Bride of Christ[7] was not brought up, regaled   40
   With blood of mine, of Linus, or of Cletus,[8]
   That she might be a means of getting gold:
Rather it was to gain this happy life
   That Sixtus, Pius, Urban and Callixtus[9]
   Shed their blood after all their tears and strife.
We did not purpose it, that on the right
   Of our successors, one part of Christ's people
   Should sit, with on the left the other part;[10]
Nor that the keys which were entrusted me[11]
   Should turn into an emblem on a standard   50
   Facing the baptized in hostility;[12]
Nor that I should be stamped upon the seal
   Of lying privileges, bought and sold:[13]
   I blush with shame and anger at such gall.

---

1   Pope Boniface VIII.
2   There is still a Pope, but not a worthy one.
3   Rome, where the remains of St Peter and other martyred Christians are buried.
4   Satan.
5   They all blush to hear of this corruption.
6   Good Friday.
7   The Church.
8   First-century Popes.
9   Popes of the second and third centuries.
10   Respectively, the Guelfs, favoured by the Pope, and the Ghibellines.
11   The keys of Heaven and Hell. See *Par.* XXIV, 35.
12   Pope Boniface VIII made war upon the Colonna family. See *Inf.* XXVII, 85–93.
13   Church offices and other ecclesiastical favours granted for money, not for desert.

Fierce wolves, but clothed like shepherds of the sheep,
 Are seen from here above in all the pastures:
 Vengeance of God, why do you lie asleep?
Men from Cahors and Gascony[1] are set
 To drink our blood. Oh such a good beginning,
 In what depravity you terminate!   60
And yet high providence, which came to save,
 With Scipio, the world's renown for Rome,[2]
 Will come to help us soon, as I believe.
And you, my son, who with your mortal load[3]
 Must sink down there again, open your mouth,
 And what I have not hidden do not hide."
Then, as at times our atmosphere rains down
 In flakes its frozen vapours, when the Goat
 Touches the sun in Heaven with its horn,[4]
Just so I saw the ether was adorned   70
 With the triumphant vapours snowing upwards,
 Who had with us a little while sojourned.[5]
My gaze was travelling with their semblances,
 Until there was such distance in between
 I could no longer follow with my eyes.
At that my lady, now I was not bound
 To look up any longer, said to me:
 "Lower your eyes, and see how far you've turned."
I saw that I had travelled, from the time
 I looked down first,[6] the whole way on an arc   80
 From midpoint to the end of the first clime,[7]
So that I saw, beyond Cadiz, the mad
 Venture of Ulysses[8] and, here, the shore
 On which Europa was a precious load.[9]
I would have seen all of our threshing floor,[10]
 But that the sun went on beneath my feet,
 Divided from me by a sign[11] or more.
My loving mind, which always more and more

---

1 Respectively, Pope John XXII and Pope Clement V. Cahors was noted for usury, and
  Gascony for greed.
2 Scipio Africanus defeated Hannibal in 202 BC and secured the supremacy of Rome,
  which later became the seat of the Roman Emperor and of the Papacy.
3 His body.
4 In the middle of winter.
5 The souls rise from the eighth sphere, the sphere of the fixed stars, into the Empyrean.
6 See *Par.* XXII, 127–54.
7 Dante has been revolving with the eighth sphere. The "climes" were latitudinal divisions
  of the known world.
8 Ulysses's voyage beyond the Pillars of Hercules, described in *Inf.* XXVI, 91–142.
9 The coast of Phoenicia, from which Jupiter, in the guise of a bull, carried off Europa.
10 The known habitable world. See *Par.* XXII, 151.
11 Of the zodiac.

Was concentrated on my lady, burned
   More than ever to turn my eyes on her: 90
All art or nature ever made, as pasture
   To take the eyes, and so attract the mind,
   In human flesh, or in a breathing picture,
United, would appear but nothingness
   To the divine delight which shone on me
   When I turned round to see her smiling face.
And I was granted from her smile such power
   As snatched me from the lovely nest of Leda[1]
   And thrust me up into the swiftest sphere.[2]
All of it is so lively and so high   100
   And uniform, I do not know which part
   Beatrice selected as the place for me.
But she, to whom my wish was obvious,
   Began to speak, smiling so joyfully
   It seemed that God delighted in her face:
"The nature of the cosmos is to hold
   The centre[3] still, while all the rest revolves:
   Here is the place from which it's all unspooled.
And yet this heaven has no location but
   The mind of God, which kindles both the love   110
   Which rolls it and the power that comes from it.[4]
As light and love surround it, it surrounds
   The other circling spheres, and this encircling
   Only the One Who does it understands.
Its own motion is measured out by none –
   And yet it measures out the others' motion,
   Even as five and two go into ten.[5]
And how time's roots in this vase have been placed,
   While all the others hold time's foliage,[6]
   Must after all by now be manifest.   120
Oh swallower of men, cupidity!
   You swallow them so deep nobody raises
   His eyes above the surface of the sea!
There is no doubt the will is there and blooms,
   But then the everlasting rain works changes,
   Leaving but bloated skins instead of plums.
And faith and innocence are only known
   In very little children: both of them

---

1   The constellation Gemini, named after the twins borne by Leda when she was impregnated by Jupiter in the guise of a swan.

2   The Primum Mobile or Crystalline Sphere.

3   The earth.

4   This sphere keeps all the others in motion.

5   With exactitude.

6   The Primum Mobile is the source of time, which is made apparent to humanity (in day and night, seasons, etc.) by the other spheres and the planets and stars they contain.

Have fled before the cheeks show signs of down.
One, while he is a babbling infant, fasts,   130
    And later, when he's adult and loquacious,
    Even at times when there is fasting,[1] feasts;
Another, babbling still, loves and pays heed
    To his dear mother, but when speaking clearly
    He has a great desire to see her dead.
In the same way, our pallid skin turns black
    In its exposure to the light – his offspring[2]
    Who leaves at evening and brings morning back.
Now you, lest this should cause you any wonder,
    Remember there's no ruler on the earth[3] –   140
    And so the human family must wander.
And yet before that hundredth of a day,
    Ignored on earth, moves Janus out of winter,[4]
    These spheres above will shoot down such a ray
That the tempest, so long in store for us,
    Will turn the sterns to where are now the prows,
    And the whole fleet will come back onto course –
And the true fruit will ripen after flowers."[5]

---

1   The times set aside by the Church for fasting and abstinence.
2   The sun.
3   No competent and conscientious Emperor.
4   The Julian Calendar was inaccurate by roughly a hundredth of a day per year, so January (Janus) was gradually moving nearer the end of winter. To move out of winter would have taken thousands of years: Dante is using litotes to denote a brief period.
5   A moral regeneration is prophesied.

CANTO XXVIII

As Beatrice prophesies a renewal of Christendom, Dante sees a brightness reflected in her eyes. He turns round and finds that it comes from a point of unbearably intense light. It is almost indescribably minute. A circle moves round it, travelling faster than the Primum Mobile itself. There are eight more spheres round that one, each of which is moving more slowly than the one before it. Similarly, the brightest light comes from the circle nearest the centre, and the brightness is less acute the farther away from the centre the circles are.

Dante is baffled by this, because it goes against what is apparent in the universe, where the outermost and therefore largest sphere – the Primum Mobile – moves fastest, and the other spheres move more slowly the nearer they are to the earth. Beatrice explains this apparent contradiction by saying that we must distinguish between what our senses perceive, where size matters, and the controlling force or virtue which, being spiritual, has no size.

As Dante realizes this truth – essentially that God is not bounded in space and not subject to His laws which govern matter – the circles send out millions of sparks and hosanna is sung.

Beatrice distinguishes between the different orders of angels which control the spheres of the universe, and she names them, according to the system credited to Dionysius the Areopagite. Dante need not wonder that a mere mortal could understand and explain these mysteries, since, she says, this and many other things were revealed to Dionysius by St Paul himself, who saw them in Heaven.

When, as against the state of humankind
    In all its wretchedness, the truth was opened
    By her who has imparadised my mind –
Like one who sees a mirrored candle flame,
    Being illuminated from behind
    Before the thought of it occurs to him,
And then turns round, for he must find out whether
    His glass tells truth, and finds it corresponds
    As words well sung accord with music's measure –
Just so my memory tells me that I did,   10
    As I was looking into those bright eyes
    From which, to capture me, Love made the cord.
And, as I turned around and mine were hit
    By what appears in that revolving sphere
    When anybody keeps his eyes on it,
I saw a point which was emitting light,
    And so intensely eyes on which it blazes
    Have to be closed, since it is so acute:
The smallest star seen by the human eye
    Would look to that star like the moon in size   20
    When all the stars are gathered in the sky.
And then, apparently no farther thence

Than the halo around the star[1] which paints it,
  When vapour which creates it is most dense,
Around that point a blazing circle wheeled
  So rapidly as to outstrip the swiftest
  Motion[2] around our universal world.
Another circle circumscribed the first,
  Round that a third, and then a fourth, and then
  A fifth, and then a sixth one, not the last.   30
The seventh followed after, so extended
  That Juno's messenger,[3] even complete,
  Would still be far too narrow to contain it.
And so the eighth and ninth – and every one
  Moving more slowly than the one before it,
  As it was more remote from number one.
That flame was shining with the clearest light
  That was least distant from the Perfect Spark,
  I think as nearest to the truth of it.
My lady, seeing me in deep conjecture   40
  And held in such suspense, said: "On that Point
  Depend the heavens and the whole of nature.
Look at that circle which is nearest it,
  And know that circle's motion is so rapid
  Through the enkindled love which pierces it."
I said to her: "If the universe agreed
  With the order as I see it in these wheelings,
  Then what you say would leave me satisfied,
But in our visible universe we can
  Only observe the spheres are more divine   50
  The farther from the centre that they turn.[4]
So, if my wish for knowledge can be met
  In this amazing and angelic temple,
  Whose only boundaries are love and light,
I must hear further, and hear you explain
  Just why the copy and the pattern differ:
  As for myself, I ponder this in vain."
"Now, if your fingers are inadequate
  To disentangle such a knot, no wonder:
  Through lack of trying, it's become hard-set!"   60
So said my lady, then she added: "Take what
  I say to you, and you'll be satisfied –
  And think it over: exercise your wit.
The bodily spheres are large, some, and some small,
  According to the greater or less virtue

---

1 The sun or moon.
2 The Primum Mobile.
3 Iris, the rainbow.
4 E.g. the moon, nearest the earth, is slowest, and the Primum Mobile, farthest from the
   earth, is fastest. Contrast ll. 34–36 above.

Which is distributed throughout them all.
Goodness affects the influence or weight,
   And there's more influence in a bigger body,
   Providing that its parts are all complete.
And so that largest sphere[1] which sweeps the rest   70
   Of the universe along must correspond
   To the circle that loves most and knows the most.
Consider now the virtue which inheres
   Within these substances, and not their seeming –
   For they appear to you simply as spheres –
And you will see a marvellous congruence
   Of more with larger, lesser with the smaller,
   In every heaven with its intelligence."[2]
Now, as the hemisphere of air is left
   Serenely brilliant when Boreas[3]   80
   Has blown from out his gentler cheek[4] to waft
Away the dissipated cloud which first
   Obscured it, so that Heaven laughs in delight
   With all its beauties in the clear at last;
So was I, instantly I had been given
   My lady's answer, for her clear response
   Made truth as obvious as a star in heaven.
And then, her words had scarcely time to settle
   Before the rings began to send out sparks,
   Exactly as sparks fly from molten metal.   90
And every sparkle circled with its blaze,[5]
   And they were many, running up to millions,
   More than the doubling on the chessboard does.[6]
I heard hosanna sung, from choir to choir
   To the Fixed Point which holds them where they are,
   And always will, there where they always were.
And she who saw the uncertainty within
   Me said: "The closest circles have revealed
   To you the Seraphim and Cherubim.
They chase their Centre with such expedition   100
   To be like Him as much as they are able,
   And are, with their sublimity of vision.
Those other loves that circle next around

---

1   The Primum Mobile.
2   The angelic order which moves it.
3   The north wind.
4   From the north-east. The image is derived from representations of the wind on medieval
    maps as a face.
5   With the blazing sphere from which it derived.
6   An allusion to the old fable of how the inventor of chess asked his king to reward him
    in grains of corn. If we begin with one on the first square of a chessboard, and then
    double the number on each square of the board (1 + 2 + 4, etc. in geometrical progres-
    sion), the final result is many billions of billions.

Are known as Thrones, because they bear God's judgement:
    They bring the primal triad[1] to an end.
And you should know that all of them rejoice
    According to how far their vision plumbs
    That Truth where every intellect finds peace.
Hence you can see how blessedness depends
    Upon the act of vision – not the act   110
    Of loving, which is vision's consequence –
And merit is the measure of their vision,
    Merit which grace begets and then good will:
    And thus from rank to rank is the progression.
The second triad, which thus germinates
    In this eternal spring whose constant growth
    The Ram does not despoil throughout dark nights,[2]
Perpetually unwinters[3] with "Hosanna"
    In trinal melodies which sound in three
    Orders of joy where all three are together.   120
In their own hierarchy are these others:
    Dominions first, and after them the Virtues –
    And then the Powers come third of these three orders.
Next, in the rings which are penultimate,
    Principalities and Archangels whirl;
    Last are the Angels who rejoice and sport.
These orders all direct their gaze upward,
    And downward they have so much influence[4]
    That all are drawn and all draw up to God.
Dionysius,[5] in his desire and love,   130
    Gave thought to all these orders, and he named them,
    And he distinguished them, just as I have.
But Gregory[6] begged to differ from him after,
    With the result that, when his eyes were opened
    In Heaven, he turned against himself his laughter.
That such mysterious truths should be revealed
    By a mortal on the earth need not amaze
    You: he[7] who saw them all up here had told
Him, with some other truths about these spheres."

---

1   Consisting of the Seraphim, the Cherubim and the Thrones.
2   The constellation Aries (the Ram) is visible in the night sky in all seasons but spring.
3   Sings, as birds do in spring.
4   On human beings.
5   Dionysius the Areopagite, converted to Christianity by St Paul (Acts 17:34). Among the theological works attributed to him in the Middle Ages was one which named and distinguished the angelic orders.
6   Pope Gregory I (r.590–604).
7   St Paul, from whom Dionysius said he derived his knowledge.

CANTO XXIX

Beatrice pauses for an instant to look at the luminous Point which has dazzled Dante. Then she continues her account of the angels, their creation and their nature. She stresses that what she is saying is accurate, because she learnt it through gazing at the Beatific Vision.

The angels were created not gradually, but in an instant, before there were any instants, before time itself was made. Before the creation there was no time and no place, God Himself being timeless and not bound to any location. And the angels were not created, as St Jerome thought, a long time before mankind: the whole of creation happened at once.

Angels were the pinnacle of creation. Some of them, led by Lucifer (whom Dante saw imprisoned in the Inferno at the centre of our globe), fell from grace through their pride. Those angels who remained with God did so because of their humility, their understanding that they owed their very existence to God. They are the ones who now circle round controlling the movement of the spheres. Beatrice stresses one difference between the angels and ourselves: they have no need of memory, because their apprehension is immediate and unchanging.

Beatrice then digresses in order to attack the many contemporary false and vain preachers, who are intent on swaying their audiences for their own vainglory and profit, rather than preaching the Gospel as Christ enjoined. This digression makes, in its fierce indignation, a sharp contrast with the calm and subtle disquisition on the angels and the nature of Creation.

Beatrice returns to the angels, and she insists on their inconceivably great number, and how they vary among themselves in the intensity of their love for God. The climax of Beatrice's account is her description of how God disperses Himself throughout Creation, and yet remains unchangeably One.

That time of year[1] when both Latona's twins[2] –
   One covered by the Ram, one by the Scales[3] –
   Have made of one horizon both their zones,
From that point when they're held in perfect poise
   Until they're liberated from the girdle,
   And both, unbalanced, change their hemispheres,[4]
So long,[5] and with a smile upon her face,
   Beatrice was silent, while she kept on looking
   Upon the Point[6] that overwhelmed my eyes.
"I tell without being asked," she then began,   10
   "What you most wish to hear, because I see it
   Where every *where* meets up, and every *when*.[7]
Not that His own goodness might be increased,
   Which is not possible, but that His splendour

---

1   At the equinox.
2   Apollo (the sun) and Diana (the moon).
3   The sun in the sign of Aries and the moon in the sign of Libra.
4   The sun drops below the horizon and the moon rises above it.
5   A very brief time.
6   See *Par.* xxviii, 16–18.
7   In the sight of God to Whom all places and times are eternally present.

In shining back might witness 'I exist',[1]
In His eternity, beyond all time,
   Beyond all comprehension, as He pleased,
   The Eternal Love allowed new love to bloom.[2]
Nor was He indolent before all this:
   In no *before* and in no *after* did   20
   God's spirit move upon the water's face.[3]
Form and matter, combined or separate, flow
   Out as existence which has no defect,
   Like triple arrows from a triple bow.[4]
As glass, or amber, or a crystal cup,
   When light shines on them, know no interval,
   But they are instantaneously lit up,
So this threefold effectiveness shone out
   From the Lord God and into this existence,
   And was not gradual, but immediate.   30
Order was set up for the substances,
   And those in whom pure act had been produced[5]
   Were at the summit of the universe.
Potentiality was lowest placed:
   Between potentiality and act
   Was such a bond as never can be loosed.
Jerome[6] insists there was a period
   When, though the angels had been long created,
   The universe itself was still unmade,
But what I tell as truth's attested by   40
   Scribes of the Holy Ghost, in many places,
   As you will find if you look carefully.
And it can be inferred by human reason,
   Which cannot think the movers of the spheres
   Should be without the use of their perfection.
Now you know accurately when and where
   And how these loves were made – and so already
   Three ardours have been quenched in your desire.
Nor would you get to twenty in your count
   As quickly as a section of the angels   50
   Fell and disturbed the lowest element.[7]
The others stayed, and then, as you have found,
   They exercised their skill with such delight
   That they are never tired of circling round.

---

1   The angels, like human beings, are conscious of their own existence.
2   He created the angels.
3   Gen. 1:2: "And the spirit of God moved upon the face of the waters."
4   Form is pure intellect, the angels; matter is the stuff which has potentiality only. Their combination is the heavens.
5   The angels.
6   St Jerome (*c.*340–420).
7   The earth.

The reason for that fall was the accursed
  Pride of that angel you have seen constricted
  By all the weights of all the universe.[1]
Those whom you see here were the ones who knew,
  In all humility, their understanding
  Came from the Goodness that had made them so: 60
Their vision is exalted in the light
  Of grace and of the merit they had earned,
  So that their wills are firm and absolute.
Be sure of this, which you must never doubt:
  Receiving grace is meritorious
  According to the love exposed to it.
By now, if you have grasped what I have said,
  I've left you with enough to contemplate
  About this gathering, with no further aid.
But since on earth throughout your various schools   70
  People are taught that the angelic natures
  Have understanding, intellects and wills,
I shall speak further, that you may be clear
  About the truth that down there's obfuscated
  By the equivocating lecturer.
These substances, once they were overjoyed
  In the face of God, have never turned their vision
  Away from Him from Whom nothing's concealed:
And since they never have their vision crossed
  By a new object, they can have no need   80
  Of memory, since nothing has been lost.
Meanwhile, down there, while not asleep, men dream,
  Whether or not they think they tell the truth –
  But the liars incur the greater shame.
You do not walk below on one straight way
  Philosophizing: for your self-delight
  And love of show lead you so far astray!
Yet even such as that is not disdained
  Up here so much as when the Sacred Scripture
  Is thrust behind or even twisted round.   90
They do not think of how much blood is shed
  To sow it in the world, or just how blessèd
  Is he who humbly keeps it at his side.
Each preacher makes a show and tries to trace
  The ins and outs of his inventions, while
  The Gospels are required to hold their peace.
One says the moon turned from her usual path
  During Christ's Passion, and was interposed

---

1   Dante has seen Lucifer, the leader of the rebel angels, imprisoned in the lowest part of
    the Inferno, at the centre of our globe, to which matter is drawn by the force of gravity.
    See *Inf.* xxxiv and especially ll. 121–26.

So that the sun's light could not reach the earth –
And saying that, he lies: the sun held back   100
   Its own light, and in Spain and India,
   As in Judaea, everything went dark.
Lapos and Bindos[1] are not commoner
   In Florence than such fabrications, shouted
   From pulpits here and there throughout the year –
And so the sheep, who know so little, come
   Back from their pasture having fed on wind,
   And not excused through ignorance of harm.
Christ did not say to His first congregation:
   'Go forth and preach your rubbish through the world',   110
   But he set them upon a firm foundation
Of truth, and truth was their whole utterance.
   So when they fought to stimulate the faith,
   They made the Gospel both their shield and lance.
Now preachers preach with many a quip and fleer,
   And just so long as they can raise a laugh
   And the hood's puffed up with pride, they ask no more.
But such a bird is nesting in that hood[2]
   That, if the crowd could see it, they would see
   The value of the pardon[3] they have had.   120
Such pardons but increase credulity,
   So that the crowds rush round to every preacher,
   Whether or not he has authority.
Anthony's pig grows fatter by this plan,[4]
   As many others do who are more swinish,
   Paying the folk who feed them with false coin.
Turn your eyes now – we have digressed enough –
   Back to the straight and narrow road, and let us
   Shorten the way, because our time is brief.
Angels progress from grade to grade more great   130
   In number, and so many that no tongue
   Or mortal concept gets as far as that;
For if you look more carefully at what
   Daniel reveals, you'll find with all his thousands
   The intended number is indefinite.[5]
The Primal Light, which shines on all of them,
   Is taken in by them as many ways

---

1   Lapo and Bindo were common Florentine names.
2   The Devil is hiding in the preacher's cowl.
3   For their sins.
4   St Anthony (c.251–356), a hermit, regarded as the father of monasticism, was often depicted with a pig (to represent the Devil tempting him, but here used as a symbol of greed).
5   Dan. 7:10: "Thousand thousands ministered unto him, and ten thousand times ten thousand stood before him."

As there are splendours[1] which can take it in.
And so, because affection follows on
    The act of understanding, all their loving   140
    Varies in its intensity in them.
Now you discern the magnanimity
    Of God, Who breaks Himself into those more
    Than many mirrors He's reflected by,
While still remaining One just as before."

---

1   Angels.

CANTO XXX

The circle of angels fades from Dante's sight. He turns to Beatrice, who is ever more beautiful, and he imagines that only God can perceive that beauty fully. Dante is unable to find words to express it.

Beatrice explains that they have now left the Primum Mobile and are in the Empyrean. They have moved from matter to the realm of pure light, which is beyond time, space and matter. Beatrice promises that Dante will see the saints and angels as they really are.

Dante is at first unable to cope with the light, but then recovers and finds that his sight has improved and there is no brightness he cannot endure. He sees a river of light, whose banks are covered with flourishing grasses and flowers. Sparks are rising from the river to fall into the flowers, and then returning from the flowers into the river. It becomes clear that these sparks represent the angels who are ministering to the saints, who are represented by the flowers. Beatrice tells Dante that this vision is but a preface to what is to come: his spiritual immaturity means that he can as yet see them only in this form.

Dante then finds the river has turned into a lake of light. Around it is an enormous amphitheatre of saints and angels. Although there are so many, and the light extends so far, Dante finds no difficulty in seeing everything: here, where God is working without intermediaries, sight is undiminished by distance.

Dante sees an empty throne with a crown above it. Beatrice says this is for the Emperor Henry VII, who will attempt to govern Italy but die before he succeeds. She blames his failure on the Guelfs, and especially the Florentines, and also on the subterfuges of Pope Clement V. Clement, she says, will die soon after Henry and be thrust into that part of the Inferno reserved for simoniacs.

Perhaps six thousand miles away high noon
    Is blazing, and this world of ours already
    Casting its shadow almost on a plane,[1]
And heaven's atmosphere, so high above,
    Begins to change, so that the fainter stars
    Are being lost to sight on our low earth,
And as the brightest handmaid[2] of the sun
    Advances, heaven closes gradually
    All of its lights, down to the loveliest one.
Just so the angelic circle which rejoices   10
    For ever round the Point which dazzled me,
    And looks embraced by that which it embraces,[3]
Little by little faded from my sight,
    Till lack of vision and my love constrained me
    To turn my eyes to Beatrice as a light.
If all that I have ever said of her

---

1   As the sun sinks the earth's shadow is lowered.
2   Aurora, the dawn.
3   See *Par.* XXIX, 9 and XXVIII, 16–18.

Were integrated in one act of praise,
   It would not be enough to serve me here.
The beauty that I saw transcends so wholly
   All human understanding, I believe   20
   Only its Maker can enjoy it fully.
At this pass I am vanquished, I confess,
   More than at any instant in his work
   Comic or tragic poet ever was;
For, as the sun strikes on the weakest vision,
   Just so the memory of that sweet smile
   Plunges my intellect into confusion.
From the first day that ever I saw her face
   On earth,[1] until this sight, no obstacle
   Hindered the singing of my song like this;   30
But now I have no choice but to desist
   From following her beauty in my verses,
   As, at his wit's end, every artist must.
Such as I leave her for a louder sound
   Than my poor trumpet gives, which strives to follow
   Its difficult material to the end,
And acting like a guide whose work's complete,
   She spoke again: "Now we have left the largest
   Of bodies[2] for the heaven of pure light:[3]
Light intellectual, light full of love –   40
   Love of true goodness, full of all rejoicing,
   Rejoicing which transcends the sum of grief.
Here you will see both kinds of soldiery[4]
   Of Paradise, and one of them appearing
   As you will see them on the Judgement Day."[5]
As lightning in a sudden flash can shatter
   The sense of sight and so take from the eye
   Its power to see the most apparent matter,
So was I circumfused with living light
   Which left me swathed in such a heavy veil   50
   Of radiance that nothing reached my sight.
"Love welcomes thus, and always, those who come
   Into this heaven, by love itself made peaceful,
   To get the candle ready for the flame."[6]
No sooner had these few words reached my ear
   And entered understanding than I realized
   That I had gone beyond my wonted power;
And my restored and renovated sight

---

1   When he was nine years old.
2   The Primum Mobile.
3   The Empyrean, beyond matter, time and space.
4   Saints and angels.
5   The saints in their risen bodies.
6   To prepare the soul for the Beatific Vision.

Was such that there was never any brightness
   Such that my eyes could not face up to it.   60
And I found light envisaged as a river
   Streaming with brightness, and between two banks
   Painted with spring more wonderful than ever.
From that stream living sparks were radiating
   To settle on the flowers on every side,
   Almost like rubies in a golden setting.
And then, as if the scents intoxicate,
   They plunge again in the amazing surge –
   And as one enters in one issues out.
"The deep desire that burns you and impels   70
   You to more knowledge of the things you see
   Pleases me all the more the more it swells,
But you must drink this stream of Paradise
   Before your raging thirst is satisfied,"
   Said she who is the sunlight to my eyes.
She said: "The river and the topazes
   Which come and go, the laughter in the grasses,
   Are but their truth's foreshadowing prefaces.[1]
Not that these things themselves are immature –
   No, rather the defect is on your side,   80
   Whose eyes are not yet strong enough and sure."
No baby ever turns so rapidly
   His face towards his mother's milk, when he
   Wakes up much later than is customary,
As I, to make an even clearer mirror
   Of both my eyes, bent down towards that stream
   Which flows with the intent to make us better.
No sooner had my eyes begun to slake
   Their thirst there from that river than its length
   Had turned, it seemed to me, into a lake.   90
As people look quite other than they did
   When they were wearing masks, if they throw off
   The borrowed semblance under which they hid,
The flowers and sparks in yet more celebration
   Had changed themselves so utterly I saw
   Both courts of Heaven[2] in this altered vision.
O radiance of God, through which I saw
   The lofty triumph of the reign of truth,
   Give me the power to utter what I saw!
There is a light that shines up there, and this   100
   Makes the Creator visible to creatures[3]

---

1 The river represents divine grace, the jewels (rubies, topazes) the angels, and the flowers
    ("the laughter in the grasses") the saints. The word "prefaces" is used in the same sense
    as the Preface of the Holy Mass, which leads on to the Consecration.

2 Saints and angels.

3 Angels and human beings.

Who only in His sight can find their peace.
It broadens out into a ring-like zone,
    And is so huge that its circumference
    Would be too wide a girdle for the sun.
Its whole appearance is of a ray
    Reflected off the Primum Mobile,
    Which draws thence all its life and potency.
And as a hill's reflected in the water
    Down at its foot, as if to admire itself,   110
    When it's adorned with all the blooms of nature,
So, rising from the light, tier after tier,
    I saw all round so many thousands mirrored,
    All those of us who have returned up there.[1]
And if the lowest rank of all receives
    So much light in itself, how vast the space
    This Rose extends to at its farthest leaves!
For all the breadth and depth of this, my sight
    Remained unbaffled, and I saw quite clearly
    The scope and quality of that delight.   120
There, far or near can neither take nor add,[2]
    For where the Lord God rules without an agent[3]
    The natural law is rendered null and void.
Into the yellow of the eternal Rose[4]
    Which spreads in rising ranks and sends its fragrance
    To the Sun of everlasting spring in praise,
Beatrice drew me, who wanted to speak out
    But held my tongue. She said: "You see how many
    Make up the council of those robed in white!
You see how far our city goes around: 130
    You see how all our seats are now so crowded
    Only a few are left to be assigned.
On that great throne on which your eyes now rest,
    By reason of the crown that's placed above it,
    Even before you're welcomed to this feast,[5]
Shall sit the soul, to be down there august,[6]
    Of noble Henry, who will come to govern
    Your Italy before she's predisposed.[7]
The blind cupidity which is your curse
    Has made you rather like the baby who,   140

---

1   The saints, who have returned to God, Who made them.
2   Distance does not affect the view.
3   The First Cause acts without any secondary causes.
4   The centre of the luminous circle, like the yellow stamens at the centre of a rose.
5   Before Dante dies and goes to Heaven.
6   Who will become Emperor on earth.
7   Henry VII of Luxembourg, elected Emperor in 1308, entered Italy to restore the imperial
    authority there, but died in 1313 without having overcome the resistance of the Guelfs,
    and especially the Florentines.

Half-dead through hunger, pushes off his nurse.
Then over Holy Church one will preside
  Who never, publicly or secretly,
  Will walk with Henry on the one straight road.[1]
But God will never suffer him to be
  Long in that sacred chair:[2] he'll be thrust down
  Where Simon Magus is, deservedly,[3]
To push him of Anagni[4] deeper in."

---

1   Pope Clement V pretended to favour Henry, but plotted against him in secret.
2   Pope Clement died less than a year after Henry.
3   In that part of the Inferno where simoniacs are punished by being placed upside down
    in holes in the rock. When a fresh sinner arrives he pushes down the one before him.
    See *Inf.* XIX.
4   Pope Boniface VIII; see *Inf.* XIX, 53 and *Purg.* XX, 85–90.

CANTO XXXI

Dante sees the Church Triumphant, the saints in Heaven, in the form of a pure-white Rose, with angels flying like bees back and forth, into the Rose and then returning to where their honey is made – the vision of God. Although there are so many angels, they do not obstruct Dante's sight. This complex vision shows how an active love permeates Heaven, and is in stark contrast to the frozen immobility in Cocytus, the lowest circle of the Inferno.

Dante tell us he was even more amazed at this sight than the northern barbarians were at their first glimpse of the splendour of ancient Rome. His exclamation of wonder includes, in a typical mixture of the ethereal with the mundane, a sideswipe at the current wickedness of Florence.

Dante still has questions to ask Beatrice. But when he turns to question her, he cannot find her. With him now is a reverend elder, who says that he has taken over the role of guide to Dante. He tells Dante where to look – up at the third tier from the top of the Rose – to see Beatrice. Dante has no difficulty in seeing her, despite the great distance between them, since the natural laws which operate in our world of time and space have no relevance here. Dante humbly thanks her for her guidance, and he sees her smile in acknowledgement.

The reverend elder reveals that he is St Bernard of Clairvaux. St Bernard was a famous twelfth-century abbot and theologian who, despite his many practical concerns in which he displayed a remarkably combative style, was also a contemplative and a mystic with a deep devotion to the Virgin. He will be Dante's mentor until the end of the journey.

St Bernard turns his gaze upon the Virgin, and the love his gaze reveals is such that he makes Dante all the more eager to gaze at her.

✳

I t was in semblance of a pure-white Rose
    That I perceived the sacred soldiery[1]
    Which, with the blood He shed, Christ made His spouse,[2]
While the other soldiery,[3] that flies and sings
    The Majesty which keeps them so enamoured,
    The Goodness fitting them for all these things –
Like bees which, having swiftly introduced
    Themselves into the flowers, have thence returned
    To where their toil achieves so sweet a taste –
Descend into that boundless bloom adorned   10
    With countless petals, then they reascend
    To where their Love is always to be found.
Every face there is like a blazing coal,
    Their wings of gold, their vestments so pure white
    That no snow ever equals them at all.
Into the flower, down through the spirallings,

---

1   The Church Triumphant, the saints in Heaven.
2   The Church is often referred to as the Bride of Christ.
3   Angels.

They proffer the tranquillity and ardour
That they acquire in fluttering their wings.
This multitudinous interpolation,
   Flying between the flower and Light above,[1]   20
   Did not obstruct the splendour and the vision:
Divine light shining through the universe,
   Affecting everything in due degree,
   Works in a way which nothing can oppose.[2]
This ever happy and secure domain
   Was thronged with folk from ancient times and modern
   With looks and love all bent upon one Sign.[3]
O Threefold Light,[4] which in a single star
   Sparkles into their eyes and makes them happy,
   Look down upon the tempest where we are!   30
If the barbarians – who had been born
   In regions Helice rules all the year,
   Revolving with her well-belovèd son[5] –
When they went into Rome, were stupefied –
   That era when the Lateran Palace[6] put
   All other mortal works into the shade –
Then I, who'd come from human to divine,
   From temporal things to things that are eternal,
   From Florence to a people just and sane,
Imagine how amazed I must have been!   40
   I wanted to hear nothing, dumb myself,
   In ecstasy and stupor, caught between.
And like a pilgrim getting his breath back,
   Gazing all round the temple of his vows,
   And wondering how he'll tell what this was like,
I went upon a journey through the light,
   Moving my eyes along each circling tier,
   Now up, now down, now looking round about.
I saw those faces speak of charity,
   Lit by Another's light and their own smiles,   50
   And actions which reveal true dignity.
The form of Paradise was in my sight,
   But as a whole: my eyes had not yet rested
   At length on any single part of it.
I turned; the longing was once more intense

---

1   The angels are moving between the human beings and God (the Greek *angelos* means
    messenger).
2   Distance in Heaven does not affect the view (see *Par.* xxx, 118–21).
3   God.
4   The Holy Trinity.
5   The barbarians came from the north, signified here by Helice, the constellation of the
    Great Bear, and the Little Bear which was her son.
6   At one time the Imperial Palace, and in Dante's day the seat of the Popes. By metonymy
    it signifies all the architectural splendour of ancient Rome.

To ask my lady all about those things
   On which my mind was still left in suspense.
I meant one thing, and came across another:
   I looked for Beatrice, but saw, apparelled
   Like all the glorious folk, a reverend elder.   60
Joyfulness was diffused through every feature –
   His eyes, his cheeks, and in his kindly manner –
   Such as is fitting for a tender father.
And suddenly "Where is she?" I exclaimed.
   He answered: "Beatrice urged me from my place
   To bring your longing to its rightful end.
If you look up to where there circles round
   The third tier from the top, you will see her
   Upon the throne her merits have assigned."
I did not answer him, but raised my eyes   70
   And saw her haloed with a crown as she
   Reflected from herself the eternal rays.
From that region which thunders up on high
   There never was an eye so far removed,
   Though plunged into the bottom of the sea,
As Beatrice was distant from my sight –
   And yet it did not matter, for her image
   Reached me, the distance not obstructing it.
"Lady in whom my hope is live and well,
   And who did not disdain, for my salvation,   80
   To leave your footprints in the depths of Hell,[1]
In all the many things that I have seen,
   By virtue of your power and loving kindness,
   I see what benefit and grace is mine.
You have drawn me, a slave, to liberty
   Along all of those paths, by all those ways
   Which lay within your great ability.
Keep all your goodness in me, that my soul,
   Which you have brought to purity and health,
   May please you when it leaves this mortal coil."   90
That was my prayer to her. She, who appeared
   So very distant, smiled and looked at me,
   Then turned back to the Eternal Fountainhead.
The elder then: "In order to conclude
   Your journey, for which prayer and holy love
   Combine to send me hither as a guide,
Let your eyes fly around this candid Rose,
   And looking at it will prepare your sight
   To mount still higher in the heavenly rays.

---

1   As Virgil explained in *Inf.* II, *52ff*, Beatrice went into Limbo to fetch him as a guide for
Dante.

And the great Queen of Heaven,[1] for whom I burn   100
   In love, will grant us every grace we need,
   Since I am faithful Bernard,[2] and her own."
Like one, a pilgrim from Croatia say,
   Who comes to look at our Veronica,[3]
   Whose ancient longing's hard to satisfy,
And wonders, while the relic's being shown:
   "O my Lord Jesus Christ, O my true God,
   And is this visage then Your very own?" –
So was I, in my wonderment at this
   Live charity of him who in this world   110
   By contemplation could enjoy that peace.
"This state of happiness, O child of grace,"
   The elder said, "will not be known to you
   If you but keep your eyes fixed on the base:
But scan those ranks that are most elevated
   Until you come to where the Queen's enthroned
   To whom this realm is subject and devoted."
I raised my eyes; and just as, in the dawn,
   The oriental side of the horizon
   Surpasses that which sees the setting sun,   120
So, as one moves from lowlands to the height,
   I moved my eyes, and saw the farthest region
   Overcome all the others with its light.
And as, on earth, the place where we await
   The pole which Phaethon ill-guided[4] glows
   Brighter, while on each side there is less light,
Just so was that pacific oriflamme[5]
   Quickening in the midst, while all around
   There was an equal lessening of the flame.
I saw at that mid-point, with wings outspread,   130
   More than a thousand angels celebrating,
   Each one distinct in splendour and what he did.
I saw there, smiling at their sports and songs,
   A beauty which reflected joyfulness
   Into the eyes of all the holy ones.
And if I had the wealth of words to write
   All that I can conceive, I would not dare

---

1   The Virgin Mary.

2   St Bernard of Clairvaux (1091–1153), who had a special devotion to the Virgin. He preached in favour of the Second Crusade, the one in which Dante's ancestor Cacciaguida died (see *Par.* XV, 13–148).

3   A cloth, kept as a relic in Rome, said to have been used by St Veronica to wipe Christ's face on His way to Calvary, and to be imprinted with His image.

4   The chariot of the sun, designated by its pole: Phaethon was allowed by his father Helios to guide the sun, but he lost control of the horses (see *Inf.* XVII, 106–8).

5   That part of the Rose where the Virgin is enthroned. It is "pacific" in contrast to the earthly oriflamme, the red war standard of the Kings of France.

To try to tell the least of that delight.
Bernard, seeing my eyes were all attention
  On her[1] the love for whom had made him blaze,   140
  Turned his eyes on her, and with such affection
They made me even more on fire to gaze.

---

1   The Virgin Mary.

CANTO XXXII

St Bernard is happy to be Dante's mentor for the last stage of his journey. He shows Dante
how Heaven is organized. The Celestial Rose is similar to an amphitheatre, with seats inside
it arranged in tiers. The Virgin is in the top tier, with saintly Hebrew women below her in
a line stretching downwards. Opposite the Virgin, on the other side of the Rose, is a similar
line of saintly Christian men, with John the Baptist on the top tier. The Rose is divided into
two equal sections, with saints from the era before Christ, figures from the Old Testament,
on one side, and saints from the Christian era on the other. On the Christian side there are
seats still waiting to be filled. Close to the heart of the Rose are children who died before
reaching the age of reason. Like the adults, they are arranged in differing degrees of beatitude.

Dante is perplexed, but he is told that the children's degrees of beatitude come from their
dispositions at birth: this is God's judgement, and must therefore be simply accepted by us
as right. What seems to us an arbitrary choice by God is illustrated by the history of Jacob
and Esau, twins who were at odds even in the womb: Jacob was the one favoured by God.

St Bernard explains that in the early world their parents' faith assured children's salvation;
later it was necessary for male infants to be circumcised; in Christian times baptism is essential.

St Bernard tells Dante to look at the Virgin, the sight of whom will make him fit to see
God. Dante sees her with the Angel Gabriel in front of her holding the palm branch that
was in his hand at the Annunciation. The saints sing the Ave Maria.

St Bernard tells Dante that they must pray to the Virgin that Dante does not fall from
grace. Then Bernard himself addresses a prayer to the Virgin.

T hat holy man, still wrapped up in his bliss,[1]
    Assumed, and willingly, the role of mentor,
    And spoke to me in sacred words, like this:
"The wound[2] which Mary closed up by anointing
    Was that the lovely lady[3] at her feet
    Had opened up in her primeval wounding.
In the third row of seats from those on high
    Rachel[4] is seated under Eve directly,
    And Beatrice seated with her, as you see.
Sarah,[5] Rebecca,[6] Judith[7] and the one[8]   10
    Who was ancestress of the singer crying
    Out *"Miserere mei"* for his sin
Are those whom you can see in their degrees

---

1   St Bernard is gazing at the Virgin.
2   The wound of original sin.
3   Eve.
4   Second wife of Jacob, symbol of the contemplative life.
5   Wife of Abraham and mother of Isaac.
6   Wife of Isaac and mother of Jacob.
7   She saved the Jews from the Assyrians by killing Holofernes.
8   Ruth, great-grandmother of King David. He composed Psalm 51, which begins "Have
    mercy upon me", in repentance for his adultery and murder.

Going downwards, as I name them one by one,
　Moving through every petal of the Rose.
And from the seventh level down, the same
　As up from it, are seated Hebrew women,
　Dividing all the petals of the bloom:
That is because, according to the view
　There was of faith in Christ, these make a wall　　　20
　To separate the stairways into two.
On this side, where the flower is in full bloom
　With all its petals, are those blessèd seated
　With faith in Christ when He had not yet come;
On the other side, where there are empty places
　Across the semicircles, saints are sitting
　Who to the risen Saviour turned their faces.
And, as Our Lady's throne upon one side,
　And all those other seats set in a line
　Below her, serve to make a great divide,　　　30
So, opposite, does that of the great John,[1]
　Who, always holy, suffered Hell two years,[2]
　After the desert and his martyrdom.[3]
Beneath him, making this division clear,
　Are Francis,[4] Benedict[5] and St Augustine,[6]
　And many others down to where we are.
Now wonder at the depth of God's decree:
　Both of the ways of exercising faith[7]
　Are set to fill this garden equally.
Know that, below the horizontal line　　　40
　Which cuts these two lines in the middle, saints
　Are seated for no merit of their own,
But others' merits, under fixed conditions;
　For all of these are souls who were released
　Before they had the power to make decisions.[8]
And this is what their faces let you see,
　And what their childish voices let you gather,
　If you but look and listen carefully.
Now you're perplexed, and don't express your doubts –
　But I shall swiftly disentangle for you　　　50
　The tightened knots which bind your subtle thoughts.
In all the amplitude of this domain
　There is no place for anything haphazard,

1　St John the Baptist.
2　He was in Limbo until rescued by Christ at the Harrowing of Hell.
3　He preached in the wilderness, and was killed by order of King Herod.
4　See *Par.* XI, 43–117.
5　See *Par.* XXII, 28–51.
6　Bishop of Hippo, one of the most famous Fathers of the Church (354–430 AD).
7　As shown in the Old and New Testaments.
8　Because they died before reaching the age of reason.

Any more than for hunger, thirst or pain.
Whatever you can see here is by act
   Of everlasting law: the correspondence
   Between the ring and finger is exact.
And so these people who were rushed into
   The true life find, and that *non sine causa*[1]
   Their places differ, whether high or low.   60
The King through Whom this kingdom nestles here
   In so much love and in such great delight
   That nobody would dare to ask for more,
Creating every mind in His glad sight,
   Gives graces differently, at His own pleasure,
   And here the fact itself shows it is right.[2]
And this is clearly noted and set down
   In Sacred Scripture, where it tells of twins
   Who came to blows inside their mother's womb.[3]
Therefore, as with the colour of their hair,[4]   70
   It is appropriate the Highest Light
   Confers on them what crown of grace they wear.
With no regard to merit they might earn,
   They are located here in varying ranks,
   According to their tendencies when born.
In far-off centuries, when your world's birth
   Was recent, innocence sufficed to gain
   Salvation, coupled with the parents' faith.
Then, when those earliest ages had gone by,
   Every male child had need of circumcision   80
   To give his innocent wings the strength to fly.
But now the centuries of grace are here,
   Then without perfect baptism in Christ
   Such innocence has Limbo for its share.
But look now at the face resembling Christ[5]
   Most clearly, for its clarity alone
   Can make you fit and able to see Christ."
I saw, raining upon her, such delight,
   Transported by those sacred intellects
   Created for such flights through such a height,[6]   90
That whatsoever miracles I had
   Seen previously had not provoked such wonder,
   Nor shown me such a semblance of the Lord;

---

1   "Not without cause", a Latin legal term.
2   The children have differing degrees of blessedness, and God's decree cannot be
    questioned.
3   Jacob and Esau were at odds before they were born, and God favoured Jacob (Gen.
    25:21–26).
4   Esau had red hair.
5   The Virgin Mary's.
6   See the angels flying into and out of the Rose at *Par.* XXXI, 1–24.

And that love which came down to her before,
    Singing, "*Ave, Maria, gratia plena*",[1]
    Spread out its wings again in front of her.
On every side of her the blessèd court
    Responded to the holy canticle,
    And all the faces there became more bright.
"O holy father, who did not disdain   100
    To come down here, relinquishing the place
    Designed eternally to be your throne,[2]
Who is that angel whose euphoria
    Is such as he looks in Our Lady's eyes,
    Enamoured, that he seems to be all fire?"
So I turned for an answer once again
    To him who drew his beauty from Maria
    Just as the morning star does from the sun.
He said to me: "All confidence and grace
    That could be in an angel or a saint   110
    Are found in him, and we would have it thus:
For this is he who brought the palm branch down
    To Mary when the weight of human flesh
    Was taken willingly by God's own Son.[3]
But come now – follow with your eyes once more
    As I am speaking: see the great patricians
    Of this most merciful and just empire.
Those two who sit in greatest happiness
    Up there, because they're nearest to the Empress,
    Are, as it were, the two roots of this Rose: 120
He who is sitting on her left, up close
    To her, is our first father,[4] whose rash taste
    Brought human kind to know such bitterness.
Upon her right you see the ancient sire[5]
    Of Holy Church, to whom the Lord entrusted
    The keys which can unlock this lovely flower.
And he who saw the dreadful times and trials,
    Before his death,[6] endured by the lovely bride[7]
    Won with the piercing of the lance and nails,[8]

---

1   "Hail Mary, full of grace" (Latin), the beginning of the most famous Marian prayer.
2   St Bernard has temporarily left his allotted place in Heaven to join Dante at the centre
    of the Rose.
3   The Angel Gabriel, often depicted with a palm branch as he announced to Mary that
    she would bear the Son of God.
4   Adam.
5   St Peter.
6   St John the Evangelist, who in his old age wrote the book of Revelation, which describes
    the persecution of the Church.
7   The Church.
8   Metonymy for the Crucifixion.

Sits next to him. By Adam sits the guide[1]   130
  Of that ungrateful, fickle, restive nation
  Nourished with manna[2] by their kindly Lord.
Across from Peter you see mother Anna,[3]
  So happy as she gazes at her daughter
  Her gaze is constant while she sings hosanna.
Then opposite the father of our race[4]
  Sits Lucy, she who first inspired your lady
  When you seemed bent upon your own disgrace.[5]
But since times flies (for you with life and breath),[6]
  We shall here make an ending, like the tailor   140
  Who cuts his coat according to his cloth,
And turn our eyes towards the Primal Love,
  To penetrate His radiance, in so far
  As this is something that we can achieve.
And yet, for fear that you may well regress
  On your weak wings, believing you go forwards,
  It is essential that we pray for grace,
Grace from the Lady who can give you aid,
  And you must follow me in all affection,
  So that your heart sticks closely to my word."   150
Then he began his sacred supplication.

---

1 Moses, who led the Jews out of Egypt.
2 Exod. 16:14–15.
3 Mother of the Virgin.
4 Adam.
5 St Lucy told Beatrice of Dante's danger in the dark wood (*Inf.* II, 97–126).
6 There is no time in Heaven, but Dante is still alive.

CANTO XXXIII

St Bernard prays to the Virgin Mary, addressing her as the perfection of creation, and the mother of God, of Whom she is also the daughter. He stresses her power as a willing intermediary between God and humankind. He begs for her help to enable Dante to have the sight of God. He begs also for her intercession to keep Dante, after he returns to earth, in a state of grace. Beatrice and all the other saints join in this prayer. Bernard now tells Dante to lift his eyes, but he has already done so.

Dante emphasizes his inability to express, or even remember, what he has seen, but all the joy of it remains in him. He prays that he may be able to provide posterity with some inkling of his vision. He sees the wholeness of the universe, where everything is bound together with love. He sees, and "understands", in so far as a human being can, the Incarnation.

Finally Dante's imaginative powers fail utterly, and he is now at peace, in perfect harmony with God.

It is here, in this final canto, where he faces his greatest difficulties as a poet, that Dante is at his greatest. We see here his subtlest use of a device which he has employed many times before in the *Comedy* – the admission that his powers are inadequate to what he wishes to express. The canto also includes some of his most striking concrete images to convey what is not only inexpressible, but also entirely spiritual. Such images are those of the universe as a book (ll. 85–87) and of his peaceful state of mind as a smoothly revolving wheel (ll. 143–45). Two of the most evocative images (the Sibyl's leaves in ll. 65–66, and the Argo's shadow in ll. 94–96) are concerned with his inability to remember the vision: they add to our sense of how overwhelming it is.

  "Virgin and mother, daughter of your Son,[1]
    More humble and more high than all created,
    The end intended in the great design,
You are the one by whom our human nature
    Was so ennobled that the One who made it
    Did not Himself disdain to be its creature.
The Love which was rekindled in your womb
    Emitted warmth that, in the eternal peace,
    Encouraged this immortal flower[2] to bloom.
You are for us in Heaven a noonday blaze   10
    Of charity[3] – you are a living spring
    Of hope down there among the human race.
Lady, you are so powerful and high
    They who seek grace and do not turn to you
    Desire but vainly, with no wings to fly.

---

1   Lines 1–9, addressing the Virgin Mother of God, express the paradoxical nature of the Incarnation.

2   The Celestial Rose.

3   Lines 10–21 address Our Lady as the intermediary between God and man.

Your loving kindness is not only there
   For those who pray to you, but frequently
   Arrives spontaneously before the prayer.
In you there's mercy, and in you compassion,
   In you munificence, in you compact   20
   Is all the goodness found in all creation.
And now this man,[1] who from the lowest pit
   Of all the universe[2] right up to here
   Has witnessed one by one the souls in it,
Begs you to beg for him in your compassion
   Such grace as may suffice to lift his eyes
   Higher and to the ultimate salvation.
And I, who never burned to see that Sight
   As now I do for him to see It, proffer
   My prayers to you, and pray they don't fall short: 30
So may you scatter every single cloud
   That clouds his mortal being, with your prayers,
   And let the Highest Pleasure be displayed.
I pray you also, Queen of Heaven,[3] able
   To compass all you ever want, to keep
   This man's will, after such a vision, stable:
Watch and restrain his all-too-human passion.
   See Beatrice! See all these saints whose hands,
   During my prayers, are clasped in supplication!"
He ceased. Those eyes the Lord loves and reveres,[4]   40
   Fixed on the supplicant, revealed to us
   How welcome to her are devoted prayers.
And then those eyes turned to the Eternal Light,
   Where no one can believe that any creature
   Can find the way as clearly as her sight.
And I, who was approaching now the End
   To which all longings tend in course of nature,
   Found my desires had reached their utmost bound.
Bernard was making signals with a smile
   To lift my eyes on high, to me who had   50
   Done that already of my own free will:
Because, as it became more clear, my view
   Was entering more and more into the beam
   Of the High Light that of Itself is true.
From that point what I saw was in excess
   Of anything that words can say, while even
   The memory falters at such overplus.
Like someone who sees something in his dreams

1   Dante. In ll. 22–33 St Bernard prays for Dante to see the Beatific Vision.
2   The Inferno.
3   In ll. 34–39 St Bernard's prayer for Dante to remain in grace is a reminder that Dante
    still has to complete his life in the world.
4   The eyes of the Virgin.

And waking finds the passion that it roused
   Is with him still, though nothing seen remains,   60
Just so am I: my vision is in flight,
   While all the sweetness that was born of it
   Remains with me, distilled into my heart.
Like that, the snow is melted in the sun –
   Like that, upon the wind and drifting leaves,
   The Sibyl's oracles are swiftly gone.[1]
O Light Supreme, so elevated, far
   Above our mortal understanding, bring
   Back to my mind somewhat of what I saw
And give such vigour to this tongue of mine   70
   That I may leave but one spark of Your glory
   Behind me for the peoples yet unborn,
Which, part-returning to my memory,
   And echoing a little in these lines,
   May give some concept of Your victory.
I think the keenness of the living ray
   I underwent then would have left me dazzled
   Had I presumed to turn my eyes away.
And I remember that I grew more bold,
   Because of this, to endure it, till my gaze   80
   United with the Everlasting Good.
O grace abounding and through which I dared
   To fix my gaze on the Eternal Light
   So that no atom of my sight was spared!
In that profundity I saw – in-gathered,
   And bound by love into a single volume –
   All that throughout the universe is scattered:[2]
Substances, accidents,[3] how they relate
   In interpenetration, and so fused
   That what I say shines but a feeble light.   90
The universal structure of this knot
   Is what I know I saw, because I feel,
   While I am speaking, greater joy in it.
One instant brings me greater memory loss
   Than five-and-twenty centuries since Neptune
   Dumbfounded saw the Argo's shadow pass![4]
Like him my mind was held in its amaze
   To gaze intently, fixedly, unmoving,

---

1   The Sibyl was a prophetess who wrote her prophecies on leaves which were easily scattered by the wind.

2   The source of everything is in God, and what holds it all together is love.

3   Substances are things which exist in themselves; accidents are qualities which exist only in substances, differentiating them.

4   The Argonauts' voyage to Colchis in quest of the Golden Fleece has left, after two and a half thousand years, more trace in the memory of mankind than the Beatific Vision has left in Dante's mind after one instant.

With always more encouragement to gaze.
Before that Light one alters so that it   100
   Would be impossible one should consent
   To turn away for any other sight;
Since all the good the will has ever sought
   Concentrates in that Light, and what is there
   Is perfect, which outside of It falls short.
Henceforth what I recall will be expressed,
   Slight though it be, with less coherence than
   The babble of a baby at the breast.
Not that the Living Light I looked at bore
   More than one simple uncompounded semblance,   110
   For it is always what it was before,
But as I grew much stronger in my vision,
   The single semblance seemed to me to change,
   In what was after all my transformation.
In luminous profundity appeared,
   In depth of light, three circles of three colours,
   While all of them were of one magnitude:
Iris by iris, so one seemed to be
   Reflected by the other, while the third
   Seemed to be fire they breathed out equally.[1]   120
How feeble is my phrasing, and how bare
   To what stays in my mind, which is itself
   The tiniest residue of what I saw!
O Everlasting Light, You who include
   Only Yourself, and love Yourself and smile,
   Self-understanding and self-understood!
That circle that appeared to be conceived
   Inside You as a light that was reflected,
   When it had been a little while observed,
Inside itself, with its own coloration,   130
   Seemed painted with the Image of Mankind[2] –
   And so attracted and absorbed my vision.
As the geometer applies his mind
   To square the circle, yet for all his efforts,
   The formula he needs is never found,
So was I, faced with that amazing sight:
   I wished to fathom how the human image
   Could fit the circle and be placed in it.
I had no wings to fly to what I wanted:
   Except that suddenly my mind was smitten   140
   By a flash of lightning and its wish was granted.[3]

---

1   Lines 115–20 are an adumbration of the Holy Trinity: the Son is the reflection of the
    Father, and the Holy Spirit is the love between the Father and the Son.
2   An allusion to the Incarnation.
3   So far as any human being can, he "understood" the Incarnation.

That was the end of lofty fantasy[1] –
  But now all my volition and desires
  Were turned, like a wheel revolving smoothly, by
The Love that moves the sun and all the stars.

---

1 The power of Dante's imagination to represent, however inadequately, what he saw
now fails him completely.

EXTRA MATERIAL

ON

THE DIVINE COMEDY

Dante Alighieri's Life

We know far more about Dante the man than we do about Shakespeare, even though Shakespeare is three hundred years closer to us. We know what Dante looked like from the several similar portraits which survive (some of which may well be contemporary), and from a detailed pen portrait by a fellow Florentine writing only a short while after his subject's death:

> Our poet was of medium height, and after he came to maturity he bent somewhat as he walked, and his gait was grave and gentle. He was always dressed in good clothes of a fashion appropriate to his years. His face was long, his nose aquiline, his eyes rather big, his jaw large, and his lower lip protruded beyond the upper. His complexion was dark, his hair and beard thick, black and curly, and his expression was melancholy and thoughtful. (Giovanni Boccaccio, *Life of Dante*)

We know about his marriage, his children, and his close friendships with men like the considerably older Brunetto Latini and the slightly older and socially superior Guido Cavalcanti (*c.*1258–1300), from both of whom he learnt so much. His public life – with first its civic responsibilities and then the torment of the lack of those responsibilities after his permanent exile from his native city – is well documented. There are myths also, of course: it may not be strictly true that, when he passed by in Verona, one woman declared that this was the man who visited hell and another saw the proof of this in the apparently singed beard and smoke-browned face; but even such myths reveal that he was the sort of man around whom myths gather. His views on an astonishing range of topics and people are available to us: he does not disappear behind his works as Shakespeare does. Shakespeare of course was a dramatic writer, but then so was Dante in a way, especially in his chief work, his *Divina Commedia* (*Divine Comedy*). The difference is that Dante is himself part of his own drama, and not just in the same manner as, say, Chaucer is with his incidental self-mockery, but as the protagonist who is always there and never afraid of putting his oar in – one of the main reasons why we know so much about him.

The Florence into which Dante was born in 1265 was a city only beginning on its progress towards the political and cultural dominance of Tuscany: indeed, five years before his birth, after the battle of Montaperti between Tuscan Ghibellines and Florentine Guelfs, the victorious Ghibellines were with difficulty dissuaded from razing the city to the ground. This is a sobering thought: it is hard to imagine what European

Early Life in Florence

495

culture would be like now without the influence of Florence, and just as hard to imagine European literature without Dante.

Dante's father was a reasonably successful businessman: the nature of his business is uncertain, but may well have involved usury (a foretaste perhaps of the later importance of Florentine banking), and the family were comfortably off. Dante had the usual formal education of his time, which involved Latin grammar, logic and rhetoric, followed by arithmetic, geometry, astronomy and music. Even the most cursory reading of his works, however, makes it apparent that his learning and, more importantly, his understanding, went far beyond the requirements of any formal education. In Florence he was able to benefit from the society of some of the most accomplished men of his time. He makes a striking comment on his education in the *Inferno*, when he comes across the shade of the diplomat, scholar and writer Brunetto Latini, damned for sodomy; even in such circumstances respect and gratitude demand to be expressed:

> ...still I have in mind, to my great pain,
> The dear, the kindly, the paternal image
> Of you who, in the world, time and again,
> Taught me how man becomes eternal...
> (*Inf.* xv, 82–85)

There is much of Dante in these few lines – his unflinching moral judgement (after all, it is in his poem that Brunetto is seen to be damned), his deep human sympathies and his strong desire (despite the overriding importance of his eternal destiny) for posthumous renown on earth.

His father's death in 1283 meant that Dante was placed under a guardian for several years until he came of age. However, he was old enough in 1289 to fight in the battle of Campaldino, where the Florentine Guelfs defeated the Ghibellines of Arezzo, so reversing the disaster of Montaperti; and he was also present some months later at the siege of Caprona, during an incursion into Pisan territory. There was never anything in Dante of the temperament which Milton was later to disparage as "a fugitive and cloistered virtue, unexercised and unbreathed, that never sallies out and sees her adversary" (*Areopagitica*): his unwillingness to walk away from a fight is as obvious in spiritual as in physical matters.

Marriage   Dante married in 1285 a certain Gemma Donati, of whom we know little except that she bore him several children and did not follow him into exile. She seems to have had property of her own which could not be affected by the sentence issued against Dante, and since there was a family to provide for, remaining in Florence probably made good practical sense. Even Boccaccio, who strongly deprecated marriage for a scholar, had to admit that he had no evidence that Dante's marriage was worse than any other he knew of. Dante's children certainly kept in touch with their father till the end of his life, and two of his sons conscientiously gathered and preserved the various parts of the *Commedia* after his death.

According to Dante's own account, the most formative event of his life *Beatrice*
occurred when, at the age of nine, he saw, at a festival, the little girl, some
months younger than he was, who has been identified as Bice (Beatrice)
Portinari. To say that he immediately fell and always remained in love
with her is a feeble way of describing what was a lifelong obsession, often
in the foreground and always in the background of his writings. Boccac-
cio discusses this event sympathetically in his *Life of Dante*, and a more
detailed account of its consequences can be read in Dante's own *Vita
Nuova* (*New Life*); but only a reading of the hundred cantos of the *Divina
Commedia* reveals the full effect of this childhood event. Beatrice died at
the age of twenty-four, and we can have no idea what she thought of it
all, or even whether she had any awareness of her importance to Dante.

When Dante came of age, it was inevitable that he should play his *Political Activities*
part in the politics of Florence. The city was violently disturbed by
disputes between the aristocrats and the merchant class, among the
aristocrats themselves, and also between the rival parties of the Ghibel-
lines and Guelfs. This last conflict especially is one where the various
interests are hard now to disentangle. Hostility between Guelfs and
Ghibellines was not confined to Florence, and it influenced that city's
foreign policy as well as its internal affairs, as it had in the battles of
Montaperti and Campaldino. Behind these party divisions, sometimes
a long way behind, was the centuries-old struggle between the Pope, as
the head of Western Christendom, and the Holy Roman Emperor, as
at least the titular head of secular power in Europe. Conflict between
the demands of religious conscience and civic duty is perennial; but
this problem was aggravated throughout the Middle Ages by the papal
claim to secular as well as religious power. As a gross oversimplifica-
tion, it may be said that the Ghibellines favoured the Emperor and
the Guelfs the Pope. Applying that simplification to Dante we can
say that he began as a Guelf and ended as a philosophical Ghibelline,
deploring the papal claims to secular power. A further complication
is that the Guelf party in Florence was split into two – the Blacks and
the Whites. This distinction may seem to us trivial, but it led to the
second most decisive event in Dante's life. Reading of all this turmoil is
likely to put one in mind of Max Beerbohm's humorous tale *Savonarola
Brown*. The eponymous hero's play on the life of Savonarola contains,
time and again and for no particular reason, the stage direction "Enter
Guelfs and Ghibellines, fighting", followed after a while by "Exeunt
Guelfs and Ghibellines, still fighting". It may well be that many at the
time in Florence, including possibly Dante himself, found it difficult
to know what was really going on. At any rate, in 1300 Dante, as one
of the seven Priors (the governing body, elected for a period of only
two months), in an attempt to pacify the city agreed to the exile of
some of the leaders of the Black and White Guelfs, including his
friend Guido Cavalcanti. In 1302 Dante as a White Guelf found him-
self condemned to death by the Blacks, and his property confiscated.
Since he was out of the city when the sentence was pronounced, he
preserved his life, but only at the cost of remaining in exile. Years
later an offer came of safe return to Florence and the restitution of

his property if he would admit the truth of the trumped-up charges against him: he spurned the offer.

Exile and death   Dante spent the rest of his life wandering from city to city in Italy, depending on the benevolence of patrons for his livelihood. Banishment came as a disaster to one who believed, as Dante so firmly did, that an individual's good was bound up with the good of his society. Although for a long time he entertained the hope of returning eventually to his native city, and even of being crowned with laurel in the place where he had been baptized (his beloved San Giovanni, the present-day Baptistery), in reality he fulfilled the prophecy which, with hindsight, he put into the mouth of his ancestor Cacciaguida when he met him in his *Paradiso*:

> You shall leave every single thing behind
> Which you hold dear; and this is but the first
> Arrow that exile shoots, and your first wound.
> You shall experience the bitterness
> Of eating strangers' bread, and feel how hard
> Going up and down another's staircase is.
> (*Par.* xvii, 55–60)

The places where he stayed included, among others, Forlì, Verona, Arezzo, Treviso, Padua, Venice, Lunigiana, Lucca, Verona again, and eventually Ravenna. It was there that he completed his *Divine Comedy*, died in 1321, and was buried.

Dante Alighieri's Works

Dante was still in his teens when he first showed his poems to his friends in Florence. Manuscript circulation was a common form of publication in the days before printing, when books were few and expensive; what was perhaps not so common was that Dante's recipients included men who were themselves accomplished poets, particularly Guido Cavalcanti: he cannot have lacked informed criticism and encouragement. The drawback of this kind of publication is that short poems, such as Dante's were at this early stage, tend to get scattered, and the relationship between them, and between them and other people's poems, tends to be forgotten, and accurate dating is now hard to achieve.

Vita Nuova   Dante's first book-length production, his *Vita Nuova* (*New Life*), was probably composed when he was nearly thirty. It is made up partly of poems which had been written years before, but which fitted in with the book's prose narrative and commentary; or perhaps they were poems he wished to preserve and which suggested the prose to him. It is in this book that Dante describes his first meeting with Beatrice and how it influenced his early life. We learn of the physical effects, tantamount to a form of illness, which his obsession had on him, how he tried to conceal the object of his passion by paying court to another lady, his joy at Beatrice's greeting and his anguish when that greeting was denied him, his suffering in sympathy with her when her father died; it is always the effect on Dante himself which his poems seem most interested in. The book can be read in many different ways. One of its most interesting features is that the poems tend to talk about themselves, and it is illuminating to read *Vita Nuova* as an *ars poetica*. Eventually Dante comes to a momentous decision – to concentrate on praising Beatrice; he even declares:

> …if it should please Him by Whom all things live that my life should last for a few more years, I hope to write of her what has never been written of any woman.

Dante may or may not have had *The Divine Comedy* already in mind when he wrote those words; but it was in the *Comedy* that he achieved that astounding ambition.

Some time in his thirties Dante began writing his *De vulgari eloquentia* (*Literature in the Vernacular*). That an essay which insists on the value of the vernacular should be written in Latin is itself an indication of why such an insistence was needed: the prestige of Latin as the language for serious matters survived long after Dante's time. Dante gives cogent reasons for valuing the vernacular: it is the language we all possess, it is more natural than Latin since we learn it at our mother's knee, and we learn it in a sense without trying consciously to learn it – unlike Latin, which we have to obtain in an artificial way through a study of its grammar. Although he is talking of Italian, many of the issues he raises are applicable to any language, and this work retains its importance today despite its unfinished state. Dante attempts to identify which of the many vernaculars in Italy presents the language in its purest form, and he comes to the conclusion that it is one which has

De vulgari eloquentia

> left its scent in every city but made its home in none… which belongs to every Italian city yet seems to belong to none, and against which the vernaculars of all the cities of the Italians can be measured, weighed and compared. (*De vulgari eloquentia*, ed. and tr. Steven Botterill)

It is as a result of Dante's own writings, and Petrarch's and Boccaccio's later, that the nearest Italy has to a standard language today is Tuscan: they wrote in Tuscan, and wrote so well as to become models of how the Italian language might be used.

It was in the early years of his exile that Dante wrote his *Convivio* (*The Banquet*), a treatise which he intended to consist of fourteen of his poems accompanied by commentaries, all of them together providing a banquet of knowledge. Of the projected fifteen books only four were completed; we can only conjecture why, but there may be a hint in the method of the *Convivio*, which was to consider the poems carefully in their literal and allegorical senses, in a way that included but went far beyond literary criticism. Possibly Dante came to realize that his ambitious project of an encyclopedic treatment of human knowledge and

The Banquet

understanding was better entrusted to fiction, and more precisely the verse epic which became *The Divine Comedy*.

The Divine Comedy

The *Comedy* is generally thought to have been started in the early years of his exile; there is a tradition however, related by Boccaccio, that he had completed the first seven cantos of the *Inferno* while he was still living in Florence; these cantos were then found by someone who realized their quality and took them to Dino Frescobaldi, a well-known Florentine poet; he had them forwarded to Dante, living at that time in Lunigiana at the court of the Malaspina family, with a request that the work should be continued; thus encouraged, Dante did continue it. At least ninety-three of the hundred cantos were composed during his exile.

It is impossible to summarize the contents of any of Dante's works and still remain fair to their quality, and this applies most of all to *The Divine Comedy*, which is possibly the greatest literary work ever produced in Europe. With that caveat in mind, it can be safely said that the poem opens in the year 1300, when Dante was middle-aged and suffering what might now be called a mid-life crisis, astray in an allegorical dark wood and unable to find the right path to lead him out of it. He is helped by the shade of Virgil, who reveals that he has been sent by Beatrice, who is now herself in heaven. Dante's rescue is represented as a journey which he has to make through the three realms of the afterlife – Hell, Purgatory and Heaven. Since the purpose of the journey is to show him the true nature of existence and thereby bring him to his senses, the physical details of it are allegorical; but these details – the geography of the realms he visits, the appearance and characters of the people he meets, his interaction with them and with Virgil – are all presented in physically realistic terms. It can be a mistake to read the poem with an obsessive eye for allegory. Often it seems best to take it as a literal fiction and allow the allegory to impinge on us in its own various ways. Dante has to scramble down into Hell, he has to climb up Mount Purgatory, and he has to float into space to get to Heaven: the significance of those movements is obvious. As with any long work, there are places where scholars may wrangle, and any reader may at times be baffled, but generally the point of what happens is crystal-clear. Dante himself, the protagonist, is seen time and again as a representative of the whole human race. The shades he meets are both sharply individualized and also generalized, in that they are actors in human history in all its untidiness while at the same time they embody sins and virtues which have their consequences in the realms where history no longer happens. Perhaps the most dramatic book is Purgatory: the souls there are striving to rise out of it, while those in Hell cannot change their place, and those in Heaven would not wish to. However, there is no lack of drama anywhere in the *Comedy*. In the face of such a powerful work it is needless to ask (although some have done so) whether it can be appreciated by a reader who does not share Dante's beliefs and presuppositions. Do we need to approve of human sacrifice in order to appreciate Homer? Or be an ancient Roman imperialist in order to enjoy Virgil? The drama of the *Comedy* is the same drama that is in the world around us here, but with its consequences brought home to us.

Inferno

After seven hundred years, and after many rereadings by individuals, Dante's *Inferno* remains a shocking poem. The physical torments of the damned are so horrific as to make the first-time reader feel that he has strayed into some extreme Grand Guignol: shades are immersed in boiling pitch, or in human excrement, or running on burning sand under a hail of fire – and these are only the first few torments that spring to mind. And those punishments are less horrifying than the ones which reveal an apparently fiendish ingenuity: the simoniac popes placed upside down in holes in the rock with only their feet showing, around which flames flicker in a parody of the haloes of the saints; or sinners like Bertran de Born, the sowers of discord, who tore apart the fabric of society, and whose bodies are now torn and mangled. One of the most ingenious punishments, and perhaps the most affecting, is that of the sinners frozen in the ice of Caïna, those who betrayed their kindred, and who are desperate to weep but cannot:

> Their eyes, which had been only moist within,
> Gushed over at the lids, until the cold
> Congealed those tears, and locked the lids again.
> (*Inf.* XXXII, 46–48)

It is apparent that the punishments are not designed to display ingenuity for its own sake. It seems fitting that those who flattered others for their own ends should wallow in excrement: after all, that is what they chose to do. Again, Bertran de Born, who stirred sons up to make war upon their father, thus wrenching apart natural and honourable ties, receives a justice which is poetic in more ways than one:

> I really saw, and still I seem to see,
> A trunk without a head, moving along
> With all the others in that company;
> It held its severed head up by the hair,
> Swinging it in one hand just like a lantern;
> The head saw us and moaned in its despair…
> And thus fit retribution is delivered.
> (*Inf.* XXVIII, 118–23, 142)

We are bound to recognize what may be, to many modern readers, the most shocking feature of all. That is, that Dante's universe is strictly moral: it is a world where no one asks whether it is nature or nurture which leads us to do what we do, one where no excuses can avail; it is a world where human beings do what they do of their own choice, and live, even when dead, with the consequences of their choices – live with what they have themselves chosen: they have what they wanted all along.

To convey this sense of a just and moral order behind the spectacle of human existence, Dante uses allegory. Many may find that word more off-putting than the idea of eternal damnation, but we need not make heavy weather of it: Dante himself does not. It can be analysed and categorized in a hundred and one ways, but it is in its essence very simple – a manner of expression, and a way of understanding, which comes naturally to human beings. Boccaccio puts it succinctly:

> What other thing is it than poetic fiction in Scripture when Christ says that He is now a lion, and now a lamb, and now a serpent, and then a dragon, and then a rock?... What else do the words of the Saviour in the Gospels contain if not a meaning different from the plain sense, a way of speaking which we call by the common term allegory?
> (*Life of Dante*, tr. J.G. Nichols)

Ordinary conversation never proceeds far without words being used in such ways. And, as with all expression, there are occasional difficulties. This is particularly so when emblems – devices whose meaning exists *only* figuratively, and often needs interpretation – are used. I mean such devices as a red cross on a field ambulance (the same emblem, but with a very different meaning, as on a crusader's chest), or a red crescent, or any number of political and commercial logos which we can think of, or – last but not least – the leopard, the lion and the she-wolf in the first canto of the *Inferno*. These creatures are hardly realistic: they appear out of the blue for no apparent purpose other than to convey something of the state of Dante's mind at that stage; above all, they need interpretation, interpretation which is often uncertain and disputed.

Most of the allegory, however, is not like that. Objects in the poem are there in their own right, as things in themselves, while they also have deeper symbolic meanings which coexist with the literal ones. This is the kind of allegory in which Dante excels. Consider the dark wood which Dante, and we, come across in the second line of the poem, or the hill which Dante then attempts to climb, or the huge hole in the ground in the shape of an inverted cone down which Dante and Virgil climb as they sink into the very depths. The single most important feature of the *Inferno*, and of the *Divine Comedy* as a whole, is that it is presented to us as fact, physical fact which bristles with spiritual, psychological and eschatological meaning.

The *Inferno* contrasts sharply with another justly famous Christian allegory. John Bunyan's *The Pilgrim's Progress* (1678) begins:

> As I walked through the wilderness of this world, I lighted on a certain place, where was a den; and I laid me down in that place to sleep: and as I slept I dreamed a dream.

Dante's journey is not a dream: it is given as history. We do not therefore have to be always interpreting: as we follow the story, the deeper significance of it enters into our minds without further effort. (This is not to suggest that, if we make the effort, even more interest will not be revealed.) Dante's "dark wood" is not labelled with an abstract word: this is something which is more likely to happen in works that are more obtrusively allegorical, or emblematic: it happens in Spenser's *Faerie Queene* (1590) in a similar situation:

> This is the wandring wood, this *Errours den*.
> (I, 1, 13)

Bunyan is always careful to explain his allegory as he goes along: when Pilgrim climbs a hill we are told that it is "Hill Difficulty". His characters have names which reveal their significance – their significance being the only reason for their appearance in the narrative. In Dante there is no one, as there is in Bunyan, called "Mr Facing-bothways". There is, however, Guido da Montefeltro, a complex historical character who does indeed face both ways and comes to grief accordingly. There is in Dante a slough of despond, where the souls of those who willed to live in sadness wallow in the mud; but Dante does not call it such. Bunyan tells us clearly that "the name of the Slough was Despond": Dante leaves us to realize that for ourselves, and his characters and their circumstances are much more than simple allegorical abstractions:

> "Beneath the surface many people sigh,
> With lots of little bubbles rising up,
> As you can see, wherever you cast your eye.
> They say, stuck in the mud: 'Our minds stayed dark
> In the sweet air enlightened by the sun.
> Inside us was a sort of sluggish smoke.
> Now we are sullen in the gloomy mud.'"
> (*Inf.* VII, 118–24).

It is here that the English reader is irresistibly reminded of Shakespeare, whose characters too are seen not only in a moral light but in all their human complexity. So, for instance, we have in the *Inferno* no one known as Pliable or Obstinate, but we do have Farinata, who is as proud in the Inferno as he was on earth, and who has other human qualities, like his snobbery and his concern with the politics of his city. And it is not just little intriguing foibles, little humanizing details, which Dante reveals along with the reasons for damnation. Farinata is allowed to manifest even in the Inferno his good qualities – the strength and determination which saved the city of Florence from destruction:

> "Yet there at Empoli I was the one –
> When all agreed on Florence's destruction –
> Who set his face against it, I alone."
> (*Inf.* x, 91–93)

Despite this, Farinata, who is an enemy of Dante's party, might seem to provide some justification for the assumption, frequently made by those who have not read the poem, that Dante placed his enemies in hell and his friends in heaven. The lie is given to this assumption most obviously when Dante, on the burning sand of the seventh circle, comes across "the dear, the kindly, the paternal image" of his old friend and mentor Brunetto Latini. Our judgements are not as God's, and so Brunetto, damned for sodomy, reveals in his damnation the qualities for which he was loved: not just his beguiling pride in his writings, but also his intellectual achievement, which is not nullified either by death or by damnation:

> "I recommend to you my *Treasury*,
> In which I'm still alive: that's all I'll say."
> Then he turned round, and looked like one of those
> Who race, to win the green cloth at Verona,
> Across the fields; and looked, among all these,
> Most like the winning, not the losing runner.
> (*Inf.* xv, 119–24)

It is well known how the eponymous hero of *Piers Plowman* (from the second half of the fourteenth century) sees at the beginning of that poem "a fair field full of folk". One could hardly describe the Inferno as a "fair field", but it is certainly full of folk in all their various human complexity. One must also bear in mind that Dante's "fair field" will come later, glimpsed at times in his *Purgatory*, and in full bloom in his *Paradise*. The greatest mistake we could make as readers of the *Inferno* would be to stop short once we had read it and go no further. Dante's vision in the *Inferno* is overwhelming, but still only partial. The best, morally and poetically, is yet to come.

Purgatory

Dante's *Inferno* is much better known than his *Purgatory*. Is that because sin is naturally more popular than repentance? Or is it because Dante, like so many before and after him, writes better about badness than about goodness? Surprisingly, Dante's writing in *Purgatory* is even more assured than in his first book of the *Comedy*. To present goodness, even if only at the stage of becoming, is not easy, and requires more subtlety than the description of evil. It may also require more subtlety on the reader's part.

When Dante arrives on the island of Purgatory, after his escape up through the earth from the Inferno, there is a strong sense of relief. The night is clear, dawn is not far off, and the very air is more breathable. The landscape has changed, and the atmosphere (both meteorologically and socially) is utterly different:

> Soft hue of oriental sapphire, clear
> Up to the very circle of the moon,
> Suffusing all the intervening air,
> Restored my joy in seeing, once I'd passed
> Clearly beyond the lifeless atmosphere
> Which was so troublesome to eyes and breast.
> (*Purg.* i, 13–18)

Everything in *The Divine Comedy*, even the slightest detail, is subordinated to the general effect: we know immediately that Purgatory will not be like the Inferno. Mount Purgatory has a purpose, while the souls in the Inferno know only purposelessness. Dante's first sight of Hell is the antechamber to the Inferno proper, where those who were not good enough for Heaven and not bad enough for Hell are racing round and round endlessly and pointlessly: while they lived they were neither for God nor against Him, and after death they remain in that state. But Purgatory is

> ...where the human spirit is made worthy
> To soar to Heaven, being purged of sin.
> (*Purg.* I, 5–6)

These are the souls of those who were not indecisive, but who sinned and repented. They are in Purgatory to cleanse themselves of the stains, the corruption left by the sin they have now abandoned. There is suffering in Purgatory as there is in Hell, but it is suffering with an end in sight. Many of the souls in the Inferno are immobile; those who do move do so in pointless anger or irritation. In Purgatory there is almost continuous movement during the daylight hours, as the souls there embrace their suffering willingly, since they so strongly desire its effects. There is a brisk, almost athletic sense (physically and mentally) in Purgatory which is poles apart from the torpor or the aimless activity of Hell. When he moves deeper into the Inferno, Dante comes "to where there is no light at all" (*Inferno* IV, 151); but when he arrives on the antipodean island of Purgatory he sees in the night a constellation of four stars, emblematic of the cardinal virtues:

> The sky appeared delighted with their light:
> Oh, northern regions, well and truly widowed,
> Because you are excluded from their sight!
> (*Purg.* I, 25–27)

Dante tacitly encourages the reader to compare the two realms, and to see therefore more clearly the difference between them. The Inferno is a hole in the ground, shaped like a funnel, and so getting narrower and narrower and more constricted as it goes down to the centre of the earth, where the worst sinners are, while Purgatory is the opposite – a mountainous cone rising up to the Earthly Paradise, a jumping-off place for Heaven. Dante and Virgil slither down farther and farther into the Inferno, but they must climb, with considerable effort, to reach the peak of Mount Purgatory. The Inferno is in perpetual darkness: there are nights in Purgatory, the hours when no one can climb, but they are simply times of rest to prepare for the next day's efforts. There is at times an apparent similarity between the suffering in both places. In Ptolomea the betrayers of guests are lying supine with their eyes frozen over:

Their very weeping will not let them weep:
Their pain, finding obstruction in their eyes,
Turns back inside them to augment their grief;
Their first tears form a cluster as they freeze,
Which like a sort of visor made of crystal,
Fills up the cavity below their brows.
(*Inf.* XXXIII, 94–99)

On the second terrace of Purgatory, those who sinned in envy have their eyes sewn up with iron wire like sparrow hawks; they cannot see, but they can, and do, cry out their prayers to Mary and all the saints. More striking still is the difference in Dante's attitude: he makes a deceitful promise to the damned that he will remove the ice from their faces. On the contrary he addresses the envious in Purgatory with the utmost friendliness and courtesy, even with a certain respect, since they are sure of Paradise. At times Dante is callous, or even cruel, to the shades in the Inferno – their sinfulness arouses the same feelings in him – but he always responds sympathetically to the souls in Purgatory: they mean well, and they encourage him to mean well also.

Of all the many parallels and contrasts between the two states, perhaps the most famous is that between the father and son, Guido da Montefeltro and Buonconte da Montefeltro, which is both highly dramatic and resonant with theological meaning. Guido, who counsels Pope Boniface VIII in fraud by urging "large promises, but minimally kept" (*Inf.* XXVII, 110) is damned, even though he has received an advance pardon from the Pope: such a pardon, which is inevitably without repentance, is invalid. Buonconte dies a brutal death and dies excommunicate, but he is saved because at the last gasp he repented (*Purg.* V, 85–129).

As Dante and Virgil descend through the Inferno there is less and less communication between them and the damned. Dante's conversations higher up in that realm could not usually be described as friendly (as an example there is his confrontation with Farinata at *Inf.* X, 22–121); but in Caïna, the lowest part of the Inferno, there is no possibility of discussing anything in any way with Lucifer, and not simply because Lucifer has his three mouths full of the traitors Judas, Cassius and Brutus: everything in Caïna is frozen stiff. On the terraces of Mount Purgatory, on the contrary, there is continual conversation, which is often amazingly charitable. Some of the most notable exchanges are with artists, and especially other poets. In the *Inferno*, perhaps the nearest we come to sympathy with the shades is in Dante's meeting with his old mentor Brunetto Latini: we can smile indulgently at Brunetto's parting words, when even in these circumstances he maintains a writer's partiality for his own productions:

I recommend to you my *Treasury*
In which I'm still alive…
(*Inf.* XV, 119–20)

That gains our indulgence; but it is admiration which is aroused on
Mount Purgatory by the reply of Oderisi da Gubbio, the celebrated
painter of miniatures, after Dante has praised his skill:

> "Brother," he said, "those leaves laugh more and shine
> Painted by Franco of Bologna's brush:
> The honour's his now; very little mine.
> I hardly would have been so generous
> While I was still alive, because my heart
> Was goaded by the urge for excellence."
> (*Purg.* XI, 82–87)

Those words are spoken on the terrace of the proud. There follows a
discourse on the transience of earthly fame, which enables Dante to
slide in what is apparently a puff for his own poetry:

> Guido from Guido has contrived to wrest
> The glory of our tongue, and now perhaps
> There's one who'll drive them both out of the nest.
> (*Purg.* XI, 97–99)

Oderisi is saved and destined for Heaven: Dante still has his human
failing of pride.

There is another outstanding encounter with a poet: that with Guido
Guinizzelli (XXVI). Guido describes Arnaut Daniel as (in words now
famous in another context) *"miglior fabbro del parlar materno"* ("A better
craftsman in his mother tongue", l. 117); and at the end of this canto
Dante the poet (as distinguished from Dante the character in his own
work) honours Arnaut by having him speak in his native Provençal.

Like the *Inferno*, the *Purgatory* abounds in vignettes that are dramatic
and colourful and revelatory of significant states of mind and soul:
Sordello greeting Virgil with enthusiasm as a fellow citizen (with that
sense of human solidarity which is so lacking in Hell and not always
evident on earth), even before he knows he is speaking to the world-
famous poet (*Purg.* VI, 58*ff*); the pathetic and yet triumphant end of
Manfredi (*Purg.* III, 118*ff*), which despite all the emphasis in the poem
on the power and authority of the Church which Dante accepts,
shows that ultimately the human soul depends for its fate on its own
decisions and on God; or the strangely affecting words of Pia, whose
mortal end is all the more striking for being so mysterious, and yet
who stays in our mind most because of her concern for Dante himself:

> "When you are in the world of living men
> Once more, and fully rested from your journey...
> Do please remember me – my name is Pia;
> Siena made, Maremma undid me:
> And he knows all about that, who before
> Had given ring and gem to marry me."
> (*Purg.* V, 130–31, 133–36)

Every reader will have his own favourites: there is a wealth to choose from.

The poem abounds also in brief images which not only move the story forward in a lively manner, but also have implications beyond the mere action. Guido Guinizzelli goes back into the blazing fire of the lustful in a way which shows how these penitent souls welcome their purgative suffering:

> Then, possibly to make way for another,
> He vanished in the burning, like a fish
> Which flashes to the bottom of the water.
> (*Purg.* xxvi, 133–35)

Then there is the strange process by which the angel who ferries souls to Purgatory (incidentally in implicit contrast to Charon, the ferryman in the Inferno) is seen first only as *"un lume per lo mar"*,

> "A light that came across the sea so swiftly
> No bird in flight could ever be so fast…"
> (*Purg.* ii, 17–18)

and then bit by bit is revealed as "the sailor sent from heaven" (ii, 43).

Not all the imagery is so sharp and dynamic. Those images which are deliberately unnaturalistic, emblematic rather than symbolic, are difficult for the modern reader and less likely to appeal. The carvings on the ground in the twelfth canto, which depict examples of the punishment of the sin of pride, are sharply drawn and dramatic, but the acrostic which comes with them (ll. 25–63) is of a different order altogether. The tableaux and processions in the later cantos are again more stately than dramatic, and some of the details – such as the representation of Christ – although they are full of meaning, are not easy for a modern to accept: the literal beast is at odds with the metaphorical gryphon. It might be argued that it would be better for us if we could appreciate such things. Possibly, but readers now are more likely to treasure in their memories from these late cantos the character of Beatrice as it comes over in her conversations with Dante – her sternness, her maternal love for him and her teasing.

Some problems are insoluble. Just as no translation can possibly be adequate to the verbal power of the original, its sound and rhythm, so no commentary, even one much more detailed than that offered in this book, can draw attention to all the meaning inherent in this poem. The *Comedy* is ultimately ungraspable as a whole by any one person (which is not to suggest that it is not rewarding to try to grasp it as a whole), and, despite the intricate organization of all three books, what stays in the mind is often this scene or that scene which appeals particularly to the individual reader – for instance Provenzano Salvani who, proud though he was and suffering for it, humiliated himself for the sake of a friend (*Purg.* XI, 118–42) and at his death went into Purgatory with no delay.

Most readers will feel themselves to be neither wholly good nor wholly bad. So Purgatory may well seem to be our natural destination. But, as the constant movement on Mount Purgatory emphasizes, it is not a permanent home: it is merely a staging post to Paradise, or in any event to Dante's *Paradise*.

Paradise

Paradise is probably the least read of the three books of *The Divine Comedy* and perhaps the least admired. It is not difficult to suggest reasons for this. We have, as Dante had, St Paul's word for it that the task Dante undertakes is impossible:

> Eye hath not seen, nor ear heard, neither have entered into the heart of man, the things which God hath prepared for them that love him. (1 Cor. 2:9)

In more prosaic terms, how can a mere mortal comprehend, let alone express, a state of pure happiness beyond time and space? Even the brief summary which Dante himself gives of his *Comedy* suggests a final book which is hard to write and hard to read. He speaks of a journey

> Down through the world of endless misery,
> Up round the Mountain to whose lofty height
> My lady's eyes raised and attracted me,
> And afterwards through Heaven from light to light...
> (*Par.* XVII, 112–15)

Endless misery most of us can imagine without difficulty: pits and mountains and a lady's eyes offer scope to our imagination which a movement from light to light does not. Dante actually warns the reader off very early on, and this is not the time-honoured ploy to gain attention:

> You who have followed in your tiny skiff,
> Eager to listen to the song I sing,
> And sailed behind my ocean-going ship,
> Turn back and seek again your native coast;
> Do not attempt to cross the open water:
> If you lose sight of me, you will be lost.
> No one has ever ventured on this sea...
> (*Par.* II, 1–7)

It becomes clear a little later that the warning is only for the less than saintly reader; but this is small comfort to most of us.

Dante does not temper the wind to the shorn lamb. The reader is not led gently by the hand into the unknown joys of Heaven. Most of the second canto of *Paradise* is devoted to an explanation of why there are dark spots on the face of the moon. Dante did not have in mind the modern reader of poetry, who is hardly likely to be enthralled by this problem or, if he were, to look for the answer in a poem. But even in Dante's own day it seems likely that many readers would be put off by such a disquisition, and perhaps never reach the beginning of the following canto with its haunting description of those faces seen like reflections in water – the point at which Heaven first seems heaven-like.

This is not Dante being obtuse. Perhaps the greatest theme in *Paradise*, indeed throughout the *Comedy*, is that everything in the created universe, down to the tiniest detail, is part of one harmonious whole. If we could see all, then everything would fit in, and we would see how love penetrates everything, even accounting for the dark spots on the moon. Dante expresses this by means of a simple, homely metaphor in the final canto of his poem:

> In that profundity I saw – in-gathered,
> And bound by love into a single volume,
> All that throughout the universe is scattered...
> (*Par.* XXXIII, 85–87)

Those lines gain much of their effect from so much that has gone before, including much abstract, and even abstruse, reasoning.

It is no surprise that Dante makes frequent use of the figure of speech known as *adynaton*, the admission that the matter is beyond his power to convey. He uses this throughout the *Comedy*, starting with the exclamation at the beginning of the *Inferno*

> How hard a thing it is to express the horror
> Of that wild wood...

but nowhere so often, and so forcibly, as in *Paradise*:

> If all those tongues were now to sound aloud
> Which Polyhymnia with all her sisters
> Had fortified with their nutritious food,
> They would not even reach a thousandth part
> Of what is true about her sacred smile,
> And how it made her sacred face so bright;
> And so, in symbolizing Paradise,
> The sacred poem has to leap at times,
> Like walkers who find obstacles to cross.
> (*Par.* XXIII, 55–63)

Dante is not admitting any inadequacy as a poet. He says only a few lines farther on:

This is no voyage for a little vessel,
These waters my audacious prow is cleaving,
Nor for a boatman who would spare his muscle.
(*Par.* XXIII, 67–69)

The *adynaton* here, as so often in Dante, is used to draw attention to
the poet's skill by emphasizing the difficulty of the task.

A variation of this figure of speech is Dante's repeated declaration
in this book that his memory cannot retain precisely what it has seen,
which adds to the difficulties of expressing it. As with all writers of
autobiography, it is remarkable how much Dante can remember, and in
what great detail. It has wittily been said that it is more important for
an autobiographer to have a good imagination than a good memory. If
so, Dante's loss of memory in *Paradise* is all the more striking. It is not
a matter of things merely slipping his mind, as he is careful to tell us in
the first canto:

Because, as it draws near to its desire,
The mind sinks into such profundity
That memory cannot pursue it there.
(*Par.* I, 7–9)

Memory, which is a necessity in our world of time, is not relevant any
more in the timelessness of Heaven.

There is much more to *Paradise* than the extended and subtle use of
devices which it has in common with the other two books. Although
metaphors and figurative language generally are used throughout the
Inferno and *Purgatory*, both those poems are presented to us as fact,
not fiction. This is in stark contrast to some other famous visionary
poems which gain in scope and freedom by being presented as dreams.
Dante is wide awake in the dark wood at the beginning of the poem,
and he remains so during most of his experiences in the Inferno and
on Mount Purgatory. Both those poems are set in carefully described
places, where time is not only present but frequently referred to. In
Paradise, which is a state and not a place, and where time does not
exist, there has to be another way of making the reader well aware
that what Dante, and he, are seeing in the poem is so much less than
the reality of Heaven. Dante, as a mere mortal, is bound to see, and
consequently describe, Heaven in a radically different way, since it is
a radically different state. As Beatrice explains to him on the moon
after he has met his first group of the blessed:

Some were apparent here, not that this star
Is their allotted place, but as a sign
That in the Empyrean their place is lower.
(*Par.* IV, 37–39)

So Dante meets not the people who are saved, but various semblances
of them, on planets which are themselves metaphors for varying states

of beatitude. This figurative way of speaking is, as Beatrice is careful to point out, adapted to the understanding of a mortal, and comparable to the language of the Bible, "assigning hands and feet to God" (IV, 44). And what better justification can there be?

The Divine Comedy begins in a dark wood, and the Inferno is dark and progressively more claustrophobic as it narrows towards its base. In sharp contrast, Paradise is for Dante more and more spacious, until he reaches the Empyrean, where space does not exist. There are lights of an astonishing variety of kinds, which form themselves into many patterns, all of them drawing their existence from the One Light which is God. The most striking appearance of light is kept in reserve until Dante and Beatrice are on the farthest sphere of the created universe, the Primum Mobile: Dante sees a glow reflected in Beatrice's eyes. It is so tiny, he says, that the smallest star we see in the sky would seem like the moon in comparison with it. There are nine spheres revolving round it. This central light, the smallest, is the brightest. Dante is baffled, because the arrangement appears to be the opposite of what exists in the universe he knows. Beatrice explains that, in Heaven, what matters is not size (in Heaven there is no size), but the controlling spiritual power (Par. XXVIII, 13–78). This is concerned with the same problem as the discussion of the marks on the moon in the second canto – God's power which is unconfined by space or time, and so not ultimately apprehensible by a mere mortal: the spiritual is here conveyed with more sensuous immediacy.

There are places where Paradise is hard-going for many modern readers. The lengthy theological discussions may be admired for their clarity and at the same time found boring. At least, they are not to everyone's taste. It may come as a relief to some readers when St Peter Damian, on the sphere of Saturn, tells Dante that some things are beyond mortal comprehension and should not be questioned (Par. XXI, 91–102). Perhaps no one ever required that admonition more than Dante, although he lived at a time when theological probing and questioning was rife, when – as with some scientists today – theologians seemed to imagine that, if only they thought hard enough, they would eventually unlock every secret of the universe. So St Peter Damian silenced Dante; but he could not stop him thinking. The fate of those who could not know, for geographical, historical or other reasons, of Christ or Redemption, and could not apparently be saved, since there was no salvation outside the Church, was a problem which kept recurring to Dante. He provides in Paradise two reactions, if not solutions, to the problem. The first is a variant of the decision reached in the book of Job: "Touching the Almighty, we cannot find him out: he is excellent in power, and in judgement, and in plenty of justice: he will not afflict" (37:23). The second reaction of Dante is simply to show that pagans and other sinners can be saved, that the facts run against the dogma. So the harlot Rahab is in the heaven of Venus (Par. IX, 115–17), the pagan Ripheus – a Trojan known only from two bare mentions plus one statement that he was "most just" in the Aeneid (II, 339, 394, 426) – is in the eyebrow of the eagle in the sphere of Jupiter, where the pagan emperor Trajan (whom we met previously depicted in a carving symbolizing humility in the first circle of Purgatory (*Purg.* x, 73–78) keeps him company. Those concrete particulars are worth any amount of abstract reasoning.

Another difficulty for the reader is that there are times when it seems that Dante is deliberately avoiding saying anything directly, if he can possibly wrap it up in periphrases, frequently astronomical or, even thornier for a modern reader, astrological. This demands the reader's close attention, but his concentration will be well rewarded. The periphrases are justified by the effect they have of showing how everything is linked to everything else, although we may not always be able to detect the links: they suggest, in fact, the essential unity of all creation. It is not merely a matter of the heavens declaring the glory of God, but the whole of creation doing so, even down to things which might seem not beyond God's scope, but unworthy to be named in connection with Him. In the very first canto Dante prays to Apollo, the pagan god of poetry:

Enter my breast with your inspiring breath,
Just as you did when you drew Marsyas
Out of his fleshly limbs as from a sheath.
(*Par.* I, 19–21)

So a fiction, a rather unsavoury classical myth, is seen as part of God's creation, where somehow nothing is wasted.

Periphrases, or any kind of delay in naming the subject, can also have the effect of keeping the reader in a state of eager suspense. St Thomas Aquinas's praise of St Francis (*Par.* XI, 43–117) runs for thirty lines before the object of his praise is named. This keeps the reader guessing: surely a Dominican cannot be praising someone who sounds like the founder of the Franciscans, when those two orders were in Dante's day so often at odds? That is precisely what he is doing, just as in the next canto the Franciscan St Bonaventura praises St Dominic. What could make it clearer, after all, that this is Heaven? But Heaven, even more than the Inferno and Purgatory, demands a deeply engaged reader with all his wits about him.

Nevertheless, difficult concepts are often expressed very simply. Dante's ancestor, Cacciaguida, sums up the problem of the apparent clash between God's foreknowledge of events and the existence of human free will in one clear image:

"Contingency, outside the written sheet
Of mortal comprehension, is depicted
Fully and clearly in the Eternal Sight:
Necessity is not implied by that,
Any more than the ship which sails downstream
Depends upon the eye observing it…"
(*Par.* XVII, 34–42)

The dogma of the resurrection of the body is another very difficult concept to grasp. It is not "explained" – how can it be? – but it is somehow clarified by another simple image (which happens to be yet one more variety of light):

> ...just as coal may generate a flame
> And by its incandescence still outshine it,
> So that it is itself not overcome –
> So will this brilliance shining all around
> Us be outshone by resurrected flesh,
> Which all this while lies hidden in the ground.
> Nor will we be offended by that light:
> The organs of our bodies will be strengthened
> To welcome all that gives us such delight.
> (*Par.* xiv, 52–60)

Just as the physical and the metaphysical are inexplicably entwined in the resurrection of the body, so in Heaven, which is beyond time and space, Dante's earthly concerns are far from forgotten. Dante himself is, of course, an important figure throughout the *Comedy*, but it is in the realms of Heaven that his earthly life is outlined in most detail, and perhaps with the strongest personal feeling. In the central canto of *Paradise* the numerous hints which Dante has been given throughout the *Comedy* of some great disaster awaiting him are finally resolved when Cacciaguida forecasts his coming exile and its harshness:

> You shall experience the bitterness
> Of eating strangers' bread, and feel how hard
> Going up and down another's staircase is.
> (*Par.* xvii, 58–60)

He does not stop there. He tells Dante of where he will be staying during his exile, and with whom, and the tribulations he will suffer from his fellow exiles. Then Dante adds to this by saying that he is in a sense in a cleft stick: he has learnt during his journey many things, not all of them in famous people's favour; he would do wrong to conceal them, and he will add to his own trials if he reveals them. If Dante ever needed any encouragement to speak out, Cacciaguida gives it, in a typical blunt manner:

> Nevertheless, no lies! Be sure your speech
> Makes manifest the wholeness of your vision:
> Then let them scratch themselves who feel the itch.
> (*Par.* xvii, 127–29)

Furthermore, the canto where Dante meets St James the Greater and is examined closely on his understanding of the theological virtue of hope is prefaced by a dozen lines where Dante expresses his wish to return to Florence and be crowned as poet in the Baptistery there (*Par.* xxv, 1–12). This does show, as a prelude to the discussion with St James, another aspect of hope, although in this case a very worldly one; but, like the other personal allusions and statements, it has a greater significance. Put simply, when earthly concerns are seen in the light of Heaven, they matter more, not less than they did.

It is then no surprise that earthly matters loom so large in Paradise. The saved are not only happy to answer Dante's many questions, but also very ready to inveigh against the sins they see being committed down on the earth. St Thomas Aquinas, after his praise of St Francis, concludes with a condemnation of those of his own order who fall short of its high standards (Canto xi). Similarly, St Bonaventura, after his praise of St Dominic, condemns the backsliders in his own order (Canto xii). For the reader, then, Dante's ascent to Heaven does not lead to any lack of interest in the earth. The severest condemnation is of corrupt prelates, including cardinals, those wearers of "that hat which always / Goes down from one bad wearer to a worse" (*Par.* xxi, 125–26). Popes themselves are even more vigorously condemned for their betrayal of their high office. Their worst faults are caused by greed, particularly when this leads to the misuse of priestly powers for worldly gain: the sanctity of the office worsens the sin against it. Even Beatrice, in the Empyrean itself, with the very last words she addresses to Dante, condemns Pope Clement V, both for his betrayal of the Emperor Henry VII, who tried to establish peace in Italy, and for his greed and corruption:

> Then over Holy Church one will preside
> Who never, publicly or secretly,
> Will walk with Henry on the one straight road.
> But God will never suffer him to be
> Long in that sacred chair: he'll be thrust down
> Where Simon Magus is, deservedly,
> To push him of Anagni deeper in.
> (*Par.* xxx, 142–48)

One of the strengths of *Paradise* is that in this poem Dante is able to draw together themes which were present in the two earlier poems of the *Comedy* and bring them to an artistic conclusion. This may also be its greatest difficulty for a reader: it is not easy to have the whole of the *Comedy* in mind at one time; for the mere earthly reader the details may preponderate over the great design, as a result of his own inadequacy, not the poet's. So *Paradise* makes even greater demands on its readers than the other two books do. With Ben Jonson's always valuable warning in mind – "rare poems ask rare friends" – all we can do is try to be a rare friend. Where the matter of *Paradise* would seem to be most recalcitrant, as in the final vision of God, the poet is at his best, particularly in powerful concrete images which the reader cannot help but respond to, even if so much is momentarily out of his mind, and he suffers from forgetfulness with Dante, as Dante does with God:

> One instant brings me greater memory loss
> Than five-and-twenty centuries since Neptune
> Dumbfounded saw the Argo's shadow pass!
> (*Par.* xxxiii, 94–96)

The Divine Comedy is a triumph of light over darkness. After their journey through the gloom of the Inferno, Dante and Virgil

> Emerged to look once more upon the stars.
> (*Par.* xxxiv, 139)

After his climb up Mount Purgatory Dante was

> Pure and prepared to rise up to the stars.
> (*Par.* xxxiii, 145)

Now, after his vision of God, Dante tells us, all his

> ...volition and desires
> Were turned, like a wheel revolving smoothly, by
> The Love that moves the sun and all the stars.
> (*Par.* xxxiii, 143–45)

Select Bibliography

Editions of Dante Alighieri's The Divine Comedy:
La Divina Commedia, ed. Natalino Sapegno, 3 vols. (Florence: La Nuova Italia, 1985)
La Divina Commedia, ed. Umberto Bosco and Giovanni Reggio, 3 vols. (Florence: Le Monnier, 2002)
The Divine Comedy, tr. Allen Mandelbaum (London: Everyman, 1995)
The Divine Comedy of Dante Alighieri, tr. Robert M. Durling, 3 vols. (Oxford: Oxford University Press, 1996–2011)

Other works by Dante Alighieri:
The Banquet, tr. Christopher Ryan (Saratoga, California: Anima Libri, 1989).
Monarchy, and Three Political Letters, trs. D. Nicholl and C. Hardie (London: Weidenfeld & Nicolson, 1954)
New Life, tr. J.G. Nichols (London: Hesperus Press, 2003)
Rime, tr. J.G. Nichols and Anthony Mortimer (London: Oneworld Classics, 2009)
De vulgari eloquentia, ed. and tr. Steven Botterill (Cambridge: Cambridge University Press, 1996)

Additional Recommended Background Material:

Barolini, Teodolinda, 'Dante and the Lyric Past', *The Cambridge Companion to Dante* (Cambridge: Cambridge University Press, 1993)

Boccaccio, Giovanni, *Life of Dante*, tr. Nichols, J.G. (London: Hesperus Press, 2002)

Burge, James, *Dante's Invention* (Stroud, Glos: The History Press, 2010)

O'Donoghue, Bernard, *The Courtly Love Tradition* (Manchester: Manchester University Press, 1982)

Reynolds, Barbara, *Dante* (London & New York, NY: I.B. Tauris, 2006)

Toynbee, Paget, *Concise Dante Dictionary* (New York, NY: Phaeton Press, 1914, reprinted 1968)

Wilson, A.N., *Dante in Love* (London: Atlantic Books, 2011)

Note on the Text
and Acknowledgements

This translation is based on the edition by Natalino Sapegno. For biblical quotations, in the notes only, I have used the Authorised Version of the Bible, as the one most familiar and congenial to English readers, checked when necessary with reference to the Vulgate.

I am very grateful to Alessandro Gallenzi, who has checked this translation throughout, and provided many valuable criticisms and suggestions. I would also like to acknowledge the patience and dedication of Alex Billington, William Chamberlain, Matt Lewis, Christian Müller and the rest of the Alma Classics team. My thanks also go to Stephen Parkin for his help with the diagrams of the Inferno, Purgatory and Paradise.

INDEX

Angels in Heaven: *Par.* xxvIII, 25*ff*; xxxI, 13–15

Angiolello (from Fano): *Inf.* xxvIII, 77

Anselmo (nephew of Ugolino): *Inf.* xxxIII, 50: 90

Antaeus (giant): *Inf.* xxxI, 100–5: 113–45; xxxII, 17

Antandros (city of Phrygia): *Par.* vI, 68

Antenor's descendants (Paduans): *Purg.* v, 75

Antenora (second zone of Cocytus): *Inf.* xxxII, 88

Antigone (daughter of Oedipus): *Purg.* xxII, 110

Antiochus (king of Syria): *Inf.* xIx, 86

Antiphon (Greek poet): *Purg.* xxII, 106

Apennines: *Inf.* xvI, 95; xx, 65; xxvII, 30 • *Purg.* v, 96: 116; xIv, 31–32: 92; xxx, 86 • *Par.* xxI, 106

Apocalypse (by St John): *Purg.* xxIx, 105: 143–44 • *Par.* xxv, 94*ff*

Apollo (god): *Purg.* xII, 31; xx, 132 • *Par.* I, 13: 19–21: 32: 36; II, 8; xIII, 25

Apostles: *Inf.* xIx, 94 • *Purg.* xxII, 78 • *Par.* xI, 102; xxIII, 74; xxv, 33

Appetite (good will): *Par.* xvI, 5

Apulia (region of Italy): *Inf.* xxvIII, 9: 17 • *Purg.* vII, 126

Aquarius (sign of the Zodiac): *Inf.* xxIv, 2

Aquino (town in the Lazio region): *Par.* x, 99

Arabs: *Par.* vI, 49

Arachne (mythical weaver transformed into a spider): *Inf.* xvII, 18 • *Purg.* xII, 43

Aragon (kingdom): *Purg.* III, 116

Arbia (Tuscan river): *Inf.* x, 86

Arca (Florentine family): *Par.* xvI, 92

Archangels: *Par.* xxvIII, 125

Archiano (Tuscan river): *Purg.* v, 95: 124

Ardinghi (Florentine family): *Par.* xvI, 93

Arethusa (nymph transformed into a spring): *Inf.* xxv, 98

Aretines (citizens of Arezzo): *Inf.* xxII, 5 • *Purg.* xIv, 46

Arezzo (city): *Purg.* xIv, 44*ff*

Argia (daughter of Adrastus): *Purg.* xxII, 110

Argo: *Par.* xxxIII, 96

Argonauts: *Inf.* xvIII, 86 • *Par.* II, 16–18; xxxIII, 96

Argus (mythical shepherd): *Purg.* xxIx, 95; xxxII, 66

Ariadne (daughter of Minos): *Inf.* xII, 20 • *Par.* xIII, 15

Aries (or the "Ram", sign of the Zodiac): *Inf.* I, 38–40 • *Purg.* vIII, 134; xxxII, 53–54 • *Par.* xxvIII, 117; xxIx, 2

Aristotle (Greek philosopher): *Inf.* Iv, 131; xI, 80: 101 • *Purg.* III, 43 • *Par.* vIII, 120; xxvI, 38

Arius (heretic): *Par.* xIII, 127

Ark (of the Covenant): *Par.* xx, 39

Arles (city in Provence): *Inf.* Ix, 112

Arnaut Daniel (Provençal poet): *Purg.* xxvI, 115*ff*: 142

Arno (river in Florence): *Inf.* xIII, 146; xv, 113; xxIII 95; xxx, 65; xxxIII, 83 • *Purg.* v, 122: 125; xIv, 17: 24: 49–51 • *Par.* xI, 107

Arrigo (possibly one of the Fifanti family): *Inf.* vI, 80

Arrigo Mainardi (lord of Romagna): *Purg.* xIv, 97

Arrigucci (Florentine family): *Par.* xvI, 108

Art: *Purg.* xxII, 49; xxxIII, 141 • *Par.* I, 127–29; II, 96; x, 43; xIII, 77–78; xxvII, 91

Aruns (Etruscan soothsayer): *Inf.* xx, 46

Asdente (cobbler from Parma): *Inf.* xx, 118

Asopus (a river of Boeotia): *Purg.* xvIII, 91

Assisi (town in Umbria): *Par.* xI, 53

Assyrians: *Purg.* xII, 58

Athamas (king of Boeotia): *Inf.* xxx, 4*ff*

Athens: *Inf.* xII, 17 • *Purg.* vI, 139; xv, 97 • *Par.* xvII, 47

Atropos (one of the Fates): *Inf.* xxxIII, 126

Attila the Hun (king of Huns): *Inf.* xII, 134; xIII, 149

Attraction of the heavenly spheres: *Par.* xxvIII, 127*ff*

Augustine (Franciscan friar): *Par.* xII, 130

Augustus (imperial title): *Inf.* xIII, 68

Augustus (Octavian, emperor): *Inf.* I, 71 • *Purg.* vII, 6; xxIx, 116 • *Par.* vI, 73*ff*

Aulis (Greek port): *Inf.* xx, 111

Aurora (the dawn): *Purg.* II, 7; Ix, 1 • *Par.* xxx, 7

Ausonia (Italy): *Par.* vIII, 61

Auster (or "south wind"): *Purg.* xxx, 89; xxxI, 72; xxxII, 99

Avellana, see Fonte Avellana

Aventine (hill of Rome): *Inf.* xxv, 26

Averroës (Arab philosopher): *Inf.* Iv, 144 • *Purg.* xxv, 63

Avicenna (Arab philosopher): *Inf.* Iv, 143

Azzo degli Ubaldini (lord of Romagna): *Purg.* xIv, 105

Azzo VIII d'Este (lord of Ferrara): *Purg.* v, 77; xx, 80

Casella (Florentine musician): *Purg.* II, 76*ff*

Casentino (region of Tuscany): *Inf.* XXX, 65 • *Purg.* V, 94: 115; XIV, 43

Cassino (town at the foot of Mount Cairo): *Par.* XXII, 37

Cassius (assassin of Julius Caesar): *Inf.* XXXIV, 67 • *Par.* VI, 74

Castel Sant'Angelo (fortress in Rome): *Inf.* XVIII, 32

Castile (kingdom of Spain): *Par.* XII, 53–54

Castor (brother of Pollux): *Purg.* IV, 61

Castrocaro (small town in Romagna): *Purg.* XIV, 116

Catalano (Frisky Friar from Bologna): *Inf.* XXIII, 76*ff*

Catalans (citizens of Catalonia): *Par.* VIII, 78

Catellini (Florentine family): *Par.* XVI, 88

Cato of Utica: *Inf.* XIV, 15 • *Purg.* I, 31*ff*; II, 119–23

Catona (town near Reggio Calabria): *Par.* VIII, 62

Catria (mountain in the Apennines): *Par.* XXI, 109

Cattolica (town near Rimini): *Inf.* XXVIII, 80

Cavalcante de' Cavalcanti (father of Guido Cavalcanti): *Inf.* X, 52–72

Cecina (town in the Maremma district): *Inf.* XIII, 8

Celestial Rose: *Par.* XXX, 117*ff*; XXXI, 1: 10: 16: 20; XXXII, 4*ff*: 109*ff*; XXXIII, 9

Celestine V (pope): *Inf.* III, 59–60; XXVII, 105

Cenchres (snakes): *Inf.* XXIV, 87

Centaurs: *Inf.* XII, 56–139; XXV, 17–34 • *Purg.* XXIV, 121–23

Centre of the earth: *Inf.* XXXIV, 93

Ceprano (town on the Liri river): *Inf.* XXVIII, 16

Cephas, see St Peter

Cerberus (three-headed monster from hell): *Inf.* VI, 13*ff*; IX, 98

Cerchi (Florentine family): *Par.* XVI, 65: 94*ff*

Ceres (goddess): *Purg.* XXVIII, 51

Certaldo (town in Val d'Elsa): *Par.* XVI, 50

Cervia (town in the Romagna region): *Inf.* XXVII, 42

Ceuta (Moroccan city): *Inf.* XXVI, 111

Chaos: *Inf.* XII, 43

Chariot (symbol of the Church): *Purg.* XXIX, 107*ff*; XXX, 9*ff*; XXXII, 24*ff*

Charity (theological virtue): *Purg.* XV, 71 • *Par.* III, 43: 71: 77; V, 105: 118; XXI, 70; XXII, 32; (Dante questioned on charity) XXVI, 7–66; XXXI, 49; see also Theological virtues

Charlemagne (emperor): *Inf.* XXXI, 16

Charles I of Anjou (king of Naples): *Inf.* XIX, 99 • *Purg.* VII, 113: 124: 127; XI, 137; XX, 67

Charles II of Anjou (king of Naples): *Purg.* V, 69; VII, 127; XX, 79 • *Par.* VI, 106; VIII, 72; XIX, 127; XX, 63

Charles Martel (king of Hungary, son of Charles II of Anjou): *Par.* VIII, 31*ff*; IX, 1–4

Charles of Valois ("Lackland"): *Purg.* XX, 71*ff*

Charon (ferryman across the Acheron): *Inf.* III, 82–117: 128

Charybdis (mythical whirlpool on the Strait of Messina): *Inf.* VII, 22

Chastity (examples of): *Purg.* XXV, 128*ff*

Chelydres (snakes): *Inf.* XXIV, 87

Cherubim: *Par.* XXVIII, 99

Chiana (river in Tuscany): *Par.* XIII, 23

Chiaramontesi (Florentine family): *Par.* XVI, 105

Chiascio (river in Umbria): *Par.* XI, 43–44

Chiavari (city in Liguria): *Purg.* XIX, 100

Children who died before the age of reason: *Par.* XXXII, 44*ff*

Chiron (centaur): *Inf.* XII, 65*ff* • *Purg.* IX, 38

Chiusi (town in Tuscany): *Par.* XVI, 75

Christ, see Jesus

Christians: *Par.* V, 73*ff*; XII, 37*ff*; XIX, 106*ff*; XXVII, 47: 51

Church of Rome: *Par.* IV, 46; V, 35: 77; VI, 22: 95; IX, 133*ff*; X, 108: 139*ff*; XI, 31; XII, 107; XVIII, 132; XXII, 82; XXV, 52; XXVII, 40*ff*; XXXI, 3; XXXII, 125: 128

Ciacco (Florentine): *Inf.* VI, 38*ff*

Ciampolo (from Navarre): *Inf.* XXII, 32*ff*

Cianfa Donati (Florentine): *Inf.* XXV, 43

Cianghella della Tosa (Florentine woman): *Par.* XV, 127

Cicero (Roman orator): *Inf.* IV, 141

Ciel d'Oro (San Pietro in Ciel d'Oro, basilica in Pavia): *Par.* X, 128

Cimabue (painter): *Purg.* XI, 94–95

Cincinnatus (Roman politician): *Par.* VI, 46; XV, 129

Circe (sorceress): *Inf.* XXVI, 91 • *Purg.* XIV, 42

Classe (former port of Ravenna): *Purg.* XXVIII, 20

Clawboys (devils): *Inf.* XXI, 37; XXII, 100; XXIII, 23; XXXIII, 143

Clemence (wife of Charles Martel): *Par.* IX, 1

Clement IV (pope): *Purg.* III, 126

Clement V (pope): *Inf.* XIX, 82*ff* • *Par.* XVII, 82; XXVII, 58; XXX, 142*ff*

Frederick II (king of Sicily): *Purg.* VII, 119 • *Par.* XIX, 131; XX, 63

Free will: *Purg.* XVI, 64*ff*; XVIII, 40*ff*; XXVII, 140*ff*

French: *Inf.* XXVII, 44; XXIX, 123; XXXII, 115

Friar Gomita (from Sardinia): *Inf.* XXII, 81*ff*

Friars Minor: *Inf.* XXIII, 3

Frieslanders: *Inf.* XXXI, 63

Frisky Friars: *Inf.* XXIII, 103

Fucci: Vanni, see Vanni Fucci

Fulcieri da Calboli (nobleman from Forlì): *Purg.* XIV, 58*ff*

Furies: *Inf.* IX, 38*ff*

Gabriel (archangel): *Purg.* X, 34*ff* • *Par.* IV, 47; IX, 138; XIV, 36; XXIII, 94: 103; XXXII, 94*ff*: 112

Gaddo (son of Ugolino): *Inf.* XXXIII, 68: 90

Gaeta (town): *Inf.* XXVI, 92 • *Par.* VIII, 62

Gaia (daughter of Gherardo da Camino): *Purg.* XVI, 140

Galaxy: *Par.* XIV, 98

Galeazzo Visconti (lord of Milan): *Purg.* VIII, 80

Galen (Greek physician): *Inf.* IV, 143

Galicia (region of Spain): *Par.* XXV, 18

Galigai (Florentine family): *Par.* XVI, 101

Galli (Florentine family): *Par.* XVI, 105

Gallura (Sardinian district): *Inf.* XXII, 82 • *Purg.* VIII, 81

Galluzzo (town near Florence): *Par.* XVI, 53

Game of dice: *Purg.* VI, 1

Ganelon (traitor): *Inf.* XXXII, 122

Ganges (river): *Purg.* II, 5; XXVII, 4 • *Par.* XI, 51

Gano degli Scornigiani (man from Pisa): *Purg.* VI, 17

Ganymede (cup-bearer of the gods): *Purg.* IX, 23–24

Garda (lake): *Inf.* XX, 65

Gardingo (area of the city of Florence): *Inf.* XXIII, 108

Garisenda (tower in Bologna): *Inf.* XXXI, 136

Gascony (French province): *Purg.* XX, 66 • *Par.* XXVII, 58

Gate of Purgatory: *Purg.* IX, 90; X, 1*ff*; XXVIII, 102

Gaville (town): *Inf.* XXV, 151

Gemini (sign of the Zodiac): *Purg.* IV, 61 • *Par.* XXII, 111: 152; XXVII, 98

Generation of Man: *Purg.* XXV, 37*ff*

Generosity (examples of): *Purg.* XIII, 28*ff*; XX, 31*ff*

Genesis (book of the Bible): *Inf.* XI, 107

Genoese: *Inf.* XXXIII, 151*ff* • *Par.* IX, 90

Gentucca (woman from Lucca): *Purg.* XXIV, 37

Geomancers (diviners): *Purg.* XIX, 4

Geri del Bello (relative of Dante): *Inf.* XXIX, 27*ff*

Geryon (winged monster): *Inf.* XVII, 97: 113*ff*; XVIII, 20 • *Purg.* XXVII, 23

Ghent (city): *Purg.* XX, 46

Gherardo da Camino (from Treviso): *Purg.* XVI, 125: 133: 138

Gherardo II della Scala (abbot of San Zeno in Verona): *Purg.* XVIII, 112*ff*

Ghibellines: *Par.* VI, 101: 103; XXVII, 48

Ghino di Tacco (Sienese bandit): *Purg.* VI, 13

Ghisolabella (sister of Venedico Caccianemico): *Inf.* XVIII, 56

Gianfigliazzi (Florentine family): *Inf.* XVII, 60

Gianni Buiamonte dei Becchi (Florentine usurer): *Inf.* XVII, 73

Gianni de' Soldanieri (Florentine): *Inf.* XXXII, 121

Gianni Schicchi (Florentine): *Inf.* XXX, 32: 42*ff*

Giano della Bella (Florentine nobleman): *Par.* XVI, 131

Giants: *Inf.* XXXI, 43*ff*; XXXIV, 30–31 • *Purg.* XII, 33

Gideon (judge of Israel): *Purg.* XXIV, 125

Gilboa (mountain in Samaria): *Purg.* XII, 41

Giotto di Bondone (painter): *Purg.* XI (95

Giovanna (wife of Buonconte da Montefeltro): *Purg.* V, 89

Giovanna Visconti (daughter of Nino Visconti): *Purg.* VIII, 71

Girault de Bornelh (Provençal poet): *Purg.* XXVI, 120

Giuda de' Guidi (Florentine): *Par.* XVI, 123

Giuochi (Florentine family): *Par.* XVI, 104

Giuseppe della Scala (abbot of San Zeno in Verona): *Purg.* XVIII, 124

Glaucus (mythical Greek fisherman): *Par.* I, 68–69

Gluttons: *Purg.* XXII, 133*ff*; XXIII; XXIV 4*ff*

Gluttony: *Inf.* VI, 7–99 • *Purg.* XXIV, 121–26

God: *Inf.* I, 40: 124: 126*ff*: 131; II, 16: 91: 103; III, 4: 39: 63: 103: 108: 122; IV, 38; V, 91; VII, 19: 73*ff*; VIII, 60; XI, 22: 26: 31: 51: 74: 81: 84: 105; XII, 119; XIV, 16: 69; XIX, 2: 10–12; XX, 19; XXIV, 119; XXV, 3; XXXIV, 35 • *Purg.* II, 29: 123; III, 36: 120, 122: 125; IV, 128; V, 56: 104; VI, 37: 93: 118; VII, 5: 26; VIII, 66;

Hautefort (fortress in France): *Inf.* xxix, 29
Hebrew women (in the Celestial Rose): *Par.* xxxii, 17
Hector (Trojan hero): *Inf.* iv, 122 • *Par.* vi, 68
Hecuba (wife of Priam): *Inf.* xxx, 16
Helen of Troy (wife of Menelaus): *Inf.* v, 64
Helice (constellation of the Great Bear, nymph): *Purg.* xxv, 131 • *Par.* xxxi, 32
Helicon (sacred mountain of the Muses): *Purg.* xxix, 40
Heliodorus (treasurer of King Seleucus): *Purg.* xx, 113
Helios (name for God): *Par.* xiv, 96
Hellespont (Dardanelles straits): *Purg.* xxviii, 71
Hellhound (devil): *Inf.* xxi, 119; xxii, 106*ff*
Henry I (king of Navarre): *Purg.* vii, 104: 110
Henry II (king): *Inf.* xxviii, 136
Henry III (king of England): *Purg.* vii, 131
Henry VI (emperor): *Par.* iii, 119
Henry VII (emperor): *Purg.* vi, 102 • *Par.* xvii, 83; xxx, 133*ff*
Henry of Segusio (bishop of Ostia, canon lawyer): *Par.* xii, 83
Heraclitus (Greek philosopher): *Inf.* iv, 138
Hercules (Greek hero): *Inf.* xxv, 32; xxvi, 107–9; xxxi, 132 • *Par.* ix, 101–2
Heresiarchs: *Inf.* ix, 126*ff*; x, 7
Hermaphrodites (sinners): *Purg.* xxvi, 82*ff*
Hezekiah (king of Judah): *Par.* xx, 49*ff*
Hierarchy of angels: *Par.* xxviii, 121*ff*
Hippocrates (Greek physician): *Inf.* iv, 143 • *Purg.* xxix, 137
Hippolytus (son of Theseus): *Par.* xvii, 46
History of the Roman Empire: *Par.* vi, 1–96
Hogwash (devil): *Inf.* xxi, 122; xxii, 55
Holofernes (Assyrian leader): *Purg.* xxii, 59
Holy Face: *Inf.* xxi, 47
Holy Land (Palestine): *Par.* ix, 125; xv, 144
Holy Mother Church: *Inf.* xix, 57
Holy Spirit: *Purg.* xx, 98 • *Par.* iii, 53; vi, 11; vii, 33; x, 1; xiii, 57; xiv, 76; xix, 100; xx, 38; xxi, 128; xxiv, 92: 138; xxvii, 1; xxix, 41; xxxiii, 119: 124
Holy Trinity: *Purg.* iii, 36 • *Par.* vii, 30*ff*; x, 1*ff*; xiii, 79; xiv, 28*ff*; xxiv, 139; xxxi, 28; xxxiii, 116
Homer (Greek poet): *Inf.* iv, 88 • *Par.* xxii, 101–2
Homicide: *Inf.* xi, 37; xii, 47*ff*
Honorius (pope): *Par.* xi, 98

Hope (theological virtue): *Par.* (Dante questioned on hope): xxv, 31*ff*; see also Theological virtues
Horace (Roman poet): *Inf.* iv, 89
Horatii (adversaries of the Curiatii): *Par.* vi, 39
Hound: *Inf.* i, 101*ff*
Hugh Capet (king of France): *Purg.* xx, 19*ff*
Hugh of St Victor (theologian): *Par.* xii, 133
Human corruption (cause of): *Purg.* xvi, 67*ff*
Humility (examples of): *Purg.* x, 44*ff*
Hungary: *Par.* viii, 66; xix, 142
Hyperion (father of Apollo, the sun): *Par.* xxii, 142
Hypocrites: *Inf.* xxiii, 58*ff*
Hypsipyle (queen of Lemnos): *Inf.* xviii, 92 • *Purg.* xxii, 112; xxvi, 95

Iarbas (king of the Gaetuli): *Purg.* xxxi, 72
Icarus (son of Dedalus): *Inf.* xvii, 109–10 • *Par.* viii, 126
Ida (mountain): *Inf.* xiv, 98 • *Purg.* ix, 22
Ilium, see Troy
Illuminato of Rieti (follower of St Francis): *Par.* xii, 130
Imola (city): *Inf.* xxvii, 50
Importuni (Florentine family): *Par.* xvi, 133
Incontinent: *Inf.* xi, 70–90
India: *Inf.* xiv, 31 • *Purg.* vii, 74 • *Par.* xxix, 101
Indians (people from India): *Purg.* xxvi, 20; xxxii, 42
Indus (river): *Par.* xix, 70
Infangati (Florentine family): *Par.* xvi, 122
Innocent III (pope): *Par.* xi, 92–93
Iole (girl loved by Hercules): *Par.* ix, 102
Iphigenia (daughter of Agamemnon): *Par.* v, 70
Iris (the messenger of Juno, the rainbow): *Purg.* xxi, 50 • *Par.* xii, 12; xxviii, 32; xxxiii, 118
Isaac (patriarch): *Inf.* iv, 59
Isaiah (prophet): *Par.* xxv, 91
Isère (river in France): *Par.* vi, 59
Ismene (daughter of Oedipus): *Purg.* xxii, 111
Ismenus (river in Boeotia): *Purg.* xviii, 91
Israel (Jacob, patriarch), see Jacob
Israel: *Purg.* ii, 47
Italian: *Inf.* xxii, 65 • *Purg.* xi, 58; xiii, 92
Italy: *Inf.* i, 107; ix, 114; xx, 61; xxvii, 26; xxviii, 72; xxxiii, 80 • *Purg.* vi, 76: 85: 105: 124; vii, 95; xiii, 96; xx, 67; xxx, 86 • *Par.* ix, 25; xxi, 106; xxx, 138

Leah (wife of Jacob): *Purg.* XXVII, 98*ff*

Leander (lover of Hero): *Purg.* XXVIII, 73

Learchus (son of Athamas): *Inf.* XXX, 10

Lebanon: *Purg.* XXX, 11

Leda (loved by Jove): *Par.* XXVII, 98

Lemnos (island): *Inf.* XVIII, 88

Leo (sign of the Zodiac): *Par.* XVI, 38; XXI, 14

Leopard: *Inf.* I, 32; XVI, 108

Lerici (city in Liguria): *Purg.* III, 50

Lérida (Lleida, city in Spain): *Purg.* XVIII, 101

Lethe (river in the Earthly Paradise): *Inf.* XIV, 131: 136 • *Purg.* XXVI, 108; XXVIII, 130; XXX, 143; XXXI, 1; XXXIII, 96: 123

Levites (Jewish priests): *Purg.* XVI, 131

Libra (sign of the Zodiac): *Purg.* II, 5; XXVII, 3 • *Par.* XXIX, 2

Libya: *Inf.* XIV, 14; XXIV, 85 • *Purg.* XXXI, 72

Lille (Flemish city): *Purg.* XX, 46

Lily (arms of the King of France), see Fleur-de-lis

Limbo (the first circle of the Inferno): *Inf.* IV, 31*ff* • *Purg.* I, 4; VII, 28; XXI, 31; XXII, 14: 103; XXVI, 133; XXXII, 84

Limoges: *Purg.* XXVI, 120

Linus (mythical Greek poet): *Inf.* IV, 140

Linus (pope): *Par.* XXVII, 41

Lion (animal): *Inf.* I, 44

Livy (Roman historian): *Inf.* XXVIII, 12

Lizio (from Romagna): *Purg.* XIV, 97

Loderingo (Frisky Friar): *Inf.* XXIII, 104

Logodoro (Sardinian region): *Inf.* XXII, 88

Loire (river in France): *Par.* VI, 59

Lombards (citizens of Lombardy): *Inf.* XXII, 99

Lombardy: *Inf.* I, 68; XXVII, 20 • *Purg.* VI, 61; XVI, 46

Looters and pillagers: *Inf.* XI, 38

Louis (name of various Kings of France): *Purg.* XX, 50

Love (theory of): *Purg.* XVII, 91–139; XVIII, 13–75

Lucan (Roman poet): *Inf.* IV, 90; XXV, 94

Lucca (city): *Inf.* XXI, 38; XXXIII, 30 • *Purg.* XXIV, 20, 35: 44

Lucifer (Satan): *Inf.* XXXI, 143; XXXIV, 89 • *Purg.* XII, 25 • *Par.* IX, 128; XIX, 46–48; XXVII, 26–27; XXIX, 56

Lucrece, see Lucretia

Lucretia (Roman woman): *Inf.* IV, 128 • *Par.* VI, 41

Luni (city): *Inf.* XX, 47 • *Par.* XVI, 73

Lustful: *Inf.* V, 32*ff* • *Purg.* XXV, 109

Lycurgus (king of Nemea): *Purg.* XXVI, 94

Maccabees (book of the Bible): *Inf.* XIX, 86

Maghinardo Pagani da Susinana (lord of Faenza): *Inf.* XXVII, 49 • *Purg.* XIV, 118

Magpies (Pierides, daughters of King Pierus): *Purg.* I, 11

Magra (river): *Par.* IX, 89

Mahomet: *Inf.* XXVIII, 31*ff*

Maia (mother of Mercury): *Par.* XXII, 144

Majorca (island): *Inf.* XXVIII, 83

Malaspina (family from Lunigiana): *Purg.* VIII, 118: 124

Malatesta da Verrucchio (lord of Rimini): *Inf.* XXVII, 46

Malatestino da Verrucchio (son of Malatesta da Verrucchio): *Inf.* XXVII, 46; XXVIII, 81: 85

Malice: *Inf.* XI, 82 • *Par.* IV, 65

Manfred (king of Puglia and Sicily): *Purg.* III, 103*ff*; IV, 14

Manto (seer): *Inf.* XX, 54*ff* • *Purg.* XXII, 113

Mantua (city): *Inf.* XX, 92 • *Purg.* VI, 72; VII, 18; XVIII, 83

Mantuans (citizens of Mantua): *Inf.* I, 69; II, 58 • *Purg.* VI, 74; VII, 86

Marcabò (fortress in the Ravenna area): *Inf.* XXVIII, 75

March of Treviso: *Par.* IX, 25: 44

Marche (region in central Italy): *Purg.* V, 68–69

Marchese degli Orgogliosi of Forlì: *Purg.* XXIV, 31

Marcia (wife of Cato of Utica): *Inf.* IV, 128 • *Purg.* I, 79: 85

Marco Lombardo (courtier): *Purg.* XVI, 25*ff*

Maremma (region in Tuscany): *Inf.* XXV, 19; XXIX, 48 • *Purg.* V, 134

Margaret of Burgundy (wife of Charles I of Anjou): *Purg.* VII, 128

Mars (god): *Inf.* XIII; 144; XXIV, 146; XXXI, 51 • *Purg.* XII, 31 • *Par.* IV, 63; VIII, 132; XVI, 47: 146

Mars (planet): *Purg.* II, 14 • *Par.* XIV, 100; XVI, 37; XVII, 77; XXII, 146; XXVII, 14

Marseille (city): *Purg.* XVIII, 102

Marsyas (satyr): *Par.* I, 20

Martin IV (pope): *Purg.* XXIV, 20*ff*

Mary (Jewish woman): *Purg.* XXIII, 30

Mary (Virgin Mary), see Virgin Mary

Mary of Brabant (queen of France): *Purg.* VI, 23

Pratomagno (massif of the Tuscan Apennines): *Purg.* v, 116

Prayer (effectiveness of): *Purg.* vi, 30*ff*

Prayers recited in Purgatory: *Purg.* ii, 47; v, 24; vii, 83; viii, 13; ix, 140; xi, 1*ff*; xiii, 50; xvi, 19; xix, 73; xx, 136; xxv, 121; xxxiii, 11

Preachers (invective against): *Par.* xxix, 94*ff*

Prescience: *Inf.* x, 97*ff*

Pressa (della, Florentine family): *Par.* xvi, 100

Priam (king of Troy): *Inf.* xxx, 15

Pride (examples of): *Purg.* xii, 25*ff*

Priscian (Latin grammarian): *Inf.* xv, 109

Procne (mythical woman transformed into a nightingale): *Purg.* xvii, 19

Prodigals: *Purg.* xix, 70*ff*, 118*ff*; xxii, 54

Prophecy of Beatrice: *Purg.* xxxiii, 34*ff*

Prophets: *Par.* xxiv, 136

Proserpine (infernal goddess): *Inf.* ix, 44; x, 80 • *Purg.* xxviii, 50

Proud people: *Purg.* x–xii

Provençals: *Par.* vi, 130

Provence (region in France): *Purg.* vii, 126 • *Par.* viii, 58–59

Provence (the dowry of): *Purg.* xx, 61

Provenzano Salvani of Siena: *Purg.* xi, 109*ff*

Psalms (recited by penitents): *Purg.* ii, 47; v, 24; xix, 73; xxiii, 11; xxviii, 80; xxix, 3; xxx, 83*ff*; xxxi, 98; xxxiii, 1

Ptolemy (Greek astronomer): *Inf.* iv, 142

Ptolemy (king of Egypt): *Par.* vi, 69

Ptolomea (third zone of Cocytus): *Inf.* xxxiii, 124

Puccio Sciancato (Florentine): *Inf.* xxv, 148

Purgatory (moral ordering): *Purg.* xvii, 85*ff*

Pygmalion (king of Tyre, brother of Dido): *Purg.* xx, 103

Pyramus (lover of Thisbe): *Purg.* xxvii, 37; xxxiii, 69

Pyrenees: *Par.* xix, 144

Pyrrhus (king of Epirus): *Inf.* xii, 135 • *Par.* vi, 44

Quarnero (gulph in the Adriatic Sea): *Inf.* ix, 113

Quintius, see Cincinnatus

Quirinus, see Romulus

Rabanus (theologian): *Par.* xii, 139

Rachel (wife of Jacob): *Inf.* ii, 102; iv, 60 • *Purg.* xxvii, 104 • *Par.* xxxii, 8

Rahab (harlot of Jericho): *Par.* ix, 115

Rainouart (medieval legendary hero): *Par.* xviii, 46

Ram, see Aries

Rape of the Sabine women: *Par.* vi, 41

Raphael (archangel): *Par.* iv, 48

Rascia (province of the Serbian realm): *Par.* xix, 140

Ravenna (city): *Inf.* v, 97; xxvii, 40 • *Par.* vi, 62

Ravignani (Florentine family): *Par.* xvi, 97

Raymond Berengar (count of Provence): *Par.* vi, 133

Rebecca (wife of Isaac and mother of Jacob): *Par.* xxxii, 10: 69

Red Sea: *Inf.* xxiv, 89 • *Purg.* xviii, 134 • *Par.* vi, 79; xxii, 94

Rehoboam (king of Israel): *Purg.* xii, 46

Reno (river in Emilia): *Inf.* xviii, 61 • *Purg.* xiv, 92

Resurrection: *Par.* vii, 146

Revelation (book of the Bible): *Inf.* xix, 106

Rhea (goddess: wife of Saturn): *Inf.* xiv, 100

Rhine (river in Germany): *Par.* vi, 58

Rhône (river in France): *Inf.* ix, 112 • *Par.* vi, 60

Rialto (island of Venice): *Par.* ix, 26

Richard of St Victor (theologian): *Par.* x, 131

Rimini (city): *Inf.* xxviii, 93

Rinieri da Calboli (nobleman from Forlì): *Purg.* xiv, 88

Rinieri da Corneto (bandit from Corneto): *Inf.* xii, 137

Rinieri de' Pazzi (bandit): *Inf.* xii, 136

Ripheus (Trojan hero): *Par.* xx, 68: 118

Rizzardo da Camino (lord of Treviso): *Par.* ix, 50–51

Robert Guiscard (Norman adventurer): *Inf.* xxviii, 14 • *Par.* xviii, 48

Robert II (king of France): *Purg.* xx, 58

Robert of Anjou (king of Naples): *Par.* viii, 76*ff*

Roland (paladin): *Inf.* xxxi, 18 • *Par.* xviii, 43

Romagna (people from): *Purg.* xiv, 99

Romagna (region of Italy): *Inf.* xxvii, 28: 37; xxxiii, 154 • *Purg.* v, 69; xiv, 92; xv, 44

Roman Church: *Purg.* iii, 137; xvi, 127; xxiv, 22; xxxii, 149*ff*; xxxiii, 45

Roman Pastor (pope): *Purg.* xix, 107

Roman prince (emperor): *Purg.* x, 74

Romano (castle in the Veneto region): *Par.* ix, 28

Romans: *Inf.* xv, 77; xviii, 28; xxvi, 60 • *Par.* vi, 44; xix, 102

Rome: *Inf.* I, 71; II, 21; XIV, 105 • *Purg.* VI, 112;
XVI, 106; XVIII, 80; XXI, 89; XXIX, 115; XXXII,
102 • *Par.* VI, 57; IX, 140; XV, 126; XVI, 10;
XXIV, 63; XXVII, 25: 62; XXXI, 34

Romée de Villeneuve (minister of Raymond
Berengar): *Par.* VI, 127*ff*

Romena (fortress in the Casentino area): *Inf.*
XXX, 73

Romulus (mythical founder of Rome, also
called Quirinus): *Par.* VIII, 131

Rubaconte (bridge over the Arno): *Purg.* XII,
101

Rubicon (river): *Par.* VI, 61

Rudolf of Habsburg (emperor): *Purg.* VI, 103;
VII, 91*ff* • *Par.* VIII, 72

Ruggieri degli Ubaldini (archbishop of Pisa):
Inf. XXXII, 125*ff*; XXXIII, 3: 14: 28

Rusticucci, see Jacopo Rusticucci

Ruth (great-grandmother of king David):
Par. XXXII, 10

Sabellius (heretic): *Par.* XIII, 127

Sabellus (one of Cato's soldiers): *Inf.* XXV, 95

Sacchetti (Florentine family): *Par.* XVI, 104

Sacred Ark: *Purg.* X, 56

Sacristy (of St Jacopo in Pistoia): *Inf.* XXIV, 138

Saladin (sultan of Egypt): *Inf.* IV, 129

Salimbeni, see Niccolò dei Salimbeni

Samaritan woman: *Purg.* XXI, 2–3

San Benedetto in Alpe (monastery north of
Forlì): *Inf.* XVI, 100–1

San Giovanni (baptistery in Florence): *Inf.*
XIX, 17

San Leo (small town in Montefeltro): *Purg.*
IV, 25

San Miniato (church in Florence): *Purg.* XII,
101

Sannella (Florentine family): *Par.* XVI, 92

Sant'Angelo Bridge (in Rome): *Inf.* XVIII, 29

Santa Fiora (town near Siena): *Purg.* V, 111

Santerno (river of the Emilia region): *Inf.*
XXVII, 50

Santo Andrea, see Jacopo da Santo Andrea

Sapia (Sienese lady): *Purg.* XIII, 100*ff*

Sapphira (wife of Ananias): *Purg.* XX, 112

Saracen women: *Purg.* XXIII, 103

Saracens: *Inf.* XXVII, 87

Sarah (wife of Abraham): *Par.* XXXII, 10

Sardanapalus (king of Assyria): *Par.* XV, 107

Sardinia: *Inf.* XXII, 89; XXVI, 104; XXIX, 48 •
Purg. XXIII, 94

Sardinians: *Purg.* XVIII, 81

Sassolo Mascheroni (Florentine): *Inf.* XXXII,
65

Satan, see Lucifer

Saturn (god): *Par.* XXI, 26

Saturn (planet): *Purg.* XIX, 3 • *Par.* XXI, 13;
XXII, 146

Saul (king of Israel): *Purg.* XII, 40

Savio (river of Cesena): *Inf.* XXVII, 52

Scala (della), see Bartolomeo and Cangrande
della Scala

Scipio (Africanus, general who defeated
Hannibal): *Inf.* XXXI, 116 • *Purg.* XXIX, 116
• *Par.* VI, 52; XXVII, 62

Scorpio (sign of the Zodiac): *Purg.* IX, 5; XXV, 3

Scot, see Michael Scot

Scrotter (devil): *Inf.* XXI, 122; XXII, 34

Scumbag (devil): *Inf.* XXI, 121; XXII, 70

Sea (ocean): *Par.* IX, 84; XII, 49; XXVII, 82

Seducers: *Inf.* XVIII

Seine (river in France): *Par.* VI, 59; XIX, 119

Semele (daughter of Cadmus, loved by Jove):
Inf. XXX, 2 • *Par.* XXI, 5

Semifonte (castle in Val d'Elsa): *Par.* XVI, 62

Semiramis (queen of Assyrians): *Inf.* V, 58

Seneca (Roman philosopher): *Inf.* IV, 141

Sennacherib (king of Assyria): *Purg.* XII, 53

Seraphim: *Par.* IV, 28; VIII, 27; IX, 77; XXI, 92;
XXVIII, 99

Serchio (Tuscan river): *Inf.* XXI, 49

Sestos (city of the Hellespont): *Purg.* XXVIII,
74

Sestri (city in Liguria): *Purg.* XIX, 100

Seven candlesticks (seven gifts of Holy
Spirit): *Purg.* XXIX, 43*ff*; XXXII, 18

Seven Kings (who besieged Thebes): *Inf.*
XIV, 68–9

Seven Kings of Rome: *Par.* VI, 42

Seven women (symbol of virtue): *Purg.* XXIX,
121*ff*; XXXII, 2: 109

Seville (city of Spain): *Inf.* XX, 126; XXVI, 110

Sextus Pompey (son of Pompey): *Inf.* XII,
135 • *Par.* VI, 72

Shades (theory of): *Purg.* XXV, 88*ff*

She-wolf (a symbol of cupidity): *Inf.* I, 49*ff*
• *Purg.* XX, 10

Shepherd of Cosenza, see Bartolomeo
Pignatelli

Shinar (country in Mesopotamia): *Purg.* XII,
36

Sichaeus (husband of Dido of Carthage):
Par. IX, 98

Sicilian Vespers: *Par.* VIII, 75

EVERGREENS SERIES
Beautifully produced classics, affordably priced

Alma Classics is committed to making available a wide range of literature from around the globe. Most of the titles are enriched by an extensive critical apparatus, notes and extra reading material, as well as a selection of photographs. The texts are based on the most authoritative editions and edited using a fresh, accessible editorial approach. With an emphasis on production, editorial and typographical values, Alma Classics aspires to revitalize the whole experience of reading classics.

 On the ORIGIN of SPECIES — Charles DARWIN

 Daniel Defoe — Moll Flanders

 CHARLES DICKENS — A CHRISTMAS CAROL

 DAVID COPPERFIELD — CHARLES DICKENS

 GREAT EXPECTATIONS — CHARLES DICKENS

 HARD TIMES — CHARLES DICKENS

 CHARLES DICKENS — OLIVER TWIST

 CHARLES DICKENS — TALE OF TWO CITIES

 the DOUBLE — Fyodor DOSTOEVSKY

 Fyodor DOSTOEVSKY — The GAMBLER

 the IDIOT — Fyodor Dostoevsky

 NOTES from UNDERGROUND — Fyodor DOSTOEVSKY

 Middlemarch — GEORGE ELIOT

 The MILL in the FLOSS — George Eliot

 PRAISE of FOLLY — ERASMUS

 The BEAUTIFUL and DAMNED — F. SCOTT FITZGERALD

 The GREAT GATSBY — F. SCOTT FITZGERALD

 TENDER the NIGHT — F. SCOTT FITZGERALD

 GUSTAVE FLAUBERT — MADAME BOVARY

 NORTH and SOUTH — ELIZABETH GASKELL

 THE SORROWS OF YOUNG WERTHER — GOETHE

 Dead SOULS — Nikolai GOGOL

 Nikolai GOGOL — Petersburg TALES

 THOMAS HARDY — FAR FROM THE MADDING CROWD

 THOMAS HARDY — JUDE THE OBSCURE

 THOMAS HARDY — TESS OF THE D'URBERVILLES

 Nathaniel Hawthorne — The Scarlet LETTER

 THE PORTRAIT OF A LADY — HENRY JAMES

 THREE MEN IN A BOAT — JEROME K. JEROME

 DUBLINERS — JAMES JOYCE

 ULYSSES — JAMES JOYCE

 FRANZ KAFKA — METAMORPHOSIS

 FRANZ KAFKA — THE TRIAL

 LADY CHATTERLEY'S LOVER — D. H. LAWRENCE

 SONS AND LOVERS — D H LAWRENCE

 Mikhail Lermontov — A Hero of Our Time

For our complete list and latest offers

visit

almabooks.com/evergreens

GREAT POETS SERIES

Each volume is based on the most authoritative text, and reflects Alma's commitment to provide affordable editions with valuable insight into the great poets' works.

Selected Poems
Blake, William
ISBN: 9781847498212
£7.99 • PB • 288 pp

The Rime of the Ancient Mariner
Coleridge, Samuel Taylor
ISBN: 9781847497529
£7.99 • PB • 256 pp

Complete Poems
Keats, John
ISBN: 9781847497567
£9.99 • PB • 520 pp

Paradise Lost
Milton, John
ISBN: 9781847498038
£7.99 • PB • 320 pp

Sonnets
Shakespeare, William
ISBN: 9781847496089
£4.99 • PB • 256 pp

Leaves of Grass
Whitman, Walt
ISBN: 9781847497550
£8.99 • PB • 288 pp

MORE POETRY TITLES

Dante Alighieri: *Inferno, Purgatory, Paradise, Rime, Vita Nuova, Love Poems*;
Alexander Pushkin: *Lyrics Vol. 1 and 2, Love Poems, Ruslan and Lyudmila*;
François Villon: *The Testament and Other Poems*; Cecco Angiolieri: *Sonnets*;
Guido Cavalcanti: *Complete Poems*; Emily Brontë: *Poems from the Moor*;
Anonymous: *Beowulf*; Ugo Foscolo: *Sepulchres*; W.B. Yeats: *Selected Poems*;
Charles Baudelaire: *The Flowers of Evil*; Sándor Márai: *The Withering World*;
Antonia Pozzi: *Poems*; Giuseppe Gioacchino Belli: *Sonnets*; Dickens: *Poems*

WWW.ALMABOOKS.COM/POETRY

ALMA CLASSICS

ALMA CLASSICS aims to publish mainstream and lesser-known European classics in an innovative and striking way, while employing the highest editorial and production standards. By way of a unique approach the range offers much more, both visually and textually, than readers have come to expect from contemporary classics publishing.

LATEST TITLES PUBLISHED BY ALMA CLASSICS

www.almaclassics.com